D1711330

Federalism and Territorial Cleavages

Federalism and Territorial Cleavages

Edited by
Ugo M. Amoretti and Nancy Bermeo

The Johns Hopkins University Press
Baltimore and London

© 2004 The Johns Hopkins University Press
All rights reserved. Published 2004
Printed in the United States of America on acid-free paper
9 8 7 6 5 4 3 2 1

The Johns Hopkins University Press
2715 North Charles Street
Baltimore, Maryland 21218-4363
www.press.jhu.edu

Library of Congress Cataloging-in-Publication Data
Federalism and territorial cleavages / edited by Ugo M. Amoretti and
Nancy Bermeo.
　　p. cm.
Includes bibliographical references and index.
　ISBN 0-8018-7408-4
　1. Federal government—Case studies. 2. Regionalism—Case studies.
I. Amoretti, Ugo M., 1969– II. Bermeo, Nancy Gina, 1951–
　　JC355.F3725 2004
　　320.4′049—dc21　　　　2003006211

A catalog record for this book is available from the British Library.

Ai miei genitori,
senza il cui affetto non avrei portato a termine questo lavoro.
                                    —*Ugo M. Amoretti*

To the memory of Vincent Wright
who taught us so much about institutions and decency
                                    —*Nancy Bermeo*

Contents

Preface

This book began in Florence, Italy, in the mid-1990s, when Ugo Amoretti became interested in federalism, a topic that had recently risen to prominence on the Italian political scene and to which he decided to dedicate his doctoral work. It developed further when Ugo became a fellow of the Center of International Studies at Princeton University in 1998 and teamed up with Nancy Bermeo, who had a long-standing interest in the political effects of institutions. The project they designed benefited greatly from the early advice and encouragement of Michael Doyle and later, from the insights of Larry Diamond and Marc Plattner. Throughout the writing of the book, both editors received inestimable assistance from the competent and kind staff of the social science division of Firestone Library, especially from the late Rosemary Little. The support of family and friends proved invaluable to the project, too. Ugo wishes to thank his parents and his sister, who have always been there when needed, for their precious teachings, and his partner, Kruskaia, a woman of incredible energy and love, for constantly encouraging and supporting him throughout this project. Nancy wishes to thank the five members of her household for providing joyful distractions from the serious business of politics. Thanks also go to Amelie von Zumbusch, who managed to remain both joyful and serious throughout the trials of coordinating and editing the text, and to Sarah Bermeo for early and immensely helpful research assistance.

The editors extend their sincere thanks to the German Marshall Fund, the Carnegie Corporation, and the National Endowment for Democracy for funding. Financial contributions from Princeton University's Center of International Studies, Center of Regional Studies, Politics Department, and Liechtenstein Institute on Self-Determination also deserve mention.

Abbreviations

AC Autonomous Communities, Spain
ACF Arewa Consultative Forum, Nigeria
AD Alliance for Democracy, Nigeria
AG Action Group, Nigeria
ANAP Anavatan Partisi (Motherland Party), Turkey
ANIPA Asamblea Nacional Indígena Plural por la Autonomía (National Pluralistic Indigenous Assembly for Autonomy), Mexico
APP All Peoples Party, Nigeria
ATR Administration du Territoire de la République, France
AV Alternative Vote
BJP Bharatiya Janata Party, India
BNG Galician Nationalist Block
CA Constituent Assembly, Nigeria
CAN Christian Association of Nigeria, Nigeria
CC Canarian Coalition, Spain
CDC Constitution Drafting Committee, Nigeria
CDS Social and Democratic Center, Spain
CE CONSTITUCIÓN ESPAÑOLA (The Spanish Constitution)
CELIB Comités d'expansions in Brittany, France
CHP Cumhuriyetci Halk Partisi (Republican People's Party), Turkey
CIS Centro de Investigaciones Sociológicas (Center for Sociological Research), Spain
CiU Convergencia i Unió (Convergence and Union), Spain
COCOPA Comisión de Concordia y Pacificación, Mexico

CNC National Peasant Confederation, Mexico
CNI Congreso Nacional Indígena (Indigenous National Congress), Mexico
CODER Regional Committees for Economic Development, France
CPSU Communist Party of the Soviet Union
CRIC Centre for Research and Information on Canada
CUP Committee for Union and Progress Party, Turkey
CVP Christian Democratic Party, Belgium
DATAR Direction à l'Aménagement du Territoire et à l'Action Régionale, France
DC Christian Democrats, Italy
DMK Dravida Munnetra Kazhagam, the Tamil nationalists, India
DSP Demokratik Sol Partisi (Democratic Left Party), Turkey
DYP True Path Party, Turkey
EA Estado de las Autonomias, Spain
EEA European Economic Area
EMU European Economic and Monetary Union
ENEG effective number of ethnic groups
ERC Esquerra Republicana de Catalunya, Spain
ETA Euskadi ta Askatasuna (Basque Fatherland and Liberty), Spain
EU European Union
EZLN Zapatista Army of National Liberation, Mexico
FDF Front démocratique des francophones, Belgium

FLNC Front National de Libération Corse,
France
FPTP first-past-the-post
GDP gross domestic product
HADEP People's Democracy Party
(Kurdish-based), Turkey
IDB Islamic Development Bank, Nigeria
IMC Interministerial Conference, Belgium
IRA Irish Republican Army
ISI import substitution industrialization
JKLF The Jammu and Kashmir Liberation
Front, India
KPE Kurdish Parliament in Exile, Turkey
LL Lombard League, Italy
]LN Northern League, Italy
LV Venetian League, Italy
MAR Minorities at Risk, Conclusion
MASSOB Movement for the Actualization
of a Sovereign State of Biafra, Nigeria
MBF Middle Belt Forum, Nigeria
MHP Milliyetçi Hareket Partisi (Nationalist
Action Party), Turkey
MMM mixed-member majoritarian
MMP mixed-member proportional
MOSOP Movement for the Survival of the
Ogoni People, Nigeria
MP Member of Parliament
NAFTA North American Free Trade
Agreement
NCNC National Council of Nigerian
Citizens
NDDC Niger Delta Development
Commission, Nigeria
NPC Northern People's Congress, Nigeria
NSC National Security Council, Turkey
OCEZ Organización Campesina Emiliano
Zapata, Mexico
OECD Organization for Economic
Cooperation and Development
OIC Organization of Islamic Conference,
Nigeria
OMPADEC Oil Mineral Producing Areas
Development Commission, Nigeria
OPC Odua Peoples Congress, Nigeria
PAN National Action Party, Mexico

PCE/IU Communists, Spain
PCI Communists, Italy
PDP Peoples Democratic Party, Nigeria
PKK Kurdistan Workers' Party, Turkey
PNV Partido Nacionalista Vasco (Basque
National Party), Spain
PP Conservatives, Partido Popular, Spain
PQ Parti Québécois, Canada
PR proportional representation
PRD Partido de la Revolución Democrática,
Mexico
PRD Partido Reformista Democrático, Spain
PRI Partido Revolucionario Institucional,
Mexico
PS Socialist Party
PSI Italian Socialist Party
PSK Kurdistan Socialist Party, Turkey
PSOE Socialists, Partido Socialista Obrero
Español, Spain
RP [Islamist] Welfare Party, Turkey
RSFSR Rossískaya Sovétskaya Federatívnaya
Sotsialistícheskaya Respúblika (the
Russian Soviet Federative Socialist
Republic), Russia
RW Rassemblement Wallon, Belgium
SDLP Social Democratic and Labour Party,
United Kingdom
SHP Social Democratic People's Party,
Turkey
SMP single-member plurality
SNC Sovereign National Conference,
Nigeria
SNP Scottish Nationalist Party
SOKAPU Southern Kaduna Peoples Union,
Nigeria
STV single transferable vote
UK The United Kingdom of Great Britain
and Northern Ireland
UN United Nations
UNICEF United Nations Children Fund
UPC Union du Peuple Corse, France
USSR Union of Soviet Socialist Republics
VNV Vlaams Nationaal Verbond, Belgium
VP Virtue Party, Turkey
VU Volksunie, Belgium

Federalism and Territorial Cleavages

Federalism and Territorial Cleavages

Ugo M. Amoretti

The term *nation-state* implies the fusion of states and nations. Though the idea of the nation-state has become commonplace in the contemporary world, states have rarely been homogeneous political organizations of a single people. More often, states have been the home of two or more identity groups, not always standing on equal footing and rarely incorporated voluntarily within the state's boundaries. Virtually everywhere, states have been built by coercive means such as annexations and military conquests, and their rulers have attributed, de jure or de facto, a different status to dominant and minority groups. This situation has not changed much over time. Though some minorities have been either assimilated or eliminated, others have resisted both processes. Moreover, new identity groups sometimes emerge and changes in borders and migrations have further increased the heterogeneity of state populations. As a result of all these trends, states that have a homogeneous *demos* and hence qualify for the nation-state label are extremely rare. One or more minorities inhabit almost all states (Connor 1994).

Within a state's territory, a minority group may be concentrated in specific regions, where it is a majority or a plurality, or it may be more evenly distributed across the territory of the state, representing a minority everywhere. Whereas this second scenario constitutes a case of "local intermingling" (Van Evera 1994), the first one is at the basis of territorial cleavages. A territorial cleavage exists when a self-conscious minority is concentrated in a specific area of a state's territory. The differences distinguishing this minority may include social, economic, ethnic, or cultural features. What matters is that the minority and the majority perceive themselves as collectively different and therefore deserving of some kind of different treatment.

The presence of minorities—whether concentrated or intermingled—does not necessarily lead to conflict. However, comparative evidence shows that conflict is much more likely to emerge when minorities are territorially concentrated. Disputes over the degree of autonomy that the territory inhabited by a minority group should enjoy are surely one of the most important and potentially difficult policy challenges facing the world community at the dawn of the new millennium. They involve tens of millions of people around the world, and their consequences, as exemplified by the breakup of the former Yugoslavia, are often unmatched by most other kinds of political divisions.

The broad objective of this collection of essays is to assess why some territorial cleavages are more easily accommodated than others. In our effort to explain variations in successful accommodation across states we are especially interested in examining whether this goal is facilitated by federal state structures, though we analyze a broad range of possible explanatory variables.

For our purposes, the term *accommodation* refers to the capacity of states to contain conflict within the mechanisms and procedures embedded in existing institutional arrangements. Accommodation has three dimensions. First and foremost, it involves minimizing violence and extrainstitutional mobilization. Second, it involves minimizing alienation or hostility toward the state itself and, relatedly, separatist party support. Whereas regional parties can easily be seen as positive contributors to accommodation, separatist parties are an indication that accommodation has fallen short. Finally, a third dimension concerns respect for minority civil and political rights. States might eliminate minority-led violence and separatist parties through outright coercion, but such a strategy would not meet the democratic standards that we consider essential for a successful accommodation of territorial cleavages.

This introduction begins by presenting the historical evolution of territorial cleavages. It then discusses the relevance of territorial cleavages to political life today, relating the project's hypotheses to the social science literature. The final section gives an overview of the volume's essays.

The Historical Evolution of Territorial Cleavages

The existence of territorial cleavages derives from the way contemporary states and the contemporary state system formed over time. To recall the well-known Weberian definition, states are political organizations characterized by a "monopoly on the legitimate use of physical force in the territory they control" (Weber 1958 [1919], 78). Today, virtually the whole world is partitioned into states. Yet, throughout most of human history this has not been the case. States appeared only at a certain point and often coexisted with other political entities such as empires, principalities, and city-states.

Before the emergence of the individual countries we are now familiar with, sovereignty was enormously fragmented and states were far from being the world's largest and most powerful political organizations. Other ways to organize political power have long represented viable alternatives. In certain areas, such as Africa, these alternatives have been prevalent until relatively recent times (Herbst 2000, 35–57). Even in Europe, where the state as organizational structure originated, and where its oldest prototypes are located, state-building processes have been long and complicated. Several of our chapters illustrate that the process of state formation and reformation is still taking place.

There are large differences in the paths of development followed by states in different times and places. Outside Europe, most contemporary states originated as a consequence of decolonization. In Europe, the birth and the success of the modern state were marked by rulers' efforts to extend the range of population, territory, and resources over which they exerted power. Virtually all European rulers devoted themselves to these tasks for centuries. Although, depending on the conditions of the surrounding environment, they could rely on alternative strategies in order to build states, most of the time state building meant war and its preparation (Tilly 1990, 28). In the long run, states that lost wars contracted or simply ceased to exist, whereas those with the strongest coercive powers prospered.

State building may be defined as a process of territorial expansion and consolidation, through which, if successful, a core area turns into a state. Because of the wide diversities among adjacent peoples, the formation of states often resulted in the extension of the same rule over heterogeneous populations living in territories originally beyond the state builders' control—a process that sowed the seeds of territorial cleavages. This happened in Europe as well as in its former colonies, where decolonization frequently led to artificial boundaries drawn without paying attention to the territorial distribution of identity groups.

Rulers engaged in the formation of a state generally delegated the administration of newly acquired territories to local patrons and notables, who enjoyed substantial autonomy in exchange for part of the revenue they extracted from local populations. Initially, state building was largely a process of territorial aggrandizement paired by the simple subordination of the inhabitants of the newly acquired territories who, in turn, normally lacked the resources to mobilize. With time, however, the broadening scope of state activity favored the emergence of sizable bureaucracies that assisted sovereigns in moving toward a more direct administration of their territories. Along with demanding taxes and the conscription of their subject populations to feed and fill standing armies, rulers' activities began to include new tasks, such as the provision of basic public services carried out by the emerging administrative apparatuses.

Sovereigns could consider the territorial segmentation and the heterogeneity of their states' population an asset to the extent that it enhanced the costs of collective action and, therefore, reduced the probability of large-scale rebellions. However, heterogeneity also represented an obstacle because it made it harder to extend a standardized administration across the whole territory. In a homogeneous context, the same administrative tools could have been employed everywhere—something obviously much more difficult in a heterogeneous setting. In order to overcome the problems posed by heterogeneity and consolidate their states, rulers generally worked to increase the cultural significance of borders by trying, with different degrees of success, to impose common languages, religions, and identities on their subjects. This homogenizing effort, commonly known as nation building, represented a watershed in modern state development, as it corresponded with a shift from an old-fashioned strategy of pure subordination to one of assimilation, aimed at transforming the *state* into a *nation-state* (Rokkan 1973). Even if the origins of nation-building processes are debatable, these efforts reached their zenith only after the French Revolution (Weber 1977).

Whereas state-building processes created territorial cleavages by incorporating diverse peoples under the same rule, nation-building policies induced their political mobilization and, thus, conflict. Standardizing strategies, in fact, promoted nationalism, both as identification of the majority people with "their" state and as resistance of the distinct minority groups to the "alien" state's demands for uniformity and integration.

Homogenizing efforts produced different outcomes in different places. Where minority identities were not very distinctive, the result was a considerable degree of assimilation. Elsewhere, where they were stronger, minority groups managed to better resist homogenization and, at least partially, keep their own particular characteristics, sometimes gaining a degree of political autonomy, depending on how their resource endowment compared to that of the central government.

The efforts of standardization triggered the processes of national integration and territorial separation. Yet, the contemporary constellation of intrastate territorial divisions is not just a legacy of century-old processes that led to the formation and the consolidation of the modern state. More recent developments, such as industrialization, the expanding role assumed by the government over time, the interaction of old territorial differences with other cleavages, the rise of supranational institutions, as well as economic globalization, all contributed to remodel patterns of territorial divisions.

Industrialization affected territorial divisions in two ways. On the one hand, by tending to reward areas enjoying natural positional advantages rather than areas surrounding state capitals, it created unprecedented tensions between new economic centers and the established political cores (Keating 1998, 22–23). On the other hand, by creating a large urban proletariat and making capital-labor relations a key social and political issue, it contributed to set states' political agendas more on class than territorial matters, thus downplaying territorial divisions and favoring their temporary political eclipse.

The escalating role of the state produced one of its major effects on territorial cleavages through the creation and expansion of educational programs. Often conceived only in the core-area language, these programs proved to be key in promoting linguistic standardization and, therefore, forging a new "national" identity. As mentioned above, this drive for linguistic homogeneity proved to be highly controversial in several countries, often contributing to mobilization around resistance to assimilation.

The creation and the development of welfare, on the contrary, affected territorial cleavages by improving, with economic modernization and political development, the quality of life of large sectors of the masses, allowing citizens once concerned almost exclusively with economic questions to gradually focus on different, postmaterialist issues, including territorial identities (Inglehart 1977, 234–43). This new attention to postmaterialist issues has contributed to both the resurgence of old identities that had been kept at the margin since the process of industrialization was set in motion, and to the creation of new ones.

Current patterns of intrastate territorial divisions have been also influenced by their interplay with other cleavages, such as those emerging from the industrialization process: urban versus agrarian interests and capital versus labor. Peasant discontent, maybe because of its ties with the land and local ownership, frequently assumed a clearly defined territorial form, thus contributing to restructure territorial cleavages. The same can be said for the urban labor movement, which was often local in its origins and achieved a statewide dimension only gradually. While it was committed to the universalistic and internationalist doctrines of proletarian solidarity and class struggle, the labor movement also influenced territorial relationships, contributing to the development of specific identities in areas of early industrialization (Keating 1998, 24–25).

In Western Europe, territorial cleavages have also been affected by their interaction with the religious differences introduced by the Reformation. In Catholic countries, the Church and its followers had to face the opposition of liberal and anticlerical groups.

This opposition frequently assumed a territorial dimension, since the anticlericals were often centralist and used state institutions to challenge the Church, which, in turn, assumed the defense of local traditions and played them against the central authorities. On the other hand, in various Protestant countries, fundamentalist groups broke away from their own church, and since the fundamentalists tended to be stronger in peripheral areas, this division over religious matters tended to assume a territorial dimension as well (Keating 1998, 25).

If the anarchy and perpetual warfare of the international arena have long contributed to dampen intrastate territorial divisions, more recent trends such as the emergent role of supranational institutions and economic globalization have produced contrasting effects. The development of supranational institutions, such as the European Union (EU), is providing territorial minorities with new constraints and opportunities. Since tasks gradually acquired by supranational institutions include matters of direct interest for territorial minorities, their growing scope alters traditional center-periphery dynamics, with consequences that are still uncertain. Globalization changes center-periphery dynamics too. As market forces become less linked with states and more connected with international organizations and particular enterprises, the nature of the relationship between territories and central authorities is bound to change (Türsan 1998, 1–16).

The Relevance of Territorial Cleavages Today

Shaped by a complex mix of long-term and short-term influences, territorial cleavages are one of the main causes of conflict in today's world. Following the end of World War II, they have been increasingly mobilized, turning into a powerful source of turmoil that has modified the political landscape in all of the world's regions. Like other sociopolitical phenomena, territorial cleavages seem to acquire salience in waves and, after their political eclipse during the centralizing trends of the 1940s and 1950s, they entered an upward trend during the 1960s. The centrality of territorial cleavages as a source of conflict, nonetheless, has produced different consequences in the advanced industrial societies and the rest of the world. In the developed West, despite the presence of territorially based minorities in most countries, conflicts have been less bloody and deadly than elsewhere. Excluding conflicts related to Northern Ireland, the Basque Country, and—to a lesser extent—Corsica, territorial cleavages have generally been managed peacefully, channeling political action and participation through the conventional avenues provided by democratic institutions (Newman 1996, 1–9). In the less institutionalized, unstable political regimes of the former communist and developing countries, the mobilization of territorial diversities has instead led to very different outcomes. Often based on ascriptive features, territorial cleavages have given way to deadly and bloody confrontations where, to quote Donald Horowitz (1985, 684), "ties of blood" have produced "rivers of blood." The growing numbers of these armed conflicts reached an unprecedented high in the early 1990s following the collapse of the Soviet bloc, and its future evolution is far from being easily predictable (Gurr 2000, 281–88; Wallensteen and Sollenberg 2001).

The contemporary relevance of territorial conflict is best understood through some simple facts. Between 1989 and 2000, 111 armed conflicts—33 of which were still ongoing in 2000—took place in 74 different locations. While only 7 of them were inter-state, a full 104 were fought between the inhabitants of a single state. Out of these 104 internal conflicts, 46.6 percent were ideological and 53.4 percent concerned territory instead (Wallensteen and Sollenberg 2001). In other words, disputes over controlling part of the territory of a certain state are the prevalent source of conflict in today's world.

Most of these armed conflicts occurred in Africa and the former Soviet bloc. Only two of them took place in the advanced industrial societies, namely, in the Basque Country and Northern Ireland. As various scholars have already stressed, the outcomes generated by the mobilization of territorial cleavages tend to be less severe in the developed West than elsewhere. Among the developing and former communist countries, the mobilization of dissatisfaction with the state and its borders often generates a considerable amount of violence. In the advanced industrial societies, where economies are developed and democracy is consolidated, it is normally contained within the mechanisms set up by the institutional system. Economic and welfare development make unconventional strategies and non-negotiable stands less attractive than in developing and former communist countries (Young 1994, 222–23; Dion 1996). By providing strong incentives to channel people's dissatisfaction with the state and its borders into the electoral arena, consolidated democratic institutions work in the same direction (Newman 1996, 9).

Among Western democracies, the salience of territorial cleavages is therefore better appreciated by looking at conventional forms of political activity such as those involving political parties. There were approximately fifty ethnic parties in the Organization for Economic Cooperation and Development (OECD) countries as of 1997 and virtually all of these had a territorial constituency (Lane, McKay, and Newton 1997, 139).

The electoral performance of territorial parties has obvious implications for party systems and for the composition and workings of democratic governments. In the seven developed countries considered in this volume, the maximum vote won by territorial parties at the national level was 16.4 percent—won by the Belgian territorial parties in the second half of the 1970s (Lane, McKay, and Newton 1997, 153). Yet, these parties do not aim at winning the votes of the whole electorate. Their goal is to maximize support in the territory they claim to represent, and if we look at their success in their own constituencies (regions, provinces, and so forth), a different picture emerges. Several of them, such as the *Partido Nacionalista Vasco* in the Basque Country and the *Convergència i Unió* in Catalonia, have achieved two-digit returns over a long span of time, thus gaining lasting and powerful positions within their home regions (De Winter 1998, 204–47).

Summarizing, territorial cleavages are today's main source of conflict and one of the principal causes of violence in the world. Among the developing and former communist countries, their mobilization often leads to armed conflicts on various scales. In the advanced industrial societies, it is mostly constrained by the institutions of consolidated democratic regimes and therefore channeled toward the electoral arena. Yet, the outcomes of territorial mobilization are not easily predictable on the basis of economic and political development alone. Whereas not all cases of mobilization in the developing and former communist countries have produced violence, a few of those within the realm of the advanced industrial societies have given way to deadly conflicts between terrorist groups and the state. Hence, the potential for conflict from territorial cleavages represents a serious policy challenge throughout the world. A deeper understanding of how territorial cleavages might be better accommodated is of profound practical as well of scholarly importance.

The Project and the Literature

The cases included in our project differ on a range of dimensions but each focuses on the same set of questions and each examines the same set of possible answers.

Our primary research question, as stated above, concerns variations in the accommodation of territorial cleavages. The variations in accommodation experiences are multiple and perplexing. Why, for example, has the United Kingdom's accommodation experience been much less successful than Switzerland's? The United Kingdom has been plagued with decades of armed conflict over the Irish question—plus a massive and ultimately successful movement for territorial devolution in Scotland. Switzerland, by contrast, has managed to accommodate three different linguistic communities and two different religious groups with no violence and virtually no movements for devolution for well over a century. Why, in another part of the world, has Turkey been unable to work out a successful formula for the accommodation of the Kurdish minority while Russia has managed to accommodate the minority in Tartarstan? Given that the Russians and the Tartars are divided by religion and are operating in a relatively new democracy one might have predicted the opposite outcome.

Empirical evidence shows that the accommodation of territorial conflicts is not an easy task. Building peace and democracy in divided countries requires a great effort. Each side needs to compromise. Governments need to acknowledge and support the rights of minority peoples so that they do not mobilize exclusively on the basis of territorial identity and so that feelings of alienation do not become prominent among them. Minority groups need to confine their actions within the channels provided by democratic institutions and accept the state's political authority.

What factors increase the likelihood of successful accommodation? The social science literature offers us a number of appealing hypotheses and these are the foundation of a series of subsidiary research questions addressed in our project. The most important of these hypotheses derives from the literature on federalism.

Federalism's Features and Varieties

The basic feature of a federal system is an institutionalized division of power between a central government and a set of constituent governments—variously denominated as states, regions, provinces, *Länder,* or cantons—in which each level of government has the power to make final decisions in some policy areas but cannot unilaterally modify the federal structure of the state (Riker 1964, 11; 1975, 101; 1993, 508–14; Dahl 1986, 114; Lijphart 1999, 4).

Federalism has other important features such as bicameralism and judicial review. Whereas the legislatures of unitary states may be unicameral or bicameral, all fully federal systems have a bicameral legislature. Though federal bicameralism varies in its organization and effects, it allows the representation of constituent units at the center and, thus, provides an arena in which central and regional authorities can interact (Lijphart 1999, 200–215; Stepan 1997, 29–40).[1] In general, the wider the policy scope of the upper chamber, the stronger the bicameralism and the greater the protection of constituent units.

The importance of judicial review in federal systems is straightforward. Because of the existence of two levels of government, intergovernmental conflicts are endogenous to federations and a supreme arbitral authority to settle disputes over the constitution and intergovernmental relations is needed. In the absence of a constitutional court charged with judicial review, legislatures would judge themselves and the balance of power between federal and constituent units could be drastically altered (Lijphart 1999, 4, 223–30).

Different institutional configurations produce different types of federalism. Federal systems, for example, vary with respect to the concrete powers attributed to each level of government. Though defense and foreign policy are always exclusive to the jurisdiction of the central government, the allocation of authority over other policy areas, especially taxation and spending, is not so obvious. Federations diverge too in the size and number of their federated units. In general terms, bigger units tend to be more powerful, and are more likely to become the constituencies of territorial conflict. Historically, federal systems with only two or very few constituent units, such as Nigeria, Czechoslovakia, Malaysia-Singapore, and Pakistan, have been notoriously unstable. The size and number of constituent units sometimes alters over time in response to demands from minorities themselves. Where ethnic divisions exist, units can be ethnically homogeneous or heterogeneous. Scholars such as Horowitz have illustrated that "the case for ethnically homogeneous states is strong" where "groups are territorially separate and sub-ethnic divisions are prominent" (Horowitz 1985, 613).

A final and highly consequential variation within the set of federal regimes concerns their mix of majoritarian and consensual institutions. As Arend Lijphart has ably demonstrated, there are two competing views on who should govern when people have diverging preferences. Both views are embodied in a distinct set of institutions and both have special ramifications where territorial cleavages are present and views are therefore likely to diverge (Lijphart 1999, 2–3). In majoritarian democracies, differences are resolved by majority rule. The principle is that the right to rule belongs to the simple majority of the people, no matter how narrow. First-past-the-post electoral systems exemplify this principle. In consensual democracies, the assumption is that governing should be in the hands of as many people as possible. Proportional representation systems exemplify this principle.

Federalism itself is an antimajoritarian mechanism for, by devolving power to smaller constituencies, it places some policy issues beyond the reach of the center's majority. R. Kent Weaver designates federalism a *delegatory* antimajoritarian mechanism and points out three other important antimajoritarian subtypes: *consociational* mechanisms, such as proportional representation, which encourage multiparty government and bargaining among elites; *arbitral* mechanisms, such as judicial review, which restrain majority rule by placing power in the hands of officials who have limited or no electoral accountability at all; and *limited government* mechanisms, such as veto points, which limit majority rule by raising the barriers to decision making in general (Weaver 1992; Lijphart, Rogowski, and Weaver 1993).

The mix of antimajoritarian institutions varies from one federal state to another. Among our case studies, Switzerland represents the paradigmatic consensual system. Canada, with its first-past-the-post voting system, is the case that comes closest to majoritarianism.

Although still unsystematic, evidence suggests that antimajoritarian devices facilitate the accommodation of territorial cleavages better than majoritarian mechanisms do (Cohen 1997; Lijphart 1999, 270–74). In a majoritarian context, minorities can be permanently but "democratically" shut out of power.[2] As Horowitz reminds us, when the size of minorities is fixed rather than fluid and the voting system is majoritarian, "the textbook case of democratic majority rule turns quickly into a case of egregious minority exclusion. In ethnically divided societies, majority rule is ... a problem because it permits domination, apparently in perpetuity" (Horowitz 1994, 46).

Federalism's Effects

The central hypothesis examined in this project is that the accommodation of territorial cleavages is facilitated by federalism, an institutional setting that a broad range of scholars has identified as a useful device in divided societies. By combining the advantages of shared rule with those of self-rule, federalism offers a range of solutions and opportunities that make it preferable to unitarism.[3] However, since claims for the merits of federalism are often accompanied by qualifications and based on single cases, its effects—and the contextual factors that shape them—have not been clearly specified. On the other hand, while some federal systems have successfully contributed to the accommodation of territorial cleavages, others have a much less positive record (Elazar 1993, 194). Hence, variations between and within federal states need to be more closely examined. Nevertheless, in states with territorial cleavages, some provision for territorial autonomy seems to be a necessary—if not a sufficient—condition for successful accommodation. As Alfred Stepan (1999, 20) has pointed out, every single long-standing democracy in a multicultural polity is a federal state.

Alternative and Complementary Explanations

Though it is clear that a state's capacity to accommodate territorial cleavages is affected by domestic institutions, we recognize that successful accommodation does not derive from institutional factors alone. The contrast between the Basques and the Catalans—in a single state—make the insufficiency of institutional explanations patently clear. Recognizing this, we asked our project participants to consider federalism versus unitarism as just one of a larger set of other factors that might explain successful accommodation. Thus, the other explanations considered here go beyond domestic institutions and include historical, social, and international factors.

All of our case studies, as well as the chapters by Valerie Bunce, Alfred Stepan, and Nancy Bermeo, examine the *history of interaction* between cleavage groups and the central state. Our assumption is that present behavior is conditioned by past experience—by what Horowitz aptly calls "the texture of group relations" (Horowitz 1981, 167). We assume, specifically, that trust and mistrust are the products of what scholars now call the "history of play" (Rothstein 2000) and that the salience and even the very existence of a people's identity derive from "the intensity of their past and ongoing conflicts with rival groups and with the state" (Calhoun 1997, 51–65; Gurr 2000, 68–69).

Another possible set of explanations examined in our project includes a series of factors related to the *depth of difference* between territorial minorities and centrally dominant groups. Are cleavages with one dimension, such as language, easier to accommodate than cleavages forged along multiple dimensions, including religion, wealth, language, and race? Do some differences have stronger explanatory power than others?

Economic differences are among the most salient of the set of explanations for the variance in accommodation. Differences in wealth, economic opportunities, and employment loom large as explanations for territorial conflicts and, particularly, the birth of secessionist movements. Michael Hechter, for instance, argues that drives for secession vary with position in the labor force.[4] Horowitz (1985, 229–88) places the relative economic position of regions and groups within a multicultural state at the center of his highly influential explanation for failed accommodation.[5] While he acknowledges that other, noneconomic variables are influential too, he argues that economically underdeveloped regions and groups are far more prone to secede than their better off counterparts. His argument has been challenged from a variety of quarters. Henry Hale, for example, argues that wealthy groups are more likely to secede (Hale 1998). But the debate simply confirms that we need to know more about how material differences shape mobilization.

The effects of cultural differences require more investigation as well. Many scholars reason that the more a regional group has a distinctive understanding of the world, the less smooth its relations with neighboring groups are likely to be. Samuel Huntington makes a case for the power of cultural variables in *The Clash of Civilizations*. In the post—cold war order, he maintains, local politics is the politics of ethnicity and the most dramatic conflicts will be between peoples belonging to different cultures (Huntington 1996, 28). Particularly risky are fault-line conflicts, which involve groups that are mainly located in a certain geographical area, since territory is at stake and conflict may degenerate into ethnic cleansing (Huntington 1996, 252). Language and religion are the main elements of any civilization, and the latter, especially in a historical phase of great change like the present one, plays a major role because it may fulfill the psychological, emotional, moral, and social needs of a disoriented people (Huntington 1996, 64–65). Thus, the difference that will determine the nature of the accommodation challenge is most likely to be a religious one.

Huntington's argument has been hotly criticized but it has also been supported by at least one quantitative multicountry study which found that religious diversity is an important predictor of territorial conflicts (Hale 1998). The weight of cultural differences, like the weight of material differences, clearly needs more investigation. The empirical materials in the essays that follow help to fulfill this need.

Because the final set of explanatory factors addressed by our project is international in character, the essays also fill the need for more research on how international actors affect cleavage accommodation. The supply of arms, the provision of safe havens, the promise of trade, and the threat of sanctions are just a few of the means through which international actors can affect the behavior of cleavage groups. Each of our case studies considers the links between territorial groups and the larger international environment in which they operate.

We designed this project assuming that successful cleavage accommodation depends on how the factors outlined above combine and shape the behavior of central and regional political elites and thought that some contexts would give them the incentives to cooperate and be accommodating while others would provide incentives for conflict instead. The challenge was to explain which combinations of institutional and noninstitutional factors lead to successful accommodation and which lead to other, less desirable, outcomes.

We reasoned that this challenge would be best met by looking at variations within states as well as between states. Thus, though our primary independent variable is system type—and the relative merits of federalism versus unitarism—our units of analysis are not states alone but, rather, territorial cleavages within states. Holding regime type constant enables us to see which noninstitutional, contextual factors are most important.

Our case studies embrace a wide range of states and an even wider range of cleavage groups. In the first part of the book, the reader will find essays on how territorial cleavages have been accommodated in seven advanced industrial societies. While these countries share similar levels of political and economic development, they differ substantially in their institutional arrangements. Switzerland and Belgium, after the 1993 constitutional reform, are cases of federalism coupled with other antimajoritarian mechanisms. Canada represents a case of federalism joined with majoritarian institutions. Belgium before 1993 and Italy until the same year are examples of consensual unitary states. The United Kingdom and France represent cases of unitary states coupled with majoritarian institutions. Spain, considered a federal state by many scholars and a "federation in the making" by others (Guibernau 1995), shares most, though not all, of federalism's basic features, combined with a variety of consensual and majoritarian institutions.[6]

All together (and with varying degrees of attention) these essays enlighten us about eighteen cleavage groups; the French, German, and Italian speakers in Switzerland; the Flemish and French speakers in Belgium; the *Québécois*, Anglophones, and Allophones in Canada, the Catalans, Basques, and Galicians in Spain; the Irish, Scots, Welsh, and English in the United Kingdom; the northern Italians in Italy; and, finally, the Corsicans and Bretons in France. The contested issues in these states, for the most part, do not involve civil war or democratic consolidation but, instead, revolve around institutional design and the quality of democracy. Because both elections and democracy are taken as givens in our first group of cases, Part I ends with an essay on federalism and electoral institutions by R. Kent Weaver and an essay on federalism and democratic representation by Ferran Requejo.

Part II examines how territorial cleavages are accommodated in developing and former communist states. Here our cases include Russia, India, Turkey, Mexico, and Nigeria, and the territorial cleavages discussed range from the indigenous peoples of Oaxaca to the Islamic peoples of Kashmir. These cases all have much lower income levels and much higher levels of political instability than those in Part I. This context makes the accommodation of territorial cleavages even more difficult and, as our essays show, the way in which accommodation has been pursued differs dramatically from the patterns of Western Europe and Canada. Though failed strategies of accommodation have given rise to terrorism in the United Kingdom and Spain, outside the advanced industrial societies they have led, in virtually all our cases, to open warfare. Unitary Turkey has been no more successful in accommodating its Kurdish minority than federal India has been in accommodating its Muslim minority in Kashmir. Curiously, though, the stories of accommodation attempts in third world and postcommunist states are not uniformly tragic.

Russia has failed to accommodate the Muslim peoples of Chechnia, but has succeeded in the Muslim republic of Tartarstan—and many other diverse regions. Mexican government elites failed to avoid armed struggle in Chiapas, but prevented it in the highly mobilized region of Oaxaca. Nigeria's territorial cleavages led, in 1967, to a gruesome civil war, but several sharp divisions have been solved without violence more recently and armed struggle has been contained. Finally, though India suffers from a deadly conflict in Kashmir, the central state has quelled heated divisions in many other regions. With the single exception of Turkey, each state has had its triumphs alongside its failures.

Explaining the differences within states, as well as between states, yields rich lessons. These lessons bear on questions of majoritarianism and consensus and each of these cases brings its own peculiar mix of majoritarian and consensual elements. But the political stakes in our third world and postcommunist cases go beyond questions of institutional design and autonomy. Failed accommodation in these contexts can lead to changes in borders and changes in regime—each accompanied by massive loss of life. Accordingly, the second part of the book ends with two essays, relating system type with democratic consolidation. One, by Valerie Bunce, focuses on how the legacy of federalism affects postcommunist regimes. Another, by Alfred Stepan, focuses on the effects of institutional design and federalism, in particular, on the viability of democracies throughout the world. The collection's concluding chapter, by Nancy Bermeo, draws together common themes from the whole volume and highlights the collection's main lessons.

A Preview of the Essays

André Bächtiger and Jürg Steiner open our collection with an essay on Switzerland— the case that comes closest to being our paradigm of success. They begin by showing that Switzerland has not always been as peaceful and harmonious as it currently seems and explain how the extraordinarily antimajoritarian, federalist constitution in place today was the result of a civil war fought in 1847 by territorially based religious groups. They attribute successful accommodation to the federal institutions that allow cleavage groups a large discretionary range of autonomous policy-making powers but argue that the success of Switzerland cannot be ascribed to institutions alone. Elites contributed to the accommodation of territorial cleavages by promoting a political discourse revolving around the political and multicultural character of Switzerland. Though Bächtiger and Steiner warn that a number of factors that have helped the management of diversity have weakened in recent times, the case remains a decidedly positive model.

In Chapter 2, Liesbet Hooghe examines the case of Belgium. She explains that territorial protest began to escalate in the 1950s and reached its zenith in the late 1970s. This evolution of territorial conflicts moved in tandem with a long process of institutional reform that eventually transformed Belgium, in 1993, from a consensual unitary system, to a consensual federal one. Hooghe holds that, in the past, consociational mechanisms helped avoid violence but also fueled the centrifugal forces of territorial conflict. These forces remain operative under federalism today but, overall, the impact of the federal reform has been positive. Territorial conflicts have declined and the erosion of the Belgian identity has stopped. Increasingly, both Flemish and Walloons seem to share the multiple identities that scholars consider essential to holding together a multicultural polity.

Richard Simeon discusses the case of Canada in Chapter 3. Simeon explains how Canada's institutional system (unlike Belgium's) has not been able to reform itself and how coupling federalism with majoritarian institutions like a single-party government, a plurality electoral system, and a virtually unicameral parliament means that entire provinces can be excluded from exerting any influence on the central government level.

Such a situation, combined with weak national parties, increases the risk of nourishing feelings of exclusion and alienation, especially where, like in Quebec, a strong separate identity exists. Despite these problems, Simeon's judgment of Canadian federalism remains comparatively positive. In fact, even if federalism helped perpetuate the very cleavages it was designed to manage, it has also proved quite effective in accommodating them. By granting provinces a substantial degree of autonomy, federalism has helped reduce conflict on potentially divisive issues and ensure that *Québécois* nationalism remained peaceful and democratic—despite the strength of the separatist movement.

In Chapter 4, Pablo Beramendi and Ramón Máiz discuss the achievements and shortcomings of the *Estado de las Autonomías* in dealing with territorial conflicts. They explain how the drafters of the Spanish constitution searched for a common denominator acceptable to all parties. Skirting the most divisive issues, they avoided ruling on the extent of regional decentralization or the extent of asymmetry among regions. They simply accorded a special status to the historical nationalities and left the other issues open for bilateral negotiations. Beramendi and Máiz argue that the openness of the Spanish constitution contributed to the successful transition to democracy but that it also sowed the seeds of later problems. Today, the level of harmonization between the powers attributed to the historical nationalities and those given to the other regions are a key issue in Spanish politics. Centrifugal drives have been set in motion by a decentralizing spiral, in which the historical nationalities push for more devolution and the other regions try to catch up in the name of harmonization. This can last until there are no more powers to be decentralized but the long-term picture may be problematic. The counterbalance to this centrifugal drive lies in the diffusion of dual identities, which are another product of the existing institutions. Dual identities have reduced the appeal of separate statehood among Catalans, Basques, and Galicians, and this bodes well for Spain's future.

Michael Keating analyzes the blueprint for majoritarian democracy in his chapter on the United Kingdom. He explains how territorial cleavages were managed through a complex and, in many ways, informal set of mechanisms, including territorial secretaries of state, Members of Parliament, and interest groups. These mechanisms of territorial management were different for each minority nation—as were the depths of difference dividing the minority nations from the English center. The mechanisms for accommodation were a conspicuous failure in Ireland from the nineteenth century on and neither the welfare state nor the trade unionist movement played an integrative role there, though they helped accommodation in Wales and Scotland. Indeed, accommodation mechanisms worked reasonably well outside of Ireland—as long as the minority nations supported the same political majority as the United Kingdom as a whole. When this did not happen, as in Scotland in 1922 and between 1979 and 1997, the majoritarian political system shut out the minority nation altogether and pressures for devolution emerged. These have turned the United Kingdom toward what Keating calls a form of de facto federalism and the government has recognized, explicitly in Northern Ireland and implicitly in Scotland, that there is no barrier to secession should people want it.

In Chapter 6 I analyze the case of Italy where, from the mid-1940s to the mid-1980s, ideological polarization and consensual institutions guaranteed the quiescence of territorial conflicts. In a fashion similar to that of the United Kingdom, territorial interests were transmitted from the periphery through party lines, while a set of informal rules guaranteed them an audience at the center. The minimally empowered regional governments set up during the 1970s proved to be ineffective and, instead, gave the periphery symbolic resources that fueled frustration and centrifugal forces. When, in the late 1980s, the communist threat finally disappeared, the Italian party system collapsed and, with it, the informal system of representation on which territorial politics had been based. When the budgetary requirements of European integration hampered the center's capacity to buy consensus through the allocation of new resources, doors to a more adversarial confrontation among diverging regional interests opened. These, in turn, changed the social and geographical bases of government support and ultimately led to a crisis of the old consensual system of territorial representation during the 1990s. The Italian case illustrates the merits and the limits of a system of territorial management based on consociational, unitary institutions.

The final case study in Part I focuses on France and the dramatic contrast between the successful and unsuccessful accommodation of the territorial cleavages in Brittany and Corsica. Marc Smyrl explains how success in the Breton case derives from the center's ability to work with hierarchical but united local elites who set their sights on the goal of local economic development and worked through unitary institutions to achieve it. The unsuccessful experience in Corsica stems from divided local elites. Traditional elites who based their power on patron-clientism never raised a serious nationalist challenge but drove the costs of accommodation higher and higher in a spiral of internal competition. They also provided incentives for the emergence of nationalist counterelites who used violence to challenge both the corruption of traditional local politicians and the legitimacy of French rule itself. The French state is trying to meet these challenges now through the creation of a Corsican territorial assembly that may represent a first step toward a federal-type arrangement.

The section on the advanced industrial societies concludes with an essay on institutions and one on the quality of democracy. R. Kent Weaver investigates how federal electoral systems affect party systems and governability in Europe and North America.

He points out that federal states vary greatly both in their electoral laws and in the role that their subunits play under bicameralism and concludes that single-member plurality elections raise the risk that territorial minorities will be excluded from sharing in government. He also argues that these majoritarian electoral systems affect the fortunes of antisystem secessionist and irredentist parties in ironic ways. Though these systems constitute barriers to small and moderately popular antisystem parties, they actually help these parties once they reach a threshold of 35 percent of the vote because of a tipping effect.

Ferran Requejo examines how liberal federalism affects the quality of democracy in states with multiple nationalities. He takes up the subject of power asymmetry—an issue that emerges throughout our cases—and argues persuasively that symmetrical models are ill suited to the accommodation of territorial cleavages. National minorities suffer under uniform rules of entry and need external protections. Liberal democracies must see national pluralism as a "value worth protecting rather than an inconvenient fact" and protect cultural as well as civil and political rights.

There is no case that parallels the success of Switzerland among third world and postcommunist regimes. Thus, the second part of the book begins with a chapter on India—a case of relative success. India has maintained the largest and most heterogeneous democracy in the world for over half a century. Atul Kohli's essay helps explain why by comparing the state's accommodation experience with three distinct territorial groups. Though pointing out that India's record of success varies over time and region, Kohli argues that a well-institutionalized federal polity provides room for territorial groups to mobilize yet sets firm limits within which such movements must operate. Concessions by secure but accommodating national leaders blunt the radical edge of ethnic movements and draw them into mainstream, if tumultuous, political bargaining. The keys to successful accommodation, according to Kohli, are the level of institutionalization of the central state and the security and ruling strategy of the center's leaders.

Kathryn Stoner-Weiss makes a case for a stronger central government in the chapter on Russia. Russia, like India, presents us with a mixed picture. It offers an example of failed accommodation in the tragic case of Chechnia, but it shows us instances of successful accommodation as well. Stoner-Weiss underscores the unpredictability of center-periphery relations and, like the authors of the Spanish case, attributes this to the bilateral bargaining that pervades them. Though the institutions that have developed to manage Russian territorial politics have proven weak, the Russian center has endured challenges to its authority from almost all quarters. Federalism has contributed to the system's asymmetry and instability but it has also allowed for the flexibility that the diversity of Russia's cleavages requires.

Rotimi T. Suberu's chapter on the accommodation of territorial cleavages in federal Nigeria highlights important contrasts with the Russian case. In Nigeria, the accommodation of territorial cleavages is hampered by a center that many find excessively strong. The risk in Nigeria comes, Suberu tells us, not from decentralization but from a concentration of power and material resources that disadvantages the peoples of the south. Though federalism has been recognized as "the indispensable basis for Nigeria's stability and survival," elites throughout the country are engaged in furious debate about how the federal system should be reformed. As in India, past reforms in Nigeria have involved the creation of new, more homogeneous states.

In the chapter on Mexico, Guillermo Trejo describes how the mobilization of indigenous groups varied across time and in different regions in the waning years of Partido Revolucionario Institucional (PRI) hegemony. Comparing the Chiapas region, where the *Zapatistas* led an armed uprising in 1994, with Oaxaca and other regions, Trejo explains that poverty was a poor predictor of indigenous mobilization. Political-institutional variables turned out to be more important in explaining when and where accommodation failed. Mexico's federal structure allowed for variations in state constitutions and state electoral cycles and these variations had dramatic effects on center-periphery relations. States, such as Chiapas, with authoritarian local constitutions, strong PRI hegemony, and high levels of electoral concurrence, were highly repressive to indigenous minorities and sowed the seeds of a violent uprising. States with more democratic local constitutions did not succeed fully in accommodating minority demands but they did provide minority leaders with other options and thus, the institutional means to avoid guerrilla warfare.

Michele Penner Angrist's essay on the Turkish-Kurdish conflict is the last of our case studies. Despite a variety of tactics (running from the banning of the Kurdish language to fighting a war that cost 40,000 lives) the central state in Turkey has found no long-term means of accommodating the country's 8 to 12 million Kurds. The author attributes this failure to three institutional factors: the highly centralized, unitary Turkish state; the state's promotion of an assimilationist nationalist ideology; and the long shadow that the Turkish military casts over civilian political decision making. Underscoring how coercion has failed in the past, she argues for alternative, more accommodationist policies, including some devolution of local powers.

The book closes with three general essays. The first, by Valerie Bunce, asks how "the contrast between unitary and federal systems affects national identities, secessionist demands, and the durability of regimes and states." After discussing some of the project's key concepts, Bunce argues that national federalism had deleterious effects on the durability of postcommunist states because it both "constructed" and "empowered" nations and "states-in-the-making" within each federal system. When these systems entered into crisis with the collapse of communism, the nationalist component of national federalism redefined the boundaries of politics organizing "political identities, political agendas, and political boundaries." Bunce concludes that if new democracies in multinational states inherit a national federal structure, they will be especially vulnerable to secessionist pressure. Democracies in India and Spain have endured, Bunce argues, because they began as unitary states.

Alfred Stepan also discusses the chronology of federalism's development in the succeeding chapter. Stepan argues that the model of federalism that emerged in the United States is unique in both its history and its content and that it should not be the blueprint for multinational states considering federalism today. Federalism in the United States emerged from the voluntary unification of sovereign polities. As a result, its institutions were both symmetrical and highly constraining of what Stepan calls the *demos*—the center majority. Multinational democratic states today are more likely to endure if they use federal arrangements to "hold together" diverse peoples, but they require asymmetrical, "*demos*-enabling" institutions to do it best.

The connection between institutions, democracy, and stability is taken up again in the concluding chapter by Nancy Bermeo. Combining the findings of the empirical and theoretical chapters of the book with a broad array of comparative materials, Bermeo shows that depth of difference is not a consistent predictor of accommodation; that successful accommodation is made much more difficult if the history of interaction between territorial minorities and dominant groups has been violent; that compromise and inclusion carry fewer risks as a formula for accommodation than coercion; and finally, that federalist institutions are preferable to unitary ones for the accommodation of territorial cleavages, though they work best within certain contexts. The contextual features that matter most are revealed in the essays that follow.

NOTES

I thank Nancy Bermeo for extensive comments on earlier drafts of this essay. Amelie von Zumbusch deserves thanks for editorial assistance.
    1. It may be worth noting that while bicameralism is crucial to the representation of constituent units at the center, in modern democracies it may be even more important to the representation of constituent units in the federal executive. Representation in the legislature was key when parliaments were the cradle of policy making; today, the locus of this function is more and more the executive.
    2. As argued by Horowitz, the peculiarities of cleft countries present particular challenges, for impeccable democratic procedures may well lead to dramatic forms of exclusion because of the

interplay between the rules of the game and the demography of countries. See Horowitz (1994, 45–48).

3. Since Alexis de Toqueville, scholars of very different schools have praised this asset of federalism. For example, see; Oates (1972, 35–45); Duchacek (1987); Horowitz (1985, 601–28); Elazar (1987; 1993, 190–95); Burgess (1993); Stepan (1997, 1999).

4. Hechter's argument (1975, 1985, 1992) is that where a "cultural division of labor" induces social stratification, thus producing an "internal colonialism," the exploited group may develop a self-consciousness that enables it to overcome the problems of collective action and act to increase its own autonomy. The willingness to go through the route of secessionism depends, however, on its economic interests which, in turn, are linked to its market position. The more groups are dependent on the union market, the less they will be eager to secede. This explains why, in general, industrial workers are less prone to secede than agricultural workers or professionals. This theory, however, has a limited applicability, since it is hardly pertinent to Western democracies, even considering Hecther's further distinction between "hierarchic" and "sectional" divisions of labor.

5. Horowitz defines secessionist groups in broad terms, embracing all movements seeking a separate region within an existing state, as well as those seeking a separate and independent state (1985, 232).

6. On the grounds that they do not have important territorial cleavages, this selection leaves prominent federal systems such as the United States and Germany off.

REFERENCES

Burgess, Michael. 1993. Federalism and Federation: A Reappraisal. In *Comparative Federalism and Federation: Competing Traditions and Future Directions*, ed. Michael Burgess and Alain-G. Gagnon, 3–14. New York: Harvester Wheatsheaf.

Calhoun, Craig J. 1997. *Nationalism.* Buckingham: Open University Press.

Cohen, Frank S. 1997. Proportional versus Majoritarian Ethnic Conflict Management in Democracies. *Comparative Political Studies* 30, no. 5: 607–30.

Connor, Walker. 1994. *Ethnonationalism: The Quest for Understanding.* Princeton, N.J.: Princeton University Press.

Dahl, Robert A. 1986. *Democracy, Identity, and Equality.* Oslo: Norwegian University Press.

De Winter, Lieven. 1998. Conclusion: A Comparative Analysis of the Electoral, Office, and Policy Success of Ethnoregionalist Parties. In *Regionalist Parties in Western Europe*, ed. Lieven De Winter and Huri Türsan, 204–47. London: Routledge.

Dion, Stéphane. 1996. Why is Secession Difficult in Well-Established Democracies? *British Journal of Political Science* 26, no. 2: 269–83.

Duchacek, Ivo D. 1987. *Comparative Federalism: The Territorial Dimension of Politics.* 2d ed. Lanham, Md.: University Press of America.

Elazar, Daniel J. 1987. *Exploring Federalism.* Tuscaloosa: University of Alabama Press.

———. 1993. International and Comparative Federalism. *PS: Political Science and Politics* 26, no. 2: 190–95.

Guibernau, Monserrat. 1995. Spain: A Federation in the Making? In *Federalism: The Multiethnic Challenge*, ed. Graham Smith, 239–54. London: Longman.

Gurr, Ted R. 2000. *Peoples versus States: Minorities at Risk in the New Century.* Washington, D.C.: United States Institute of Peace Press.

Hale, Henry E. 1998. Secession from Ethnofederal Systems: A Statistical Study of Russia, India, and Ethiopia. Paper presented at the 1998 Annual Meeting of the American Political Science Association, Boston, Mass., September 3–6.

Hechter, Michael. 1975. *Internal Colonialism: The Celtic Fringe in British National Development, 1536–1966.* Berkeley: University of California Press.

———. 1985. Internal Colonialism Revisited. In *New Nationalisms in the Developed West*, ed. Edward A. Tiryakian and Ronald Rogowski, 267–83. Boston: Allen and Unwin.

———. 1992. The Dynamics of Secession. *Acta Sociologica* 35, no. 4: 267–83.

Herbst, Jeffrey. 2000. *States and Power in Africa: Comparative Lessons in Power and Control.* Princeton, N.J.: Princeton University Press.

Horowitz, Donald H. 1981. Patterns of Ethnic Separatism. *Comparative Studies in Society and History* 23, no. 2: 165–95.

———. 1985. *Ethnic Groups in Conflict.* Berkeley: University of California Press.

———. 1994. Democracy in Divided Societies. In *Nationalism, Ethnic Conflict and Democracy*, ed. Larry Diamond and Marc F. Plattner, 35–55. Baltimore: Johns Hopkins University Press.

Huntington, Samuel P. 1996. *The Clash of Civilizations and the Remaking of World Order.* New York: Simon & Schuster.

Inglehart, Ronald. 1977. *The Silent Revolution: Changing Values and Political Styles Among Western Publics.* Princeton, N.J.: Princeton University Press.

Keating, Michael. 1998. *The New Regionalism in Western Europe: Territorial Restructuring and Political Change.* Cheltenham: Edward Elgar.

Lane, Jan-Erik, David McKay, and Kenneth Newton. 1997. *Political Data Handbook: OECD Countries.* 2d ed. Oxford: Oxford University Press.

Lijphart, Arend. 1999. *Patterns of Democracy: Government Forms and Performance in Thirty-Six Countries.* New Haven, Conn.: Yale University Press.

Lijphart, Arend, Ronald Rogowski, and R. Kent Weaver. 1993. Separation of Powers and Cleavage Management. In *Do Institutions Matter? Government Capabilities in the United States and Abroad*, ed. R. Kent Weaver and Bert A. Rockman, 302–44. Washington, D.C.: The Brookings Institution.

Newman, Saul. 1996. *Ethnoregional Conflict in Democracies: Mostly Ballots, Rarely Bullets.* Westport, Conn.: Greenwood.

Oates, Wallace. 1972. *Fiscal Federalism.* New York: Harcourt, Brace, Jovanovich.

Riker, William H. 1964. *Federalism: Origin, Operation, Significance.* Boston: Little, Brown.

———. 1975. Federalism. In *Handbook of Political Science.* Vol. 5, *Governmental Institutions and Processes*, ed. Fred J. Greenstein and Nelson Polsby, 93–172. Reading, Mass.: Addison-Wesley.

———. 1993. Federalism. In *A Companion to Contemporary Political Philosophy*, ed. Robert Goodin and Phillip Pettit, 508–14. Cambridge, Mass.: Blackwell.

Rokkan, Stein. 1973. Cities, States, Nations: A Dimensional Model for the Study of Contrasts in Development. In *Building States and Nations*, ed. Stein Rokkan and S. Eisenstadt, 1:73–97. Beverly Hills, Calif.: Sage

Rothstein, Bo. 2000. Trust, Social Dilemmas and Collective Memories: On the Rise and Decline of the Swedish Model. Paper presented at the 2000 Annual Meeting of the American Political Science Association, Washington, D.C., August 31–September 3.

Stepan, Alfred. 1997. Toward a Comparative Analysis of Democracy and Federalism: Demos Constraining and Demos Enabling Federations. Paper presented at the XVII World Congress of the International Political Science Association, Seoul, Korea, August 17–22.

———. 1999. Federalism and Democracy: Beyond the U.S. Model. *Journal of Democracy* 10, no. 4: 19–34.

Tilly, Charles. 1990. *Coercion, Capital, and European States: AD 990–1990.* Cambridge, Mass.: Basil Blackwell.

Türsan, Huri. 1998. Introduction: Ethnoregionalist Parties as Ethnic Entrepreneurs. In *Regionalist Parties in Western Europe,* ed. Lieven De Winter and Huri Türsan, 1–16. London: Routledge.

Van Evera, Stephen. 1994. Hypotheses on Nationalism and War. *International Security* 18, no. 4: 5–39.

Wallensteen, Peter, and Margareta Sollenberg. 2001. Armed Conflict, 1989–2000. *Journal of Peace Research,* 38, no. 5: 629–44.

Weaver, R. Kent. 1992. Political Institutions and Canada's Constitutional Crisis. In *The Collapse of Canada?* ed. R. Kent Weaver, 7–75. Washington, D.C.: The Brookings Institution.

Weber, Eugene. 1977. *Turning Peasants into Frenchmen: The Modernization of Rural France, 1870–1914.* London: Chatto & Windus.

Weber, Max. 1958 [1919]. Politics as a Vocation. In *From Max Weber: Essays in Sociology,* ed. H. H. Gerth and C. Wright Mills, 77–128. New York: Oxford University Press.

Young, Robert A. 1994. The Political Economy of Secession: The Case of Quebec. *Constitutional Political Economy* 5, no. 2: 221–45.

Part I/Advanced Industrial Democracies

CHAPTER ONE

Switzerland

Territorial Cleavage Management as Paragon and Paradox

André Bächtiger and Jürg Steiner

Karl Deutsch (1976) once described Switzerland as a "paradigmatic case of political integration," and, compared to other countries with such linguistic and religious diversity, the modern Swiss polity does appear well integrated. Apart from the Jura conflict, it has experienced no violent and disruptive territorial conflicts since a short civil war between Protestant liberals and Catholic conservatives in 1847. Yet, the absence of disruptive conflicts does not necessarily indicate harmonious relationships between the different cleavage groups. French and Italian speakers have regularly expressed feelings of distance, marginalization, and incomprehension toward German speakers (du Bois 1999; Ceschi 1991). While the religious cleavage has gradually withered away since World War II, the linguistic cleavage, particularly between French and German speakers, has deepened considerably over the past decades. Not only do French speakers have political preferences that differ from those of the majority of German speakers, they are also often outvoted in a number of crucial policy areas. The vote against the European Economic Area (EEA) in 1992, for example, led to violent polemics from French speakers. Nonetheless, political stability in Switzerland has remained high and none of its cleavage groups has ever sincerely questioned the unity of the federation or engaged in disruptive protest. This leaves us with a strangely divided situation: the comparativist, concentrating on the happy outcomes, might still consider Switzerland a paragon of conflict management; yet the presence of recurring divisions and serious management failures, which in other contexts are at the root of disruptive territorial conflict, make Switzerland an ambiguous, indeed paradoxical, case of cleavage management.

This chapter begins by examining the Swiss paradox and asks how political institutions, in particular federalism, made their imprint on the management of the territorially based cleavages of religion and language. It will then analyze Swiss cleavage management from a sociological or constructivist perspective and from the perspective of historical institutionalism. Here, the focus is first on the discourse surrounding and legitimizing the multicultural political order and the related process of identity building. Then, we will examine whether historical patterns of institution building yielded longer-term effects. Finally, the chapter asks to what extent other noninstitutional factors (crosscutting cleavages, socioeconomic differences) contributed to the favorable outcomes in Switzerland.

We argue first that Switzerland's institutional setting (strong delegatory mechanisms, strong legislative veto points, and consociational arenas) provided for a large discretionary range of autonomous policy making for cleavage groups and their strong influence on the politics of the central state. Second, a discourse revolving around the political and multicultural character of the Swiss nation enhanced conciliation and coexistence among the different cleavage groups. Third, at the critical juncture of state building in Europe, Switzerland retained its medieval polycephalic structure, rejecting the model of the strong, hierarchical state suppressing cultural differences. We end with an argument that helps to resolve the Swiss paradox: while the success of Swiss cleavage management owes much to formal institutions, it cannot be explained without taking into account the informal and constructivist aspect of its institutions. The identity-based preferences of political elites for the maintenance of a multicultural Switzerland—coupled with the support of large majorities in all cleavage groups for the political order and its institutions—has led to a willingness to contain growing divisions rather than engaging in disruptive conflict.

Historical Evolution of Territorial Cleavages

When "Switzerland" began to evolve as a loose alliance of *Orte* (cantons) in the thirteenth century,[1] it was culturally quite homogeneous. The founding *Orte* were all Catholic and German-speaking. The most serious conflict was that between the rural agricultural *Orte* and the urban manufacturing *Orte*. With the Reformation in the sixteenth century, this division was overlaid by the religious cleavage between Catholics and Protestants. From the sixteenth to the eighteenth centuries, four civil wars were waged between the Protestant and the Catholic *Orte*. Each ended with an advance in consociational mechanisms and a precarious balance between the two religious blocs, with the Protestants being slightly more numerous than the Catholics (Altermatt 1989, 134).[2]

Linguistically, Switzerland remained overwhelmingly German-speaking until the French Revolution. French- and Italian-speaking territories were either allies without equal rights or subject territories. By the eighteenth century, a total of thirteen cantons had joined the Swiss Confederation. The Confederation of the thirteen "old" cantons was an extremely loose political system, more a system of alliances than a political system (Mesmer 1997, 14). It was based on federal treaties (*Bundesbriefe*) that contained provisions for mutual military and legal help as well as an arbitral court to settle disputes among the *Orte* in an accommodative way (Körner 1983, 37). There were no central authorities except a Diet where the delegates appointed by the *Orte* met. Decisions of the Diet had to be unanimous and decision making was slow and prone to deadlock. The implementation of decisions was left to the *Orte*, and even unanimous decisions were frequently ignored. State-building activities, such as tax collection and the buildup of military forces at the central level, were completely absent. Distinguishing itself from the vigorous state-building efforts in many parts of Europe, the Confederation retained its medieval polycephalic structure with a chain of distinctive centers with no first-city dominance. Nevertheless, patriotic feelings toward the Confederation can be traced back to late medieval times (Im Hof 1991, 19).

When the armies of Napoleon invaded Switzerland in 1798, France installed a new regime recasting Switzerland as a centrally governed satellite republic; the *Orte* were abolished and the country was reorganized into administrative units. It was also at that time that Switzerland really became multilingual, with the French-speaking territory of Vaud and the Italian-speaking Ticino obtaining independence. Confronted with the choice of remaining in the Swiss fold or joining France or the Italian Cisalpine Republic, the elites of the French- and Italian-speaking territories opted for the former, hoping to gain more participation rights and more political influence in Switzerland. In addition, the Protestant French speakers in Switzerland felt culturally distant from Catholic France (Schoch 1998, 21–22). The trilingual Grisons (German, Italian, and Romansch speakers), a confederation of independent communes loosely allied with the Confederation, also joined the Helvetic Republic. The government of the Helvetic Republic extended far-reaching equality to all three languages. The Helvetic Republic tried to overcome the denominational question by proclaiming freedom of conscience and emphasizing principles such as concord and freedom (Stadler 1987, 86). Still, the new state faced fierce resistance. The Catholic territories of central Switzerland, fearing atheism, had to be forced into the new state. Moreover, a large part of the citizenry revolted against the uniformity of the new state and viewed the Helvetic Republic as an artificial and foreign creation.

Napoleon Bonaparte, who at the time tried to consolidate his rule by relying on traditional legitimization forms, decided to end the central state experiment. He declared that unless Switzerland existed as a federal state it would not exist at all (Mesmer 1997, 21) and ordered in the *Mediationsakte* (Mediation Act) of 1803 that the cantons should regain their sovereignty. The former subject territories such as the Vaud and the Ticino preserved their independence and became new cantons. At the Congress of Vienna in 1815, the old political order of strong and autonomous cantons within a loosely organized confederation was confirmed. The Congress of Vienna also allowed the return to Switzerland of its ancient allies, Valais, Neuchâtel, and Geneva, which took their place as independent cantons. The language composition of Switzerland became about 75 percent German speakers, 20 percent French speakers, 5 percent Italian speakers, and less than one percent Romansch speakers; the figures have barely changed since.

The restored old order was only short-lived. The emerging entrepreneurial and bourgeois elites did not accept its illiberal social and economic elements. During the Enlightenment and the French Revolution, they had organized in numerous, mostly multilingual associations that aimed at the consolidation of Helvetic bonds and established a common set of national and liberal values among the new Swiss elites. When the July Revolution broke out in France in 1830, they took advantage of the moment: several cantons adopted new constitutions proclaiming popular sovereignty, division of powers, and freedom of trade. However, a proposal for a renewal of the federal treaty (*Bundesvertrag*) in 1832, with a national Swiss executive, an independent court, and federal competencies for a number of economic issues, found no approval. The conservative forces considered it too far-reaching while the liberal forces considered it too moderate (see Maissen 1999, 66ff.).

In the 1840s, Switzerland was on the verge of civil war. The confrontation revolved around the appropriate political, social, and economic order (Mesmer 1997, 25)—with linguistic conflicts playing no role. The liberal movement, mainly Protestant, was challenged by the Catholic and conservative forces who wanted to preserve the status quo with largely independent cantons and saw unbridled "liberalism" and the drive toward Swiss unification as a threat to their religiously anchored way of life and their traditional forms of societal and political organization (Moos 1997).

In 1845, seven Catholic and conservative cantons signed a separate treaty, the *Sonderbund*, to defend their common interests. The subsequent decision of the *Sonderbund* cantons to leave the Diet was interpreted by the progressive cantons as a step toward secession. Fearing the intervention of conservative foreign powers, the liberal cantons decided to go to war. In a short civil war in 1847, the *Sonderbundskrieg*

(War of Secession), the liberal forces vanquished the Catholic and conservative forces. It was a war with few casualties and the principle of moderation prevailed (Remak 1997, 223). General Dufour, the commander of the liberal forces, even asked his troops to be tolerant toward the Catholic religion.

The victors of the war immediately engaged in drafting a new constitution. The drafting committee consisted largely of liberal politicians. Only three moderate conservative representatives were involved in the deliberations (Kölz 1992, 547–50) and Catholic extremists were completely excluded. Although the emerging state was clearly the product of liberal societal formation, the results of the constitutional deliberations nevertheless suggest that conservative forces were not ignored (Jorio 1998, 98–99). The drafters did not adopt extreme centralist positions and greatly limited the competencies of the new central state (Jorio 1997, 157). Cantons would retain their autonomy, freedom of worship was secured,[3] and it was unanimously proposed that the Swiss federation be trilingual:[4] no language could claim exclusiveness. These were mainly tactical moves to further the acceptance of the new state among the conservative federalists and to win them over for the planned referendum on the constitution (Kölz 1992, 578).

The new constitution was written in only a few weeks and then put to referendum: fifteen and a half of the cantons were in favor, six and a half against (all cantons of the *Sonderbund* with the exception of Lucerne and Fribourg)—a sign of Catholic opposition that was not to disappear. In Lucerne, the nonvoters were counted as votes in favor; in Fribourg the new liberal government did not even dare to take a vote. The notion of cantons "coming together" voluntarily (Stepan, this volume) does not stand up to historical scrutiny: the integration of the Catholic cantons conforms rather to a "coerced" coming together.

The Development of the Religious and Linguistic Cleavage

In the first years of the new federal state, relations between the liberals and the Catholic conservatives were by no means harmonious. The Catholics felt like second-class citizens, a barely tolerated, underprivileged minority. Religious conflict rose again in the *Kulturkampf* (cultural struggle) in the 1870s, when the Catholic Church tried to enforce the authority of the pope in all aspects of Catholic life. But, in the following decades, tensions slowly cooled off, and by the 1960s, relations between the denominational groups were quite harmonious.

The linguistic cleavage followed a different course. Tensions between the French and German speakers were particularly high during World War I, when the French speakers sided with France, and the German speakers sided with Germany. The relationship between the Italian speakers and the central state was occasionally quite turbulent, plagued by complaints of marginalization and neglect. In the 1920s and 1930s, the

Italian-speaking canton confronted the federal authorities with demands for enhanced economic and cultural protection (*rivendicazioni ticinesi*). The most severe language problem, however, arose in connection with the Jura, a Catholic, French-speaking minority in the Protestant, German-speaking canton of Berne. The relationship between the Jura and the majority of the canton was already stormy in the nineteenth century and continued to be so until the 1970s. Though conflict among the linguistic groups never achieved the centrality of the religious conflict, it has become salient since the 1990s, which we will discuss in the concluding section.

The Institutional Setting of the Swiss Federal State

Self-Rule

The constitution of 1848 introduced a symmetrical federalist arrangement with a large degree of autonomy for the cantons. While article 1 of the constitution guarantees the existence and sovereignty of the cantons,[5] article 3 involves a general subsidiarity principle, assigning all tasks not explicitly delegated to the central state to the cantons. Cantons are free to elect their authorities and are not politically controlled by the federal state. However, the state builders at the same time wanted to eradicate the sources of the *Sonderbund* (Maissen 1999, 251). They ruled that cantonal constitutions could not breach the federal constitution, and forbade special political treaties among the cantons. In addition, cantons are required to have a republican form of government (art. 6). Initially, the Confederation was only responsible for foreign affairs, national defense, the currency, customs, and the postal and the railway services. But, with the establishment of the welfare state after World War II and the adoption of the constitutional provisions on economic policy in 1947, broad responsibilities in these fields were attributed to the Federation (Vatter 1999).

The tasks and competencies of cantons are primarily education, religion, the police, churches, health, energy, regional construction and planning, and regional economic policy. With regard to language policies, the *principle of territoriality* guarantees the cantons linguistic sovereignty, granting the right of each language territory to protect and defend its own linguistic character and to ensure its survival. Furthermore, cantons play a very prominent role in the implementation of federal law. Since the Swiss federal administration has no regional offices in the cantons—central state actors also refrained from following the American model of developing a parallel central administration—it is the cantons that implement federal laws. In 1848, the drafters of the constitution had a model of dual federalism in mind that would assign exclusive competencies to either the central state or the cantons (Bucher 1977, 996). However, the principle of dual federalism was never fully realized in practice, and with the rising of the intervention and welfare state, the system of administrative federalism increasingly began to resemble the model of *cooperative federalism,* with the center providing the basic legislation and the cantons in charge of the implementation. Cooperative federalism has simultaneously led to broad financial transfer payments from the federation to the cantons—a massive transfer of about 29 percent of all federal expenditures is allocated to cantons. About 70 percent of these transfers is linked to clearly specified tasks; the remaining 30 percent of transfers is allocated according to the discretion of the cantons. Swiss federalism, furthermore, is marked by a vision of solidarity rather than by competition. The solidaristic side of Swiss federalism was further institutionalized in 1958–59, when a constitutionally anchored system of financial transfers from rich to poor cantons was introduced (see Schild 1971, 193ff.). Finally, fiscal autonomy is very high in comparative perspective (Lane, McKay, and Newton 1997, 86): only about a third of all public monies is currently spent at the federal level; the other two-thirds is spent at either the cantonal or the community level.

Shared Rule
LIMITED GOVERNMENT INSTITUTIONS

— *Bicameralism.* The bicameral Swiss legislative system was mainly an institutional copy of the American bicameral system (see Netzle 1998). The adoption of bicameralism was the most controversial issue when the new constitution was drafted, since many drafters feared that a second chamber might lead to slow decision-making processes or even to deadlock (Kölz 1992, 557ff.). Still, representatives from smaller, rural cantons insisted that a second chamber be established to better protect their interests. The council of states is composed of two representatives from each canton, designated by the cantonal parliaments until the 1920s, since then elected by the people according to majoritarian rule (see Heger 1990, 111–14).[6] Unlike the Diet, its representatives are not bound by instructions; each votes independently. This rule was also controversial, but it was adopted for the sake of effective decision making. Unlike in many other federal states, the council of states and the national council have equal power—the people's chamber's decisions cannot be denied. Since every full canton elects two councilors to the small chamber, small cantons are greatly overrepresented and the Swiss system is highly *demos*-constraining.[7]

Legislative Veto and Innovation Points. In 1848, a mandatory referendum was introduced for a total revision of the constitution and for the adoption of new constitutional amendments. For passage a referendum needed support from both a majority of the national electorate and a majority of the cantons. The mandatory referendum now also applies to decisions concerning some international treaties as well as membership in supranational organizations and systems of collective security. Since 1874, most parliamentary acts and regulations can be challenged in an optional referendum if the necessary number of 50,000 signatures is collected. While referendums are often considered a majoritarian instrument, the ability of a small group of voters to launch a referendum has proved to be an important power device for minorities and the true veto point in the system (see Vatter 2000). Moreover, a minimum of eight cantons can challenge parliamentary bills and 100,000 citizens can demand a constitutional amendment or propose the alteration or removal of an existing constitutional provision by signing a formal petition. Cantons also have the right to make petitions to the federal chambers. If one chamber rejects a cantonal petition or both chambers do not find a common position, the petition fails.

Consociational Mechanisms

A first consociational mechanism is the preparliamentary consultation procedure, where bills are submitted to a number of political and societal actors, among them the cantons. In a first stage, an expert commission crafts a first draft of the bill; next, the political and societal actors evaluate the draft. Although the federal administration only collects the different opinions and then prepares a bill, the consultation procedure is the locus where corporate actors express their interests and where consensual solutions are crafted.

A second consociational mechanism is found in the composition of the federal council. The federal council, elected by a joint session of the two chambers of the parliament, is a collegial body chosen on a consociational rather than a federal basis (Elazar 1987, 208). An unwritten rule requires that it include at least two French or Italian speakers. This "voluntary" proportional rule was adopted within both the executive and the federal administration, but did not apply, initially, to the Catholic minority (Altermatt 1989, 129). It was only in the 1950s that the Catholic conservatives attained parity with the Free Democrats (the former liberals) in the federal council.[8]

Analysis of Conflict Management

Self-rule

The large degree of self-rule embodied in Swiss federalism proved to be an important means of conflict management. Far-reaching cantonal autonomy compensated for the fact that symmetrical arrangements grant no special rights to the cleavage groups. It allowed both the Catholics and the linguistic minorities to manage the affairs in their cantons independently, especially with regard to such sensitive issues as education and religion. The Catholics, after their defeat in the civil war and the subsequent installation of liberal governments in the cantons that attempted to secede, quickly managed to regain executive and legislative majorities in their homelands. Not only did the homeland cantons serve them as refuges in the unwanted new central state, the Catholic elites also made use of the substantial cantonal autonomy to seize control of the cantonal socialization apparatus (particularly the education curriculum) to preserve their grip on the Catholic population and to develop a Catholic subculture (Altermatt 1989, 1995; Kriesi 1995, 319). For the linguistic minorities, in turn, the territorial principle and the educational autonomy allowed them to preserve their linguistic and cultural differences. The territorial principle stipulates that people who live in another linguistic region have a duty to assimilate and learn the language of the respective canton with no possibility of being instructed in another official language (the exceptions are the linguistically mixed cantons, where bilingual schooling is the rule). In the eyes of the French and Italian speakers, the territorial principle always constituted an essential protective barrier against "Germanization" (see Schoch 1998, 51ff.; Ceschi 1991, 62).

Although the central state has gained power over time (Germann 1999, 392), there has not been a general centralization trend (Nüssli 1985).[9] Indeed, the Swiss constitution prevents the central state from assuming new powers without a constitutional amendment (Linder 1994, 42–43). With no implementation apparatus at its disposal, the major means of federal control are the subsidies offered to the cantons. This leaves much discretionary power to the cantons, for they can reject a particular subsidy if they do not want to implement the goals of the federation. Thus, cantons have the power to adapt federal policy programs to their particular needs and preferences (Schenkel and Serdült 1999, 472; see also Kissling-Näf and Knöpfel 1992). The institutional framework induces the federal authorities to negotiate with the cantons (Linder 1999, 347) and, given the necessity to maintain cooperation over the long term, the federation prefers cooperative to conflictual strategies (Kissling-Naef and Knöpfel 1992; see also Neidhart 1975, 22).

Furthermore, a considerable share of tax revenues, together with the transfer payments from the federation, provides the cantons with the financial means needed to pursue their own policy projects. The system of financial transfers reallocates substantive resources to poorer cantons—among them a number of French-speaking, rural, and mountain cantons. This helps to reduce economic disparities among cleavage groups. However, the solidaristic side of Swiss federalism should not be exaggerated: not only have economic disparities among rich and poor cantons continued to grow (Dafflon 1995, 93ff.), there is also considerable tax competition among the cantons, often to the detriment of poorer cantons who cannot afford to have lower levels of taxation than the rich cantons.

Shared Rule

LIMITED GOVERNMENT INSTITUTIONS

Bicameralism. Though intended to protect the interests of cantons, councilors of state rarely make use of their blocking power and the relationship between the council of states and the national council does not appear to be very conflictual (Trivelli 1974). Members of the two chambers frequently defend the same group and party interests (Heger 1990). The nonconflictual relations of the national council and the council of states can be ascribed mainly to institutional details and actor constellations. Because councilors of state are not bound by instructions, they do not have to represent cantonal executive interests. Since both national councilors and councilors of state are elected in the same district, they have to be responsive to the same constituent interests. Finally, the two chambers have never differed in their partisan majorities.

However, it would be false to present the council of states as a mere partisan chamber unwilling to protect and forward cantonal interests. First, there have been occasions when the council of state did use its blocking power and furthered the interests of cleavage groups (e.g., when opposing the establishment of the Federal University in Zürich in 1854). Second, the council of states is generally less centralizing than the national council (Trivelli 1974, 513–14), and more receptive to cantonal status quo interests as well as regional economic interests (Wiesli and Linder 2000, 40).[10] Third, due to its composition, the council of states protects rural cantons far better than the national council (Vatter 1999, 85ff.;). Finally, the councilors of state feel much more responsible toward their cantons and less to parties and interest groups than do members of the national council. This is particularly true for French-speaking councilors (Wiesli and Linder 2000, 20ff.; see also Hertig 1980). Overall, the council of states plays an ambivalent role in managing territorial conflicts: it is not the prime venue for territorial interests, but occasionally it has functioned as a veto institution for territorial cleavage groups.

Legislative Veto and Innovation Points. In the initial stages of the federation, politics at the central state level conformed closely to the majoritarian model. However, the introduction of the optional referendum gave Catholics and linguistic minorities the opportunity to counteract the majoritarian features of the early federation. Forming a veto coalition was easy, as its mobilization required only the common rejection of a proposal and not a common political position (Neidhart 1970, 65–66). The effects of the optional referendum were immediate: within two decades twenty federal bills were challenged by way of referendum, and the liberal government was defeated fifteen times (Trechsel 2000, 142). This forced the governing liberals to become more conciliatory and compromising. Needing the permanent support of the Catholic conservatives, the liberals also ceded a seat in the federal council in 1891. This inclusion and co-optation strategy succeeded (Neidhart 1970, 75–77) because it was a symbolic first step toward equality and recognition, a major goal of the Catholic minority. In the following years, a closer, more cooperative relationship between the liberals and Catholics developed, with the goal of building a bourgeois bloc against socialism (Altermatt 1995, 437–38). In the long term, the introduction of the referendum produced a steady danger of a veto for policy proposals in a popular vote (Neidhart 1970, 292). Evidence suggests that political parties have only partial control over their voters in referendum votes, as voters frequently view policy issues differently than political and interest group representatives. Furthermore, referendum votes are frequently negative: the rejection rate in optional referenda between 1947 and 1995 was 43 percent (23 percent in case of the mandatory referendum; Trechsel and Sciarini 1999, 106).

Two subsidiary factors exacerbate these effects: first, it is easier to mobilize the opponents of legislation than its proponents; second, voter turnout in referenda votes is low, which means that the voters who turned out may be skewed samples of the rest of the population. Uncertainty creates institutional pressures for risk-averse policy makers to adopt cooperative strategies and build large supporting coalitions for policy proposals (Neidhart 1970; Linder 1999, 295–97).

The system of direct democracy and the referendum in particular have proven to be major barriers to centralization efforts, as citizens have been very reluctant to extend competencies of the federal state. While the optional referendum means that cleavage groups' interests are taken into account when policies are designed, the system of direct democracy still involves pitfalls for cleavage management. First, a policy proposal favoring the interests of minorities may be challenged or subject to a mandatory referendum; second, a policy proposal (even a compromise solution) might not match the preferences of minorities but still may be accepted by a majority of voters. A study by Kriesi et al. (1996, 31ff.) reveals that such failures of cleavage management do occur, but not frequently. In an analysis of popular votes between 1872 and 1994, there were twenty-nine cases where clear-cut voting differences between French- and German-speaking cantons appeared (calculated as voting differences between the two groups exceeding 25 percent); in fifteen of the twenty-nine cases, the French-speaking cantons were outvoted. Yet, in the period from 1870 and 1920, French speakers managed to outvote the German speakers more frequently than vice versa (eight against six cases). However, this only occurred when French and Italian speakers formed a closed bloc with a high voter turnout and the issue was hotly disputed among the German speakers (Wili 1988, 231–32). As time passed, both the French- and Italian-speaking cantons (Kriesi et al. 1996, 20ff.) and the cantons that seceded in the civil war (Wili 1988, 229) came to be outvoted less often. Direct democratic votes thus did not undermine cleavage management by regularly forcing cleavage groups to bend to the desires of the majority.

The other institutional devices designed for the protection of cleavage groups—the majority of the cantons clause, the cantonal referendum, the cantonal and the popular initiative—have not proven critical to cleavage management. The majority of the cantons clause, aimed at protecting cantonal interests in direct democratic votes, played a minor role. Between 1848 and 2000, there were only eight collisions of a popular majority and a federalist majority. Yet, in the few cases when the popular majority was overruled by a majority of the cantons, it was mainly the smaller, rural cantons of the former *Sonderbund* that benefited (Wili 1988, 211, 210). Cantonal referenda are also extremely difficult to orchestrate and they have never been successfully used (see Wili 1988, 341). Cantonal initiatives were rarely used before the 1970s, but since then have become more numerous, even though their success rate remains low (Vatter 1999, 90–92). The popular initiative was rarely used by the Catholics and linguistic minorities as a power device, though, as mentioned, the Catholic conservatives (together with the Social Democrats) made use of the popular initiative to bring about a change in the electoral system from winner-take-all to proportionality.

CONSOCIATIONAL MECHANISMS

The consociational mechanism of the preparliamentary consultation procedure is a direct consequence of the threat of the referendum. Research shows that the influence of cantons in this process is generally strong. Cantonal authorities were called to participate in more than three out of four expert commissions and nine out of ten consultation procedures in the 1970s (Germann 1981, 63; 1986, 350). Though economic interest groups are better armed to influence policy designs than the cantons,[11] cantons can exert considerable influence on federal policies, especially when their administrations are equipped with sufficient resources (Neidhart 1975, 34) and central state authorities depend on the cantons for implementation. The small and economically weak cantons, however, often lack the necessary expertise to evaluate complex federal projects and thus may not always be able to defend their interests (Vatter 1999).

The exact contribution of the federal council to cleavage management is difficult to evaluate, as no systematic empirical studies are available. Nonetheless, two points can be stressed: although the federal council is elected by the parliament, federal councilors, once in office, are almost always reelected (only two were dismissed in the nineteenth century) and the parliamentary actors seem to have given up their right to dismiss them (Riklin and Ochsner 1984, 81). Secure in their offices, Swiss federal councilors can play a mediating role in conflict management and be receptive to the claims of cleavage groups—which, at least in recent times, occurs frequently. Though votes are taken by majority rule and there is no guarantee that all interests are taken into consideration (Linder 1999, 226–27), there is a tradition of collegial decision making. On the other hand, the federal council is heavily constrained by institutions of direct democracy and the actors in parliament, who are free to support the proposals of the council or reject them. From this perspective, the Swiss central government is a rather weak actor with no possibility of enforcing its political goals and preferences.

Besides institutional veto points, cleavage group protection and integration can be greatly furthered by the party system (Horowitz 1985). Switzerland, unlike Belgium or Canada, has no parties organized around the linguistic cleavages. All major parties are represented in the different linguistic regions and this prevents linguistic differences from being used for political goals (Ladner 1999, 218). The fact that the party system is weakly centralized matters too. Cantonal parties are much stronger than central parties and exert a strong influence on national politics (Kriesi 1995, 144). Whenever a national party takes a position on an important issue, it has to be approved by the cantonal party organizations, which means that the interests of cleavage groups can never be ignored (Armingeon 2000).

We conclude that the institutional setting of the Swiss federal state did indeed contribute to the successful management of territorial cleavages. While the limited scope of federal competencies enables cleavage groups to engage in autonomous policy making and helps to preserve their cultural differences, the legislative veto point of the referendum sets the consensus barriers at the federal level very high and results in policies that incorporate cleavage groups' interests. While, historically, federalist self-rule avoided conflicts by putting sensitive policy issues in the hands of cleavage groups, it was not, in itself, the panacea for managing territorial conflicts. In its early stages, the federal polity had strong majoritarian features and the Catholics could not always prevent unwanted policies from being adopted at the central level. Only the introduction of the optional referendum turned the Swiss polity into a negotiation democracy with consociational arenas and the ubiquitous practice of negotiated compromises (Neidhart 1970). Thus it is strong cantonal autonomy coupled with the veto point of the optional referendum that provides for the comprehensive protection of cleavage groups' interests.

On the other hand, institutions per se did not determine policy outcomes. Their effects were always connected to a specific constellation of actors and behavioral logics, or they were dependent on institutional details. The bicameral chamber, the council of states, for example, turned out to be a rather mute veto institution for territorial interests. The optional referendum as a power device for minority groups did not constitute a strict veto point. The cleavage groups depended—at least in the beginning—on specific constituencies in direct democratic votes to block policies (later on, due to the uncertain outcomes of direct democratic votes, their demands were mostly included from the beginning of the process of legislative design). The cantonal implementation process constitutes a third example: the federal authorities refrained from developing more powerful controls over policy outcomes. This was not an institutional necessity, but rather a conscious strategy to avoid massive political resistance and subsequent policy deadlocks (see Wälti 1996, 133). Thus, the Swiss case strongly suggests that cleavage management through federalist and other nonmajoritarian institutions can be successful only if political actors choose to make them work.

Multicultural Nation-building

To function effectively, any political order must enjoy legitimacy and the loyalty of those groups and individuals who are in the domain of its authority (e.g., Rokkan and Urwin 1983, 166). As John Dryzek (1996, 104) puts it, no institution can operate without an associated, supportive discourse. This takes us to sociological or constructivist institutionalism with its focus on the identity- and preference-building effects of institutions (DiMaggio and Powell 1991; March and Olsen 1989, 126; see also Hall and Taylor 1996, 939). However, one should not see rationalist and constructivist conceptions of institutions as mutually exclusive. Legitimizing techniques and supportive discourses can also be described as economizing devices—introduced as deliberate strategies by political entrepreneurs in order to further their political goals and ambitions—by which individuals come to terms with their environment and are provided with a "worldview" so that the costs of maintenance of an existing order are significantly reduced (North 1981, 49; see also Rothstein 2000).

One of the key legitimizing and integrating devices of the modern age was nationalism. With the decline of religiosity, the rapid changes brought on by industrialization, and the rise of the hierarchical state, a new rationale for community, a new legitimization of the state, and a new integration ideology was needed (Schulze 1994, 172). What is often overlooked, however, is the interplay between nationalism (a process of internal cultural homogenization and external cultural boundary building [Flora et al. 1983, 16ff.]), and cleavage management in multicultural societies. When the conception of *Kulturnation* or ethnolinguistic nationalism is applied to a multicultural setting, this often means that the dominant ethnic group pursues policies that are designed to repress and eliminate multilingualism and multiculturalism systematically (Linz and Stepan 1996, 33ff.). Will Kymlicka's (normative) ideal is that states should develop a politics of multiculturalism to support diverse cultural groups and take an active interest in their societal reproduction (1999, 20ff.). This captures what happened in the Swiss context, where multilingualism and multiculturalism were turned into central pillars of nationhood.

When the new political order was formed in 1848, the conception of the "Swiss nation" was not very explicit: it rested mainly on principles such as unity, popular sovereignty, and liberal political rights while cultural elements such as language, ethnicity, and race were almost completely absent. The industrialization process and the rise of cultural nationalism in the neighboring states, however, prompted a process of nation building in Switzerland as well. The producers of the new national discourse were the liberal elite (Kriesi 1999, 23). Their goal was legitimizing and stabilizing the political order they had created in 1848. The conception of *Kulturnation* with its stress on linguistic and cultural homogeneity was hardly relevant to a setting like Switzerland, where the linguistic minorities had participated in the creation of the new state. Instead, multilingualism was encoded as an essential and even sacred attribute of "Swissness." The liberal Swiss constitutional lawyer, Carl Hilty (1875, 169), defined the Swiss nation as follows: "Neither race, nor tribal cooperation, neither common language and custom, nor nature of history have created the state of the Swiss Confederation. It has been formed rather as a contrast to all these great powers, originating in an idea, in a political thought and will." This voluntaristic and political conception of the Swiss nation was combined with a neutrality discourse in foreign politics, again with the goal of holding the various linguistic groups together (Schoch 1998, 35).

With the rapprochement of the liberals and the Catholic conservatives at the beginning of the 1890s, the new nationalism of the late nineteenth century adopted interconfessional characteristics as well (Jost 1998, 67). The year 1891 was used to commemorate the 600th anniversary of the mythical pact between the Confederates of central Switzerland in 1291. The elites stressed myths about the heroic struggles of the old Confederation, accompanied by images of alpine nature and direct democratic traditions. The nation builders could employ historical traditions to better integrate the public and appropriate patriotic feeling toward the old Confederation. Since the 1930s, the Swiss nation was also increasingly presented as federal and canton-friendly (von Greyerz 1953, 271). In the wake of World War II, we find the full elaboration of the political discourse on the Swiss nation with the "holy trinity" of direct democracy, federalism, and neutrality combined with the multicultural definition of Switzerland as a four-language nation (see also Sciarini, Hug, and Dupont 1997).

Switzerland's multicultural nationhood was enhanced by a discourse of mutual understanding and conciliation. The Swiss have always been able to reconcile their differences through mediation. Its basic feature was to define mutual understanding as the appropriate behavioral norm for coping with the diverse cleavage groups, and to stress that despite political quarrels and wars, the Swiss have always been able to reconcile and find a compromise through talking and mediation. As Carol Schmid notes, Swiss textbooks not only present consensus as the panacea of Swiss policy making, they also treat all of Switzerland's cultural groups with respect. Schmid found this not to be true of the textbooks of other multilingual countries, such as Canada (Schmid 1981, 80).

The question now is whether these discourses had an imprint on the cognitive scripts and the identities of the actors. Of course, we cannot track the evolution of identities, as data only exist for the most recent period, nor can we measure the relationships between discourses and identities. Yet, we can try to inventory traces of the discourses in the identities of actors. Dual identities seem to be very important. In fact, communal, cantonal, and regional identities outweigh national allegiance—especially among French and Italian speakers. In a 1996 survey, the majority of respondents in French- and Italian-speaking territories said that they belong foremost to their commune, canton, or linguistic region (61 percent and 58 percent, respectively), while only 18 percent and 22 percent of the French and Italian Swiss felt they belonged to Switzerland as a whole. The corresponding percentages for Swiss Germans were 43 percent and 34 percent, respectively (World Value Service 1995–96) However, it would be misleading to interpret these figures as hostile feelings toward the national state. To the contrary: as other studies suggest, there seems to be not much incompatibility among the various allegiances (e.g., Frei and Kerr 1974, 30–31). Moreover, large majorities (70–90 percent) in all linguistic groups declare that they are proud to be Swiss (Brunner and Sgier 1997, 111). This attachment and pride is based on a political rather than a cultural understanding of the nation, reflecting the discourse on the political character of the Swiss nation. Survey data indicate that people from all linguistic groups are particularly proud of the peculiarities of the Swiss institutional system (Univox Data Set 1991; see Armingeon 1999, 226): More than 70 percent say that they are proud of the institutions of direct democracy (78 percent of the initiative, 72 percent of referendum), 70 percent of the coexistence of diverse linguistic groups, 63 percent of federalism, 55 percent of the government including all major parties (*Konkordanz*). Neutrality is also highly valued (see Melich 1991, 8). Furthermore, the diverse linguistic groups do not feel very distant from each other. Although all linguistic groups feel closest to members of their own group, a majority in all linguistic groups state that they feel rather close to their confederates (Kriesi et al. 1996, 60–62). Moreover, Swiss Germans, who constitute a numerical majority, do not possess a majoritarian outlook. In a survey on young Swiss Germans, Schmid found that they not only underestimate their numerical strength but also seem willing to acknowledge Switzerland's diversity (Schmid 1981, 121). However, positive attitudes toward diversity and mutual understanding seem to be more prevalent among elites than among the public at large (McRae 1983, 107).

These findings suggest that Swiss nation builders have effectively created a discourse on the political nation that unites cleavage groups together through an emphasis on shared political values, while explicitly allowing cleavage groups to preserve their cultural identities. Moreover, they constructed cultural diversity as an opportunity and a source of enrichment rather than a problem. They constructed a "history of play" among the cleavage groups that "excluded" the "bad" past of conflict and violence, and instead emphasized the "good" past of mutual understanding, compromise, and conciliation. These discourses on the political, multicultural, and conciliatory nation were not the only existing discourses. Not only do we find a number of negative stereotypes among the linguistic groups; linguistic minorities also regularly exhibited feelings of being marginalized, misunderstood, and ignored (du Bois 1999, 35ff.; Ceschi 1991, 57). However, counterdiscourses have never dominated the public sphere, and when dissension grew, elite actors usually supported the moderation and depoliticization of intergroup differences (see Im Hof 1991, 206–8).[12]

History's Long Shadows

Following historical institutionalism, institutional analysis has to be susceptible to the critical role of timing as well as to path-dependent effects (Pierson 1996, 2000). The basic thrust of the historical institutionalist argument is that initial institutional choices can transform the environment in a way that produces institutional lock-in and groups that benefit from an institutional arrangement will resist change.

As described in our historical section, Switzerland retained its medieval polycephalic structure with a chain of distinctive centers, each with its own profile of elite groups. The abolition of the *Orte* during the Helvetic Republic met with fierce opposition from the old elites who lost their traditional power bases (see Braun 1984, 310–11) and the new centralized order did not find much acceptance among the citizenry either. However, the notion of a Switzerland deeply rooted in a federal political culture (e.g., Elazar 1993) captures only one part of the story. Federalist positions were often contested by centralists, but the latter were not politically powerful enough to enforce their vision on the new state emerging in 1848. For the management of territorial cleavages, this meant that the model of the strong, hierarchical state suppressing cultural differences had been rejected at an early stage of Swiss history.

The Nature of Cleavages

Territorial cleavage management can also be facilitated if the cleavages do not overlap with one another and if socioeconomic differences among cleavage groups are not too large (see Lijphart 1985, 1996; Horowitz 1985; Siaroff 2000).

It has become standard to comment upon the fortunate accident that linguistic and religious cleavages did not coincide in Switzerland (e.g., Kälin 1997; Linder 1997). However, this is not really relevant if one cleavage is perceived to be much more salient than the other (Steiner 1974, 265–68), as was the case in Switzerland. The evidence for the period since 1848 suggests a considerably greater salience of religious, social, and ideological divisions, and a correspondingly lower salience of linguistic divisions (McRae 1983, 114–15). Therefore, the crosscutting cleavage hypothesis may not fit Switzerland as well as is often thought.

It is significant that there were no outstanding disparities among the different cleavage groups in economic terms. For the French and German speakers, economic disparities are far greater within each group than between them. Nonetheless, one should not overlook the fact that there was constant talk among French and Italian speakers of economic colonization and "Germanization," as many key posts in Swiss industry were monopolized by German speakers. Moreover, the Ticino falls clearly below the economic averages for French and German Switzerland. Although the economic backwardness of the Ticino gave rise to claims for enhanced economic protection in the interwar period (*rivendicazioni ticinesi*), it did not lead to disruptive conflict or to the birth of autonomist or secessionist movements. The difficulties of the crosscutting and the socioeconomic difference hypotheses in accounting for the success of cleavage management in the Swiss context suggest the importance of the institutional, constructivist, and identity factors.

Current Strains in Cleavage Management

After World War II, Switzerland seemed to take a decisive turn toward the paradigmatic case of political integration that Karl Deutsch identified in 1967. First, external pressure during World War II had greatly strengthened Swiss national unity. This continued during the cold war, when the communist threat and the massive immigration of workers served to strengthen national unity again (see Kriesi 1999, 18). Second, due to a trend toward secularization, the religious cleavage slowly dissolved. The Catholic subculture left its cantonal and societal "ghettos" (Altermatt 1989), increasingly participated in the hitherto liberal-dominated federal political arena, and gained acceptance and complete integration into society at large. Third, economic prosperity with high GDP growth rates and extremely low unemployment rates (below one percent) not only provided the financial resources for redistributive politics, but also contributed to the strong identification of all cleavage groups with the Swiss state.

The only thing that marred this happy state of affairs was the Jura problem, which had troubled the canton of Berne for a long time. The Jura region is an example of unsuccessful cleavage management in Switzerland and lacks a number of factors that have contributed to the integration success of the other cleavage groups. The Jura region had a double minority—French-speaking Catholics in a canton populated by Protestant German speakers—and it had already developed a distinct identity when it was

awarded to the canton of Berne in 1814. The Jurassians claimed to be economically neg-
lected and feared "Germanization." In addition, the Jura region did not enjoy much autonomy, had little influence on cantonal politics, and was frequently outvoted in
cantonal direct democratic votes (Ganguillet 1998). Throughout the nineteenth century, the insensitivity and oppressiveness of the Bernese elites served to aggravate the
situation, leading to open conflicts and separatist claims. For many years, the conflict
centered on religion with linguistic issues mostly in the background; but in 1947 the linguistic issue gained sudden prominence when the appointment of a Jurassian to a key
post in the Bernese government was opposed on the grounds that a German speaker
ought to hold such an important post. This action incited indignation from the French
speakers in the Jura and memories of past repression were rekindled.

A jurassian movement formed which, after a popular initiative for a separate canton
was defeated in a referendum, deliberately chose to escalate the conflict in order to draw
attention to its plight. Although the Bernese authorities subsequently recognized the
identity of a *peuple jurassien* and provided for permanent power-sharing devices in the
cantonal executive, these policies and techniques were put in place too late to prevent
the conflict. What followed was a series of violent incidents and terrorist bombings.
Then, in 1979, the Catholic part of the Jura became its own canton and the remainder
of the Jura received increased autonomy within the canton of Berne. Now, the situation
in the Jura has become quite calm although Catholics and French speakers in the
southern districts still complain about being a minority, cut off from the ethnic group
to which they feel they belong. The Jura conflict shows that nonaccommodative elites
from the majority segment, coupled with partly hostile identities on the part of the minority segment toward the center (nurtured by a "bad" history of interaction and perceived economic disparities) as well as the absence of institutional protections, can spur
disruptive territorial conflict.

Since the late 1970s, there has been increasing talk of a divide between German and
French speakers (the so-called *Röstigraben*). The language cleavage is particularly
salient in the eyes of the French speakers, who sense a certain antagonism between the
linguistic groups (Kriesi et al. 1996, 63–66). The salience of the linguistic cleavage was
also revealed in an analysis of 51 recent federal referenda in the 1990s. The ratio of
German to French speakers turned out to be the most important variable, being statistically significant for 35 of the 51 referenda. By contrast, religion was statistically significant only for 16 referenda (Linder, Riedwyl, and Steiner 2000).

Several factors have contributed to the growing division between the linguistic
groups. The first is the decreased importance of religious and class-based identities,
turning language into a key identity marker (Altermatt 1997). The second factor is the
differences in the political preferences of the linguistic groups: French and Italian

speakers are more inclined to social and federalist policies and less inclined to ecological policies than German speakers. On foreign policy issues, French speakers take a more internationalist position than German speakers.[13] The French-German division found its symbolic expression in 1992, when a proposal interpreted as a first step toward Switzerland's adherence to the European Union (EU) was defeated, with French speakers strongly in favor and 56 percent of the German-speaking electorate against it (particularly in the rural areas). This led to the outbreak of violent polemics from many French speakers, backed by the media in the French-speaking areas.

The majority of the cantons clause—originally conceived as an institutional safeguard for cantonal interests—has increasingly become a "trap" for cleavage management. Different paths of demographic development in the cantons and migration from rural to urban areas have dramatically increased the voting strength of citizens in small cantons. The voting strength of each citizen of a small canton can be up to thirty-eight times greater than that of a citizen in a large canton. Thus, a minority of the population (20–30 percent) in smaller, rural cantons has veto power when the majority of the cantons clause is necessary for a proposal to pass.[14] There have been a total of eight cases where a majority of cantons outvoted a majority of the people, six of them occurring in the past thirty years. The working of the cantons clause mainly benefits the small and medium-sized rural cantons in the German-speaking part of Switzerland (the cantons of the former *Sonderbund*) and particularly hurts the French-speaking cantons and the Ticino, as well as urban areas and large cities (Vatter and Sager 1996, 176). As the population in rural, German-speaking areas strongly opposes European integration, the working of the cantons clause—obligatory in any vote concerning the membership in supranational organizations—makes it impossible for French speakers to be on the winning side in a direct democratic vote on European integration.

The bleak prospects the linguistic minorities face in achieving their preferred outcomes are exacerbated by two other factors. French and Italian speakers are, in absolute terms, more often outvoted in crucial policy questions than in former times—which, of course, brings latent tensions to the forefront (Kriesi et al. 1996, 22–23). Also, Switzerland experienced an economic crisis in the 1990s, with negative GDP growth and growing unemployment rates, which hit the French and Italian areas hardest and revived long-standing fears of economic inferiority.

However, rising divisions, disputes over the EU, frequent outvotings, bleak prospects for achieving preferred outcomes, and growing economic disparities have not translated into disruptive conflict on part of the linguistic minorities. Certainly, the fractures are serious: survey data show that the allegiance of French and Italian speakers to Switzerland declined during the 1990s (Brunner and Sgier 1997). Nonetheless, the divisions have not been the top priority according to the linguistic minorities, and over the course of the 1990s (Kriesi et al. 1996, 53–54), they partially cooled off. This brings us back to the paradox formulated at the start: why has Switzerland—in comparative terms—been so successful in preventing territorial conflicts from becoming disruptive, despite deteriorating circumstances and obvious failures?

A key factor was the insistence of political elites on the maintenance of the multi-cultural political order, leading to a willingness—especially among German-speaking elites—to contain growing divisions, to be receptive to the claims of other cleavage groups, to engage in conciliatory activities, and to find policy solutions that alleviate grievances. This is not to say that French- and Italian-speaking elites have not occasionally politicized the cleavage (Büchi 2000, 267ff.), but they eventually agreed to co-operate rather than engage in disruptive protest. After the negative vote on the EEA and the ensuing violent polemics of the French speakers, political elites tried to develop a new overall consensus by increasing the level of general and linguistic knowledge about other regions and providing more infrastructural and economic aid to peripheral regions. The federal council—when reporting its policy priorities in 1996—also made reinforcing national cohesion a central goal. Moreover, the federal authorities immediately tried to find a new arrangement with the EU, resulting in the bilateral accords—a more shallow form of integration than the EEA—which passed in a referendum in 2000.

While other political elites have to perform a difficult balancing act between compromising with ethnic rivals and maintaining the support of their own followers, Swiss political elites had broad support to pursue accommodating policies. The majority of their electorate values (or at least is not opposed to) efforts for understanding and agreement among the various groups (Church 2000, 99), which can be ascribed to the discourses of multiculturalism, mutual understanding, and conciliation. Efforts for accommodation were also facilitated by the enduring support of linguistic minorities for the political order and its institutions and by a party system that is not organized along cleavage lines.

Institutions, while giving rise to current strains, simultaneously contributed to their curbing. The large measure of cantonal autonomy still has conflict-defusing capability.[15] Furthermore, Swiss policy making still has consensual features: although the steep increase in the use of the optional referenda and the related increase in sanctioning votes on important policy issues force political elites to take the majority's preferences more into account (Hug and Sciarini 1995, 67), Swiss politics still produces many policy outcomes that do not pass over minorities' interests. Finally, macroeconomic management had improved by the end of the 1990s, with higher economic growth and lower unemployment rates in the whole country.

To conclude, we would like to add a word of caution: although the current strains have been partially defused, the future might not necessarily be bright. Differences in preferences along territorial lines persist and if linguistic minorities continue to be out-voted in crucial policy issues, their support for the political order might eventually decrease, providing fertile soil for political entrepreneurs to politicize the situation and play the card of ethnic conflict. Moreover, institutional reforms (such as the abolishment of the cantons clause) that would favor linguistic groups' interests are hard to come by. As Clive Church (2000) rightly notes, contemporary Switzerland might be best understood as "a paradigm in evolution."

Conclusion

In his essay "Whither the Modern Nation-State?" Daniel Elazar (1987, 223ff.) suggested that while the Westphalian order might have been appropriate for the modern era, the dawn of the postmodern era with its multiculturalism and "ethnic" revival requires the development of an entirely new governmental arrangement: a federal matrix model geared toward partnership, negotiation, and sharing, structuring relationships in a way that would permit diverse groups to coexist within the same political system. This vision is a stunningly accurate description of the modern Swiss polity. The Swiss federal polity lacks most of the standard features of the classical state paradigm: sovereign, yes, but nonhierarchical, noncentralized, engaging in partnership-like arrangements with its member units and relying heavily on negotiated agreements. These "postmodern" features lie at the root of Switzerland's success in managing territorial cleavages. Not only do cleavage groups enjoy considerable autonomy, the evolving non-majoritarian features at the central level also secure their influence on federal politics. But while formal institutions were indeed important for managing territorial conflicts in Switzerland, they alone cannot sufficiently explain the outcomes. Especially when divisions between the linguistic cleavage groups were growing, formal institutions were not much of a help and even aggravated the situation (as in recent times). To understand the Swiss paradox of favorable outcomes despite recurring divisions and serious management failures, it is necessary to focus on the informal and constructivist aspect of institutions and the related identities of actors as well.

Resolving the paradox of Swiss cleavage management, however, does not suggest that Switzerland is, in the end, a paragon. To the contrary: no simple formula can be handed over to the political engineer. The mix of factors and particularly the inter-twining of formal and informal institutions cannot be easily transferred to another setting. But what we can learn from the Swiss experience is that a "postmodern" setting with strong nonmajoritarian devices, a development of multicultural identities, topped by a willingness of elite actors to contain growing divisions, seem to be key factors for successfully managing territorial cleavages.

NOTES

1. The founding *Orte* were the three mountain cantons in central Switzerland, Uri, Schwyz, and Unterwalden.

2. This Protestant edge survived for centuries. Since the 1970s, however, figures have reversed and Catholics have a slight numerical edge.

3. The only restrictions were that no new monasteries could be founded and that the Jesuits were not allowed to exercise any activities in the church and in schools.

4. In 1938 Romansch was recognized as the fourth official language. This has to be seen mainly as a reaction to* fascist language politics in Italy (Im Hof 1991, 200).

5. This status, however, should certainly not be exaggerated and is more of symbolic value: cantons are sovereign only insofar as their sovereignty is not restricted by the central state and, as it is the central state that decides on the distribution of competencies, the status of sovereignty becomes questionable (Bucher 1977, 995).

6. With the exception of the canton of Jura, all cantons follow the majority principle.

7. In an international comparison of inequalities of representation in bicameral systems Switzerland ranks second behind the United States (Lijphart 1999, 208).

8. There is no arbitral veto point for federalist claims in Switzerland. The Supreme Court, the federal tribunal, does not have the right to scrutinize federal legislation judicially. Instead, the federal tribunal is an appeal court for all cantonal laws, since it can evaluate the constitutionality of every cantonal decision.

9. Rather, it is important to look at particular policy fields: on the welfare state issue, there is a tendency toward (financial and legal) centralization, while in the field of traditional framework policies, there is a tendency toward decentralization.

10. An interesting result is, however, that cultural interests of cantons and regions are better secured in the national council (Wiesli 2000, 43).

11. Lehmbruch (1993, 54) even concludes "that the cantons themselves, as institutionalized corporate actors, have no strong influence in federal policy making.... They certainly play a role in decentralized issue areas, such as education policy, and ... cantonal actors may exert some influence in specific fields, such as territorial planning, but their role is relatively marginal to the central domains of economic and social policy." This picture, however, is not based on empirical studies and is overdrawn.

12. A good example is the famous German-speaking poet Carl Spitteler who, in view of the growing divisions between French and German speakers in World War I, declared that French speakers are not only neighbors, but also brothers.

13. However, one should not overlook that this cleavage partly crosscuts linguistic groups and also represents a cleavage between a traditional, pastoral, inward-looking Switzerland and a modern, urban, and outward-looking Switzerland (Sardi and Widmer 1993).

14. Theoretically, the "smallest possible blocking minority" lies at about 9 percent of the voting population, if their votes are distributed "optimally" among the small cantons (Germann 1991, 262f.).

15. A good example is the introduction of a maternity insurance scheme in the canton of Geneva. After the proposal—seen as a crucial policy issue by most French speakers—was defeated in a national referendum in 1999, the canton of Geneva decided to adopt a maternity insurance scheme by itself.

References

Altermatt, Urs. 1989. *Katholizismus und Moderne: Zur Sozial- und Mentalitätsgeschichte der Schweizer Katholiken im 19. und 20. Jahrhundert.* Zürich: Benziger.

———. 1995. *Der Weg der Schweizer Katholiken ins Ghetto: Die Entstehungsgeschichte der nationalen Volksorganisationen im Schweizer Katholizismus 1848–1919.* Freiburg: Universitätsverlag Freiburg Schweiz.

———. 1997. Viersprachige Schweiz: anderthalbsprachig plus Englisch? Debate: Language Policy Perspectives in Switzerland. *Swiss Political Science Review* 3, no. 1:135–56.

Armingeon, Klaus. 1999. Nationalismus und Verfassungspatriotismus: Die Schweiz im internationalen Vergleich. In *Traditionen der Republik-Wege zur Demokratie,* ed. Peter Blickle and Rupert Moser, 219–38. Bern: Peter Lang.

———. 2000. Swiss Federalism in Comparative Perspective. In *Federalism and Political Performance,* ed. Ute Wachendorfer-Schmidt. London: Routledge and Kegan Paul.

Braun, Rudolf. 1984. *Das ausgehende Ancien Régime in der Schweiz: Aufriss einer Sozial- und Wirtschaftsgeschichte des 18. Jahrhunderts.* Göttingen: Vandenhoeck und Ruprecht.

Brunner, Martin, and Lea Sgier. 1997. Crise de confiance dans les institutions politiques suisses? Quelques résultats d'une enquête d'opinion. *Revue Suisse de Science Politique* 3, no. 1:105–13.

Bucher, Erwin. 1977. Die Bundesverfassung von 1848. In *Handbuch der Schweizer Geschichte,* Bd. 2, 987–1018. Zürich: Verlag Berichthaus.

Büchi, Christophe. 2000. "Röstigraben": Das Verhältnis zwischen deutscher und französischer Schweiz. Geschichte und Perspektiven. Zürich: Verlag Neue Zürcher Zeitung.

Ceschi, Raffaello. 1991. Un Ticino poco svizzero? L'epoca dei malintesi 1880–1940. *Neue Studien zum Schweizerischen Nationalbewusstsein,* Fasc. 13, 53–65. Basel: Schwabe.

Church, Clive H. 2000. Switzerland: A Paradigm in Evolution. *Parliamentary Affairs* 53, no. 1:96–113.

Dafflon, Bernard. 1995. *Fédéralisme et solidarité: Etude de la péréquation en Suisse.* Fribourg: St-Canisius Fribourg Suisse.

Deutsch, Karl W. 1976. *Die Schweiz als paradigmatischer Fall politischer Integration.* Bern: Haupt.

DiMaggio, Paul J., and Walter W. Powell. 1991.* Introduction. In *The New Institutionalism in Organizational Analysis,* ed. Walter W. Powell and Paul J. DiMaggio, 1–38. Chicago: University of Chicago Press.

Dryzek, John S. 1996. The Informal Logic of Institutional Design. In *The Theory of Institutional Design,* ed. Robert E. Goodin, 103–25. Cambridge: Cambridge University Press.

Du Bois, Pierre. 1999. *Alémanniques et Romands entre unité et discorde.* Lausanne: Favre.

Elazar, Daniel J. 1987. *Exploring Federalism.* Tuscaloosa: University of Alabama Press.

———. 1993. International and Comparative Federalism. *PS: Political Science & Politics* 26 (June): 190–95.

———. 1997. Contrasting Unitary and Federal Systems. *International Political Science Review* 18, no. 3:237–25.

Flora, Peter et al. 1983. *State, Economy, and Society in Western Europe. 1815–1975: Data Handbook in two Volumes.* Vol. 1. Frankfurt: Campus.

Frei, Daniel, and Henry H. Kerr. 1974. Wir und die Welt: Strukturen und Hintergründe aussenpolitischer Einstellungen. Bern: Pädagogische Rekrutenprüfungen.

Ganguillet, Gilbert. 1998. *Le conflit jurassien: Genèse et trajectoire d' un conflit ethno-régional.* Thèse. Zürich: bokos druck.

Germann, Raimund E. 1981. *Ausserparlamentarische Kommissionen: Die Milizverwaltung des Bundes.* Bern: Haupt.

———. 1986. Die Beziehungen zwischen Bund und Kantonen im Verwaltungsbereich. In *Handbuch Politisches System der Schweiz,* ed. Raimund Germann and Ernest Weibel, Bd. 3, 343–69. Bern: Haupt.

———. 1991. Die Europatauglichkeit der direktdemokratischen Institutionen der Schweiz. *Schweizerisches Jahrbuch für politische Wissenschaft* 30:257–69.

———. 1994. *Staatsreform: Der Übergang zur Konkurrenzdemokratie.* Bern: Haupt.

———. 1999. Die Kantone: Gleichheit und Disparität. In *Handbuch der Schweizer Politik,* ed. Ulrich Klöti, Peter Knoepfel, Hanspeter Krisei, Linder Wolf, and Yannis Papadopoulos, 387–420. Zürich: NZZ Verlag.

Greyerz, Hans von. 1953. *Nation und Geschichte im Bernischen Denken: Vom Beitrag Berns zum schweizerischen Geschichts- und Nationalbewusstsein.* Bern: Lang.

Hall, Peter A., and Rosemary C. R. Taylor. 1996. Political Science and the Three New Institutionalisms. *Political Studies* 44:936–57.

Heger, Matthias. 1990. *Deutscher Bundesrat und Schweizer Ständerat: Gedanken zu ihrer Entstehung, ihrem aktuellen Erscheinungsbild und ihrer Rechtfertigung. Beiträge zum Parlamentsrecht,* Band 17. Berlin: Duncker und Humblot.

Hertig, Hans-Peter. 1980. *Partei, Wählerschaft oder Verband? Entscheidfaktoren im eidgenössischen Parlament.* Bern: Francke.

Hilty, Carl. 1875. *Politik der Eidgenossenschaft (Vorlesungen).* Bern: Friedrich-Emil-Welti- Stifung.

Horowitz, Donald L. 1985. *Ethnic Groups in Conflict.* Berkeley: University of California Press.

Hug, Simon, and Pascal Sciarini. 1995. Switzerland—Still a Paradigmatic Case? In *Towards a New Europe: Stops and Starts in Regional Integration,* ed. Gerald Schneider, Patricia A. Weitsman, and Thomas Bernauer, 55–74. Westport, Conn.: Praeger.

Im Hof, Ulrich. 1991. *Mythos Schweiz: Identität-Nation-Geschichte, 1291–1991.* Zürich: NZZ Verlag.

Jorio, Marco. 1997. "Wider den Pakt mit dem Teufel": Reaktion und Gegenwehr der Konservativen. In *Im Zeichen der Revolution: Der Weg zum schweizerischen Bundesstaat 1798–1848,* ed. Thomas Hildbrand and Albert Tanner, 139–60. Zürich: Chronos.

———. 1998. Zwischen Rückzug und Integration—die Katholisch-Konservativen und der junge Bundesstaat. In *Etappen des Bundesstaates: Staats-und Nationsbildung der Schweiz, 1848–1998,* ed. Brigitte Studer, 89–108. Zürich: Chronos.

Jost, Hans-Ulrich. 1998. Der Helvetische Nationalismus: Nationale Identität, Rassismus und Ausgrenzungen in der Schweiz des 20. Jahrhunderts. In *Nationalismus, Multikulturalismus und Ethnizität: Beiträge zur Deutung von sozialer und politischer Einbindung und Ausgrenzung,* ed. Hans-Rudolf Wicker, 65–78. Bern: Haupt.

Kälin, Walter. 1997. Federalism and the Resolution of Minority Conflicts. In *Federalism against Ethnicity? Institutional, Legal and Democratic Instruments to Prevent Violent Minority Conflicts,* ed. Günther Bächler, 169–83. Chur: Rüegger.

Kissling-Näf Ingrid, and Peter Knoepfel. 1992. Politikverflechtung dank zentralstaatlichem Immobilismus? Handlungsspielräume kantonaler Vollzugspolitiken im schweizerischen politisch-administrativen System. In *Staatätigkeit in der Schweiz,* ed. Heidrun Abromeit and Werner W. Pommerehne, 43–69. Bern: Haupt.

Kölz, Alfred. 1992. *Neuere Schweizerische Verfassungsgeschichte: Ihre Grundlinien vomEnde der Alten Eidgenossenschaft bis 1848.* Bern: Stämpfli.

Körner, Martin. 1983. Glaubensspaltung und Wirtschaftssolidarität (1515–1648). In *Geschichte der Schweiz- und der Schweizer,* Bd. 2, 7–96. Basel: Helbing und Lichtenhahn.

Kriesi, Hanspeter. 1995. *Le système politique suisse.* Paris: Economica.

————. 1999. Introduction: State Formation and Nation Building in the Swiss Case. In *Nation and National Identity: The European Experience in Perspective,* ed. Hanspeter Kirsei, Klaus Armingeon, Hannes Siegrist, and Andreas Wimmer, 13–28. Grüsch: Rüegger.

Kriesi, Hanspeter, Boris Wernli, Pascal Sciarini, and Matteo Gianni. 1996. *Le clivage linguistique: Problèmes de compréhension entre les communautés linguistiques en Suisse.* Bern: Bundesamt für Statistik.

Kymlicka, Will. 1999. *Multikulturalismus und Demokratie: Über Minderheiten in Staaten und Nationen.* Hamburg: Rotbuch.

Ladner, Andreas. 1999. Das Schweizer Parteiensystem und seine Parteien. In *Handbuch der Schweizer Politik,* ed. Ulrich Klöti, Peter Knoepfel, Hanspeter Kriesi, Wolf Linder, and Yanni Papadopoulos, 213–59. Zürich: NZZ Verlag.

Lane Erik, David McKay, and Kenneth Newton. 1997. *Political Data Handbook OECD Countries.* 2d ed. Oxford: Oxford University Press.

Lehmbruch, Gerhard. 1993. Consociational Democracy and Corporatism in Switzerland. *Publius* 23 (spring):43–60.

Lijphart, Arend. 1985. *Power-sharing in South Africa.* Policy Papers in International Affairs, no. 24. Berkeley: University of California Press.*

————. 1999. *Patterns of Democracy: Government Forms and Performance in Thirty-Six Countries.* New Haven, Conn.: Yale University Press.

Linder, Wolf. 1987. *Politische Entscheidung und Gesetzesvollzug in der Schweiz.* Bern, Haupt.

————. 1994. *Swiss Democracy: Possible Solutions to Conflict in Multicultural Societies.* London: Macmillan.

————. 1997. Federalism and Power-Sharing as a Means to Prevent Internal Conflict. In *Federalism against Ethnicity? Institutional, Legal and Democratic Instruments to Prevent Violent Minority Conflicts,* ed. Günther Bächler, 186–93. Chur: Rüegger.

————. 1999. *Schweizerische Demokratie: Institutionen–Prozesse–Perspektiven.* Bern: Haupt.

Linder, Wolf, Hans Riedwyl, and Jürg Steiner. 2000. Konkordanztheorie und Abstimmungsdaten: Eine explorative Aggregatsanalyse auf Bezirksebene. *Swiss Political Science Review* 6, no. 2:27–56.

Linz, Juan J., and Alfred Stepan. 1996. *Problems of Democratic Transition and Consolidation: Southern Europe, South America, and Post-Communist Europe.* Baltimore: John Hopkins University Press.

Maissen, Thomas. 1999. *Vom Sonderbund zum Bundesstaat: Krise und Erneuerung 1798–1848 im Spiegel der NZZ.* Zürich: NZZ Verlag.

March, James G., and Johan P. Olsen. 1989. *Rediscovering Institutions: The Organizational Basis of Politics.* New York: Free Press.

McRae, Kenneth D. 1983. *Conflict and Compromise in Multilingual Societies: Switzerland.* Waterloo: Wilfrid Laurier University Press.

Melich, Anna, ed. 1991. *Die Werte der Schweizer.* Bern: Lang.

Mesmer, Beatrix. 1997. Die Modernisierung der Eidgenossenschaft—Sattelzeit oder bürgerliche Revolution? In *Im Zeichen der Revolution: Der Weg zum schweizerischen Bundesstaat 1798–1848*, ed. Thomas Hildbrand and Albert Tanner, 11–28. Zürich: Chronos.

Moos, Carlo. 1997. Im Hochland fiel der erste Schuss: Bemerkungen zu Sonderbund und Sonderbundskrieg. In *Im Zeichen der Revolution: Der Weg zum schweizerischen Bundesstaat 1798–1848*, ed. Thomas Hilbrand and Albert Tanner, 161–77. Zürich: Chronos.

Neidhart, Leonhard. 1970. *Plebiszit und pluralitäre Demokratie: Eine Analyse der Funktion des schweizerischen Gesetzesreferendums*. Bern: Francke.

———. 1975. *Föderalismus in der Schweiz*. Zürich: Benziger.

Netzle, Simon. 1998. Die USA als Vorbild für einen schweizerischen Bundesstaat. In *Revolution und Innovation: Die konflikreiche Entstehung des schweizerischen Bundesstaates von 1848*, ed. Andreas Ernst, Albert Tanner, and Matthias Weishaupt, 49–60. Zürich: Chronos.

North, Douglass C. 1981. *Structure and Change in Economic History*. New York: Norton.

Nüssli, Kurt. 1985. *Föderalismus in der Schweiz: Konzepte, Indikatoren, Daten*. Grüsch: Rüegger.

Pierson, Paul. 1996. The Path to European Integration: A Historical Institutionalist Analysis. *Comparative Political Studies* 29 (April):123–63.

———. 2000. Increasing Returns, Path Dependence, and the Study of Politics. *American Political Science Review* 94, no. 2:251–67.

Remak, Joachim. 1997. *Bruderzwist nicht Brudermord: Der Schweizer Sonderbundkrieg von 1847*. Zürich: Orell Füssli.

Riklin, Alois, and Alois Ochsner. 1984. Parlament. In *Handbuch Politisches System der Schweiz*, ed. Ulrich Klöti. Bern: Haupt.

Rokkan, Stein, and Derek W. Urwin. 1983. *Economy Territory Identity: Politics of West European Peripheries*. London: Sage.

Rothstein, Bo. 2000. Trust, Social Dilemmas and Collective Memories. *Journal of Theoretical Politics* 12, no. 4:477–501.

Sardi, Massimo, and Eric Widmer. 1993. L'orientation du vote. In *Citoyenneté et démocratie. Compétence, participation et décision des citoyens et citoyennes suisses*, ed. Hanspeter Kriesi. Zürich: Seismo.

Schenkel, Walter, and Uwe Serdült. 1999. Bundesstaatliche Beziehungen. In *Handbuch der Schweizer Politik*, ed. Ulrich Klöti, Peter Knoepfel, Hanspeter Kriesi, Wolf Linder, and Yannis Papadopoulos, 469–507. Zürich: NZZ Verlag.

Schild, Andreas 1971. *Föderalismus-Zentralismus, Partikularismus-Unitarismus: Eine Untersuchung über den Föderalismus in der Schweiz anhand wichtiger Volksabstimmungen von 1935 bis 1953*. Diss. Bern.

Schmid, Carol L. 1981. *Conflict and Consensus in Switzerland*. Berkeley: University of California Press.

Schoch, Bruno. 1998. *Die Schweiz—ein Modell zur Lösung von Nationalitätenkonflikten?* HSFK-Report (April). Frankfurt: Hessische Stiftung Friedens- und Konfliktforschung.

Schulze, Hagen. 1994. *Staat und Nation in der europäischen Geschichte*. München: Beck.

Sciarini, Pascal, Simon Hug, and Cédric Dupont. 1997. *Example, Exception, or Both? Swiss National Identity in Perspective*. EUI Working Papers 97/32. Florence: EUI.

Siaroff, Alan. 2000. Lessons from Consociational Theory and System Performance. *Comparative Politics* (April):317–32.

Stadler, Peter 1987. Konfessionalismus im schweizerischen Bundesstaat 1848–1914. In *Auf dem Weg zu einer schweizerischen Identität 1948–1914: Probleme-Errungenschaften-Misserfolge,* ed. François de Capitani and Georg Germann, 85–92. Freiburg: Universitätsverlag.

Steiner, Jürg. 1974. *Amicable Agreement versus Majority Rule: Conflict Resolution in Switzerland.* Chapel Hill: University of North Carolina Press.

Trechsel, Alexander H.. 2000. *Feuerwerk Volksrechte: Die Volksabstimmungen in den schweizerischen Kantonen 1970–1996.* Basel: Helbing & Lichtenhahn.

Trechsel, Alexander H., and Pascal Sciarini. 1999. Direct Democracy in Switzerland: Do Elites Matter? *European Journal of Political Research* 33:99–124.

Trivelli, Laurent. 1974. *Le Bicamérisme, Institutions comparées, Etude Historique, statistique et critique des rapports entre le Conseil national et le Conseil des Etats.* Thèse. Lausanne: Payot.

Vatter, Adrian. 1999. *Föderalismus.* In *Handbuch der Schweizer Politik,* ed. Ulrich Klöti et al. Zürich: Verlag.

———. 2000. Consensus and Direct Democracy: Conceptual and Empirical Linkages. *European Journal of Political Research* 38:171–92.

Vatter, Adrian, and Fritz Sager. 1996. Föderalismusreform am Beispiel des Ständemehrs. *Swiss Political Science Review* 2, no. 2:165–200.

Wälti, Sonja. 1996. Institutional Reform of Federalism: Changing the Players Rather Than the Rules of the Game. *Swiss Political Science Review* 2, no. 2:113–41.

Wiesli, Reto, and Wolf Linder. 2000. *Repräsentation, Artikulation und Durchsetzung kantonaler Interessen in Stände-und Nationalrat.* Bern: Institut für Politikwissenschaft Universität.

Wili, Hans-Urs. 1988. *Kollektive Mitwirkungsrechte von Gliedstaaten in der Schweiz und im Ausland: Geschichtlicher Werdegang, Rechtsvergleichung, Zukunftsperspektiven.* Bern: Stämpfli.

CHAPTER TWO

Belgium

Hollowing the Center

Liesbet Hooghe

Territorial conflict in Belgium has primarily pitted the Flemish region against the Walloon region, with a Brussels center caught in the middle and a small, peripheral German region as bystander. When Belgium seceded from the Netherlands in 1830, there were few indications that Flemish-Walloon conflict would profoundly shape politics and polity throughout much of the twentieth century.[1] Yet disruptive, nonviolent territorial protest became widespread in the 1950s and 1960s. It topped in the late 1970s, and it has declined since. Through much of the postwar period Flemish and Walloon identities gained strength at the expense of a Belgian identity, but in the 1990s Belgian and regional identities appear to have become more inclusive. The ebbing of disruptive, territorial protest and of exclusive identities coincides with the transformation from a unitary to a federal state in 1993. Is this a coincidence?

Nonmajoritarian rule has been a constant feature of Belgian politics, and this has most certainly facilitated territorial conflict management (Cohen 1997). Yet nonmajoritarian institutions have varied over time. This chapter compares the influence of these different institutional configurations on territorial conflict. Until the late 1980s, territorial conflict was managed in a unitary framework, largely by resorting to consociational rules that constrained one group from dominating the other. In 1993, the unitary state was transformed into a federal one. To what extent has federalism been a more effective buffer against disruptive territorial conflict than nonterritorial consociationalism? What are the threads of continuity and change between unitary consociationalism and federalism, and how do these influence conflict management?

I will show that nonterritorial (mainly consociational) limits to majority rule contained disruptive violence in exchange for a gradual hollowing of the center, in which resources and competencies were bartered away to maintain peace. So while nonterritorial rules successfully avoided violence, they helped fuel centrifugal territorial conflict. I also demonstrate how the legacy of nonterritorial limits to majority rule smoothed the transition to a federal regime. Though federal rules appear more robust in avoiding disruptive conflict and in strengthening a Belgian identity, incentives to hollow the center in exchange for peace remain strong.

Historical Profile

Territorial conflict in Belgium has linguistic roots. Dutch (or Flemish) has always been the mother tongue of a majority of the population, even while in the nineteenth century French was the dominant official language. The fact that Dutch and French speakers were to a large extent geographically segregated facilitated the territorialization of demands and, in the event, solutions. After the Second World War, the reversal of Walloon economic fortunes and rapid economic growth in the Flemish region reinforced linguistic conflict between the two regions, and this consolidated the territorialization of Flemish-Francophone conflict. By 1970 the conflict had been transformed from one between Dutch speakers and French speakers into one between the Flemish region on the one hand and the Walloon region—with primarily French-speaking, but officially bilingual Brussels—on the other.

Sociodemographic Profile of Groups
LINGUISTIC PROFILE

The contemporary Belgian federation has just over 10 million inhabitants divided over three regions: the Flemish region (58 percent), the Walloon region (32.6 percent), and Brussels (9.4 percent). The three official languages are Dutch (56 percent), French (43.5 percent), and German (0.5 percent). Since the early 1900s, the Flemish and Walloon regions have been virtually unilingual, while Brussels has evolved from a town that spoke predominantly Flemish dialects to a primarily French-speaking city after the Second World War. Most German speakers are located in the East cantons (now the German region), which were acquired from Germany after the First World War. Except for Brussels and the German cantons, the linguistic ratio has barely changed over 170 years of Belgian independence (Hooghe 1991; McRae 1986).

The proportions of Dutch, French, and German speakers are rough estimates, because after 1960, population censuses ceased to carry language questions. Yet linguistic homogeneity has further increased in the Flemish and Walloon regions. A strict policy of unilingualism in the two regions since the 1930s, and reinforced in the 1960s, has contributed to this outcome. Increased linguistic homogeneity in the two main regions has helped to put language usage as an issue to sleep.

The one major exception is in and around Brussels. Various alternative measures of language use indicate that assimilation to the French language and culture increased at least until the mid-1980s. As a result, in the Brussels region, the proportion of Dutch speakers is estimated to be between 10 and 20 percent of the population.[2] Passions run particularly high in six Flemish municipalities south/southeast to Brussels, where French speakers constitute up to 30 to 50 percent of the population. These formally Flemish areas form a narrow territorial corridor between the predominantly French-speaking Brussels metropolis to the north and the unilingually French-speaking Walloon region to the south.

SOCIOECONOMIC PROFILE

Language has always been a socioeconomic marker. In the nineteenth century, until perhaps as late as the Second World War, those with power, money, or aspirations spoke French. The roles are reversed in contemporary Belgium.

The tide began to turn in the 1950s. Economic success in the Walloon region had depended to a large extent on the heavy steel and coal industries, which were rapidly losing importance. Light industry moved out and new industry went elsewhere, discouraged by a militant workforce, high wages, and unreceptive public authorities. The Walloon region deindustrialized. In contrast, industrial modernization took off in the Flemish region. Much of it was financed by foreign investment, and the region also benefited from capital diversion from Wallonia by the big Belgian holding companies. The Flemish region overtook the Walloon region between 1963 and 1966 in terms of gross regional product per capita. This reversal of fortunes is clear from Table 2.1.

Stages in Territorial Mobilization

Ethnic—and eventually territorial—conflict has been intense, but it has been confined to electoral competition and nonviolent street protest.

STAGE ONE: FROM LINGUISTIC GRIEVANCES TO TERRITORIAL GRIEVANCES

The constitution of 1831 guaranteed linguistic liberty, but French became the only official language. Soon after independence, intellectuals in the Flemish urban centers

Table 2.1 *Regional Structure of the Belgian Economy*

		Flemish Region	Walloon Region	Brussels	Belgium
Agriculture	1949	15.5	9.3	1.5	10.5
	1995	1.9	2.2	0.0	1.7
Industry	1949	51.6	62.3	46.6	54.4
	1995	32.6	27.6	19.2	29.2
Services	1949	32.9	28.4	52.1	35.1
	1995	65.5	70.2	80.8	69.1
GDP per capita	1949	88	103	132	100
	1963	90	93	148	100
	1988	102	81	153	100
	1995	101	80	161	100

Sources: Nationaal Instituut voor Statistiek; Jones 1998.

began to advance language grievances. The nineteenth-century Flemish movement was an urban-based phenomenon generally concerned with individual language rights, not with group rights (Murphy 1995; De Schryver 1981). But the intransigence of the French-speaking elite radicalized the movement. The first series of language laws, adopted in the late nineteenth century, imposed asymmetrical bilingualism. The Flemish region became in principle bilingual, while the rest of the country remained unilingual. The legislation was limited in scope, and much of it remained dead letter. The most significant measure was the Equalization Act of 1898, which made Dutch an official language on equal footing with French.

In the 1930s, new laws reinforced territorial unilingualism in Flanders and Wallonia and bilingual institutions in Brussels as well as in areas with linguistic minorities. The laws were more comprehensive than their nineteenth-century predecessors, and, except in Brussels, more evenly implemented. This choice for territorial unilingualism set the country on course for territorial rather than group conflict. The switch to territorial unilingualism was convenient for all parties involved, though Walloon parties had insisted upon it most adamantly. Walloons and French-speaking residents of Brussels feared that nationwide bilingualism would take jobs away from French speakers. Territorial unilingualism secured a unilingual Wallonia, and poor implementation of bilingualism in Brussels sabotaged Flemish aspirations in the capital. But unilingualism was also convenient for the Flemish, who anticipated that this would accelerate the assimilation of the small, but strategic French-speaking bourgeois minority in the Flemish urban centers.[3]

The laws of the 1930s were pivotal in transforming Flemish society into a Dutch-speaking community with a Dutch-speaking elite. They also transformed prior linguistic concerns into territorial claims. Flemish nationalists now perceived a Francophone threat on their borders. The main source of this was the population census. On the basis of questions on language usage, parliament adjusted territorial boundaries every ten years. As a result of the first two censuses many more "Flemish" parcels of land had become "French-speaking" or "bilingual" than the other way around. Flemish territory was lost around Brussels, partly to the Walloon region and partly to Brussels. During the 1947 census Flemish politicians accused census takers of pressuring Dutch speakers to report themselves as French speakers. In the subsequent census in 1960–61, Flemish local authorities boycotted the language questions in the census and forced the government to drop questions on language usage.

Grievances on the language questions in the census, along with gaps in previous language laws, led to another series of laws in the 1960s reinforcing unilingualism. A 1963 law divided Belgium into four language areas: unilingually Dutch-speaking (Flemish region), unilingually French-speaking (Walloon region), unilingually German-speaking, and the bilingual area of Brussels.[4] The 1963 law froze the linguistic frontier between the three major regions and halted the expansion of the bilingual Brussels region.

Despite the regional transfer of forty-nine municipalities and very small bits of territory, the 1963 laws could not engineer perfectly homogeneous regions. Six communes around Brussels and some municipalities on either side of the border retained limited bilingual facilities. Many Francophones have never accepted the freezing of the linguistic frontier around Brussels. Attempts to negotiate a permanent settlement for boundaries and linguistic minority rights around Brussels have failed consistently, most recently in 2001. The most contested area outside Brussels is Voeren, a conglomerate of six villages, which was transferred from the Walloon region to the Flemish region.[5]

Until the First World War, advocates of Flemish grievances worked through existing parties, especially the Christian Democratic wing of the Catholic Party. The first separate Flemish party was the *Frontpartij* in 1919, which rose on postwar pacifism among Flemish ex-soldiers and benefited from the introduction of universal manhood suffrage to gain some short-lived electoral success. Its successor in the 1930s was the *Vlaams Nationaal Verbond* (VNV). It formed a direct electoral threat to the Catholic Party in the Flemish region. The Belgian Catholic Party responded by reorganizing itself into a Flemish wing and a Francophone wing within a unitary structure, which gave Flemish Catholics some room to call for Flemish cultural autonomy.

The Flemish movement was originally primarily concerned with cultural equality within the existing institutions, but it became gradually more nationalist and autonomist in response to the slow adaptation of the Belgian-Francophone institutions and growing anti-Flemish sentiment among French-speaking politicians. The transformation was complete after the Second World War. A new party, *Volksunie* (VU), entered parliament on a federalist platform in 1954. Its zenith of success was in 1971, when it obtained 18.8 percent of the Flemish vote. By that time, Walloon nationalism had entered the scene with its own grievances.

STAGE TWO: FROM TERRITORIAL GRIEVANCES TO TERRITORIAL CONFLICT

Walloon nationalism was sparked by regional economic decline. Uneven economic development after the Second World War and an increasingly unfavorable demographic balance caused widespread resentment. Walloons feared that in a unitary state their economy would be restructured on Flemish terms. Within Belgium, political parties in the Walloon region have traditionally been more supportive of state intervention. The Socialist Party (PS) has been by far the strongest political party, sometimes obtaining an absolute majority of votes and seats.

The first serious challenge to the Belgian unitary state came from the Walloon movement. At a conference of all major Walloon and French-speaking leaders in 1945, an overwhelming majority opted for an autonomous Wallonia in a federal Belgium. However, the dust settled quickly.

The economic expansion program of the 1950s and 1960s and subsequent decentralization of industrial policy and regional development in 1970 were in part a response to Walloon socialist demands. But political regional autonomy did not come about until the constitutional reform of 1980.

Walloon grievances crystallized in a separate party in 1961, when a popular trade union leader broke away from the Socialist Party to establish the *Mouvement Populaire Wallon* on a radical federalist and socialist platform. Four years later, two Walloon nationalist parties each won a seat in the national parliament. In 1971, the *Rassemblement Wallon* (RW) won 21 percent of the regional votes, which was also the high point of political regionalism. While the Flemish movement constituted from the start primarily a political threat to the Catholic Party, and after the Second World War to its successor the Christian Democratic Party (CVP), the Walloon movement was a direct electoral competitor to the PS.

STAGE THREE: TERRITORIAL CONFLICT TAKEN TO BRUSSELS

In the 1960s and 1970s the Flemish and Walloon movements transferred the battle about the appropriate constitutional structure to Brussels, where a separate Brussels movement also emerged.

As the Flemish region became solidly Dutch-speaking in the 1960s and 1970s, the Flemish movement shifted its attention to Brussels. It seemed a logical step, because the expansion and *verfransing* of Brussels echoed the earlier Francophone threat to Flemish culture in Flanders. The Flemish movement won the first round in the 1960s.

Expansion was stopped by the 1963 law, which defined the linguistic frontier. Creeping *verfransing* was made more difficult by bolstering official bilingualism in the capital. But the Francophones reacted against this *cordon sanitaire* and the restraints upon their majority position in the capital. Brussels produced its own Francophone nationalist movement, the *Front democratique des francophones* (FDF, founded in 1964), which obtained at the height of its success in the 1970s more than 35 percent of the votes in the Brussels metropolitan area. The FDF had ideological connections with the Liberal Party, which had traditionally been strong in the capital.

By the 1970s all three movements endorsed federalism, but of different kinds. French speakers in Brussels favored an autonomous Brussels region as part of a three-partite Belgian federation. The Walloon nationalist movement supported this plan; the socialist-oriented movement was not keen on absorbing a largely free-market Brussels in the Walloon region. The Flemish movement argued instead for federalism based on the two large linguistic communities, with special arrangements for Brussels. In an autonomous Brussels region the small Flemish minority would be cut off from the Flemish region, and in a three-partite federation the Flemish region feared being a permanent minority.

By 1970 ethnic conflict in Belgium had taken a decidedly territorial turn. Policy decisions in the cultural-linguistic and socioeconomic field had consolidated the Flemish-Walloon/Francophone boundaries, and this induced conflict managers to diffuse authority along spatial lines to lower the temperature.

The three major political parties were torn apart by conflicting nationalist pressures. In 1967, the Christian Democrats split into a Flemish party and a Francophone party in the wake of an acrimonious linguistic confrontation around the Catholic University of Leuven/Louvain. Flemish and Francophone Liberals separated relatively amicably in 1968. The unitary Socialist Party held out until 1978, though the two wings gained de facto autonomy in the early 1970s.

The breakup of the major parties undercut the nationalist parties (Table 2.2). Under pressure of the Flemish nationalists, Flemish Christian Democrats and Socialists wrote federalism into their party programs in the 1980s. Deprived of its primary issue, the VU has been declining since, obtaining its lowest result since 1965 in the November 1991 parliamentary elections: 9.4 percent of the Flemish vote. After that, its fortunes waxed and waned; it obtained just over 10 percent of the vote in 1999 and finally ceased to exist in 2002. The VU also suffered from the defection of more extreme elements: in 1978, a breakaway group, the *Vlaams Blok*, entered parliament on a separatist and traditionalist platform. In the 1980s, elements moved the party to the radical right, espousing, in addition to separatism, xenophobia, Euro-skepticism, traditionalism, and support for law and order. Its support jumped from 3 percent of the Flemish vote in 1987 to 10.4

Table 2.2 *Electoral Evolution in Flemish and Walloon Regions for Selected Years since 1961*

	Flemish Region			Walloon Region[a]		
	1961	1968	1971	1961	1968	1971
Christian Democrats	50.9	39.1	37.8	30.5	20.9	20.5
Socialists	29.7	25.7	24.2	47.0	34.5	34.4
Liberals	11.6	16.2	16.3	11.7	26.7	17.7
Nationalists	6.0	16.9	18.8	0.2	10.5	20.9
Greens	—	—	—	—	—	—
Extreme Right	—	—	—	—	—	—

[a] Votes for the Communist Party in the Walloon region: 6.3 percentage (1961), 6.9 percentage (1968), 5.8 percentage (1971).

	Flemish Region			Walloon Region[b]		
	1981	1991	1999	1981	1991	1999
Christian Democrats	32.3	27.0	22.1	19.6	22.5	17.1
Socialists	20.6	19.6	15.0	36.2	39.2	29.5
Liberals	21.1	19.1	22.0	21.7	19.8	24.7
Nationalists	16.0	9.4	10.2[c]	7.1	1.2	—
Greens	3.9	11.9	11.6	6.1	13.5	18.2
Extreme Right	1.8[d]	10.4[d]	15.5[d]	—	2.4	4.0

[b] Votes for the Communist Party in the Walloon region: 4.2 percentage (1981), 0.3 percentage (1991), none (1999).
[c] This includes 0.9 percentage for the Union des Francophones, a party defending the interests of French speakers in the Flemish region.
[d] The extreme right party is the Vlaams Blok, which propagates Flemish separatism in addition to an extreme right-wing agenda.

percent in 1991 and 15.5 percent in 1999. In the Walloon region, a similar evolution occurred. In the 1980s, the nationalist RW became almost completely absorbed by the Francophone Socialists (PS) when the PS endorsed a radical federalist program for economic autonomy. The nationalists in Wallonia obtained less than 2 percent of the regional vote in the elections of 1991, and they have disappeared since. Finally, the Brussels-based FDF, which at its zenith in the 1970s obtained more than 35 percent of Brussels votes, saw its support dwindle to 12 percent by 1991. In the 1990s, the party merged with the local Liberal Party.

Conceptualizing Territorial Conflict

Are some institutions more effective in accommodating territorial cleavages than others? Before we compare the role of consociational versus federal institutions in territorial conflict management in Belgium, let us first acquire a clear picture of the evolution of territorial conflict—the dependent variable. I consider two components.

The first component concerns disruptive territorial protest since 1945, which is detailed in Table 2.3. The events in *italics* refer to violent incidents, including death and injury, sabotage, and major property damage. Violence has not been completely absent in territorial conflict, especially in the first postwar decades. However, violent disruption has been primarily associated with nonterritorial conflict: the royal question, the religious school "war," the coal mining crises, and the steel crises. The words in bold in the last column describe the geographical spread of protest. Territorial conflict was mobilized most extensively in conjunction with powerful nonterritorial issues.

Table 2.3 *Major Instances of Disruptive Protest Concerning Territorial Conflict, 1945–2000*

Time	Description of Events	Location and Spread of Mobilization
1946	Monument for Flemish soldiers in Diksmuide (symbol of Flemish national movement) blown up, *sabotage*	Flemish region **local**
1950	Return of King Leopold (royal question); strikes, street demonstrations, *three deaths* in clashes with police, one *politician murdered, property damage*	Country, but mainly Walloon region **widespread**
1955	School war (financing of Catholic education): strikes, mass demonstrations (some illegal), disruption, *property damage*	Country, but mainly Flemish region **widespread**
1960	Civil disobedience: 300 Flemish local authorities (including large cities) boycott language questions in census	Flemish region **widespread**
1960–61	Winter strike of 1960–61 against Economic Recovery Law (budget cuts, closing of Walloon mines): *sabotage, four deaths* in clashes with police. Breakaway by Walloon trade unionists to form Movement Populaire Wallon	Country, but mainly Walloon region **widespread**
1961, 1962	2 × Mars op Brussel (Flemish demonstration to extract freezing of linguistic border); counter-demonstrations by Mouvement Populaire Wallon	Brussels (for Flemish), Walloon region (for Walloons)
1965–66	Strikes against closing of Limburg mines; socio-economic, but strong Flemish nationalist flavor. *Two deaths* in clashes with police	Flemish region **province**
1966–68	"Leuven Vlaams/Walen buiten" to oust Francophone university: mass demonstrations, street riots, *property damage;* strikes in Flemish education sector	Flemish region **widespread** demonstrations; riots mainly **local** in Leuven

(Continued)

Table 2.3 — Continued

Time	Description of Events	Location and Spread of Mobilization
1970s	High number of strikes, mostly for economic reasons, but often taking on a territorial flavor	Country **widespread**
	Flemish in Brussels: regular acts of civil disobedience (nonappliance of language regulations) by Francophone local government in some Brussels communes (bilingualism) and in some *faciliteitengemeenten* around Brussels (formally Flemish, with special language regime for Francophones)	Brussels capital and Brussels periphery **local**
1977–81	Steel question: major strikes, demonstrations, *property damage*, disruption against reduction of steel production in Walloon region	Walloon region (Liège and Charleroi), **widespread**
1980s	Voeren issue: frequent small-scale demonstrations and counterdemonstrations; occasional skirmishes on transfer of Voeren to Walloon region	Voeren (Flemish commune in east, with special language regime for Francophones) **Local**
	Comines/Mouscron issue: occasional small-scale demonstrations defending implementation of minority rights for Flemish	Comines/Mouscron (Walloon communes in west, with special language regime for Flemish) **Local**
	Faciliteitengemeenten—six communes around Brussels with special language regime for Francophones: occasional small-scale demonstrations and counterdemonstrations; occasional acts of civil disobedience by Francophone local governments	Six Flemish communes around Brussels (special language regime for Francophones) **Local**
1990s	Voeren issue: occasional small-scale demonstrations and counterdemonstrations; rare skirmishes	Voeren **Local**
	Faciliteitengemeenten—six communes around Brussels: occasional small-scale demonstrations and counterdemonstrations; occasional acts of civil disobedience by Francophone local governments	Six Flemish communes around Brussels **Local**

These data allow us to draw three conclusions. First, territorial conflict has only occasionally given rise to disruptive protest. Second, it was most disruptive and most mobilizing in conjunction with religious or socioeconomic conflict. Third, territorial conflict reached its peak in the 1970s. Since then, it has become less frequent, less reliant on mass mobilization, less disruptive, and increasingly confined to a few local areas (six communes around Brussels, Voeren, Comines/Mouscron).

The transition to less disruptive and infrequent territorial conflict has been accompanied by changes in territorial identities, the second element of territorial conflict considered here. Though methodological flaws make direct comparisons of the absolute strength of each category difficult, the trends are clear (De Winter 1998; Maddens, Beerten, and Billiet 1994).[6] First, local attachments to town and village have been consistently stronger than regional and national attachments, and they have been strongest of all in the Flemish region. This may change in the future because local identities declined in the 1990s. Second, since 1975, Flemish identity has been stronger than Belgian identity. It reached its peak in the early 1980s. In the Walloon region, Belgian identity was consistently favored over Walloon/Francophone identity. But from the mid-1980s, Belgian identity has gained ground on regional and local identities. The development of regional governance institutions in Belgium has not gone hand in hand with a deepening of regional identity.

The data show, instead, that a system of multilevel governance may encourage the development of complementary multiple identities. Regional identity is present, but it is not a dominant primary territorial identity in Belgium. Rather, citizens indicate allegiance to one of multiple optional territories. This was confirmed by a 1999 survey. Respondents were asked to indicate their first and second identities from the following list: own town or village; region; Belgium; Europe; the whole world. While a primacy effect pushes up town or village identities, (39 percent for Flemish, 30 percent for Walloons, and 21 percent for Brusselers), the Flemish are almost equally likely to identify first with Belgium (22 percent) as with the Flemish region (24 percent). Walloons are more than two times more likely to identify first with Belgium (34 percent) than with the Walloon region (15 percent). Francophone Brusselers are 1.4 times more likely to identify with Belgium (27 percent) than with the Brussels region (19 percent). Between 12 (Flemish) and 30 percent (Brusselers) identify first and foremost with territorial entities larger than Belgium, that is, Europe or the world (Billiet, Doutrelepont, and Vandekeere 2000).

The survey results also confirm that, like in Spain and the European Union (EU), regional and national identities are not exclusive, but complementary (Billiet, Doutrelepont, and Vandekeere 2000). The stronger one feels Flemish or Walloon, the more likely one also feels strongly about Belgian identity. The correlations between factors expressing frequency, intensity, and value of identity are high: 0.46 for Flemish and Belgian identity, and 0.55 for Walloon and Belgian identity. The typical Belgian citizen—Walloon or Flemish—holds multiple identities.

The existence of multiple identities does not preclude significant differences in national consciousness between Flemish and Walloons as well as within the two regions. In a 1991 survey of five items measuring national consciousness (Maddens, Beerten, and Billiet 1994), the Flemish region shows much greater polarization than the Walloon region and broader attachment to regionalism. At one end stand "unitarists" (31 percent), who consistently prefer Belgium to Flanders and oppose giving more autonomy to the regions. At the other extreme stand 10 percent who reject Belgian identity and want independence for Flanders. This "autonomist group" shares many of the same concerns with a larger group of "regionalists," who rank Flemish identity more highly than Belgian identity and want more autonomy for the Flemish region, though they stop short of full independence. In the Walloon region, the "autonomist" category is essentially absent, and support for regionalism is generally more conditional. While a little less than 20 percent prefer Walloon identity to Belgian identity and demand more Walloon autonomy, 15 percent support Walloon autonomy but not if the economic cost would be too great. Almost one out of five Walloons give inconsistent answers; these "neutrals" have not made up their minds about the nationality problem (Maddens, Beerten, and Billiet 1994, 1996).

At the level of public opinion, regional nationalism is moderate, and has become more so over time. Regional identity is surpassed by local identity in all three regions, and by Belgian identity in two of the three; only in Flanders is regional identity somewhat stronger than Belgian identity. Moreover, regional identity is nonexclusive in that most Flemish, Walloons, or Brusselers have multiple territorial identities of which their regional identity is only one. Yet regional nationalism is asymmetrical in Belgium; it is more widely anchored in the Flemish region than in the Walloon or Brussels region.

At first it seems odd that nationalist conflict could become salient in a country where regional nationalism has had rather limited public support. However, political movements are often the products of active minorities with intense preferences. These active minorities existed and had easy access to strategic political elites in the three parts of the country. Their conflicting demands became particularly salient from the 1960s on. Why have political leaders responded to these minorities by engaging in a radical "hollowing out of the Belgian center" in favor of extensive regional autonomy, while most citizens prefer to maintain Belgian institutions and identity?

Conceptualizing Institutional Change: Consociational versus Federal Institutions

It is common wisdom that majority rule exacerbates conflict in deeply divided societies. This is particularly so for territorially divided countries.

Yet, in Belgium, territorial conflict resolution was never hindered by majority rule. Nonmajoritarianism has been the main feature of the Belgian political regime from its independence in 1831. Lijphart considered it to be a typical example of a consociational democracy, where potential instability is countered by prudent elite accommodation and techniques of power sharing among segments (Lijphart 1969, 1999; Deschouwer 1996). At the same time, Belgium was, until 1970, a textbook case of a territorially centralized unitary state. In response to territorial conflict, Belgium changed from one nonmajoritarian regime with strong consociational characteristics into another—federalism. Yet the current constitutional architecture has inherited many nonmajoritarian features of the prefederal period.

I will show that, notwithstanding the radical constitutional transformation of the Belgian political institutions since 1970, the fundamental feature of territorial conflict management is continuity. It is possible to trace the roots of twenty-first-century mechanisms for conflict management in nineteenth- and early-twentieth-century nonmajoritarian innovations.

Before 1970: *Nonterritorial Nonmajoritarian Rules in a Consociational Regime*

Territorial conflict emerged in a regime that tended to co-opt challengers rather than exclude them; that depended on broad agreement rather than minimal winning majorities; that tolerated systemic opposition and had mechanisms to take the sharp edges off conflict. It also emerged in a regime where one set of actors—political parties—had disproportionate power.

Belgium was a classical example of consociationalism. A consociational system refers to a closed, but consensual system, which rests on four important rules: groups or segments govern themselves as much as possible; each group or segment receives a proportional share of common resources; group leaders mediate links between state and citizens; active public participation is discouraged in order not to disrupt elite accommodation. That places segmental elites in a pivotal position. In Belgium, these were the political parties, or more precisely, the party leaderships.

Because of the critical role of political parties, some have labeled pre-1970 Belgium a consociational partitocracy (Dewachter 1987; Deschouwer 1996, 1998; Deschouwer, De Winter, and Della Porta 1996). Parties connected societal segments with decision making among elites. Parties "are much more than purely political organizations. They are the political expression of a subcultural network of organizations. ... At the same time, the parties are the structures that organize the seeking of consensus at the level of the political elites. It is actually the parties' elites that must be 'prudent leaders' in order to prevent the subcultural divisions (which they themselves organize and mobilize) from becoming the source of centrifugal conflicts. The political agreements then also have to be implemented, and therefore the parties need a firm control over the parliament and over the public administration. ... A consociational democracy tends to be a partitocracy" (Deschouwer 1996, 296).

If one travels down from the regime level to the level of institutional mechanisms, it is clear that even in the heyday of consociationalism, majority rule was not only limited by purely "Lijphartian" consociational measures. Several techniques relied on the arbitral, delegatory, and limited government principle (see Table 2.4). For example, the 1831 constitution declared that a two-thirds majority (after the dissolution of the parliament and a special election) was necessary for any constitutional revision—a measure of limited government. Such a large majority assured that no parliament could change the constitution unless proposals had the support of the major segments. In the nineteenth century the constitution maker's intention was to reassure Catholics and Liberals, the two alternating governing powers. In the twentieth century, this supermajority protected Christian Democrats against potential socialist domination, and vice versa. In 1970, it was not much of a stretch to adjust this provision to give the new segmental forces—Flemish and Francophones—the same reassurance on constitutional issues.

Table 2.4 Limits to Majority Rule.

	Consociational Era, Pre-1970	Territorialization, 1970–1980	Federal Era, 1981–
Consociational mechanisms	-PR electoral system (since 1899)	-idem	-idem
	-1930s, 1963: linguistic minority rights in mixed communes	-idem	-idem
		-linguistic parity rules in cabinet and parliament	-idem
		-cabinet decides by consensus	-idem
			-1989: linguistic parity rules in Brussels region
			-symmetrical coalitions (informal) (Francophone + Flemish member of party family; same parties at federal and subnational level)

Table 2.4 — Continued

	Consociational Era, Pre-1970	Territorialization, 1970–1980	Federal Era, 1981–
Delegatory mechanisms	-de facto partitioning of some central administrations from 1950s	-idem	-subsumed in larger decentralization
	-partitioning of cultural policy: Dutch and Francophone ministers (1965)	-idem	-subsumed in larger decentralization
		-1970: creation of cultural councils; separate meetings of some Dutch and Francophone ministers; no separate executives -partitioning of education policy: Dutch and Francophone ministers (1970)	-1980: communities and regions: indirectly elected councils, separate executives -1989: Brussels region: directly elected council, separate executive/more competencies for communities and regions -1993: dual federalism: directly elected councils for regions; residual powers; exclusive competencies
Arbitral rules	-corporatist institutions (trade unions distributing unemployment benefits; segmental health organizations allocating health benefits, etc.)	-idem	-idem
			-1980: court of arbitration (partial constitutional review); considerably strengthened in 1989 -1992: central bank independence -1993: Maastricht Treaty: Commitment to EMU, and in 1999: entry to EMU

(Continued)

Table 2.4 — Continued

	Consociational Era, Pre-1970	Territorialization, 1970–1980	Federal Era, 1981–
Limited government	-constitutional revision: two-thirds majority needed	-idem, but more demanding "special majority" for language policy legislation and for some constitutional laws	-idem
	-1963 law: linguistic border irrevocably fixed	-idem	-idem
		-alarm bell procedure	-idem, also applicable in Brussels region (since 1989)

Note: This table summarizes consociational, delegatory, arbitral, and limited government rules since the 1960s that have direct relevance to territorial conflict management.

1970–1979: *Gradual Territorialization of Nonmajoritarian Rules*

The reform of 1970 put in place primarily nonterritorial mechanisms for managing growing territorial conflict. The constitution entrenched four measures of power sharing between the two language groups. The government was to consist of an equal number of Dutch- and French-speaking ministers, who were to take decisions by consensus. Second, members of the national parliament were subdivided into separate Dutch and French language groups. Third, language policy legislation and certain constitutional laws were made subject to special voting requirements (a majority of each language group had to be present, a majority in each language group had to support the law, and there had to be an overall two-thirds majority in favor). Finally, an alarm bell procedure was approved: a legislative proposal was to be postponed if considered harmful for Flemish-Francophone relations by 75 percent of a language group, and the parliament was to instruct the national government to formulate a compromise.

In a departure from nonterritorial mechanisms, the 1970 reform also entrenched two models of territorial devolution in the constitution. To accommodate demands for cultural autonomy, the constitution defined three communities (Francophone, Dutch-speaking, and German). The Francophone (later renamed as French) community referred to all Belgian citizens in the Walloon region and Brussels who spoke French; French speakers in the Flemish region were excluded. The Dutch-speaking (later renamed as Flemish) community indicated all persons in the Flemish region or in Brussels who spoke Dutch. The German community referred to all German speakers in the eastern cantons. So the communities had fluid territorial boundaries. The lawmakers also wrote the principle of regional autonomy into the constitution. The creation of regions accommodated demands for socioeconomic autonomy. In contrast to the communities, these regions—the Flemish, Walloon, and Brussels regions—had clearly identifiable, though contested boundaries. The proposed regional autonomy remained dead letter, but a limited form of cultural autonomy was put into effect in 1971. The special law set up cultural councils for the two largest communities, which consisted of the Flemish and Francophone members of the national parliament, respectively, and these councils monitored small executives composed of ministers accountable to the national government. This was a timid response to the process of regional realignment that had just begun.

The two components of the constitutional reform fit neatly in a nonmajoritarian approach to conflict management. The first four features assured that each segment had a fair share in joint activities and could not be overruled by the other segment, while the second component promised cultural self-rule where possible. As Table 2.4 shows, these two steps creatively employed consociational, delegatory, and limited government mechanisms. The 1970 reform was an attempt to co-opt nationalist challengers by applying familiar nonmajoritarian principles to a new cleavage.

1980–1992: *Protofederal Rules*

The second constitutional revision in 1980 set Belgium on the path of territorial devolution. The 1980 reform created separate executives and a separate administrative apparatus for regions and communities, but no independently elected councils. The Brussels region was exempt from the reform. Regions and communities spent approximately 8 percent of the overall state budget. Presciently the reformers labeled the reform "interim, but irreversible."

The third constitutional reform of 1989 stopped short of creating a federal state. The new Belgian constitutional structure resembled a subdued form of dual federalism, in which regions, communities, and national government had exclusive rather than concurrent or joint competencies, and in which the division of labor was primarily jurisdictional rather than functional. However, two features induced cooperation to temper these dual characteristics. An extensive network for executive and bureaucratic collaboration was created. Also, the regional and community parliaments remained composed of the members of the national parliament. For example, the Walloon regional council was composed of all members of the national parliament elected in Walloon constituencies and the French council consisted of all members of the national parliament elected in Walloon constituencies, plus French-speaking members of parliament elected in Brussels.

The 1989 reform intentionally limited fiscal devolution (Stienlet 1999). Regions and communities obtained only circumscribed fiscal autonomy in the form of some fiscal powers, a mechanism for automatic funding, and a solidarity mechanism, though they received considerable financial autonomy. That is, they gained limited powers to tax, but they received considerable discretion to spend their share of the total national budget, which was increased from less than 10 percent in 1980 to 33 percent.[7] The financial arrangement was complicated. A transition period of more than ten years (until 2000) eased the shock for the French-speaking part of the country, which stood to lose from greater financial and fiscal autonomy based on a *juste retour.*

At first, it seems difficult to understand why Flemish and Walloon politicians settled for a financial compromise that was suboptimal for both sides. One explanation could be that the negotiators were determined to gain political autonomy irrespective of the economic costs. A more plausible explanation posits strategic economic calculations. The compromise was the second-best solution given that likely alternatives—status quo and separatism—were economically less palatable.

The economic benefits of separatism were real and transparent. For the Flemish, partition would end transfers from the richer Flemish region to the poorer Walloon region, and it would create the prospect of lower taxes in an independent Flemish state. For the Walloons, independence would allow them to pursue more redistributive policies than in Belgium as a whole. So either side could reap economic benefits from separatism. So why was separatism avoided in Belgium in 1989?

Bolton and Roland (1997) suggest that high uncertainty concerning the costs of secession may have compelled both the Flemish and Walloon voters to forego secession. On the Flemish side, opponents of secession feared that the Flemish economy would take a hit if its domestic market shrunk by two-fifths, and they pointed out that the taxpayers would probably have to shoulder the lion's share of the huge Belgian public debt. The most obvious loss for the Walloon region was that secession would end considerable transfers through taxation and social security as well as future transfers through the health and pension system.

The confrontation between Flemish and French-speaking negotiators on financial autonomy took the form of a game of chicken, in which either side could credibly threaten to blow up the country if its demands were not met and yet where secession was unpalatable to both sides. The compromise, then, can be seen as a Nash equilibrium, where each side reaps some benefits from hollowing the center while avoiding the worst-case scenario—abolishing the center. French-speaking politicians accepted phasing in a reduction of redistributive transfers in return for greater immediate control over key redistributive policies: education, regional policy, transport, public utilities. The Flemish accepted delaying a reduction of transfers in return for some immediate financial autonomy, an automatic phasing in of *juste retour,* and a promise of future fiscal autonomy.

Several factors made it easier for French-speaking negotiators to accept a deal that appeared to make them gradually worse off financially. First, the full financial impact of the 1989 reform would not be felt until ten years later—well beyond the normal time horizon of elected politicians. Some observers even anticipated that an economic recovery in the Walloon region might turn the *juste retour* principle to its advantage by that time. Even if the economy did not change for the better, many French-speaking negotiators calculated that they could probably extract a better financial deal in return for greater fiscal autonomy in 2000—a core demand for Flemish politicians. But second, and most important, the financial rules of the 1989 reform created far greater financial penury for the French community institutions than for the Walloon region. From the perspective of Walloon regionalists, then, the 1989 compromise was a pretty good deal. Walloon regionalists had a powerful grip over the main negotiator on the Francophone side, the PS, which owed its 1989 electoral victory to their support. It was payback time for the PS leadership, which privileged Walloon regional interests over Francophone community interests.

The 1989 reform also worked out a solution for the Brussels region with strong consociational overtones. Various mechanisms inspired by the 1970 arrangements for the national parliament protected the small Dutch-speaking minority against French-speaking majority rule on regional matters. In addition, the two cultural communities gained autonomy on most cultural and person-related matters (such as youth policy and education,) while they were to co-decide under linguistic parity rules on joint matters (such as hospital policy). The reform also provided for the direct election of the Brussels regional council. This made the Brussels regional council the only directly elected subnational council (Witte 1992).

From 1993: *Nonmajoritarian Rules in a Federal Regime*

The constitution of May 1993 formally characterized Belgium as a federal state. In June 2001, a mini-reform further extended federalization. The revisions put in place the full range of institutions and mechanisms typical of a modern federation: direct election of subnational councils; a senate representing subnational interests; residual competencies with subnational units; fiscal federalism (changes in financing mechanism and more fiscal autonomy); constitutional autonomy of each level over its working rules; international competencies and treaty power; coordination machinery and conflict resolution.

The list of subnational competencies is extensive. Regions have competencies with a territorial logic. These consist of regional economic development, including employment policy; industrial restructuring; environment; nature conservation and rural development; housing, land-use planning, and urban renewal; water resources and sewage; energy policy (except for national infrastructure and nuclear energy); road building; waterways; regional airports and public local transport; local government; agriculture; external trade. However, framework rule making remains federal in most of these areas. The communities have responsibility for matters related to individuals: culture (including arts, youth policy, tourism); language policy (except in communes with a special language regime); education (three-quarters of the community budget); health policy and welfare (but not social security); and international cooperation in these areas. The communities set the normative framework for culture and, with some exceptions, education autonomously. The list of exclusive federal competencies is short, though substantial: defense, justice, security, social security, fiscal and monetary policy. Under the Economic and Monetary Union (EMU), monetary policy has largely shifted to the EU and fiscal policy is considerably constrained by EMU criteria.

The net effect of this division of labor was that in 1992, regions and communities spent 34 percent of the overall government budget, the federal authorities 29 percent, and the EU 4.4 percent. The remaining 32.6 percent was absorbed by interest payments on public debt, predominantly borne by the federal government.

The constitutional reform of 1993 entrenches dual federalism ("two worlds model"), but it does so with a particular Belgian twist. Very few competencies are concurrent; most competencies are exclusive. This reduces opportunities for the federal level to interfere with the regions and communities and vice versa. But, the division of powers running along jurisdictional lines is weak. In several areas, from environment to health to energy policy, the federal government retains control over the general legislative and fiscal framework, while detailed legislative and executive work is transferred to regions or communities.

The input of subnational interests in the current political system is extremely complex. The contribution is probably greater than in most federal systems, including Canada, Germany, and Switzerland. This greater input increases the risk of conflict, but the laws provide four arenas in which territorial conflicts between federal and subnational interests or between Flemish and Walloon/Francophone interests can be addressed.

Federal institutions remain the prime venue for the resolution of much horizontal Flemish-Francophone conflict, and here the familiar consociational mechanisms are unchanged. The most important provision is that the federal cabinet must have an equal number of Flemish- and French-speaking ministers. And because the cabinet decides by consensus, this ensures the two large linguistic groups a veto. The other non-majoritarian measures introduced by the 1970 state reform are also still in place: the federal house of representatives and the senate are divided into two language groups, sensitive legislation needs to pass with supermajorities, and an aggrieved language group can invoke the alarm bell procedure. These practices are not very different from the ones found in Switzerland. However, while these practices in the Swiss confederation are counterbalanced by the fact that the language groups are dispersed across twenty-six cantons, the Belgian federation has formally only five components: Flemish community, French community, German community, Brussels region, and Walloon region.[8] In real political terms, it has only two-and-a-half: the Flemish community, the Walloon region, and the somewhat less weighty Brussels region. The Belgian federation has de facto a bipolar structure, which is moreover asymmetrical in that the components are a community and a region. This tilts the system toward confederalism.

The second arena is the reformed senate, a hybrid of the American and German senates. It consists of 3 groups: 40 directly elected senators (25 elected in the Flemish community and 15 in the French community); 21 delegated from regional and community councils, with 10 Flemish, 10 French speakers, and 1 German member; 6 Flemish and 4 French-speaking individuals appointed by the previous 2 groups. The main task of the senate is to advise on conflicts of interest between the various governments. Although its decisions are not binding, its advice carries considerable political weight. It is not involved in ordinary legislation, in budgetary control, or in parliamentary control over the federal government, but it plays a full role, together with the house of representatives, in constitutional reform and legislation on the organization of the state.

The third arena for conflict regulation is the complex maze of intergovernmental relations. Subnational and federal governments are intertwined through an elaborate network of collaborative agreements. This is modeled on German cooperative federalism, but there is a major difference. In Germany, functional interdependence evolves from the fact that the federal government is the superior normative authority and the *Länder* are the prime authorities for implementation. In Belgium, the dual federalism model usually enables the federal and subnational levels to implement what they have legislated, each in their spheres of competencies. There is no legal equivalent for *Bundesrecht bricht Landesrecht* because the constitution avoids concurrent competencies. Nevertheless, unilateral action is often ineffectual because of the way in which policy areas are carved up among federal and subnational governments; it often happens that another authority has crucial policy instruments, that one government's action interferes with the competencies of other levels, or that externalities are created (Alen and Peeters 1989; Alen and Ergec 1994). Mutual dependency is thus of a quite different nature than in the German federation: it depends on the assumption that governments are rational in that they seek optimal policy outcomes, and it does not depend on legal provisions.

The central institution in this executive network is the Deliberation Committee for the Government and the Executives (*Overlegorgaan,* or *Comité de concertation*). This twelve-member committee conforms to the double parity rule: an equal number of federal and community/regional representatives, and an equal number of Flemish and Francophones. The German community votes on matters of its concern. The committee takes decisions by consensus and, although its decisions are not legally binding, its recommendations are difficult to reject because it consists of the political heavyweights of each government. The Deliberation Committee established more than a dozen interministerial conferences (IMCs) of functional ministers. They are authorized to conclude collaboration agreements, which are legally enforceable. Each IMC can set up working groups consisting of public servants, political aides of the minister (members of the cabinet), experts, or interest group representatives.

This executive system also regulates the international relations of subnational authorities (Devuyst 1993; Hooghe 1995; Ingelaere 1994). The core component is a 1993 cooperation agreement in the interministerial conference for external affairs by the federal government, the three regional governments, and the three community governments. It lays down the composition of the Belgian representation in the EU council of ministers and decision rules concerning negotiation strategy and voting in the absence of agreement among the governments from Belgium. Regions and communities are fully qualified to regulate international cooperation within the scope of their competencies. That includes the power to conclude treaties. Detailed machinery arranges the coordination of a partitioned Belgian foreign policy. For EU policy, for example, the agreement classifies the EU councils in four categories, depending on the relative importance of federal and regional competencies in a policy area. This categorization is then used to determine whether federal or subnational officials represent Belgium in the council of ministers and related council working groups. For areas with regional or community competence, regions and communities rotate the chair.

A final arena for territorial conflict resolution is the Court of Arbitration (set up in 1980, but significantly strengthened in 1989), a quasi-constitutional court composed of an equal number of judges/legal authoritative figures and former politicians (and an equal number of Dutch and French speakers). It guards the legal division of competencies between the various levels of government, and it checks the conformity of federal laws and regional or community decrees with specific constitutional provisions (equality of all Belgians, protection of ideological and philosophical minorities, and the freedom of education). However, it is considerably less powerful than the German, Canadian, or U.S. constitutional courts. For example, it cannot scrutinize the constitutionality of laws and decrees beyond the aforementioned three provisions.

Contrary to the three previous reforms, the reformers announced that the 1993 reform would be the final round. And yes, the intensity of territorial conflict has abated, and the pace of centrifugal change has slowed down. Nevertheless, senior politicians on either side still plead regularly for further devolution, and some do not exclude full independence. Particularly among Flemish politicians of the center-right (Christian Democrats, some liberals, nationalists, and the *Vlaams Blok*), separatism is discussed as a viable option. A broad consensus has emerged among the political parties on either side of the linguistic divide to siphon off a few portions—in areas as diverse as education, agriculture, trade, and immigrant policy—from federal to regional or community control. This would strengthen the jurisdictional features of federalism. In June 2001, the parliament passed a near-complete federalization, including rule making, of agriculture and trade. Yet the most important changes are financial: regions obtain extensive fiscal autonomy, and the budget for the communities is increased considerably. Most financial changes will be phased in, but the bottom line is that the Belgian center is set to shrink considerably, and federalism is due to take a decidedly dual-type turn.

The transition from a unitary state to a federation in two decades constitutes radical institutional change. Nonterritorial mechanisms for conflict resolution within a unitary state have been substituted by a territorial mechanism par excellence: federalism, and more particularly, by a form of dual federalism. If one examines more closely the mix of institutions in the subsequent regimes, one discerns continuity. Throughout, territorial conflict management in Belgium has been characterized by a preference for limiting majority rule. Table 2.4 understates this continuity because it reviews only those rules that are directly relevant to territorial conflict.

Hollowing the Center in Return for Peace

Territorial conflict peaked around 1980 and has subsided since. Moreover, indicators of national consciousness appear to suggest that integrative forces have gained strength. More Flemish, Walloons, and Brusselers profess primary attachment to Belgium. Fewer vote for separatist or nationalist parties. To what extent have these changes been a consequence of the introduction of federal institutions?

Nonterritorial Mechanisms and Hollowing Out

While nonterritorial devices to constrain majority rule have been useful in containing violent, disruptive territorial conflict, they have facilitated the "hollowing of the center." The literature on consociationalism usually emphasizes the dimension of shared

rule (Lijphart 1985, 1993), or to use the typical consociational term, elite accommodation. However, students of consociationalism underestimate incentives for a centrifugal
course that are embedded in a consociational logic. When the conflict is territorial, these
centrifugal features lead elite conflict managers to hollow out the center.

Classical nonterritorial devices to constrain majority rule specialize in maximizing
benefits to the groups while minimizing loss from the center. Several of these mechanisms were developed to deal with religious and class conflict in Belgium (Huyse 1970,
1980), and from the 1960s they became widely used to contain the growing nationalist
challenge.

CARVING UP THE CENTER

One way to achieve peace among competing groups is to give each group control
over those central policies that matter most to them. Belgian conflict brokers traditionally applied this technique to the allocation of ministerial portfolios. They often
gave big expenditure departments like defense, public works, or public housing to
Walloon socialist ministers, who could thereby create jobs for the declining Walloon
economy. And they allocated agriculture and culture to Flemish Christian Democrats,
who wanted to satisfy their sizable rural constituency or felt pressure from cultural nationalists.

MUTUAL CHECKS

Mutual checks may be used when parties are not keen to vacate an area. This technique was introduced first in education policy after the school war in the 1950s to alleviate tensions between Catholics and non-Catholics. From then on, a deputy minister
representing the other side of the religious cleavage assisted the minister of education.
When in the early 1970s the Ministry of Education was divided into a Dutch-speaking
and a French-speaking ministry, each minister was assigned a deputy. A non-Catholic
became minister of education in the Flemish community with a Catholic deputy-
minister on his side; for French-speaking Belgium, a Christian Democratic minister
had a non-Catholic deputy. In the 1960s and 1970s, mutual linguistic checks became a
more general feature when several ministerial departments introduced linguistic
deputies.

ALLOCATING NEW RESOURCES

The center may also buy off disaffected groups by putting more resources on the
table. This technique was widely used to soften conflict between Catholics and non-
Catholics, and at a high financial cost, to settle educational conflict in 1958 after the
school war. It quickly became a widely used technique for buying nationalist peace as

well. The Belgian center released additional resources to fund linguistic quotas in public service and public procurement. One famous package deal was the construction of a new university in Louvain-la-Neuve to put to rest Flemish/Francophone conflict over the bilingual University of Leuven (early 1970s). Another, in the 1980s, concerned the construction of a highway connecting two Walloon towns in exchange for a Flemish kindergarten in Comines (a Francophone commune with special language rights for Flemish).

Each technique affects political cohesion differently. The first two—carving up policy making over center resources and mutual checks—increase interdependence among actors. One cannot move without the consent of the other; this is *interlocking*. The latter strategy—to share new resources—unties actors' hands as groups agree to go separate ways; this is *unlocking*. While the former two manipulate the balance of power *at the center*, the latter manipulates power *between* center and group. If there is more of the latter than the former, it leads to an ever more hollow center.

These nonmajoritarian devices are expensive. Partly as a result of this, Belgium ran up the highest public debt per head in the EU by the early 1980s. Public finance ran out of control in the late 1970s—a period of chronic nationalist conflict and social friction, paralyzed governments, and expensive deals between parties in power. As money ran out, conflict managers introduced a new currency for making deals: while they used to trade goods (jobs, subsidies, infrastructure), penury forced them to start trading competencies (slices of authoritative decision making in culture, education, regional policy, environmental policy, etc.). It is not difficult to understand why this transition from goods to competencies occurred. In the late 1970s, nationalist conflict appeared close to descending into violence. Consociational techniques had successfully abated potentially violent religious conflict; they promised to achieve the same for potentially violent nationalist conflict.

Conflict management through the above techniques gradually created an incentive structure in which nationalism became an attractive strategy for political actors. Even non-nationalist actors were tempted to raise the nationalist banner to get what they wanted. This challenges the traditional argument of scholars of consociationalism, who assume that elites always prefer compromise to conflict unless constituents force them into conflict (Tsebelis 1990). It is their prudent wisdom that justifies the elitist style of governance in consociational regimes. In contrast, as George Tsebelis has argued forcefully, given a certain incentive structure it may be rational for elites to initiate nationalist conflict so as to maximize electoral utility. By the late 1970s, this situation had emerged in Belgium (Tsebelis 1990; Covell 1982, 1986). Nationalist demands became part of the standard competitive game between regional parties in Belgium (Deschouwer 1996).

The consociationalist legacy was crucial to elite capacity to contain territorial conflict. They successfully exported consociational devices from religious to territorial conflict, and they flexibly changed the currency for compromise from goods/money to competencies. The upshot of this is that territorial conflict in Belgium avoided violence. However, this efficient and flexible response made it profitable for contending groups to perpetuate territorial conflict. Consociational cooperation and territorial benefit became intimately linked to separatism. As a result, the center was being hollowed out.

Consociationalism and the Gradual Transition to Federalism

Consociationalism and federalism have both been defined as regimes that combine self-rule and shared rule (Elazar 1987; Lijphart 1984, 1985). The similarities between a consociational regime and a federal regime have facilitated the transition to territorial mechanisms of conflict resolution.

Why did the major political parties in Belgium finally replace consociationalist devices with federal rules? One reason is that federalism offered them an opportunity to curb the creeping separatism embedded in consociationalist politics. Federalism became Belgium's best chance for survival. Another reason is that unchecked nationalist conflict had become a threat to the major parties' predominant position. Belgium has been a partitocracy, with a preponderant role for Christian Democrats and Socialists since the first half of the twentieth century. Party leaders—not governments, the electorate, or societal actors—have been the architects of all major reforms. A top-down federal reform allowed these party leaders to design the rules in ways that would help them sustain their positions in authority.

From the standpoint of political party leaders traditional consociational devices appear less effective in contending with territorial conflict than federalism. First of all, consociational conflict resolution requires that elites represent monolithic segments with near-consensual support for their leaders; opposition within a segment is destabilizing. Yet interparty competition within the same segment undermines the dominant parties' authority. The Flemish Christian Democrats' capacity to deliver a deal was threatened by Flemish nationalist parties and even by the nationalist outbidding from the Liberal and Socialist parties. The Walloon Socialists faced similar challenges in Wallonia. In a federal system, opposition within a territorial segment is institutionalized. Governments backed by a majority in the regional legislature make or break deals. The Flemish Christian Democrats and the Walloon Socialists could anticipate being major coalition partners in governments of their respective regions.[9]

Second, consociationalism works best when the central decision load is low. This is why consociational elites usually hive off functions to semiprivate segmental organizations. However, this logic collides with a nationalist logic where nationalists usually demand an expanding role for public authority and not limited government. Federalism is better equipped to accommodate subnational demands for greater authoritative autonomy. The Flemish Christian Democrats wanted and received extensive community autonomy in education and cultural policy; the Walloon Socialists wanted and obtained extensive regional autonomy in economic development, industrial policy, and public housing.

Third, as Ian Lustick (1979; see also Barry 1975) has argued persuasively, consociationalism requires a secure equal status among the segments. If the institutional mechanisms to prevent one segment from dominating the other are insecure, consociationalism may become a control regime. A potentially destabilizing situation emerged in the 1970s, when the Flemish demographic majority was briefly tempted to pursue a majoritarian logic within a unitary Belgian framework. Federalism blocked these ambitions.

Other Influences on the Level of Territorial Conflict
ECONOMIC FACTORS

Theories of nationalism are ambivalent about the role of economic factors in territorial conflict. Economic factors do not predict the dynamics of territorial conflict in Belgium (Hooghe 1991; Maddens, Beerten, and Billiet 1994).

Even straightforward economic explanations linking territorial conflict to the business cycle fall flat. A grievances-based explanation would suggest greater conflict in times of economic downturn because competition for scarce resources is sharper. A resource-based explanation would expect intensification of conflict during economic prosperity because there are more resources available for the mobilization of territorial protest. However, Belgian history provides little support for either hypothesis. Territorial conflict was highest in the 1960s—a period of unparalleled prosperity—and in the late 1970s to early 1980s—a period of negative or stagnant growth, high unemployment, and deficit spending.

EUROPEAN INTEGRATION

Territorial conflict is usually conceptualized as primarily a domestic matter. However, some authors have linked the rise in regionalism and separatism to the erosion of national sovereignty by economic globalization and by rule setting through international institutions (Alesina and Spolaore 1997; Alesina, Perotti, and Spolaore 1995; Bolton and Roland 1997; Hooghe and Marks 1996, 2001; Marks and Hooghe 2000). The most tangible expression of these twin transnational developments for Belgium has been European integration. Paulette Kurzer has argued that EU membership has intensified the Flemish-Walloon conflict because it has exacerbated divergent economic developments between the regions (Kurzer 1996).

Though it is correct that European integration as a market-making process has made the preferences of Flemish and Walloon actors more divergent, it has also lowered the stakes of territorial conflict. It has eased the terrain for federal reform, and as a polity-building exercise it has increased incentives for cooperation among these territorial units.

European membership has made the implications of a split-up of the country more predictable and less consequential. Independent Flemish or Walloon states would find themselves restricted by EU membership in ways that are similar to the Belgian state. The potential costs of separatism for social actors in terms of economic uncertainty and policy unpredictability are lower. An independent Flemish or Walloon region will incur smaller efficiency losses from separation within a EU where free trade can be enforced across countries (Alesina and Spolaore 1997). That is why some have predicted that "a country like Belgium is more likely to break up when it is an integral part of a single European market" (Bolton and Roland 1997, 1066). But the potential benefits of separatism for political actors in terms of policy autonomy are also considerably smaller than in a world of sovereign nation-states. European regulations limit the range of policy choices at the domestic level, whether that is the federal, regional, or community level. At the extreme, incentives for separation may evaporate (Bolton and Roland 1997).

The rules of EU decision making induce Flemish and Walloon actors to search for common ground in the European arena. The most important formal institutional constraint is that the EU recognizes only member states, which makes it difficult for the regions or communities to act officially. Since 1993 (Maastricht Treaty) regional ministers may negotiate and vote for their country in the council of ministers (art. 203, formerly art. 146). This made it possible for the Belgian constitutional reformers in 1993 to extrapolate subnational autonomy to the European level for policy areas within their competence. However, member states are not allowed to split their votes in the council, so the various Belgian governments have strong incentives to agree on a common position. If they fail, Belgium has to abstain, and this supports de facto the "no" side in the council of ministers.

Membership of the EU is a double-edged sword for territorial conflict in Belgium. On the one hand, EU membership provides the most powerful external discipline on territorial conflict in Belgium. It reduces the expected benefits of separatism; it constrains policy divergences among Belgian actors; and it induces moderate and cooperative behavior among subnational and federal actors. At the same time, it reduces the cost of separatism as the benefits of free trade no longer vary with country size. Small countries such as Ireland or Luxembourg benefit as much from European integration as do Germany or Spain.

GENERATIONAL TURNOVER

Some sociologists argue that generational turnover may weaken the support base for territorial conflict. Survey data of the mid-1990s demonstrate that the generation younger than forty years is distinctly less interested in Flemish-Walloon conflict. However, the implications for regional nationalism are different for Flemish and Walloons.

For Flemish citizens, there appears to be a relatively weak, but growing interaction effect between age and education. Young, educated people tend to feel more Belgian (or European) than the average Flemish citizen. This seems to point to the emergence of a pro-Belgian movement among Flemish intellectuals, despite the fact that Flemish nationalism has been historically strongest among intellectuals. Hard-core Flemish nationalism appears to be on the decline (Martinielli and Swyngedouw 1998; Maddens, Beerten, and Billiet 1996). To the extent that it exists, it is concentrated in two groups. One category concerns the less educated, mostly male, young Flemish. Another, declining category consists of the sons and daughters of traditionally Flemish-nationalist families.

Some contribute this generational effect to differential socialization experiences. Flemish older than forty years are likely to have had firsthand experience of linguistic (and economic) discrimination; they lived as young adults through the sharpest linguistic conflicts: school war, *Leuven Vlaams*, conflict around Brussels. These life experiences induced them to become Flemish nationalists in the 1950s and 1960s. The younger Flemish generation, however, grew up in an affluent, linguistically self-confident Flemish region. For these people, the grievances that initially fueled Flemish nationalism have an unreal quality. Economic and political discrimination had been most acutely felt in traditionally Flemish nationalist families, many of whom were affected by the repression after the Second World War. It is therefore not surprising that anti-Belgian feelings etched on Flemish grievances die hardest among sons and daughters of these Flemish-nationalist families. Yet even here, family socialization appears to be losing force (Maddens, Beerten, and Billiet 1994, 1996).

The effect of age is more pronounced in Wallonia, and it works in the other direction (Maddens, Beerten, and Billiet 1994). Walloon regional identity is significantly stronger among the younger cohort than the older generation. That effect is present across all educational and occupational categories, but Walloon nationalism is much less concentrated in intellectual circles than it is in Flanders. Antiunitarist sentiment is strongest among uneducated workers, and radical regionalism is powerful among the self-employed. Moreover, there is a shift from moderate to radical regionalism among younger Walloons, though few regionalists are yet willing to embrace separatism.

Observers have again linked this generational effect to particular socialization experiences. Pro-Belgian unitarist sentiment is heavily concentrated among the oldest cohorts, who grew up during the Walloon economic boom and French-speaking dominance in Belgium during and just after the Second World War. This sentiment began to erode among the next generation, which reached adulthood during the dramatic reversal of economic fortunes in the Walloon region in the 1960s and 1970s. They were mobilized in the mix of territorial-linguistic and social protest that accompanied the strike of 1961, the closure of coal mines throughout 1960s, and the cutbacks in the steel industry in the 1970s and early 1980s. The youngest generation is growing up in a postindustrial Wallonia, an area with an aging population, endemic high unemployment, and a considerably lower standard of living than the Flemish region. However, the region has also patches of high-tech industry and an extensive third sector, which could form the basis of an economic revival. One may argue that, among the younger Walloon generation, anti-Belgian (and anti-Flemish) resentment has combined with regional confidence to produce a more radical strand of Walloon regionalism (for an early argument, see Collinge and Quévit 1988). So while in the Flemish region generational turnover appears to weaken radical regionalism and separatism, radical regionalism in Wallonia seems on the rise.

These generational factors are unlikely to transform politics overnight. The current political elite belongs overwhelmingly to a generation socialized by salient Flemish-Walloon conflict in the 1960s, 1970s, and 1980s. This elite is the gatekeeper for the next generation of political leaders. In the Belgian partitocracy—weakened, though not mortally wounded—party leaders weigh disproportionately on the selection of aspiring elites, not only in the party-political arena, but also in the administrative, judicial, cultural, and socioeconomic sectors.

Generational change also exacerbates a curious mismatch between Flemish- and French-speaking defenders of Belgian unity. An analysis of elite discourses demonstrates contrasting conceptions of Belgian and regional identity in Flanders and Wallonia (Van Dam 1996). In the Flemish region, defenders of Belgian unity conceive of the Belgian state as a model of peaceful coexistence of different ethnic groups (i.e., Flemish, Walloons and immigrants) and of solidarity between these groups. A choice for the Belgian model is presented as a choice against xenophobia and narrow-minded nationalism. This republican depiction of Belgian identity contrasts sharply with the dominant ethnocentric representation of Flemish identity, developed in the prewar period by the authoritarian VNV, and now propagated most vigorously by the *Vlaams Blok*. In contrast, Walloon identity is primarily associated with republican values such as the socioeconomic emancipation of the Walloon region, and the construction of an open, nonracist regional identity. In Brussels and Wallonia, the extreme right has continued a tradition of ethnic Belgian nationalism; in that sense, the *Front national* stepped into the footsteps of the prewar semifascist and ardently Francophone-Belgicist party Rex. This elite discourse analysis finds considerable support in survey research, where "multivariate analysis confirms that autonomist Flemish identity attracts citizens tending towards ethnocentrism and repels those tending towards ethnopluralism," even when one controls for socioeconomic indicators and party preference (Maddens, Beerten, and Billiet 1996, 14–15). In Wallonia, ethnocentrists are more likely to adopt a Belgian identity and ethnopluralists a regionalist identity, while authoritarian attitudes are positively correlated with pro-Belgian views and nonauthoritarian views with regionalist identity (Maddens, Beerten, and Billiet 1996; Maddens, Billiet, and Beerten 2000).

The fact that, in Flanders, defenders of Belgian unity are primarily found among progressive political actors but, in the Walloon region, mainly associated with traditionalist, ethnocentric values makes the mobilization of a national pro-Belgian countermovement more difficult. Some Flemish and Walloons feel strongly about maintaining Belgian unity, but they promote very different models of Belgian society. Generational change is not likely to salvage Belgian unity.

Strong institutional incentives in dual federalism continue to induce politicians in Belgium to emphasize territorial conflict and deemphasize cooperation. For rulers seeking to sustain their positions in authority, the benefits reaped by magnifying territorial difference appear greater than the costs of endemic conflict. Even aspiring leaders socialized differently may learn this lesson. Here lies the fundamental explanation for why nationalist conflict has been—and will be—more salient among elites than among the population (Kerremans 1997; Maddens 1994; Murphy 1995). There is a gap between the political preferences of the population and those of the country's elites, and the gap is the product of an incentive structure that has rewarded political elites who play the nationalist card. In that fundamental sense, there is continuity between the consociational era and the federal era in Belgium.

Under prefederal nonterritorial rules, the costs of unresolved territorial conflict could run up astronomically, because Flemish-Walloon conflict was capable of paralyzing the national government. Nonterritorial devices of conflict management made it relatively easy to "buy off"—at least temporarily—nationalist dissent and so to avoid government paralysis. It was rational for politicians to provoke nationalist conflict to extract more benefits for their constituencies (Tsebelis 1990). The price was the gradual hollowing of the center.

Under the rules of dual federalism, the costs of unresolved territorial conflict are relatively low for the subnational levels but considerable for the federal level. A weak federal level, composed of representatives of the subnational levels, has an interest in preventing deadlocks. In a framework of dual federalism, it can do so most easily by shifting more competencies to the subnational level. For example, throughout the 1990s Flemish politicians demanded the federalization of social security, and particularly of the national health system, on grounds of the principle of dual federalism. With health policy a competence for the Flemish and Francophone communities, they argue, it would be more efficient to devolve all levers of health policy, including national health insurance, to the communities. While the federal government has held out so far, the logic of the Flemish argument is a powerful one in a context of dual federalism with a weak federal level. In 2001, the federal level gave way in two contentious policy areas—agriculture and external trade. And it made significant financial concessions. The federal government took out a mortgage on its recently regained financial solvency in return for greater fiscal autonomy and greater financial resources for education policy. Greater fiscal autonomy delivers Flemish nationalists a long-demanded good and new resources for education policy save the French community from bankruptcy. It is not clear how the federal government is going to make up for lost funding in its own budget. The financial deal, observers agree, constitutes a total victory for communities and regions (Van Waterschoot 2001). It buys Flemish-Francophone peace at a considerable price for the federal treasury. The hollowing of the Belgian center is likely to continue in federal Belgium—be it perhaps at a slower pace than under consociationalism.

NOTES

1. There is much confusion about whether the people in the Flemish region speak Flemish or Dutch. Both are correct, but it makes much sense to use the word *Dutch (nederlands)* to emphasize that the language is the same as the one spoken in The Netherlands. I reserve the label *Flemish* to refer to the culture and identity of the people considering themselves members of the Flemish community; they live in the Flemish region, though most Dutch speakers in the Brussels region would also describe themselves as Flemish. Flemish, then, is an ethnic term. Similarly, *Walloon (wallon)* refers to the culture and identity of the people living in the Walloon region; the language spoken there is French, the same as in France. They share this language with the large majority of Brusselers; Brussels is primarily a French-speaking region, though there is an active Dutch-speaking minority. The label *Francophone,* which simply means French-speaking, is the preferred self-characterization of French-speaking inhabitants of the Brussels region; they only secondarily describe themselves as *Bruxellois.* Hence French-speaking Brusselers identify first and fore-

most with the linguistic community they share with Walloons; yet Walloons identify first and foremost with their region, and only secondarily with other French speakers. These self-descriptions are indicative of the weak common identity between Walloons and Francophone Brusselers.

I use the political-legal terms *Flemish region* and *Walloon region* instead of the cultural terms *Flanders* and *Wallonia,* even though the former terminology did not exist legally until 1970. The boundaries of the cultural concepts *Wallonia* and *Flanders* are much fuzzier than those of the regions.

Later I will also explain the distinction between communities and regions, of which there are three each. In twenty-first-century Belgium only four units play a political role: the Flemish community, the German community, the Brussels region, and the Walloon region. For reasons that will become clear, Flemish politicians have chosen to merge regional and community institutions and they have called this amalgam the Flemish community. The territorial boundaries of the Flemish community are less clearly delineated in legal terms than in practice: the Flemish community consists of the Flemish region, though it also exercises limited authority over the 10—15 percent of Dutch speakers who live in the Brussels region. The German community has unambiguous territorial boundaries; for all practical purposes it functions as a region. The Walloon and Brussels regions have clear territorial boundaries. Rather than using the label *community* for the Flemish and German autonomous institutions and *region* for the Walloon and Brussels institutions I have chosen to simplify matters where I can, and I call all *region.*

2. A figure somewhere in between these was suggested by the first direct election of the council for the Brussels capital region in 1989, when the Dutch-speaking parties obtained 15.3 percent of the vote; all parties had been required to submit unilingual lists. Because linguistic issues were salient in the capital's politics at the time, very few voters crossed linguistic lines, so that it seems reasonable to extrapolate these 15/85 proportions among voters to the population. There was more linguistic cross-voting during subsequent elections in 1994 and 1999. Note that the figures refer here to Belgian citizens only; close to 30 percent of Brussels population is non-Belgian, and most prefer French in public life. In October 2000, EU citizens among these non-Belgians were able to vote for the first time in local elections, but only 10 percent did. Mainly because of the electoral implications in and around Brussels, Flemish parties were extremely reluctant to support the provision in the 1993 Treaty of European Union that grants EU citizens voting rights in local and European elections. They finally agreed, though not before the Belgian government negotiated some exemptions on this provision. Registration for participation in these elections is extremely laborious, which is why so few voters registered on time.

3. In the 1930s, French remained highly attractive for the upper classes in the Flemish region. The spread of French as "the language spoken only or most frequently," in the terminology of the population census, reached a maximum in the 1920s and 1930s: between 6 and 12 percent in the Flemish urban centers.

4. These were incorporated in the Belgian constitution in 1970.

5. *Voeren* (*Fourons* in French) is a commune of 5,000 people near the German-Dutch border. Since 1963, it has been under Flemish administration and most inhabitants have historically spoken a Flemish-Germanic dialect. But it is geographically cut off from the Flemish region. To the extent that contemporary Voerenaars speak a standard language, most now prefer French to Dutch, though the commune is deeply divided between Dutch speakers and French speakers. Since the early 1960s, Voeren politics has been consumed by the question whether the small com-

mune should remain under Flemish administration or be transferred back to the Walloon region, and this conflict has regularly spilled over into national politics. Voeren dominated national headlines most prominently throughout the 1980s, when the Walloon socialist party (PS) decided to provide Voeren's French-speaking mayor José Happart with a national platform.

6. From 1975 to 1995, surveys used a variant of the following question: "Which political group do you identify with in the first place: all Belgians (or Belgium), with the Dutch-speaking/ French-speaking community, with the Flemish/Walloon/Brussels region, with your province, with your town (or village), or other? And which one in the second place?" These surveys demonstrated fluctuations in territorial identity in the range of 15 to 20 percent, which can to a large extent be explained by the ordering of the various identities. Research indicates that a primacy effect gives an artificial boost to the first category of approximately 10 percentage points, especially among respondents who lack strong opinions (De Winter 1998; De Winter, Frognier, and Billiet 1998; Billiet 1999).

7. These figures include interest payments on the national debt, which by then was at 140 percent of annual GDP. The financial arrangement provided that regions and communities would contribute to repaying the national debt.

8. In 1988, the Flemish community and the Flemish region decided to merge their institutions into one council, one government, and one administration. On the Francophone side, the French community and the Walloon region maintained separate institutions, though financial pressures forced the French community to cede much of educational policy to the Walloon region (and for Brussels, to the Brussels region). As a consequence, the real players are the Flemish community and the Walloon region, with a secondary role for the Brussels region. The small German community does not play a national role, but it enjoys extensive home rule because it has been able to add to the traditional community competencies some regional competencies. The Walloon region ceded to the German community authority for local development, urban planning, and other regional competencies. It is the only community with a directly elected council.

9. That proved to be a miscalculation for the Flemish Christian Democrats, who were relegated to the opposition banks after the 1999 election. But few would have anticipated their electoral demise at the time of the negotiations for federalization in the late 1980s and early 1990s.

References

Alen, André, and Rusen Ergec. 1994. *La Belgique fédérale après la quatriéme réforme de l'état de 1993.* Brussels: Ministère des Affaires étrangères.
Alen, André, and Patrick Peeters. 1989. België op zoek naar een cooperatief federaal staatsmodel. *Tijdschrift voor Bestuurswetenschap en Publiek Recht* 6:343–71.
Alesina, Alberto, Roberto Perotti, and Enrico Spolaore. 1995. Together or Separately? Issues on the Costs and Benefits of Political and Fiscal Unions. *European Economic Review* 39:751–58.
Alesina, Alberto, and Enrico Spolaore. 1997. On the Number and Size of Nations. *Quarterly Journal of Economics* 112:1027–56.
Barry, Brian. 1975. The Consociational Model and its Dangers. *European Journal of Political Research* 3:393–412.

Bélanger, Sarah, and Maurice Pinard. 1989. *Ethnic Movements and the Competition Model: Some Missing Links*. McGill Working Papers in Social Behaviour, no. 89/5. Montreal: McGill University.

Billiet, Jaak. 1999. Les opinions politiques des Flamands. *La Revue Générale* 134, no. 2:9–17.

Billiet, Jaak, R. Doutrelepont, and M. Vandekeere. 2000. Types van sociale identiteiten in België: Convergenties en Divergenties. Mimeo.

Bolton, Patrick, and Gérard Roland. 1997. The Breakup of Nations: A Political Economy Analysis. *Quarterly Journal of Economics* 112:1057–89.

Cohen, Frank. 1997. Proportional versus Majoritarian Ethnic Conflict Management in Democracies. *Comparative Political Studies* 30, no. 5:607–30.

Collinge, Michel, and Marcel Quévit. 1988. Wallonnie 87: les enjeux économiques, politiques et culturels. *Res Publica* 30, no. 1:257–77.

Covell, Maureen. 1982. Agreeing to Disagree: Elite Bargaining and the Revision of the Belgian Constitution. *Canadian Journal of Political Science* 15:451–69.

———. 1986. Regionalization and Economic Crisis in Belgium: The Variable Origins of Centrifugal and Centripetal Forces. *Canadian Journal of Political Science* 19, no. 2: 261–82.

Deschouwer, Kris. 1996. Waiting for the 'Big One': The Uncertain Survival of the Belgian Parties and Party Systems. *Res Publica* 38, no. 2:295–306.

———. 1998. Falling Apart Together: The Changing Nature of Belgian Consociationalism 1961–1998. Paper prepared for presentation at the Conference "The Fate of Consociationalism in Western Europe, 1968–98," Harvard University.

Deschouwer, Kris, Lieven Dewinter, and Donatella Della Porta. 1996. Partitocracies between Crises and Reforms: The Cases of Belgium and Italy. Special issue of *Res Publica*, 38, no. 2.

De Schryver, Reginald. 1981. The Belgian Revolution and the Emergence of Belgium's Biculturalism. In *Conflict and Compromise in Belgium: The Dynamics of a Culturally Divided Society*, ed. Arend Lijphart, 13–33. Berkeley: Institute of International Studies.

Devuyst, Youri. 1993. De omzetting van EG-richtlijnen in de Belgische rechtsorde en de Europeanisering van de Belgische politiek. *Res Publica* 35:39–54.

Dewachter, Wilfried. 1987. Changes in Particracy: The Belgian Party System from 1944 to 1986. In *Party Systems in Denmark, Austria, Switzerland, the Netherlands and Belgium*, ed. Hans Daalder. London: Pinter.

De Winter, Lieven. 1998. Etnoterritoriale identiteiten in Vlaanderen: verkenningen in een politiek en methodologisch mijnenveld. In *De (on)redelijke kiezer: Onderzoek naar de politieke opvattingen van Vlamingen—Verkiezingen van 21 mei 1995*, ed. Marc Swyngedouw, Jaak Billiet, Ann Carton, and Roeland Beerten, 159–80. Leuven: Acco.

De Winter, Lieven, André-Paul Frognier, and Jaak Billiet. 1998. Y a-t-il encore des belges? Vingt ans d'enquêtes sur les identités politiques territoriales. In *Où va la Belgique? Les soubresauts d'une petite démocratie européenne*, ed. Marc Swyngedouw and Marc Martinelli, 122–37. Paris: Editions L'Harmattan.

Elazar, Daniel. 1985. Federalism and Consociational Regimes. *Publius* 15:17–33.

———. 1987. *Exploring Federalism*. Tuscaloosa: University of Alabama Press.

Hechter, Michael. 1975. *Internal Colonialism: The Celtic Fringe in British National Development, 1536–1966*. London: Routledge & Kegan Paul.

Hooghe, Liesbet. 1991. *A Leap in the Dark: Nationalist Conflict and Federal Reform in Belgium in the 1980s*. Ithaca: Cornell Occasional Papers.

————. 1995. Belgian Federalism and the European Community. In *Regions in the European Community*, ed. Barry Jones and Michael Keating, 135–65. Oxford: Clarendon.

Hooghe, Liesbet, and Gary Marks. 1996. Europe with the Regions? Regional Representation in the European Union. *Publius: The Journal of Federalism* 26, no. 1:73–91.

————. 2001. *Multi-level Governance and European Integration*. Boulder: Rowman & Littlefield.

Horowitz, Donald. 1981. Patterns of Ethnic Separatism. *Comparative Studies in Society and History* 28, no. 2:165–95.

Huyse, Lucien. 1970. *Passiviteit, pacificatie en verzuiling in de Belgische politiek*. Antwerpen: Standaard Uitgevery.

————. 1980. *De gewapende vrede: politiek in België na 1945*. Leuven: Acco.

Ingelaere, Frans. 1994. De Europeesrechtelijke raakvlakken van de nieuwe wetgeving inzake de internationale betrekkingen van de Belgische Gemeenschappen en Gewesten. *Sociool-Economische Wetenschoppen*, 2:67–82.

Jones, Erik. 1998. Consociationalism, Corporatism, and the Fate of Belgium. Paper prepared for presentation at the Conference "The Fate of Consociationalism in Western Europe, 1968–98," Harvard University.

Kerremans, Bart. 1997. The Flemish Identity: Nascent or Existent? *Res Publica* 39, no. 2:303–14.

Kurzer, Paulette. 1996. Rescue of the Nation-State? Belgium in the European Community/Union. *Journal of Common Market Studies*.

Lijphart, Arend. 1969. Consociational Democracy. *World Politics* 21:207–25.

————. 1984. *Democracies: Patterns of Majoritarian and Consensus Government in Twenty-One Countries*. New Haven, Conn.: Yale University Press.

————. 1985. Non-Majoritarian Democracy: A Comparison of Federal and Consociational Theories. *Publius* 15:3–15.

————. 1999. *Patterns of Democracy: Government Forms and Performance in 36 Countries*. New Haven, Conn.: Yale University Press.

Lijphart, Arend, Ronald Rogowski, and R. Kent Weaver. 1993. Separation of Powers and Cleavage Management. In *Do Institutions Matter? Government Capabilities in the United States and Abroad*, ed. R. Kent Weaver and Bert A. Rockman, 302–44. Washington, D.C.: The Brookings Institute.

Linz, Juan. 1986. *Conflicto en Euskadi*. Madrid: Espasa Calpe.

Llera, F. J. 1993. *Conflicto en Euskadi* Revisited. In *Politics, Society, and Democracy: The Case of Spain*, ed. Richard Gunther. Boulder, Colo.: Westview.

Lorwin, Val. 1972. Segmented Pluralism: Ideological Cleavages and Political Cohesion in the Smaller European Democracies. *Comparative Politics* 3:141–75.

Lustick, Ian. 1979. Stability in Deeply Divided Societies: Consociationalism versus Control. *World Politics* 31:325–44.

Maddens, Bart. 1994. *Kiesgedrag en Partijstrategie*. Leuven: KULeuven Afdeling Politologie (Doct. Thesis).

Maddens, Bart, Roeland Beerten, and Jaak Billiet. 1994. *O Dierbaar België? Het natiebewustzijn van Vlamingen en Walen*. Leuven: Departement Sociologie.

————. 1996. *Ethnocentrism and Nationalism: Towards a Contextual Approach*. Leuven: Departement Sociologie, ISPO.

Maddens, Bart, Jaak Billiet, and Roeland Beerten. 2000. National Identity and the Attitude towards Foreigners in Multi-National States: The Case of Belgium. *Journal of Ethnic and Migration Studies* 26, no. 1:45–60.

Marks, Gary. 1999. Territorial Identities in the European Union. In *Regional Integration and Democracy*, ed. Jeffrey Anderson, 69–91. Boulder: Rowman & Littlefield.

Marks, Gary, and Liesbet Hooghe. 2000. Optimality and Authority: A Critique of Neo-Classical Theory. *Journal of Common Market Studies* 38, no. 5:795–816.

Marks, Gary, and Ivan Llamazares. Forthcoming. Multi-level Governance in Southern Europe: European Integration and Regional Mobilization. In *The Changing Functions of the State in the New Southern Europe*, ed. P. Nikiforos Diamandouros, Richard Gunther, and Gianfranco Pasquino. Baltimore: Johns Hopkins University Press.

Martinielli, Marco, and Marc Swyngedouw, eds. 1998. *Où va la Belgique? Les soubresauts d'une petite démocratie européenne*. Paris: l'Harmattan.

McRae, Kenneth. 1986. *Conflict and Compromise in Multilingual Societies: Belgium*. Waterloo: Wilfrid Laurier.

Melich, Ana. 1986. The Nature of Regional and National Identity in Catalonia: Problems of Measuring Multiple Identities. *European Journal of Political Research* 14, nos. 1–2: 149–70.

Murphy, Anthony. 1995. Belgium: Regional Divergence along the Road to *Federalism*. In *Federalism: The Multi-Ethnic Challenge*, ed. Graham Smith. London: Longman.

Nagel, Joan. 1986. The Political Construction of Ethnicity. In *Competitive Ethnic Relations*, ed. Susan Olzak and Joan Nagel. Orlando: Harcourt Brace Jovanovich.

Nagel, Joan, and Susan Olzak. 1982. Ethnic Mobilization in New and Old States: An Extension of the Competition Model. *Social Problems* 30, no. 2:127–43.

Nairn, Thomas. 1981. *The Break-up of Britain: Crisis and Neo-Nationalism*. London: New Left Books.

Nielsen, François. 1980. The Flemish Movement after World War II: A Dynamic Analysis. *American Sociological Review* 45, no. 1:79–94.

———. 1985. Toward a Theory of Ethnic Solidarity in Modern Societies. *American Sociological Review* 50, no. 2:133–49.

Obler, Jeffrey, Jurg Steiner, and Guido Dierickx. 1977. *Decision-Making in Smaller Democracies: The Consociational "Burden."* London: Sage.

Reif, Karlheinz. 1993. Cultural Convergence and Cultural Diversity as Factors in European Diversity. In *European Identity and the Search for Legitimacy*, ed. Soledad García. London: Pinter.

Risse-Kappen, Thomas. 1996. Exploring the Nature of the Beast: International Relations Theory and Comparative Policy Analysis Meet the European Union. *Journal of Common Market Studies* 34, no. 1:53–80.

Stienlet, Georges. 1999. Institutional Reforms and Belgian Fiscal Policy in the 90s. In *Institutions, Politics and Fiscal Policy*, ed. Rolf R. Strauch and Jürgen von Hagen, 215–34. Boston: Kluwer Academic.

Tsebelis, George. 1990. Elite Interaction and Constitution Building in Consociational Democracies. *Journal of Theoretical Politics* 2, no. 1:5–29.

Van Dam, Denise. 1996. *Blÿven we buren in België? Vlamingen en Wolen over Vlomingen en Wolen*. Leuven: Van Holewyck.

Van Waterschoot, Jerry. De verzwegen aderlating van Lambermont. *De Standaard,* August 8, 2001.

Weaver, R. Kent. 1992. Political Institutions and Canada's Constitutional Crisis. In *The Collapse of Canada?* ed. R. Kent Weaver, 7–75. Washington, D.C.: The Brookings Institution.

Witte, Els. 1992. Belgian Federalism: Towards Complexity and Asymmetry. *West European Politics* 15, no. 4:95–117.

CHAPTER THREE

Canada

Federalism, Language, and Regional Conflict

Richard Simeon

For those seeking a deeper understanding of the implications of federal institutions for
the management of conflict in divided or multinational societies Canada is a puzzle.
On the one hand, Canada is one of the world's longest lived and most decentralized
federations. Few would dispute that historically federalism has been an important—
though not the only—institutional device for managing linguistic and regional conflicts. Yet, in recent decades many Quebec nationalists have rejected federalism and
struggled to achieve an independent, sovereign Quebec state. In October 1995, they
came within a few thousand votes of winning a referendum calling for secession, with
a continuing economic and political "partnership" with the remaining Canada. More
generally, Canada appears to illustrate the Janus-faced quality of federalism. It is at
once a vehicle for accommodation, a way of reconciling the minority nations and
groups to the larger whole, and a device for perpetuating and institutionalizing the very
cleavages it is designed to manage, which may provide the institutional resources from
which to launch a successful secession movement. Canada adopted federalism in large
measure as a means to accommodate its linguistic duality and regional differences. In
2003, the prospect of a secession has considerably receded, but the capacity of federalism to continue to provide a framework for accommodation remains in question.

The fundamental questions for this chapter are these: First, what explains the capacity of federalism to manage and accommodate the dualist and regionalist character of Canada? The answer primarily lies in social and political changes in Quebec and in the rest of country as they have interacted with the institutions and practices of federalism. Second, is it possible to imagine reforms to the federal system that could bring about more effective accommodation in the future? The most promising possibilities lie in the direction of greater asymmetry, but the dynamics of constitutional politics makes this very difficult to achieve.

The Canadian federation was born in 1867, bringing together the British North American colonies. Several factors drove this alliance. One was defensive: the economic and political power of a resurgent United States threatened the small, vulnerable individual colonies. A second was economic: the colonies needed to unite in order to mobilize capital for economic development, and to counteract the loss of British economic preferences. The third was political: relations between French and English within a single colony, the United Province of Canada, were at an impasse.

The original federation, negotiated in a series of conferences among leaders of all the colonies, only included Ontario, Quebec, New Brunswick, and Nova Scotia (which passed a secession resolution shortly after Confederation was achieved). British Columbia joined a few years later, on the promise of a railroad to the west coast, as did Prince Edward Island. The western province of Manitoba was created out of a small settlement west of Ontario on the Red River in 1870. In 1905, the prairie provinces of Saskatchewan and Alberta were created out of what had been a western territory administered from the federal capital. The present federation was completed only in 1949, when Newfoundland joined following a closely contested referendum. Canada also includes three northern territories, still administered by the federal government, but increasingly taking on the powers and responsibilities of provinces. They include the Yukon, the Northwest Territories, and the recently created Nunavut, the first Canadian jurisdiction to have an absolute majority of aboriginal peoples, the Inuit, and thus the first Canadian experiment in full-fledged aboriginal self-government.

Federalism and Changing Political Cleavages in Canada

Language and region have historically been the dominant political divisions in Canada. The ways in which these identities have been articulated and mobilized have been shaped by the federal institutional structure, just as the territorial character of these divisions has helped to shape the character of Canadian federalism. The causal arrows run both ways. Language and region ensured that the Canadian system would be federal; but the design and operation of the federal system have had profound effects on how language and region have played out in national politics.

Language

When Britain sent its commissioner, Lord Durham, to investigate conditions in the British North American colonies in 1838, he discovered "two nations warring in the bosom of a single state." His solution was to propose that English- and French-speaking Canada, then concentrated in separate colonies, be merged into a single political entity, the United Province of Canada. This would ensure, he believed, that over time the Catholic, conservative French-speaking community would eventually be assimilated into a British identity and British political institutions, with "English laws and language ... and a decidedly English legislature" (McNaught 1982, 94, 95).[1] English was to be the language of the legislature, and each region was to have equal representation, despite the fact that Lower Canada's population was larger.

The result, however, was neither the assimilation nor the subordination of the French-speaking community. Instead the two communities rapidly established a regime remarkably akin to Lijphart's consociational democracy (Lijphart 1984). Key to this development was an alliance between leaders of a reform movement in both linguistic communities seeking responsible government, which would require the appointed governor to take instruction from elected Canadian ministers, rather than from the British Colonial Office. French was restored as an official language in 1848. Parallel ministries led by French- and English-speaking ministers were established with largely separate administrations, often passing laws that applied only to one of the sections. Voting on key legislation was by double majorities (Careless 1967).

By the early 1860s, this consociational accommodation had broken down. The rapid growth of English and Protestant Canada West led to demands for "Representation by Population," fueling Francophone fear of dominance by an English-speaking majority. A series of divisions over issues such as sectarian education led to deadlock and paralysis (McNaught 1969, 121).

Federalism became an increasingly attractive way out of the impasse. Disengagement allowed each group to pursue its basic goals, without fear of veto by the other; the dangers of deadlock in a two-unit system were reduced by bringing into the federation the other British North American colonies. The chief architects were one leader from each group, Sir John A. Macdonald and Georges-Etienne Cartier, working in close partnership.

Language was also a major reason why the federalism that developed was relatively decentralized. But by the 1880s, Quebec, along with Ontario, was pushing successfully for limits on federal power and increased autonomy for the provinces. For Quebec the primary issue was the power to preserve its own language and culture in the face of an English-speaking majority at the national level. For Ontario the issue was not language, but a combination of partisan differences and a struggle among rival economic elites over free trade versus protectionism in relations with the United States. Together they elaborated the more confederal compact theory of Canadian federalism, seeing the national government as the creature of the provinces. But even if Canada were to be seen in this way, the question has persisted: is it to be a compact between two language groups, or ten provinces?

Confederation was also a nation-building exercise aimed at creating a Canada "from sea to sea." This creation of new provinces had an important effect on the development of French Canadian and Quebec identity. First, it reduced the overall weight of Quebec in the federation—from one of four provinces at the outset, to eventually one province in ten. Second, the new western provincial governments proved hostile to French-Canadian interests. The legislation establishing the provinces of Manitoba, Alberta, and Saskatchewan included protections for their French-speaking minorities, including minority-language education rights, the translation of provincial statutes, and the right to use either official language in the courts. These provisions were systematically ignored by the new legislatures.[2] Ontario also placed limits on French- language schools in the province. These developments helped reshape Francophone identities, from the original *Canadiens*, the first white settlers of what is now Canada, to *French-Canadians*, defined primarily by language and religion, and eventually to the contemporary *Québécois*, a national identity centered on the Quebec state. With the exception of parts of Ontario and much of New Brunswick, French speakers were concentrated in Quebec, where today they make up just over 80 percent of the population; they constitute small and rapidly assimilating proportions of the population in most other provinces. The autonomy conferred by federalism not only had the effect of opening an institutional space from which Francophones could pursue self-government within the province of Quebec, but also provided the space for other provinces to limit the use of the French language. Hence the French-English cleavage is in Canada today expressed almost entirely as a Canada-Quebec conflict, a conflict between two "nations" (Richards 1999, 84–143). That it came to take this form is a powerful institutional consequence of federalism.

Region

Regional differences constitute the second set of cleavages that have dominated Canadian politics. Here too, important historical, cultural, and economic differences sustain regional identities and regional politics. Indeed, there is some evidence that globalization and North American economic integration are weakening the economic linkages that tie the Canadian regions together (Courchene and Telmer 1998). Here too federalism is not only a response to regional difference, but also institutionalizes and perpetuates it. Regionalism, while often expressed in parties of regional protest in national politics, is most often articulated by provincial governments using the institutional resources provided by federalism. Federalism means that regional conflicts tend to be played out in the arena of competitive intergovernmental relations. Moreover, the institutionalization of region through provincial governments creates an image of homogeneity within regions, while blurring both their internal heterogeneity (especially in large, diverse provinces like Ontario) and the convergence among regions in terms of social structures, attitudinal patterns, and the like.[3]

On most important policy issues, regional differences are small, and declining. Canadians in all provinces, including Quebec, positively identify with both the national and provincial political communities. In a recent survey, 81 percent of Canadians outside Quebec felt "profoundly attached" to Canada; 59 percent felt the same way about their province. Here, however, there are differences: Quebecers tend to give primacy to their Quebec identification. Forty percent of Quebecers feel profoundly attached to Canada; 52 percent to Quebec (CRIC 2000, 14–16). In 2000, 46 percent of all Quebecers identified themselves as Quebecers first or Quebecers only; 30 percent as Canadians and Quebecers equally; and 22 percent as Canadians first or only. On another question, 54 percent of Francophone Quebecers defined themselves as *Québécois,* 30 percent as French-Canadian, and 13 percent as Canadian (Mendelsohn 2003, slides, 1, 2, 4).

Residents of the largest province, Ontario, identify most with a national government in which they exercise significant political weight; westerners tend to value both identifications equally, but often perceive themselves as excluded from power at the center. Citizens in the poorer Atlantic Canada have similar views, tempered in their case by the recognition that their well-being continues to depend heavily on financial support from Ottawa (Beauchamp, Dugas, and Graves 1999, 307–54).

Nevertheless, strong regional grievances persist. For example, in 2000 respondents were asked whether their province has its fair share in making important national decisions and whether their province is treated with the respect it deserves. In eight provinces (all but Quebec and Ontario), majorities ranging from 54 to 74 percent said their province has less than its fair share of influence; and majorities from 50 percent (in Manitoba) to 76 percent (in Newfoundland) said they were not treated with sufficient respect (CRIC 2002, 19). The salience of regional grievances varies over time and according to the dominant public issues of the day. When the national project was the federally led construction of the welfare state, regional concerns were muted. In the 1970s the energy crisis sharply divided Canadians along regional lines. Regional identities took center stage, and the ensuing battles paved the way for the emergence of the latest and strongest western regional party, the Reform Party, which in 1999 renamed itself the Canadian Alliance. When the party failed to extend its base in the November

2000 election, there was a brief resurgence of western separatist movements, but the overwhelming emphasis of western protest has been a call for "we want in"—more influence in Ottawa—rather than for "we want out."

In recent years newer divisions have emerged to challenge the dominance of territory in Canadian politics. First are aboriginal peoples seeking self-government. Their call for a "Third Order" of aboriginal government is strongly informed by the logic of federalism, but their image of Canada is for obvious reasons deeply opposed to any conception of Canada as a partnership between English and French. Like Quebec, many aboriginal leaders seek to relate to Canada on a "nation" to "nation" basis (Cairns 2000; Tully 1999, 413–42; Abele 1999, 443–62). Second is the increased ethnic diversity of Canada, leading to the embrace of multiculturalism in legislation and in the constitution. This too challenges the "two founding peoples" image with the image of many constituent groups. It is sometimes seen as a threat by Francophones, who fear being relegated to the status of just another ethnic group. Finally, the emergence of social movements such as feminism, empowered by the Charter of Rights and Freedoms adopted in 1982, challenged the legitimacy of a constitutional agenda dominated by issues of territory and language and contested a constitutional process monopolized by the institutions of executive federalism.

These changes have led the rest of Canada to be less willing to view Canada as a binational or dualist system. Quebec increasingly has come to be seen as just one element of Canadian diversity; and increasingly it seemed to be fainter on the national radar screen than newer manifestations of diversity. Moreover, changes since the 1960s have significantly reduced the disparities in economic and political power between French- and English-speaking Canadians that had been thoroughly documented as recently as the 1960s by a federal Royal Commission (Canada 1969). This improvement—the result of both provincial and federal policies—undermined the perception of Quebecers as a group with legitimate grievances that should be redressed.

These multiple cleavages, as they interact with federalism, are closely related to a set of competing images of the Canadian polity that have dominated recent debates. Language leads to a sense of Canada as a dualist, bicommunal, or binational entity, and focuses attention on accommodations that will recognize a distinct status for Quebec in an asymmetrical federal system. That is in tension with a provincialist conception of Canada, seeing it as composed of ten equal provinces, each distinctive in its own way. This image focuses attention on constitutional symmetry, and on Canadian governance as a collaboration or partnership between federal and provincial governments. Both of these are in tension with the aboriginal vision of Canada as a partnership between Europeans and the First Nations, leading to the idea of aboriginal self-government as a third order of government alongside national and provincial governments. And all of these are in tension with the liberal vision of Canada as made up of 30 million equal citizens, a conception strongly reinforced by the adoption of the Charter of Rights and Freedoms. The central constitutional challenge for Canada in recent years has been to find a way to reconcile these "three equalities"—of nations, provinces, and citizens (Cairns 1991).

The Institutional Design of Canadian Federalism

Canada combines federalism with the Westminster model of parliamentary government. Powers and responsibilities are divided into two sets of watertight compartments; constitutionally, at least, there are few areas of concurrent jurisdiction. The federal government was given the powers to build a national polity and economy—interprovincial and international trade and commerce, currency and banking, and the like. Provinces were allocated powers more linked to social and cultural development, but some of these, including health, education, and welfare, later emerged as fundamental building blocks of the modern welfare state.

Each level of government has a high degree of autonomy in the raising and spending of revenues. There are considerable financial transfers between federal and provincial governments. The significance of these transfers in provincial budgets has been steadily declining in recent years, though equalization payments—unconditional federal payments to ensure that poorer provinces are able to maintain comparable levels of public service with comparable levels of taxation—constitute more than 40 percent of the budgets of some Atlantic provinces (Lazar 2000).

Federal and provincial governments see themselves as equals rather than in a hierarchical relationship. Though in its early years the federal government used its powers over the provinces with little restraint (Wheare 1946, 19, 20), this centralist model did not persist. By the early twentieth century, Canada functioned as a fully federal polity. The pendulum shifted back to Ottawa between the 1930s and 1950s, the result of depression, war, and the building of the welfare state. Since then, the predominant forces have been in a decentralizing direction (see Simeon and Robinson 1990).

There are many reasons for these shifts. First, throughout much of Canadian history, Ottawa was unable to establish the hegemony of a national vision. Provincial and regional identities and interests remained strong. The most powerful of these was Quebec, which consistently argued for greater provincial autonomy, and which has resisted federal "intrusions" into provincial jurisdiction. Ontario and the wealthier provinces in western Canada have also often argued for greater provincial autonomy. Provincial political and bureaucratic competence and self-confidence, together with their share of total government spending, grew in the 1950s and 1960s since most of the postwar expansion of government took place in areas of provincial jurisdiction, such as health, education, and welfare. The disallowance and reservation powers, while remaining in the constitution, have long since fallen into disuse, and are now considered essentially defunct. The most important power to influence the provinces that remains in federal hands is spending power—the ability to provide grants to the provinces with conditions attached. Quebec, along with some other provinces, has always opposed this power as an unwarranted license for Ottawa to invade provincial jurisdiction. Various constitutional proposals have attempted to place limits on its use, and a recent "Framework Agreement on the Social Union" (1999) requires Ottawa to secure the prior consent of a majority of provinces before initiating new shared-cost programs in areas of provincial jurisdiction. Over time, the conditions attached to federal transfers have been steadily relaxed. By 1996, only 4.3 percent of Canadian federal transfers to the provinces had significant conditions attached to them (compared with 100 percent in the United States and 53 percent in Australia) (Watts 1999, 49).

Judicial interpretation has also played a major role in the evolution of Canadian federalism. Until 1949, the Judicial Committee of the Privy Council (JCPC) in Britain remained Canada's final court of appeal. It sharply limited the scope of the "peace, order, and good government" clause, turning it into an emergency power. It also narrowed the scope of federal powers over trade and commerce and foreign affairs. More recently, the Supreme Court of Canada has taken a balanced approach, sensitive to federalism values. For example, in the "secession reference," in 1998, it found that Quebec has no right under domestic or international law to a unilateral secession, but that in the event of a "clear majority" on a "clear question," there is a constitutional obligation on the rest of the Confederation partners to negotiate with Quebec (*Re Secession of Quebec* [1998] 2 S.C.R. 217).

A third set of institutional factors that reinforces the competitive, divided pattern of Canadian federalism is the weakness of provincial representation within the central government (Smiley and Watts 1985). The Canadian senate is structured along regional, rather than provincial lines, with equal numbers of senators from the Atlantic provinces, Ontario, Quebec, and the west. Members are appointed for life by the national government alone,[4] making the senate a patronage body, which cannot provide effective representation for either provincial governments or their populations. A wide range of proposals for reform of the senate has been discussed. They include modeling it on the German Bundesrat as a council representing provincial governments, or on the U.S. Senate, with members elected equally from each province. A version of the latter was included in the failed Charlottetown Accord.

In order to manage the interdependence among governments, a complex network of intergovernmental institutions has been established. But this machinery is only weakly institutionalized. It does not appear in the constitution, and has no legislative mandate, little bureaucratic support, and few rules and procedures. It is an add-on to the basic federal structure, rather than an integral part of it.

Canadian governments at both levels are executive-dominated majority governments, exercising powerful party discipline. There is little opportunity for MPs to act as advocates of regional or provincial interests. More seriously in this winner-take-all system, one or more regions or provinces may have little or no representation in the governing caucus or cabinet, and hence feel frozen out of political power at the center. This in turn makes it more difficult for the national government to bridge and integrate regional interests, and makes it more likely that disaffected regions will instead look to powerful provincial governments to defend their interests.

This effect is compounded by the increasing regionalization of the Canadian party system. Throughout most of the twentieth century, the Canadian party system was comprised of three main parties. The centrist Liberals and Progressive Conservatives competed to form the party of government; the social democratic New Democratic Party generally played a minor (but sometimes influential) role on the left. The two major parties sought to build pan-Canadian electoral coalitions though the practice of brokerage politics, in which regional party barons were influential. By the 1970s a combination of highly divisive conflicts over the constitution, energy, and Quebec, together with internal changes in party structure emphasizing the dominance of the party leader and small cadres of party professionals, effectively destroyed the brokerage pattern. The result was "the triumph of regionalism" in the contemporary party system (Tanguay 1999, 217–54).

In the 1993 and 1997 elections, the three traditional parties' share of the popular vote dropped from about 90 percent of the total to about two-thirds. The 1993 election "tore up this [pan-Canadian] pattern and left the country balkanized, with a set of regionally distinctive party systems" (Carty et al. 2000, 34). Two regional parties took center stage. In 1997, the Reform Party formed the Official Opposition, with sixty seats, all of them in western Canada. The Bloc Québécois, the federal wing of the sovereignist PQ in Quebec, won forty-four seats, every one in Quebec. This pattern continued in the November 2000 federal election.

The Liberal Party maintained its claim to be the only national party. It won seats in all provinces, but again its support was concentrated in central Canada, where it won 100 of Ontario's seats and 36 of Quebec's. It remained weak in western Canada, winning only 14 of the 74 seats in the region. The renamed Alliance Party of Canada remained concentrated in the west, where it won 60 seats. It managed to win only 2 seats in Ontario, and none farther to the east. Most of the Conservatives' 12 seats came from Atlantic Canada. NDP seats were scattered across the country. The Bloc Québécois lost some ground in Quebec but still managed to win 38 of the province's 75 seats. Overall, "the ability of broadly based parties to aggregate interests and demands across the entire country has been become increasingly narrow" (Carty and Wolinetz 2001, 14). Canada thus no longer has an integrative party system. "The rise of regionally based parties in Canada makes nonsense of the very concept of a national election. The country is in the midst of a series of coordinated regional contests" (Greenspon 2000, A1, A8).

The single-member district electoral system accentuates these regional differences by rewarding parties whose votes are concentrated in specific regions, and harming those whose votes are more evenly distributed. In the 2000 election, for example, the Liberals won between a fifth and a third of the vote in all the western provinces; the Alliance won a quarter of the vote in Ontario. The regional composition—and hence the internal dynamics—of both the government and opposition caucuses would have looked very different if Canada had a more proportional electoral system.

Several other factors undermine the integrative capacity of the party system. First, parties do not tie national and provincial politics together: while in 2002 the federal Liberals governed in Ottawa, they did so in only one province. Second, even when parties share the same name, the federal and provincial wings have few organizational, financial, personnel, or ideological linkages. Third, there is little mobility of leaders between federal and provincial governments. Fourth, national, provincial, and local elections take place at different times. National elections are conducted on national issues, with little connection to provincial politics; provincial elections are carried out in terms of internal provincial political dynamics, with little reference to national issues.

Fifth is the constitutional amending formula. The Constitution Act of 1982 established a domestic formula for amendments. Most amendments require the assent of the parliament of Canada and seven provincial legislatures, representing 50 percent of the population. Some key amendments call for unanimity. This high hurdle has made agreement on constitutional change extremely difficult. The hurdle was raised higher by the precedent set in 1992, when a package of proposed changes agreed to by the eleven governments—the Charlottetown Accord—was put to a national referendum and defeated. It is plausibly argued that ratification by popular referendum has now become a constitutional convention.

This greatly undermines the effectiveness of elite accommodation as the means for managing linguistic and regional difference. Both Meech Lake and Charlottetown initially embodied unanimous agreement among governments to accommodate both provincialism and Quebec as a distinct society. Both, however, were defeated after mobilization from below. If elite accommodation depends on elite commitment to perpetuating the system and on mass deference to elites, neither of these conditions now holds in Canada (Nevitte 1996).

Sixth, for most of its history, the two fundamental pillars of the Canadian constitutional order were federalism and parliamentary government. In 1982, a third pillar was added—the Canadian Charter of Rights and Freedoms. The charter has empowered nonterritorial minorities, shifted the discourse of Canadian politics to a focus on rights, and increased the judicialization of Canadian politics. There are significant tensions between the premises of parliamentary government, with its emphasis on majority rule; federalism, with its emphasis on the power of regionally based collectivities; and the charter, with its emphasis on individual citizen rights.

Two sets of institutional characteristics thus combine to shape the dynamics of Canadian federalism. On the one hand, there is the character of federalism itself, emphasizing separate federal and provincial powers and financial autonomy, with a relatively underinstitutionalized structure of intergovernmental relations. On the other hand is a national political structure—Westminster parliamentary government, a weak senate, the single-member district electoral system, and so on—that reduces the integrative capacity of central institutions. These two sets of factors contribute to the distinctive Canadian pattern of intergovernmental relations. Interregional and federal provincial accommodation occur not through legislatures or the party system, but through government-to-government negotiations—"executive federalism," or "federal-provincial diplomacy" (Smiley 1974; Simeon 1972). This is structured as a highly competitive relationship, in which the institutional interests—defending their status, seeking credit, and avoiding blame—of the executives is a central element.

Constitutional Politics and Federalism

Through much of Canadian history, Quebecers used federalism not so much to advance a nation-building project, but as a defensive mechanism to protect French language and culture. This was especially evident in Quebec's rearguard action against the federally led postwar development of the Canadian welfare state, exemplified by the report of the Tremblay Commission (Quebec 1954). However, the basic design of the 1867 constitution provided a reasonably effective accommodation until the modernizing and democratizing "Quiet Revolution" of the 1960s (McRoberts and Posgate 1983; Gagnon 1999). Now Quebecers wished to compete on the same terrain as the Anglophones, who were dominant both within Quebec and nationally. Quebecers embraced the interventionist state, but it was to be on their own terms—"maîtres chez nous"—with the government of Quebec, representing the French-speaking majority, as the instrument for nation building.

In the early 1960s, Quebec made significant gains. The provincial share of major tax revenues was increased; the conditions attached to federal shared cost or conditional grant programs were greatly relaxed; Quebec was permitted to opt out of a number of such programs with full financial compensation; and when Canada adopted the Canada Pension Plan, one of the final building blocks of the Canadian welfare state, Quebec was able to establish its own separate scheme. Through such devices, and without constitutional change, Quebec achieved a considerable degree of de facto asymmetry within Canadian federalism.

Nevertheless, nationalist ideas continued to develop in Quebec, and increasingly came to be framed in constitutional language—"Egalité ou indépendance." In 1968, a group of dissident Quebec Liberals formed the Parti Québécois, whose goal was a sovereign Quebec with a continued "association" with the rest of the country.

Partly in response to these developments, the federal Liberals recruited a group of leading Quebec intellectuals, led by Pierre Trudeau, to bolster the federalist cause. Trudeau became prime minister in 1968. Deeply opposed to nationalism in all its forms, he came to Ottawa, he said, to arrest what he saw as a drift toward secession.

The Quebec nationalist position—federalist and sovereignist—saw Quebec as a sociological nation, and Canada as a partnership between two equal "founding peoples." The provincial government was the primary political expression of the French-Canadian people; Ottawa was the primary government of English Canada. The constitution must reflect this fundamental asymmetry, if not by according Quebec a special status within the federation, then by independence itself.

To this Trudeau made several replies (Trudeau 1968). Nationalism was retrograde and dangerous. Distinct, or special status for Quebec, he believed, would inevitably lead to a slippery slope, in which Quebecers' links to the national government and political community would be cut one by one, leading inevitably to eventual separation. Hence his emphasis on the equality of the provinces.

His own vision was of a Canada that was bilingual from sea to sea, and of a federal government that was as much a center of loyalty for Francophones as for others. He strenuously rejected the identification of the Quebec people with the Quebec state. His strategy was to increase the presence of Francophones within the upper reaches of the central government, and to strengthen the position of minority-language groups by extending education and other services to minority-language communities across the country, "wherever numbers warrant." Many of these reforms were enshrined in the

Official Languages Act of 1969. In the words of one Quebec scholar, Trudeau "was implicitly asking his fellow Quebecers to trade their identity as a people against the promise of bilingualism" (Balthazar 1997, 45–60). It is an interesting puzzle of the Canadian case that the movement for an independent Quebec grew simultaneously with an increased presence and influence of Francophones in the central government.[5]

Thus the stage was set for the extended search for a new constitutional accommodation that could reconcile the competing visions of Canadian federalism and the role of Quebec in Canada. Federalism provided the forum for these negotiations. The constitution was debated by the prime minister and the provincial premiers, together with senior ministers and advisers, in a series of First Ministers' Conferences. There was remarkably little involvement of political parties or legislatures and few attempts to mobilize popular participation.

In June 1971, the first ministers unanimously agreed on a draft set of changes that represented an uneasy compromise among the competing values (Simeon 1972, 118–20). This "Victoria Charter" was initialed by all eleven first ministers, including Quebec premier Robert Bourassa. But in Quebec a wave of opposition argued that the agreement did not go far enough to satisfy its demands, leading Bourassa to retract his agreement. This episode set the pattern for future attempts at a resolution. First, the actors were participating in a two-level game: in the intergovernmental conference, the Quebec representatives were under strong pressures to agree with their federal and provincial counterparts; but in the Quebec political setting, they were in danger of being accused of selling out. Second, it illustrated the tensions between federalists in Quebec, whose attention had to be focused on preempting the opposition of the Quebec sovereignists, and the federalists in Ottawa, whose attention was focused on building support across the country. These tensions within the federalist camp have persisted to the present day, seriously undermining the federalist cause in Quebec. Third, on some items on the constitutional agenda, Quebec would have strong allies among the other provinces, but on others, there remained profound differences. Finally, in the absence of imminent crisis, the incentive to agree was low: the default position was the status quo, which would always appear preferable to the proposed alternatives for at least some of the actors.

The political stakes were dramatically raised when, in October 1976, the Parti Québécois was elected. Now secession was on the table as a constitutional option. The new government, headed by René Lévesque, was committed to a double referendum process—the first asking for a "mandate to negotiate" Quebec sovereignty accompanied by an economic and political "association" with the rest of the country; and the second to confirm any sovereignty arrangement that had been negotiated.

The election set in motion a widespread search among federalists for a third option between status quo federalism and Quebec sovereignty. The most important was the Pepin-Robarts task force, whose report (1979) argued that the central facts of Canadian political life are duality and regionalism, that "politically regions were best understood as provinces and that, with respect to duality, the key issue was the status of Quebec in Confederation" (Cameron 1993, 344). This analysis undercut the Canada-centered model of national bilingualism advocated by Prime Minister Trudeau. In 1980, the Quebec government held its first referendum calling for a mandate to negotiate sovereignty with continued association, "égal a égal." It was supported by only 40 percent.

During the campaign, Trudeau had promised that rejection of sovereignty would be followed by a commitment to a "renewed federalism." For many Quebecers this meant greater recognition of Quebec within the constitution. Trudeau, of course, had an alternative vision. Many of the other provinces had begun to generate their own constitutional demands for enhanced provincial powers, partly in response to the deep regional cleavages promoted by the energy crises of the decade, which sharply divided central and western Canada.[6]

The federal government responded by undertaking an act of *force majeure*. Faced with the impossibility of agreement on constitutional change, Ottawa acted unilaterally—to strengthen national unity by "patriating" the constitution to make it a fully Canadian document, thus cutting the last colonial ties with Britain; to constitutionalize a Charter of Rights and Freedoms, embodying values all Canadians held in common, and to be enforced by the Supreme Court; and to impose a formula for future amendment of the constitution. In the face of provincial intransigence, argued Trudeau, Ottawa had no alternative but to exercise its right to request that Britain amend the British North America Act of 1867 one last time.

All but two of the provinces (Ontario and New Brunswick) joined with Quebec in the "gang of eight" to oppose this initiative. They argued that it provided no response to provincial demands for constitutional change, and that unilateral action violated an established convention that provincial consent was necessary before any amendment affecting them was adopted.

The ensuing battle was played out in many political arenas. Eventually Ottawa was forced to submit a reference to the Supreme Court to ascertain whether or not provincial assent to change was constitutionally required. In a politically astute judgment, the Court replied that according to black letter law, Ottawa did have the right to seek the amendment, but that a constitutionally enforceable convention requiring "substantial provincial consent" was also in force (Russell 1983, 210–38).

When the parties came back to the bargaining table in the fall of 1981, the provincial alliance broke down. Ultimately the English-speaking provinces could not sustain their alliance with a separatist Quebec government. In a late night agreement, Ottawa and the other provinces agreed on a compromise that left Quebec out.

The compromise, embodied in the Constitution Act of 1982, reflected the blend of Canada- and province-centered visions of federalism. It did patriate the constitution, along with a Charter of Rights and Freedoms. But it also adopted some limitations on the scope of the charter advocated by provinces (for example, a "notwithstanding clause" permitting any government to set aside certain sections of the charter for a limited period); and it adopted a highly provincialist formula for constitutional amendment. The agreement did not include any recognition of or increased powers for Quebec, or a Quebec veto over future constitutional change. It was thus an enormous defeat, not only for Quebec sovereignists, but also for Quebec federalists who had pinned their hopes on a renewed federalism. Quebec made a final appeal to the courts—arguing that the constitutional convention for provincial consent also required the assent of Quebec—but the court rejected the argument (Romanow, Whyte, and Leeson 1984).

The charter added a third pillar to the Canadian institutional structure of parliamentary government and federalism. The constitution was now as much about the relations of citizens to governments as it was about federal-provincial relationships. And it gave recognition to groups and identities not captured within the prism of federalism—equality for women, affirmation of aboriginal treaty rights, and multiculturalism. But the absence of Quebec was a gaping hole. What long-term legitimacy could the settlement have as long as Quebec was excluded?

In 1984, the federal Liberals were replaced by a Progressive Conservative majority government elected in a massive landslide. The new prime minister, Brian Mulroney, had built his winning coalition by combining traditional western support with the support of many "soft nationalists" from Quebec. His goal was to bring Quebec back into the constitutional family "with honor and enthusiasm." The timing seemed propitious, since a federalist Liberal government was now back in power in Quebec, support for sovereignty in Quebec seemed to be declining, and regional tensions elsewhere were in retreat.[7]

The resulting negotiations led to unanimous agreement on the Meech Lake Accord of 1987. It responded to an earlier set of "minimum conditions" outlined by the Quebec government, adding to the constitution an interpretive clause recognizing Quebec as a "distinct society" within the Confederation; a veto for Quebec over constitutional amendment; a constitutional guarantee of Quebec representation on the Supreme Court of Canada; a limitation on the federal power to spend in areas of provincial jurisdiction through an opting-out provision; and a constitutionalizing of informal arrangements giving Quebec a greater voice in immigration.

Under the amending formula, governments had a three-year window to pass the accord through their legislatures. At first, public opinion was strongly supportive, but soon a massive mobilization against it developed. Some came from the western provinces, angered that their constitutional concerns such as the need for a reformed senate had not been addressed, and that the principle of equality of the provinces had been broached. Some came from groups concerned with social policy, worried that the limitations to the federal spending power would spell an end to federally led social policy innovation. But the strongest opposition came from "charter Canadians"—those who had been recognized and empowered in the charter of rights. Women's groups argued that distinct society status might allow Quebec to erode gender equality, and multicultural groups argued that their status might be impaired. More generally, the charter and its great popularity had given many Canadians the sense that the constitution belonged to them; it was not the property of governments. Hence the idea that the constitution could be amended by the decisions of "eleven men in suits" meeting behind closed doors violated newly dominant ideas of democratization. Fear that a "distinct" Quebec might violate charter values was heightened by Quebec's invoking the notwithstanding clause to protect its law respecting the use of English on commercial signs in Quebec.[8]

This opposition was crystallized by the election of two new provincial governments, which had not been party to the original agreement. An extraordinary First Ministers' Conference was called to try to rescue the accord in April 1990. Originally scheduled to last for one evening, it eventually lasted a full week, as the supporters tried to cajole the recalcitrant governments. Eventually the effort failed; in the end two legislatures did not pass the accord.

This failure was a pivotal event. To many the accord had represented a moderate, limited attempt to balance the competing views, especially when read in conjunction with the 1982 changes. For Quebecers the "exclusion" of 1982 was now compounded by a second rejection. Support for the sovereignty option shot up to more than 50 percent. Quebec leaders argued that the result demonstrated that the rest of Canada would not make any new accommodation with Quebec; it would respond only with a knife to its throat—the imminent possibility of Quebec independence. The (federalist) Quebec government established a commission—the Bélanger-Campeau Commission—to explore the options, and promised a referendum for the fall of 1992, which would choose between any offers of a renewed federalism from the rest of Canada, or sovereignty. Quebec federalists proposed changes in the federal system that would drastically reduce federal powers. Thus, Quebec opinion was becoming more polarized. So was opinion in the rest of Canada.

The practices of executive federalism were also increasingly under challenge. More groups were arguing that constitutional discussion should be removed from the closed, elitist, processes of executive federalism, and subjected to much more open discussion, including ratification of any agreements through referenda, or even the calling of an independent, elected constitutional assembly.

There was to be one more attempt at megaconstitutional change. This time there would be more public involvement, through extensive parliamentary hearings and a series of national conferences. The intergovernmental bargaining table was to be extended to include leaders of the two northern Canadian territories[9] and representatives of aboriginal groups. The agenda was also expanded to include not only Quebec, but also a wider review of the division of powers, protection of the Canadian economic and social unions, senate reform to make it "equal, elected, and effective," the right of aboriginal peoples to a "third order" of government, and a Canada clause that would try to set out the common values shared by all Canadians. The idea was inclusion: all groups should find their concerns reflected in the outcome.

The result was the cumbersome, complex Charlottetown Accord of 1992. At the last moment governments agreed to submit it to a national referendum. It was defeated by substantial majorities in eight of the ten provinces, including Quebec, winning only small majorities elsewhere (McRoberts and Monahan 1993; Blais, Gidengil, Johnston, and Nevitte 1993, 919–43).

Thus Canadians failed to reconcile the competing models of federalism—dualist, provincialist, and nation-centered—discussed at the outset. Moreover, the middle ground was eroding. Quebec opinion was now distributed along a continuum from recognition of distinct society and special status to outright independence; opinion outside Quebec increasingly rejected any departure from provincial equality.

Meanwhile, the PQ had regained power in Quebec, and it called a second referendum on sovereignty for October 1995. Premier Jacques Parizeau was impatient both with a gradualist approach to sovereignty and with proposals coupling sovereignty with a continued economic and political partnership. Others in the PQ argued that Quebecers retained a strong attachment to Canada, and would reject a clear break.[10] The final question asked Quebecers to support sovereignty, along with a partnership. If the rest of Canada refused to negotiate a partnership, Quebec could decide to go it alone.

The referendum lost by less than one percent of the vote, in a very high turnout. Again, the result changed the nature of the debate. First, it revealed the deep fissures within Quebec society itself. Despite PQ efforts to define its goal as one of inclusive civic rather than ethnic nationalism, support for sovereignty remained almost entirely confined to the Francophone majority. Following the referendum, many Anglophones argued for partition: if Canada was divisible, they argued, then so was Quebec. Aboriginal groups, who occupy large areas of the resource-rich northern Quebec, argued that their treaties were with the federal government, which had a constitutional responsibility for them. They held their own referendum, securing a 95 percent majority to remain in Canada.

Second, the referendum revealed an enormous gulf between Quebecers and non-Quebecers regarding how to view sovereignty. Survey data from Quebec show that both support for outright independence and for status quo federalism are minority positions. Opinion is grouped around either renewed federalism or sovereignty-partnership (CRIC 2000, 35), and most Quebecers seem to view the difference merely as a few steps along a continuum, with no sharp break between them. Many continue to believe that once sovereignty-partnership is achieved, they will continue to share in many aspects of continued Canadian citizenship.[11] Non-Quebecers tend to see sovereignty as a fundamental step, a Rubicon, with all federalist options on one side, and all sovereignist options on the other (Simeon 1999).

Indeed, Quebecers remain profoundly ambivalent about their preferred constitutional options. A recent survey shows that only 25 percent of Quebecers would support the province becoming a fully independent country, but 58 percent would support sovereignty if accompanied by an assured partnership (CRIC 2002, 28).

Third, the referendum demonstrated how ill-prepared the government of Canada, and Canadians generally, were for a successful "yes" vote. Few had thought about the immediate or long-term consequences if a few thousand votes had gone the other way. There was thus an urgent demand for more consideration and planning.

Federalist thinking in the aftermath of the referendum fell into three categories, often labeled plans A, B, and C (Cameron 1999). Plan A represented the continuing search for accommodation within the federal system. Its prospects have been limited both by the bitter experience of years of failed constitutional negotiations and by the continued antipathy to asymmetrical solutions outside Quebec. Now the search was for options that did not involve constitutional change. For example, in 1997, all the provincial governments agreed on the Calgary Declaration, a broad statement of principles in support of "the unique character of Quebec society, including its French-speaking majority, its culture, and its tradition of civil law," and the resulting recognition that "the legislature and government of Quebec have a role to protect and develop the unique character of Quebec society in Canada." The declaration was ratified in most legislatures, but it was a much watered down expression of Quebec's distinctness than either Meech Lake or Charlottetown, and had no constitutional status. It had little impact in Quebec. In addition, the federal parliament promised that it would not agree to any future amendments without the support of Quebec. It too had little impact.

The more substantial element of plan A was to demonstrate to Quebecers and others that federalism works, that it allows provinces considerable freedom to pursue their own priorities and to manage their interdependence through intergovernmental cooperation. A number of initiatives illustrate this collaborative model of decision making. (Cameron and Simeon 2000). For example, Ottawa and the provinces agreed in 1995 on an Agreement on Internal Trade, aimed at reducing barriers that interfere with the Canadian Economic Union. Governments also agreed on cooperative arrangements with respect to child care and regulation of the environment. In 1999, they signed a Framework Agreement on the Social Union, designed to establish more harmonious relationships in social policy; to secure provincial consent before Ottawa can initiate new shared programs in areas of provincial jurisdiction; and to achieve greater accountability in intergovernmental relationships. These developments respond to a public mood: large majorities of both Quebecers and non-Quebecers agree that more federal-provincial cooperation is the best way "to make the country work better" (CRIC 2000, 22). These efforts to enhance the workability of Canadian federalism open up the possibility of increasing the scope of de facto, rather than constitutional, asymmetry.

Plan B is a set of strategies designed to convince Quebecers that secession would be messy, costly, and very difficult to achieve, and that it is quite wrong for them to believe that life would go on as before. It is also designed to demonstrate that Quebec has no unilateral right to secession, and that it cannot expect that the rest of Canada would be prepared to negotiate a partnership in the aftermath of a secession. Plan B also tells Quebecers that among the many items on any negotiating table would be the very borders of Quebec itself. If plan A options are the carrot designed to win Quebecers over to federalism, plan B is the stick to make secession appear undesirable and infeasible (Cameron 1999).

The first major step to implement B was a reference by the federal government to the Supreme Court of Canada in 1996. It asked whether Quebec has a right to unilateral secession either under existing Canadian law or under international law; and if these differ, which should prevail. The court determined that neither Canadian nor international law suggests such a right.[12] Quebec does not fall into the category of oppressed or colonial peoples that would justify self-determination under international law. Secession would be a constitutional change of profound importance that could only be achieved in accordance with the Canadian constitution. Any movement toward secession would have to respect the fundamental principles of constitutionalism and the rule of law, federalism, democracy, and respect for minorities. But, having rejected the legality of unilateral secession, the court went on to level the playing field. It said that if Quebecers were to vote for secession according to a "clear question" and a "clear majority," then other Canadian political actors would have a *constitutional* obligation to negotiate the matter, taking into account the fundamental principles and the questions that would be on the table, including debts, borders, and the like. Canada was divisible. It was a remarkable decision. But crucial questions remained. What constitutes a clear question? What is a clear majority? And who decides?

The PQ position has been that a question that links sovereignty and partnership is fair, because it represents what Quebecers actually want (Simeon 1999). The federal government asserts that such a question is fundamentally misleading and unfair, since it includes a partnership that can be delivered only with the consent of the rest of the country. It also suggests that partnership is a ruse, to convince Quebecers sovereignty is a safe option, when the PQ's real desire is a complete break. Or it is a knife to the throat, using the threat of secession to blackmail the rest of Canada into reform of federalism.

The federal government argues that for a decision as momentous as secession, a simple majority of 50 percent plus one is insufficient. As with constitutional amendment in most countries, some form of supermajority would be required. The PQ response is that 50 plus one is the standard decision rule in a democracy, and that there can be no principled or nonarbitrary way to set an alternative rule.

Many other procedural questions would need to be resolved. If there were to be negotiations on secession, who, in addition to the federal government and Quebec, would be at the table? Would the negotiation be about simply the terms for secession, or some form of reconstituted federal system? What specific issues would need to be negotiated? And would any results need to be ratified by referenda in Quebec and the rest of Canada?

In 1999, the federal government sought to answer such questions by tabling Bill C-20, "An Act to give effect to the requirement for clarity as set out in the opinion of the Supreme Court of Canada in the Quebec Secession Reference." The bill acknowledged that any province is free to put any question to its people. But it asserted that "the House of Commons as the only political institution elected to represent all Canadians, has an important role in identifying what constitutes a clear question and a clear majority sufficient for the Government of Canada to enter into negotiations in relation to the secession of a province from Canada." The act specifies that the national parliament will determine whether or not the question is clear, and that the government must be satisfied that there has been "a clear expression of a will by a clear majority of the population" of the seceding province. It does not specify how high the bar should be: the assessment would have to take into account the size of the majority achieved, the turnout, and "any other" relevant circumstances (S 2.2).

Finally, the act states that no constitutional amendment bringing about secession can be considered unless it has addressed issues such as "the division of assets and liabilities, any changes in the borders of the province, the rights, interests and territorial claims of the Aboriginal peoples of Canada, and the protection of minority rights" (S. 3).

The Quebec government deemed the federal bill an offense to the "democratic values all Quebecers hold dearest." It denies the basic right of Quebecers and Quebecers alone, to determine the choice between sovereignty or a reformed federalism that respects Quebec identity. "We subscribe, of course, to the obligation of clarity, but we maintain it is a responsibility that only the (Quebec) national Assembly can and must assume" (Government of Quebec 1999). The provincial government retaliated with its own legislation, asserting the right of Quebecers alone to decide their future, the sanctity of the 50 percent plus one majority, the inviolability of Quebec's current boundaries, and Quebec's respect for diversity.

Thus positions about the basic rules that might determine Canada's future remain starkly polarized. The irony is that both sides have an enormous interest in prior agreement on the rules and the consequences that would flow from different outcomes. The politics of the situation, however, render such agreement impossible.

Faced with stagnant support for independence, the failure of the Bloc Québécois to make gains in the November 2000 federal election, and divisions within his own party on the pace of change and the nature of the nationalist movement, Premier Lucien Bouchard resigned early in 2000. His replacement was Bernard Landry, who promised a more aggressive approach to building support for sovereignty. He too, however, had to contend with a difficult policy agenda and the apparent "constitutional fatigue" of Quebec voters, and once again put off another referendum.

Whether and when there will be a third referendum remains uncertain but unlikely in the near future. The Quebec government has been caught up in difficult and contentious policy issues at home, and surveys suggest support for sovereignty has been on a downward trend since the referendum of 1995, from 51 percent in 1995 to 40 percent early in 2001 (CRIC 2002, 27). Polls also show that most Quebecers have little appetite for the stress of another referendum campaign. The winning conditions seem increasingly remote.

Some commentators have suggested that this signals that secession is no longer a live option in Quebec. But as a recent study of support among various social groups in Quebec concludes, a "rebound in support should not be ruled out." Support for sovereignty continues to be above 50 percent for Francophone Quebecers between eighteen and fifty-four. Events in either English Canada or Quebec could yet produce the winning conditions (Gagne and Langlois 2000, 29–45).[13] For the moment, the tough love approach of the federal government appears to have the upper hand, but it remains possible that another setback such as the defeat of the Meech Lake Accord in 1990 could increase support for sovereignty in the future.

Yet the current situation is deeply frustrating for many Quebecers. As Alain Noel puts it: "Quebec ... is not free because constitutional amendments can be adopted without its consent [as in 1982], because it cannot in practice seek constitutional recognition [as in the defeat of Meech Lake], and because it would be bound, following a referendum by constitutional rules it has not approved. ... The choices are stark: You take Canada as it is, and learn to love it (Plan A) or you accept that you cannot leave it (Plan B)" (Noel 2000, 34). Or as a distinguished Quebec federalist leader, Claude Ryan, put it: "linguistic duality and the distinct reality of Quebec remain the two principal axes around which gravitate all searches for a solution to the relationship between Quebec and Canada within a federal regime." The challenge is to reconcile these realities with the reinforcement of the economic union, the status of the aboriginal peoples, the balance among the regions, and the expectations of the multicultural communities (Ryan 2000, 45).

Canadians have yet to find ways to reconcile alternative constructions of Canada and the federal system. They have not yet managed a way to get "Beyond the Impasse" (Gibbins and Laforest 1998).

In an analysis published in 1990, this writer had the temerity to write the heading "An end to Quebec nationalism?" in the conclusion to a history of Canadian federalism (Simeon and Robinson 1990, 311). He was saved from acute embarrassment only by the question mark. In 2003, few would claim that nationalism in the sense of a deep identification with Quebec as a national community is in decline. But it can be argued that nationalism in the form of a claim for sovereignty or formal independence may be losing its appeal. There could be both positive and negative reasons for this. On the positive side, one might cite the successes of nationalism since the Quiet Revolution of the 1960s. They include the emergence of Quebec as a modern industrial society, with levels of education and income at least as high as their English-speaking compatriots, and the ability of Quebec, within the flexible framework of Canadian federalism, to pursue distinct policy preferences in many fields, notably in social policy, and to develop a more consensual style of bureaucratic and legislative decision making than that which prevails in most other Canadian jurisdictions. More generally, the words *distinct society* may not have been enshrined in the Canadian constitution, but there can be little doubt that in almost all aspects of lived experience, Quebec is secure as a highly distinct society, not only in language, but also in terms of its arts, culture, and media. In this context, it is not easy to argue that federalism has proved to be a straitjacket, blocking the ability of the Quebec government to preserve and promote the province's distinctiveness.

On the negative side, it seems likely that the federal campaign to ensure clarity has succeeded in convincing many Quebecers that sovereignty and full disengagement from Canada would indeed be very difficult to achieve, that it would involve high costs, and that partnership or association with the rest of Canada cannot be assumed. Moreover, in the context of globalization and North American economic integration, and in the broader global context of eroding sovereignty and multilevel governance, it is less clear what sovereignty in the classical sense actually entails, or what greater scope for independent action it would provide.

Thus there is little reason to proclaim the death of Quebec nationalism, but much reason to believe that it may take different forms in the future—for example, in a greater emphasis on asymmetrical federalism, if not in law, then in practice (Gagnon 2001, 337). Whatever the final outcome, Canada's major achievement may be that it has managed to conduct a fundamental debate about its very existence as a united country openly, peacefully, and democratically. With one exception—a brief outbreak of violence in 1970, the "October Crisis"—the debate has been played out in the framework of democratic politics.

The more serious challenge to the political economy of Canadian federalism may come from elsewhere. Western disaffection is deeply entrenched, flowing from a sense that western Canadian interests are not effectively heard in Ottawa. Only half of western Canadians feel that federalism "has more advantages than disadvantages," and a majority feels that their province does not have a fair share of influence in national decision making (Berdahl, in CRIC 2002, 20)

In large part this is simply a function of population, with almost two-thirds concentrated in Ontario and Quebec. But this alienation is also fueled by some of the institutional characteristics we have discussed: the distortion between seats and votes engendered by the electoral system, the distribution of senate seats, and the winner-take-all pattern of Westminster-style parliamentary government with strict party discipline. These are the issues that preoccupy western critics of the Canadian federal system, unlike the basic claim for greater autonomy characteristic of Quebec.

Conclusion

Federal institutions have had a deep influence on conflict and its management in Canada. Language and regional differences ensured that the Canadian polity would be federal; but federalism, in turn, has influenced the ways in which these divisions are structured and articulated, the nature of the discourse that surrounds them, the arenas and sites where they are played out, and the solutions that are explored.

In many ways federal institutions have proved effective in managing the divisions. In Canada's highly decentralized model, Quebec governments have had broad scope to engage in a successful nation-building project. It has also permitted a considerable degree of asymmetry—a separate Quebec system of civil law, a separate provincial income tax system, a greater voice than other provinces in the concurrent area of immigration policy, and separate Quebec and Canadian pension plans. Despite the primacy of their identification with the province, most Quebecers, even sovereignists, retain a psychological attachment to Canada, and Quebecers have played a major role in national governance. This why sovereignist leaders realize that any successful referendum for independence must be coupled with the idea of association and partnership. It may also be argued that federalism—both in terms of the autonomy it provides to Quebec and in terms of the channels it provides for negotiation—has helped ensure that Quebec nationalism has remained peaceful and highly democratic, and that the Canadian unity debate has been conducted with remarkable civility.

But there is another side of the balance sheet. In successive rounds of constitutional discussion, Quebec's search for constitutional recognition as a distinct society and for a special status that would recognize the Quebec government as having a special role as the primary government of the Francophone community, or nation, within Canada has been rejected. Recognition of Canadian duality in the constitution has been trumped by the ideas of the equality of the provinces, national bilingualism, and Canada as a site of multiple diversities, of which Quebec is only one. The declining weight of French-speaking Canada in the Canadian population, along with the changing demographic makeup of Canada outside Quebec, suggest that it is unlikely that this will change. Hence the impasse and the polarized choice between opting for the status quo or for sovereignty.

Regional conflict is also salient in Canada, though it has not had the potential to create a viable secessionist movement. Here too, federalism has a double-edged character. It has permitted a broad range of provincial diversity in politics and policy, hence reducing conflict. On the other hand, it has institutionalized and hence helped perpetuate and accentuate this diversity. At various times in Canadian history, commentators have suggested that modern cleavages such as class or a politics based on nonterritorial social movements will displace region and language as the dominant fault lines of Canadian politics. That they have not done so is largely a function of the federal institutional structure.

The effect of federal institutions depends greatly on their interaction with other elements of the institutional structure—notably with the effects of Westminster-style parliamentary government. Together they institutionalize intergroup relations as a confrontation between rival state institutions, federal and provincial. The parliamentary system combined with the single-member electoral system and a weak senate means that the central government is poorly designed to represent, accommodate, and reconcile divergent regional interests at the center. Canadian provinces are strong and assertive not only because of the institutional resources that federalism provides them, but also because they are frequently the voice of provinces that feel frozen out of influence in Ottawa.

As in other federations, federalism in Canada is less a state than a process. Over its history, the pendulum has swung between more and less decentralization; regional conflict has varied greatly in its intensity. These changes suggest an important limitation on using the institution of federalism as the only explanation of regional and linguistic conflict in Canada. The institutions themselves have changed very little since 1867. Change must therefore be explained by changes in the underlying society and economy: in the salience of provincial and national identities, in regional economic interests, and in the issues on the public agenda, some of which trigger and highlight the regional dimension, while others transcend or cut across it. The causal arrow between federal state and federal society runs both ways.

This analysis suggests some other observations about the relationship between federalism and the management of conflict in multinational societies.

First, the Canadian experience suggests that federal institutions may respond to two quite different dynamics. On one hand is the impulse of coming together, the "building" dynamic, as previously separate entities explore the advantages of closer association. The alternative dynamic is federalism as a coming apart, as entities find it impossible to remain in a single unit. This is the dynamic at work in Belgium; it may be the dynamic at work with respect to Scotland in the United Kingdom, and it has been central to recent Canadian discussion.

We need to understand more about these alternative dynamic processes. The key question is when, and how, federalism becomes the logical stopping point. Under what conditions is it a stable outcome; under what conditions is it a way station either between separateness and unity (in the building scenario) or between association and separation (in the disbuilding scenario)?

The Canadian case also suggests the need to understand more about symmetry and asymmetry in federalism. Under what conditions is asymmetry acceptable or unacceptable? Is asymmetry achieved informally and in political practice more acceptable than explicit, constitutionally entrenched asymmetry? Why is it that the United Kingdom seems to have moved to a dramatic degree of asymmetry with little conflict when it appears to remain an anathema in Canada? Does asymmetry lead to secession? Or does it permit national minorities to feel more secure within a larger union, rendering full independence unnecessary? (Simeon and Conway 2001).

This debate has not been resolved in Canada. For Quebecers no avenues short of recognition as a nation functioning within a fundamentally reformed Quebec-Canada economic and political union could ever lead to a lasting solution to the continuing constitutional crisis (Gagnon 1999, 279–99). This implies a high degree of asymmetry. Meanwhile, in the rest of Canada, the political dynamic has hardened against such a vision (Young 1999). Some English Canadians argue, in parallel with Quebecers, that there is an emerging sense of English Canadian nationhood, centered on the federal government, and looking toward a reassertion of federal influence. They realize that this is not acceptable in Quebec, and therefore could only be achieved by considerable asymmetry (Kymlicka 2000, 48). Such an outcome is, however, highly unlikely to emerge from the intergovernmental processes of executive federalism that institutionalize provincial equality.

Finally, the Canadian experience suggests a dilemma. It turns out to be very difficult to write down, in constitutional language, all the relationships that must exist within a diverse society. The impulse to frame them in precise language is likely to generate irreconcilable conflicts. Hence the attraction of nonconstitutional solutions, and of constitutional silences and ambiguities.

In any case, placing the burden of accommodation on federal institutions alone is not enough. Federalism does not resolve the problem of minorities within minorities such as Anglophones in Quebec and Francophones outside the province. The devolution of authority outward to constituent units must be accompanied by the reform of national institutions to provide accommodation at the center. Canadian debates have focused on change within the federal system, and have given too little attention to reform of the larger institutional context.

NOTES

1. The error, he argued, would be the "vain endeavor to preserve a French-Canadian nationality in the midst of Anglo-American colonies and states."

2. Not until 1985 did the Supreme Court of Canada declare that Manitoba must fulfill the obligations of the Manitoba Act by translating all its statutes into French.

3. See Roger Gibbins, *Regionalism: Territorial Politics in Canada and the United States* (Toronto: Butterworth's, 1982). The argument is that regionalism is no greater in Canada than in the United States; the difference is that it is more institutionalized in Canada. See also David J. Elkins and Richard Simeon, *Small Worlds: Provinces and Parties in Canadian Political Life* (Toronto: Methuen, 1980).

4. In an attempt to force the issue of appointment, Alberta has held senatorial elections, challenging Ottawa to appoint them formally.

5. With only very brief interludes, the prime minister of Canada since 1968 has been a Quebecer.

6. Perhaps the defining moment was when Newfoundland premier Brian Peckford in- formed the prime minister that he felt more comfortable with René Lévesque's view of federal- ism than Trudeau's.

7. Declining oil prices reduced the east-west conflict, and the Mulroney government dis- mantled virtually all of the National Energy Program that had provoked so much anger in west- ern Canada.

8. Quebec's hostility to the charter is not based on hostility to its values, but on its imposi- tion by the federal government.

9. Yukon and the Northwest Territories.

10. One survey, just before the 1995 Referendum, found that 29 percent identified as Quebecers only, 29.1 percent as "Quebecers first, but also Canadian," 28.1 as Quebecers and Canadians equally, and 6.7 percent as "Quebecers only." In Kenneth McRoberts, *Misconceiving Canada: The Search for National Unity* (Toronto: McClelland and Stewart, 1997), 247.

11. A 1999 survey, for example, found that 30 percent believed that a "sovereign" Quebec would "still be a province of Canada"; 26 percent believed they would still be sending MPs to Ottawa (Centre for Research and Information of Canada 1999).

12. Reference re Secession of Quebec. [1998] 2 S.C.R.

13. An average of seven polls conducted between April and December 1999 showed support for sovereignty at 42.1 percent, but more than 50 percent of Francophones aged eighteen to fifty- four continued to support the yes side.

REFERENCES

Abele, Frances. 1999. The Importance of Consent: Indigenous Peoples' Politics in Canada. In *Canadian Politics 3*, ed. James Bickerton and Alain-G. Gagnon, 443–62. Peterborough: Broadview.

Balthazar, Louis. 1997. Quebec and the Ideal of Federalism. In *Quebec Society: Critical Issues*, ed. Marcel Fournier, Michael Rosenberg, and Deena White, 45–60. Scarborough: Prentice-Hall Canada.

Beauchamp, Patrick, with Tim Dugas and Frank L. Graves. 1999. Identity and National Attachments in Contemporary Canada. In *Canada: The State of the Federation 1998-9 (13: How Canadians Connect)*, ed. Harvey Lazar and Tom McIntosh, 307–54. Kingston: Institute of Intergovernmental Relations.

Bickerton, James, and Alain-G. Gagnon, eds. 1999. *Canadian Politics*. 3d ed. Peterborough: Broadview.

Blais, André, Richard Johnston, Elisabeth Gidengil, and Neil Nevitte. 1993. The People and the Charlottetown Accord. In *Canada: The State of the Federation 1993*, ed. Ronald L. Watts and Douglas M. Brown, 919–43. Kingston: Institute of Intergovernmental Relations.

Cairns, Alan C. 1991. Constitutional Change and the Three Equalities. In *Options for a New Canada*, ed. Ronald L. Watts and Douglas Brown. Toronto: University of Toronto Press.

———. 2000. *Citizens Plus: Aboriginal Peoples and the Canadian State*. Vancouver: University of British Columbia Press.

Cameron, David. 1993. Not Spicer and Not the B and B: Reflections of an Insider on the Workings of the Pépin-Robarts Task Force on Canadian Unity. *International Journal of Canadian Studies* 3:344.

Cameron, David, ed. 1999. *The Referendum Papers: Essays on Secession and National Unity.* Toronto: University of Toronto Press.

Cameron, David, and Richard Simeon. 2000. Intergovernmental Relations and Democratic Citizenship. In *Governance in the Twenty-first Century: Revitalizing the Public Service*, ed. B. Guy Peters and Donald Savoie, 58–118. Montreal: McGill-Queen's University Press.

Canada. 1969. Royal Commission on Bilingualism and Biculturalism. *Report.* 3 vols. Ottawa: Queen's Printer.

Careless, J.M.S. 1967. *The Union of the Canadas.* Toronto: University of Toronto Press.

Carty, R. Kenneth, William Cross, and Lisa Young. 2000. *Rebuilding Canadian Party Politics.* Vancouver: UBC Press.

Carty, R. Kenneth, and S. Wolinetz. 2001. "Political Parties and the Canadian Federation." Paper for the State of the Federation Conference, Institute of Intergovernmental Relations, Queen's University, Kingston, November.

Centre for Research and Information of Canada (CRIC). 1999. Portraits of Canada. http://jefflab.queensu.ca.

——— . 2000. *Portraits of Canada 2000: An Analysis of the Results of CRIC's National Tracking Poll.* Ottawa: Council for Canadian Unity.

——— . 2002. *Portraits of Canada 2001.* Ottawa: Council for Canadian Unity

Courchene, Thomas J., with C. Telmer. 1998. *From Heartland to North American Region State.* Toronto: Center for Public Management, University of Toronto.

Gagné, Gilles, and Simon Langlois. 2000. Is Separatism Dead? Not Quite Yet. *Policy Options* 21, no. 5:29–45.

Gagnon, Alain-G.. 1999. Quebec's Constitutional Odyssey. In *Canadian Politics 3*, ed. James Bickerton and Alain-G. Gagnon, 279–300. Peterborough: Broadview.

——— . 2001. The Moral Foundations of Asymmetrical Federalism: A Normative Exploration of the Case of Quebec and Canada. In *Multinational Democracies*, ed. Alain-G. Gagnon and James Tully, 319–37. Cambridge: Cambridge University Press.

Gagnon, Alain-G., ed. 1994. *Quebec: State and Society.* 2d ed. Toronto: Nelson Canada.

Gibbins, Roger, and Guy Laforest, eds. 1998. *Beyond the Impasse: Toward Reconciliation.* Montreal: Institute for Research on Public Policy.

Government of Quebec. 1999. Notes for a Statement by the Premier of Quebec upon the Tabling of a Bill Respecting the Exercise of the Fundamental Rights and Prerogatives of the People of Quebec and the State of Quebec. December 15.

Greenspon, Edward. 2000. Liberals, Like Their Foes, Aren't a National Party. *The Globe and Mail,* November 3, A1, A8.

Kymlicka, Will. 1998. *Finding Our Way: Rethinking Ethnocultural Relations in Canada,* Toronto: Oxford University Press.

——— . June 2000. What English Canada Wants. *Policy Options* 48, no. 21:20.

Lazar, Harvey. 2000. *Canada: The State of the Federation 1999/2000—Toward a New Mission Statement for Fiscal Federalism.* Montreal: McGill-Queen's University Press.

Lazar, Harvey, and Tom McIntosh, eds. 1998. *Canada: The State of the Federation 1998— Non-Constitutional Renewal.* Montreal: McGill-Queen's University Press.

Leger Marketing. 2001. Survey prepared for *The Globe and Mail* and *Le Journal de Montreal*, reported February 9.

Lijphart, Arend. 1984. *Democracies: Patterns of Majoritarian and Consensus Government in Twenty-one Countries*. New Haven, Conn.: Yale University Press.

McNaught, Kenneth. 1982. *The Pelican History of Canada*. Rev. ed. London: Pelican Books.

———. 1969. *The Pelican History of Canada*. Harmondsworth, U.K.: Penguin Books.

McRoberts, Kenneth, and Patrick Monahan, eds. 1993. *The Charlottetown Accord, the Referendum and the Future of Canada*. Toronto: University of Toronto Press.

McRoberts, Kenneth, and Dale Posgate. 1993. *Quebec: Social Change and Political Crisis*. Toronto: McClelland and Stewart.

Mendelsohn, Matthew. 2003. Quebecers National Identities. http://www.queensu/cora/trends.

Nevitte, Neil. 1996. *The Decline of Deference Canadian Value Change in Cross National Perspective*. Peterborough: Broadview.

Noel, Alain. 2000 . Canada: Love It or Don't Leave It! *Policy Options* 34, no. 21:34–36.

Quebec, Royal Commission of Inquiry on Constitutional Problems (the Tremblay Commission). 1954. *Report*. Quebec: Editeur officiel.

Richards, John. 1999. Language Matters: Ensuring that the Sugar Not Dissolve in the Coffee. In *The Referendum Papers: Essays on Secession and National Unity*, ed. David Cameron, 84–143. Toronto: University of Toronto Press.

Romanow, Roy, John Whyte, and Howard Leeson. 1984. *Canada Notwithstanding: The Making of the Constitution 1976-1982*. Toronto: Carswell/Methuen.

Russell, Peter. 1983. Bold Statecraft, Questionable Jurisprudence. In *And No One Cheered: Federalism, Democracy and the Constitution Act*, ed. Keith Banting and Richard Simeon. Toronto: Methuen.

———. 1993. *Constitutional Odyssey*. 2d ed. Toronto: University of Toronto Press.

Ryan, Claude. 2000. Le Dossier Constitutionnel: Perspectives de Changement. *Policy Options* 45, no. 21:42–45.

Simeon, Richard. 1972. *Federal-Provincial Diplomacy: The Making of Recent Policy in Canada*. Toronto: University of Toronto Press.

———. 1998. Considerations on the Design of Federations. *SA Public Law* 13:42–72.

———. 1999. The Limits of Partnership. In *The Referendum Papers: Essays on Secession and National Unity*, ed. David Cameron, 384–428. Toronto: University of Toronto Press.

Simeon, Richard, and Daniel Conway. 2001. "Federalism and the Management of Conflict in Divided Societies." In *Multinational Democracies*, ed. Alain-G. Gagnon and James Tully, 338–65. Cambridge: Cambridge University Press.

Simeon, Richard, and Ian Robinson. 1990. *State, Society and the Development of Canadian Federalism*. Toronto: University of Toronto Press.

Smiley, Donald V. 1974. *Constitutional Adaptation and Canadian Federalism*. Document 4, Royal Commission on Bilingualism and Biculturalism. Ottawa: Queen's printer.

Smiley, Donald, and Ronald L. Watts. 1985. *Intrastate Federalism in Canada*. Toronto: University of Toronto Press.

Tanguay, Brian. 1999. Canada's Political Parties in the 1990s. In *Canada: The State of the Federation 1998-1999. How Canadians Connect*, ed. Harvey Lazar and Tom McIntosh, 217–44. Montreal: McGill-Queen's University Press.

Taylor, Charles. 1991. Shared and Divergent Values. In *Options for a New Canada*, ed. Ronald L. Watts and Douglas Brown. Toronto: University of Toronto Press.

Trudeau, Pierre-Elliot. 1968. *Federalism and the French-Canadians*. Toronto: Macmillan of Canada.

Tully, James. 1999. Aboriginal Peoples: Negotiating Reconciliation. In *Canadian Politics 3*, ed. James Bickerton and Alain-G. Gagnon, 413–42. Peterborough: Broadview.

Watts, Ronald L. 1999. *Comparing Federal Systems*. 2d ed. Kingston: McGill-Queen's University Press.

Wheare, K. C. 1946. *Federal Government*. Oxford: Oxford University Press

Young, Robert. 1999. Quebec's Constitutional Futures. In *Canadian Politics 3*, ed. James Bickerton and Alain-G. Gagnon, 301–21. Peterborough: Broadview.

CHAPTER FOUR

Spain

Unfulfilled Federalism (1978–1996)

Pablo Beramendi and Ramón Máiz

The Spanish constitution is often celebrated as a model of how successful transitions can, or even should, be made. Paradoxically enough, this picture is blurred precisely in the arena in which the results of the constitution-making process were most daring and innovative: the design of a new territorial distribution of power. The almost unanimous assumption that the constitution can provide the present and future skeleton for Spanish democracy turns out to be problematic when one takes into consideration its actual performance in the management of territorial cleavages in Spain. The aim of this chapter is to understand the achievements and shortcomings of the *Estado de las Autonomías* (EA)[1] in the broader, comparative context of the capacities of federalism to deal appropriately with territorial conflicts.

Spain's federal institutions have been generally successful in managing territorial conflicts. In fact, their very design reflects the commitments that were integral to the new constitution's initial success during the transition. However, as time passed, these same features evolved in such a way that, while still contributing to effective management, became problematic. While the overall record of the EA in the management of territorial conflicts is a positive one, we will argue that the existing debates about the EA are mainly a consequence of those features that facilitated its initial success. The ambiguous nature of the constitutional contract was a necessary condition to complete the transition. Ambiguity in 1978 nurtured a short-term solution for problems among the different actors involved. However, some major institutional features agreed upon in the early stages of the process and the very dynamics generated by the EA itself are causing a change in the preferences of major actors within the system. As a result, several proposals to reform the system have emerged, pointing both to the weakness of an otherwise rather successful institutional design and to the possible directions of its evolution.

The essay has four sections. The first presents the major features of the historical evolution of the relevant actors and institutions. The second section offers a brief description of the constitution of 1978. Section 3 focuses on two indicators of the performance of the EA: its institutional stability and the evolution of territorial identities. The final section analyzes the capacity of the EA to deal with territorial conflicts, based on the interplay between the intended and the unintended consequences of its original institutional design.

Actors and Institutions in Historical Perspective

The 1978 constitution brought far-reaching historical change to Spain. Centralism had been a dominant characteristic of the institutional organization of Spanish politics since 1810. Thus, the process of decentralization initiated with the constitution must be seen as a path-breaking moment, especially after nearly forty years of strongly centralized dictatorship. In fact, the EA represents the first enduring noncentralized polity in Spanish history and a direct political response to the existence of several competing identities in Spain. In what follows we account very briefly for the key factors that led to their emergence.[2]

Though our limited space leads us to focus almost exclusively on the nineteenth and twentieth centuries, we must take into account a number of elements inherited from previous periods. One such element was the survival of other identities, linked to the former territories of the Crowns of Castilla and Aragon, due to socioeconomic, ethnic, political, and institutional factors. Another factor accounting for the multiple identities in Spain derived from the fact that the notion of a Spanish identity was constructed differently by Liberals and Absolutists.

Thus, Spanish nationalism was doomed to be weakened from its very early stages. On top of this, the performance of the different governments between 1845 and 1876 did not contribute very much to the expansion and consolidation of a strong, widely accepted Spanish national identity.[3] The lack of administrative efficiency, increasing political conflict, and, last but not least, the slow and imbalanced pattern of economic development of the country also failed to make positive contributions to that process.

Despite the state's inability to forge a single national identity, a first step toward democratization was taken with the constitution of 1869. Four years later, another constitutional text proclaimed the First Federal Republic, linking, quite remarkably from our perspective, the processes of federalization and democratization. The constitution of 1873 established a federation with seventeen states, including Cuba and Puerto Rico. Each member state had its own constitution, parliament, and executive and judicial powers, guaranteed in the original constitutional contract. A senate, in this case a second chamber of territorial representation, was also considered. The localism of the left and the militarism of the fight doomed the First Republic to an almost immediate crisis, with two important consequences. First, the Spanish conservatives came to strongly associate any notion of decentralization with chaos, disorder, and anarchy. Second, regionalist movements were boosted by this experience, because, like significant sectors of the Spanish left, they saw in the federal formula an institutional solution to the need for democratization and the integration of opposed regional identities.

From 1860 on, a change occurred in the pace of the formation of other competing national identities. The three main instances—the Basque Country, Catalonia, and Galicia—shared two major similarities. Between 1850 and 1890, all three regions witnessed similar developments. On the basis of historical and ethnic differences, cultural movements, driven mainly by literature and historiography, aimed at the recovery of some common roots of identity. Parallel to this cultural awakening, some early ideological formulations and political movements emerged. This was the moment of regionalism. Finally, after the disaster of 1898, the consolidation of nationalist platforms, organizations, and parties took place. The three regions also shared concerns about the inadequacy of Spanish governmental institutions, which were ultimately an underlying factor in any claim in favor of an increase of self-government. Nevertheless, despite these common factors, the experiences of the three regions differ substantially (Beramendi 1999, 83–88).

It may very well be argued that the Basque Country was the only region with a well-developed sense of identity during the first two-thirds of the nineteenth century. The Basque elites, composed mainly of rural nobility and clergy, had special privileges in their relations with the Church as well as their own institutional framework, the Diputaciones Forales. The Liberal Revolution erased the former and threatened the latter. As a consequence, these elites massively supported the Absolutist reaction and Carlism and were defeated in three wars (1833–39, 1846–48, and 1872–75). Progressively, as a result of these defeats, the Basque elites followed the path of Fuerism, an ideologically diverse regionalist movement, quite successful in expanding a sense of territorial identity among significant sectors of the population. The ultimate failure of Carlism forced the Basque traditionalist elites to seek alternative ways to accommodate their political preferences (De Pablo, Mess, and Rodríguez 1999). Switching their national identity from Spanish to Basque would eventually be their way ahead. Therefore, this traditionalist and very religious sector of the Basque Country would play a crucial role in the ultimate development of the Basque nationalist ideology and movement, conditioning quite heavily their further development (Aranzadi 1981; Azurmendi 2001; Juaristi 1987; Elorza 2001).

The experience in Catalonia was far less dramatic. The movement of cultural recovery, the *Renaixença*, was quite successful in boosting the use of the regional language. The processes of agrarian modernization and early industrialization transformed the social structure of the region, launching more effective means for socialization and transmission of political ideas. However, despite its cultural expansion and ideological pluralism, Catalanism had hardly any political or electoral support at this stage.[4]

Finally, and in contrast with the other two cases, Galicia represents a case of continuity. The lack of significant economic changes facilitated the continued survival of structures belonging to a mainly rural society. The *fidalguía*, or lower nobility, were at the same time profiting from their land rents (*foros*) and were well positioned in the thick network of political clienteles around Madrid. Thus, they had no incentive at all to switch to another ethnic or territorial identity and, therefore, the regional language and culture became a drawback for those aiming at upward social mobility. For Galicia, regionalism was an issue only for a few isolated groups, incapable of attracting more significant sectors of society.

The final decade of the nineteenth century as well as the first three decades of the twentieth century witnessed the final stages in the articulation of the territorial conflict in Spain. In 1898, a new, more intense phase in the development of such conflict began. The loss of Cuba and the Philippines was the ultimate indicator of the ongoing crisis of the political machine of the *Restauración*, built upon an enormous patronage system disguised as a parliamentary regime, administratively inefficient, economically ominous, and, not surprisingly, with a declining legitimacy as a territorial reference point. The so-called *Disaster* had two major consequences. It provoked a remarkable reaction and spawned changes in the formulation of Spanish nationalism, which in turn triggered the transformation of many regionalist movements into nationalist platforms and organizations. Eventually, the basic structure and participants in the territorial conflict in Spain would emerge from the convergence of these two processes.

Spanish nationalism was once again ideologically divided (Alvarez-Junco 2001). Though all the factions of the *Regeneracionismo* shared an organic conception of Spain, the two major branches trying to boost the pride of a nation humiliated by its failing political system had opposing strategies. On one side stood a clearly right-wing authoritarian vision, radically opposed to the claims of an increasingly organized working class and unwilling even to consider any regionalist or protonationalist idea. The defense of Spanish unity, at any cost, was their leit-motif, which achieved an initial success during the dictatorship of Primo de Rivera (1923–29) and would eventually be supported *ad pedem literae* by Franco and the Church and all the forces behind the coup d'état in 1936. On the other hand, a more liberal and democratic vision of the *Regeneracionismo*, closer to the left side of the ideological spectrum, tried to promote intellectual renewal through the modernization of the educational system at all levels. It supported the social and economic demands of the working class and was open to interaction with regionalist and nationalist movements, which were increasing in salience.

The differences between the three major regional experiences continued to be significant, affecting both the scope and the ideological profile of each of the three nationalist movements. In the case of the Basque Country, the aforementioned switch from Carlism was coupled with nationalism and rapid industrialization. This process, driven by the production of capital goods (Díez-Medrano 1995), proved to be an enormous shock to the social structure of the region. Foremost among its consequences were a massive inflow of immigrants coming from other regions, especially Galicia, Extremadura, and Andalusia, and the emergence of the first working-class organizations. Over time, the rapid industrialization in the Basque Country generated a level of economic development well above the Spanish average. Preindustrial elites with rural lifestyles and values faced the erosive power of modernization and urbanization while extremely dynamic capitalist elites integrated thoroughly with the dominant Spanish elite. At the same time, a left-wing working class drawn from the underdeveloped regions of Spain maintained a popular culture that differed from that of the Basque.

The social base of Basque nationalism was principally composed of the traditional segments of society that had been hurt by the region's economic modernization and the liberal policies of the homogenizing Spanish state. These policies involved a range of political and cultural changes, including organizing the country into provinces following the French model and establishing a national educational system and linguistic uniformity policies built around Castilian history and language. Other social groups joined the Basque nationalist movement later on, but the founding principles remained the same. The racist, antiliberal, and military character of the nationalist myths, symbols, and narratives elaborated by the movement's founding intellectuals gave Basque nationalism a radical, separatist, anticapitalist, and traditional Catholic discourse. Not surprisingly, the majority of the industrial bourgeoisie distanced itself from the Basque nationalist phenomenon. Basque nationalism achieved its support in the old rural and urban strata. Nationalism expanded, but did not achieve an overwhelming acceptance in society at large. The final incarnation of Basque nationalism can be understood as a reaction to both industrialization and immigration by the traditional groups linked to Carlism and Fuerism. Major aspects of this discourse still underpin the message of many Basque Nationalist Party leaders and members, even though democratic principles, moderation, and pragmatism have been incorporated for the purpose of electoral competition.

The Catalan nationalist movement experienced an impressive political takeoff during the first decades of the twentieth century, reflected by the growing political and electoral presence of the *Lliga Regionalista* (Riquer 1977). Between 1914 and 1923, the expansion of Catalan nationalism achieved institutional recognition in the first experience of self-government worthy of that name: the *Mancomunidad*, led by Prat de la Riba. In fact, Catalonia would be the only region in which the institutionalization of political autonomy foreseen in the constitution of the Second Republic was to be implemented, though very briefly (1932–34). So, what was the engine behind that process? Quite simply, the answer lies in the fact that the Catalan bourgeoisie, unlike the Basque, built upon a process of industrialization based on consumer goods (Díez Medrano 1995) The loss of the colonies in 1898 reduced the markets for their products and made it very risky to leave the regulation of their affairs to be managed exclusively from Madrid. They could not ally with Madrid as their counterparts did in the Basque country. So, they opted for an alternative national identity regarded as more appropriate for the promotion of their material interests.

As in the Basque Country, Catalonia's industrialization created a level of economic development far above the Spanish average. However, its social and political consequences were rather different. The economic transformation in Catalonia generated an increasingly modern social structure that gradually incorporated preindustrial segments of society into the capitalist context. Catalan nationalism was designed and directed by a dynamic, modern bourgeoisie that found the parties and representative mechanisms of a centralist national state unresponsive to Catalan attempts to influence the Spanish political system. This bourgeoisie led and encouraged the economic modernization process, but perceived a lack of any real representation of its interests in the policies of Madrid's government. Its political autonomy as well as the development of the Catalan language and culture were hindered by the centralist political and cultural homogenization imposed by the Spanish liberal state. This gave rise to a civic, moderate, negotiating, and nonsecessionist nationalism, which from the former political party, the *Lliga,* to the present-day *Convergencia i Unió* (CiU) has always sought to combine its demands for self-government with a significant participation in Spanish national politics. Most sectors of the Catalan society followed that pattern and, as a result, the ideological and organizational profile of Catalan nationalism became more and more plural, as shown by the convergence of several parties and organizations into the *Esquerra Republicana de Catalunya*, a left-wing organization which, before the civil war (1936–39), would manage to surpass the *Lliga* in terms of political and electoral support.

Galicia presents a strong contrast with the Basque and Catalan cases. The absence of modernization, industrialization, and urbanization resulted in territorial disarticulation, a heavily agrarian social structure, and a level of development below the Spanish average. Galician nationalism was led by intellectuals, the local petit bourgeoisie, and the liberal professions. These groups felt both sidelined within the Spanish state and hindered by economic backwardness and lack of opportunities, which caused a massive migration toward more developed areas of Spain, Latin America, and eventually other European countries. Galician society was also negatively affected by the cultural and linguistic homogenization instituted by the Spanish state, which forced the Galician language out of the schools, reducing it to a language "of peasants," regarded as unacceptable for the purposes of national modernization. Nationalism flourished culturally and intellectually along traditional lines, evolving into moderate liberalism and then, after some internal fragmentation, into democratic republicanism. But its limited social support resulted in a precarious organizational and electoral base that, for a long time, left Galician nationalism a second-tier force within the Galician party system. Only after 1931, in the midst of the political mobilization generated by the Second Republic, would the *Partido Galeguista* become a representative force, though far less successful than its Basque or Catalan equivalents.[5]

When the Second Republic came into existence in April 1931, the demands for decentralization were strong enough to require constitutional recognition.[6] Thus the Estado Integral as designed in the constitution can be understood as an intermediate solution between the traditional centralist polity, in a never-ending crisis, and a full federal solution, which was considered far too hazardous at the time for nearly everyone (Beramendi 1999, 79–100). In this respect, the Estado Integral can be considered the direct precursor of the solutions adopted in 1978, as it was the first institutional attempt to accommodate the tense relationships between different national identities. It also shared the 1978 constitution's open and flexible design, its recognition of non-Spanish political identities, and its subnational self-government institutions. The collapse of the Republic and the civil war prevented the Estado Integral from being fully developed. However, it was on the basis of this precedent that (despite the efforts by the Franco regime) the demands for autonomy and decentralization would reemerge after 1975.

After 1978, the evolution of nationalist parties is characterized by two different experiences. From the very beginning they dominated the Basque and Catalan regional elections. In the Basque country, the *Partido Nacionalista* Vasco/Basque Nationalist

Party (PNV) received over 30 percent of the vote in regional elections, while, in Catalonia, the CiU has averaged 40 percent. The Galician nationalist party had an almost insignificant record at the beginning of the period, but gained votes progressively, ending the 1990s with 25 percent of the vote. Table 4.1 presents the evolution of nationalist voting in the regional elections in the Basque Country, Catalonia, and Galicia.

In Catalonia, nationalist parties consistently rank first in regional elections while non-nationalist parties are systematically ahead in national elections. In the internal competition between nationalist parties, CiU's moderation and bargaining style representing center-right nationalism consistently triumphs over the radical secessionist nationalism of Esquerra Republicana de Catalunya (ERC), which attracts 8 percent of the vote in contrast to CiU's 40 percent. Under Jordi Pujol's leadership, the CiU has ruled the region since the first regional elections and, thus, has been able to organize a solid nationalism, identifying itself as the true defender of regional interests. In terms of center-periphery relations, Catalan nationalists have followed, according to their previous historical experiences and ideological background, a very pragmatic and moderate strategy in their relations with the central government and the parties supporting it (Socialist Party, Popular Party). Bargaining, collaboration, and exchange have dominated open conflict in the pattern of relations between the Catalan and the central government since 1978.

The Basque Nationalist Party has also been hegemonic since its beginning, establishing a solid organizational, electoral, and clientelist base in the early 1980s and controlling the regional institutions either alone or in coalition with Socialists or other nationalist parties. In this highly competitive pluralist electoral system, polarized between statewide parties (Popular Party and Socialist Party) and nationalist ones (PNV, Herri Batasuna, and Eusko Alkartasuna), each of the two groups occupies roughly 50 percent of the political space, with the regionalist parties slightly stronger. Whenever polarization is intensified, Euskadi suffers the threat of two potentially irreconcilable communities. The weakness of the right (Popular Party) until the 1990s and the decline in support for the Socialist Party helped the regionalist PNV to remain in government. Popular support for *Euskadi ta Askatasuna's* (ETA—literally, Basque Country in Freedom) activities has been waning: the regional vote for its political organization, Herri Batasuna, declined from 18 to 10 percent in the last elections. The PNV's political stance had been increasingly moderate since the 1930s due to its Christian Democratic agenda. However, in a recent attempt to end ETA violence, it changed course in 1998 and began to reject the EA framework, demanding the right to self-determination, and seeking the construction of a European Union (EU)-based Basque state separate from Spain and France. In this sense, the PNV reached an agreement with Herri Batasuna and also with ETA to stop terrorism as part of a broader joint political

Table 4.1 *Nationalist Vote Share in Galicia, the Basque Country, and Cataluña*

Galicia

1981	(%)	1985	(%)	1989	(%)	1993	(%)	1997	(%)
BNPG+PSG	6.2	PP	41	PP	43.65	PP	52.2	PP	52.1
EG	3.3	PsdeG-PSOE	28.6	PsdeG-PSOE	32.4	PsdeGPSOE	23.47	PsdeG-PSOE	19.4
PG	3.2	**PSG-EG**	5.7	**PSG-EG**	3.7	**BNG**	18.7	**BNG**	24.7
		EU		BNG	7.9	UG-EG	3.1		
		BNG	4.2	CG	3.6				
		CG	13	CDS	2.86				
		CDS	3.32						

Pais Vasco

1980	(%)	1984	(%)	1986	(%)	1990	(%)	1994	(%)	1998	(%)
PNV	38.1	**PNV**	42	**PNV**	23.6	**PNV**	28.5	**PNV**	29.3	**PNV**	27.6
HB	16.5	**HB**	14.7	EA	15.8	EA	11.4	EA	10.1	EA	8.6
EE	9.8	EE	8.0	**HB**	17.4	**HB**	18.3	**HB**	16.0	**HB**	17.7
PSE-EE	14.2	PSE-EE	23.0	EE	10.8	EE	7.8	PSE-EE	16.8	PSE-EE	17.3
PCE	4.0	PCE	1.4	PSE	22	PSE	19.9	PCE	9.0	PCE	5.6
UCD/CDS	8.5	AP-PP	9.4	PCE/IU	1.0	PCE/IU	1.4	AP-PP	14.2	AP-PP	19.8
AP-PP	4.8			UCD/CDS	3.5	UCD/CDS	0.7	UA	2.7	UA	1.2
				AP-PP	4.8	AP-PP	8.2				
						UA	1.4				

(Continued)

Table 4.1 — Continued

	1980		1984		1988		1992		1995		1999	
		(%)		(%)		(%)		(%)		(%)		(%)
Cataluña	**CIU**	27.68	**CIU**	46.56	**CIU**	45.49	**CIU**	46.19	**CIU**	41.00	**CIU**	37.70
	PSC-PSOE	22.33	PSE-PSOE	29.95	PSC-PSOE	29.63	PSC-PSOE	27.52	PSC-PSOE	24.80	PSC-CPC	30.33
	PSUC	18.68	AP-PDP-UL	7.66	IC	7.72	PP	5.96	PP	13.10	**ERC**	8.67
	CC-UCD	10.55	PSUC	5.55	AP	5.29	IC	6.51	ERC	9.50	PP	9.51
	ERC	8.87	**ERC**	4.39	**ERC**	4.12	**ERC**	7.96	IC-Els Verds	9.70	EUiA	1.42
	PSA	2.64			CDS	3.81					IC-V PCC+ICV	7.52

Sources: Galicia: (Beramendi 1997). Catalonia: Parlament de Catalonia. Basque Country: Department of Politics, UPV.

CIU: Convergència i Unió.
PSC-PSOE: Partido Socialista de Cataluña, PSOE
PSOE: Partido Socialista Obrero Español
ERC: Esquerda Republicana de Cataluña
AP: Alianza Popular—PP: Partido Popular
PSUC: Partido Socialista Unificado de Cataluña
IC: Iniciativa per Catalunya.
Note: Nationalist parties are marked in **bold**.

PP: Partido Popular
EG: Esquerda Galega
PG: Partido Galeguista
CG: Coalicion Galega
PsdeG PSOE: Partido de los Socialistas de Galicia

EAJ-PNV: Partido Nacionalista Vasco
PSE: Partido Socialista de Euskadi
EE: Euskadiko Ezkerra
IU-EB: Izquierda Unida
EA: Eusko Alkartasuna
HB: Herri Batasuna
UCD: Union de Centro Democrático

UA: Unidad Alavesa

132

agenda. This strategy failed badly and the agreement was subsequently rescinded due to the continuation of terrorist acts by ETA, which has been responsible for more than 800 murders since democracy was ushered in. As a result of this development, the level of polarization in the Basque Country has increased both between parties within the region and between the regional and the central governments, in what constitutes a much more unsettled pattern of center-periphery relations. Meanwhile, terrorism remains at the center of the political scene.

During the democratic transition, Galician nationalism was organized in small groups with radical Marxist-Leninist and secessionist agendas. These positions became increasingly moderate during the 1980s and 1990s. This process of moderation includes the acceptance of the constitution and the EA as the vehicle with which to pursue their political platforms and the participation in the regional parliament and local governments. The demand remains for greater self-government and defense of new Galician interests based in the modernization and urbanization processes of the 1980s and 1990s. The Galician Nationalist Block (BNG) has gradually incorporated a number of nationalist groups and parties that developed in the 1970s, forming a broad nationalist front spanning from extreme left wing to neo-liberal positions in which social-democratic positions seem to be the dominant ones. This catch-all strategy increased the percentage of the vote in regional elections to a high of 25 percent. The BNG earned a favorable position within the structure of political competition at the regional level by becoming the only Galician nationalist option, moderating its ideological position, leaving behind secessionist ideas, and accepting the EA, though occasionally demanding self-determination to please its supporters. The BNG also took advantage of the Galician Socialist Party crisis in the 1990s and increased its impact due to excellent organization, a catch-all discourse, and charismatic leadership. Still, the BNG had no impact on the center-periphery relations. Galicia has been ruled almost continuously by the conservative Popular Party (PP) since the beginning of the process of decentralization, with the exception of a brief period between 1987 and 1989. As a result, relations between Galicia and the central government had a very low profile until the PP took over the central government in 1996. They intensified after that date, but largely as an internal affair for the PP.

The Institutional Setting of 1978

The features of the 1978 constitution that bear most on the territorial cleavages described above are:[7] (1) an openness and flexibility in the distribution of political powers, (2) a multidimensional asymmetry, and (3) an absence of institutionalized cooperation in center-periphery relations.

Openness and Flexibility in the Distribution of Political Capacities

Perhaps the most important way the Spanish constitution of 1978 organized the territorial distribution of power is the fact that the final text did not reflect any coherent model of state. Actors at the time were much more aware of what they did not want to be reflected in the constitution than anything else. The very notion of the *Estado de las Autonomías* is not even recorded in the constitutional text, but was coined later. Thus the constitutional design of 1978 remained open, indeterminate, and ambiguous. Like most other constitutions, the Spanish one was an incomplete contract with lacunae to be closed by normal politics (Dixit 1996; Rodden and Rose-Ackermann 1997, 1527). But in this case, the degree of incompleteness was remarkably high by comparative standards.

Rather than stating clearly who does what, the constitution lists those subjects and fields over which the state has exclusive jurisdiction (art. 149) and those subjects and fields over which regions (*autonomous communities* [AC]) are "entitled to assume exclusive jurisdiction" (art. 148). It does not say that the political capabilities and jurisdictions listed in that article are in fact allocated to the AC—thus, the initial level of power to be adopted by each AC is not precisely defined.[8] Each of the seventeen AC had to write an *Estatuto de Autonomia*, a sort of regional basic law. The concrete contents of each of those *Estatutos* was an open issue, subject to political contention. They were not fixed a priori (art. 148.3). Second, the system contemplates some "catching-up" mechanisms, allowing the revision and expansion of the levels of decentralization initially achieved. So, for instance, the state has the capacity to decentralize those domains that happen to be susceptible to delegation (art. 150.2). Moreover, every AC has the right to expand its level of power five years after the approval of the Estatuto (art. 148.2). But the constitution also includes some clauses that could well allow the state to slow down, or even undo, part of the decentralization process on behalf of the general interest. The constitution is silent as to which path to pursue. This silence made the initial distribution of political capacities particularly significant, which leads us to the subject of asymmetry.

Multidimensional Asymmetry

Asymmetry implies an uneven, unequal distribution of resources or capacities within a given set of actors. One can argue that the Spanish federalization process has nurtured, from the very beginning, a highly asymmetrical political system involving electoral asymmetry, asymmetry of access, and fiscal asymmetry.

Electoral asymmetry refers to the differences in the electoral success of political forces representing exclusively regional interests. It depicts differences in the presence and political capacity of different nationalist parties in the national political institutions. The Spanish electoral system is one of proportional representation, built upon the D'Hondt Law. It was originally aimed to overrepresent rural provinces, with lower population density and a higher likelihood to opt for conservative forces. It also aimed to ensure the generation and stabilization of a two-party political system at the national level (Montero 1998, 53–80). In both respects it must be regarded as successful. For instance, the Communists (*Partido Communista de España*/Spanish Communist Party [PCE]/*Izquierda Unida*/United Left [IU]) have never been able to obtain any representation in thirty-four out of the fifty-two provinces of Spain, despite being a fairly stable political force in the national parliament. The examples of the *Centro Democrático y Social* (CDS) and the notorious failure of the *Partido Reformista Democrático* (PRD) also support this argument.[9] This electoral system has allowed for those nationalist parties with a high presence in their regions, first the PNV and CiU, and later on the *Coalición Canaria* (CC), to have an almost constant and growing presence in the central parliament. Between 1977 and 1996, the CiU jumped from 2 seats to 16, the PNV jumped from 2 to 6 seats, and the regionalist parties in the Canary Islands and Galicia jumped from 0 seats to 4 and 2 seats, respectively. From 1993 to 1996 and from 1996 to 2000, the political capacity of certain nationalisms has increased remarkably. Due to a combination of several factors, which we will discuss later, region-based nationalist parties have become key factors in the achievement of any stable government when neither the Socialist Party nor the conservative party has been able to achieve an absolute majority. As Linz and Montero (1999) have pointed out recently, PNV, CC, and CiU share the double condition of having a strong coalition potential in the central parliament and holding office in their regions.

Asymmetry of power refers to the existence of substantial variations in the degrees of autonomy enjoyed by different provincial governments. Every regional government's *Estatutos* enjoyed the same level of constitutional protection, but their content and scope varied considerably. The Basque Country, Catalonia, Galicia, and Andalusia achieved much higher levels of autonomy than the rest of the regions. As we will see below, the consequences of this gap were to be far-reaching for both the political dynamics of the system and its capacity to deal with territorial conflicts.

Finally, *fiscal asymmetry* refers to the constitutional facilitation and further political development of a twofold system of fiscal federalism in Spain. Two fiscal regimes are at work: the general or common one, applied to fifteen out of seventeen AC, and a special one, only applied in the Basque Country and Navarra (Aja 1999, 172–98; Monasterio et al. 1995). These two autonomous communities collect their own income, corporate, and value-added taxes and then contribute a fixed amount to the central government. The central government received over 95 percent of the revenues collected by the other fifteen AC,[10] until the situation was partially amended, allowing the AC to collect and manage a greater share of the income tax (15 percent in 1994, 30 percent in 1996).

Together with the presence of three nationalist movements, each with varying levels of political mobilization and party organization, the presence of a violent terrorist organization claiming independence in the Basque Country must be regarded as a fourth and special source of asymmetry. Violence has changed the parameters of the political process, altered the structure of the bargaining process, and modified the relative position that one major actor, the PNV, would have otherwise had. In fact, the evolution of both the political profile and the strategies of this party illustrate our case clearly.[11] The ETA's violence puts the PNV in the position of a gatekeeper, with one foot in each world. It generates both costs and constraints (the impossibility of full acceptance for the constitution, the possibility of blame from both sides) and further bargaining resources (a monopoly in the management of any possible solution, in the relations with Madrid, in the relations to the social network of ETA) which have allowed the Basque Country to achieve and maintain the highest levels of political autonomy.

Absence of Institutionalized Cooperation in Center-Periphery Relations

Traditional and well-established definitions of federalism present it as a mix of self-rule and shared-rule (Elazar 1987). After twenty years of permanent decentralization, Spain qualifies as "federal" in all respects related to self-rule. But, in terms of shared rule, Spain does not qualify as federalist at all. Shared rule implies a coordinated and institutionalized means for making all those decisions affecting both realms of power in such a way that both nationwide and regionally bounded interests are represented and protected. Yet, there is no institution performing such a function in the Spanish political system. There are only two regular forums that constitute arenas for cooperation: the fiscal and financial policy council and the regular meetings of all the national and regional ministers for education (Colomer 1998, 49–50). However, they are limited to their specific policy areas. There is also a senate. However, while the constitution presents it as "the Chamber for territorial representation" (art. 69.1), neither the way it is elected nor the array of its functions is characteristic of a federal second chamber. The vast majority of its members are elected at the same time and on the same territorial basis as the members of the national parliament (arts. 69.2–69.4). Each province is allocated four seats, combining to provide 208 of the 256 seats. The remaining seats are appointed by the different AC regional parliaments. Each AC must appoint one senator by default plus one more per million inhabitants within its boundaries (art. 69.5). This adds up to between forty-four and forty-eight seats, depending on the year. As a result of this method of election, the senate's composition resembles that of the national parliament. This, in turn, makes its real institutional influence very small and its capacity as a realm to represent territorial interests nonexistent. In the event of disagreement, the lower house always prevails (art. 90.2).

Some minor devices to promote cooperation and coordination among the different levels of government have been launched. But they are far from being a real alternative to the absence of a proper institution. Among all of the devices, two deserve attention: the *Conferencias Sectoriales* (sector conferences) and the *Acuerdos de Cooperación entre el Estado y las Comunidades Autónomas* (cooperation agreements between the states and the AC). The former are basically policy-specific realms for the exchange of information and carry out consultative functions (Cruz Villalón 1990; STC 76/1983). The latter have been established as a joint effort in specific fields or projects (such as public works or joint programs; see Albertí Rovira 1996, 616–36). But neither can be considered an alternative form of institutionalized cooperation.

The absence of institutionalized cooperation was bound to bring two major consequences. First, actors engaged in an endless process of bilateral negotiations. Second, the constitutional court remained the final venue to resolve conflicts over policy domains, jurisdictions, and duties. The openly incomplete nature of the constitutional contract, together with the absence of an institution in which territorial contentions could be politically solved, forced the court to assume increasing importance in determining the evolution of the system.

Spain is, thus, a rather peculiar case. From the perspective of the political capacities of its constituent units we can hardly deny its federal and highly asymmetrical character. However, federalism in Spain is also incomplete. The dual character of its fiscal dimension and, most important, the lack of an arena for territorial representation and cooperation are the major sources of this incompleteness.

The Evolution and Performance of Federalism in Spain

Before exploring how Spain's unique federal structures affect its capacity to deal with territorial conflicts, a discussion of our criteria for evaluation is in order. Identifying criteria to evaluate federal systems is not an easy task, for every choice is susceptible to bias. The optimal choice for criteria would be to include all the significant dimensions along which there has been contention over federal policies. These would include what Simeon and Mintz (1982) call conflicts of taste, which regard identity-related issues, and conflicts of claim, which regard distributive issues. Since this project is concerned primarily with the capacity of federal systems to accommodate conflicts of taste, we chose two indicators related to these. Our first is institutional stability. By looking at institutional stability, we aim to capture the extent to which Spanish federal institutions have managed to be self-enforced. We assume that the lower the levels of contention and contestation in the institutional design, the greater the success of Spanish federal institutions in promoting their own self-enforcement and the greater their success as an integrative device. A similar logic underlies our second criterion for evaluation, namely, the evolution of identities. As long as we observe a robust association between the development of the EA, the expansion of dual identities, and the shrinking of exclusive ones, the Spanish federal institutions may be regarded as successful (Stepan 1997).[12]

The Endogenous Character of Institutions: Patterns of Political Decentralization

The evolution of the Spanish *Estado de las Autonomías* took place in three major stages: 1978–83, 1983–93, and 1993 until the present. All share a similar feature: institutions are at the root of the bulk of the political contention among major political actors.

1978–1983

The period from 1978 to 1983 is the most intense of the institutional game. After the initial steps of the EA, the first big inflection point came with the launching of the *I Acuerdos Autonómicos* (autonomous agreements), signed by both the *Partido Socialista Obrero Español* (PSOE) and *Unión de Centro Democrático* (UCD) in 1981. These were the very first attempts to control the emerging dynamics of the system, since the early stages of Spanish democracy could not afford any avoidable instability. The failed coup d'état in February 1981 provides us with a good indicator of the complexity of the environment at the time. The objectives pursued by the two major parties are easily traceable through the contents of the agreements (MAP-1982): the clarification and generalization of the institutional designs of all Spain's autonomous communities, the adoption of a common position regarding the fiscal arrangements to be implemented, and, last, but certainly not least, the creation of a law aimed at harmonizing the decentralization process, namely, through the *Ley Organica de Armonización del Proceso Autonómico* (LOAPA). This law was the first big step in what we interpret below as a permanent tension between harmonization and asymmetries. It created a conflict about the real meaning of the process of decentralization. As a response to this conflict, the constitutional court formulated two far-reaching rulings on the subject of autonomy. In its ruling 37/1981, the court legitimated differences in the way citizens are treated by the different realms of power. Civil rights are regarded as the only field in which absolute equality must be guaranteed. Subsequently, in its ruling 73/1983, it overrode most of the LOAPA and established that the *Estatutos de Autonomia* enjoyed a constitutional status well above ordinary legislation. Autonomy was constitutionally protected thereafter (Aja 1999, 65). The *I Acuerdos Autonomicos* ended the first phase of the federalization and became embodied in the newly elected institutions. Following the elections on May 8, 1983, thirteen new regions (AC) were finally created.

1983–1993

These years were marked by the expansion and consolidation of the *Estado de las Autonomías*, driven mainly by the three consecutive socialist governments of Felipe Gonzalez, who benefited from an absolute majority in the parliament. Table 4.2 presents a general picture of the evolution of the transfer of powers from the central government to the AC between 1978 and 1997.

As Table 4.2 illustrates, the process of decentralization developed rapidly between 1983 and 1986. Most of the transfer of powers involved the construction of regional political institutions and the transfer of some elementary services formerly provided by the central government. After 1986, the process slows down significantly. In the particular case of the Basque Country, this is very much related to the issue of violence. For the rest of the AC, it just indicates an intensification of the institutional conflict between several levels of government. These involved complaints about the constitutionality of central and state governments lodged by both administrations against each other and conflicts of jurisdiction. There are two kinds of such conflicts: the positive (when two administrations claim control over any given policy field) and the negative (when both levels of governments claim not to have the responsibility to provide some particular good or service). As mentioned in the first section of this essay, the constitutional court had to assume the key political role of resolving many of the open aspects of Spanish federalism during these years. The levels of tension over who had the right to do what, as measured by the evolution of the positive conflicts of jurisdictions, rose rapidly during the mid-1980s. The Socialists' strong parliamentary majority during this period facilitated bringing issues to the constitutional court, if bilateral negotiations failed. If the disagreement was about legislation approved by either level of government and the other disagreed, the expected outcome was an appeal regarding the constitutionality of the law. Alternatively, if the conflict regarded the sharing of powers, conflicts of jurisdiction were expected. In this case, most of the conflicts had their origins in the definition of the meaning of "basic" jurisdictional areas to be guaranteed by the central government in the fields of concurrent legislation. These involved some of the most important policy fields, such as education, environment, and health. Not surprisingly, the high number of conflicts between 1983 and 1991 introduced significant delays in the development of such programs and, in turn, in the overall pace of the process of decentralization (Table 4.2).

Table 4.2 *Development of Autonomous Communities*

	78–79	80–81	82–83	84–85	86–87	88–89	90–91	92–93	94–95	96–97	98–99	Total
Basque C.	3	34	8	21	7	0	0	0	9	6	3	91
Cataluña	7	34	23	15	8	6	6	4	16	10	12	141
Galicia	2	2	38	30	7	10	1	2	16	17	13	138
Andalucia	2	8	38	32	7	0	7	4	10	4	0	112
Navarra	0	0	0	16	17	3	4	0	0	10	6	56
Canarias	1	3	25	32	6	1	7	2	17	8	8	110
Castilla y León	0	6	24	23	5	3	0	3	16	7	5	92
Castilla-La Mancha	1	3	31	19	2	3	0	2	14	5	5	85
Extremadura	1	3	27	18	1	4	0	1	22	3	5	85
Madrid	0	0	4	32	3	6	0	1	18	8	8	80
Aragón	3	4	23	21	3	0	0	7	21	3	10	95
Valencia	3	4	35	33	9	6	0	2	7	10	11	120
Baleares	2	4	23	19	4	0	0	8	19	8	9	96
Murcia	0	3	29	20	4	2	1	2	26	2	7	96
Asturias	1	3	29	20	3	3	0	0	20	0	0	79
Cantabria	0	0	35	15	2	0	0	0	0	25	9	86
La Rioja	0	0	15	17	3	2	0	0	11	10	5	63

Source: Ministry for Public Administration data set.
Note: Figures represent the number of transfers from the central government to AC during each two-year period.

In this context, Spain's entry into the European Economic Community (EEC) (1986) became one more source of political conflict. Before Spain's entrance into the EEC, the central government was the only acknowledged realm of power with full political capacities. Nonetheless, many of the choices made during the integration process affected both the interests and jurisdictions of all the AC. This change in the external political environment created the problem of how the AC could represent their interests before the EU. As long as representation was not possible, nationalist parties would perceive Europeanization as a hidden means of centralization within a constantly open institutional agenda.

At the end of this period, Socialists (PSOE) and Conservatives (PP) shared the view that the level of instability, the increasing demands for further decentralization, and the practice of bilateral exchanges demanded some sort of coordinated reaction by the two countrywide parties. As a result, the *II Acuerdos Autonómicos* were adopted.

Retrospectively, these pacts can also be seen as a temporary commitment by these two national parties not to use issues concerning the institutional design of the country as a partisan tool. The major effects of this agreement were twofold: on the one hand, they meant a great step forward in the overall levels of decentralization. The reform of the *Estatutos de las Autonomía* gave the AC with slower access to autonomy (art. 143) the potential to receive most of the transfers enjoyed by those that achieved autonomy earlier and faster, namely, the Basque Country, Catalonia, Galicia, and Andalusia. This explains the increase in the transfer of power over the past few years represented in Table 4.2. By 1994, the process was almost concluded except for health transfers. Somewhat paradoxically, the center-rooted parties provided, in the early 1990s, an average increase in the levels of decentralization. As we will see in the following section, this very fact contradicts some conventional expectations about the processes of decentralization. But implicit in this expansion was the pursuit of the horizontal equalization of power. When the nationalist parties reacted against this harmonizing change, the system polarized further.

1993–1999

The results of the general elections in 1993 opened a new stage in the development of Spanish federalism. The structure of political competition at the central level prevented both the Socialists (1993) and the Conservatives (1996) from achieving enough seats to rule on their own. This change implied significant shifts in the relationship between the central and the nationalist state governments.[13] The political case against higher levels of harmonization was now much stronger. Therefore, important policy changes were to be expected. The evolution of Spanish fiscal arrangements illustrates this point well. In 1994, tax policy was finally reformed to allow AC to collect and manage 15 percent of the general income taxes. The Conservatives at the time accused the socialist government of "selling" Spain. After 1996, when the conservative government needed nationalist support, the reform was expanded to include 30 percent of general income taxes. It is hard to think of any of these reforms being implemented under the political conditions existing prior to 1993.[14]

However, harmonization is still perceived as a risk by nationalist parties. They have repeatedly argued that blanket decentralization is no solution. In addition, the issue of terrorist violence and the aforementioned complex position of the PNV (who decided to link any step toward the achievement of peace with deep constitutional changes) increased the levels of polarization. During these years the number of appeals before the constitutional court increased. In fact, it was during this period that some of the major ideas for the substantial reform of the EA were proposed.

So, even though "self-determination," "sovereignty," and even independence have been present in the discourses of nationalist parties throughout the period, it is only recently that the BNG, PNV and CiU have adopted a common platform in order to pursue a constitutional reform toward some sort of indeterminate "confederal" arrangements.[15] Leaving aside the vagueness of their statements, these three parties have recently agreed upon a set of *minima* for the constitutional reform. These can be summarized as follows: (1) explicit acknowledgment of the plurinational character of Spain, with the only subjects of sovereignty to be the three historical AC and the rest of Spain; (2) the transformation of the senate into an asymmetrical, territorial chamber; (3) the establishment of the special fiscal regime currently enjoyed by the Basque Country and Navarra in Galicia and Catalonia; (4) a reform of the constitutional court, incorporating both regional representation and input on the appointment of its members; (5) the achievement of full external representation before the EU; and finally (6) the decentralization of the social security system.

These positions provoked two different responses: while the Conservatives (PP) sought to defend the constitution in its current state, the Socialists (PSOE) sought to reform the constitution along a federalist path.[16] The contents of the PSOE proposal shared very little with the nationalist proposals. The only real points of agreement concerned the representation of the AC in the EU. But even these were dubious, given their fundamental disagreement as to who the major collective actors should be. The nationalists argued that not all the AC should be entitled to EU representation. The Socialists argued that each of the seventeen existing AC must have representation. Moreover, the rest of the Socialists' proposals had even less in common with the nationalists' ideas. They argued that solidarity, as opposed to asymmetry, should guide a general reform of fiscal federalism in Spain. Cooperation and intergovernmental coordination were the principles needed for a stable development of the system. The reform of the senate should be as symmetrical as possible. At first sight, then, the prospects for an agreement between the federalist proposals of the PSOE and the nationalist claims were rather low.

2000–2003

In March 2000 the PP won the national election by a margin that allowed it to rule alone, without the support of the nationalist parties (CiU, PNV). Meanwhile, the reactivation of terrorism after the 1998–99 truce and the growing disagreements with the Basque Nationalist Party as to how to pursue peace in the Basque Country, exacerbated debates about both the EA and the path toward its reform. As a result, positions became more extreme. While the Basque Nationalists (PNV and Eusko Alkartasuna) openly advocated a radically new institutional framework that would situate the Basque Country outside the EA framework, albeit still "associated" with the Crown,[17] the PP declared the constitution untouchable and warned against any discourse proposing its reform, regardless of its content. After 2000, such discourse became the axis of a neo-centrist approach to institutional reform. In this framework, the federalist solution proposed by the PSOE was considered a dangerous game that objectively facilitated the ultimate goals of those aiming to destroy the EA. The neo-centralist approach to the EA has not stopped the plea for a reform of the *Estatuto de Autonomia* in Catalonia. In fact, both the Catalan nationalists (CiU) and the Catalan Socialists (PSC-PSOE) have put forward proposals that advocate direct representation at the EU, adoption of a fiscal regime similar to the one in the Basque Country and Navarra, and recognition of Catalonia as a nation within a plurinational state.[18] In brief, due to the neo-centrist twist of the PP in the last legislative term, the disagreements regarding the EA have become more bitter and more visible.

Identities

As mentioned earlier in this section, we take identities as one more indicator of the evolution of the tension between different nationalisms in Spain (Stepan 2001, 315–62). Our empirical strategy to cope with them is twofold: first we map their change over time using several surveys collected by the CiS in 1979, 1985–86, and 1996. For each of the years we map identities using the standard scale of the ordered answers to the question: "How do you consider yourself? Exclusively Spanish, more Spanish than from your AC, as Spanish as from your AC, more from your AC than Spanish, and exclusively from your AC." It must be noted from the very beginning that the data for 1979 are not strictly comparable, since they are answers to the question: "When you are abroad, how do you consider yourself?" In our view, the most useful information from the 1979 survey concerns exclusive AC identities. The underlying assumption is that only those people with extremely strong regional identities would declare themselves to be Basque, Catalan, or Galician if approached, for instance, in Picadilly Circus.

As a second means of assessing identities, we carry out a binomial logistic regression model of the determinants of political identities in 1996, checking the extent to which identities are actually driven by institutional and discursive factors (namely, the effects of the presence of nationalist parties) when controlling for education and labor market position. The dependent variable takes the value 1 if the individual shows dual identities in either order and 0 if she or he presents any of the exclusive identities. Our major concern is with the degree of development of dual identities as opposed to either of the two exclusive ones.

Table 4.3 shows that the levels of non-Spanish exclusive identities have remained fairly constant in Catalonia and Galicia. We observe also a significant drop in the Basque Country (from 29 percent in 1985 to 20 percent in 1996). This appears to be related to the growing rejection of terrorist violence among the nationalists. It is also related to the growing electoral presence of the Socialists and, more recently, the Conservatives (PP) in the Basque area. The relative success of nationalist mobilization strategies can also be traced through the changes in the internal distribution of dual identities: in Galicia and Catalonia there is a significant shift from those who see themselves as both Spanish and either Catalan or Galician toward a more intense identification with the regional nationality associated with their AC. In the Basque Country, however, the distribution remains practically unchanged.

The rest of the table shows that the development of the *Estado de las Autonomías* has also had important consequences for the evolution of territorial identities in the rest of Spain. In spite of their internal changes, the levels of dual identity have remained significantly high in Galicia, the Basque Country, and Catalonia.[19] Moreover, in the rest of the country, the EA has diminished the weight of exclusively Spanish identities. Even in Madrid and La Rioja, two of the AC where there was no competing reference in terms of political identities, the dual ones represent the biggest share of the population in 1996. In the case of Valencia, dual identities seem to be quite consistent, despite the political expansion of regionalist/nationalist parties. On the contrary, in Aragon, we observe an increase in the proportion of people who see themselves more identified with their AC than with Spain (from 11 to 17 percent between 1985 and 1996). Finally, Andalusia and Canarias constitute two interesting cases. Andalusia experienced a centripetal movement from a more strongly AC identity toward an identity equally Spanish and Andalusian. In Canarias, the centripetal shift comes from both sides. Strong preexisting exclusive identities have given way to an increase in the proportion of groups showing dual identities (both equal and skewed toward the AC).

Table 4.3 Mapping Evolving Identities

	1979			1985–1986					1996				
	EX SP	DUAL	EX.	EX. SP	More SP	Equal	More	EX.	EX. SP	More SP	Equal	More	EX.
Cataluña	33.97	52.86	13.16	11.0	19.0	48.0	8.0	11.0	11.9	11.5	36.5	25.7	11.0
Galicia	n.a.	n.a.	n.a.	5.0	7.0	52.0	27.0	6.0	4.8	7.8	43.7	35.7	7.0
Basque Country	19.75	53.25	26.98	10.0	4.0	36.0	28.0	28.0	5.3	4.0	36.3	29.8	20.7
Canarias	25.20	57.74	14.38	13.6	2.1	37.1	16.4	27.9	5.5	2.7	45.6	33.6	10.9
Andalucia	n.a	n.a.	n.a.	7.0	7.0	63.0	18.0	2.0	5.0	10.1	67.9	12.6	3.2
Aragon	n.a.	n.a.	n.a.	13.0	5.0	66.0	11.0	2.0	8.9	10.1	63.3	17.7	0
Valencia	46.42	48.0	0.03	17.0	18.0	53.0	9.0	1.0	19.4	14.8	55.5	9.8	1.3
Madrid	n.a.	n.a.	n.a.	n.a.	n.a.	n.a.	n.a.	n.a.	31.1	20.4	44.0	2.2	0
La Rioja	n.a.	n.a.	n.a.	n.a.	n.a.	n.a.	n.a.	n.a.	0	5.9	82.4	11.8	0

Sources: CIS 1979; CIS 1985–86; Moreno 1997; CIS 1996.
Notes: Calculations by the authors. **EX.SP**: Exclusively identified with Spain. **EX.**: Exclusively identified with the AC. **More SP**: more identified with Spain than with the AC. **More**: more identified with the AC than with Spain. In 1979 **Dual** means that there was no distinction between these two categories. In 1985–86 and 1996 **Equal** means "as identified with Spain as with the AC." Numbers are percentages.

Are these results really linked to the development of nationalist parties and the *Estado de las Autonomías?* Could they not result from other factors? In order to find out, we have estimated a simple binomial logistic regression model whose results are presented in Table 4.4.

According to the model, three variables have a significant effect on the development of dual identities. The scale of nationalism[20] and the presence/absence of a strong nationalist party in the region have a strong, negative impact on the development of dual identities. The variable tracking the degree of development of the process of decentralization in each AC in 1996 shows the expected results. The implications of the model reinforce the interpretation we drew from Table 4.3. Controlling for nationalism, education, and labor market position, the EA has a net positive, though not very strong, effect on the development of dual identities.

In conclusion, it may well be said that Spanish federalism has been relatively successful in maintaining and nurturing dual, compatible identities. However, nationalist parties have also succeeded in skewing the distributions in Catalonia and Galicia in favor of positions closer to the AC, while essentially holding constant the levels of

Table 4.4 Modeling Dual Identities

Variable Exp (B)	B	S.E.	Wald
LEVEL 1.0252	.0249*	.0060	17.4636
NATION .2601	-1.3467*	.2748	24.0115
NATSC .8451	-.1683*	.0465	13.0988
UNEMPL 1.1330	.1249	.2995	.1738
EDUCAT 1.0782	.0753	.1051	.5123
Constant	.7591	.8667	.7671

N= 4322   R-squared: 0.439

Source: CIS (*Center for Sociological Research*) survey no. 2228 on *National and Regional Consciousness* 1996.

Notes: Binomial logistic regression model. The variables included in the model have been defined as follows. LEVEL: continuous variable that represents the degree of the development of the process of decentralization in a particular AC in 1996. Data from the Ministry of Public Administration. NATSC: is a scale of nationalism that goes from 0, self-perception as fully non-nationalist, to 10, self-perception as fully nationalist. NATION: dummy variable capturing the presence(1)/absence(0) of strong nationalist parties in each of the seventeen AC. UNEMPL: dummy variable capturing the labor market position of the interviewee (1: unemployed; 0: at work). EDUCAT: continuous variable that measures the number of years in education of the interviewee.

*Significant at $p < 0.001$ level.

exclusive identities. Finally, a quick look at these levels in Catalonia and in the Basque Country shows that neither are a priori high enough to allow any credible push toward secession at present.

Nonetheless, our model also shows that identities are shaped by the strategies of actors, rather than the other way around. This suggests that this threat may become more credible as long as hegemonic nationalist parties push their discourses and strategies in that direction. This very possibility is, in itself, an extremely powerful political source of instability (backed in the Basque Country by the activities of ETA) which influences to a great extent the present and the future of Spanish politics.

Institutional Choices and Unintended Consequences: Federalism and the Management of Territorial Conflicts in Spain

How can the empirical evidence provided in the previous sections shed some light on the more general questions addressed by this project?

In line with other contributions to the project, it must be first noted that the Spanish experience points to the interactive relationship between the design and performance of federal institutions and the specific articulation of historical, economic, and identity-related differences within Spain. The institutional design of 1978 is not independent of the existing structure of territorial cleavages and the subsequent pattern of territorial conflicts was not independent of the consequences of the EA.

The EA's ability to manage territorial conflicts can be assessed by combining two different perspectives. Relative to experiences in other countries and to Spanish history, the capacity of the EA to integrate different clusters of economic and identity-related differences has been impressive. From this perspective, the EA must be regarded as a success. Conflicts about linguistic rights, the control of policy domains, health care funding, the design of curricula, or foreign policy decision making, to mention only a few, will continue to exist as long as there are several layers of government. The major success of EA lies in that, however contested at the ideological/discursive level, all actors (but ETA) act within the rules of the system. Additionally, the EA itself has managed to modify the structure and depth of identity-related differences, by reducing mutually exclusive differences and nurturing dual ones in Catalonia, Galicia, and, to a lesser extent, the Basque Country. The practice of decentralization had important effects in the rest of Spain as well, where dual identities have increased in relation to Spanish exclusive ones.

However, while regional and national incumbents, and all other salient political actors, follow the system's rules, they have been trying to adjust the scope and nature of decentralization from 1978 on. Spain presents us with an open-ended process in which a general picture of success hides complex internal dynamics, causally linked to the intended and unintended consequences of the original institutional design.

It is fairly well known that the conditions under which the EA was designed were not optimal. In the context of the transition to democracy from a heavily centralized dictatorship, any maneuvering room was strictly limited. Retrospectively speaking, the sources of success can be found in the combination of a twofold strategy: the acknowledgment and satisfaction of demands affecting mainly symbolic and identity-related issues in the constitution itself,[21] and the deliberate omission of major issues on which full agreement was impossible. In this latter respect, to quote the current president of the constitutional court, important aspects of the central state's boundaries were de facto *"deconstitutionalized"* from the very beginning (Cruz-Villalón 1990, 71–103). In turn, in order to attract nationalist parties to the constitutional consensus, asymmetry had to be implicitly or explicitly present in the constitutional text. Hence, the distinctions analyzed above were introduced to both reflect the existing differences and facilitate their future reinforcement beyond the constitutional arena.

However, there was a price to be paid for such a strategy. The EA lacks institutions of shared rule (as explained above), and conflicts about asymmetry have been ongoing since 1978. Given the initial conditions of openness, asymmetry, and lack of institutionalized cooperation, bilateral exchanges and pressures became the engine of the system. This dynamic has generated two factors that have increased the tension between harmonization and asymmetry and kept the system far from the perfect institutional stability described above. The first is an expansion in the number of regionalist and cryptonationalist parties in AC where they had previously had virtually no political presence. Table 4.5 presents the evolution of the voting share of those parties in the regional elections for all the AC except for Galicia, the Basque Country, Navarra, and Catalonia.

These parties foster the tension between harmonization and asymmetry because they pressure incumbents in their ACs to demand that their local region's autonomous powers match those of the original nationalist ACs.

The second factor increasing the tension between harmonization and asymmetry is the fact that the process of decentralization has come closer and closer to its constitutional limits. Paradoxically, as the design of EA becomes more complete, the trade-offs become harder. As the system approaches its final form and the case for higher levels of harmonization is supported both by statewide and new regionalist parties, it loses

Table 4.5 Share of Regionalist and Nationalist Voting in Regional Elections of the AC plus the Canary Islands

	1983	1987	1991	1995	1999
Aragón	19.8	26.0	26.4	24.8	24.38
Baleares	13.92	9.19	3.98	11.02	10.97
Asturias	0.7	1.3	3.1	3.1	9.76
Canarias	23.1	29.0	38.8	42.4	42.1
Cantabria	8.6	13.6	41.3	33.1	16.6
Castilla-La Mancha	0.0	0.3	0.7	0.8	0.8
Castilla Yleón	2.8	2.4	2.5	5.1	6.7
Extremadura	10.4	7.0	4.6	5.3	3.9
Madrid	0.4	0.1	0.9	0.9	–
Murcia	2.7	3.4	3.0	1.3	2.7
Valencia		9.14	10.37	7.01	8.9
La Rioja	7.5	6.5	5.5	7.6	7.02

Sources: Oñate et al. 1999 and Ministry of Internal Affairs.
Note: Figures are percentages.

flexibility and thus pushes nationalist parties to move toward a different strategy. As illustrated by the empirical evidence provided in the third section of this essay, these actors have turned from arguments about shares within the system to questions about the overall structure of the system. System stability is still elusive.

This said, the EA has, by historical and comparative standards, worked rather well as an institutional device to manage the coexistence of multiple identities. It has also helped Spain complete the transition to democracy.

On a more theoretical level, the Spanish experience raises some interesting questions about the interaction between federalism and nationalism (Linz 1997; Watts 1998). On the one hand, the experience of the EA shows that federalism is the most successful institutional device in integrating several nationalisms within the same polity. Its advantages in relation to its alternatives, especially in relation to a centralized/unitary system, are illustrated by the long-term historical analysis of the Spanish experience. On the other hand, the evolution of EA also shows how nationalism introduces an additional, entirely independent dimension into the relationships between several levels of government: asymmetry (and its opposite, harmonization). While decentralization concerns the sharing of powers between the center and the regions, asymmetry is a function of nationalism, and applies to the horizontal differences between regions in terms of their power and capabilities. In this sense, our chapter shows that when federalism and nationalism are combined, the political system will never be at equilibrium.

NOTES

The authors appreciate the comments and suggestions by the editors and participants at the conference "Does Federalism Matter?" Princeton, February 2000, as well as the help at various stages by Justo Beramendi, Francisco Caamaño, Marta Conde, Santiago Lago, and Martha Peach. The usual disclaimer applies.

1. EA is the specific name given by academics and politicians to the institutional design agreed upon in 1978. This denomination is not recorded as such in the constitution and is the result of the need to avoid the word *federalism* for both academic and theoretical reasons in reference to the design of 1978.

2. What follows in this section is a broad summary of the work produced by many historians whose research interest focused on the evolution of different nationalisms in Spain. Certainly, the summary does not do justice to the richness of their contributions, and thus we apologize in advance for that. A general summary is to be found in Moreno (1997). For more recent general accounts, see Beramendi (1999, 79–100) and De la Granja et al. (2001).

3. For an overall synthesis of the process of formation of a Spanish national identity, see Alvarez-Junco (2001).

4. Further insights on Catalan nationalism can be found in Balcells (1996) and Termes (2000).

5. A study of the different phases in the origins of Galician nationalism can be found in Beramendi (1997). An analysis of its process of political mobilization is offered in Máiz (1994, 173–209).

6. The different aspects of the conflict between different nationalisms during the Second Republic have been treated at length in Beramendi and Máiz (1991).

7. Aja (1999) and Bañón and Agranoff (1998) offer good overviews of the formal institutional aspects of the EA.

8. Article 148 states that the potential exclusive domains for the AC are: institutional organizations (executive, parliament, ombudsman); industry; handicrafts; commerce; urbanism; tourism; agriculture and livestock; social assistance and services; rivers and lakes; transportation within the AC; culture, language, and research policies; museums and libraries related to the AC. For more details, see articles 148 and 149.1.

9. The founding of the PRD was an attempt to construct from Catalonia a reformist, countrywide party. The CDS was a party created by Adolfo Suarez after the collapse of the UCD, the center-right party heading Spain.

10. For more detailed information about the structure of fiscal revenues in Spain, see Valle (1996, 2–26). On page 18, he analyzes the structure of fiscal revenues. The AC percentage is 1.72 percent, whereas local councils' is 2.76 percent.

11. For an excellent analysis of the political process leading to autonomy in the Basque Country and the position of the PNV, see Corcuera (1991, 70–125).

12. By dual identities we refer to the consideration by people of more than one territorial referent (for instance, Spain and the Basque Country), regardless of how they rank their attachment to it. On the contrary, exclusive identities are characterized precisely by ruling out that possibility.

13. In order to explain the privileged position of nationalist parties in the 1993–96 period, one must understand that their electoral success is a necessary, though not sufficient condition given the fact that the total sum of the votes of PSOE and IU would be enough to support a stable government. The enormous difference between the Socialists and the Communists regarding the

EU process and the guidelines of economic policy must be brought into the picture in order to understand why the nationalists of CiU were able to achieve a much higher political capacity to impose their preferences. For further references, see Maravall (1999, 154–97) and Linz and Montero (1999).

14. Ruiz-Huerta and López-Laborda (1996, 582–614) present an excellent review of the major issues after these reforms took place.

15. The contents and principles of these proposals can be found in the background documents of the subsequent meetings of Barcelona, Gasteiz, and Santiago. They are available at the CiU website: www.convergencia.org/declaraciones. For an elaborate exposition of the logic underlying these proposals, see Requejo (1998).

16. The contents of the socialist proposal are available at length in their document *La Estructura del Estado: Politica Autonomica y Municipal del PSOE* (The Structure of the State: Regional and Local Policy), 1998.

17. The core of the PNV position consists of considering the fulfillment of this agenda as the only feasible path toward the eventual dissolution of ETA and, ultimately, the achievement of peace. In this spirit, they formally agreed in the *Pacto de Extella-Lizarra* (October 12, 1998) to cooperate with HB (the radical nationalist party recently banned by the Supreme Court for its support for ETA) for the achievement of peace and the establishment of a set of procedures such that "Euskadi could freely have the final word about its future." The full text of the agreement is available from http://www.lizarra-garazo/org/01default.htm.

18. A comparative analysis of these proposals can be found in EL PAIS (March 26, 2003, 30). The full version of the proposal by the Catalan Socialists is contained in the document *Bases per a l'elaboració de l'Estatut Catalunya.*

19. Much more detailed accounts of the problem of identities in the Basque Country and Catalonia in earlier periods can be found in Linz (1986) and Llera (1985).

20. For details about the model estimated as well as about the sources and definition of the variables used, see Table 4.4.

21. So, for instance, the army was acknowledged as a guarantor of the unity of the country and Spain was declared a unitary and indivisible nation. On the other hand, ACs were distinguished between *nacionalidades* and mere regions and three languages, Catalan, Euskera (Basque), and Galician, were declared co-official in their respective AC s.

REFERENCES

Aja, E. 1999. *El Estado Autonómico: Federalismo y Hechos Diferenciales.* Madrid: Alianza Editorial.

Albertí Rovira, E. 1996. El Régimen de los Convenios de Colaboración entre Administraciones: un problema pendiente. In *Informe Comunidades Autónomas,* ed. E. Aja, 616–37. Barcelona: Civitas-Instituto de Derecho Público.

Alvarez-Junco, J. 1997. The Nation-building Process in Nineteenth-Century Spain. In *Nationalism and the Nation in the Iberian Peninsula,* ed. M. Molinero and A. Smith, 89–106. Oxford: Berg.

——— . 2001. *Mater Dolorosa.* Madrid: Taurus.

Aranzadi, J. 1981. *El Milenarismo Vasco*. Madrid: Taurus.

Azurmendi, M. 2001. *Y se limpie aquella Tierra*. Madrid: Taurus.

Balcells, A. 1996. *Catalan Nationalism*. London: Macmillan.

Bañón, R., and R. Agranoff. 1998. *El Estado de las Autonomías. ¿Hacia un nuevo Federalismo?* Bilbao: IVAP.

Beramendi, J. G. 1997: *El Nacionalismo Gallego*. Madrid: Arco/Libros.

——— . 1999. Identity, Ethnicity and State in Spain: 19th and 20th Centuries. *Nationalism and Ethnic Politics* 5, nos. 3–4: 79–100.

Beramendi, J. G., and R. Máiz, eds. 1991. *Los Nacionalismos en la España de la II República*. Madrid: Siglo XXI.

Calsamiglia, X., et al. 1991. *La Financiación de las Comunidades Autónomas: Evaluación del Sistema Actual y Criterios para su Reforma*. Barcelona: Generalitat de Catalunya.

Colomer, J. M. 1998. The Spanish State of Autonomies: Non Institutional Federalism. In *Politics and Policy in Democratic Spain: No Longer Different?* ed. P. Heywood, 50–53. London: Frank Cass.

Corcuera, J. 1991. *Política y Derecho: La Construcción de la Autonomía Vasca*. Madrid: Centro de Estudios Constitucionales.

Cruz-Villalón, P. 1990. La Doctrina Constitucional sobre el Principio de Cooperación. In *Comunidades Autónomas e Instrumentos de Cooperación Interterritorial*, ed. J. Cano Bueso, 71–103. Madrid: Tecnos.

De la Granja, J. L., J. Beramendi, and P. Anguera.2001. *La España de los Nacionalismos y de las Autonomías*. Madrid: Editorial Síntesis.

De Pablo, S., L. Mess, and J. A. Rodriguez. 1999. *El Péndulo Patriótico*. Barcelona: Crítica.

Díez-Medrano, J. 1995. *Divided Nations*. Ithaca: Cornell University Press.

Dixit, A. K. 1996. *The Making of Economic Policy: A Transaction Cost Politics Perspective*. Cambridge, Mass.: MIT Press.

Elazar, Daniel. 1987. *Exploring Federalism*. Tuscaloosa: University of Alabama Press.

Elorza, A. 2001. *Un Pueblo Escogido*. Barcelona: Crítica.

ERA-CECS. 1997. *Informe España 1996: Una interpretación de su Realidad Social*. Madrid: Fundación Encuentro.

Giménez Montero, A. 1996. Autonomía y Dependencia Financiers en el nuevo modelo de financiación de las Comunidades Autónomas de Régimen Común. *Cuadernos de Información Económica* 116:100–110.

Juaristi, J. 1987. *El Linaje de Aitor*. Madrid: Taurus.

Linz, J. 1986. *Conflicto en Euskadi*. Madrid: Espasa-Calpe.

——— . 1997. *Democracy, Multinationalism and Federalism*. Working Paper, no. 103, CEAS Juan March.

Linz, J., and J. R. Montero. 1999. *The Party Systems of Spain: Old Cleavages and New Challenges*. Working Paper, no. 138, CEACS Juan March.

Llera, F. 1985. *Postfranquismo y Fuerzas Políticas en Euskadi: Sociología Electoral del Pais Vasco*. Bilbao: Universidad del Pais Vasco.

Máiz, R. 1994. The Open-Ended Construction of a Nation: The Galician Case in Spain. In *Nationalism in Europe: Past and Present*, vol. II, ed. J. Beramendi, R. Máiz, and X. M. Nuñez, 173–209. Santiago de Compostela: USC-Press.

——— . 1999a. Cuando los efectos devienen causas: déficit federal y nacionalismos institucionalmente inducidos en la España de los noventa. *Revista Española de Ciencia Política* 1, no 1:173–85.

————. 1999b. Nationalism, Federalism and Democracy in Multinational States. *Nationalism and Ethnic Politics* 5, nos. 3–4.

Maravall, J. M. 1999. Accountability and Manipulation. In *Accountability and Representation,* ed. A. Przeworski et al., 154–97. Cambridge: Cambridge University Press.

Ministerio de Administraciones Públicas. 1992. *Acuerdos Autonómicos de 28 de Febrero de 1992.* Madrid.

————. 1995. *La Descentralización del Gasto Público en España: Período 1984-1993.* Dirección General de Coordinación con las Haciendas Territoriales, Ministerio de Economía y Hacienda.

Ministerio de la Presidencia. 1982. *Acuerdos Autonómicos de 1981.* Madrid: Colección Informe.

Monasterio, C., et al. 1995. *Informe sobre el actual sistema de financiación y sus problemas.* Madrid: Instituto de Estudios Fiscales.

Monasterio, C., and J. S. Pandiello. 1996. *Manual de Hacienda Autonómica y Local.* Barcelona: Ariel.

Montero, J. R. 1998. Stabilising the Democratic Order: Electoral Behaviour in Spain. In *Politics and Policy in Democratic Spain: No Longer Different?* ed. P. Heywood, 40–53. London: Frank Cass.

Moreno, L. 1997. *La Federalización de España.* Madrid: S. XXI.

Oñate, P., and F. Ocaña. 1999. *Análisis de Datos Electorales.* CiS, Cuadernos Metodológicos 27/1999.

Portero Molina, J. A. 1997. *Constitución y Jurisprudencia Constitucional.* Valencia: Tirant Lo Blanc.

Requejo, F. 1998. *Federalisme per a qué?* Valencia: 3 i 4.

Riquer i Permanyer, B. 1977. *Lliga Regionalista: la burgesia catalana I el Regionalisme.* Barcelona: Edicions 62.

————. 1996. Nacionalidades y Regiones: Problemas de la débil nacionalización de la España del Siglo XIX. In *Historia Contemporánea de España,* ed. A. Morales Moya and M. Vega. Salamanca: University of Salamanca Press.

Riquer, B., and E. Ucelay. 1994. An Analysis of Nationalism in Spain. In *Nationalism in Europe. Past and Present,* ed. J. Beramendi, R. Máiz, and X. M. Núñez. Santiago de Compestela: Santiago University Press

Rodden, J., and S. Rose-Ackermann. 1997. Does Federalism Preserve Markets? *Virginia Law Review* 1521–73.

Rose-Ackermann, S. 1981. Does Federalism Matter? Political Choice in a Federal Republic. *Journal of Political Economy* 89, no. 1:152–65.

Ruiz-Huerta, J., and J. López-Rueda. 1996. Catorce Preguntas sobre el nuevo sistema de financiación autonómica. In *Informe Comunidades Autónomas,* ed. E. Aja. Barcelona: civitas-Instituto de Derecho Público.

Sánchez Cuenca, I. 2001. *ETA contra el Estado.* Barcelona: Tusquets.

Simeon, R., and J. Mintz. 1982. *Conflict of Taste and Conflict of Claim in Federal Countries.* Kingston, Ont.: Institute of Intergovernmental Relations, Queen's University.

Solé Tura, J. 1985. *Nacionalidades y Nacionalismos en España: Autonomías, Federalismo, Autodeterminación.* Madrid: Alianza.

Stepan, Alfred. 2001 Toward a New Comparative Politics of Federalism, Multinationalism and Democracy. In A. Stepan, *Arguing Comparative Politics.* Oxford: Oxford University Press.

STC 76/1983. Sentencia del Tribunal Consitucional sobre el Proyecto LOAPA de 5 de Agosto.

Termes, J. 2000. *Historia del Catalanisme.* Barcelona: Pórtico.

Valle, V. 1996. La Hacienda Pública de la Democracia Española: Principales Rasgos. *Papeles de Economía Española* 68:2–26.

Velilla Lucini, P. 1993. *El Proceso de Descentralización del Gasto Público en España: comportamiento fiscal y decisiones de gasto de los gobiernos autonómicos.* Fundación BBV.

Watts, R. 1998. Federalism, Federal Political Systems and Federations. *Annual Review of Political Science* 117–37.

Weingast, B. R. 1995. The Economic Role of Political Institutions: Market-Preserving Federalism and Economic Development. *Journal of Law, Economics and Organisation* 11, no. 1:1–32.

Weingast, B. R., and R. De Figueirido. 1998. *Self-enforcing Federalism: Solving the Two Fundamental Dilemmas.* Unpublished manuscript quoted with permission from the authors.

CHAPTER FIVE

The United Kingdom

Political Institutions and Territorial Cleavages

Michael Keating

Center-Periphery Relations

The case of the United Kingdom is unusual in that, while territorial politics have long been an important factor in public life, the state is not federal and, indeed, it is only since 1999 that devolved parliamentary institutions have been introduced. To appreciate the dynamics and issues of territorial politics it is therefore necessary to survey the arrangements to govern the multinational state before 1999. Judgment on the performance of the new institutions themselves must wait a little longer.

Nation and Nationalism in the United Kingdom

The United Kingdom of Great Britain and Northern Ireland[1] consists of England which, with 48 million inhabitants, dominates the union; Scotland (population 5 million); Wales (population 3 million); and the six counties of Northern Ireland (1.5 million). The twenty-six southern counties of Ireland broke away in 1922 to form the Irish Free State, which later became the Republic of Ireland (population 3.5 million). Each part was incorporated in the United Kingdom in a different way, preserving its own features and characteristics but, in contrast to other states so constructed, like France or the Netherlands, there was no national revolution to unite nation and state and forge a shared identity. Instead, consistent with the British tradition of pragmatism, this differentiated structure persisted into the modern era to constitute what Rokkan and Urwin (1983) called a "union state." This is a form neither federal nor unitary, in which the constituent parts, "fragments of states" (Jellinek 1981), retain many of their old rights and privileges.

Wales was the most fully incorporated, after the failure of efforts to found an independent principality in the thirteenth century. Under the Tudors, a Welsh dynasty, it was merged with England by the Acts of Union of 1536 and 1542, retaining only the courts of Great Session into the nineteenth century. Ireland's relationship with the Crown was more colonial in nature. It was first conquered by Anglo-Normans in the twelfth century, although the Crown's hold was ever more precarious until the sixteenth century, as the settlers gradually assimilated with the Old Irish. The Reformation introduced a sharp division between the Irish (Gaelic and Norman), who remained largely Catholic, and the Protestant settlers from England and Scotland, who were planted in both north and south during the seventeenth century. There was an Irish parliament, representing the Protestant ascendancy class[2] until the Union of 1800, but the executive was never accountable to it and after 1800 the country was managed by the lord lieutenant and the chief secretary, appointed from London. Scotland beat off attempts at conquest in the thirteenth and fourteenth centuries but was linked to England in 1603 when King James VI succeeded to the English Crown as James I. In 1707 there was a negotiated union in which both England and Scotland surrendered their parliaments in favor of a new parliament of Great Britain. Provision was made for Scotland to keep its own system of law and courts, its established church, and its education and local government systems.

Each of the smaller nations of the United Kingdom preserved its distinctive traits within the union. Wales was least distinct institutionally but retained its own language, spoken until the nineteenth century, by the majority of the population. In the eighteenth century most of the Welsh broke away from the Church of England, creating a social cleavage in the countryside between the small farmers and the anglicized and Anglican gentry. In the late nineteenth century a distinct Welsh political culture emerged, rooted in religious nonconformity, egalitarianism, and radicalism (Morgan 1980). In Ireland, the peasantry were distanced from the Anglo-Irish landlord class by religion and nationality, and the two issues of religion and land were to dominate Irish politics for much of the nineteenth century. Government was in the hands of appointees sent over from London. Scotland, by contrast, enjoyed a large degree of informal self-government as its native elites found their own place within the union (Paterson 1994; Harvie 1994). Until the 1830s power was in the hands of the Scottish "manager" who, in return for delivering Scottish MPs to the government of the day, had a free hand in the distribution of patronage. Such administration as was needed was provided by the burghs, appointed boards, or the Kirk (Church of Scotland). As the state expanded its role from the late nineteenth century, it took on a Scottish form, notably with the appointment in 1885 of a secretary for Scotland, who gradually took on responsibility for most domestic policy in Scotland. The secretary (of state) was a Scottish MP of the ruling party who acted as a broker between the Scottish and U.K. levels of politics, applying government policy in Scotland while defending Scotland's interests in the cabinet.

It is impossible to assign a date to the start of territorial mobilization in the United Kingdom. While territorial/national conflicts do have deep roots, anachronistic myths such as that of "Ireland's 800-year struggle" are an effort to put a contemporary gloss on historical conflicts. The dynastic struggles of the seventeenth and eighteenth centuries have also been given a nationalist slant, with the Jacobites being presented as proto-Scottish nationalists and even, at one time, Irish nationalists.[3] The religious wars of the seventeenth century, which should rightly be seen as part of a wider European conflict around the Thirty Years' War, have also been pressed into service by nationalist and antinationalist historiography. The first explicitly nationalist movement, however, was the United Irishmen of 1798, inspired by the Jacobin ideals and civic nationalism of the French Revolution. Like other parts of Europe, the United Kingdom in the nineteenth century saw a series of upheavals as the politics of territory, religion, and class intersected in the context of state building and consolidation. After the Napoleonic Wars, a renewed Irish movement, associated with Daniel O'Connell, sought the repeal of the Union. This failed with the famine of 1847 but was followed by the home rule movement, which reached its peak under Charles Stewart Parnell in the 1880s. By the end of the nineteenth century, this moderate tradition was rivaled by more radical ideas, often tied in with use of violence, and the consequent division between peaceful and "physical force" nationalism has persisted to our own day. Irish nationalism was linked to the movement for Catholic advancement and land reform and its progress was matched by a mobilization of the Protestant community, especially in the north, dedicated to the Union and Protestant supremacy. Although many of the leaders of the United Irishmen (like Wolfe Tone) and the home rule movement (like Isaac Butt and Parnell) were Protestant, and the Catholic Church had never given its open support, Irish nationalism came to be increasingly identified with the aspirations of the Catholic community and the religious and national divisions became ever more identical. A movement for Scottish home rule took off in the late nineteenth century, in response to the expansion of the British state and the example of Ireland. Its main support was among the more advanced Liberals and radicals and it was to draw in Highland land reformers and the early labor movement (Keating and Bleiman 1979). The religious element was weaker, although advanced Liberals did support disestablishment of the Church of Scotland, and sympathy with Ireland had to coexist with an undercurrent of anti-Catholicism.[4] A weaker movement developed in Wales, also based on the radical wing of the Liberals, playing on issues of land and language but above all on opposition to the Anglican Church establishment and its control of the education system.

Mobilization reached a peak in the 1880s and again in the years before and after the First World War, causing constitutional crises and even a danger of civil war. Before the war, the main division was between Gladstonian Liberals and the emerging left on the one hand, and the Conservatives and Unionists on the other. Gladstone's conversion to the cause of Irish self-government in 1886 split the Liberal Party and kept it out of power for most of a generation. The breakaway Liberal Unionists took not only most of the Liberal aristocrats and the right wing, but also a section of the radicals under Joseph Chamberlain, and gave the Conservatives, with whom they eventually amalgamated, a lower-class Protestant base in urban centers in Scotland and northern England.

The Gladstonian home rule concept, soon extended to Scotland (Finlay 1997) and then home rule all round, envisaged the creation of subordinate parliaments in Ireland, Scotland, Wales, and, in some versions, England, to manage local affairs, leaving the imperial Parliament to deal with the great affairs of state. Its main objective was to contain nationalist pressures, especially in Ireland, but it was also promoted as a form of constitutional modernization to relieve the burden on central government and foster national efficiency. It was federal in its implications although Gladstone, presenting his home rule bill for Ireland, went out of his way to distinguish it from the old O'Connellite demand for repeal of the Union, which would have restored a measure of sovereignty to the Irish parliament. Like all subsequent home rule governments down to Tony Blair's, he insisted that nothing would abridge the sovereignty of Westminster. There has also been a federalist movement in the United Kingdom (Kendle 1997) proposing variously a federation of the British Isles or of the empire, but since the First World War it has survived largely within the Liberal Party, itself a minority force in British politics.

On the other side, there developed the ideology and politics of unionism, again initially in Ireland but later in the rest of the United Kingdom. Irish Unionists were to a large degree concerned with preserving Protestant power but their supporters on the mainland were more concerned with the principle of the Union itself. Their intellectual apologists, from A .V. Dicey (1886, 1912) to antidevolutionists in the 1970s (Wilson 1970) and 1990s have argued that we must not devolve power to subordinate legislatures precisely because the United Kingdom is a multinational state. Any Irish or Scottish parliament, or even a Welsh assembly, would of necessity consider itself to embody the will of a nation and thus abrogate to itself full sovereignty. Local municipal self-government, recognition of special conditions, administrative distinctions, and policy differentiation, on the other hand, were acceptable. Unionists are not Jacobins and have not sought to promote an overriding U.K. national identity. Unlike in France, there was no consistent program for cultural homogenization, although in practice the peripheral cultures did suffer neglect and depreciation. Instead, the main propaganda effort went into sustaining support for the empire, a concept that subsumed the United Kingdom but took in a lot else besides. From the late nineteenth century, British Unionists approached Ireland with a combination of concession and coercion, addressing the land issue with quite radical reforms, but setting their faces against constitutional change and bringing in special legislation to clamp down on disturbances.

Struggles over home rule peaked in the years before the First World War. Irish home rule bills sponsored by Liberal governments had been thrown out by the House of Commons in 1886 and the House of Lords in 1893,[5] so when the Liberals returned with a massive majority in 1906 they proceeded with circumspection. Only after they had lost their majority in 1910 and were reliant on the Irish members in the Commons did they produce a new home rule bill. With the lords' veto removed following the constitutional crisis of 1910, there was no legal obstacle to its passage, but the Unionists remained intransigent. Militias emerged on both sides in Ireland and the Conservative and Unionist leadership declared that military resistance to home rule would be justified. Irish Unionists for their part took the view that, if home rule could not be avoided altogether, then the province of Ulster or its Protestant parts should be allowed to opt out. Only the outbreak of the First World War avoided a slide into civil war or a coup d'état. The year 1916 saw the Easter rising whose suppression boosted the republican forces dedicated to secession and physical force. Sinn Féin swept aside the moderate home rulers in the postwar election of 1918, heralding a violent conflict that ended in the partition of Ireland and the establishment of two home rule governments, the Irish Free State and the Province of Northern Ireland. The Free State evolved into independence, ultimately as the Republic of Ireland (1949), while Northern Ireland remained in the United Kingdom but under the dominance of the Ulster Unionist Party dedicated to Protestant supremacy.

These years also witnessed a rise in Scottish nationalism, although this was overshadowed by the Irish crisis. A series of home rule bills was presented to Parliament and in 1913 one of them even gained a second reading. During the war, Labour and the trade unions campaigned hard for home rule, culminating in a great mobilization between 1918 and 1922 (Keating and Bleiman 1979). Then the movement went into rapid decline. The parliamentary breakthrough of 1922 showed Labour that Westminster was open to them. The collapse of the Scottish economy after the postwar boom emphasized Scotland's dependence on U.K. markets and financial support; and the independent Scottish trade unions gradually merged with their English counterparts and Scottish civil society generally found a secure niche within the union state.

In Wales, local grievances never quite crystallized into a great movement for home rule. The educational issue was resolved by the Liberal government elected in 1906 and the Church in Wales disestablished by an act of 1913, which took effect after the war. Prominent figures in the Welsh revival, notably David Lloyd George, found a niche in British politics, while the rising labor movement, like its Scottish counterpart, looked to London for redress (Jones and Keating 1985).

The Institutional Environment

Territorial Management in the Union State

Political scientists in the 1960s and 1970s often portrayed the United Kingdom as a unitary state without any federal features and with a homogeneous political culture (Blondel 1974; Finer 1970). In reality it was a highly differentiated polity in which the numerical dominance of England and the absence of devolved parliamentary institutions except in Northern Ireland masked considerable divergences. Managing this differentiated polity involved a complex exercise in statecraft in each of the constituent nations. After a period of stability, these arrangements broke down from the late 1960s, heralding another outbreak of territorial politics comparable to that of the years 1880–1920.

After 1922, British politicians sought to externalize the question of Northern Ireland. Ironically, the province that had most resisted home rule was the only place to experience it before the 1990s in the guise of the Stormont regime. This was a devolved parliament and government with extensive social, economic, and fiscal competences over all matters not expressly reserved to Westminster.[6] In practice it was a vehicle for maintaining the Protestant ascendancy, despite the fact that around a third of the population was Catholic. The Ulster Unionist Party abolished the proportional representation that been bequeathed by the British and consequently won all the elections.[7] Local government boundaries and electoral constituencies were gerrymandered, to keep the majority Catholic city of Derry under Unionist control. The Royal Ulster Constabulary was an instrument of Protestant domination. Catholics suffered systematic official and social discrimination and authoritarian measures were passed that had no counterpart on the mainland.

Nationalists had widely assumed that Northern Ireland would prove unviable, allowing Irish unification in due course. In practice, as Stormont was unable to pay its way, the "imperial contribution" to cover the cost of U.K. services diminished and then became negative. After the Second World War, Stormont shadowed the welfare state measures of the new Labour government in London, secure in the knowledge that London would pay the bill. This had two opposite consequences. It helped legitimize the Stormont regime by giving Northern Ireland citizens a higher level of welfare services than that available in the Republic,[8] but without ever winning the positive support of Catholics. Surveys indicate that Catholics are more preoccupied with their immediate situation within Northern Ireland. Rose's 1968 survey showed 21 percent of Catholics in favor of retaining the border and only 14 percent in favor of immediate unification (Rose 1971). Surveys in the late 1970s confirmed that northern Catholics were more concerned with power sharing than reunification (Moxon-Browne 1983). On a very soft question in 1995, just 53 percent of Catholics preferred Irish unity, although only 13 percent were opposed (Breen 1996). A 1996 survey showed 15 percent of Catholics in favor of remaining within the United Kingdom while 34 percent wanted to join the Republic (Evans and O'Leary 1997). Protestants, on the other hand, consistently come out as massively opposed to Irish unity.

On the other hand, the British subvention kept the Stormont regime in existence and the British never demanded equal civil rights as a condition for support. So Northern Ireland remained a divided society, in which the Catholics felt discrimination while the Protestants felt themselves under constant threat from Irish irredentism. For the most part, Catholics retreated into political quiescence and nonparticipation, punctuated by sporadic campaigns by the republican movement whose stated goal was to overthrow the regimes of both Northern and southern Ireland in favor of a unified Republic. There was a complex interplay of class and ethnic/religious cleavages. Sporadic efforts were made to organize labor and socialist parties across the sectarian divide, but the institutionalization of the communitarian and nationalist division consistently frustrated this (Bew, Gibbon, and Patterson 1996; Ruane and Todd 1996; O'Leary and McGarry 1993).

Scotland was governed through a modified form of the management system that had existed since the mid-eighteenth century. The secretary of state for Scotland, always a Scottish MP from the ruling party, enjoyed full cabinet status from 1926 and gradually took over the management of most domestic policy in Scotland. Around the Scottish office there developed an array of specifically Scottish administrative institutions and agencies, while the local government system took a distinct form. Separate legislation was passed at Westminster where Scottish conditions or the needs of the Scottish legal system required this. So there developed a distinct Scottish layer of politics within the U.K. political system, with Scottish MPs having to decide whether to take a Scottish or a U.K. career path (Keating 1975). The centralizing force of cabinet government, of party loyalty, and of the policy leadership exerted by the big Whitehall departments limited policy autonomy to areas where there was a strong Scottish tradition, where the issue was of low political salience, where party ideology was weak, and where the Scottish office controlled the resources needed for policy development (Keating and Midwinter 1984; Midwinter, Keating, and Mitchell 1991). Education, social work, and local government structure were areas of higher autonomy than economic development, expenditure priorities, or health. Most important, Scottish politicians saw a trade-off between autonomy for Scotland and access to the center. Scotland was overrepresented in the House of Commons (McLean 1995; Rossiter, Johnston, and Pattie 1997). The Scottish office, linked into Whitehall networks, the secretary of state in cabinet, and the overrepresentation of Scotland in Parliament provided material advantages that could be jeopardized by adopting home rule. These advantages were real enough. Scotland, whose economy went through a series of structural crises from the 1930s, benefited from regional policies designed to bring in new industry, while expenditure levels were consistently higher than in England or Wales.[9] The bargaining and brokerage between Scotland and the U.K. treasury and economic departments was conducted discreetly so as not to arouse undue suspicion in other regions and Scottish parties and interests were able to cooperate in pursuing Scottish interests without attenuating their primary partisan or class loyalties. It was precisely the institutional structure around the Scottish office and its agencies that allowed the articulation of a territorial economic interest, which was notably lacking, for example, in the regions of England. This institutional arrangement served to tie Scotland into the United Kingdom, while at the same time maintaining and even reinforcing the idea of a distinct Scottish political and administrative identity. The role of the Scottish office and its agencies in shaping issues and instruments further invited people to frame issues, such as economic development, in a Scottish context. So, despite regular campaigns for home rule or devolution (Mitchell 1996) the political elite were able to contain the pressures without constitutional change.

In Wales there was much less administrative differentiation. Wales does not have its own legal system and only in 1965 was the Welsh office established on the lines pioneered by the Scottish office in 1885. The secretary of state for Wales was a less senior minister than his Scottish counterpart and played less of a role as a broker between Whitehall and local civil society, as shown by the fact that Conservative governments in the 1980s and 1990s were able to appoint MPs from English constituencies to the office—this would be unthinkable in Scotland. From the 1960s, however, Wales also benefited from regional policy initiatives and gradually a Welsh political-administrative arena emerged. The Welsh language was an important identifier but it also divided Welsh society since only about 20 percent of population used it. From the

1960s, Westminster made quite generous provisions for the language, a process that continued even under the centralizing Conservative governments of the 1980s and 1990s (Snicker 1997) in a characteristic British move to defuse peripheral nationalism by showing that centralized government could address the substantive grievances of the minority nations.

The Collapse of Territorial Management

The United Kingdom's system of territorial management was based, as were other elements of the constitution, on unwritten understandings and balances. From the 1960s it began to collapse under the influence of external and internal change. Loss of empire exposed the weakness of British national, as opposed to imperial, identity, while economic decline sapped confidence in the superiority of British ways. The 1960s and 1970s saw a frenzy of institutional reforms, informed by the new managerialism, none of which touched the essence of the constitution, and new economic ideas from Keynesianism, through indicative planning, to monetarism, were tried in rapid succession. The two big political parties were challenged by new parties and social movements, while the social deference that had underpinned much of the old practice declined.

In Northern Ireland, a new generation of Catholics, products of the postwar welfare state and education system, challenged the Stormont regime, initially to demand the civil rights to which they were entitled as British citizens. This strategy of confronting the state with the inconsistencies in its own positions paralleled that of the civil rights movement in the United States, but was soon to give way to a more traditional nationalism aimed at overcoming the division of Ireland. As before, nationalism was divided into a constitutional/moderate wing represented by the Social Democratic and Labour Party (SDLP) and a physical force/extreme wing represented by Sinn Féin, political wing of the paramilitary Irish Republican Army (IRA). Faced with the prospect of civil war, the British government sent in troops, initially to protect the Catholics against a Protestant pogrom, and insisted on a program of reform. Yet, unwilling to take direct responsibility, it left the institutions of the Stormont regime, including most of its policing apparatus, intact. With the introduction of interment without trial and the Bloody Sunday massacre of 1972, this robbed the British of their credentials as honest brokers[10] and rapidly pitched them into conflict with the republican movement and a large part of the Catholic community. Stormont collapsed in 1972 as the Unionists were unwilling to push through reform and the British government imposed direct rule through a secretary of state for Northern Ireland. Like the secretaries for Ireland in the nineteenth century, but unlike the secretary of state for Scotland, this is never a locally elected politician, but a member of the government of the day sent over from London.

Policy has followed three tracks in a manner that is not always entirely consistent. The first is based on the need to combat violence from paramilitaries and has involved a return to exceptional measures that have further alienated much of the Catholic community. There have been suggestions of a shoot-to-kill policy and collusion with Protestant paramilitary organizations as well as widespread civil rights violations. The high point of the definition of the problem as one of law and order was the handling of the IRA hunger strikers by the Thatcher government, which gave Sinn Feín a massive boost within the Catholic community and provided a recruiting bonanza for the IRA (Taylor 1997). The second strand is the search for a consociational solution by bringing both communities in Northern Ireland together in a power-sharing arrangement. Two of these resulted in agreement. The Sunningdale Agreement of 1973 brought in moderate nationalists and unionists but not the republicans or loyalists; it was brought down by a strike of loyalist workers. The Good Friday Agreement of 1998 brought in all the parties except for the Paisley Unionists, but it has led a precarious life since. The third strand, since the mid-1980s, is to bring in the government of the Republic of Ireland in the search for an all-Ireland dimension that could satisfy some of the aspirations of the nationalist community. This strategy, seriously launched with the Anglo-Irish Agreement of 1985, also fed into the Good Friday Agreement.

The undermining of the union arrangement in Scotland was slower and less dramatic but very real. From the 1960s, the Scottish National Party scored some spectacular by-election victories and increased its general election vote to over 30 percent, with eleven MPs in October 1974. Thereafter its vote has fluctuated but in recent years has not fallen below 20 percent. In the 1990s it reestablished itself as the second party in Scotland. At the same time, a more diffuse nationalism has developed in Scotland and the Labour Party has returned to its old home rule traditions. Economic arguments for the Union have become less compelling as regional policy has been run down and dependency on the U.K. state has partly given way to dependence on the European Union (EU) and multinational capital. For a while in the 1970s, the nationalists made a lot of mileage out of the issue of "Scotland's oil,"[11] but this is less salient now. Scottish nationalism is historically not a product of periods of deprivation—when Scots veer to the parties of the left who can get resources from London—but of periods of relative prosperity like the years around the First World War, the 1970s, or the 1990s, when the arguments about dependency were less compelling. Polls in recent years show that the Scots are not convinced that the Union is working in their economic interest or that the benefits of prosperity are being evenly divided, and nationalists have played this into an image of productive Scots being deprived of the fruits of their labor.

Nationalists and home rulers have also taken advantage of the attack on the welfare state by the Conservative governments of the 1980s and 1990s. It is not that Scots are more attached to the welfare state than their co-citizens to the south. Evidence shows that they are slightly more in favor of redistribution but otherwise quite similar to the English on most issues; in any case, we know that support for the welfare state in England held up through the Thatcher years. Rather, Scottishness is used as a basis for mobilizing around defense of the welfare state, with nation perhaps replacing class as the rationale for social solidarity. This interpretation is supported by the finding that Scottish identity predicts support for redistribution better than the other way around (Brown et al. 1998). So, because of the institutional framing of political issues in Scotland, social welfare issues, as well as economic ones, are now seen through a territorial/national lens. The social bases of the Union have been weakened with the decline of the trade unions and their exclusion from policy consultation under the Conservatives. Business remains strongly antinationalist and has generally opposed home rule, but is less concerned with losing markets given the European commitment of all the parties.

The traditional upper classes were an important pillar of unionism in the Conservative Party, tied into all four nations of the United Kingdom,[12] but they have declined in social importance and have been marginalized within modern Conservatism, with its reliance on business and the middle classes. The role of the parties as brokers has also declined. Until the 1960s, the party balance in Scotland was not radically different from that in England and until the 1980s, Scotland had rarely been run by a party for which it had not voted. After 1979, Scottish secretaries of state governed with such a narrow parliamentary base that it became difficult to find enough MPs to staff the posts in the Scottish office. In 1997, the Conservatives lost all their remaining seats outside England. Europe has been a powerful influence in Scotland as in other stateless nations, positing an alternative external support system for Scottish autonomy. In the mid-1980s the Labour Party, the trade unions, and the Scottish National Party (SNP) were all converted to Europe. The SNP supports independence in Europe, with Scotland as a full member state, while Labour is closer to the Europe of the Regions model, but both have made a critical link between European integration and substate mobilization.

State responses to Scottish nationalism have been of three types. The most traditional is to extend administrative devolution. In the 1970s, a Scottish Development Agency was set up and the Scottish office received new powers in economic development. The Conservative governments of the 1980s and 1990s continued this trend, with transfers of responsibility for all regional aid and the universities. At the same time, the role of the secretary of state as territorial gatekeeper was reinforced with the introduction of formula-based funding that prevents the secretary of state from coming back to the treasury when pressures in Scotland are getting out of hand. Threats to cut

Scotland's relative funding levels never materialized. The rationale for administrative devolution is partly to offload the political management of the periphery but also seems to owe something to a naïvely technocratic belief that, given efficient government, Scots will forget about home rule. In practice, by strengthening the Scottish framework for politics and policy, it raises the salience of home rule and points to the democratic deficit in having a whole tier of administration run by ministers with no local mandate.

A second response has been to deny nationalism and stress other, universal forms of politics. This was the dominant position within the Labour Party after the 1920s, as it emphasized class solidarity. By the 1970s, it had difficulty explaining why class solidarity should extend as far as, but no farther than, the borders of the United Kingdom, a position that it has modified over time with an acceptance of both Europe and devolution, although it has never quite worked out the connection between the two. Under the Thatcher government, territorial politics was denied in the name of the universal values of neo-liberalism, markets, and deregulation. Thatcher herself put a particular spin on this by accusing Scots of being peculiarly dependent on the state and of having abandoned the values of Adam Smith and the eighteenth-century Enlightenment. Yet what Thatcher could only see as collectivist institutions oppressing the individual were otherwise regarded as vital elements in the civil society whose preservation was a central part of the Union settlement. Her combination of state centralization and deregulation was presented as an attack on the informal autonomy of Scottish society, and her efforts to hijack the Enlightenment and present it as a form of proto-Thatcherism caused particular resentment.

The third response to Scottish pressures is to concede home rule on Gladstonian lines, in which powers are devolved, but with parliamentary sovereignty retained and without federalism. Interestingly, the first party to accept this in the contemporary era was the Conservative Party under Edward Heath but the party's attempt to combine this with untrammeled parliamentary supremacy resulted in a contrived scheme for a Scottish assembly to share legislative power with Westminster. How this would work when the two were under different party control was never quite explained, and the Scottish Conservatives themselves abandoned the scheme after Heath came to power. In 1974 the Labour Party, which was seriously divided on the issue, opted for a legislative Scottish assembly but its bill was sabotaged by parliamentary opposition and the final one was saddled with a requirement for a referendum with a threshold of 40 percent of the entire electorate to approve it. The referendum came at the very end of the government's term in 1979 and, while it was approved, the vote fell well short of the 40 percent requirement. Labour nevertheless persisted with the policy. By the late 1980s it was committed to a bill setting up a legislative assembly during the first parliamentary session of a Labour government. Pressure was maintained, especially during the 1980s by the cross-party campaign for a Scottish parliament. After the 1987 election, Labour agreed to enter alongside the Liberal Democrats into the Scottish Constitutional Convention, a body rooted in Scottish civil society and which had the support of the trade unions, local government, social movements, and even a small section of the business community. This pressure ensured that Labour stuck to the policy even after Tony Blair succeeded the Scottish John Smith in the leadership. Blair's main contribution was to insist on another referendum, duly held and won by a large majority in 1997 (Taylor and Thomson 1999).

Nationalism and home rule sentiment in Wales have been inhibited by the divisions within the society, sometimes summed up as the "three Wales" (Balsom and Jones 1984). There is the Welsh-speaking heartland of the north, dominated since the 1970s by the Welsh nationalists of Plaid Cymru; the English-speaking but Welsh lands of the valleys and industrial areas, a Labour heartland; and English Wales to the east, an area of large-scale English immigration. A devolution bill for Wales was passed along with that of Scotland in 1978 but, largely due to these divisions, it was defeated by margin of four to one in the referendum of 1979. Since the 1980s, however, there has been a process of institution building in which a new Wales has emerged, focused on modernization and the needs of competition as a European region. The extension of administrative devolution through the Welsh office has reinforced this institutional framework, while the language is increasingly accepted as a badge of identity even by people who do not speak it, as evidenced by the decision to make the study of Welsh compulsory even in English-speaking schools in the principality. Conservative secretaries of state Peter Walker and David Hunt, both sent in from England, sought to build up the office and give the rather misleading impression that they were saving Wales from the excesses of Thatcherism. As in Scotland, a territorial lobby developed around the administrative institutions, framing economic and social demands in a territorial mode. Gradually, the idea of Welsh devolution was brought back into Labour Party thinking and by the 1990s Labour was proposing a Welsh assembly, which as in the 1970s version, would have administrative powers only. This was incorporated into the Labour manifesto and approved by referendum in 1997 by the narrowest of margins (Taylor and Thomson 1999).

The New Constitutional Settlement

Since 1997–98, the United Kingdom has had a radically new constitutional settlement based on political devolution to elected assemblies. The cases of the three minority nations are all different, and the rationale for devolution is a little different in each case. In Scotland, it is seen as a response to Scottish nationalist pressure articulated by the Scottish National Party, and to home rule sentiment within the Labour Party. It is also justified as part of a broader program of democratization and constitutional reform, and has gained a broad consensus among Scots. Welsh devolution is much more contentious, because of the divisions within Welsh society and the relative weakness of nationalism. It was brought in by the Labour Party on the coattails of Scottish devolution, and as part of the overall program of constitutional reform and decentralization, which includes an elected mayor for London and the possibility of regional assemblies in England. In both Scotland and Wales, the European issue was relevant, the argument being that they needed stronger autonomous institutions to compete in the new "Europe of the Regions." Northern Ireland was different again, since the governments had consistently been trying to devolve power on a consocational basis there since the fall of the Stormont regime, in an effort to deal with the communitarian conflict. Since these situations were so different and the reasons for devolution so distinct, the new arrangements present considerable contrasts. The novelty of this arrangement makes it difficult to assess it or to relate it to specific outcomes. The basic principles can, however, be explained (Keating 1998).

The Scotland Act of 1998 established a Scottish parliament and an executive headed by a first minister. The parliament has primary legislative powers over all matters not explicitly reserved to Westminster. Major reserved powers include defense and foreign affairs, taxation and monetary policy, company law and regulation of financial institutions, employment legislation, social security,[13] and a range of regulatory matters. The main areas thus devolved to Scotland include health; education and training; local government; social work; housing; economic development; transport; criminal law; civil law (except in reserved matters); judicial appointments; the environment; agriculture, forestry, and fishing; and sports and the arts.

As in the 1970s, the Labour government has insisted that sovereignty remains with Westminster, which will thus be able to legislate in nonreserved matters or override Scottish legislation. The list of reserved items is reasonably clear, largely following existing areas of Scottish law and administration, although there has been some criticism of the details.[14]

The financial powers of the Scottish parliament are not up to the measure of its legislative competence. The main source of funding is a block grant from Westminster. The Scottish parliament may raise or lower the basic rate of income tax by 3 percentage points. It also has full control of local taxation, which presently is limited to property taxes set by local governments for residential property and by the Scottish government for commercial property, but in practice there is little scope for changing this. If it is tempted to raise money for itself by squeezing transfers to local governments, there is provision for Westminster to claw back the block grant.

The Scottish parliament is elected by a mixed-member semiproportional system with regional party lists competing in the eight European constituencies in Scotland, providing fifty-six members to top up the seventy-three elected in the constituencies. This was a major concession by Labour to bring on board the Liberal Democrats and rebut accusations that the parliament would be dominated by the Labour machine of west-central Scotland. It was not intended to achieve ethnic balance, although the Labour Party did successfully aim for gender parity in its representation.

The Government of Wales Act provides for a national assembly for Wales with executive powers and some powers of secondary legislation, corresponding to existing ministerial powers. There is no definitive list of powers but rather a list of existing Welsh office powers that can be transferred over time to the assembly. It has no powers of taxation but depends entirely on block grants. Although there is an executive with ministers known as secretaries, they have to work within a committee system some-what akin to that of local government. In practice, Wales has moved toward a parlia-mentary system, with an ever clearer distinction between the assembly and what is known as the Welsh assembly government. The electoral system is the same as in Scotland. The executive responsibilities of the secretary of state for Wales transferred to the assembly include economic development; agriculture, forestry, fisheries, and food; industry and training; education; local government; health and personal social serv-ices; housing; environment; planning; transport and roads; arts, culture, the Welsh lan-guage; the built heritage; sport and recreation.

The Northern Ireland Act of 1998 is a great deal more complex, corresponding to the complexity of the problem. The Northern Ireland settlement, as embodied in the Good Friday Agreement, seeks to accommodate radically opposed positions in order to bring all parties into the constitution and stop political violence. It encompasses three di-mensions: the intracommunity dimension within Northern Ireland, the relationship between Northern Ireland and the Republic of Ireland (the north-south dimension), and the relationship between Ireland and the United Kingdom (the east-west dimen-sion). The first dimension is addressed through a consociational arrangement. There is a Northern Ireland assembly with legislative powers, elected by proportional represen-tation but using the single transferable vote, rather than the semiproportional mecha-nisms used in Scotland and Wales. Members are invited to designate themselves as nationalist or unionist and certain matters require qualified or concurrent majorities. There is to be an executive headed by a first minister and deputy first minister, and in which all parties represented in the assembly are entitled to have ministers. The aspira-tions of nationalists are addressed through a provision that, should a majority of the electorate wish at some time in the future to join a united Ireland, then the secretary of state must lay an order to give effect to it. The role of the Republic in the meantime is recognized, and a whole range of institutions are put in place to allow the people of Ireland to express multiple loyalties and forms of identity and to secure the north-south and east-west dimensions. There is a North-South Ministerial Council to link Northern Ireland and the Republic, an Intergovernmental Conference linking the British and Irish Republic governments, and a British-Irish Council (sometimes referred to as the Council of the Isles) bringing together the British and Irish governments, the Northern Ireland assembly, the Scottish parliament, the national assembly for Wales, and even the Channel Islands and the Isle of Man.

Competences are divided into excepted matters, which remain with the U.K. Parliament; reserved matters, which may be devolved to the assembly provided it asks for them by concurrent majority; and transferred matters, which cover everything else. The excepted matters are similar to those reserved in the Scotland act, but there are differences in substance and tone, reflecting the political preoccupations and concerns that the United Kingdom has over the two cases. In Northern Ireland, the list of reserved powers covers most matters dealing with security and policing, a highly sensitive area in which competences will be transferred only when the assembly has demonstrated its ability to use them without discrimination. There are lengthy sections on equal rights and nondiscrimination provisions. On the other hand, it is silent on many "common market" and "common standards" matters. It is notable that there is no commitment to maintaining a single currency as in Scotland, so that Northern Ireland could probably move into the European single currency without the rest of the United Kingdom (O'Leary 1999). The conclusion is that in the case of Scotland, maintaining the economic and social union is paramount, while the British government's main concerns in Northern Ireland are related to security. The list may also reflect the fact that the former Stormont parliament (1922–72), established before the interventionist welfare state, was not barred from a wide range of economic and social fields and developed parallel provisions; Scotland on the other hand has always had its own criminal law.[15]

An innovation in U.K. politics is the introduction of judicial review for the legislation of the Scottish parliament and Northern Ireland assembly. This is open to challenge on *ultra vires* grounds and cases are ultimately decided by the Judicial Committee of the Privy Council. Laws of the devolved assemblies can also be overturned where they violate the European Convention on Human Rights. While the Labour government has also incorporated the convention into the law of England and Wales, it was not prepared to allow the courts to overturn Westminster laws, citing the doctrine of parliamentary sovereignty. As Westminster remains the legislature for England and Wales, this means an identical law would be subject to judicial review in Scotland and Northern Ireland but not in England or Wales.

Other intergovernmental matters are to be managed by concordats negotiated between the center and the devolved governments. Given the lack of entrenchment of the powers of the assemblies, these have tended to reflect continuing Westminster supremacy. Indeed, they look more like the arrangements previously in place to regulate territorial politics within U.K. government than agreements between autonomous administrations.

Explaining (and Predicting) the Outcomes

It is difficult to assess the effect of the new constitutional changes in the United Kingdom, since they are so recent and, in some cases, have yet to come into effect. It is possible, however, to make some judgments about the effects of institutions on territorial politics under the previous dispensation. The British union state was neither unitary nor federal but preserved the distinctive institutions of its various components under the rule of a single Parliament. This ensured that territorial politics would continue, but provided a complex and, in many ways, informal set of mechanisms to manage it. Institutional mechanisms included the territorial secretaries of state with their dual role of representing the center in the periphery and the periphery in the center; Members of Parliament; and functional interest groups that were able to combine sectoral and territorial claims. Administrative devolution for Scotland and later Wales helped forge territorial lobbies and to present economic and social issues in a territorial framework; this could not happen in Northern Ireland because of the fundamental division between the two communities on the existence of the province itself and the political polarization caused by sectarian practices. Differentiated policies could, within limits, address the substantive grievances of the various territories. Underlying the system was the same set of understandings that underpinned the unwritten constitution as a whole, notably the understanding that parliamentary sovereignty be accompanied by limitations on the scope of government and respect for the institutions of civil society. The system also depended on a reasonable degree of consensus and the expectation that the political majorities in the various territories should more or less coincide most of the time. When Scotland elected one majority and the United Kingdom as a whole elected a government of a different complexion, as in 1922 or between 1979 and 1997, there were demands for devolution. Success in territorial management was a function both of the tractability of the issues with which it had to deal, and of the efficacy of the institutions set up to deal with them.

The regime saw its most conspicuous failure in Ireland in the nineteenth century. The problem, based in a religious/ethnic cleavage as well as social and economic discontents, was difficult and institutional management was hampered by the lack of territorial collaborators. Instead, Ireland was governed in a quasi-colonial mode. The refusal of the British political establishment to accept moderate reform of the Union in the Gladstonian program put Ireland on the road to outright secession.

Management succeeded for many years in Scotland, where the main grievances were social and economic. There were territorial intermediaries rooted in the local society and the U.K. parties were able to combine distinctively Scottish appeals with a role at the center. The labor movement and the welfare state served as further integrating factors. These conditions also existed in Wales, although institutional distinctiveness was less marked. In Scotland, however, the U.K. state was slow to respond to changing conditions from the 1970s. Throughout the 1980s and most of the 1990s, Conservative governments, in a repeat of their attitude to nineteenth-century Ireland, insisted that the issue was not constitutional but had to do with getting the policies right. As in Ireland this provoked a countermovement in civil society, a questioning of the legitimacy of the state itself, and a decline in British identity. Stormont represents another failure of territorial management. Given the circumstances of its foundation, it is unlikely that the Stormont regime would ever have gained the allegiance of the Catholic population. In practice it made no attempt to do so, so entrenching national divisions within the society. British strategy was to ignore this as long as the problem did not intrude into Westminster politics and order was maintained, and then to seek to reform the regime rather than abolishing it outright.

Evidence on national identities in the United Kingdom supports this differentiated picture. In Scotland, where identity has long been sustained by indigenous institutions, in fields like education, law, and local government, the strongest identity is the Scottish one, although there is also a strong attachment to the United Kingdom as a whole (Table 5.1). This dual identity is captured by a regular question about strength of identities on a spectrum from purely Scottish to purely British. When the same question is asked in Wales, the middle point of equal territorial and British identities scores exactly

Table 5.1 National Identity, Scotland and Wales, 1997

	Scotland (in percent)	Wales (in percent)
Scottish/Welsh, not British	23.1	13.1
More Scottish/Welsh than British	38.7	29.1
Equally Scottish/Welsh and British	25.8	25.8
More British than Scottish/Welsh	4.0	10.4
British, not Scottish/Welsh	3.5	15.3
Other	2.4	4.3
No response	2.1	0.2

Source: Scottish Election Survey.

the same as in Scotland, but the rest of the distribution is skewed more heavily toward a British identity. This reflects the fact that English people make up around a fifth of the population in Wales but less than 5 percent of those in Scotland, but also the fact that Welsh identity is often associated with the language and is thus less assimilative than its Scottish counterpart. Asking the same question in Northern Ireland would be of little use, given the polarization of identities between the two communities.

Table 5.2 gives the responses to a question that aims to tap the existence of exclusive or shared identities in a different way. The categories *British* and *Ulster* have been shown to overlap almost completely, reflecting the strong unionist position. The category of *Irish* taps a nationalist identity. The intermediate category here captures those voters whose identity is more fluid and is the nearest we have to the dual identity questions in the Scottish and Welsh surveys. The polarization of the communities between the British/Ulster and Irish identities is striking. The main exception is the 28 percent of Catholics with a fluid identity. These tend to be Catholics repelled by Republican violence and already there is evidence that since the launching of the peace process, they have been moving in a more nationalist direction (NILT 2000). This seems to be reversing a long tradition in which Catholics were less likely to feel strongly nationalist than were Protestants to feel strongly unionist (Evans and Duffy 1997). If the devolved assembly works, it may be easier to adopt a dual Northern Ireland and all-Ireland identity and Irish identity may become somewhat less politicized.

The new constitutional arrangements represent continuity in that they are an ad hoc and differentiated response to distinct problems in the nations of the United Kingdom. Government has insisted that the essence of the constitution, the sovereignty of the Westminster Parliament, is unaffected. On the other hand, power has been transferred to elected institutions in a way that previous governments resisted and the Gladstonian solution, which divided the country so deeply in the past, has at last been carried through. Secession is now a real issue in Scotland as well as in Northern Ireland, and the government has recognized, in law in Northern Ireland and in fact in Scotland, that there is no barrier to this should the people want it. In this situation, parliamen-

Table 5.2 National Identity, Northern Ireland, 1992

	Protestant (in percent)	Catholic (in percent)
British/Ulster	82	10
Northern Irish/Sometimes British	15	28
Irish	3	62

Source: Richard Breen, "Who Wants a United Ireland? Constitutional Preferences among Catholics and Protestants," *Social Attitudes in Northern Ireland*, 5th Report, Appletree, 1996.

tary sovereignty, already undermined by European integration, loses even more of its meaning. The question therefore is whether the new dispensation will serve to preserve the Union or facilitate its dissolution.

One can only speculate about the effects of the new institutional arrangements. Clearly the Labour government hopes that they will bring a new stability as the diverse aspirations of the nations are met within a restructured United Kingdom. This is indeed a likely outcome, although it comes in two versions. In one, there is an acceptance of diffused power and a form of de facto federalism, in which the devolved assemblies pursue their own policies, while the minority nations continue to be represented in U.K. politics. The other version holds that devolution will work because it no longer makes much difference whether the nations have devolved assemblies and governments. The pressures of globalization, market competition, and European regulation, together with the end of the old ideological cleavages, have, in this view, emptied politics of its meaning, while power has retreated into new and ill-understood networks. A real cynic might claim that devolution has happened now precisely because it cannot make much difference.

Critics of the whole process claim that devolution is a slippery slope, which will lead inexorably to the breakup of the United Kingdom. Some people have always argued this on rather general grounds, ignoring the experience of successful federations around the world (Dalyell 1977). Others argue that devolution and federalism cannot work in multinational states because the devolved parliaments will always arrogate sovereignty to themselves, an argument that, as we have noted, goes back to the nineteenth century. Some argue that frustration with the lack of powers of the new assemblies, notably in economic and financial matters, will lead to them pressing for ever more powers, to the point of separatism. The slippery slope argument is given more credence by the pattern of politics in the devolved assemblies. As a result of the elections of 1998–2003, the main line of cleavage in all three is between nationalists and unionists. This is formalized in Northern Ireland, where a noncompetitive political system has been instituted. In Scotland and Wales, the system is competitive, the Labour Party straddles the political center, the Conservatives are impotent, and the only alternative government is the nationalists. There is some evidence in Wales that the nationalists are responding to their role by moderating their policy, perhaps to the extent of transforming themselves into a party of territorial defense combined with moderate social democracy. In Scotland, there are some voices within the SNP who see this as their future, adopting a postsovereignty strategy similar to that of the Catalan nationalists.

Public opinion on the new institutions will take time to evolve but at the time of writing there are some interesting data (Keating 2001). Polls have shown that the very high expectations that the Scottish parliament has more influence over their lives than

Westminster fell in the early phase of the devolved institutions. Since all the political parties now support Scottish devolution, the cleavage is between nationalists and home rulers. Polls between 1998 and 2000 regularly showed that, in a referendum on independence, around 50 percent of Scotland would vote Yes. Yet polls taken on the old questions, posing a range of options from independence to centralization, showed home rule within the United Kingdom to be the most popular option, with independence support falling to around 20 percent. These findings are seemingly in stark contradiction. A more detailed examination, however, shows that Scottish voters, like those in Quebec, give their own meaning to independence and do not necessarily associate it with traditional statehood. In particular they associate it with membership in the EU. Scottish political elites are strongly pro-European, in contrast to those in England. Scottish voters are less enthusiastic and only slightly less anti-European than the English. They do differ, however, in their expectations, being much more likely to think that Europe will evolve and that the United Kingdom will enter the single currency. In these circumstances, they seem to have a rather open mind on the future of Scottish statehood.

There are some signs of a similar evolution in Northern Ireland, although it must be emphasized that as this book went to press Northern Ireland had still not had any sustained experience of consociational, power-sharing government. Support for Irish unity, according to recent polls, has actually fallen while expectations that it will come about have increased (NILT 2000). As in Scotland, electors are less inclined to see the issue as one of stark alternatives and there is a surprisingly large middle ground. Of those against Irish unity, only 19 percent felt that a united Ireland would be impossible to live with. This included 29 percent of the Protestant unionists but only one percent of Catholic antiunity electors. Conversely, 68 percent of those wanting either to unify with the Republic or declare an independent state could happily accept a majority decision never to unify with the Republic and only 2 percent would find this impossible to live with. These results may be difficult to interpret, but they do suggest that belief in the absolutes of British and Irish sovereignty is rather weak, especially on the Catholic side. This is consistent with longer-term evidence suggesting that discrimination and political exclusion have encouraged support for the absolutes of nationalism and unionism, while given alternatives, many people will take them. The new institutions, which deliberately blur the question of sovereignty and encourage people to express multiple identities, may reinforce this trend, if they survive in the long term. To date they have proved more popular on the Catholic and nationalist side, despite not promising Irish unity. Yet they do provide a generalized system for minority protection, which could be used by Protestants within a future united Ireland and it seems that some proagreement Unionists are looking toward such a future.

NOTES

1. Many of us have grown weary of correcting the North American and European habit of referring to the whole as England. The United Kingdom refers to England, Scotland, Wales, and Northern Ireland. Great Britain (so-called to distinguish it from little Britain, or Brittany) does not include Northern Ireland. The Channel Islands and the Isle of Man do not form part of the United Kingdom but have a link to the British (sic) Crown.

2. Catholics were given the vote in the late eighteenth century but could not sit in the Parliament.

3. The Jacobites, supporters of the Stuart dynasty unseated in 1688–90, sought to restore their claimant to the thrones of all three kingdoms (England, Scotland, and Ireland). The legend of Bonny Prince Charlie as a Scottish national hero is a product of nineteenth-century romanticism. The Jacobites did support a repeal of the Union, but the Catholicism of the Stuarts alienated them from most Scots, including most antiunionists.

4. An important symbol for some Scottish nationalists is provided by the Covenanters, extreme Protestants (and opponents of the Stuarts) in the seventeenth century.

5. The Conservatives held a permanent majority in the House of Lords until the abolition of most of the hereditary peers' vote in 1999.

6. The main powers not devolved were in defense and foreign affairs and the currency. In practice, as I explain, Stormont did not choose to exercise all its autonomous powers.

7. This was not so much to keep out the Catholics and nationalists, who were in a permanent minority, but to fend off the threat of class-based parties within the Protestant community.

8. Incomes and welfare services were consistently higher in Northern Ireland, the former because it was more industrialized than the Republic, the latter because of the British subsidy. Since the 1990s, living standards in the Republic have overtaken those in the north.

9. This is a contentious and highly politicized issue. From the late nineteenth century, most Scottish expenditure levels were determined as a proportion of English levels under the Goschen formula. This gradually died out and was replaced after the Second World War by a system under which the Scottish office bargained with the treasury function by function for changes at the margin. As Scotland's population was falling relative to England's, the continuing effect of the Goschen formula on the base allowed per capita increases while, at the margin, further increases could be negotiated. Scotland did rather better at times when it was politically marginal and the secretary of state was well placed in the cabinet. By the 1970s, the advantage was around 20 percent per capita over England and Wales (Heald 1994; Heald et al. 1998). From the late 1970s, a new formula was introduced, the Barnett formula, under which marginal changes in Scottish expenditure are a population-based proportion of the corresponding English change. This was intended to produce a gradual convergence of expenditure levels, although the "Barnett squeeze" was repeatedly postponed until the late 1990s.

10. British troops were initially welcomed by Catholics and there was strong support in the Catholic community for direct rule as an alternative to Stormont. The governing Labour Party, particularly Prime Minister Harold Wilson, was traditionally sympathetic to the Catholics. This, as I have emphasized, does not mean that there was a positive preference for British rule among Catholics, merely that the British were not doomed by primordial sentiment to be seen as the enemy.

11. They appealed to naked self-interest with the slogan "Rich Scots or Poor Britons?"

12. They were arguably the only truly United Kingdom-wide social class, owning estates in all parts of the Union and sharing a common culture and educational experience.

13. In the United Kingdom, this includes welfare, unemployment benefits, family support, and pensions.

14. Matters reserved for the Crown include the Union of the Kingdoms of Scotland and England, the Parliament of the United Kingdom, and international relations (with the exception of implementing EU matters); defense; national security; antiterrorism; fiscal policy; currency; immigration; extradition; enforcing laws on drugs and firearms; nonlocal elections; regulating companies, business associations, monopolies, mergers, financial institutions and services; intellectual property; industrial relations; equal opportunities; workplace health and safety; consumer and data protection; postal and telegraph services; most energy matters; transportation and transportation safety; social security; regulating certain professions; research councils; nuclear safety, broadcasting; reproductive medicine and abortion; control and safety of medicines.

Functions devolved to the Scottish parliament include health; education; local government; social work; housing; planning; economic development; the administration of the European Structural Funds; most civil and criminal law; the criminal justice and prosecution system; police and prisons; agriculture, fisheries and forestry; sport and the arts.

15. Extraterrestrial readers may take comfort from the fact that both the Scottish parliament and the Northern Ireland assembly are explicitly excluded from intervening in outer space. The functions given to the Northern Ireland assembly include health; education; social work, housing; planning; economic development; the administration of the European Structural Funds; the environment; agriculture, fisheries and forestry; sport and the arts.

Reserved matters include navigation; aviation; natural resources; domiciles; postal services; requirements for assembly membership; criminal law; extradition to the Republic of Ireland; public order; police; firearms and explosives; civil defense; the Emergency Powers Act (Northern Ireland) of 1926 or any similar enactment; court procedure; foreign trade; regulation of monopolies, mergers, banking, and the investment and securities businesses; intellectual property; consumer safety; some environmental matters; data protection; telecommunications; reproductive medicine; nuclear installations; research councils.

Exempted matters include international relations (with the exception of all-Irish institutions and EU matters); defense; national security; antiterrorism; immigration; taxes under U.K. law; social security; the appointment of judges; elections; currency; the National Savings Bank; any matter for which provision is made by this act or the Northern Ireland Constitution Act of 1973.

REFERENCES

Balsom, Denis, and Barry Jones. 1984. *The Faces of Wales. In The Nationwide Competition for Votes: The 1983 British General Election,* ed. Ian McAllister and Richard Rose. London: Pinter.

Bew, Paul, Peter Gibbon, and Henry Patterson. 1996. *Northern Ireland 1921-1996: Political Forces and Social Classes.* London: Serif.

Blondel, Jean. 1974. *Voters, Parties and Leaders.* Harmondsworth: Penguin.

Breen, Richard. 1996. Who Wants a United Ireland? Constitutional Preferences among Catholics and Protestants. *Social Attitudes in Northern Ireland, 5th Report.* Appletree.

Brown, Alice, David McCrone, Linsday Paterson, and Paula Surridge. 1998. *The Scottish Electorate: The 1997 General Election and Beyond.* London: Macmillan.

Dalyell, Tam. 1977. *Devolution: The End of Britain?* London: Jonathan Cape.

Dicey, A. V. 1886 [1973]. *England's Claim against Irish Home Rule.* Richmond: Richmond Publishing.

————. 1912. *A Leap in the Dark: A Criticism of The Principles of Home Rule as Illustrated by the Bill of 1893.* 3d ed. London: John Murray.

Evans, Geoffrey, and Mary Duffy. 1997. Beyond the Sectarian Divide: The Social Bases and Political Consequences of Nationalist and Unionist Party Competition in Northern Ireland. *British Journal of Political Science* 27:47–81.

Evans, Geoffrey, and Brendan O'Leary. 1997. Frameworked Futures: Intransigence and Flexibility in the Northern Ireland Elections of May 30 1996. *Irish Political Studies* 12:23–47.

Finer, Samuel. 1970. *Comparative Government.* Harmondsworth: Penguin.

Finlay, Richard. 1997. *A Partnership for Good? Scottish Politics and the Union since 1880.* Edinburgh: John Donald.

Harvie, Christopher. 1994. *Scotland and Nationalism: Scottish Society and Politics, 1707-1994.* London: Routledge.

Heald, David. 1994. Territorial Public Expenditure in the United Kingdom. *Public Administration* 72:147–75.

Heald, David, Neal Geaughan, and Colin Robb. 1998. Financial Arrangements for UK Devolution. In *Remaking the Union: Devolution and UK Politics in the 1990s,* ed. Howard Elcock and Michael Keating. London: Frank Cass.

Jellinek, Georg. 1981. *Fragmentos de Estado,* trans. Michael Forster, Miguel Herrero de Miñon, and José Carlos Esteban. Madrid: Civitas.

Jones, Barry, and Michael Keating. 1985. *Labour and the British State.* Oxford: Oxford University Press.

Keating, Michael. 1975. *The Role of the Scottish MP.* Ph.D. thesis, Glasgow College of Technology.

————. 1998. Reforging the Union: Devolution and Constitutional Change in the United Kingdom. *Publius : The Journal of Federalism* 28, no. 1:217–34.

————. 2001. *Plurinational Democracy: Stateless Nations in a Post-Sovereignty Era.* Oxford: Oxford University Press.

Keating, Michael, and David Bleiman. 1979. *Labour and Scottish Nationalism.* London: Macmillan.

Keating, Michael, and Arthur Midwinter. 1984. *The Government of Scotland.* Edinburgh: Mainstream.

Kellas, James. 1984. *The Scottish Political System.* 3d ed. Cambridge: Cambridge University Press.

Kendle, John. 1997. *Federal Britain: A History.* London: Routledge.

McLean, Iain. 1995. Are Scotland and Wales Over-Represented? *Political Quarterly* 66, no. 4:250–68.

Midwinter, Arthur, Michael Keating, and James Mitchell. 1991. *Politics and Public Policy in Scotland.* London: Macmillan.

Mitchell, James. 1996. *Strategies for Self Government: The Campaigns for a Scottish Parliament.* Edinburgh: Polygon.

Morgan, Kenneth. 1980. *Rebirth of a Nation: Wales, 1880-1980.* Oxford: Oxford University Press.

Moxon-Browne, Edward. 1983. *Nation, Class and Creed in Northern Ireland.* Aldershot: Gower.

NILT. 2000. Northern Ireland Life and Times Survey, Queen's University of Belfast.

O'Leary, Brendan. 1999. The 1998 British-Irish Agreement: Power-Sharing Plus. *Scottish Affairs* 26 (winter):14–35.

O'Leary, Brendan, and John McGarry. 1993. *The Politics of Antagonism.* London: Athlone.

Paterson, Lindsay. 1994. *The Autonomy of Modern Scotland.* Edinburgh: Edinburgh University Press.

Rokkan, Stein, and Derek Urwin. 1983. *Economy, Territory, Identity: Politics of West European Peripheries.* London: Sage.

Rose, Richard. 1971. *Governing Without Consensus: An Irish Perspective.* London: Faber and Faber.

Rossiter, David, Ron Johnston, and Charles Pattie. 1997. The Evolution and Partisan Impact of Scottish and Welsh Over-Representation in the Redrawing of British Parliamentary Constituencies. *Regional and Federal Studies* 7, no. 3:49–65.

Ruane, Joseph, and Jennifer Todd. 1996. *The Dynamics of Conflict in Northern Ireland.* Cambridge: Cambridge University Press.

Snicker, Jonathan. 1997. Strategies of Autonomist Actors in Wales. In *Remaking the Union: Devolution and UK Politics in the 1990s,* ed. Howard Elcock and Michael Keating. London: Frank Cass.

Taylor, Bridget, and Katarina Thomson. 1999. *Scotland and Wales: Nations Again?* Cardiff: University of Wales Press.

Taylor, Peter. 1997. *Provos: The IRA and Sinn Féin.* London: Bloomsbury.

Wilson, C. 1970. Note of Dissent. *Scotland's Government: Report of the Scottish Constitutional Committee.* Edinburgh: Scottish Constitutional Committee.

CHAPTER SIX

Italy

Political Institutions and the Mobilization of Territorial Differences

Ugo M. Amoretti

The political mobilization of the territorial cleavage between north and south has perhaps been the central question of Italian politics throughout the past decade. Although Italy went through a deep transformation during the 1990s (Bull and Rhodes 1997) that generated intense public debate over many issues, no matter has been discussed as widely and energetically as the north-south divide. The roots of this cleavage are deeper than those of the Italian unitary state (Putnam 1993). Yet, after unification in 1861–70, the political relevance of the north-south fracture gradually declined, and territorial questions remained marginal until the late 1980s, when Umberto Bossi's Northern League (LN) appeared on the political scene and succeeded in translating the differences between the two parts of the country into a political resource and, ultimately, into consensus and votes.

This chapter examines the evolution of territorial politics in Italy and its interaction with political institutions. While it provides a survey of the period preceding World War II, its main focus is on the time following the establishment of the Italian Republic in 1946. Italy's territorial differences remained politically quiescent for decades, yet the record of republican institutions seems bifurcated: highly effective until the mid-1980s and definitely problematic since. By examining the interplay between territorial politics and political institutions, this chapter seeks to shed light on how the latter have influenced the evolution of one of the most important issues of Italy's turbulent 1990s, and to answer the more general research questions of this book project.

The chapter begins by delineating the historical profile of territorial fragmentation in Italy, and then surveys the Italian institutional setting, highlighting its principal characteristics with regard to the accommodation of territorial conflicts. The chapter then analyzes how institutions have affected the mobilization of territorial differences, and closes by discussing the results and the implications of the analysis.

Territorial Fragmentation in Italian History

The term *Italy* was introduced by the ancient Greeks and meant only the very southern part of the Italian peninsula, roughly corresponding to the lower half of today's Calabria. The Romans extended it to include all the territory south of the Alps. However, from the fall of the Roman Empire in the fifth century C.E. until unification in the second half of the nineteenth century, Italy was little more than a geographical expression.

During the centuries between Rome's last emperor and Italy's first king, the polities that formed on the peninsula out of the ruins of the Roman Empire developed in a largely independent way. Some, like the Republics of Venice and Genoa, grew fully autonomous and actually played a major role on the international scene (Tilly 1990). Others did not manage to became more than protectorates of foreign powers. This diverse array of historical experiences—including the free communes in central and northern Italy and the Norman Kingdom in the south—sowed the seeds of a territorial differentiation that political unification could not fully sweep away (Putnam 1993, 121–62).

One reason why political unification could not wholly overcome the existing territorial differences was its top-down character. Taking advantage of the favorable international scenario following the Crimean War, unification was undertaken by the Piedmontese elites—with the support of the upper strata of the then Italian population, but not that of the masses.[1] As Lucy Riall (1994, 70) puts it: "United Italy was the creation of kings, not of people."

Even after political unification, Italy remained far from united. Regional and local identities, rooted in the fragmented political and social past of the peninsula, persisted (Lyttleton 1996, 33). The more developed north was much stronger economically (Clough 1964, 163–64); and only 2.5 to 10 percent of the population could speak Italian (Lepschy, Lepschy, and Voghera 1996). In short, as former Sardinia-Piedmont's prime minister Massimo D'Azeglio once stated, political unification had made "Italy but not Italians."[2]

After 140 years as a constitutionally unitary state, contemporary Italy is still territorially diversified in many respects. Despite a series of nation-building policies designed to overcome regionalism with a supreme sense of shared "Italianness," the Italians never developed a sense of national identity strong enough to stand comparison with what one finds in countries such as France (Connor 1991). Except for the displays of patriotism evident during the major soccer tournaments such as the World Cup, Italy remains an entity toward which most Italians show little obvious attachment.

Although Italy's regional differentiation is highly complex (Bagnasco and Oberti 1998), the economic divide between the developed north and the less fully modernized south—a major feature of Italy's economic history (Clough 1964, 8)—remains remarkable.[3] While the central and northern regions all have a per capita income above the European average (with the exception of Umbria, where the per capita income is 98 percent of the European average), the southern regions continue to lag behind (Eurostat 2001). In addition, while the northern regions are home to about 44 percent of Italy's population of 57 million, they produce 55 percent of the national income, as compared to 21 percent from the central regions (with 19 percent of the population) and 24 percent from the southern regions (with 36 percent of the population) (ISTAT 2000, 182, 199).[4]

Finally, though the rise of literacy and the spread of television over the past half century have somewhat homogenized the country, they have not extinguished cultural localism. Today, nearly everyone can speak standard Italian, but local languages or dialects remain popular. As recently as the 1990s, slightly less than a fifth of the population used Italian exclusively, and more than three-fifths switched between Italian and a local language according to the social setting. Moreover, 36 percent said that they never used standard Italian at home as compared to 34 percent who spoke only Italian and a remaining 30 percent who switched between standard Italian and a dialect in the family circle (Lepschy, Lepschy, and Voghera 1996, 75).

The Institutional Setting of the Republic

The constituent assembly elected in 1946, which drafted the 1948 constitution, was split along the ideological line that was polarizing Italy, with the Christian Democrats (DC) and its small centrist allies facing off against the pro-Soviet left—which at this time included not only the Italian Communist Party (PCI) but also the Italian Socialist Party (PSI). While the former were a majority both in the assembly and in the country, the latter constituted a sizable 40 percent minority.[5] The political uncertainty resulting from this balance suggested a compromise constitution that spread power as much as possible and served each camp as a kind of political insurance policy. These circumstances explain why the constitution featured such a broad array of antimajoritarian decision-making mechanisms. However, because in the aftermath of World War II territorial devolution was not seen as a key concern, these mechanisms were meant to prevent one branch of the central government (and by extension the party or parties in charge of it) from wielding too much power over the others. They had little to do with restraining the authority that the central government could exert over lower levels of government such as regions, provinces, and municipalities. At least until the 1993 electoral reform, the Italian Republic may be regarded as a case of antimajoritarian, but centralized, democracy.[6]

Horizontal Antimajoritarian Decision-making Mechanisms

The most important horizontal antimajoritarian mechanisms set up in 1948 were the privileged position of the legislature in relation to the executive and the adoption, albeit by ordinary law rather than the constitution, of proportional representation (PR).[7] Together, these mechanisms restrained majority rule by encouraging executive power sharing, a multiparty system, and balanced executive-legislative relations—with a tilt in favor of parliament (Morlino 1998, 259–60).

The favorable position of the parliament vis-à-vis the executive, witnessed by the fifty-four cabinets that Italy has had since 1948, rested on several factors, in particular the absence of any provisions allowing the government to lead the assembly in daily politics. The constitution, for instance, gave no special status to cabinet-sponsored bills, which could be easily amended by the parliament. This was especially true until the 1980s, when the use of secret ballots allowed party defectors to alter legislation originating from the cabinet.

A second element that weakened the cabinet was its internal structure. By giving the prime minister the status of a mere *primus inter pares,* in charge of coordinating the many parties and factions represented within the executive, the constitution allowed the latter to become the cabinet's real sources of power and loyalty, undermining the cohesion of the executive. In addition, under the PR voting system that existed until 1993, the prime minister's authority over the ministers was further restricted by his or her limited legitimacy, due to the absence of any relationship with the electorate (Hine and Finocchi 1991). People could vote for any given party, but could not foresee who would be the head of the executive formed after the general elections.

By allowing any party with some electoral support to gain parliamentary representation, the system of PR adopted in 1948 led to the fractionalization of the party system. From a low 2.9 in 1948, when the tension between the DC and the left was high, the effective number of parties (Laakso and Taagpera 1979) grew to about 4 during the 1960s, and reached a high of 6.6 in 1992, the last general elections held with PR.[8]

This fractionalization induced by PR was antimajoritarian because it prevented the formation of single-party governments, forcing the DC to share the executive power with their small centrist allies. From 1976 to 1979, to combat the problem of terrorism, the parliamentary majority was broadened to include even the PCI, giving the government the support of the whole legislature with the exception of the far right.

In addition, the structure of the Italian parliament, whose houses were organized in a number of powerful standing committees that could pass into law or veto a wide range of legislation, further encouraged consensual policy making.[9] Because these committees worked in relative obscurity (Furlong 1990, 63), government-opposition relations were much less adversarial than they might appear at first glance, allowing a great deal of logrolling—that often ended in particularistic laws (*leggine*) passed by coalitions that crossed the majority-opposition line (Di Palma 1976, 1977; D'Onofrio 1979; Furlong 1990; Giuliani 1997).[10] Thus, although electoral competition was inspired by the logic of polarized pluralism (Sartori 1976), the actual organization of the legislative assembly encouraged an extensive collaboration between parliamentary majorities and minorities that resulted in continued power sharing.

Besides these antimajoritarian mechanisms, the constitution provided additional tools to further restrain majority rule: bicameralism and judicial review. By endowing both houses with equal powers, including legislative veto privileges and political control over the executive, bicameralism resulted in a supplementary veto point (Tsebelis 1995) that made it very difficult for the government to pass legislation.[11] Judicial review also worked as a constraint on majoritarian policy making, particularly after 1956 when the constitutional court was set up, preventing legislation not compliant with constitutional provisions.

The picture changed in 1993, when the electoral reform turned PR into a mixed, but largely majoritarian, system (D'Alimonte and Chiaramonte 1995; Bartolini and D'Alimonte 1996, 105–8; Katz 1996). Though this new system has not been effective in reducing the number of parties, which grew past seven in 1996, the introduction of plurality rules for the election of three-quarters of the deputies has encouraged the formation of preelectoral alliances and the bipolarization of the party system. Parties (with the possible exception of the LN) now enter into elections in preelectoral coalitions and, given the possibility of winning an absolute majority of parliamentary seats, disclose their candidate for premier to the electorate.

This has been a remarkable majoritarian turn in Italian politics. The possibility that a clear parliamentary majority might emerge after a general election is now much greater. Meanwhile, the new link between the premier and the electorate has increased the premier's legitimacy and authority, contributing to strengthen the executive vis-à-vis the parliament. Moreover, because the electoral reform was passed through a popular referendum, in a context of corruption scandals and antipolitical feeling for which consociational practices—not without reason—have been blamed,[12] this change has been commonly understood as a majoritarian twist to the consensual philosophy underpinning the constitution. However, though some consensual practices, such as the allocation of one of the parliamentary speakers' posts to the opposition, have been terminated, no comprehensive constitutional revision has been enacted. Thus, although the system is no longer consensual it has not yet become coherently majoritarian.

Vertical Antimajoritarian Decision-making Mechanisms

In 1948, Italy's territorial differentiation was recognized for the first time since unification. Under the pressure coming from several areas, including Sardinia (Petrosino 1992), and, above all, Sicily (Finkelstein 1998), the new constitution allowed for the creation of regional governments, granting a privileged autonomy and the status of "special regions" to the areas where the quest for self-rule was most active—namely, Sicily, Sardinia, Valle d'Aosta, Trentino-Alto Adige, and Friuli-Venezia Giulia.

Yet, the vertical antimajoritarian mechanisms included in the constitution were by no means comparable to the horizontal ones. They neither delegated meaningful powers from the central state to the regions (self-rule), nor allowed the regional governments to have a say in central politics (shared rule).

SELF-RULE

The constitution established a parliamentary system in each region based on a legislative assembly (elected every five years with PR), an executive, and a president, and endowed them with a number of concurrent powers.[13]

Whereas the constitution allowed for the existence of regional governments, decades of centralization, first under the monarchy and later under fascism, meant that the regions had no structure or personnel. Therefore, their de facto establishment depended on the passage of enabling legislation by the central parliament. However, while the constitutional mandate was soon carried out in the special regions, it was delayed until the 1970s in the rest of Italy.

The main obstacle to the establishment of regional governments came from the opposing views of the DC and the PCI over regionalism. In the second half of the 1940s, the DC favored regionalization because it was consistent with Catholic social teaching, which commends subsidiarity, whereas the PCI opposed it because regionalism has never had a place in Marxist thought and they believed that centralization would have fostered economic development. With time, however, the two parties reversed their original stances. The PCI, excluded from government access in the statewide political arena, looked for regionalism as its best hope of being able to take control of some administration—as happened after 1970. The DC, fearing precisely that, turned centralist in response.

By the early 1970s, this dynamic led to the implementation of regional governments (as the PCI wanted), albeit of a very weak nature (as the DC wanted). A number of legal and administrative caveats successfully restrained their autonomy.

During their first five years, about one-quarter of regional legislation was vetoed by the central administration (Putnam 1993, 21). Moreover, regional governments enjoyed virtually no fiscal autonomy. In 1975, for example, five years after the first regional elections, subnational governments (regions, provinces, and municipalities) were still accountable for only 0.9 percent of the fiscal revenue, a percentage lower than in any other OECD country except Portugal (OECD 2001, 23). During the second half of the 1970s, the scope of regional governments increased slightly; yet controls and limits imposed by the basic legislation of the central state proved to be so detailed that regional autonomy remained remarkably narrow.[14]

The debate on regional devolution, driven since the early 1990s by the electoral rise of the LN, has produced a number of attempts to decentralize the Italian state and strengthen the regions. After the collapse, in April 1998, of the bicameral commission that was established in February 1997 to federalize the state, a modest innovation has been the promulgation, between 1997 and 1998, of the so-called Bassanini laws, "a half way house in the local government reform" (Gilbert 2000). A more significant change has been the "presidentialization" of regions, whose presidents are now directly elected by the regional electorates. Employed for the first time in the April 2000 regional elections, this new system has given regional presidents new visibility and legitimacy, which has strengthened their position vis-à-vis the central state.[15]

The major reform in the direction of a greater decentralization was approved by popular referendum on October 7, 2001. Due to the center-left majority that governed Italy between 1996 and 2001, the reform package made it through parliament in March 2001, just a few days before the end of the center-left parties' governing spell. Yet, because it was passed by much less than the two-thirds majority that is required in order to amend the constitution without facing the challenge of a popular referendum, it took a popular vote to finally turn it into law.

In essence, the October 7 reform redistributes certain lawmaking powers from the central government in Rome to the twenty regions. After establishing that all legislation has to be consistent with the constitution as well as European Union (EU) and international norms, the new version of article 117 lists the matters under central jurisdiction, enumerates the areas of concurrent legislation, and grants all residual powers to the regions.[16] In addition, the package introduces changes regarding subsidiarity, taxation, and intergovernmental relations. It devolves powers and responsibilities to the lowest feasible level of government, encourages officials to involve citizens in public affairs, gives regions a nominal and still somewhat hazily defined "fiscal autonomy," and ends the central government's power to suspend new regional legislation pending a constitutional court ruling on its constitutionality.

While this package has a few shortcomings—like leaving the senate in its original form—it is obviously too early to assess its consequences fully. Many of its changes have not even been implemented yet. Nonetheless, by expanding the concurrent jurisdiction of the regions and the central government, and by reserving residual powers to the former, it appears safe to say that, without actually making Italy a federal state, it will move Italy closer toward federalism.[17]

SHARED RULE

The degree of shared rule allowed by the constitution was even more modest than that of self-rule. One of the main institutional devices through which substate units may have a voice in statewide politics is bicameralism. A parliament divided into two houses gives the substate units the possibility of being represented in the upper house—endowed with powers directly related to substate matters. The importance of this device is such that all major federations, since the birth of the American federal system, have had a bicameral parliament (Lijphart 1999, 203).

The Italian constitution, following the logic of unitary states, does not provide regions with any institutional channels to play a significant role at the center. Although the parliament is bicameral, neither the chamber of deputies nor the senate can be regarded as a territorial chamber. Moreover, there is no form of territorial representation institutionalized within the executive and regions have no role in the constitutional amendment process or in the selection of neutral institutions.[18]

Outside the constitution, one must note the existence of the state-regions standing committee (*conferenza stato-regioni*). Created in 1983, this forum is composed of the prime minister (or the minister of regional affairs) and the presidents of all the twenty regions plus those of the two autonomous provinces of Trento and Bolzano, and is the only device that can enhance the profile of regions at the center. Its function is to provide a forum for coordinating state and regional policies and allowing regions to advise the central government on decisions important to them. So far, however, it has not been particularly relevant, as regions have often found themselves divided and unable to score any important decisional success.

The Mobilization of Territorial Differences and the Role of Political Institutions

For a long time, Italy's territorial differentiation did not constitute a basis for polit-ical mobilization. The cultural and economic diversity of the country existed without generating any urgent political issues. However, the 1990s saw this equilibrium imper-iled, especially in the north. There, surveys reported that nearly a fifth of all residents no longer identified with Italy as a whole—a position, by contrast, shared by a mere 6 percent of southerners (Biorcio 1999, 68–69).

In the aftermath of unification, when the Italian state was still new and somewhat weak, the potential for the political exploitation of territorial cleavages was high. The Italian government, however, put territorial mobilization down *manu militari*. A mas-sive armed action, which produced more casualties than the fighting against Austria before unification, was undertaken to defeat southern Italy's *brigantaggio*, a form of banditry born out of some southerners' disaffection for what they saw as an alien regime.[19] Soon after, the parliament rejected a bill for regional devolution sponsored by the minister of interior, Marco Minghetti.

However, although the consistency of regionalist forces during these times is not clear, territorial differences continued to make themselves felt politically. Political par-ties were divided along regional lines (Morandi 1997, 16) and, when a group of Tuscan deputies was sufficiently powerful to provoke the fall of the central government in 1876, the importance of regional interests became clear (Lyttleton 1996, 46). Moreover, the bases of the two-party system of the time were territorial: the right dominated the north, while the left had its stronghold in the south.[20]

Nonetheless, by the end of the nineteenth century, the politicization of territorial differences was a waning force in Italian national life. Elites in nearly every region of the country were coming to sense a common interest in a united Italy and a number of other trends diminished the political saliency of regionalism (Hine 1996). These in-cluded economic modernization, the gradual rise of popular political participation, the sharpening of church-state tensions, and the growing influence of nationalist ideolo-gies, with their emphasis on scale and bulk as factors in the competition for power and wealth among Europe's ambitious nation-states.

The 1922 fascist takeover hampered regionalism even further. The authoritarian and centralized fascist regime repressed regional differences and boosted Italian national-ism. It was not until its demise in 1943 and the replacement of the monarchy with the Republic—declared by referendum on June 2, 1946—that territorial differences would gain institutional recognition for the first time since 1861.

Yet, while the diverging views of the DC and the PCI over regionalism produced a timid regional devolution, the ideological polarization (Sartori 1976) that characterized the political life of the new Italian Republic ensured that any political expressions of regionalism would remain informal and sublimated for the duration of the cold war. It also secured the dominance of the DC and their small centrist allies as a legitimate anticommunist bulwark.

The stark division between pro-Western and pro-Soviet forces that dominated Italian politics in the years after World War II meant that the very identity of Italy was at stake in each national election. With the DC-led camp looking to the Atlantic alliance, democracy, and the free market, and the PCI-led camp looking to the Soviet bloc, its dictatorships, and the command economy, there was no room for any parties or movements competing along regional or territorial lines.

While the northeast was known as "white" and central Italy as "red," the divisions were first and foremost ideological, rather than regional. The way in which the famous journalist Indro Montanelli once rallied his readers—"hold your nose and vote for the DC"[21]—conveys the political state of postwar Italy.

The institutions created by the constituent assembly also contributed to this end. Due to the incentives set up in 1948, including the organization of the parliament in powerful standing committees, the daily workings of Italian democracy were much less adversarial than one might gather from inspecting the records of electoral competition alone. Since antimajoritarian mechanisms encouraged accommodation and power sharing, covert bargaining among rival elites—despite the high ideological polarization—usually produced a consociational decision-making process that rested on oversized majorities.

Under this unwritten constitution, relations between the central government and the geographic subunits of the Republic revolved around the informal practices adopted by the political parties. For instance, regional factors were nearly always taken into account in the composition of new cabinets (Calise and Mannheimer 1982, 27–68; Amoretti 2002b).

Though this system denied the regions *qua* regions any explicit role, it was fairly effective in giving territorial interests some say in the decisions emanating from Rome. Because the regions could not make policy, territorial politics was chiefly distributional. Following a custom that had its roots in the Kingdom of Sardinia-Piedmont (Meriggi 1997, 61–63), local or regional party bosses—particularly those from places that produced strong voter support for the governing parties—could arrange to have the central government transfer considerable flows of resources back to their home areas. Moreover, since the size of the ministerial contingent from any given region—and thus the likelihood that that region's desires would be fulfilled—depended on the electoral support for the governing party or parties in that region, the system discouraged the transmission of regional demands to the center through alternative channels, undercutting regionalist movements and effectively preventing the overt political mobilization of clashing territorial interests.

To manage competing demands, those who wielded power at the center used several devices typical of consociational democracy (Lijphart 1968, 1977). First and foremost, there was logrolling. Since the regions' interests were obviously heterogeneous, policy makers frequently crafted (usually working in the relative obscurity of parliamentary committees) complex deals granting various benefits to different interests. Whenever an agreement proved elusive, other approaches could be brought into play. A favorite was to increase the total quantity of resources to be distributed. This strategy was very costly, however, and it fed Italy's growing public debt to the point that it became the second largest in all of Western Europe, ranking behind only Belgium's as a percentage of gross domestic product.

The supremacy of the DC and the other "insider" parties and the demobilization of territorial cleavages were products not only of ideological polarization and these parties' skill at informally representing regional interests but also of party control over the institutions and resources of the central government—a crucial lever that gave the established parties an edge over potential challengers. Consociational decision making allowed the governing parties—and to a lesser extent, given the *conventio ad excludendum*, the PCI—to build elaborate patron-client networks that enabled them to take advantage of public resources through shrewd personnel appointments and the distribution of benefits to loyal districts, groups, and individuals. Especially in the south, where ideology had less weight on electoral behavior, such networks permitted the DC and, later, the PSI to exchange resources for votes (Parisi and Pasquino 1977).

The implementation of regional governments in the early 1970s first undermined this system, as the regions became vulnerable arenas for the DC and the PCI. For one thing, ideology mattered less at the regional level and a large part of the voting for both the DC and the PCI was ideology-driven. Second, being closer to citizens, regions were also more accessible to parties challenging the bipolar logic of the DC-PCI competition. It is not a coincidence that, shortly after the implementation of regional governments, new parties, including regional parties, began scoring some local and regional successes.

At first, however, nothing seemed to have changed at the national level. Regional devolution was still a timid affair while the major parties' creation of nationwide networks of social and cultural organizations, from trade unions to youth groups, strengthened and reproduced ideological loyalties, and virtually colonized civil society. As a consequence, in the 1976 general elections, the DC and the PCI won a combined

73.1 percent of the total vote—an all-time high. Thanks to ideological polarization and each party's skillful use of central resources, any potential competitors found themselves blocked from gaining influence. Along with their parallel penetration of central government institutions and Italian society, this made them so powerful and their presence so pervasive that some observers began to speak of Italy as a partitocracy (*partitocrazia*). This dominance also contributed, at least to some extent, to the territorial integration of the country (Calise 1993). On the whole, however, the Italians seem to have been far from pleased with this situation. Their dissatisfaction with the workings of their political system was unmatched anywhere else in Europe (La Palombara 1965; Morlino and Tarchi 1996).

The crisis of the Italian system of polarized consociationalism, undermined by the implementation of regional governments in the first half of the 1970s, began in the second half of that decade. As the PCI joined the parliamentary majority supporting the fourth government formed by the DC's Giulio Andreotti in 1976, more voters began to find the DC-PCI divide less relevant. As a consequence, new parties began to win votes. These new parties, including several regional movements, gained support especially in the north, where urbanization and postwar prosperity had created a new middle class that no longer identified with either the communist or the Catholic political subcultures and increasingly turned away from associations with traditional parties (Woods 1992).

Initially, the small regionalist movements that had begun forming in several regions in the north during the late 1970s were weak and poorly funded, with little voter support. After this slow start, the most successful appeared to be the Venetian League (LV) in the Veneto region. Building on the comparatively strong cultural identity of the region, the LV won 4.2 percent of the vote in Veneto in the 1983 general election, enough to earn one deputy and one senator.

Within a few years, however, the most popular regionalist organization became the Lombard League (LL) in the Lombardy region. Under the leadership of Umberto Bossi, the LL gained ground year by year, sending Bossi to Rome as a senator in 1987 and winning almost half a million votes in the 1989 elections for the European Parliament. This success lifted the LL into a position of leadership among the northern regionalist groupings, which together commanded 3.7 percent of the vote across all of northern Italy. In 1989, several of these movements joined the LL to form the LN.

The rise of regionalism in the north upset the traditional regional balance within the established parties, which as late as 1979 had been able to sway the votes of nearly equal numbers of citizens north and south. To face the challenges posed, especially in the north, by new competitors and an increasingly unpredictable electorate, the governing parties took to handing out more and more resources as the national debt mounted.

When the cold war ended and the Soviet Union collapsed, voters no longer had a reason to vote along the lines of the communism-anticommunism divide and the inherently centrifugal logic of Italy's PR system reasserted itself. Both the DC and the PCI (which officially embraced social democratic politics and renamed itself the Democratic Party of the Left, or PDS) found themselves hard-pressed to retain support as a number of smaller new parties claimed votes and parliamentary seats.

In 1992, the DC and the PDS combined won just under 46 percent of the national vote, a full 25 percent lower than only five years before. It was in the net-taxpaying north, not in the tax-absorbing and therefore more party-dependent south, where the worst hemorrhaging took place. One consequence of this change in Italian electoral geography was the formation, between 1992 and 1994, of governments that were increasingly southern-based, while two different oppositions, one regionalist and one leftist, prevailed in northern and central Italy, respectively.

The system that had dominated Italy since the late 1940s, however, did not come to an end just because of decreased polarization and PR. An additional factor was the process of European and monetary integration (Dyson and Featherstone 1996). By setting economic standards as a precondition for further integration, the European Community (EC) put severe limits on the use of lavish public spending as a means of building political support. The days of the growing public pie were over and politicians from Italy's established parties found themselves facing a hard choice: they could keep spending, which would hurt Italy's prospects to stay at the forefront of monetary integration, or they could cut back and watch their electoral base erode even further. Until the early 1990s, the choice was to keep on spending. Italy's standing worsened and it took a decade-long effort, initiated by the draconian budget under Giuliano Amato's first government in 1992, for Italy to be able to join the European single currency.

Voters, especially in the economically thriving, net-taxpaying north, reacted accordingly. Distributional and territorial conflicts overlapped, offering new opportunities for regionalist political entrepreneurs. The LN capitalized on them by reinterpreting the classic themes of regionalism through its own brand of antiparty, antiestablishment rhetoric. Boosted by massive public corruption scandals implicating numerous figures from the traditional parties, the LN skyrocketed. The politicization of territorial difference and federalism moved to the heart of the Italian political agenda.

Conclusion

The above analysis offers several lessons about the role played by the Italian institutional setting in the management of territorial cleavages. For more than thirty years, from the mid-1940s to the mid-1970s, regional mobilization was prevented by the ideological polarization resulting from the international context and by the consensual institutions of the Republic. This does not mean that territorial politics were not significant in Italy. Territorial interests were transmitted from the periphery to the center along party lines; a set of informal rules guaranteed them an audience that for a long time secured their depoliticization. From this point of view, the antimajoritarian mechanisms embedded in the Italian constitution seem to have played a positive role, offering policy makers a set of devices that kept territorial politics quiescent. Although impossible to prove, it is likely that, given the high polarization, a more majoritarian system would have generated less satisfactory outcomes. Thus, in broad terms, the analysis of the first thirty years of the Italian Republic is consistent with the results of other works (Lijphart 1994, 1999; Cohen 1997), which have shown that consensual democracy outperforms majoritarian democracy in many respects.

The virtues of antimajoritarian institutions are further illustrated by the events of the late 1970s and the 1980s, when consociational practices prevented territorial conflict from escalating in the presence of unfavorable conditions such as a reduction of ideological polarization. These years also witnessed an important institutional innovation, namely, the implementation of regional decentralization, however timid. Even if the resources devolved from the center to the periphery were modest, the mere creation of this intermediate level of territorial government accentuated the differences among the various regions (Nanetti 1988, 5). If the powers transferred from Rome to the regions were meaningful, the creation of regional governments might have favored the management of territorial conflict by allowing each regional society to govern itself to some extent. However, the limited policy competences granted to the regions simply stressed the differences, without granting regional actors the authority to deal with them with substantive and creative policy making. They devolved to the periphery symbolic resources that fueled frustration and centrifugal forces.

In the late 1980s, when the communist threat disappeared, freeing electors from prior constraints, the pervasive Italian party system—and with it the informal system of representation upon which territorial politics had been based—collapsed. This collapse was provoked also by many factors, among which were the changing territorial bases of governments and the waning power of the traditional consociational devices. The elimination of an antimajoritarian mechanism, such as the link between resource allocation and votes, opened up the doors to confrontation among diverging regional interests. This further changed Italy's geopolitics and ultimately led to the crisis of the old consensual system of territorial representation and the emergence of a more adversarial style, as seen in the rise of the LN and the presence of increasingly exclusive substate identities.

As the workings of the Italian institutional system have been remarkably problematic since the late 1980s, the examination of the Italian case stresses the merits but also the limits of consociational institutions. Whereas the conflict management capabilities of consociational democracy are undeniable in a stable environment, its effectiveness in a changing context appears to be more problematic. This inconsistent performance is, in some ways, accounted for by the fact that consociational institutions protect those interests and actors already relevant prior to their introduction, but do not perform equivalently with those that emerge later, whose access to political power they obstruct.

Notes

I thank Nancy Bermeo, Larry Diamond, Alberta Sbragia, and Marc F. Plattner for comments on earlier drafts of this essay. Jordan Branch, Philip J. Costopoulos, Stephanie Lewis, and Amelie von Zumbusch deserve thanks for editorial assistance.

1. Nationalist activists—such as intellectuals, entrepreneurs, and bureaucrats—were a minority of the already tiny portion of the population of that time (2 percent) that was enfranchised.

2. Quoted in Holsti (1996, 52).

3. On the different features of the northern and southern economies and, particularly, on the redistributive role of the public sector, see Alesina, Danninger, and Rostagno (2001).

4. To take but another economic indicator, Italy's 11.8 percent unemployment rate is unevenly distributed among its three main areas: 6.1 percent in the north, 9.5 percent in the center, and 21.9 percent in the south (ISTAT 2000, 189).

5. On June 2, 1946, the PCI and the PSI obtained, respectively, 19 and 21 percent of votes.

6. The only exceptions to this pattern were the special regions created to accommodate the mobilized minorities along the borders, which enjoyed a larger degree of autonomy from the outset of the Republic.

7. The constitutional character of the electoral system, although not included in the constitution, is well witnessed by the exceptional controversy created, in the early 1950s, by the DC's attempt to modify it by introducing a majority bonus. The left-of-center parties mobilized the public opinion, labeling this bill "swindle law" (*legge truffa*), and eventually managed to defeat it (Morlino 1998, 78–79). Likewise, the constitutionality of the electoral system has been underlined by the use of the term *Second Republic*, which, as reported, for example, by Calise (1993, 556), has been employed by many commentators and politicians after the 1993 electoral reform, even though no formal constitutional change took place.

8. I computed these figures with reference to the votes cast for each party. For figures calculated with reference to parliamentary seats, which are generally slightly smaller, see Morlino (1996, 19).

9. According to the article 72 of the Italian constitution, only constitutional amendments, voting laws, delegations of legislative function to the government, international agreements, and budget decisions must be referred to the floor.

10. For an alternative interpretation of the *leggine* and their role within the legislative process, see Kreppel (1997).

11. This because of party factionalism and lack of parliamentary discipline, rather than for the formation of different political majorities in the two chambers. Despite article 57 of the constitution, which states that "the senate is elected on regional basis," the upper house has never been elected with criteria significantly different from those adopted for the chamber of deputies, resulting in its carbon copy most of the time.

12. The negative attitudes of Italians toward politics are shown by a number of works covering the period of the 1950s on. For example, see La Palombara (1965) and Morlino and Tarchi (1996). Eurobarometer data, however, show that the percentage of Italians dissatisfied with the workings of their democracy steadily rose from about 70 percent to about 90 percent in the period preceding the electoral reform (1988–93). By the late 1980s, antiparty feelings also increased (Bardi 1996).

13. These were listed in article 117 of the constitution and included the organization of regional administration; communal boundaries; local urban and rural police; fairs and markets; public charities, health, and hospital assistance; vocational training and financial assistance to students; local museums and libraries; urban planning; tourism and the hotel industry; regional transport networks; regional roads, aqueducts, and other public works; lake navigation and ports; mineral and spa waters; quarries and mines; hunting; inland fisheries; agriculture and forestry; and craftsmanship.

14. One of their major outcomes were the so-called 616 decrees issued in June 1977, which transferred to the regions about 20,000 offices from the central administration, including portions of several ministries. These measures were, at least partly, the result of the electoral rise of the PCI and a concession by the DC prime minister Giulio Andreotti to keep the PCI support for his government (Putnam 1993, 22–23).

15. Especially between April 2000 and May 2001, regional presidents (mainly northern) gained particular relevance on the political scene at the national level. This activism, however, was due also to party factor, since all northern regional presidents were expressions of a coalition between the center-right parties and the LN—at a time in which the central government was instead run by the center-left. Significantly, after the center-right parties and the LN took control of the central government following the May 2001 elections, regional presidents' activism has dropped.

16. The principal state powers now include: foreign policy, international relations and relations with the EU, right of asylum and juridical conditions of citizens of non-EU states; immigration; relations between the Republic and religions; defense and armed forces; state security, weapons, munitions, and explosives; currency, protection of savings, and financial markets; protection of competition; monetary system; the state's fiscal and bookkeeping systems; equalization of financial resources; organs of the state and relative electoral laws; state referenda; election of the EU Parliament; administrative organization of the state and national agencies; law and order, with the exclusion of the local administrative police; citizenship and register; jurisdiction and trial norms; civil and penal law; administrative justice; determination of the essential levels of civil and social rights that have to be guaranteed in the entire national territory; social security; electoral legislation, governmental structure and essential functions of municipalities, provinces, and metropolitan cities; customs and protection of national borders; weights, measures, time, statistical coordination of data related to the state, regional, provincial, and local administration;

environment and culture. Among the remaining areas, instead, the main ones subject to concurrent jurisdiction are regions' international relations and relations with the EU; foreign trade; labor; education; professions; scientific research; public health; alimentation; sport organization; territorial governance; ports and airports; transportation and navigation networks; communication organization; energy; complementary and integrative pensions; harmonization of public budgets and coordination of public finance; promotion and organization of cultural activities; saving, rural, and regional banks.

17. For a more detailed discussion of the October 7 referendum, see Amoretti (2002a).

18. To be sure, the president of the Republic is elected by a body made of the whole parliament (630 deputies, 315 elective senators, and 5 nonelective senators) plus three representatives for each of the twenty regions but Valle d'Aosta, which has only one. This norm, however, is far from giving any significant power to the regions as, all together, they have less than 6 percent of the total electoral body (58 out of 1008).

19. Not without reason, given the House of Savoy's decision to extend to the entire territory of the newborn Italian state the Kingdom of Sardinia-Piedmont's system of centralized administration, with no regard to the differences there were between it and the newly acquired territories.

20. Istituto Centrale Statistica e Ministero per la Costituente (1947, 120–22). It is worth recalling that the meaning of left and right was at that time radically different from today's, being just tendencies within an electorate made of a mere 2 percent of the population.

21. Quoted in Morlino and Tarchi (1996, 61).

REFERENCES

Alesina, Alberto, Stephan Danninger, and Massimo Rostagno. 2001. Redistribution through Public Employment: The Case of Italy. *IMF Staff Papers* 48, no. 3:447–73.

Amoretti, Ugo M. 2002a. Italy Decentralizes. *Journal of Democracy* 13, no. 2:126–40.

———. 2002b. Da Andreotti a Berlusconi: la rappresentatività territoriale dei governi italiani, 1976–2001. *Rivista Italiana di Scienza Politica* 32, no. 2:269–304.

Bagnasco, Arnaldo, and Marco Oberti. 1998. Italy: Le 'trompe-l'œil' of Regions. In *Regions in Europe*, ed. Patrick Le Galès and Christian Lequesne, 150–65. London: Routledge.

Bardi, Luciano. 1996. Anti-Party Sentiment and Party System Change in Italy. *European Journal of Political Research* 29, no. 3:345–63.

Bartolini, Stefano, and Roberto D'Alimonte. 1996. Plurality Competition and Party Realignment in Italy: The 1994 Parliamentary Elections. *European Journal of Political Research* 29, no. 1:105–42.

Biorcio, Roberto. 1999. La Lega Nord e la transizione italiana. *Rivista Italiana di Scienza Politica* 29, no. 1:55–87.

Bull, Martin, and Martin Rhodes. 1997. Between Crisis and Transition: Italian Politics in the 1990s. *West European Politics* 20, no. 1:1–13.

Calise, Mauro. 1993. Remaking the Italian Party System: How Lijphart Got It Wrong by Saying It Right. *West European Politics* 16, no. 4:545–60.

Calise, Mauro, and Renato Mannheimer. 1982. *Governanti in Italia: Un trentennio republicano 1946-1976*. Bologna: Il Mulino.

Clough, Shepard B. 1964. *The Economic History of Modern Italy*. New York: Columbia University Press.

Cohen, Frank S. 1997. Proportional Versus Majoritarian Ethnic Conflict Management in Democracies. *Comparative Political Studies* 30, no. 5:607–30.

Connor, Walker. 1991. From Tribe to Nation? *History of European Ideas* 13, nos. 1–2:5–18.

D'Alimonte, Roberto, and Alessandro Chiaramonte. 1995. Il nuovo sistema elettorale italiano: le opportunità e le scelte. In *Maggioritario ma non troppo: le elezioni politiche del 1994*, ed. Stefano Bartolini and Roberto D'Alimonte, 373–400. Bologna: Il Mulino.

D'Onofrio, Francesco. 1979. Committees in Italian Parliament. In *Committees in Legislatures: A Comparative Analysis*, ed. Malcolm Shaw and John D. Lees, 61–101. Durham, N.C.: Duke University Press.

Di Palma, Giuseppe. 1976. Institutional Rules and Legislative Outcomes in the Italian Parliament. *Legislative Studies Quarterly* 1, no. 2:147–79.

————. 1977. *Surviving without Governing: The Italian Parties in Parliament*. Berkeley: University of California Press.

Dyson, Kenneth H. F., and Kevin Featherstone. 1996. Italy and EMU as a '*Vincolo Esterno*': Empowering the Technocrats, Transforming the State. *South European Society & Politics* 1, no. 2:279–99.

Eurostat. 2001. *Regional Gross Domestic Product in the European Union*. Statistics in Focus, 1–3/2001.

Finkelstein, Monte S. 1998. *Separatism, the Allies and the Mafia: The Struggle for Sicilian Independence, 1943-1948*. Bethlehem, Pa.: Lehigh University Press.

Furlong, Paul. 1990. Parliament in Italian Politics. *West European Politics* 13, no. 3:52–67.

Gilbert, Mark. 2000. The Bassanini Laws: A Half Way House in the Local Government Reform. In *Italian Politics: The Return of Politics*, ed. David Hine and Salvatore Vassallo, 139–55. Oxford: Berghahn.

Giuliani, Marco. 1997. Measures of Consensual Law-making: Italian *Consociativismo*. *South European Society & Politics* 2, no. 1:66–98.

Hine, David. 1996. Federalism, Regionalism, and the Unitary State: Contemporary Regional Pressures in Historical Perspective. In *Italian Regionalism. History, Identity and Politics*, ed. Carl Levy, 109–29. Oxford: Berg.

Hine, David, and Renato Finocchi. 1991. The Italian Prime Minister. *West European Politics* 14, no. 2:79–96.

Holsti, Kalevi J. 1996. *The State, War, and the State of War*. New York: Cambridge University Press.

Istituto Nazionale dell'Informazione. (Various editions). *La Navicella*. Rome: Editoriale italiana.

ISTAT. 2000. *Rapporto sull'Italia: Edizione 2000*. Bologna: Il Mulino.

Istituto Centrale Statistica and Ministero per la Costituente. 1947. *Compendio delle statistiche elettorali italiane dal 1848 al 1934*. Rome: Istituto Poligrafico dello Stato.

Katz, Richard S. 1996. Electoral Reform and the Transformation of Party Politics in Italy. *Party Politics* 2, no. 1:31–53.

Kreppel, Amie. 1997. The Impact of Parties in Government on Legislative Output in Italy. *European Journal of Political Research* 31, no. 3:327–50.

La Palombara, Joseph. 1965. Italy: Fragmentation, Alienation, and Isolation. In *Political Culture and Political Development,* ed. Lucian W. Pye and Sydney Verba, 282–329. Princeton: Princeton University Press.

Laakso, Markku, and Rein Taagepera. 1979. "Effective" Number of Parties: A Measure with Application to Western Europe. *Comparative Political Studies* 12, no. 1:3–27.

Lepschy, Anna Laura, Giulio Lepschy, and Miriam Voghera. 1996. Linguistic Variety in Italy. In *Italian Regionalism: History, Identity and Politics,* ed. Carl Levy, 69–80. Oxford: Berg.

Lijphart, Arend. 1968. Typologies of Democratic Systems. *Comparative Political Studies* 1, no. 1:3–44.

——— . 1977. *Democracy in Plural Societies: A Comparative Exploration.* New Haven, Conn.: Yale University Press.

——— . 1994. Democracies: Forms, Performances, and Constitutional Engineering. *European Journal of Political Research* 25, no. 1:1–17.

——— . 1999. *Patterns of Democracy: Government Forms and Performance in Thirty-Six Countries.* New Haven, Conn.: Yale University Press.

Lyttelton, Adrian. 1996. Shifting Identities: Nation, Region and City. In *Italian Regionalism: History, Identity and Politics,* ed. Carl Levy, 33–52. Oxford: Berg.

Meriggi, Marco. 1997. Centralismo e federalismo in Italia: Le aspettative preunitarie. In *Centralismo e federalismo tra Otto e Novecento: Italia e Germania a confronto,* ed. Oliver Janz, Pierangelo Schiera, and Hannes Siegrist, 49–63. Bologna: Il Mulino.

Ministero di Agricoltura, Industria e Commercio. 1873. *Annali. II, III, e IV Trimestre 1872, n. 51 e Annata 1873.* Rome: Tipografia Barbera.

Morandi, Carlo. 1997. *I partiti politici in Italia: Dal 1848 al 1924.* Florence: Le Monnier.

Morlino, Leonardo. 1996. Crisis of Parties and Change of Party System in Italy. *Party Politics* 2, no. 1:5–30.

——— . 1998. *Democracy between Consolidation and Crisis: Parties, Groups, and Citizens in Southern Europe.* Oxford: Oxford University Press.

Morlino, Leonardo, and Marco Tarchi. 1996. The Dissatisfied Society: The Roots of Political Change in Italy. *European Journal of Political Research* 30, no. 1:41–63.

Nanetti, Raffaella Y. 1988. *Growth and Territorial Policies: The Italian Model of Social Capitalism.* New York: Printer Press.

OECD. 2001. *Revenue Statistics of OECD Member Countries, 1965-2000.* Paris: OECD.

Parisi, Arturo, and Gianfranco Pasquino. 1977. Relazioni partiti-elettori e tipi di voto. In *Continuità e mutamento elettorale in Italia: le elezioni del 20 giugno 1976 e il sistema politico italiano,* ed. Arturo Parisi and Gianfranco Pasquino, 215-49. Bologna: Il Mulino.

Petrosino, Daniele. 1992. National and Regional Movements in Italy: The Case of Sardinia. In *The Social Origins of Nationalist Movements: The Contemporary West European Experience,* ed. John Coakley, 124–46. London: Sage.

Putnam, Robert D. 1993. *Making Democracy Work: Civic Traditions in Modern Italy.* Princeton: Princeton University Press.

Riall, Lucy. 1994. *The Italian Risorgimento: State, Society and National Unification.* London: Routledge.

Sartori Giovanni. 1976. *Parties and Party Systems: A Framework for Analysis.* Cambridge: Cambridge University Press.

Tilly, Charles. 1990. *Coercion, Capital, and European States: AD 990–1990.* Cambridge, Mass.: Basil Blackwell.

Tsebelis, George. 1995. Decision-Making in Political Systems: Veto Players in Presidentialism, Parlimentarism, Multicameralism and Multipartitism. *British Journal of Political Science* 25, no. 3: 289–325.

Woods, Dwayne. 1992. The Centre No Longer Holds: The Rise of Regional Leagues in Italian Politics. *West European Politics* 15, no. 2:56–76.

CHAPTER SEVEN

France

Challenging the Unitary State

Marc Smyrl

It may seem odd, at first glance, to include France in a comparative study of federal systems. Yet, it is precisely the strong unitary character of the French state that makes the case a valuable source of comparison. Studying how unitary states cope with the challenges of territorial differences enables us to tease out how much coping is due to federalism and how much to other factors. Clearly, France is a country that matches the other cases in this collection by having deep-seated territorial cleavages. The situation of the island of Corsica, regularly erupting into violence over the past thirty years, is only the best known of these. Other peripheral areas, such as Alsace, Brittany, and the French Basque Country, have also maintained a significant degree of social and cultural distinctiveness.

On a conceptual level, these observations provide a dual starting point for analysis. Most obviously, it is interesting to investigate the interaction of a unitary system of government and administration with a geographically diverse society. This chapter does this through case studies of two distinctive regions: Brittany and Corsica. Since even the most superficial observation of this interaction reveals significant variation in outcomes across the regional cases—smooth integration in Brittany contrasts with violent confrontation in Corsica—a second, and theoretically more important, question emerges. Why do French territorial institutions function effectively in some cases but not in others? This, in turn, leads directly to consideration of one of the central theoretical questions proposed by the broader project to which this essay is a contribution: when (and why) do unitary systems succeed or fail in managing territorially based political cleavages?

Center-Periphery Relations in France

It is a fundamental principle of French law and public philosophy that the Republic is one and indivisible. It is at the same time an inescapable fact of history and geography that France is as socially and culturally diverse as any nation in Europe; the political territory of France overlaps systematically the cultural spheres of its neighbors. This is directly attributable to the success of a thousand years of military and political expansion, which brought under the control of Parisien authority peripheries whose culture was Celtic, Flemish, German, Italian, Corsican, Catalan, and Basque.

The Republic and Its Regions

The monarchy of the ancien régime accommodated the diversity of its realm largely through inaction. Requiring of its subjects only political obedience, the royal government made little effort to impose social or cultural—or even linguistic—uniformity. Nor, for that matter, did it act to impose economic unity; regulatory diversity and even internal tariff barriers were the norm until the Revolution. From the time of the Jacobins on, by contrast, political, economic, and cultural harmonization has been central to the ideology of all successful republican regimes.[1]

The historical provinces of France were antithetical to the new regime.[2] Linked to the feudal past, they were perceived as a political threat—a rallying point for royalist nostalgia. Beyond this, the very notion of republican citizenship, unlike the loyalty of subject to monarch, seemed to foreclose any identity other than national. The division of France into artificial administrative units, the *départements,* followed from this logic. Such was its practical value as an instrument of central control that neither the restored monarchy between 1815 and 1848 nor the imperial regime of Louis-Napoleon Bonaparte, in power from 1850 to 1870, sought to revise it.

With the stabilization of the Third Republic in the 1870s, the struggle against regional particularism took on renewed vigor. To the elimination of political regionalism, the Republic added the struggle against cultural particularism. Most direct was the assault on regional languages, carried on largely through the expanded system of primary schools. In the space of half a century, the patchwork of patois that had characterized France was eradicated, and the local dialects relegated to the domain of folklore (Weber 1976). The literary success of such regionalist intellectuals as the Provençal author Frederic Mistral notwithstanding, significant linguistic resistance at the popular level was largely limited to the extreme periphery—including the two regions that will serve as case studies for this essay, Brittany and Corsica.[3]

It would be wrong to conclude from this, however, that postrevolutionary France was a regime in which an oppressive center dominated a resentful periphery. Ruthless in their elimination of any collective identity other than at the national level, the regimes that succeeded the fall of Napoleon Bonaparte were open to the individual ambitions of provincial political figures. The century from 1815 to 1914 was the golden age of the *notables,* local elites whose influence in national politics was based on a secure social and political base in their provincial home. To men like this, the highest political careers were open. This tendency was, if anything, accentuated after 1870; the political bedrock of the Third Republic was in its local-level institutions. Between these and the national center, however, no political space existed for regional representation in any meaningful way.

Decentralization and Deconcentration

The success of the Third Republic's campaign against local particularism was due in large part to its ability to co-opt most of the local elites who might otherwise have led a territorially based opposition. Nevertheless, we should not conclude from this necessarily oversimplified summary that the Republic's efforts at political and cultural harmonization met with no resistance at all. Prior to World War II, however, regionalist sentiment was found chiefly among those on the antirepublican right of the political spectrum who, by their own political choice, excluded themselves from the national political establishment. Far from advancing the cause of regionalism, this ensured that nothing short of a radical change of regime would bring it about.

After World War II, a number of important changes took place. Most obviously, the antirepublican right, hopelessly compromised by its collaboration with fascism, was out of action for a generation. Regionalists abandoned it along with everyone else, with the consequence that, for the first time since the early nineteenth century, the notion of regionalism was no longer dangerous by association. The mobilizing potential of regional identity was once again available to support legitimate political projects (Berger 1972; Mény 1974). This opportunity was seized in a number of regions by business leaders, who created unofficial but influential *comités d'expansions,* linking the old idea of territorial identity with the new ideology of economic modernization.

It is in this context that a new generation of political and economic reformers in Paris came to associate a certain degree of functional decentralization not with nostalgia for the past but rather with economic and social modernization. Imbued with the ideology of indicative planning, these men needed partners on the ground to implement their vision. They controlled, moreover, the critical resource needed for economic growth: investment capital, still scarce in the postwar French economy. The convergence of interests between central planners and territorial economic leaders was, for a time at least, very close.[4] Politicians followed, and focused squarely on economic opportunity. Political autonomy was evoked, if at all, primarily as an instrumental means to the end of economic growth, while the old cultural regionalist agenda was relegated to the (thriving) world of poets and folk singers.

Under the Fourth Republic, from 1946 through 1958, thus, two distinct movements were evident. The first was a renewed bottom-up mobilization of elites and interest groups in some (not all) regions, largely around economic issues. The second was a limited but important embrace of functional decentralization on the part of some central state administrations (Wright 1979). These trends came together over the course of the 1950s as central authorities encouraged the systematic creation of regional *comités d'expansions.* Comprised of regional political and economic leaders, the first of these, such as the justly famous CELIB in Brittany (about which more below), were genuinely spontaneous expressions of the desire for economic modernization. As such, they were very much in the spirit of the times.

It is typical of the policies of that period, however, that the regional committees were not allowed to proceed far on their own. By the early 1960s they had been harmonized and generalized into regional committees for economic development (CODER), firmly under the tutelage of central authority. The creation of the *Direction à l'Aménagement du Territoire et à l'Action Régionale* (DATAR) in 1963 gave an explicitly territorial dimension to the planning effort, while ensuring that it would remain firmly controlled and coordinated from the center.

Indeed, the creation of the DATAR was part of a larger effort by the Gaullist government of the nascent Fifth Republic to gain control of political and economic decision making in the periphery—a task that proved considerably more difficult than winning national elections. Having analyzed their political difficulties as being caused, at least in part, by the entrenched conservatism of local political elites, the Gaullists sought by a number of means to circumvent these. One tactic, repeated under various guises, was to promote and seek alliance with an alternative set of local elites, the so-called *forces vives*, presumably made up of political or economic leaders with an interest in modernization and efficiency. In the hoped-for alliance between the *forces vives* and the national authority, however, there was to be no doubt as to which was the senior partner (Ashford 1982).

All of the reforms dating from this period that were to have direct consequences for our study were intended to increase the capacity of the national administration to intervene in local affairs. This was the case of the DATAR. It was also the case of the regionalization of the national planning exercise beginning with the IVth Plan in 1962 (Quinet 1990). An increase in central control through alliance with peripheral elites, finally, was clearly the goal of the creation of regional-level administrative units, under the authority of a regional prefect (*préfet de région*) who was to have authority over departmental colleagues (Grémion 1976).

These purely administrative reforms, however, did not altogether satisfy the growing political demands of peripheral elites. Indeed, the technocratic logic of the reforms, while embracing the participation of local economic actors, explicitly kept territorial politicians at arm's length (Quermone 1998). After the political and social rupture of 1968, this was increasingly difficult. Political as well as economic decentralization was a central element of the demands of the "second left" that emerged in the late 1960s. Men as diverse in their ideas and origins as the new left socialist Michel Rocard, the modernizer Jean-Jacques Sevant-Schreiber, and social Catholic Jacques Delors shared a commitment to breaking the political monopoly of the center.

A second and ironic result of "68," however, was a rehabilitation of traditional, territorial *notables* as a direct result of the weakening of central authority following the departure from power of General De Gaulle in 1969.[5] While decentralization was a hardy perennial of the political agenda throughout the 1970s, little progress was made in actually bringing it about. Until the election of François Mitterrand to the presidency in 1981, the political, as opposed to technical, aspects of this issue remained largely at the level of rhetoric (Mény 1974). Peripheral government institutions remained largely unchanged. Elected councils at the level of the municipality and the *département* had existed since the days of the Third Republic.[6] While the former elected its own executive, the mayor, the latter did not. The *préfet*, in addition to other functions, was *ex officio* the executive of the *conseil général* of his *département*. Although regional units had been created in 1960s by bringing together groups of *départements* for planning and administrative purposes, they were a purely administrative unit, devoid of representative institutions of their own.

In 1972, these preexisting administrative regions were given an indirectly elected regional council made up of all the region's members of the national parliament along with members of the councils elected at the level of the *départements* and municipalities selected by their peers. Following the model established for the *départements*, the regional *préfet* acted as executive for the new body.

Sweeping change was brought to this system as the result of the election of François Mitterrand to the presidency in 1981. While the coalition that brought him to power was a broad one, including all of the left and parts of the political center, an important component was made up of the heirs of the new left 1968, led by Michel Rocard. Also behind Mitterrand was a phalanx of socialist *notables,* mayors of large cities or leaders of their respective *département*. For all of these men, albeit for somewhat different reasons, the time for decentralization was long overdue. Mitterrand promised it to them and delivered.[7] Beginning in 1982, a series of laws, known collectively as the *lois Defferre*,[8] thoroughly revamped the French system of territorial government. As a result of these laws, regions were put on a legal footing equivalent to that long enjoyed by the municipalities and *départements;* all of these were now established as *collectivité territoriale*. As a result, the regional council was to be directly elected.[9] In regions as well as *départements,* additionally, the executive was henceforth to be a president elected by the council rather than the *préfet*.[10] The task of the *préfet* was altered from *ex ante* political control over the actions of the territorial councils to *ex post* legal control, the responsibility for seeing to it that their actions are consistent with national law.

Institutional Environment

There is a sense in which the narrative given above, with its well-marked moments of institutional reform, is misleading. If we broaden the concept of institutions to include not just juridical rules but also the unwritten realm of norms and operating procedures the picture becomes one of gradual evolution rather than abrupt change. To this end, the following sections suggest two elements of correction. The first concerns the political dimension of decentralization. With respect to this topic, it is important to underline the ongoing mutual penetration of French governing elites at all territorial levels, and the consequent analytic danger of drawing sharp boundaries either of power or of responsibility that do not conform to actual practice. Territorial administration, and in particular the prefectoral system, provides a second dimension. Here too, it is important to distinguish practice from theory and to discount at least in part the distinction, clear in legal theory but murky in social practice, between politics and administration.

The Politics of Territory

The extent to which the political-administrative efforts of the 1960s bore their intended fruit is contested. For Grémion, whose study of this episode is by far the most thorough, the experience was a clear failure. The very title of his book, *Le Pouvoir Périphérique,* stands as testimony to his conclusion that peripheral elites succeeded in sabotaging the attempts by the Gaullist center to impose on them a "renewed Jacobinism." Ashford's analysis is more nuanced, concluding that "in France, the functional requirements of the welfare state overcame the resistance of the préfets and the mayors by devising a new relationship to the local political elites and by appealing to economic self-interest" (1982, 93, 94).

Moving beyond the political and analytic quarrels of the 1960s, moreover, it is now clear that the opposition (and, indeed, the very distinction) between center and periphery noted by all of these analysts was, in large part, an artifact of time and place, caused by the temporary division between the Gaullists in power at the national level and local elites dominated either by men of the left or by traditional conservatives. Despite this opposition, the one and the other remained in place and continued to wield considerable influence over the years.

For territorially based elites, the road to political power remained until very recently the *cumul de mandats,* the widespread practice of combining one or more local offices (mayor or member of a departmental *conseil général*) with membership in the national parliament or even a ministerial portfolio. In this way, the most powerful men of the Fifth Republic's first generation combined, rather than opposing, national and peripheral power bases.[11] Far from shutting out the representatives of the periphery, the Fifth Republic was systematically colonized by the very provincial *notables* that De Gaulle had initially tried to supplant. In this context, the decentralization of the early 1980s was seen by many observers not as a progressive reform but rather as the consolidation of peripheral elite power. In the words of one group of critics, it was *"le sacre des notables."*[12]

Supporting this point of view was the undeniable fact that, for tactical reasons, the *lois Defferre* transferred power to local and regional elected officials before the exact contents and limits of the authority in question were defined. Even after additional laws and regulations sought to bring order to the new system, moreover, the outcome of the 1982 reforms was far from simple. While it clearly increased the status of the regions, it also gave new powers to *départements* and municipalities. The share-out of tasks among the various territorial assemblies proved to be the most complex and contentious aspect of the reform.[13]

Adding to the overall uncertainty is the general legal principle that all units of territorial government (*collectivité territoriale*) are equal under the law. Municipality, *département,* and region each administer freely the affairs pertaining to their area of jurisdiction. None of these has precedence, or is permitted to exercise control, over any of the others.[14] In practice, overlapping and conflicting claims of authority have proven the rule.

Administering the Republic

In theory, the French prefectoral system is a perfect example of an arbitral institution. Its function is precisely to act as arbiter of local interests in pursuit of the general interest. In practice, as always, the truth is more complicated. Following the seminal study by Jean-Pierre Worms, a generation of French political sociologists have noted that the relation between the *préfet* and local elites is characterized as much by what Worms labeled "complicity" as by arbitration (Worms 1966). It is precisely this network of close informal relations that was seen to be threatened by the Gaullist reforms of the 1960s.

Over the course of the 1960s and 1970s, the DATAR gained considerable, albeit indirect, power through its role in designating the areas that would be eligible for special financial assistance through the *Prime à l'Aménagement du Territoire*. Although it had no budgetary power of its own the DATAR became an effective gatekeeper standing between local elites and the national treasury. It is not surprising that it would seek to replicate this role at the European level, when European Community (EC) regional policy came on the scene.

The regional *préfecture*, meanwhile, although contested, remained in place and scored significant gains in influence over the course of the 1970s and especially the 1980s. In addition to being, ex officio, the departmental *préfet* for the regional capital, the *préfet de région* maintained considerable powers of coordination and control. He was the regional participant in the regionalized aspects of the national planning process, and was responsible for implementation of the plan once it was in place. He presided over all administrative commissions whose scope exceeded a single *département*. After indirectly elected regional councils were established in 1972, the *préfet de région* served as the council's executive (Turpin, 1987).

Although the *lois Defferre* of 1982 stripped the *préfet de région* of his executive functions, other developments over the following decade worked in the opposite direction, reinforcing the power of the office. The method retained for administering regional development funding from the European Union (EU) after the major reforms of that policy in 1988 put the *préfet de région* squarely in charge of the "European" planning process (Smyrl 1997; Behrens and Smyrl 1999). In 1992, a set of administrative reforms known collectively as the ATR laws (for *Administration du Territoire de la République*) reinforced the power of the *préfet de région* not only over his departmental colleagues but also over the specialized agents of central administrations in his region such as the local agents of the Ministries of Agriculture or Industry.[15] Less well known than the 1982 decentralization laws, these deconcentration measures have had a highly significant impact on the institutional balance of power in the regions.

An Institutional Balance Sheet

It is tempting, at the dawn of a new century, to attempt an assessment of fifty years of reform. Easiest, perhaps, is to list what did not happen. The decentralization that followed the reforms of 1982, first of all, has not led to the blossoming of participatory local democracy for which some had hoped. As explored in the detailed studies of the

Observatoire Inter-régional de Politique, leadership of directly elected regional councils has in almost every case followed the trend long established by the departmental *conseil généraux,* to wit, domination by established elites[16] (Dupoirier 1998). The particularly pure system of proportional representation chosen for regional elections, moreover, ensures the control of political parties over nominations, reducing the prospects of independent candidates. Political continuity through institutional change seems to be the watchword of decentralization to date.

It does not follow, however, that the territorial reforms of the 1980s and 1990s should be dismissed. While they did not lead to the creation of significant new political opportunities, they have most certainly brought new institutional opportunity for existing actors. To what extent, and to what end, these opportunities have been seized has proven to be a complex question, the answer to which varies a good deal with time and place. It is to this dimension that we turn in the remainder of this essay.

Explaining Diverse Outcomes

Institutional constants by themselves cannot explain variation in outcomes. We must therefore bring in additional elements. For this study, these are found in the social and political history of the two regions to be studied. It is in their interactions with these very different social realities that the institutions of the French state have their true impact on observable outcomes.

The Puzzle of Brittany and Corsica

A number of similarities are evident in the historical evolution of Brittany and Corsica. Most obviously, both are economically and socially peripheral with respect to the French heartland. On the purely economic front, problems of distance and transportation were historically important in both regions. Not only were producers isolated from external markets, but poor internal communications made even a regional market impossible. The result was the persistence of subsistence agriculture and, in the nineteenth and twentieth centuries, substantial outmigration of the most active segments of the population.

Both regions also share a feeling of social distinctiveness, tied to historical events and, more concretely, to the persistence of linguistic particularism. Here, however, we find a first difference. While clearly a unifying factor in Corsica, language is potentially a divisive element in Brittany, since only the western half of the region is historically Gaelic-speaking.[17] The region's political centers of gravity, moreover, whether the historic capital of Nantes or the present center of Rennes, have always been in the non-Gaelic region, where romance dialects have long since given way to French.

Both regions, finally, have known a revival of nationalist agitation, including violence, immediately after World War II. In Brittany, this was the work of groups going by labels such as the *Front de Libération Breton* and the *Armée Révolutionnaire Bretonne* in the 1960s and early 1970s. The latter, especially, did not eschew violent methods, carrying out some thirty attacks with explosives against public buildings in those years. Faced with a near-total lack of internal support, however, these organizations largely disbanded in the later 1970s, and are not presently active. In Corsica, on the other hand, the rise of the *Front National de Libération Corse* (FLNC) in the 1970s marked the beginning of a campaign of violence which, if sporadic, has nonetheless persisted until the present.

Responses from the Center

Both Corsica and Brittany are regions that have sought special attention from Parisien authorities. To a certain degree, both have received it. The nature and scope of this attention, however, has been quite different. With Brittany we see, in a sense, the outer limits of normal regional policy, at least since World War II. Because Brittany has never been considered legally distinct, policy toward the region has tended to take to the farthest permissible point programs available in principle to all. Corsica, on the other hand, has always been seen as different. As we shall see, however, central reaction to this perceived difference has not been consistent.

Since the 1950s, Brittany has been a showplace for *aménagement de territoire*. Massive investment in road and rail infrastructure, in particular, has gone far to ease the problem of geographical remoteness. This has been done, however, in the context of a politically and administratively ordinary set of policies. No official concession has been made to regional distinctiveness; Brittany has done well out of programs and policies available to all regions.

Such is not the case for Corsica. While the island was an ordinary part of France for political and administrative purposes, it has long been the target of distinct economic, political, and fiscal treatment. In part, this was involuntary or at least unplanned. The French state in the early twentieth century began transferring resources to the island in the form of disproportionate spending on public works but also and especially pensions and support for a bloated public payroll. Transfers from the national government have been estimated at 40 percent of aggregate income on the island as early as the 1930s (Andreani 1999, 168) The comparable figure for the 1990s is nearly 50 percent.[18]

On the political and administrative dimension, Breton elites were at the forefront of those calling, from the 1950s through the 1980s, for a devolution of practical decision-making authority to the regions in general, and have made good use of that authority once received. There was never a serious demand, however, that Brittany be formally accorded a distinctive legal or constitutional status.

The question of a formal special status for Corsica, on the other hand, has been open for two centuries, but until recently it remained without any concrete answer. Nineteenth- and early-twentieth-century regimes, including those of the two Bonapartes, limited themselves to confirming limited fiscal advantages to the island and maintaining certain aspects of legal distinctiveness, especially in matters of inheritance and land tenure. Under the Fifth Republic, matters have gone farther. Corsica was recognized as an administrative region in 1970, and after 1981 the government of François Mitterrand put in place a series of reforms in the island's legal status.

The first of these, in 1982, did little more than anticipate in Corsica the regionalization that would be applied to all of France as of 1986. A regional council was elected and its president invested with the executive powers previously held by the *préfet*. The regional council was accorded a limited power of taxation and responsibility for areas such as secondary education, economic development, and transport.

In 1991, a second reform law went farther, granting to the regional council— now renamed *assemblé de la Corse*—a unique organizational model and additional powers not granted to "ordinary" regions.[19] Alone among regional representative bodies, the *assemblé de la Corse* separates executive from legislative functions. When it first convenes after a general election, the assembly elects an executive council consisting of seven members. Members of the council must forthwith resign their assembly seats and function as a ministerial cabinet, electing their own chairman (distinct from the president elected by the assembly as a whole). Once in place, the council cannot be sanctioned or removed by the assembly for the remainder of its five-year term.

In addition to the responsibilities common to all regions, the Corsican assembly has jurisdiction over cultural and linguistic questions (although the status of French as the sole official language cannot be questioned), and, most important from the financial point of view, broad authority over transportation infrastructure including the so-called *routes nationales* on the island.

In fiscal matters, a series of measures has contributed to creating a regime quite different from that of continental regions. Corsica depends far less on direct taxation than most regions, making up for this by broad powers of indirect taxation on items ranging from tobacco to motor fuel. When combined with direct transfers from the center, many of these also unique to Corsica, the result is a budget out of all proportion to the island's population.[20] Last among the twenty-one metropolitan French regions in terms of population, Corsica ranks thirteenth in terms of global budget and first in terms of per capita budget.[21]

Toward an Explanation for Diversity: The Role of Elite Cohesion

Description of state action in the two regions raises as many questions as it answers. Why was the state's limited economic intervention in Brittany so successful, while a much greater effort in Corsica has brought little lasting economic benefit and seems actually to have aggravated social tensions? The answer, I suggest, lies in the first instance not with the national state, its policies or its institutions, but rather within the regions themselves. It is to the study of regional society and politics that we therefore turn.

CORSICA: A DUAL SOCIAL FRACTURE

Observers of Corsican politics since the early nineteenth century are unanimous in underlining its clientelist nature. For Briquet (1997, 41), "any political analysis of Corsica is immediately confronted with the study of the 'clan.' " We must be wary of false analogies in adopting this terminology. A clan in this context does not connote, as it would in the Scottish highlands, an extended kinship group. What is designated, rather, is very precisely a multilevel network of political patron-client relations.

After the stabilization of parliamentary democracy in France in the 1870s, the clans took on party labels, corresponding roughly to the leading forces of the left and right in French politics of the time. With a few exceptions, however, these were little more than flags of convenience thinly veiling the realities of clientelism. Illustrative of this was the fact that the fortunes of parties in Corsica seldom followed that of their continental namesakes. The strength of the Radical Party on the island well into the 1980s, long after it had been reduced to insignificance elsewhere, stands as a recent, but by no means unique, example of this phenomenon.

Party labels notwithstanding, the clans of Corsica were and remain personalistic in nature, primarily the instruments of power of a given individual or family. Conflict among them was the result not of ideological difference but of competition for clients or of purely personal conflicts among leaders—Corsica is, after all, home to a deep-seated tradition of personal vendetta. Barring conflicts of this sort, it was entirely possible for clans to coexist and even to form alliances.

Partial exceptions to this rule in the twentieth century were the Gaullist and communist movements, each of which, at least initially, represented a genuine ideological groundswell and seemed to embody the potential for a crosscutting ideological opposition to the clan system. In each case, however, the clan system survived and what had begun as ideological movements were co-opted as labels for local *notables*. Gaullists and Communists, in other words, became clans in their own right.

An important and historically consistent feature of Corsican clientelism is its fragmentation. On no occasion has a single clan ever attained island-wide hegemony. The most common pattern has been for two meta-clans of roughly equal strength, each owing allegiance to a local politician of national stature, to share power more or less amicably. In addition to the effects common to all clientelist systems, thus, Corsican clanism has consistently been a force for political and social fragmentation.

The central state, through its regulatory and economic support functions, has unwittingly provided the lifeblood of the clan system for the past century. Since the mid-nineteenth century, clan leaders have derived the bulk of their power from control over the distribution of state resources. The institutional resources exploited by the clans are not unique to Corsica. Allocating public employment, issuing licenses and permits, and determining eligibility for various state subsidies and development programs are all normal functions of local elected officials throughout France. What is different on the island is the systematic use of these resources as the currency of political exchange.

To students of comparative clientelism, this description of the clans of Corsican politics and their tactics is likely to be unsurprising. Corsican politics analyzed at this level seem entirely typical of the clientelist degradation of economically dependent peripheral areas. That it is considered unusual to the point of pathology in France speaks well of the political and administrative practices and mores of the rest of the Republic.

An essential point to bear in mind when considering the role of the clans is that their position as the obligatory intermediary between citizens and public power means that their power is not tied to the perpetuation of a traditional society or economy. Quite to the contrary, they have been the principal beneficiaries of a generation of efforts on the part of French authorities to develop the island economically. Clientelism, we must insist, is not a form of archaism; it is not likely to be overturned by modernization.[22]

It is precisely because it has benefited from economic modernization—or more accurately, from state efforts intended to promote modernization—that the clan system is fundamentally conservative in its political role. Whether they choose, for tactical reasons, to fly the flag of the parties of the left or right, Corsican politicians have traditionally been united in defense of the status quo. As things stand, the clan system is superbly adapted to its principal function of mediating between Corsica and Parisien authority—and not coincidentally of ensuring long and prosperous careers for its leaders.

For this reason, the traditional politicians of Corsica have never been anti-French. Nor, until very recently, have they sought special status for the island—the reforms of the 1980s and, in particular the creation of a single regional assembly with significant power, were largely carried out against their wishes (Briquet 1997, 284). Once it was in place, nevertheless, the traditional elite quickly succeeded in taking control of the newly created regional assembly. Jean-Paul de Roca Serra, a third-generation clan leader from

Porto Vechio, in southern Corsica, became its president in 1984 and served in that capacity until his death. His successor, Jose Rossi, is a "new man" in the sense that he is not directly heir to an existing clan, but his personal career path, expanding a local base to regional prominence, mirrors that of his predecessor (Briquet 1997, 198).

Against this backdrop of a century of profoundly conservative republican clientelism, the rise of militant separatist movements since the 1960s should be seen as a dual revolt against the clans and the political system they embody on the one hand, and against externally imposed modernization on the other.

The birth of the modern separatist movement in Corsica is linked directly to one of the earliest attempts of the French state to promote economic development in Corsica by putting into production coastal lands traditionally left unworked due to the threat of malaria. Although this program was, in principle, open to anyone, it is undeniable that among the first to take advantage of it were not native Corsicans but rather French refugees from newly independent Algeria, the so-called *pieds noirs*. The first violent manifestations of separatist sentiment in Corsica came with bomb attacks against *pied noir* property in the mid-1960s (Loughlin and Daftary 1998).

From these beginnings, various clandestine groups emerged in the late 1960s, among which the most important was the *Union du Peuple Corse* (UPC), led by Max and Edouard Simeoni. It was this group that engaged in the occupation of the *pied noir*-owned winery at Aleria in 1974 in which the heavy-handed response of the French security forces led to the first deaths of the separatist campaign. Although the Simeoni brothers themselves renounced violent means soon thereafter, becoming the intellectual leaders of a more moderate autonomist ideology, many others did not. By 1976, the *Front de Liberation National Corse* (FLNC) was created, bringing together the groups most dedicated to armed struggle (Loughlin and Letamendia 2000). The targets of the FLNC soon expanded beyond the *pied noirs* to include tourist facilities (another symbol of externally imposed development that profited outsiders) and the symbols of public authority such as government buildings both in Corsica and on the French mainland.

Far from embracing the separatist struggle against modernization, the traditional clans adapted themselves easily to economic development. Development funds proved just as easily manipulated to political advantage as any other public money. Nor are the separatists united among themselves. Over the course of the 1990s, the FLNC split into no fewer than five mutually hostile groups. Their rivalry briefly escalated into what has been called—with considerable hyperbole—"civil war." From 1993 to 1996, a series of murders and reprisals among nationalist group left some twenty persons dead (*Le Monde*, August 10, 1999). The reasons behind this breakdown remain obscure. In addition to genuine divisions between those seeking outright independence (a minority even of the separatists) and those wanting some sort of autonomous status for the island, purely personal considerations were certainly at work. The various splinter groups accused each other not only of betrayal but also of collusion with criminal elements. Whatever its original cause, violence was escalated through the time-honored pattern of personal revenge. Such was clearly the case in the murders of Jean-Michel Rossi in August 2000 and Michel Santoni in August 2001. Former leaders of the armed independence struggle, the men were co-authors of a memoir critical of that movement, its excesses, and its alleged links to organized crime (Rossi and Santoni 2000).

On the political level, meanwhile, the special status legislation of the 1990s placed the separatists in a dilemma. Was it to be denounced as one more sham, worked up by collusion of central authorities and their local allies in the clans, or should it be embraced as a genuine opportunity? In effect, the separatists kept both options open. While pursuing their campaign of violence (albeit largely against each other), they also participated in electoral politics through an array of more or less ephemeral parties. The most successful of these since 1992 has been *Corsica Nazione,* the legal front organization of the most extreme wing of the FLNC.

In practice, the electoral fortunes of the separatists have depended not so much on fluctuations in their popular support, which remained throughout the 1990s at roughly 20 percent of the island's electorate, as on their relative unity in any given election. Thus, the separatists did well in 1992, electing thirteen members to the Corsican assembly, but were badly defeated in the 1998 assembly elections largely because they presented a number of competing lists, most of which failed to reach the 5 percent threshold necessary for representation. A year later, after the result of the 1998 election was voided due to charges of fraud, roughly the same number of overall votes as the year before secured for the separatists—once again united around the banner of *Corsica Nazione*—nine assembly seats. In no case, however, have the separatists come close to breaking the monopoly of the traditional clan's control of the island's official institutions. Politically, the situation at the turn of the twenty-first century was locked in stalemate.

BRITTANY: FROM REGIONAL IDENTITY TO POLICY COMMUNITY

In stark contrast to the divisions typical of Corsica, Brittany is a region well known for its more recent organizational successes. The strength and cohesion of the Breton agricultural sector, the fruit of organizational efforts dating back slightly over a century, is well documented (Berger 1972). More recent is the concerted effort on the part of regional elites to encourage industrial development (Phlipponeau 1993; Pasquier 2002). The outcome of this organizational effort is the existence at the regional level of something very much like the territorial policy community described by British political scientists (Rhodes 1986; Marsh and Rhodes 1992).

The origins of the present Breton policy community can be traced directly to efforts by Breton elites in the 1950s and 1960s to break the traditional isolation and fragmentation of their region by organizing to take advantage of the national territorial development programs then underway in France (Le Lanou, 1983). The *comité d'étude et de liaison des intérêts bretons* (CELIB), a coordination committee bringing together politicians, businesspeople, and academics, was organized in 1950 for the explicit purpose of presenting a common front to the authorities in Paris. Its strategy was constructed around three central principles (Pasquier 2002):

• mobilization of all regional actors across party lines
• an explicit focus on economic development, rather than on political or cultural issues
• a commitment to work with central authorities, rather than to oppose or compete with them, with the short-term goal of ensuring priority for Brittany in national planning and investment schemes

In its initial period, roughly through the mid-1970s, this policy community was remarkably successful in meeting its self-imposed objectives. Brittany, as noted above, became the model region for *aménagement du territoire*. Concretely, this period witnessed the implantation of industry, such as electronics and telecommunication, as well as a major improvement of transport infrastructure.

In addition to its considerable success in directing public and private investment to Brittany, this organizing effort left an institutional legacy of systematic cooperation and solidarity toward the outside world whose effects are still observed and acknowledged (Sainclivier, 1991). This heritage has provided a set of institutional as well as interpersonal relations on which regional authorities in the 1980s and 1990s have based their European policy. This is the case, moreover, despite the decline in importance of the CELIB itself, a victim of personal splits and political competition among its founders (Martray 1983; Phlipponeau 1986). Once in place, the Breton policy community has become self-reproducing; it is no longer dependent on any given organizational structure.

NATIONAL ADMINISTRATION: AN AMPLIFIER OF DIVERSITY

In Brittany, the fact that the administration was faced with a cohesive and insistent, but constructive and fundamentally nonthreatening, regional interlocutor gave it considerable incentive to collaborate with regional elites rather than seek to oppose them. No motivation beyond self-interest and a certain degree of careerism on the part of administrators is necessary to explain this. The *préfet* remains vulnerable to attack by well-connected *notables*.²³ Regional "successes," on the other hand, are so many feathers in the cap of the *préfet* fortunate enough to preside over them, even if his role is merely to facilitate local initiative.

In Corsica similar motivation in different circumstances has led to very different behavior. Here, the internal division of regional elites—and the presence of hostile counterelites—calls for a very different set of strategies for administrators. Several possibilities, all of them suboptimal, have been tried repeatedly. Over and above the shortcomings of each of these tactics, perhaps the greatest weakness of central strategy in Corsica has been the inability to stick with any one of them. Instead, the pattern has been for the state to cycle among periods of repression, dialogue, and more or less malign neglect, with the direct consequence of undermining whatever legitimacy might potentially have been gathered by any of them. The main episodes of this policy cycle include:

1. *Divide and rule:* Corsican *préfets* did this for years, but when applied to the separatists the outcome has been a multiplication of largely unknown opponents.
2. *Indirect rule through local bosses:* Again, this was standard operating procedure, but has become increasingly unsatisfactory, as the bosses themselves have proven unable to control radical elements.
3. *Impose order through repression:* A continuing temptation, but one whose limits are quickly reached—passive support of the population makes it extremely difficult to apprehend suspects while remaining within the bounds of legality. There seems to be good reason to believe that Corsican separatists have been more successful in infiltrating police than the other way around. Meanwhile, the courts and public opinion are increasingly unwilling to countenance any overstepping of legal limits on the part of security forces. This became abundantly clear in the summer of 1999, when the behavior of the *préfet* Bernard Bonnet burst onto the media scene. Sent to Corsica in large part to bring order after the murder of his predecessor, Erignac, presumably by nationalist terrorists, Bonnet proceeded not only to carry out his own parallel investigation of the assassination, but also to take heavy-handed measures against the widespread practice of operating unlicensed bars and restaurants on the island's beaches. Following the revelation that he had employed police to burn down one such *paillote,* Bonnet was sacked and faced criminal charges.

Predictably, the response of the state to the Bonnet affair was to switch from hard to soft tactics. A parliamentary report denounced the excesses and the ineffectiveness of previous policy (*Le Monde,* November 18, 1999). On the heels of this embarrassment, Prime Minister Lionel Jospin opened yet another round of dialogue with Corsican leaders, including both nationalists and traditional politicians. Judged narrowly on public safety grounds, Jospin's initiative cannot be said to have been a resounding success. In addition to the spectacular murders of Rossi and Santoni killings and, more frequently, bombings have continued to be a regular feature of Corsican life.

In fairness, however, the prime minister's emphasis was on a longer-term project. Unlike previous attempts at a soft line, Jospin's initiative succeeded, in the summer of 2000, in producing the outlines of an accord accepted by all but the most intransigent forces on each side (*Le Monde*, July 12, 2000; July 19, 2000; July 21, 2000; August 5, 2000). The principal thrust of the reform was the creation of a single territorial assembly in Corsica (superseding the two *départments*) and, in a significant departure from past French practice, the delegation to this assembly of the power to pass secondary legislation—that is, to adapt national laws to the special conditions of the island. This key aspect of the reform, however, was subsequently overturned by the French constitutional council (Conseil Constitutionel, 2002), which held that this was an impermissible delegation of the national assembly's constitutional monopoly on legislative authority. Remaining in place were provisions encouraging the teaching of the Corsican language in public schools and generally reinforcing Corsica's cultural autonomy and, ironically perhaps, bringing land-use regulations on the island in line with those in force in the rest of France. Thus watered down, the law was finally promulgated by President Chirac in January 2002.

It is far too early, as of this writing, to know what the long-term consequences of the new law will be or even whether it will ever be fully implemented. Taken to its extreme conclusion, it might represent the first step in a quasi-federal arrangement for the island, although the decision of the constitutional council makes this prospect even more remote. More probably, if past experience is any guide, it may be yet another episode in the cycle of repression, neglect, and opening.

A potentially hopeful sign, nevertheless, is that, for the first, time, the traditional political elite of Corsica have taken the lead in calling for institutional innovation (*Le Monde*, July 13, 2000). While it is tempting for the cynical observer to attribute their born-again regionalism to political expediency, this in itself may not be a bad thing. As they are gradually implemented, the reforms of 2000 may create for the first time in Corsica's modern history a situation in which it is politically more profitable for men of personal and political ambition to seek a role as a unifier and genuine regional leader than to play the time-honored game of fragmented clientelism. At this point, however, such a development lies in a highly uncertain future. If we take the past as a guide, the conclusions of this study are less optimistic—although of considerable analytic interest.

Conclusion: The Importance and Limits of Institutional Explanations

The discussion above leaves us with two obvious questions. The first concerns ultimate causes: why did Breton elites succeed in their quest for regional unity while those of Corsica have, to date at least, failed? The second concerns the organizing question of this volume: did national institutions matter at all in this case? With respect to the first question, a definitive answer is, without a doubt, beyond the bounds of this, and perhaps of any, essay. A few preliminary reflections, nevertheless, may be in order. These, in turn, shed light on our second question.

In the first place, we can note some important differences in premodern society in the two regions—bearing in mind that, in both cases, the premodern period extends well into the twentieth century. Of the two, ironically, Breton society seems originally to have been the more fragmented, lacking even the clan structures that characterized Corsica. While respect for traditional hierarchies, and most especially for the Catholic Church, remained very strong in Brittany, agrarian reformers in the late nineteenth century were forced to struggle for decades with the deep-seated suspicion of the rural population of *any* form of organization (Berger 1972). Brittany's nineteenth-century elites, meanwhile, were distinctly more antirepublican, indeed antidemocratic, than their Corsican opposite numbers. Brittany remained a stronghold of monarchism and clericalism long after Corsican *notables* had happily accommodated themselves to the new regime.

Putting these two observations together, what is striking is the lack in Brittany of the democratic clientelism that became the bedrock of Corsican political society over the course of the nineteenth century. Breton elites dominated society by virtue of their predemocratic position in lay or clerical society, not as a result of trading votes for political favors—favors that, in any case, their permanent opposition to the government in place left them singularly ill-equipped to provide. From a sociological point of view, the outcome can be seen as benign neglect. Breton society did not modernize, but neither did it degenerate into clientelism. Elites, for their part, emerged with their social prestige largely intact—untarnished by sordid political exchanges.

As such, conditions did not rule out a priori elite-led organizing efforts of the sort spearheaded by agrarian reformers in the late nineteenth century and the CELIB in the mid-twentieth century. The negative construction of the preceding sentence is intentional. If elite-led organizing efforts were not ruled out, neither were they by any stretch of the imagination assured. The element of voluntarism, and thus of contingency, involved must not be minimized. Regional society provided a necessary but insufficient condition for political mobilization around economic objectives. It is tempting to conclude, however, that it is precisely this necessary condition that has persistently been lacking in Corsica.

For this, the French state and its institutions clearly must bear a share of responsibility. Not only did the same national institutions that brought integration and economic development to Brittany fail spectacularly to do so in Corsica, but attempts in the latter case to use institutional adjustment to meet social and political contestation have proven at best ineffective and at worst counterproductive.

It is in their interaction with diverse patterns of territorial society that French national institutions reveal their full significance. The prefectoral system, it turns out, is much better suited to meeting some types of challenges than others. It can deal well with a unitary interlocutor, even a hostile one. Alternatively, it is able to manage division, if the parties involved are fundamentally nonthreatening.[24] The case of Corsica suggests, however, that the institutions of territorial control available to the French state are particularly ill-suited to dealing with a society that is both hostile and internally divided.

Having reached this conclusion in the context of France and its institutions, it is important to point out that there is, in fact, nothing peculiarly French about it. What emerges from a careful study of the interactions between regional societies and national institutions in France is an illustration of a much more general pattern. Problem regions, according to this line of reasoning, are those where center-periphery conflict is superimposed on a deep-seated local cleavage. Conflicts of class, religion, ethnicity, or ideology, alone or in combination, can be at the source of the cleavage. What seems to matter is less the nature or source of the infraregional antagonism than its permanence and intensity. The worst case is presented when anticenter forces are in opposition both to the national center and to the local elite. From a starting point of twofold marginalization, such forces have little reason to place their hopes in institutional compromise, and every incentive to follow a *politique du pire*—seeking instability for its own sake. Elite-led opposition to central authority, on the other hand, would seem much less prone to deteriorate into violence if not provoked beyond measure by the center itself. In a mirror image of the logic proposed above, peripheral elites have every reason to seek and uphold institutional compromise with the center if this serves to consolidate their local position.

This contrast, I would suggest, is perfectly illustrated in the United Kingdom by the difference between the largely self-enforcing institutional compromise between central and Scottish authorities on the one hand, and the ongoing chaos of Northern Ireland on the other.[25] It is no surprise, in this context, that the Scottish parliament has gotten off to a smooth and largely consensual start, while home rule for Northern Ireland remains stalled.[26]

On a more abstract level these case studies provide a useful illustration of the distinction between institutionally induced preferences (the same in Brittany and Corsica) and context-dependent strategies (very different in the two cases). In both cases, the *préfets* as territorial representatives of the state have sought above all to maintain order and political tranquility. In Brittany, the easiest way to do this has been to collaborate with the unified regional elite, becoming on numerous occasions its ambassador in Paris—and, increasingly, in Brussels. The result, as explored above, has been quite positive from the standpoint of good government. In Corsica, by contrast, the lack of a credible interlocutor has left *préfets* to oscillate between efforts at repression and periods of retrenchment. Neither has proven successful to date.

Should we conclude from this that some other set of institutions might have been—or may still be—more successful in dealing with the island's problems? This is, of course, the thesis of the various autonomist and separatist movements. Their many practical and personal differences notwithstanding, these are unanimous in the claim that Corsica will overcome its internal divisions only when it is granted a much greater degree of political autonomy. Experience to date suggests, to this author at least, a skeptical view of such claims. Existing elites have been remarkably successful to date in co-opting the institutions of autonomy, as these were created in the 1990s. Equally adept is their use, in Paris, of the rhetoric of independence while pursuing, in Corsica, a policy of self-interested accommodation with central authority. There seems little reason to believe that these strategies would not be equally successful if the power of these institutions were extended to the level of genuine autonomy or even sovereign independence.

The nationalist opposition might have to find a new cause in these circumstances, but there is little reason to believe that it would be any less marginalized and aggressive. Their fundamental quarrel is not with France, but with a Corsican elite that excludes them. The institutional mismatch between the French Republic and Corsican society has doubtlessly aggravated the social and political problems of the island, but it is not at their root. Institutional reform by itself is not likely to bring about their solution.

NOTES

1. The qualifier *successful* is intended to exclude the Girondin opposition of the 1790s, defeated by the Jacobins, as well as the federalist movement of 1870, crushed in the defeat of the Paris Commune.

2. The French historian Pierre Deyon goes so far as to speak of the "diabolisation" of the old provinces not only by the revolutionary regime but by all of its republican successors. Reactionary and royalist politicians and thinkers from the restoration of 1815 through the Vichy

regime, by contrast, proclaimed consistent attachment to them—a fact that further ensured the hostility of all republicans (Dupoirier 1998, 21–23).

3. A special case of linguistic resistance is Alsace, under German rule from 1870 to 1918, where the local German dialect remains very much alive to this day.

4. We must be careful, of course, not to equate convergence of interests with automatic success. The record of is mixed with respect both to what was attempted and what was actually done. Particularly good descriptions of these developments in all their nuances are those of Grémion (1976) and Ashford (1982). The regions selected for study in the second half of this chapter include one of the most successful (Brittany) and one of the least (Corsica) in this context.

5. It is a further irony, of course, that the event that precipitated the general's departure was the defeat of a referendum one provision of which was a limited move toward regionalization. This final attempt by De Gaulle to adapt to the changing spirit of the times, however, seems in retrospect to have received little consideration on its merits. The true subject of the referendum was De Gaulle himself, and in 1969 French voters wanted a change at the top.

6. Assemblies elected at the subnational level in France are never referred to either as governments or as legislatures. Of these, France can have only one.

7. It is worth underlining that the demand for decentralization in 1981 came from established political elites. Although Mitterrand spoke clearly of his intentions along these lines during the presidential campaign of 1981, there is little reason to believe that the issue was a particularly salient one for the electorate at large.

8. The main lines of the reform were contained in the law of March 2, 1982. This was followed by the law of July 17, 1982, which dealt with regional planning; of December 31, 1982, which dealt with the particular status of the cities of Paris, Lyon, and Marseille; and of January 7, 1983, and January 25, 1985, which dealt with the distribution of tasks among the various types of territorial assemblies (Greffe, 1992).

9. The method of election retained was proportional representation, with the *département* serving as electoral districts.

10. Change at the level of the *département* was, if anything, more significant than developments at the regional level. Almost twenty years later, the debate over who the real winners of the decentralization reform have been remains open.

11. In this category are found big-city mayors such as Jacques Chaban-Delmas, Pierre Maurois, and Gaston Defferre, all of whom were also long-serving members of parliament, leaders in their respective parties, and holders of major ministerial posts. Even politicians whose principal activity was at the national level felt the need for a local base. In this way François Mitterrand was the long-serving mayor of the small town of Château-Chinon, while Jacques Chirac was active in the politics of the *département* of Coréze.

12. *Le Sacre des Notables* was the title of a 1985 book written under the pseudonym Jacques Rondin by a group of academics and senior civil servants.

13. The all-important area of economic development provides numerous illustrations of this problem. While the regions were given general responsibility for economic planning (in partnership with the state's central planning agencies) and a general mandate to promote economic development, the *département* retained responsibility for *aménagement rural*—a term including the promotion of agriculture as well as rural infrastructure (Documentation Française, 1985). The social responsibilities of the *département*, in addition, include numerous areas such as education and training with obvious links to economic planning. The precise boundaries between these areas of responsibility remain ill-defined and controversial.

14. For this reason, to speak of higher or lower levels of territorial units is, strictly speaking, incorrect to the extent that it implies the sort of hierarchy typical of federal systems.

15. A clear institutional winner from all of the developments noted above has been the *Secrétariat Général aux Affaires Régionales* (SGAR). Headed by a senior civil servant, this unit is responsible in each regional *préfecture* for coordinating all regional activities of the state, including the management of the European structural funds.

16. The reform that, more than any other, could break this domination would be the abolition of the *cumul de mandats*. Although much spoken of, however, this remains elusive.

17. The Breton language is closely related to Welsh Gaelic and, much more distantly, to Irish. The linguistic divide separating the *pays Breton* in the west from the French-speaking *pays Gallo* in the east is one of the most studied and, seemingly, most stable sociolinguistic features of France. So far as can be established, it has shifted to the west by less than 100 kilometers since the time of its farthest extension, around the year 1000. More concretely, the line has remained almost perfectly stable since the mid-nineteenth century (Le Lanou 1983).

18. These numbers are admittedly vague. The recent figure, estimated for the year 1994, was arrived at by comparing Corsica's aggregate GDP for that year, 25.5 billion francs, with an estimate of total central transfers to the island (including pensions as well as wages and benefits of public servants), approximately 12 billion francs. It is this last figure, drawn from a 1994 parliamentary report (cited by Adreani 1999, 207) that requires careful interpretation. Since it considers only spending and not tax revenue drawn from the island (5 billion francs, according to the same source) it is clearly not a fair measure of the cost of Corsica to the French state. For our purposes, however, it seems a reasonable illustration of the weight of central transfers in the local economy.

19. The change of name was symbolically significant, the designation *assembly* having heretofore been applied only to the lower house of the national parliament. The original text of the reform went even further, referring in its first article to the existence of a "Corsican people" (*peuple Corse*), but this clause was invalidated by the constitutional council as being incompatible with the constitutional provision that the French Republic is "one and indivisible."

20. Among the unique transfers is the *prime de continuité territoriale*, a subsidy on transport costs intended to offset the excessive costs associated with insularity. In principle, this subsidy brings the cost of shipping freight and passengers to the island to the level of shipping an equivalent distance over land.

21. These figures are based on budgets for the year 1997, as reported in Huguenin and Martinat (1998).

22. The successful adaptation of the clan system to modern politics and society is the principal thesis of Briquet (1997). The dynamic he depicts is one of convergence between traditional patrons who have learned to manipulate the outputs of the modern French state and would-be reformers who find themselves with no option but to develop a client network of their own if they wish to succeed electorally. In the end, Briquet notes, the two types become indistinguishable to the naked eye.

23. As one prefectoral official put it in conversation with me, "Le préfet est nommé en Conseil des Ministres . . . tout les Mercredis"—implying that he can be revoked at any time by the government without explanation if sufficient political pressure is applied.

24. Although not considered in this essay, illustrations of this dynamic can be found in the experience of regions such as Languedoc-Roussillon and Provence-Alpes-Côte d'Azur. For analysis of these regions (and comparison with Brittany), see Smyrl (1997).

25. Catalonia provides an obvious additional example of successful elite-led peripheral nationalism while the Spanish Basque Country illustrates an oppositional dynamic. Belgian Flanders and Quebec represent interesting hybrid cases in which peripheral forces that began as opposition to indigenous elites have now achieved political supremacy—solid in Flanders, still tenuous in Quebec.

26. The case of Wales, divided but nonthreatening, is analogous to the southern French regions evoked above.

REFERENCES

Adreani, Jean-Louis. 1999. *Comprendre la Corse.* Paris: Folio Actuel.

Ashford, Douglas. 1982. *British Dogmatism and French Pragmatism.* London: Allen and Unwin.

Behrens, Petra, and Marc Smyrl. 1999. A Conflict of Rationalities: EU Regional Policy and the Single Market. *Journal of European Public Policy* 6, no. 2:419–35.

Berger, Suzanne. 1972. *Peasants Against Politics: Rural Organization in Brittany, 1911-1967.* Cambridge, Mass.: Harvard University Press.

Briquet, Jean-Louis. 1997. *La Tradition en Mouvement: Clientelisme et Politique en Corse.* Paris: Belin.

Conseil Constitutionel. 2002. *Décision N°2001-454 DC.* La Loi sur la Corse.

Documentation Française. 1985. La Décentralisation en Marche. *Cahiers Français* 220.

Dupoirier, Elizabeth, ed. 1998. *Régions, la Croisée des Chemins: Perspectives Françaises et Enjeux Européens.* Paris: Presses de Sciences Po—Collection Références.

Greffe, Xavier. 1992. *La Décentralisation.* Paris: Editions de la Découverte.

Grémion, Pierre. 1976. *Le Pouvoir Périphérique.* Paris: Editions du Seuil.

Huguenin, Jacques, and Patrick Martinat. 1998. *Les Régions: Entre l'Etat et l'Europe.* Paris: Le Monde Editions.

Le Lannou, Maurice. 1983. *La Bretagne et les Bretons.* 2d ed. Paris: Presses Universitaires de France (Que Sai'je).

Loughlin, John, and Farimah Daftary. 1998. *Insular Regions and European Integration: Corsica and the Aland Islands Compared.* Helsinki: European Center for Minority Issues.

Loughlin, John, and Francesco Letamendia. 2000. Peace in the Basque Country and Corsica? In *A Farewell to Arms? From Long War to Long Peace in Northern Ireland,* ed. Mick Cox, Adrian Guelke, and Fiona Stephens. Manchester: Manchester University Press.

Marsh, David, and R.A.W. Rhodes. 1992. Policy Communities and Issue Networks: Beyond Typologies. In *Policy Networks in British Government,* ed. David Marsh and R.A.W. Rhodes. Oxford: Clarendon.

Mény, Yves. 1974. *Centralisation et Décentralisation Dans le Débat Politique Français.* Paris: Librairie Generale de Droit et de Jurisprudence.

Pasquier, Romain. 2002. Territorial Elites and Regional Identity. In *Between Europeanization and Local Society: Political Actors and Territorial Governance,* ed. Jeanie Bukowsi, Simona Piattoni, and Marc Smyrl. Lanham, Md.: Rowman and Littlefield.

Phlipponeau, Michel. 1986. *Géopolitique de la Bretagne.* Rennes: Ouest France.

Quermone, Jean-Louis. 1998. La Genèse Institutionelledes Régions en France au Regard des Principaux Pays Européens. In *Régions, la Croisée des Chemins: Perspectives Françaises et Enjeux Européens,* ed. Elizabeth Dupoirier. Paris: Presses de Sciences Po—Collection Références.

Quinet, Emile. 1990. *La Planification Française.* Paris: Presses Universitaires de France (Que Sais-je?).

Rhodes. R.A.W. 1986. *Beyond Westminster and Whitehall: The Sub-central Governments of Britain.* London: Urwin Hyman Ltd.

Rondin, Jacques. 1985. *Le Sacre des Notables.* Paris: Fayard.

Rossi, Jean-Michel, and Santoni, François. 2000. *Pour Solde de Tout Compte: Entretiens avec Guy Benhamou.* Paris. Denoël.

Sainclivier, Jacqueline. 1991. The Economic Structure and Development of Brittany since the 17th Century. In *Centre and Periphery: Brittany, Cornwall and Devon Compared,* ed. Michael Havinden, Jean Queniart, and Jeffrey Stanyer. Exeter: University of Exeter Press.

Smyrl, Marc. 1997. Did EC Regional Policy Empower the Regions? *Governance* 10, no. 3:287–309.

Turpin, Dominique. 1987. *La Région.* Paris: Economica.

Weber, Eugen. 1976. *Peasants into Frenchmen.* Stanford: Stanford University Press.

Worms, Jean-Pierre. 1966. Le Préfet et ses Notables. *Sociologie du Travail* 8, no. 3.

Wright, Vincent. 1979. Regionalization Under the French Fifth Republic: The Triumph of the Functionalist Approach. In *Decentralist Trends in Western Democracies,* ed. L. J. Sharpe. London: Sage.

CHAPTER EIGHT

Electoral Rules and Party Systems in Federations

R. Kent Weaver

Federalism and electoral rules are usually seen as two distinctive mechanisms for managing societal conflict in general and territorial conflicts in particular (see, for example, Lijphart, Rogowski, and Weaver 1993; Lijphart 1999). Electoral rules that provide for some element of proportionality in legislative elections, for example, are frequently viewed as consociational mechanisms that allow the concerns of many different groups and interests to be expressed rather than polarizing around a single dominant cleavage. This can be particularly effective at protecting minority interests when it is combined with other consociational mechanisms such as oversized coalitions and informal norms of cabinet selection (in parliamentary systems) that reach across major cleavage lines.

Federalism, on the other hand, is viewed as a quite different mechanism for limiting the rule of national majorities: instead of consensus building across cleavage lines at the national level, conflict is managed by *devolving* decisions to geographic subunits, where decision making in turn may be managed either through majoritarian or majority-limiting mechanisms. Devolution may in fact leave regional minority groups—Spanish speakers in Catalunya, Francophones in Ontario and the Canadian prairie provinces, Catholics in Northern Ireland, for example—less well protected than they would be if the central government took a more active role.

As this simple example suggests, federalism and electoral rules need to be examined not just in isolation, but also in interaction. This chapter analyzes that interaction. It has four sections. First, I lay out some simple propositions about the effects that electoral systems have on various aspects of party systems and conflict management. Second, I review quickly the patterns of choices of electoral rules that emerge as we look across federations, especially those in the industrialized world. For example, are there similarities across systems in the electoral rules that federal countries utilize? Are there similarities in electoral rules within systems, that is, do countries tend to use the same electoral rules in national and subnational elections, or do different rules arise at each level? Third, I draw some tentative conclusions about how different electoral rules affect the integration of political parties and party systems across levels of governments within countries. I suggest several indicators that can be used to measure these phenomena cross-nationally. Fourth, I examine the impact of different sets of electoral rules on conflict management and governability in federal countries. While some of the data in the chapter draw on a variety of countries with federal institutions, the bulk of the analysis focuses on what can be called the older, richer, Organization for Economic Cooperation and Development (OECD) countries of Western Europe, North America, and Australasia.

Varieties of Electoral Systems

Electoral systems can differ in an almost infinite variety of ways (for more complete discussions, see Taagepera and Shugart 1989, Sartori 1997, Lijphart 1999). In reviewing the institutional effects of different sets of electoral rules, it is helpful to begin with the polar opposite cases, single-member plurality (SMP), also known as first-past-the-post (FPTP), and closed list proportional representation (PR), and then discuss intermediate cases. The focus here will be on legislative elections rather than selection rules for chief executives, in systems where the latter are separately elected.

Single-member plurality electoral rules, as the name implies, involve one-person legislative districts, in which the person who receives the most votes is declared elected, regardless of whether that vote share is a majority or not. The very large literature on electoral systems has identified a number of consequences associated with SMP electoral rules:

1. SMP tends to restrict the number of political parties that are potential contenders for office, and creates a tendency toward a two-party system—for example, in the United Kingdom, the United States, and New Zealand prior to 1996 (see Gaines 1999).

2. SMP facilitates creation of single-party majority governments by turning pluralities of votes into a majority of legislative seats, although this outcome is by no
   means guaranteed and is less likely to occur when territorially based cleavages
   allow minor parties to gain a significant share of legislative seats because their
   supporters are concentrated in specific regions.

3. SMP leads to some votes being worth more than others in vote-to-seat conversions. In particular, relatively small parties whose support is diffused across the
   whole political system without a territorial stronghold are likely to be severely
   punished in vote-seat conversions, while parties of similar size with geographically
   concentrated support may get a bonus.

4. SMP tends to lead to centrist, nonideological pragmatic or brokerage politics as
   parties compete for the median voter. However, significant policy swings may
   occur when there is a change in government if parties move away from median
   voter positions on some issues.

5. SMP increases incentives for strategic voting, since a vote for a minor party candidate may be wasted, leading to a voter's least preferred candidate getting elected.

In addition to these general effects, critics of SMP have noted that it may have a
number of (mostly harmful) additional effects as well. When used at the national level,
it may lead to the exacerbation of regional cleavages, since it tends to exaggerate the advantage enjoyed by the largest political party in a region in vote-seat conversions and
to punish relatively smaller parties. In combination with the tendency of SMP to promote single-party majority governments (in parliamentary systems), one danger in a
country with strong territorially based cleavages is that one region may end up dramatically overrepresented in the governing party, while another region may end up
with virtually no representatives in the governing party caucus and cabinet.
Perceptions of regional exclusion and grievance are therefore reinforced (see the chapters on the United Kingdom and Canada in this volume, as well as Cairns 1968;
Wiseman 1991; Weaver 1997; Bakvis and Macpherson 1995).

When used at the state/provincial level, SMP electoral rules may allow the majority
social group in that territory to govern alone, while facilitating consistent exclusion of
ethnic, linguistic, or religious minorities from political power (e.g., in Northern Ireland
prior to the imposition of direct rule from London). SMP may also allow a political
party that is at best ambivalent or even hostile to national unity to gain a strong power
base through control of a single-party majority government in that state or province,
which can then be used to reinforce autonomist or even proseparation policies and
popular sentiment (Cairns 1977).

It should be noted that SMP is something of a dinosaur: most parliamentary systems in the advanced industrial world—even those without severe territorially based cleavages—have moved away from strict single-member first-past-the-post systems, generally to some sort of proportional representation. New Zealand, for example, recently moved to a German-style system of mixed-member proportional representation, which will be discussed further below. Even the United Kingdom has adopted various forms of proportionality for elections to the Scottish parliament, Welsh assembly, and European Parliament, and opened a debate about introducing it for House of Commons elections (Farrell 2001)

At the other end of the electoral systems spectrum are those using proportional representation (PR). In the party list form of PR, voters choose a party in a multimember district rather than an individual candidate in multimember districts, and the party is awarded seats based on its share of the vote in that district. There are, of course, many variations among proportional representation systems, most notably in (1) the number of seats filled in each electoral district (district magnitude), (2) whether or not there is a legal minimum threshold that a party must pass to win any seats, and (3) whether voters have any choice over individual candidates or must simply endorse a preordered party list. Overall, proportional representation generally has the following effects:

1. Compared to SMP, PR may increase the number of parties that compete in elections, and it almost certainly increases the number of parties that win seats, although how much it does so depends on the electoral rules, notably thresholds and size of electoral districts.

2. Following from #1, PR increases the number of party choices that are available and are likely to be seen by voters as "nonwasted" choices, although the number again varies depending on district magnitude and legal thresholds.

3. PR makes it extremely unlikely that a single party will hold a majority of seats in the legislature, and thus makes either minority or coalition governments the norm in parliamentary systems.

4. Following from point #3, PR increases the probability that the composition of a government, and the policies of that government, will be decided not by the election, but after it, as the result of negotiations among party leaders. However, this attribute may be mitigated by preelectoral alliances and common electoral programs.

5. In most cases, PR weakens the ability of legislators in parties that operate nationwide to act (and be perceived by constituents to act) as regional representatives, since they are likely to be bound by party discipline. Closed-list PR also weakens individual legislators' incentive to act as providers of constituency services, since

the ability of voters to reward individual MPs is lessened. Open-list PR, however, may increase legislators' incentives to provide constituency services and undercut their susceptibility to party discipline.

6. Closed-list PR tends to lead to programmatic parties that seek to make distinctive appeals to relatively narrow shares of the electorate. Open-list PR may undercut parties' programmatic consistency.

Proportional representation may also have important interaction effects with federalism. For example, we might expect that the tendency of proportional representation to produce a profusion of parties might be enhanced by the combination of PR and federalism. Movement toward territorially focused parties in particular may be stimulated by this combination, since the entry barriers for small parties are relatively low and the chance of a modestly sized party sharing in government power at one or both levels of government is higher than under SMP.

There are a number of alternative electoral systems to SMP and PR. The alternative vote (AV), used in elections for the Australian house of representatives, uses single-member districts, but compels voters to list not just a single choice but a ranked set of choices; votes for least-favored candidates are redistributed in stages until one candidate wins a majority. The two-round majority system used in elections for the French chamber of deputies also employs single-member districts and produces majority support for a single candidate in most cases. Both systems are likely to stimulate the existence of more than two parties in a given district and across districts, but fewer than under PR rules. The single transferable vote (STV) operates in multimember districts as in PR, but voters rank individual candidates without regard to party; thus it weakens party leaders' control over whom is elected. Because of the practical difficulties of vote counting and allocation under STV, however, both district magnitude and the number of parties resulting are only modestly larger than under SMP.

Complexities in vote counting under AV and STV, and the added expense of two-round elections, have limited the appeal of these intermediate options. Thus much of the focus of electoral reform in recent years has been on the development of mixed electoral systems, with a combination of single-member districts and seats awarded by proportional representation. Two attributes of such systems are critical in determining the incentives for party fragmentation and the prospects for single-party majority government: (1) the ratio between the number of single-member seats and PR seats, and (2) whether PR seats are awarded as a completely separate tier from the SMP tier or on a basis that compensates parties that did poorly in vote-seat conversions in the SMP seats. Where the two types of seats are relatively equal in number and awarded on a compensatory basis, as in the Federal Republic of Germany and New Zealand, something close to full proportionality in translation of seats into votes is achieved. Indeed, such systems are generally known as mixed-member proportional (MMP) systems (see, for example, Kaase 1984; Shugart and Wattenberg 2001).

While MMP tends to lower the number of parties over that found in most pure proportional systems (especially when combined with high electoral thresholds as in Germany), the prospects for single-party majority government under MMP are nonetheless minimal. Where the percentage of PR seats is small and awarded parallel to SMP seats rather than on a compensatory basis, the number of political parties is likely to be smaller and prospects for single-party majority government higher. This option is generally referred to as mixed-member majoritarian (MMM).

Patterns

Before examining how electoral rules affect party systems and governance in federations, it is important to get a general lay of the land. Table 8.1 provides a preliminary list of electoral rules for national first and second chambers, national executives, and provincial legislatures in a number of federal systems. Several patterns and nonpatterns are evident in this table. Most generally, there is no clear relationship cross-nationally between having a federal system and a particular set of electoral rules at either the national or subnational level. Federalism is consistent with a variety of electoral systems—with separation of powers or parliamentarism, with varying degrees of proportionality, and with concurrent or nonconcurrent elections—at the national level and at the territorial level.

First Chambers

Not only is federalism consistent with many electoral systems, Table 8.2 shows that it is also consistent with a very wide variation in the effective number of parties in the lower chamber of national legislatures (on the definition and calculation of the effective number of parties, see Taagepera and Shugart 1989, 78–80). Previous research suggests that both institutional variables (notably district magnitudes, electoral thresholds, and presence or absence of concurrent presidential elections decided by plurality) and the degree of ethnic-linguistic fractionalization in a country have a very strong effect on the effective number of parties: more complex social fragmentation and electoral rules that do not discriminate against relatively small parties expand the number of legislative parties (see, for example, Taagepera and Shugart 1989; Ordeshook and Shvetsova 1994; Amorim Neto and Cox 1997).

We might also expect that federalism could have an impact on the effective number of parties. In particular, federalism may stimulate the growth of province- or region-

Table 8.1 Types of Electoral Systems

Electoral System Type	Examples	Comments/Important Characteristics
Single-Member Plurality (SMP): candidates run in single-member districts; highest vote-winner (first-past-the-post) wins seat	U.K. and Canadian House of Commons; U.S. Congress; New Zealand prior to 1996	Tends to produce single-party majority government with plurality of popular vote; usually produces least proportional outcomes of all electoral systems because smaller parties (especially those with geographically diffuse support) are highly disadvantaged
Alternative Vote (AV): candidates run in single-member districts; voters rank candidates and votes of candidates with fewest votes are redistributed until one candidate wins a majority	Australian House of Representatives; some Canadian provincial elections prior to 1950s	Encourages development of more than two parties; facilitates single-party majority government or small coalitions
Two-Round Majority: candidates run in single-member districts; two (or more) top vote-winners run in run-off election	French National Assembly (most elections)	Disadvantages small parties with geographically diffuse support
Mixed-Member Majoritarian: most seats awarded by SMP; small percentage of total seats awarded by P.R. as additive or compensation seats	Mexico prior to 1990s; Italian Chamber of Deputies; proposed for United Kingdom	Prospects for single-party majority depend heavily on geographic division of major party vote and (in Italy) rules on cross-party coalition formation
Single Nontransferable Vote (SNTV): voters choose one candidate in multimember district; candidates with most votes wins	Japan prior to 1994	Prospects for single-party majority government depend partially on district size as well as skill of parties in nominating right number of candidates and allocating votes among them to avoid wasting votes
Single-Transferable Vote (STV): Voters rank candidates in multimember districts; excess votes for winning candidates and votes of least popular candidates are redistributed to fill seats	Ireland; Australian Senate; Northern Ireland	Minimizes role of party leaders in choosing which of a party's candidates are elected; allows voter to allocate preferences across parties

(Continued)

Table 8.1 — Continued

Electoral System Type	Examples	Comments/Important Characteristics
Mixed-Member Proportional: substantial percentage of seats awarded by SMP; substantial percentage of seats awarded by P.R. as additive or compensation seats	Germany; New Zealand since 1996; Scottish and Welsh assemblies (planned)	Single-party majority governments highly unusual; degree of proportionality depends on whether PR seats are additional or compensatory, as well as district magnitude, minimum threshold for winning seats, and electoral formula used in awarding seats
Proportional Representation (PR): Seats awarded in multimember districts by party share of popular vote	Israel; Netherlands; Sweden	Single-party majority governments highly unusual; degree of proportionality depends on district magnitude, minimum threshold for winning seats and electoral formula used in awarding seats. Level of party leadership control depends on whether lists are open or closed

Note: The electoral systems presented are roughly ordered by degree of proportionality.

specific parties that then compete and win seats federally, fragmenting party representation in the national legislature. This effect is likely to be mediated, however, by whether federal and provincial elections take place simultaneously or not. In general, we would expect concurrent elections to stimulate votes for parties that operate at and have some prospect for winning at both levels of government. It may also allow for some efficiencies in campaign organization and advertising.

There is little evidence, however, that federalism has an *independent* effect on the degree of fragmentation in a legislature. Indeed Anckar (1999) has found that it does not, while Mainwaring and Shugart (1997, 417), using evidence from Latin America, argue that party fragmentation is most likely to occur in separation-of-powers systems combined with party list PR, where parties "grow up around local gubernatorial races." Mixed results of the impact of federalism on party fragmentation are not surprising, because (1) a very high degree of variance in the level of party fragmentation is already explained by other variables, such as population size and degree of ethnic/linguistic fractionalization that may be correlated with the existence of federalism, and (2) the level of variation in the effective number of parties in federal systems is so high. Indeed, two federations with concurrent federal and state elections—the United States and Brazil—currently have among the lowest and highest effective numbers of legislative parties, respectively. Federations with nonconcurrent federal and provincial elections also vary dramatically in their effective numbers of parties.

Bicameralism

There is a very strong association, evident in Table 8.2, between federalism and having a two-chamber national legislature, with the provinces/states generally playing a distinctive role in the upper chamber. While unicameralism is common at both the national and subnational levels worldwide, all of the countries shown in Table 8.2 are bicameral at the national level, as are virtually all federations worldwide—the tiny Federated States of Micronesia is a rare exception (Anckar 1999). Canada is also a partial exception, since its second chamber is a vestigial body appointed by the federal prime minister, and it is no accident that the senate has persistently been seen as a problematic political institution in Canada. The United Kingdom, with its hereditary and appointive House of Lords—also a vestigial body—is another partial exception.

Second chambers in national legislatures vary widely both in their selection rules and in the degree to which their powers approach or equal those of first chambers (Sharman 1987; Lijphart 1987; Patterson and Mughan 1999). Despite these differences, electoral rules in upper chambers almost always reinforce the role of those legislators as representatives of state/provincial interests by having them selected on a province-wide basis, even where the lower chamber elections occur in much smaller electoral districts. The most common situation is that states/provinces serve as the electoral district for second chamber elections, either in single-member districts, as in the United States, or multimember districts, as in Australia and Switzerland. In several countries, provinces play a direct role in selecting members of the national upper chamber. This can take several forms. In the case of the German Bundesrat, the *Länder* delegations are direct appointees of the *Länd* governments. Provincial legislatures (rather than executives) choose most members of the Indian Rajya Sabha, and autonomous community legislatures choose a minority of members of the Spanish senate; the Belgian senate is a hybrid of directly elected members, those delegated by regional councils, and additional members appointed by the first two groups.[1] This, then, suggests a third conclusion about upper chambers in federations: that they are more likely than first chambers to be hybrids of members selected in several quite distinct ways (as opposed to the distinctive but integrated mechanisms in mixed-member systems that are increasingly used in national first chamber elections).

Table 8.2 *Legislative Characteristics in Selected Federations*

Country	National First Chamber		National Upper Chamber		National Executive	Provincial/State Legislature	Synchronization of National and Provincial Elections
	Electoral Rules	Effective Number of Legislative Parties	Electoral Rules	Disproportionality in Representation of Territorial Subunits			
Australia	AV	2.38	STV by states; equal representation of states	Moderate	Leader of party(ies) with plurality or majority of seats	Bicameral legislatures in five of six states: mostly AV in lower chamber, upper chambers are AV in some states, STV in others	No
Belgium	PR	7.01	Combination of directly elected, indirectly elected by linguistic community councils and co-opted	Low	Leader of a party in a coalition having majority of seats	PR	No, except in 1999
Brazil	PR; very highly disproportional representation of states	8.69	PR by states; equal representation of states	Extremely high	Separately elected by two-round majority	Statewide PR	Yes

(Continued)

Table 8.2 — Continued

| Country | National First Chamber | | National Upper Chamber | | National Executive | Provincial/ State Legislature | Synchronization of National and Provincial Elections |
	Electoral Rules	Effective Number of Legislative Parties	Electoral Rules	Disproportionality in Representation of Territorial Subunits			
Canada	SMP in highly disproportional districts	1.69	Vestigial body is appointed by federal prime minister	Moderate	Leader of party with plurality or majority of seats; always single-party cabinets	SMP with moderately disproportional seat allocation	No
Germany	MMP	3.16	Appointed by *Länd* governments; weighted representation of *Länder*	Moderate	Leader of party(ies) with plurality or majority of seats	MMP in all but three *Länder*, where PR is used	No
India	SMP	1.69	Mostly elected by state legislatures by STV for fixed terms; minority nominated by president; weighted representation of states	Low	Leader of party(ies) with plurality or majority of seats	SMP; some states have two chambers	No

(Continued)

Table 8.2 — Continued

Country	National First Chamber		National Upper Chamber		National Executive	Provincial/State Legislature	Synchronization of National and Provincial Elections
	Electoral Rules	Effective Number of Legislative Parties	Electoral Rules	Disproportionality in Representation of Territorial Subunits			
Spain	PR	2.81	208 directly elected; forty-four appointed by parliaments of autonomous communities; weighted representation; fixed terms	Moderate	Leader of party(ies) with plurality or majority of seats	PR	Varies
Switzerland	PR by cantons	5.26	Weighted representation of cantons (one or two members); cantons set their own selection rules	High	Collegial executive chosen for fixed term by bicameral legislature	Varies; mostly PR	No

(Continued)

Table 8.2 — Continued

Country	National First Chamber		National Upper Chamber		National Executive	Provincial/State Legislature	Synchronization of National and Provincial Elections
	Electoral Rules	Effective Number of Legislative Parties	Electoral Rules	Disproportionality in Representation of Territorial Subunits			
United Kingdom	SMP	2.09	Vestigial hereditary and appointive body	N.A.	Leader of party(ies) with plurality or majority of seats	MMM	No
United States	SMP in highly proportional districts	1.95	Two-seat SMP with staggered elections	Very high	Plurality election in highly disproportional state-focused system	Bicameral legislatures in forty-nine of fifty states: all SMP in highly proportional districts	Partial

Sources: Data on effective number of legislative parties are from Octavio Amorim Neto and Gary W. Cox, "Electoral Institutions, Cleavage Structures, and the Number of Parties," *American Journal of Political Science* 41, no.1: 149–74. Data on disproportionality in second chambers are from the Gini indexes in Alfred Stepan, "Federalism and Democracy: Beyond the U.S. Model," *Journal of Democracy* 10, no.4: 19–34. Indexes of less than. 15 are coded as low disproportionality, those of 0.16 to 0.40 as moderate, 0.41 to 0.50 as high; and those of 0.51 or greater as very high.

Notes: AV: alternative vote; MMM: mixed-member majoritarian MMP: mixed-member proportional; SMP: single-member plurality; STV: single transferable vote.

Fourth, states/provinces are frequently represented disproportionately to population in upper chambers, either with complete equality across units, as in the United States and Australia, or with rules that divide states into a small number of categories that tend to overrepresent the smallest and underrepresent the largest units, as in Germany.[2] Table 8.2 verifies Stepan's conclusion (Stepan 1999) that the degree of disproportionality in representing territorial units in upper chambers varies broadly, ranging from close to perfect proportionality in Belgium, Austria, and India to extreme disproportionality in Brazil and Argentina.

There are probably two distinct reasons for the strong affinity between federalism and disproportional upper chambers in the national legislature. The first is that federal systems frequently have major ethnic, religious, or linguistic divisions in which minority groups seek protection not just through consociational mechanisms (if they exist) but also through the limited government checks and balances of a second chamber in which minority regions (if not minority groups) are overrepresented. The second reason is that many federations (notably Australia, Canada, and the United States) were formed from the union of preexisting political units. Politicians from those units did not want to see their influence extinguished in the new national institutions, and those from smaller units were particularly concerned not to see their jurisdictions being subsumed and potentially pushed around by the larger units in the new federation.[3]

Fifth, the electoral rules within first and second chambers are almost always uniform across territorial subunits: that is, representatives from all states/provinces are elected following the same sets of rules, even though they may not represent equal numbers of voters. There are exceptions: perhaps the best known example is the use of the single transferable vote in Northern Ireland for elections to the House of Commons, while single-member plurality is used in other areas (see Michael Keating's chapter in this volume). In the United States, many states moved to direct election of senators before passage of the Seventeenth Amendment to the U.S. constitution: thus two different systems existed simultaneously during this transition. In Switzerland, most members of the lower chamber are elected by proportional representation, but plurality elections are used in five small cantons. In addition, the cantons set their own election rules for the council of states, although all currently use proportional representation (Massicotte 2000, 102–3). A similar arrangement to the Swiss one was proposed but not adopted in the 1993 Charlottetown Accord in Canada. It would have allowed provinces to choose (within federally established limits) their own method of selecting members of the reformed Canadian senate, which would have allowed Quebec to send a block of government representatives, Bundesrat-style, while other provinces used proportional representation. But asymmetrical electoral rules for specific provinces/states in upper chambers is definitely the exception rather than the rule, even in countries with strong ethnic, linguistic, and religious divisions that are felt very differently across territorial subunits.

The extent to which legislators in second chambers actually function as representatives of regional interests varies substantially, however, even if they are elected from province-wide districts. Although second chambers normally do not function as confidence bodies sustaining or bringing down the executive, party discipline is nevertheless fairly high in most of these bodies, meaning that representation of regional interests takes place primarily (1) in the formulation of legislation rather than in votes on its adoption, and /or (2) through the development of regionally focused parties. In Australia, for example, the fact that a different electoral system is used for the senate (STV rather than the alternative vote, as in the house of representatives) has had a clear impact on policy—the governing party or coalition has never had a senate majority in recent years, and has therefore had to negotiate with smaller parties to win approval for its legislative program. But party discipline, the prevalence of class and ideological cleavages over regional ones, and the absence of regionalist parties means that Australian senators do not act primarily as representatives of state interests (Sharman 1977; Uhr 1999).

Finally, it should be noted that because representation ratios for state or provincial units tend to be embedded in constitutions (as Steiner and Bachtiger note in the Swiss context), small rural units (and interests) may become increasingly overrepresented over time relative to urban interests—regardless of whether or not that overrepresentation maps and helps to protect significant ethnic, linguistic, or other minority interests.

State/Provincial Legislatures

Several patterns (and nonpatterns) are also evident in looking at state/provincial legislatures. First, as noted earlier, there is, at a minimum, a strong family resemblance between legislative chamber electoral rules at the national level and those at the state/provincial level within the same country (Watts 1999, 86–87). The most obvious cross-level similarity is in the choice of parliamentary versus separation of executive and legislative powers: countries almost always make the same choice at the other level as well. But even within the broad categories of parliamentarism versus separation of executive and legislative powers, there is a tendency to make very similar choices in terms of degree of proportionality, or openness of lists in proportional representation systems, and so on. In some cases, notably Brazil, there is a common electoral law that operates at both the national and state levels. More frequently, however, these similarities appear to result simply from common institutional inheritances, and perhaps from a reluctance on the part of political elites to make electoral rules too difficult for ordinary voters to understand.

Family resemblances have been strained in recent years, however, by several inter-acting factors that have led to increasingly diverse choices of electoral systems within individual countries. One particularly important factor behind this trend is the rise of a supranational parliamentary institution, the European Parliament. With a directive to use proportional representation throughout the European Union (EU), countries like the United Kingdom that had formerly used SMP found themselves hosting elec-tions on a regular basis using a different set of rules. Second, a move toward devolution in many countries, especially in Western Europe, has created a need for new electoral arrangements—sometimes with different cleavage management tasks at the subna-tional level that appear better suited to different sets of rules than those operating at the national level. Third, the growth of mixed systems, and widespread perceptions among electoral experts that these rules might be an effective middle road between SMP and PR, have also fueled increased diversity of rules within countries. Fourth, perceptions in countries like Japan and Italy that current electoral rules have had negative conse-quences have spurred a search for new electoral rule arrangements that are not always pursued at all levels of government. Thus the United Kingdom, for example, currently uses SMP in elections for the House of Commons and proportional representation in elections for the European Parliament (except in Northern Ireland, where STV is used for both), STV for the Northern Ireland assembly, and MMP for the Scottish parlia-ment and the Welsh assembly (Farrell 2001, 530).

A second pattern evident in looking at state/provincial legislatures is the strong de-gree of uniformity between the electoral rules of individual states/provinces within countries. Again, there are exceptions: Louisiana with its two-round majority elections, some experiments with the alternative vote and single transferable vote in western Canadian provinces prior to the 1960s, differences across Australian states in whether all choices must be filled out in their alternative vote ballots, the use of straight pro-portional representation rather than a mixed-member system in elections for three *Länd* legislatures, and so on (Massicotte 2000, 102–3). But uniformity is the norm, even in multinational federations that are asymmetrical in the constitutional powers that they assign to specific territorial subunits.

A third very clear pattern is the low degree of synchronization between national elections and state and local elections. In general, we would expect that simultaneous elections at the two levels would foster closer cooperation between candidates and po-litical apparatuses at the two levels, and a lower disjunction between party systems and the messages conveyed by parties operating at the two levels. The low degree of inter-level electoral synchronization observed here appears to be largely a byproduct of the fact that most of the federations listed here are parliamentary systems at both levels, with the length of electoral cycles at each level varying (within fixed outer limits) based on the seeking of electoral advantage by those holding the reins of government and their capacity to maintain the confidence of majorities in their legislatures. Parliamentarism and federalism need not necessarily lead to nonsynchronized elections, however. This is shown by the case of Sweden, where electoral rules require elections by a specific date even if an intermediate, unplanned election has been held since the last scheduled election. This system has preserved a high degree of certainty in electoral timing and complete synchronization of national and communal elections.

Electoral Rules and Integration of Party Systems across Levels of Government

Unfortunately, there has been very little work done cross-nationally on the effects of electoral rules on party systems in federations. The degree to which voters choose the same party labels across levels in their partisan identification and in federal and state/provincial elections (partisan consistency) has not received sustained attention. The degree to which career paths of politicians are integrated across levels of politics or confined to a single level (career path integration) has not been widely studied either.

Partisan Consistency

Voters do not necessarily identify with the same party, and vote for the same party, in national and subnational elections. We would expect that differences in party identification and voting behavior might be especially strong in systems in which (1) national and state/provincial elections are not concurrent, (2) territorially based cleavages contribute to the development of political parties that operate at one level of government but not at the other, and (3) SMP electoral rules are used, since they may lead to the crowding out of a voter's first-choice party at one of the two levels in some regions, leading to a tactical shift in voting to another party to avoid a wasted vote. Evidence to support this proposition can be found in the case of Canada, where a study of party identification in 1974 found that almost one-third of voters with some party identification either identified only at one level (14 percent) or identified with different parties at the federal and provincial levels. As might be expected, split-identification was especially strong in British Columbia (35 percent), where the Liberal and Progressive Conservative parties had ceased to be competitive at the provincial level until the Liberals rebounded in the 1990s (Clarke et al. 1980).

Integration of Politicians' Career Paths

Vertically integrated career paths—that is, serving at both the federal and state/provincial levels of government over the course of a political career—can have important benefits for integration of a political system. In particular, politicians may develop added appreciation for the problems faced by the other level of government rather than seeing that government simply as a self-interested "other."

Although there is little systematic cross-national data, a variety of country-specific data suggests that federations vary greatly in the degree to which their career paths are integrated across the federal/provincial divide. The United States is usually seen as having one of the most integrated career paths for politicians, in part because concurrent federal and state legislative elections in most jurisdictions facilitate relatively seamless transitions across levels. Indeed, a path from state legislature to the House of Representatives to governorship to the U.S. Senate is probably as close to the modal career path as exists in the United States. Close to half of members of the U.S. House of Representatives in recent decades have experience in state legislatures, and an increasing number of those members come directly from state legislatures to Congress.[4]

The pattern in other federations is quite different, however. In Canada, for example, politicians are much more frequently confined to either provincial or federal legislative experience.[5] Moreover, changes in levels tend to be a one-way street, from provincial to federal politics. The most prominent current exceptions to this pattern reflect a similar dynamic to the American case, with federal politicians jumping directly from prominent Ottawa roles as leader of the largest opposition party (Lucien Bouchard of Quebec) or a post as a federal cabinet minister (Brian Tobin of Newfoundland) to the premier's office in their home province, just as members of the U.S. Congress sometimes move to the post of governor. Germany is probably an intermediate case in terms of career paths. Many leading federal politicians, including federal chancellors, have served as the minister-president of one Germany's *Länder* before taking on prominent federal roles.[6]

Electoral Rules, Party Systems, and the Governability of Federations

Perhaps the most important question about the effect of electoral rules on party systems in federations concerns democratic stability. A number of writers have focused on the degree to which different political institutions promote a variety of aspects of democratic stability and various indicators of democratic quality. It is unclear how much effect institutional and constitutional engineering can have in promoting either dem-

ocratic stability or the quality of democracy. Even Arend Lijphart (1999, 306–7), a force-
ful advocate of nonmajoritarian political institutions, concludes at the end of *Patterns
of Democracy* that it "appears more plausible to assume that both consensus democracy
and these kinder, gentler policies stem from an underlying consensual and communitarian culture than that these policies are the direct result of consensus institutions"—
although he argues that over the long term consensual political institutions may help
to create a more consensual culture.

Here I examine three issues concerning the governability of federations: the degree
to which various electoral rules are associated with (1) severe and persistent underrepresentation of some regions in the institutions of the central government, (2) the
growth of antisystem parties, and (3) the level of political violence surrounding ethnic,
religious, or linguistic conflict.

Underrepresentation in Government

As noted earlier, SMP electoral rules may cause parties with a broad national appeal
but not enough support to win pluralities in any region to be severely punished by the
electoral system, while regionally concentrated parties may be rewarded disproportionately by the electoral system if they are able to win plurality victories throughout
their region. An even more serious problem associated with plurality electoral rules in
countries with severe regional cleavages is that because the system requires winning
pluralities in individual districts, even political parties that win a majority of seats in
the legislature overall may be shut out entirely from regions where their popular support is relatively weak (Cairns 1978; LeDuc 1987).

This electoral system effect is particularly troubling when it involves the governing
party, for weak representation of a region in the caucus of the governing party may feed
a vicious cycle in which a region's perceived underrepresentation in government further exacerbates regional alienation. Perhaps the clearest and most persistent case of
such regional underrepresentation in government is in Canada. The Canadian electoral
system has produced severe underrepresentation of one or more regions in the governing party much of the time, most notably of the Conservatives in Quebec prior to
1984 and of Liberals in the west (Weaver 2001).

These patterns are evident in Table 8.3, which shows the share of seats won in each
region by the party or coalition of parties forming the government after each election
in five countries with varying degrees of federalism. Overall, the two countries with
proportional or semiproportional elections—Germany and Spain—are far less likely
to experience severe regional underrepresentation in the governing party caucus than
countries with SMP (United Kingdom., Canada) or alternative vote (Australia) systems. The Conservative government elected in the United Kingdom in 1992, for

example, had very few MPs in either Wales or Scotland—let alone Northern Ireland, where a distinctive party system operates. Canada stands out as particularly problematic in terms of regional underrepresentation, with the Liberals heavily overrepresented in Ontario in recent elections and heavily underrepresented in several western provinces. In earlier periods, the underrepresentation in the governing party caucus has been even more spectacular. In 1979, for example, the Progressive Conservative Party under Joe Clark won only two of seventy-five seats in Quebec in the lead-up to an expected 1980 referendum in that province on sovereignty for Quebec.[7]

Several factors in addition to electoral rules seem to affect the prospects for severe underrepresentation in government, however. One is the size of the subnational jurisdiction that forms the electoral district in PR or MM systems: extremely small jurisdictions, with one or only a few members of the legislature (e.g., the city-state of Bremen in Germany, La Rioja and Islas Baleares in Spain), are far less likely to achieve proportionality in electoral outcomes than those in larger jurisdictions. This may in turn lead to greater exclusion from the governing party caucus.

A second factor, not surprisingly, is the degree to which cleavages have a strong regional component. In Australia, despite the alternative vote electoral system, severe regional underrepresentation is a phenomenon confined largely to very small (in population terms) jurisdictions, because cleavages are stronger along class and ideological than regional lines.

Stimulation of Antisystem Parties

Federalism can clearly lead to the development of territorially based subnational parties, usually based on linguistic differences or strong regional cultural identities. In Spain, for example, the phenomenon of regionally oriented parties to new regions followed the spreading of grants of regional autonomy to Spain's various autonomous communities, although the regional parties only dominate in two regions (Catalunya and Pais Vasco) with exceptionally strong regional identities (Hamann 1999). Regionally focused parties won close to 10 percent of the seats in the Spanish chamber of deputies elected in March 2000. Moreover, the Catalan nationalist party Convergencia i Unió provided essential support to prop up a minority socialist government in Madrid between 1993 and 1996, and a minority Popular Party government between 1996 and 2000. Regionalist parties like the South Tyrolean People's Party in the South Tyrol province of Italy and the Convergencia i Unió electoral coalition in Catalonia frequently participate in, and sometimes dominate, regional assemblies in some regions of Europe where minority languages are dominant.

Of more importance for issues of governability, however, are situations in which such parties do not merely represent the interests of a particular territorially based

Table 8.3 Regional Exclusion in Lower Chamber of National Legislatures in Selected Countries

Country	Governing Party or Coalition Seat Share (in percent)	Number of Seats in Jurisdiction	Number of Seats Won by Governing Party or Coalition	Governing Party or Coalition Seat Share (in percent)	Number of Seats in Jurisdiction	Number of Seats Won by Governing Party or Coalition	Governing Party or Coalition Seat Share (in percent)	Number of Seats in Jurisdiction	Number of Seats Won by Governing Party or Coalition
Australia	1996 Election			1998 Election					
New South Wales	58	50	29	54	50	27			
Victoria	57	37	21	49	37	18			
Queensland	85	27	23	70	27	19			
Western Australia	57	14	8	50	14	7			
South Australia	83	12	10	75	12	9			
Tasmania	40	5	2	0	5	0			
Australia Capital Territory	0	2	0	0	2	0			
Northern Territory	0	1	0	0	1	0			
Total	63	148	93	54	148	80			
Canada	1993 Election			1997 Election			2001 Election		
Alberta	15	26	4	8	26	2	8	26	2
British Columbia	19	32	6	18	34	6	15	34	5
Manitoba	86	14	12	43	14	6	36	14	5
New Brunswick	90	10	9	30	10	3	60	10	6
Newfoundland & Labrador	100	7	7	57	7	4	71	7	5
Nova Scotia	100	11	11	0	11	0	36	11	4

(Continued)

Table 8.3 — Continued

Country	Governing Party or Coalition Seat Share (in percent)	Number of Seats in Jurisdiction	Number of Seats Won by Governing Party or Coalition	Governing Party or Coalition Seat Share (in percent)	Number of Seats in Jurisdiction	Number of Seats Won by Governing Party or Coalition	Governing Party or Coalition Seat Share (in percent)	Number of Seats in Jurisdiction	Number of Seats Won by Governing Party or Coalition
	1993 Election			1997 Election			2001 Election		
Ontario	99	99	98	98	103	101	97	103	100
Prince Edward Island	100	4	4	100	4	4	100	4	4
Quebec	25	75	19	35	75	26	48	75	36
Saskatchewan	36	14	5	7	14	1	14	14	2
Yukon	0	1	0	0	1	0	100	1	1
Northwest Terr./ Nunavat	100	2	2	100	2	2	100	2	2
Total	60	295	177	51	301	155	57	301	172
Spain	1996 Election			2000 Election					
Andalucia	39	62	24	45	62	28			
Aragon	62	13	8	62	13	8			
Asturias	44	9	4	56	9	5			
Canarias	36	14	5	50	14	7			
Cantabria	60	5	3	60	5	3			
Castilla la Mancha	55	20	11	60	20	12			
Castilla y Leon	67	33	22	67	33	22			
Catalunya	17	46	8	26	46	12			
Ceuta	100	1	1	100	1	1			

(Continued)

Table 8.3 — *Continued*

Country	Governing Party or Coalition Seat Share (in percent)	Number of Seats in Jurisdiction	Number of Seats Won by Governing Party or Coalition	Governing Party or Coalition Seat Share (in percent)	Number of Seats in Jurisdiction	Number of Seats Won by Governing Party or Coalition	Governing Party or Coalition Seat Share (in percent)	Number of Seats in Jurisdiction	Number of Seats Won by Governing Party or Coalition
	1996 Election			2000 Election					
Communidad Valenciana	47	32	15	59	32	19			
Extremadura	45	11	5	55	11	6			
Galicia	56	25	14	64	25	16			
Islas Baleares	57	7	4	71	7	5			
La Rioja	50	4	2	75	4	3			
Madrid	50	34	17	56	34	19			
Melilla	100	1	1	100	1	1			
Murcia	56	9	5	67	9	6			
Navarra	40	5	2	60	5	3			
País Vasco	26	19	5	37	19	7			
Total	45	350	156	52	350	183			
Germany	1994 Election			1998 Election					
Schleswig-Holstein	50	24	12	54	24	13			
Hamburg	43	14	6	62	13	8			
Niedersachsen	49	67	33	57	69	39			
Bremen	33	6	2	80	5	4			
Nordrhein-Westfalen	47	148	70	56	148	83			
Hessen	49	49	24	53	43	23			

(*Continued*)

Table 8.3 — Continued

Country	Governing Party or Coalition Seat Share (in percent)	Number of Seats in Jurisdiction	Number of Seats Won by Governing Party or Coalition	Governing Party or Coalition Seat Share (in percent)	Number of Seats in Jurisdiction	Number of Seats Won by Governing Party or Coalition	Governing Party or Coalition Seat Share (in percent)	Number of Seats in Jurisdiction	Number of Seats Won by Governing Party or Coalition
	1994 Election			1998 Election					
Rheinland-Pfalz	52	33	17	50	34	17			
Baden-Wurttemberg	57	79	45	43	88	38			
Bayern	61	92	56	43	93	40			
Saarland	44	9	4	63	8	5			
Berlin	41	27	11	52	25	13			
Brandenburg	30	23	7	57	23	13			
Mecklenburg-Vorpommern	53	15	8	50	14	7			
Sachsen	56	39	22	38	37	14			
Sachsen-Anhalt	48	23	11	54	26	14			
Thuringen	54	24	13	48	25	12			
Total	51	672	341	51	675	343			
United Kingdom	1992 Election			1997 Election			2001 Election		
England	61	524	319	62	529	328	61	529	323
Wales	16	38	6	85	40	34	85	40	34
Scotland	15	72	11	78	72	56	78	72	56
Northern Ireland	0	17	0	0	18	0	0	18	0
Total	52	651	336	63	659	418	63	659	413

cleavage segment, but seek to alter national borders, either through secession to form a new state, or through irredentism, joining another state. I will refer to such parties as antisystem parties. The boundary line between regionalist and separatist-irredentist parties is not always clear in practice, of course: the Social Democratic and Labour Party in Northern Ireland, for example, supports eventual union of that region with the Irish Republic, but eschews violence and thinks that any change in status must be consensual, while Sinn Feín, the political wing of the Irish Republican Army, has only recently moved toward a more gradualist position. Italy's Northern League, which has vacillated between support for northern separation and federalism, is another ambiguous case.

In general, we might expect that proportional representation systems would be more likely to stimulate the growth of antisystem parties (especially where electoral thresholds are low), because the barriers to entry of new parties are relatively weak.

Evidence on this point from the Western industrial countries does not permit any firm conclusions on this issue, however. Table 8.4 shows patterns of representation of antisystem parties in national and provincial legislatures in a variety of Western industrial countries, as well as whether or not those parties were part of the executive. There is no clear relationship between electoral rules and outcomes. In Belgium, for example, the Vlaams Blok has become a significant presence in both the federal and Flanders legislatures, but is not a part of the government in either. In Scotland, the SMP electoral system for elections to the U.K. Parliament has consistently discriminated against the Scottish Nationalist Party: the SNP received 14 percent of Scottish votes but only 4 percent of Scottish seats in Westminster in 1987, 21.5 percent of votes but only 3 percent of seats in 1992, 22 percent of votes but only 8 percent of seats in 1997, and 20 percent of the vote but only 7 percent of seats in 2001. And the SNP did indeed fare much better in elections to the Scottish parliament in Holyrood held in 1999 under mixed-member proportional rules: with 29 percent of first preference (constituency) and 27 percent of second (proportional) votes, the Scottish Nationalists managed to win 35 of 144 seats, or 24 percent of the total. Only seven of their thirty-five seats were won in individual constituencies (Jones et al. 2001, 272). Thus single-member plurality electoral rules do appear to have dampened both votes for and vote-to-seat conversions for the Scottish Nationalists. The use of MMP in elections for the Scottish parliament clearly has forced a change in the dominant style of governing—Labour governs in Scotland in a coalition with the Liberal Democrats rather than ruling alone—but the Scottish Nationalists are still outside of government and are likely to remain so.

Evidence regarding the impact of Canada's SMP electoral rules on growth of antisystem parties suggests that SMP electoral rules can cut both ways, however. In the 1960s and early 1970s, Canada's SMP electoral rules clearly discriminated against

Table 8.4 Antisystem Party Strength in Legislatures after Recent Elections

National Legislature				Territorial Legislature			
Country	Antisystem Party	Seat Share in National Legislature (in percent)	Part of Government	Territory	Antisystem Party	Seat Share in Territorial Legislature (in percent)	Part of Government?
Belgium	Vlaams Blok	10	No	Flanders	Vlaams Blok	17	No
Canada	Bloc Québécois	18 ('93) 15 ('97)	No	Quebec	Parti Québécois	60 ('98)	Yes
Switzerland	–	N.A.	–	–	–	–	N.A
United Kingdom	Scottish Nationalist	0.9 ('97) 0.8 ('01)	No No	Scotland	Scottish Nationalist	27 ('99)	No
	Plaid Cymru	0.6 ('97) 0.6 ('01)	No	Wales	Plaid Cymru	34 ('99)	No
	Sinn Fein	0.3 ('97) 0.6 ('01)		Northern Ireland	Sinn Fein	17 ('98)	Yes

N.A.= Not applicable.

political parties promoting Quebec sovereignty. In 1976, however, those same rules gave the Parti Québécois control of Quebec's national assembly on the strength of a plurality of the overall vote and an electoral platform that emphasized "good government" over attaining Quebec sovereignty. Since that time, the Parti Québécois has won three more national assembly majorities, but never a majority of the popular vote. Indeed, single-seat district plurality electoral rules particularly benefit the PQ, since under this system immense majorities for the Liberals in Montreal-area constituencies with many Anglophone and Allophone (persons whose first language is neither French nor English) voters are wasted: in the 1994 provincial election, for example, the PQ won a comfortable majority in the Quebec national assembly with a vote share less than one percentage point higher than that of the Liberals. The results were even more dramatic in the November 30, 1998 provincial election: the Parti Québécois won 76 of 125 seats in the Quebec national assembly although the Quebec Liberal Party won 1 percent more of the popular vote. Indeed, political scientist Louis Massicotte (1999a, 1999b) has estimated that because of geographic vote concentration and resulting wasted votes, the Liberal Party must now have an overall lead of 7 percent in popular vote over the PQ to win a majority of seats in Quebec's national assembly. In federal politics, the prosovereignty Bloc Québécois won the second largest number of seats in the house of commons in the 1993 federal election, using its concentration of plurality victories (it ran candidates only in Quebec) to win 18 percent of all commons seats—54 of 75 in Quebec—with only 13.5 percent of the national vote. In short, SMP electoral rules may discourage secessionist parties in their early stages, but provide a major boost once these parties attain sufficient size to start winning a substantial number of victories in individual constituencies.

The Italian situation of electoral coalitions within a mixed-member majoritarian system suggests that such a system may in fact be the most likely to promote parties with antisystem proclivities. Because there are strong incentives to build a broad coalition that can win a majority of seats in the two chambers of the Italian parliament, relatively small parties that do not fit clearly on one side of the left-right divide in Italian politics but have a concentrated regional base along them to win single seat districts in the plurality part of the election contest may be in a strong position to (1) provide the majority for either of two fairly evenly divided coalitions, or (2) win good deals in electoral coalition pacts, and thus be in a good position to share in power if their coalition wins. This is in fact what happened with the Northern League in 1994 and 2001, respectively (D'Alimonte 2001; Carroll 2001a, 2001b).

Stimulation of Political Violence

Defining and developing plausible measures of political violence that are reliable cross-nationally is extremely difficult. Moreover, expectations about the effects of electoral rules on the prevalence of political violence are far from obvious. One plausible hypothesis is that the lower prospects that political minorities and groups outside the political mainstream have for making major headway under SMP electoral rules may stimulate political violence by groups that see no prospect for achieving their objectives through normal political channels.

Evidence for this proposition is quite limited, however. Lijphart (1999, 271), for example, finds in a study of thirty-six democracies that once level of economic development, level of social pluralism, and population size are controlled for, relationships between "consensus democracy" institutions and the level of political violence are quite weak, with much of the variance accounted for by two outliers: the United Kingdom (because of Northern Ireland) and Jamaica (because of violence surrounding the 1980 election). Majoritarian electoral rules for the Northern Ireland parliament in Stormont, along with widespread gerrymandering practices designed to marginalize Catholic influence, have been at least partially blamed for the emergence of widespread political violence in Northern Ireland. But many other factors, such as widespread employment discrimination, seem at least as important as electoral rules. And the argument seems much less true in other countries. The movement to gain additional autonomy for Quebec, for example, has been almost entirely devoid of violence, except for a brief outburst in the period from 1968 to 1970 that culminated in two kidnappings and the murder of a Quebec cabinet minister. The revulsion to these events was extraordinarily strong, and there has been almost no violence since that time. As Liesbet Hooghe's chapter illustrates, political violence has been far more evident in Belgium than in Canada. Italy, too, underwent a bout of political violence in the 1960s in the German-speaking South Tyrol region. In short, majoritarian electoral rules may contribute to the emergence of political violence, but other factors are probably far more important in explaining a cleavage segment's turn to political violence. And reforms other than electoral reforms (e.g., increased autonomy for regionally dominant national minorities) are probably more important in containing it.

Conclusion

This review of electoral systems and their effects on party systems and governability in European and North American federations suggests several conclusions. First, federalism is compatible with a variety of electoral rules at both the national and territorial levels. Federalism has been employed with both parliamentarism and separation of powers, proportional and single-member plurality elections, and concurrent and nonconcurrent elections. There is generally a very strong family resemblance between the choices that countries make in the first chambers of their national legislatures and territorial legislatures. Countries that choose more proportional electoral rules for their national legislatures generally make similar choices for territorial legislatures as well. However, many countries in Europe are developing increasingly diverse sets of electoral rules across levels of governments.

Second, federalism is very strongly associated with bicameralism, with the territorial subunits playing a distinctive role in the selection of members for that chamber. Again, however, the role that territorial units plays varies broadly, from serving simply as the election district within which they are selected—the most common pattern—to direct appointment by territorial legislatures in the case of the German *Länder.*

Third, single-member plurality electoral rules do have some of the advantages and disadvantages associated with them in terms of governance. In particular, SMP electoral rules do appear significantly more likely to create a high risk of territorial exclusion from the governing party caucus at the national level in parliamentary systems than do more proportional electoral rules. The effect of SMP electoral rules in fostering antisystem secessionist or irredentist parties is more complex, however: they appear to both raise the barriers to antisystem parties that enjoy moderate levels of support, and stimulate them in a "tipping effect" once those parties reach a level of around 35 to

40 percent of voter support. Both of these effects are highly contingent on other factors, however—notably on the existence of strong and persistent regionally based cleavages. And the effects of electoral arrangements on stimulating political violence appear to be weak at best. Why some territorially based groups turn to and persist in political violence while others do not remains a subject that is both poorly measured and poorly understood.

Notes

The author would like to thank Matthew Shugart for his extensive and thoughtful comments on an earlier version of this essay.

1. See Liesbet Hooghe's chapter in this volume. As noted earlier, state legislatures (rather than executives) also elected U.S. senators until the passage of the Seventeenth Amendment to the U.S. constitution.

2. Article 50 of Germany's Basic Law provides that each state or *Länd* "has at least three votes; States with more than two million inhabitants have four, states with more than six million inhabitants five, and states with seven million inhabitants six votes." Brazil provides both a minimum and maximum of seats (eight and seventy seats, respectively) for seats in its lower house and represents states equally in its upper house.

3. Riker makes this point, but as Stepan (1999) has noted, it is not true of all federations. Some federations are designed to hold together previously more unitary states rather than being the result of the coming together of previously autonomous units.

4. The percent of members with experience as members of state legislatures ranged from a low of around 30 percent in the 1930s and 1940s to close to 50 percent in the 1980s. See Canon 1990, 54.

5. After the 1993 federal election, for example, only 7 percent of Liberal, no Progressive Conservative, 11 percent of New Democratic Party, and 4 percent of Reform MPs had prior provincial legislative experience. The number of provincial legislators with prior house of commons experience was even lower. See Dyck 1996. For a discussion of earlier data showing similar patterns, see Franks 1987, 72.

6. See Ordeshook and Shvetsova 1997. A 1980s study found that professional politicians, including members of the *Länd* legislatures as well as employees of parties, assistants to politicians, and so on, constituted the largest background group of Bundestag members: 25 percent in 1983. See Kaack 1990.

7. Weak representation of a region in the governing party caucus also leaves the governing party with very few qualified and/or experienced MPs available for putting together a regionally balanced cabinet. Joe Clark's Progressive Conservative government of 1979–80 had only two Quebec MPs to draw upon, and Pierre Trudeau had only two western MPs (both from Manitoba) to tap as cabinet ministers after the 1980 election. In both cases, they were forced to make cabinet appointments from the nonelected senate to create a more regionally balanced cabinet.

REFERENCES

Amorim Neto, Octavio, and Gary W. Cox. 1997. Electoral Institutions, Cleavage Structures, and the Number of Parties. *American Journal of Political Science* 41, no. 1:149–74.

Anckar, Carsten. 1999. Try Federalism. *Scandinavian Political Studies* 22, no. 2:99–119.

Bakvis, Herman, and Laura G. Macpherson. 1995. Quebec Block Voting and the Canadian Electoral System. *Canadian Journal of Political Science* 28, no. 4:659–92.

Cairns, Alan. 1968. The Electoral System and the Party System in Canada. *Canadian Journal of Political Science* 1, no. 1:55–80.

———. 1978. The Governments and Societies of Canadian Federalism. *Canadian Journal of Political Science* 10, no. 4:695–725.

Canon, David T. 1990. *Actors, Athletes and Astronauts: Political Amateurs in the United States Congress.* Chicago: University of Chicago Press.

Carroll, Rory. 2001a. Italian Nationalist Bossi Frozen Out as His Vote Collapses. *The Guardian.* May 16.

———. 2001a. Berlusconi Gives Extremists Key Cabinet Posts. *The Guardian.* June 11.

Clarke, Harold D., Jane Jenson, Lawrence LeDuc, and Jon H. Pammett. 1980. *Political Choice in Canada.* Abridged ed. Toronto: McGraw-Hill Ryerson.

D'Alimonte, Roberto. 2001. Mixed Electoral Rules, Partisan Realignment, and Party System Change in Italy. In *Mixed Electoral Systems: The Best of Both Worlds?* ed. Matthew Soberg Shugart and Martin Wattenberg, 323–50. Oxford: Oxford University Press.

Dyck, Rand. 1996. Relations Between Federal and Provincial Parties. In *Canadian Parties in Transition,* 2d ed., ed. Alain-G. Gagnon and A. Brian Tanguay, 160–89. Scarborough: Nelson Canada.

Farrell, David. 2001. The United Kingdom Comes of Age: The British Electoral Reform "Revolution" of the 1990s. In *Mixed Electoral Systems: The Best of Both Worlds?* ed. Matthew Soberg Shugart and Martin Wattenberg, 521–41. Oxford: Oxford University Press.

Franks, C.E.S. 1987. *Parliament of Canada.* Toronto: University of Toronto Press.

Gaines, Brian. 1999. Duverger's Law and the Meaning of Canadian Exceptionalism. *Comparative Political Studies* 32, no. 7:651–74.

Hamann, Kerstin. 1999. Federal Institutions, Voting Behavior and Party Systems in Spain. *Publius* 29, no. 1:111–37.

Jones, Bill, Dennis Kavanaugh, Michael Moran, and Philip Norton. 2001. *Politics UK.* 4th ed. Harlow: Pearson Education.

Kaack, Heino. 1990. The Social Composition of the Bundestag. In *The U.S. Congress and the German Bundestag,* ed. Uwe Thaysen, Roger H. Davidson, and Robert Gerald Livingstone, 129–54. Boulder: Westview.

Kaase, Max. 1984. Personalized Proportional Representation: The "Model" of the West German Electoral System. In *Choosing an Electoral System: Issues and Alternatives,* ed. Arend Lijphart and Bernard Grofman, 155–74. New York: Praeger.

Katz, Richard S. 1993. Reforming the Italian Electoral Law. In *Mixed Electoral Systems: The Best of Both Worlds?* ed. Matthew Soberg Shugart and Martin Wattenberg, 98–122. Oxford: Oxford University Press.

LeDuc, Lawrence. 1987. Performance of the Electoral System in Recent Canadian and British Elections: Advancing the Case for Electoral Reform. In *The Logic of Multiparty Systems,* ed. M. J. Holler, 341–58. Dordrecht: Martinus Nijhoff.

Lijphart, Arend. 1987. Bicameralism: Canadian Senate Reform in Comparative Perspective. In *Federalism and the Role of the State,* ed. Herman Bakvis and William M. Chandler, 101–12. Toronto: University of Toronto Press.

———. 1999. *Patterns of Democracy: Government Forms and Performance in Thirty-Six Countries.* New Haven, Conn.: Yale University Press.

Lijphart, Arend, Ronald Rogowski, and R. Kent Weaver. 1993. Separation of Powers and Cleavage Management. In *Do Institutions Matter?: Government Capabilities in the U.S. and Abroad,* ed. R. Kent Weaver and Bert A. Rockman, 302–44. Washington, D.C.: The Brookings Institution.

Mainwaring, Scott, and Matthew Shugart. 1997. Conclusion: Presidentialism and the Party System. In *Presidentialism and Democracy in Latin America,* ed. Scott Mainwaring and Matthew Shugart, 394–439. Cambridge: Cambridge University Press.

Massicotte, Louis. 1999a. Les Libéraux du Québec devraeient-ils prôner une réforme du mode de scrutin? Presentation to the Conseil général of the Parti Libéral du Quebec. Saint-Hyacinthe, May 29.

———. 1999b. Quebec's Electoral Bias. Presentation at the annual meeting of the Canadian Political Science Association meeting, Sherbrooke, Quebec, June 8.

———. 2000. Elections in Federal Countries. In *International Encyclopedia of Elections,* ed. Richard Rose, 101–4. Washington, D.C.: Congressional Quarterly Press.

McCormick, Peter. 1996 Provincial Party Systems, 1945–1993. In *Canadian Parties in Transition,* 2d ed., ed. Alain-G. Gagnon and A. Brian Tanguay, 349–72. Scarborough: Nelson Canada.

Ordeshook, Peter C., and Olga V. Shvetsova. 1994. Ethnic Heterogeneity, District Magnitude, and the Number of Parties. *American Journal of Political Science* 38, no. 1:100–123.

———. 1997. Federalism and Constitutional Design. *Journal of Democracy* 27–42.

Patterson, Samuel C., and Anthony Mughan. 1999. *Senates: Bicameralism in the Contemporary World.* Columbus: Ohio State University Press.

Rayside, David. 1978. Federalism and the Party System: Provincial and Federal Liberals in the Province of Quebec. *Canadian Journal of Political Science* 11:499–528.

Sartori, Giovanni. 1997. *Comparative Constitutional Engineering: An Inquiry into Structures, Incentives and Outcomes.* 2d ed. New York: New York University Press.

Sharman, Campbell. 1977. The Australian Senate as a State's House. In *The Politics of New Federalism,* ed. Dean Jaensch, 64–75. Adelaide: Australian Political Science Association.

———. 1987. Second Chambers. In *Federalism and the Role of the State,* ed. Herman Bakvis and William M. Chandler, 82–100. Toronto: University of Toronto Press.

Shugart, Matthew Soberg, and Martin Wattenberg, eds. 2001 *Mixed Electoral Systems: The Best of Both Worlds?* Oxford: Oxford University Press.

Stepan, Alfred. 1999. Federalism and Democracy: Beyond the U.S. Model. *Journal of Democracy* 10, no. 4:19–34.

Taagepera, Rein, and Matthew Soberg Shugart. 1989. *Seats and Votes: The Effects and Determinants of Electoral Systems.* New Haven, Conn.: Yale University Press.

Uhr, John. 1999. Generating Divided Government: The Australian Senate. In *Senates: Bicameralism in the Contemporary World,* ed. Samuel C. Patterson and Anthony Mughan, 93–119. Columbus: Ohio State University Press.

Watts, Ronald L. 1999. *Governing Federal Systems.* 2d ed. Kingston: Queen's University Institute of Intergovernmental Relations.

Weaver, R. Kent. 1997. Electoral Reform for the Canadian House of Commons. *Canadian Journal of Political Science* 33, no. 3:473–512.

————. 2001. Electoral Rules and Electoral Reform in Canada. In *Mixed Electoral Systems: The Best of Both Worlds?* ed. Matthew Soberg Shugart and Martin Wattenberg, 542–69. Oxford: Oxford University Press.

Wiseman, Nelson. 1991. Cairns Revisited—The Electoral System and the Party System in Canada. In *Politics: Canada,* 7th ed., ed. Paul W. Fox and Graham White, 265–74. Toronto: McGraw-Hill Ryerson.

CHAPTER NINE

Federalism and the Quality of Democracy in Multinational Contexts

Present Shortcomings and Possible Improvements

Ferran Requejo

In the field of political theory, there can be few who doubt that the main emancipatory watersheds in the contemporary political sphere have been associated with liberal democratic revolutions. Questions regarding the regulation and guarantee of certain rights and freedoms, the rule of law and political pluralism, the separation of powers and other limiting mechanisms such as federalism and constitutionalism, as well as the legitimacy of governmental institutions established by means of periodical and competitive elections, are clear attempts to make the modern concepts of liberty, equality, and dignity concrete within the public sphere. The concretization of these concepts has usually been far from easy to establish. At the same time, however, it has been the very success of these historical products that has underlined the distance between the universal values intrinsic to their principles and legitimizing language and the practical consequences that these have had on specific and culturally complex political realities. We could say, ironically, that progress in some liberal democracies means illuminating and transforming the darker side of humanity's emancipatory revolutions. The study of multinational democracies and their relation to federalism illustrates the point.

In certain liberal democratic federations (or regionally decentralized polities) there are various coexisting national groups. The members of a national group recognize themselves as such because they share some cultural patterns. They also share a sense of historical distinctiveness in relation to other groups. They are situated in a more or less clear territory and display a will to maintain their distinctiveness in the political sphere. When there are different national groups living together within the same federation or regional state, we call it a multinational federation (or a multinational regional state). This is the case in, for example, Belgium, Canada, India, and Spain. Multinational federations or regional decentralized polities have institutional and regulatory challenges distinct from those faced by uninational federations such as Germany, Austria, and Australia.[1]

This chapter outlines analytical and moral elements pertaining to the current revision of liberal democratic legitimacy within multinational contexts that are relevant to democratic federalism. It then presents the basis of a proposal for a liberal democratic federal organization that is more suitable to the needs of multinational societies, which I call plural federalism. If it seems necessary to revise some of the theoretical bases of democratic liberalism in multinational societies, it would also probably be necessary to revise the kind of federalism linked to this democratic liberalism. The key question addressed here is how liberal federalism affects the quality of democracy in multinational contexts.

Political Liberalism and National Pluralism

Analytical Aspects

THE DISCONNECTION BETWEEN DIFFERING TYPES OF THEORETICAL ANALYSES

In general terms, there has been little connection between the analyses of federalism, democracy, and the various types of nationalism. In comparative federal studies, there is not always a distinction made between federal systems that are democratic and nondemocratic, or between those that are uninational and those that are multinational. Analyses of nationalism do not usually assess its relation to democracy in any great depth, while theories of democracy—particularly those of a more philosophical character—have not paid significant attention to the analysis of federal systems or empirical multinational realities.

NATIONAL PLURALISM AND DEMOCRACY

Although we may say that cultural pluralism is a general trend of current liberal democracies, national pluralism is certainly not. It is a reality that is not shared by all democracies. However, despite the fact that national pluralism is a question related to the quality of some democracies, only in recent times has it received sufficient attention in democratic theory. At least three normative and institutional questions must be addressed in these democracies: the constitutional recognition and regulation of minority rights; the institutional framework of the polity; and the self-government of minority national entities.

NATIONAL PLURALISM AND FEDERALISM

In comparing the political makeup of federal democracies, we do not find a great many multinational democratic federations. The group consists of Canada, Belgium, India, and, to a lesser extent, Spain (which is not, technically speaking, a federation). In dealing with these cases, we need to be particularly careful in making judgments, avoiding inferences that are based on limited information, and drawing generalized conclusions. The basic issue here is the accommodation of diverse national realities within the same federal democracy within the public sphere. Distinct national groups are habitually characterized by perceptible differences (demographic, linguistic, income-related, cultural, in civil law, etc.) which have consequences for their self-perceptions. We also need to bear in mind other factors such as whether or not populations with distinct national identities are territorially intermixed and the importance of dual national identity in relation to the federated entity and the federation.

NORMATIVE AND NATIONAL PLURALISM

In all liberal democracies and federations, decision makers often find themselves faced with a plurality of competing legitimizing goals based on different functional or moral perspectives (liberal, democratic, national, technical, etc.). Efficiency, stability, and political participation versus the protection of individual and collective rights and liberties are classical competing goals in all federal democracies, but they are especially complex in multinational federations.

NATIONAL PLURALISM, GLOBALIZATION, AND SUPRASTATE POLITIES (E.G., THE EUROPEAN UNION)

Stateless nations like Quebec, Catalonia, Flanders, the Basque Country, and Scotland illustrate the connections between globalization and national pluralism in Western democracies. In the European context, there are some difficulties in empirical and theoretical analysis when we are dealing with concepts like democratic accountability in the suprastate decision-making networks or the recent notion of European citizenship (Treaty of Maastricht 1992). Federalism is directly influenced by these suprastate processes. In liberal democratic theories, citizenship has been approached from the perspective of the state. The dilution of the state monopoly on the principle of territoriality and the competitive dualism between state and nonstate nationbuilding processes are likely two prerequisites for implementing (1) a new institutional and democratic accommodation of national pluralism in a more globalized economic and political context and (2) a revision of the unitarian-secessionist duality in nation-building processes.

Political Liberalism and Legitimacy in Multinational Polities: Some Moral Shortcomings

Globalization and cultural pluralism constitute the two main challenges for present-day liberal democracies and federalism. In some of the more influential theoretical liberal democratic conceptions, the relationship between liberalism and nationalism has been presented as an irreconcilable opposition. Yet this view is becoming increasingly obsolete, particularly in a world dominated by globalization and liberal national pluralism. In today's context, the debate is no longer between democratic liberalism on the one hand and nationalism on the other, but, rather, between two basic and essential ways of understanding democratic liberalism itself or, if we prefer, between two different variants of democratic liberalism. The first variant defends a concept based, essentially, on individual rights of a universal kind, on a nondiscriminatory idea of equality for all citizens, and on a series of procedural mechanisms that regulate institutional principles and the collective processes of decision making. It is a form of political liberalism that distrusts the very notion of collective rights, suspecting such a concept of presenting authoritarian risks. I call this liberalism 1. The second variant, or liberalism 2, adds to these elements the protection and development of specific cultural and political differences in the public and constitutional spheres for distinct national groups living within the same democracy. It holds that the absence of such recognition, and of broad-ranging self-government, results in a discriminatory bias against national minorities and violates the principle of equality.[2]

One of the traditional criticisms leveled at political liberalism—from both conservative and socialist positions—was the contrast between the ideas described in liberal theory and what was actually carried out by those polities calling themselves "liberal." Today, such criticism extends from purely social or socioeconomic components to include the cultural components that are to be found in democracies.[3] The choice between these two versions of political liberalism will bring about variations of the formulation of possible federal solutions and the constitutional accommodation within multinational contexts.[4]

It seems that questions of interculturality and multinationality have posed a new agenda of issues for democratic debate no longer limited to the traditional liberal language of individual rights and notions of liberty, equality, and pluralism. This new agenda has led to the discussion of key elements for a special theory of democratic legitimacy and federalism in multinational contexts that overcomes the traditional approach of seeing national minority rights as unjust, discriminatory, and morally arbitrary.

Among the cultural and moral biases of the traditional approach that condition both the implementation of democratic values and the practical constitutional federal regulations of democracies in multinational societies, the following stand out:

INEQUALITY VERSUS DIFFERENCE

Traditional liberal democratic theories have usually understood public sphere justice using the paradigm of equality (equality versus inequality) rather than the paradigm of difference (equality versus difference). In multinational societies, the mere concept of equality becomes more plural than it is in uninational societies. If cultural differences are ignored or marginalized, cultural minorities will lose self-esteem and self-respect, even if their civil, political, and social rights of citizenship are guaranteed. We can even talk of a potential fourth wave of rights in liberal democracies, after the civil, political, and social stages: the cultural wave. The juxtaposition of these two paradigms is necessary in the context of historical and territorial cultural pluralism, as in the case of multinational societies. It implies a new approach to the notions of dignity and individual self-esteem, as well as to the notion of pluralism itself in liberal democracies. The political accommodation of national minorities—the regulation of minority rights, constitutional arrangements, and self-government—is currently an increasingly recognized claim that must be taken into account in the criteria of justice in theories of multinational democracy.[5]

THE MONIST CONCEPTION OF THE *DEMOS*

One of the questions that has never been resolved by the different liberal theories of democracy is that of the *demos* to which they refer. The majority of liberal democratic conceptions make no effort to define the term. We know that in the empirical world, the *demos* of democratic systems has not usually been established using the procedural rules of liberal democracies, but through a historical process full of wars, conquests, annexations, exterminations, or marginalizations of whole peoples. These are far from being sound bases for liberal democratic legitimization. Moreover, these bases usually justify the constitutional rules in universal and impartial terms, despite the implicit and unavoidable assumption of particular cultural values linked to a specific democracy and to the pretended "national" interest of its *demos*. From this perspective, the challenge of multinational democracies is "one polity, several *demoi*." In fact, theories of democracy have traditionally been theories of the democratic state and have usually assumed a uniform *demos*. Multinational democracies show the need to revise, for moral as well as functional reasons, some of the traditional statist assumptions that the hegemonic national groups have often imposed under homogenizing versions of the notions of democratic citizenship and "popular sovereignty."

THE MARGINALIZATION OF THE ETHICAL DIMENSION

Within the theories of democratic legitimacy, at least three dimensions of practical rationality have stood out: the pragmatic (or instrumental), the ethical, and the moral. The pragmatic dimension aims at the satisfaction of goals and objectives. In the political sphere it is characterized by negotiation and compromise and its guiding principles are effectiveness, efficiency, and stability. From a pragmatic perspective, a federal agreement that satisfied the ethical and moral concerns of all the parties involved, but was unstable could not be described as a good agreement. Ethical rationality is linked to the interpretation of specific cultural values and identities that provide a framework for an unavoidable particularist normativity, whether it be a special normative set of values or a specific interpretation of a more general (or universal) normativity. This is a rationality that is prescriptively characterized by contextual interpretation. The regulation of symbols, institutions, self-government, and the mechanisms of representation in a multinational federation must take into account this ethical dimension. If this regulation is based on the cultural components of only one of the national collectivities and excludes or marginalizes the others, it would be difficult to call it a good federal accommodation. A good accommodation demands that almost all citizens of the federation feel comfortable in terms of identity (and self-esteem) regardless of the national collectivity they feel they mainly belong to. Finally, moral rationality is aimed at the impartial and equitable resolution of conflicts by means of a number of principles that aspire to universal recognition regardless of the context in which they are applied. A good federal agreement needs to incorporate a clearly liberal democratic moral dimension—a dimension that respects and guarantees transcultural human rights, as well as the other principles of the rule of law (the principles of legality, constitutionality, the separation of powers, frequent and competitive elections, civil liberties, etc.).

Liberal democratic theories have tended to consider normative regulations from the perspective of pragmatic and moral rationalities. Ethical considerations of a historical and linguistic nature have tended to be marginalized, relegated to the private sphere (as with territorial minority national identities), or simply accepted implicitly as a kind of hermeneutic horizon of the public sphere (as with majority or hegemonic national identities). Political institutions have not been culturally neutral, but have leaned toward the identities and cultural patterns of the national majority or hegemonic groups. At the very least, liberal democratic theory has tended to accept and defend an implicit form of state communitarianism of a national nature.[6]

The Defense of the Nation-building Process in All Liberal Democracies

In multinational democracies, competing nation-building processes are forced to coexist. All liberal democracies have defended and continue to defend cultural particularisms of a linguistic, historical, and the like, nature. From the perspective of minority nations, two general objectives should be achieved at the constitutional level: (1) a formal political recognition of the multinationality of the state in its constitutional rules and (2) a level of political self-government and legal protections proportional to that recognition. There would probably be cultural consequences for a notion of nation-building based on the application of a universalistic legitimizing language to a particular state group that itself possesses a plurality of national groups.[7]

Universalism and Particularism as Legitimizing Criteria

The consideration of the previous points involves a revision of the role of normative universality in democratic legitimation and of its relation to values of a more particular nature in multinational federations. A normative and institutional redefinition of liberal democracy in multinational societies means seeing national pluralism as a value worth protecting and not just as an inconvenient fact that must be borne as stoically as possible. This brings an end to the notion that a form of universalism based on egalitarian components of human dignity and a form of pluralism based on the cultural dimensions that individuals acquire through processes of socialization are mutually exclusive. In a pluralist society, while universalistic values are part of the identities of particular individuals, particular cultural values influence the concept of dignity itself. Therefore, the valid criticisms that liberal universalism has regularly directed at particularist positions—that they lean toward conservatism and lack clear decision-making references—should be complemented by the no less accurate criticisms that culturally rooted particularism aims at traditional universalism, that it lacks a realistic understanding of the normative links that individuals maintain with the collectivities that they belong to, and, above all, that its alleged universalism is nothing more than a set of specific cultural particularities.[8]

In reality, we always argue from the position of cultural inheritances that have facets of both a universal and a particular nature. Understood from this point of view, the majority of claims made by stateless democratic national movements (like those in Catalonia, Scotland, or Quebec) represent a deepening of the universal suppositions of political liberalism—in particular, the values of equality, liberty, and pluralism. The key task is to understand that, in a multinational democracy, multiple public spheres coexist, engaged in diverse processes of nation building. This idea affects current discussions of whether federalism offers an adequate framework from which to

proceed to a practical and constitutional accommodation for multinational polities
in which diverse processes of nation building share the same arena.[9] The political
and constitutional regulation of this variety of pluralism thus becomes a demand
of liberal and federal normativity themselves at the beginning of the twenty-first
century.

Democratic Federalism: Present Shortcomings and Possible Improvements

Federalism and National Pluralism

We can now ask ourselves the following question: is the federal system an effective
model for the accommodation of multinational societies according to our revised liberal democratic patterns?

Federalism has traditionally been seen as one of the ideal institutional devices best
suited to the territorial organization of those political groups characterized by a high
degree of social complexity. Daniel Elazar, one of the most renowned scholars of
federalism, observed that more than a third of all countries make use of some kind of
federal agreement for their territorial organization. He even goes so far as to talk of a
worldwide "federal revolution." This does not mean that all countries are becoming
federal states or federations. In recent study, Ronald Watts argued that only 13 percent
of current states are federal.[10]

Analyzing the most widespread typologies within the current study of federalism
we can distinguish, in very general terms, four main classes of federal agreement:
regional states, symmetrical federations, asymmetrical federal agreements, and con-
federations.[11] Table 9.1 lists current examples of these classes of federal agreements.

However, there is no historical or moral connection between federalism and the regulation of national pluralism. Moreover, both institutional and normative analyses of
federalism have been dominated by the historical example of the United States. This
empirical case is not historically linked to national pluralism. If we limit ourselves to
American federalism, the answer to the question about the possibilities of accommodating multinational societies seems to be basically a negative one. The reasons are
both historical and organizational. It is a fundamentally uninational model that neither
defines "the people" nor determines who has the authority to come up with such a definition. In my view, these presuppositions make it practically impossible to accommodate the different *demoi* of a multinational society within the constitutional rules of the
game.[12]

The history of federalism has been characterized chiefly by the development of

Table 9.1 *Examples of Federal Agreements in Contemporary Democracies*

Regional States	Symmetrical Federations	Asymmetrical Federal Agreements			
		Asymmetrical Federations	Federacies	Associated States	Confederations
Spain[a]	South Africa	Belgium	Denmark-	France-	Commonwealth
Italy	Germany	Canada	Faröe Islands	Monaco	of Independent
Portugal	Argentina	India	Finland-	India-	States
UK	Australia	Malaysia	Aaland Islands	Bhutan	Caribbean
	Austria		United	Italy-	Community
	Brazil		Kingdom-	San Marino	
	United States		Jersey	Netherlands-	
	Mexico		United States-	Antilles	
	Switzerland		Puerto Rico	New Zealand-	
				Cook Islands	
				Switzerland-	
				Liechtenstein	

Source: Own elaboration from Watts 1999 and Elazar 1991.
[a]With Federal trends.

symmetrical models. These models have been fundamentally linked to uninational entities and their processes of nation building. They have encountered problems in their attempts to accommodate distinct national realities into the liberal democratic model. Such models have proven to be particularly promising in cases of coexisting or juxtaposed processes of nation building within the same polity. Symmetry stimulates uniformity in the rules of entry to a given political system. This makes it particularly difficult to achieve real accommodation, because national minorities want recognition of multinationality and minority national self-government to be established by these very rules of entry. The symbolic, institutional, and policy-making challenges that multinational societies present to the notion of federalism are, by and large, significantly different from the challenges presented by uninational societies. In addition to the search for common positions within the federation, multinational societies are preoccupied with establishing liberal institutions and mechanisms of protection on a constitutional scale, to safeguard the minority national *demoi* from the decisions of the majority.

The increasing complexity of an ever more plural and globalized world demands greater complexity from federal agreements in democratic polities. One of the historical advantages of federal agreements is their potential flexibility and adaptability to different specific realities. In fact, comparative politics since the end of the Second World War shows that adaptability is an essential requirement for the stability and success of established federal agreements.[13] This adaptability also extends to the group of multinational federations that, despite sharing certain common traits, also display important differences of a historical, cultural, constitutional, and party-political nature.

The new kind of federalism we need to improve the quality of democratic multinational federations must include the final aspects related to liberalism 2 mentioned in the first section: (1) a more complex notion of equality that takes national differences into account; (2) a pluralist conception in national terms of the *demos* of the federation; (3) the incorporation of the ethical dimension of practical rationality; (4) the accommodation of a variety of nation-building processes that are partially competitive; and (5) the combination of universal and particular legitimizing normativities.

Plural Federalism

The standardizing frameworks of uninational federations do not seem the most suitable principles for the political accommodation of multinational realities, especially when the number of federated units is high in relation to the number of national collectivities living in the same federation. The "tyranny of the majority" has also shown its perverse effects in its failure to recognize the internal national pluralism of some polities. The intergroup regulation of a multinational state requires constitutional guarantees of negative liberal liberty at the collective level or, in Kymlicka's terms, the regulation of a number of institutional external protections—constitutional rights, veto powers in upper chambers, Supreme Courts or constitutional courts, a clear and decentralized distribution of powers, and the like—that accompany the lack of internal restrictions on intragroup relations. The collective rights and values of national minorities must be recognized at the same level as the collective rights and values of the majority, which usually occurs through traditional constitutionalism.[14]

It is for these reasons that I propose plural federalism—which includes certain asymmetrical or confederal regulations—as a better model for multinational realities.

Essentially, plural federalism includes three basic types of federal agreements:

1. An explicit and satisfactory constitutional recognition of the national pluralism of the federation acceptable to the main political actors.
2. The establishment of a series of agreements, of an asymmetrical or confederate nature, for the regulation of those aspects decisive to the recognition and self-government of minority national groups and those related to the shared government of the federation. The aim of these agreements is the defense and development of such groups, both in relation to the federation and in relation to the international arena.

3. The regulation of more symmetrical agreements in other areas of self-government.

The first type of agreement is based more on the perspective of the constitutional recognition of multinationality, while the other two are more concerned with the national self-government of federated units and the shared government of the federation. The basic aim of plural federalism is to regulate different types of federal agreement in accordance with both the functional sphere and the characteristics of the federated units.[15] The basic nucleus of plural federalism is constituted by the first two types of agreement outlined above.

The application of the three types of federal agreement covers five basic areas: the symbolic-linguistic, the institutional, the fiscal-economic, the international, and responsibilities and powers. The three agreement types and five areas of application allow fifteen possible combinations. In the symbolic-linguistic area, for example, the first two types of agreement (regulation of multinationality at a federal level and asymmetrical or confederal agreements) include questions such as the regulation of plurilingualism in the federation's name, currency and personal identity documents (passports, etc.), the choice of national sports teams for international representation, the use of flags, anthems, and the like, within the various national territories, and innumerable other sensitive matters. Other intersections between types of plural federal agreement and areas of regulation would be asymmetrical regulations in institutional and responsibility spheres. This could require specific regulations related to the electoral and political-party system, second chambers that regulate national minority parliamentarians' right of veto on given issues, and a specialized and symmetrical bicameralism, as well as the potential role of multinationality in the process of constitutional reform. Regulation of the composition of Supreme Courts or constitutional courts and the federalization of the judicial power would also have to be addressed. Table 9.2 summarizes some examples of these intersections.[16]

The specific regulation of these fifteen intersections will vary from one multinational federation to another. However, as the basic aim of plural federalism is the political accommodation of diverse national collectivities in a single, high-quality democracy, it will always require the articulation of rules and procedures based on political guarantees for the recognition and national self-government of minority national groups. It is aimed more at maintaining the unity of multinational societies already in existence than at paving the way for new ones to develop. In this sense, it is essential to keep in mind the importance of theoretical revision and experimentation in the institutional design of the federation, as well as the analytic aspects outlined in the first section.[17] This flexibility is one of the advantages of classic federalism.

Table 9.2 *Spheres and Regulations in Federal Democracies*

	Linguistic-Symbolic Sphere	Institutional Sphere	Powers Sphere/Fiscal Sphere/International Sphere
Regulation of the plurinational character of the state	Constitutional recognition of the plurinational character of the state Plurilingualism: -Official name of the state -Coins and bank notes -Personal identification documents (passport, driving license, etc.) -Official documents -Stamps Symbols that reflect the plurinational character of the state (hymn, flags)	Plurilinguism in the federal parliament (documents and oral speeches) Plurilinguism in the institution of the monarchy or the presidential republican institution	Inclusion of the plurinationality and plurilinguism in the educational curricula of the whole state (primary and secondary education) Creation of departments for the study of linguistic and cultural minorities at the public universities Plurilinguism in the policies of the federation addressed to all the citizens of the state Plurilinguism in the state's embassies and consulates Plurinationality in the state's foreign policies related to language and culture

(Continued)

Table 9.2 — Continued

	Linguistic-Symbolic Sphere	Institutional Sphere	Powers Sphere/Fiscal Sphere/International Sphere
Asymmetrical or confederal regulations of the subunits' self-government (federal and international level)	Economic and civil law registers	One electoral district for the subunits of the national minorities in federal elections (including suprafederal elections, i.e., EU) Only two administrative levels in the subunit of the national minority: substate and local Possibility of horizontal federal agreements among the subunits of the federation Senate: • veto right for the members of the national minorities in specific areas • symmetrical bicameralism Constitutional court: composition with a special presence of the national minorities of the state	Own national sport selections and Olympic committees Representation of the national minorities in international sport competitions Specific representation in international organizations (EU, Council of Europe) Specific representation in UNESCO Specific representation in the international arena (embassies and consulates) Exclusive legislation and policies with regard to local power, civil law, electoral regulations, linguistics, culture, universities, infrastructure, education, immigration, social security, telecommunictions
Symmetrical regulations		Federalization of the judicial power	Fiscal federalism (legislation, taxation, and spending) Foreign policy with regard to the exclusive powers of the subunits

271

Two additional remarks must be added here concerning the concept of federal asymmetry included in this plural model. First, in all federations there are de facto differences between the subunits, which brings us to the distinction between political asymmetry and constitutional asymmetry. In each federation, the federated parts differ, for example, in population, in territory, and in economic and natural resources. These differences can be of political importance, as they may affect the weight of a given federated part within the federation. Comparative studies have shown that great disparities with respect to the political asymmetries within a federation tend to produce yet greater instability. This would be the case, for example, in a federation in which one of the federated parts contains more than half the overall population. Constitutional asymmetries, on the other hand, differ in the status of self-government for each federated part and are not present in all federations. Constitutional asymmetry involves a nonuniform division of powers across all the subunits. A specific example of constitutional asymmetry can be found in the Canadian federation, where the province of Quebec has political competence in the area of immigration policy.

The second aspect to bear in mind when we speak of asymmetry is the distinction between constitutional asymmetry and asymmetry produced by the exercise of self-government. The federal guarantee of a certain level of self-government is, in itself, a potential generator of diversity among the federated subunits. Nevertheless, it should not be confused with constitutional asymmetry, which establishes diversity within gateway mechanisms, or the federation's rules of play, rather than only within outlet mechanisms, or the different results produced by the exercise of self-government. Differences based on the exercise of self-government are common to all federations and regional decentralized states, asymmetrical or not. For example, if the federated subunits have political competence in the question of environmental policy, their policies could well differ greatly. For instance, in reducing levels of urban traffic, certain federated subunits might give priority to the construction of cycle lanes, others might promote the use of public transport, while yet others might decide to do nothing at all. This kind of diversity is intrinsic to the liberal working of the federal system and is the result of the practical exercise of the political self-government of the different subunits of the federation.[18]

In addition to the advantages associated with the competition between federated units, it is necessary to consider the advantages associated with the accommodation of different nation-building processes. However, these advantages may not always be compatible in practice. The flexibility of a federal system depends on its ability to adapt the balance between the self-government of the federated units and the level of cooperation and presence of the federation in these units according to the evolution of political life. In fact, all federations include mechanisms of cooperation between the two

levels of government, both to promote the unity of the federation and to share responsibilities. In multinational federations, it seems convenient to establish a division of
powers that will ensure a high degree of self-government for those units that display
specific national characteristics.[19]

Obviously, a good democratic accommodation for multinationality must be more
than a mere adaptation of a formal model; it requires political content and constitutional regulation stemming from the notion of *multinationalism*. When the national
reality of a federation is asymmetrical, the regulation of federal asymmetries does not
in itself constitute a guarantee of the accommodation of factual national asymmetries.
Such regulation represents a necessary precondition to constitutional accommodation,
but cannot guarantee the sufficient conditions for such accommodation. Based on the
social and historical conditions in multinational societies, one can argue that, in the absence of the constitutional regulation of the recognition of multinationality, and without asymmetrical or confederate regulations in the field of self-government, it is
particularly difficult to obtain a satisfactory federal resolution of the national question
or the different national questions.

The rigidity of the procedures of constitutional reform often hinders the operation
of institutions and the creation of new political decision-making procedures within
federations. General mechanisms such as "opting in" and "opting out"[20] offer alternatives that do not entail constitutional reforms and can be established without damaging the economic and fiscal equilibrium of the federated units. Therefore, the
relationship between the federal power and the different federated entities would end
up including more asymmetrical mechanisms than those formally recognized by the
legal framework of the federation.[21]

In general terms, we might say that while liberal, democratic, functional, and national values are desirable for the quality of a multinational democratic federation, they
are not always univocal, nor do they always attempt to achieve the same aims.[22] Liberal
protections of individual rights and liberties, democratic participation, efficiency, and
stability are competing goals in classical federal polities. Multinational federations face
additional challenges whose final objective is to form a better democratic union, avoiding the sometimes unintended culturally biased or perverse consequences linked to traditional liberalism 1 approaches. In multinational contexts, the basic demand is that
values of liberty, equality, and individual dignity be allowed to develop in a more deliberate manner and that these values be implemented through the effective accommodation of the different national realities coexisting within one and the same
democracy (Gibbins and Laforest 1998; Gagnon and Tully 2001). Certainly, we are
nowhere near the end of history as far as federalism in multinational polities is concerned.

NOTES

1. This basic distinction between uninational and multinational federations is sometimes accompanied by another distinction that is highly significant to the regulatory and institutional quality of liberal democracies within the context of cultural pluralism: the existence of indigenous minorities, or national groups (First Nations). This is the case in Brazil, the United States, and Canada. This chapter only considers federalism in relation to the first distinction.

2. According to the liberalism 2 position, the first variant of political liberalism provides incentives for restricting minority national differences to the private sphere, all the while accepting the national cultural characteristics of the majority (language, history, traditions, etc.) as an implicit common reality within the public sphere of the polity. I develop this point in Requejo 2001a, where I maintain the terms *liberalism 1* and *liberalism 2*, following the well-known expression formulated by C. Taylor and M. Walzer. It is certainly not without significance that, in multinational polities, the supporters of liberalism 1 are the majority in Ottawa, Toronto, London, and Madrid; whereas the supporters of liberalism 2 are more likely to be found in cities such as Montreal, Edinburgh, and Barcelona.

3. For the relationship between democratic liberalism and nationalism, see Canovan 1996; Norman 1996; Keating 1996; MacCormick 1996; Miller 1995; Smith 1995; Yack 1995; Tamir 1993; Nodia 1992. See also Requejo 1999a

4. This accommodation includes two basic dimensions of the national plurality of a liberal democratic polity: explicit recognition of its internal national plurality at a constitutional level, and the rules that regulate the democratic self-government of those groups. See Tully 1994. For a broader discussion of multiculturalism and liberal democracy, see also Kymlicka and Norman 2000; Williams 1995; Kymlicka 1995; Spinner 1994; Raz 1994; Taylor 1992. For a panoramic analysis of the concept of democratic citizenship within the ambit of political theory, see Norman and Kymlicka 1994.

5. A brief criticism of Rawls's and Habermas's positions in relation to multinational democracies in Requejo 1998b.

6. I have developed this idea in Requejo 1998a.

7. See Linz 1993. In the field of political thought, for a criticism of colonial and imperialist "liberal" legitimation (?) in the writings of thinkers like Locke and Mill, see Parekh 1995.

8. See Taylor 1992, 1989. See also the debate between what we may refer to as "liberal interculturalism" (B. Parekh) and "intercultural liberalism" (W. Kymlicka), in *Constellations* 4, no. 1 (April 1997). I have developed the relationship between universalism and particularism as legitimizing criteria, as well as the contrast between the impartial and partial applications of these two kinds of normativity, in Requejo 2001a (see table)

9. Requejo 1999b, 1998b; Gibbins and Laforest 1998; McRoberts 1997. For a broader view of the debate surrounding asymmetrical federalism and its political and constitutional possibilities within multinational states, like Canada, Belgium, and Spain, see Fossas and Requejo 1999.

10. Elazar 1987, 6; 1991, xvi; Watts 1999, 4.

11. Here I basically follow Daniel Elazar's and Ronald Watts's comparative analysis of federalism, only introducing certain changes to the examples summarized in the table, such as the consideration of Spain as a regional state and not as a strict federation (Watts 1999; Elazar 1987, 1991). As this point has been developed in other chapters of this volume, I do not develop it here.

12. It is worth noting that federalism does not necessarily fit with other concepts like decen-

tralization or subsidiarity from either a theoretical or an institutional perspective. I have developed this point elsewhere, Requejo 1999a, 1998. See Noël 1998; Lemieux 1996; Bermann 1994; Rubin and Feeley 1994; Teasdale 1993.

13. Watts 1995; Burgess and Gagnon 1993; Elazar 1991.

14. In Rawlsian terms: there are many sizes and shades of "veils of ignorance," but there is no a single "meta-veil" to decide from the outside which one is more suitable. The "primary goods" do not seem to be independent of the context. Moreover, the "reflective equilibrium" always takes us back to contexts that produce veils of ignorance and negotiations about which primary goods should be taken into account. In a multinational state, culture and history are partially shared. But sharing them does not automatically mean that national collectivities reconstruct their position in this culture and history in the same way. In these reconstructions, different rational and sentimental elements are present in the transition from the "I" to the different "we" in which identities are constructed. Identities contextualize our "moral autonomy." In other words, Hegel within Kant. See Rorty 1997.

15. This is not, therefore, a question of comparing a global federal model of an essentially asymmetrical character with another (also global) model of a symmetrical kind. Rather, it is an issue of combining both types, and, in the case of nationally plural societies, assessing the territories in which they are to be applied. See Requejo 1998b, ch. 2; McRoberts 1997.

16. For simplicity, the third column of the table includes the last three last basic areas mentioned above. I have also presented federal applied examples of potential agreements in these intersections for the Spanish case (Requejo 2001b).

17. In this institutional design it is important to experiment with the degree of political recognition and practical national self-government finally achieved by the national federated units according to different institutional patterns: the party system in the federation and in the federated entity, the presidential-parlimentarian system of government, the congruence of the majorities in the lower and upper chambers, or lack thereof, the system of appointment of the members of the supreme or constitutional courts, and so on. An important question for the discussion in the years to come is secession: should there be constitutional regulation of procedural mechanisms that would allow for national groups to secede from a multinational federation? This includes questions such as the majority required in such cases, the rules of procedure, the time-scale involved, the possible economic compensations, and so on. In principle, it would seem that there is no moral superiority implicit in maintaining the unity of a federation. The fact of sharing liberal democratic values does not, in itself, indicate anything about the wish of national groups to live together within the same polity. In relation to national secession, see Moore 1998; Lehning 1998; Buchanan 1997; McKim and McMahan 1997; MacCormick 1996; Philpott 1995; Margalit-Raz 1994.

18. See Webber 1994; Peeters 1995; and Fossas 1999 for the cases of Canada, Belgium, and Spain, respectively

19. F. Scharpf, in an analysis of the relation between federal policy making and multiparty systems, has insisted that "the joint-decision structure resembles a trap which, under its own decision rules, cannot be changed by the actors who are caught in it" (Scharpf 1995, 28).

20. Opting in procedural mechanisms depend on the establishment of specific programs by the federal government and the federated entities' decision whether or not to take part in them. In opting out procedures, some federated entities might decide not to take part in a federal program, instead receiving the payments that the central government would have spent in the

federated unity if it took part in that program. Canada has implemented these procedures in several areas in recent times. As R. Watts points out, "in recent decades far-reaching changes in the structure and operation of the Canadian federation have come through the impact of fiscal circumstances and the normal interactions of the policies of federal and provincial governments rather than through formal constitutional amendment.... What is more, such incremental non-constitutional adaptation may be much easier to achieve when the higher stake deliberation of mega-constitutional politics are avoided" (Watts 1999, 122–23).

21.   This seems to be more likely, however, in the areas related to self-government than in areas related to the recognition of multinationality. In any case, it is important to distinguish between those procedures that are designed to carry out the decentralization of the federation and those designed to accommodate the multinationality of the federation. In some cases, these two objectives cannot be achieved by means of the same federal techniques. This duality of objectives has been confused in the practical processes of some devolutionary multinational federations. For an analysis of the Spanish case, see Requejo 1999b.

22.   The proposed model fits the general reasoning of the recent important advisory opinion established by the Canadian Supreme Court on the constitutionality of the potential secession of Quebec (25506, 1998). This advisory opinion establishes that both the constitutional text and the procedure for its reform should be interpreted using the four general principles built into the Canadian constitution: federalism, democracy, constitutionalism, and the respect for minorities.

REFERENCES

Bermann, G. 1994. Taking Subsidiarity Seriously: Federalism in the European Community and the United States. *Columbia Law Review* 94, no. 2:331–455.

Buchanan, A. 1997. Theories of Secession. *Philosophy and Public Affairs* 26, no. 1:31–61.

Burgess, M., and A. Gagnon, eds. 1993. *Comparative Federalism and Federation.* Toronto: University of Toronto Press.

Canovan, M. 1996. *Nationhood and Political Theory.* Elgar: Chetelham.

Carens, J., ed. 1995. *Is Quebec Nationalism Just?: Perspectives from Anglophone Canada.* Montreal.

De Villiers, B., ed. 1995. *Evaluating Federal Systems.* Cape Town: Martinus Nijhoff.

Elazar, D. 1987. *Exploring Federalism.* Tuscaloosa: University of Alabama Press.

———. 1991. *Federal Systems of the World.* Essex: Longman.

Fossas, E. 1999. Asimetría y plurinacionalidad en el Estado Autonómico. In *Asimetría Federal y Estado Plurinacional: El debate sobre la acomodación de la diversidad en Canadá, Bélgica y España,* ed. E. Fossas and F. Requejo, 275–301. Madrid: Trotta.

Fossas, E., and F. Requejo, eds. 1999. *Asimetría Federal y Estado Plurinacional: El debate sobre la acomodación de la diversidad en Canadá, Bélgica y España.* Madrid: Trotta.

Gagnon, A., and J. Tully, eds. 2001. *Multinational Democracies.* Cambridge: Cambridge University Press.

Gibbins, R., and G. Laforest, eds. 1998. *Beyond the Impasse.* Montreal: IRPP.

Keating, M. 1996. *Nations Against the State: The New Politics of Nationalism in Quebec, Catalonia and Scotland.* Macmillan.

Kymlicka, W. 1995. *Multicultural Citizenship: A Liberal Theory of Minority Rights.* Oxford: Clarendon.

Kymlicka, W., and W. Norman, eds. 2000. *Citizenship in Diverse Societies.* Oxford: Oxford University Press.

Lehning, P., ed. 1998. *Theories of Secession.* London: Routledge.

Lemieux, V. 1996. L'analyse politique de la decentralization. *Canadian Journal of Political Science* 29, no. 4:661–80.

Linz, J. 1993. State Building and Nation Building. *European Review* 1, no. 4:355–69.

MacCormick, N. 1996. Liberalism, Nationalism and the Post-sovereign State. *Political Studies* 44:553–67.

Margalit, A., and J. Raz. 1994. National Self-Determination. In *Ethics in the Public Domain: Essays in the Morality of Law and Politics,* ed. J. Raz. Oxford: Clarendon.

McKim and McMahan, eds. 1997. *The Morality of Nationalism.* Oxford: Oxford University Press.

McRoberts, K. 1997. *Misconceiving Canada: The Struggle for National Unity.* Toronto: Oxford University Press.

Miller, D. 1995. *On Nationality.* Oxford: Clarendon.

Moore, M., ed. 1998. *National Self-determination and Secession.* New York: Oxford University Press.

Nagel, T. 1991. *Equality and Partiality.* New York: Oxford University Press.

Nodia, G. 1992. Nationalism and Democracy. *Journal of Democracy* 3, no. 4:3–22.

Noël, A. 1998. The Federal Principle, Solidarity and Partnership. In *Beyond the Impasse,* ed. R. Gibbins and G. Laforest, 241–72. Montreal: IRRP.

Norman, W. 1996. The Ideology of Shared Values: A Myopic Vision of Unity in the Multi-Nation State. *Is Quebec Nationalism Just?: Perspectives from Anglophone Canada,* ed. J. Carens, 137–59. Montreal.

Norman, W., and W. Kymlicka. 1994. Return of the Citizen: A Survey of Recent Work on Citizenship Theory. *Ethics* 104:352–81.

Parekh, B. 1995. Liberalism and Colonialism: A Critique of Locke and Mill. In *The Decolonization of Imagination,* ed. J. Nederveen-Parekh, 81–98. London: Zed Books.

Peeters, P. 1995. Federalism: A Comparative Perspective. Belgium Transforms from a Unitary to a Federal State. In *Evaluating Federal Systems,* ed. B. De Villiers, 194–207. Cape Town: Martinus Nijhoff.

Philpott, D. 1995. In Defense of Self-Determination. *Ethics* 105:352–85.

Preuss, U., and F. Requejo, eds. 1998. *European Citizenship, Multiculturalism and the State.* Nomos: Baden-Baden.

Raz, J. 1994. Multiculturalism: A Liberal Perspective. *Dissent* (winter):67–79.

Requejo, F. 1998a. European Citizenship in Multinational States. Some Limits of Traditional Democratic Theories: Rawls and Habermas. In *European Citizenship: Multiculturalism and the State,* ed. U. Preuss and F. Requejo, 29–50. Nomos: Baden-Baden.

———. 1998b. *Federalisme, per a què?* Tres i Quatre: València.

———. 1999a. Cultural Pluralism Nationalism and Federalism: A Revision of Democratic Citizenship in Multinational States. *European Journal of Political Research* 35, no. 2:255–86.

———. 1999b. La acomodación "federal" de la plurinacionalidad: Democracia liberal y federalismo plural en españa. In *Asimetría Federal y Estado Plurinacional: El debate sobre la acomodación de la diversidad en Canadá, Bélgica y España,* ed. E. Fossas and F. Requejo, 303–44. Madrid: Trotta.

———. 1999c. Pluralisme polític i legitimitat democràtica: El refinament de l'universalisme en les democràcies plurinacionals. In *Pluralisme nacional i legitimitat democràtica,* ed. F. Requejo, 9–29. Barcelona: Proa.

———, ed. 2001a. *Democracy and National Pluralism.* London: Routledge.

———. 2001b. Political Liberalism in Multinational States: The Legitimacy of Plural and Asymmetrical Federalism. In *Multinational Democracies,* ed. A. Gagnon and J. Tully, 110–32. Cambridge: Cambridge University Press.

Requejo, F., and S. Wynants. 2000. Democracia, federalisme i plurinacionalitat: una perspectiva des de Catalunya. In *Govern i Polítiques Públiques a Catalunya,* ed. R. Goma and J. Subirats. Barcelona: Ariel.

Rorty, R. 1997. Justice as Larger Loyalty. In *Justice and Democracy: Cross-Cultural Perspectives,* ed. Bontekoe and Stepaniants. Honolulu: University of Hawaii Press.

Rubin, E., and M. Feeley. 1994. Federalism: Some Notes on a National Neurosis. *UCLA Law Review* 41:903–52.

Scharpf, F. 1995. Federal Arrangements and Multi-Party Systems. *Australian Journal of Political Science* 30, Special Issue:27–39.

Smith, A. 1995. *Nations and Nationalisms in a Global Era.* Cambridge: Polity.

Spinner, J. 1994. *The Boundaries of Citizenship: Race, Ethnicity and Nationality in the Liberal State.* Baltimore: Johns Hopkins University Press.

Tamir, Y. 1993. *Liberal Nationalism.* Princeton: Princeton University Press.

Taylor, Ch .1989. *Sources of the Self.* Cambridge, Mass.: Harvard University Press.

———. 1992. The Politics of Recognition. In *Multiculturalism and the "Politics of Recognition."* Princeton: Princeton University Press.

Teasdale, A. 1993. Subsidiarity in Post-Maastricht Europe. *The Political Quarterly* 64, no. 2: 187–97.

Tully, J., ed. 1994. *Strange Multiplicity: Constitutionalism in an Age of Diversity.* Cambridge: Cambridge University Press.

Watts, R. 1995. Contemporary Views on Federalism. In *Evaluating Federal Systems,* ed. B. De Villiers, 1–29. Cape Town: Martinus Nijhoff.

———. 1999. *Comparing Federal Systems.* 2d ed. Montreal: McGill-Queen's University Press.

Webber, J. 1994. *Reimagining Canada: Language, Culture, Community, and the Canadian Constitution.* Kingston: McGill-Queen's University Press.

Williams, M. 1995. Justice towards Groups. *Political Theory* 23, no. 1:67–91.

Yack, B. 1995. Reconciling Liberalism and Nationalism. *Political Theory* 23, no. 1:166–82.

Part II/Developing Democracies and Postcommunist Regimes

CHAPTER TEN

India

Federalism and the Accommodation of Ethnic Nationalism

Atul Kohli

Editor's note: This essay was written before the attack on the World Trade Center in New York City that led to important developments in South Asia generally and in Kashmir specifically. While the author believes that the argument of the essay is consistent with recent developments, the essay has not been updated to take account of the unfolding events.

India's multicultural federalism provides laboratory-like conditions for examining the organizing question of this volume, namely, the conditions under which ethnic and territorial cleavages are successfully accommodated within states. Over the years numerous territorially based ethnic groups have demanded a greater share of power and wealth from the central Indian state. While most of these demands have been accommodated successfully, a few have not, leading to political disaffection and violence. A comparative analysis of the main instances of successful and unsuccessful accommodation can help tease out the conditions under which federalism works, at least in this one case. In what follows, I undertake such an analysis of three major ethnic movements in India: those of Tamils in Tamilnadu during the 1950s and the 1960s, a case of successful accommodation; those of Sikhs in the Punjab during the 1980s, a more mixed case, which was also eventually successfully accommodated but only after a decade-long phase of terrorist and state violence; and of Muslims in

Kashmir during the 1990s, an unsuccessful case of continuing political and even violent strife.

What factors help explain why some group demands have been more successfully accommodated within the Indian federal structure than others? In the analysis that follows I emphasize the conditioning role of the changing national political context, though group characteristics around which movements emerge, and the resources these groups control—especially via international contacts—are also consequential. More specifically, I argue that two dimensions of the changing national political context are especially relevant, namely, how well central authority is institutionalized within the federal democracy, and the willingness of the ruling groups to share some power and resources with mobilized groups. Given well-established central authority and firm but compromising leaders in a federal system, ethnic demands are typically accommodated successfully following a more-or-less prolonged process of power negotiation. This is because group mobilization and accommodation constitutes a "normal" political process whereby the central state and a variety of ethnic groups discover their relative power balances within a federal polity.

The organization of the essay is straightforward. After a few conceptual comments I provide a sketch of India's changing political context in the first section. The core of the essay then comparatively analyzes the three ethnic movements of Tamils, Sikhs, and Muslims in Kashmir in turn. I conclude with some general observations that address the main themes of this volume.

The Changing Political Context

The core proposition of this essay is that, given a federal polity, variations in the state's capacity to accommodate mobilized ethnic nationalism is a function of two proximate variables: level of institutionalization of the central state,[1] and the degree to which the ruling strategy of leaders accommodates mobilized demands. A well-institutionalized federal polity both provides room for identity-based territorial groups to mobilize and sets firm limits within which such movements must operate. Once mobilized, central leaders may turn out to be more or less accommodating. This may result from something as simple as the type of leader in power, or something more complex, such as a different set of ruling ideas and coalition. Whatever the underlying reasons, accommodating leaders are likely to offer some real concessions, though within limits, leading to a political process whereby more extreme demands are repressed, moderate elites are co-opted, and, following a period of power negotiation, some combination of exhaustion and genuine compromise leads to successful accommodation (Kohli 1997, 326–30).

If institutionalization of state authority and leadership strategies influence the pattern of ethnic movements, prior to a comparative analysis of such movements in India, a few comments concerning how these contextual conditions have varied in India over time are in order. India in the 1950s was a relatively well institutionalized polity, especially compared to other developing countries. This was manifest most strongly in a fairly well organized central state—especially in a highly professional national civil service and armed forces—but also in a well-functioning national political party, the Congress Party, which generally controlled the state. In addition, India possessed such effective institutions as a parliament, an independent judiciary, and a free national press. How and why India came to have such effective institutions is clearly a complex issue, well beyond the scope of this essay. Suffice it to say that some state institutions were inherited from a colonial past and other more political ones were products of a fairly prolonged and cohesive nationalist movement (Weiner 1967, 1989; Kohli 2002). India's rigid and segmented social structure—especially the elaborate caste hierarchies, organized among numerous, relatively isolated villages—kept levels of political mobilization low and ironically may have further helped new institutions to take root in the early postindependence phase.

Over time some of India's political institutions weakened. In terms of periodization, if the 1950s was a decade of relatively effective institutions, the 1960s is best thought of as a decade of transition during which the nationalist legacy declined, political competition and challenges to the hegemony of the Congress Party increased, and a new type of political system—a more populist one with noninstitutional methods of securing electoral majorities—was created by Indira Gandhi. During the two following decades, the 1970s and 1980s, some of India's well-established institutions were battered, especially by leaders in power.

Since levels of institutionalization are relative, it is important to remember that even during the 1970s and 1980s, India's central state authority in comparison to most African and many Latin American countries was relatively well institutionalized. Nevertheless, in comparison to its own past, a fair amount of deinstitutionalization had occurred: the Congress Party as an organization was largely destroyed; the civil service, police, and even the armed forces became less professional and more politicized; parliament became less effective; and the autonomy of the judiciary was reduced. Once again, how and why these political changes occurred constitute a complex story, far beyond the scope of this essay.[2]

As to the other variable of leadership strategy, India has had four main prime ministers who have ruled for more than two to three years each: Nehru ruled India for nearly seventeen years (from 1947 until his death in 1964); his daughter Indira Gandhi dominated India for nearly as long as the father (1966–77 and 1980–84); then her son,

Rajiv Gandhi, ruled from 1985 to 1989; and Prime Minister Narasimha Rao was in power during 1991–96.[3] The political strategy of Atal Bihari Vajpayee, who became India's prime minister in the late 1990s, is still unfolding and too early to assess. Characterizing the strategies of these leaders briefly is clearly to grossly oversimplify a fairly complex reality. I do so only reluctantly.

The main analytical concern here is how leaders typically respond to oppositional challenges, especially demands of mobilized groups for greater self-determination. On a dimension of leadership strategy that varies from accommodating to unaccommodating, Nehru was closer to the accommodating end of the spectrum. This was in part a function of his own personality and in part a reflection of his relatively secure power position; a concession from Nehru here or there enhanced his magnanimity rather than threatened his hold on power. The political situation during his daughter's reign, however, was quite different, as were her political instincts. Congress's hegemony had by then declined and Indira consolidated her power against considerable odds. She was always suspicious of power challenges. She re-created a powerful political center in India mainly by portraying herself as a champion of the poor. As her personal popularity soared, opposition to her also became strident, culminating in the "Emergency" in 1975, when democratic rights in India were suspended for about two years. When Indira Gandhi returned to power in 1980, she was less populist; yet still needing to mobilize electoral pluralities, she started flirting with communal themes, occasionally courting India's Hindus (more than 80 percent of India's population) by railing against religious minorities, especially Sikhs. This strategy made her increasingly less accommodating toward minorities, lest she be viewed as appeasing them. Overall, therefore, Indira Gandhi, in contrast to Nehru, was closer to the unaccommodating end of the leadership spectrum.

Both the subsequent leaders, Rajiv Gandhi and Narasimha Rao, were more flexible than Indira Gandhi.[4] Rajiv Gandhi was especially accommodating toward self-determination movements in the first two years of his rule. As his political situation became less secure, however, he too, like his mother, flirted with communalism, tilting occasionally in a pro-Muslim direction, but mainly courting the Hindu vote, becoming more and more indecisive and unaccommodating in the second half of his rule. Narasimha Rao in the 1990s portrayed himself as a nonpersonalistic, flexible leader who, at a minimum, was not bent on a further centralization of power in his own hands. After the assassination of two prime ministers (both Indira and Rajiv were assassinated for political reasons), this ruling strategy appeared to have calmed an agitated polity, at least until 1998, when the right-wing, Hindu nationalist party, the Bhartiya Janata Party (BJP), came to power.

Thus, to oversimplify a rather complex reality, the Nehru period in India, say, from 1950 to 1964, is best understood as a period when India's central state was relatively well institutionalized and leadership strategy, though firm, was also flexible and accommodating to demands for self-determination. Subsequently, especially since the mid-1960s, India's political institutions weakened, though they remain relatively effective by developing country standards. The leadership strategy over the past three decades has varied. Whereas Indira Gandhi was quite unaccommodating toward demanding groups, both Rajiv and Rao appeared to be, at least less threatening, if not actually more accommodating. With this context in mind, we are now in a position to turn our attention to a few specific self-determination movements within India.

Tamil Nationalism

Tamilnadu is one of India's important states, an integral part of the Indian federal system. Today no one, not even those who live in Tamilnadu, question whether they are fully a part of the Indian union. However, it was not always so. During the 1950s and the 1960s, Tamil leaders argued that Tamils were a distinctive people. They mobilized considerable support for a "Tamil Nation" and demanded, at minimum, greater power and control over their own affairs vis-à-vis New Delhi or, at maximum, secession from India. The movement's history is well recorded (Barnett 1976), so a very brief recapitulation of the rise and decline of this movement will serve our broader analytical interests.

Tamil is a language and Tamils as a social group are, therefore, mainly a linguistically defined group. Tamil, along with a few other languages in south India, but unlike most languages spoken in northern India, does not derive its roots from classical Sanskrit with its Indo-Germanic roots. Rather, Tamil is a Dravidian language. Tamil nationalists also used to insist that Tamils are a separate racial and cultural group, with their roots in a Dravidian society that was indigenous to southern India prior to the historic arrival of and domination by "northern Aryans." Brahmans in Tamil society could thus be viewed, not as natural hegemons of a caste society, but rather as agents of northern domination. That some of the Tamil Brahmans were of lighter skin color than much of the darker-skinned Tamil society only added to the plausibility of such an interpretation. Two other sets of "facts-on-the-ground" are important for understanding the dynamics of Tamil nationalism. First, Brahmans in Tamil society constitute a relatively small caste group: less than 5 percent of the total (in comparison, say, to parts of northern India, where Brahmans often constitute nearly 10 percent of the total population). Second, for a variety of historical reasons, the area that is now Tamilnadu was more urbanized by midcentury than many other parts of India.

The Congress Party in this part of India, as elsewhere, built its preindependence base on the Brahmans. That the Brahmans were few in number and that the non-Brahman castes were already active in city life provided the necessary conditions for the early rise of an anti-Brahman movement. Democratization and related power conflicts, in other words, came relatively early to this region of India. The first institutional manifestation of that movement was the Justice Party, which was led by the elite of the non-Brahman castes and sided with the British against both Brahmans and Congress in the hope of securing concessions in government jobs and in education. The Justice Party eventually was delegitimized both because of its elitist nature and because of the rising tide of nationalism. That had significant consequences, especially because Congress became identified as a Brahman party in a region where Brahmans had not been able to establish cultural and political hegemony. The early development of a cleavage between the Brahman and anti-Brahman forces opened up the political space for subsequent anti-Congress developments.

The link between Congress and the Brahmans became the target of Tamil nationalists in the postindependence period. The Congress Party in Madras could not easily break out of that mold. The continued Congress-Brahman alliance enabled the regional nationalists to mobilize simultaneously against both caste domination and domination by north Indians. Hammering on the theme of the distinctiveness of the Tamil tradition, and linking that with an opposition to northern Hindi rule and its allies the southern Brahmans, the leaders of the Dravidian movement found a ready audience among the numerous backward castes that were already concentrated in the cities. To simplify a complex picture, Tamil nationalism and a petit bourgeois base among the urban backward castes provided the core support for a regional nationalist movement.

The early demands of this self-determination movement were for greater power and control. Over time, the broader movement came to include a separatist movement demanding a "Dravidistan," or a land for the Dravidian people. A number of Indian states in the early 1950s argued for reorganizing the Indian federation along linguistic lines. Most such demands, of course, were not separatist. Nevertheless, in the aftermath of India's separation from Pakistan, Nehru in the early 1950s was reluctant to implement a linguistic redesign, lest it strengthen secessionist tendencies and lead to a further breakup of India. Tamil nationalists and their mobilized supporters were a case in point, insofar as they pressed their identity politics hard through demonstrations that occasionally turned violent and included public burning of the Indian flag and constitution. When pressed by several states, Nehru recalculated that the dangers of not devolving power to linguistic groups were greater than of doing so. Fully in control at the national center and widely considered to be India's legitimate leader, Nehru set firm limits on what powers the newly constituted states would have and what would be controlled by New Delhi (which, by the way, was substantial). Within these limits, then, India's federal system was reorganized along linguistic states in 1956. This reorganization gave Tamil nationalists a Tamil state, taking a fair amount of the separatist steam out of the movement.

Having gained a separate state of their own (first called Madras, subsequently relabeled Tamilnadu, or home of the Tamils), the goal of the Tamil nationalist struggle shifted to ousting Congress from power within the state. For this, the Tamil nationalists utilized a political party, the Dravida Munnetra Kazhagam (DMK), and sought to broaden their power base. They adopted a radical rhetoric of land reform and eradication of the caste system, which further threatened the Brahmans. Many of the intermediate and lower caste dwellers in villages thus came to be attracted to the DMK. The DMK also successfully mobilized cultural themes. In this they were fortunate insofar as many Tamil nationalists were playwrights, literary figures, and theater and movie actors. Movies were the new emerging medium and they were used successfully by the DMK to popularize such themes as the injustices of the caste system, the glories of Tamil history, and the social need for Robin Hood heroes, who would deliver the poor, weak, and dispossessed from the clutches of the rich and the wicked.

As Tamil nationalism became more populist it simultaneously became less coherent yet more capable of winning elections. Following Nehru's death, for example, India's national leaders for a brief moment attempted to once again impose Hindi as a national language on all states. Many states reacted negatively, with Tamilnadu reacting the most violently. Well-mobilized to confront precisely such national policy shifts, language riots broke out all over the state. Several students burned themselves to death, protesting the moves of the national government. For another brief moment the national government used a heavy coercive hand to deal with protests. As matters got worse, the national government backtracked. The principle was conceded that regional languages, such as Tamil, were coequal to two other national languages, namely, Hindi and English. This was a major victory for the DMK. Enjoying considerable popularity, the DMK ousted the Congress from power within Tamilnadu in the 1967 elections, and the Congress has never returned to power in that state since.

The rise and consolidation of power by the DMK had a profound impact on Tamilnadu's politics. The highest leadership posts in the state slipped out of the hands of Brahmans and went to the well-educated elite of the non-Brahman castes. The intermediate and local leadership more accurately reflected the real power base of the DMK: the intermediate castes. Many of them gained access to more power and resources. As the DMK settled down to rule, the predictable happened. Over time, the DMK lost much of its self-determination, anticenter militancy, and commitment to socioeconomic reforms. The reasons for that deradicalization in Tamilnadu were the same as elsewhere. Once national leaders made important concessions (though within firm limits) and the DMK achieved its major goal of securing increased power, realpolitik concerns took over and mobilizing ideologies slowly lost their relevance for guiding governmental actions. Ethnic nationalism slowly declined, leading to successful accommodation.

Sikh Nationalism

Punjab, the home of the green revolution, is one of India's most prosperous states, and Sikhs constitute about half of that state's population (the other half being Hindus). Sikh nationalism was a powerful political force in the state throughout the 1980s. Demands of Sikh groups varied from greater political and economic control within the Indian federation to secession from India and the creation of a sovereign state, Khalistan. The national government under Indira Gandhi, especially during the 1980s, was not only unaccommodating but actively sought to divide and rule the Sikhs. The strategy backfired, as some Sikh groups turned sharply militant. The central state, in turn, met the militancy with considerable force. Because they were in a border state with Pakistan, Punjab's militant Sikhs were able to secure arms and support from across the border. Militant nationalists and a repressive state thus confronted each other in a vicious cycle of growing violence. Violence took its toll throughout the 1980s, as nearly 1,000 people died every year, peaking in 1990 when some 4,000 people were killed in political violence. Since then, however, the situation has changed. Brutal state repression succeeded in eliminating many of the militants, and a more politically flexible Rao allowed state-level elections in Punjab in the early 1990s. As an elected government settled down to rule, an exhausted state went back to work and both militancy and state repression fell into the background. In 1993 only seventy-three people died in political violence, and in the decade since investment flows into Punjab have grown dramatically and violence has remained at a relatively low and sporadic level.

The underlying story behind the rise and decline of Sikh nationalism is complex and is discussed in detail elsewhere (Brass 1990, 169–213). What follows, therefore, is only a brief account. Sikhs are a religious group, concentrated mainly in the Punjab. Sikh men are distinctive in that they wear religiously prescribed long hair and turbans. Sikhs and Hindus lived side by side, peacefully, for several centuries. Like the Hindus—from which Sikhism was initially derived in the late medieval period—Sikhs are internally differentiated along castelike groups. Most Sikhs are relatively prosperous agriculturalists. A sizable minority are urban traders and entrepreneurs; until recently intermarriage between these groups and their Hindu counterparts was common in the Punjab.

Sikhs also have their own version of untouchables, the equivalent of the lowest Hindu castes that generally tend to own no land and be very poor.

Prior to the political turmoil that arose in the 1980s, caste and community divisions in Punjab had given rise to easily identifiable political divisions. In the past, the Hindus generally supported the Congress Party, though a significant minority had also been loyal to a Hindu nationalist party. The Akali Dal (a predominantly Sikh party in the state), by contrast, had consistently counted on the Sikh vote but seldom succeeded in mobilizing all the Sikhs as an ethnic political bloc.

Given internal divisions among Sikhs, Congress during the 1960s and 1970s was often in a position to form a government in Punjab with the help of Hindus and a significant Sikh minority. The Akalis, by contrast, could only form a coalition government, and that only with a seemingly unlikely partner: the pro-Hindu party. These basic political and community divisions provide the background essential for understanding the intensified political activities of the Sikhs during the 1980s. Akali militancy was aimed at mobilizing as many Sikhs as possible around a platform of Sikh nationalism. The analytical issue here is why those fairly normal political ambitions generated so much chaos and turmoil.

The Akali Dal as a political party has always exhibited a mixture of religious fervor and hard-nosed political realism aimed at capturing power. Being a primarily Sikh party, there is a close relationship between the party and Sikh religious organizations. The Sikh political elite thus periodically utilize religious organizations to influence the political behavior of the laity. Over the years, the Akalis have been in and out of power. They first came to power in 1966, when they spearheaded a successful movement for a separate *Punjabi Suba* (or the land where Punjabi is spoken) and the current boundaries of the state of Punjab were drawn. Given the electoral arithmetic, however, the power position of the Akalis was never secure. Sikhs constituted a bare majority in the state and Congress leaders consistently sought to draw away part of the Sikh vote through one machination or another. Unlike Tamilnadu, therefore, where Tamil nationalists came to power around the same time, consolidated their hold, and settled on a slow but steady road toward deradicalization, Akalis in the Punjab have consistently needed to whip up religious and nationalist issues that would keep Sikhs united politically.

During the 1970s, as Indira Gandhi's popularity grew across India, Congress leaders in the Punjab undertook aggressive efforts to divide Sikhs and to consolidate their own hold over state politics. A threatened Akali Dal had little choice but to raise the ante; they started demanding even greater control over the affairs of Sikhs, coming closer and closer in their formal statements to wanting a sovereign state for the Sikhs that they could control. Indira Gandhi countered by a combination of repression—labeling secessionists as seditious—and by further attempts to divide the Sikhs. During the "Emergency" many Sikh leaders were imprisoned. When Indira returned to power in 1980, and another round of elections was held in Punjab, Congress won a clear majority while the Akalis secured only 27 percent of the popular vote. Congress leaders considered themselves the legitimate, elected rulers. The Akalis, by contrast, viewed Punjab as "their" state, which they ought to control. The Akalis were thus cornered in their own state and decided they had to fight for their political life. Much of what followed— some anticipated but most of it unanticipated—makes sense mainly from this retrospective logic of competitive mobilization.

The battle lines were drawn. Indira Gandhi had the popular support and decided to use her position of advantage to launch a political offensive and consolidate her position vis-à-vis the Akalis. If she could use Sikh militants to split the ranks of the Akalis still further between the moderates and the extremists, victory would be hers. And this is what she attempted. The Akali Dal possessed another set of political resources, however, whose efficacy Indira Gandhi apparently underestimated. The Akalis still could organize around the issue of Sikh nationalism like no other party in Punjab. The chain of Sikh temples, moreover, provided a ready organizational network with money, personnel, and the proven ability to sway public opinion. A populist, centralizing, and unaccommodating national leader, Indira Gandhi, thus came to be pitted against a regional party, the Akali Dal, which had considerable potential to mobilize the forces of religious nationalism.

Both Indira Gandhi and the Akalis assembled militant forces for political ends. In retrospect, it is clear that over the next several years, the militancy led to civil disorder that took on a political life of its own, increasingly out of the control of both the Akalis and the national government. Whether that simply was not foreseen or was brazenly ignored under the short-term pressure to seize political advantage may never be known. What we do know is that, once mobilized, Sikh militants very quickly gained political advantage over moderate Sikh leaders. If the political aim was indeed to create a separate Sikh state, namely, a Khalistan, then moderate Sikh leaders had little to contribute toward achieving such ends. A move toward secession was mainly a political ploy for most moderate Akalis. Having shifted the political discourse in that direction, however, any and all efforts to work with New Delhi simply undermined the legitimacy of this moderate leadership; normal politics made the moderates look like opportunists, unworthy of a leadership mantle. True believers, instead, became heroes of the day and gained public sympathy. Flush with arms that often came from Afghanistan via Pakistan, Sikh militants unleashed a holy war, aimed at establishing a sovereign Sikh state. Indira Gandhi countered by increasing governmental repression. As a militancy and repression cycle set in, Punjab, one of India's most prosperous states, became engulfed in a long decade of violence.

There were at least two important occasions during the 1980s when Congress and Sikh moderates came close to a compromise. Among the demands of Akalis were a number of concrete "bread and butter" issues that fell well short of secession: enhanced access to river waters, control over the capital city of Punjab, and more agricultural subsidies. Indira Gandhi during 1982–84 refused these compromises lest she be viewed nationally as appeasing minorities. This weakened Sikh moderates and privileged those who wanted to use more militant tactics. A second and more important occasion arose when Rajiv Gandhi came to power in 1985. Flush with victory and committed to resolving the Punjab conflict, Rajiv offered broad compromises to Akalis. The results were dramatic. Elections were held in the state, Akalis came to power, and political violence dropped sharply during 1985. Unfortunately, all this was short lived. Very quickly Rajiv Gandhi found it impossible to implement the compromises he had offered to the Akali leaders. While the details are complex, the major obstacle to implementation were Rajiv's own growing political vulnerabilities: as his national popularity declined, starting sometime in 1986, he was increasingly pressed within his own party to make no further concessions to minorities. Once it became clear, therefore, that concessions from Delhi were more apparent than real, the position of elected Akali leaders was again undermined and the cycle of militancy and repression reappeared.

Had India been a weaker state during this period, it is conceivable that Sikh secessionists would have succeeded in establishing yet another state on the subcontinent. As it was, however, even though its political institutions had weakened considerably over the previous decades, India remained a relatively well-established state. The national legitimacy of elected leaders, an effective civil and police bureaucracy, and, most important, a loyal armed forces are critical components of the state. They were all utilized, especially brute force, to contain and repress the Sikh militants, who also became marginalized over time and lost popular support. Repression and political marginalization led to a dwindling number of Sikh militants undertaking violent acts to accomplish secessionist goals.

Narasimha Rao finally called elections in the Punjab in the early 1990s. The Akalis boycotted the election but a Sikh-led Congress government came to power. The Akalis eventually joined the government after municipal elections were held. Subsequently, the militancy and repression of the 1980s fell into the background.

To sum up, Sikh nationalism in the Punjab was eventually accommodated, but only after a decade-long phase of violence and repression. Among the important underlying contrasts with the earlier movement of Tamils was the contrasting approach of Nehru and Indira Gandhi, as Nehru was accommodating and Indira was not. Of course, there were other factors at work: (1) Tamils dominate Tamilnadu, whereas the Sikhs constitute only half of the Punjab's population; (2) Tamils are a linguistic group, whereas Sikhs are a religious group and, given the close marriage of politics and religion in Sikhism, the Sikh religion probably provides a more encompassing identity than does attachment to a language; (3) the threat posed by rapid socioeconomic change in the Punjab to Sikhism as a religious community was more serious than that posed to the linguistically defined community of Tamils; and (4) Tamils did not have as easy an access to arms and across-the-border sanctuaries as did Sikh militants. All of these factors played some role but none of them on their own varies as neatly with the rise and decline of movements as do the relative degrees of institutionalization of state authority and the contrasting strategies of national leaders. Within a more turbulent polity, Indira Gandhi's commitment to dominate Punjab politics pushed Akalis into aggressive mobilization. Once mobilized, professional politicians lost control and militants took over. Finally, over time, militants were repressed out of existence and a tired population was relieved to accept some concessions from a more accommodating national leadership and to vote an elected provincial government back to power.

Muslim Nationalism in Kashmir

Since 1989 the state of Jammu and Kashmir, especially its northern valley of Kashmir, has been gripped by a cycle of militancy and repression. The main protagonists of the conflict are Islamic groups that do not want Kashmir to be part of India, and a variety of Indian security forces. The dimensions of the conflict are quite severe: in a relatively sparsely populated state of some 8 million people (approximately 65 percent Muslim), some 10,000 to 40,000 people died as a result of political violence over the 1990s; security forces deployed in the state consist of more than 300 paramilitary companies and several army divisions. At least 100,000 Hindus have migrated away from the Muslim-dominated Kashmir valley, mainly to Jammu, the southern, Hindu-dominated part of the state. During the second half of the 1990s, India's central government pursued a two-pronged strategy: it came down very hard on recalcitrant Islamic militants; and the electoral process was resumed, strengthening the hands of those leaders who are willing to respect "constitutional boundaries." The hopes that this may generate a result similar to that in the case of the Sikhs in Punjab, namely, a return to normalcy, have not been borne out, at least not at the time of writing. Moreover, with a more hard-line BJP government in power, that may well rescind the special status that Kashmir enjoys within the Indian federation, the prospects of successful accommodation do not appear bright.

Once again, the full story behind this specific Indian case of ethnic politics has been explored elsewhere and need not be recalled here (Widmalm 2002). The condensed account below suggests that this case challenges the argument developed above. I explain this anomaly as partly a result of the fact that the conflict is more internationalized than the other two cases and partly that the conflict is still unfolding. The decline of ethnic militancy and of the related fratricide may still set in over the next few years. Whatever the eventual outcome, some elements of how and why ethnic conflict flared up in Kashmir are still broadly consistent with the propositions developed above.

Ever since India and Pakistan emerged as sovereign states in the late 1940s, Kashmir has been a focus of dispute. As a Muslim majority state that was contiguous to Pakistan, it is arguable that Kashmir should have become a part of Pakistan. The Hindu head of the Kashmiri state instead chose to join India. Pakistan contested the legality of this decision and, as often happens in interstate relations, it was not legality but might that determined what was right; India and Pakistan fought two wars over the issue and a large part of Kashmir was incorporated into India. What is important for our analytical purposes is that, in spite of these international problems, for much of this period, say 1950 to 1980, ethnic nationalism in Kashmir remained relatively mild. The memory and stories of ethnic injustices were probably kept alive. Nevertheless, Kashmir was accorded a special status by the Indian constitution, giving it considerable autonomy within India's federal system; India's central government also provided a substantial financial subsidy to facilitate the economic development of Kashmir. This seemed to have succeeded. While both New Delhi and Kashmiri leaders, especially Muslim leaders, viewed each other with suspicion, a working arrangement of sorts operated well into the early 1980s.

Several new factors came into play in the early 1980s. As discussed above, the Indian polity as a whole was by now relatively more turbulent. Old nationalist institutions like the Congress Party were in decline. A whole new postnationalist generation demanded a greater share of political and economic resources. Indira Gandhi was at the helm nationally. In her postpopulist phase, she in the early 1980s increasingly flirted with pro-Hindu themes to re-create a new national electoral coalition. This shift in strategy bode ill for states with considerable non-Hindu populations, such as the Sikhs in the Punjab and Muslims in Kashmir. Given Indira Gandhi's centralizing and unaccommodating instincts, moreover, states like Kashmir came under increasing political pressure.

Within Kashmir, the state's "founding father" and much-revered leader Sheikh Abdullah died in 1982. His son Farooq Abdullah moved into the resulting political vacuum, both as the leader of the state's main non-Congress political party, the National Conference, and as the head of the state government. State-level elections in 1983 turned out to be quite important. Farooq successfully campaigned on an anti-Congress, anti-Delhi, and pro-Kashmiri autonomy platform. The campaign caught the imagination of a large majority, especially Kashmir's Muslim majority. Indira Gandhi herself campaigned in Kashmir on behalf of the state Congress Party, often appealing to the fears of Jammu Hindus. Communal polarization, while hardly new to Kashmir, increasingly came to be sponsored by competing elites and grew. Farooq's platform fell well short of secessionist demands. Nevertheless, his emphasis on regional autonomy for Kashmir turned out to be very popular, propelling the National Conference to a handsome electoral victory against the Congress.

Farooq in Kashmir had to tread a thin line between emphasizing Kashmiri autonomy on the one hand and not appearing as an antinational, Muslim Kashmiri secessionist on the other hand. In order to bolster this precarious position, he joined hands with other non-Congress heads of state governments. Hoping to be one of the many who were part of the "loyal opposition," Farooq hosted a well-publicized conference in Kashmir of all major opposition leaders. Unfortunately, this was precisely the type of move that truly threatened Indira Gandhi. Hoping to clip Farooq's growing political wings, Indira appointed a close and tough personal aide, Jagmohan, to be Kashmir's governor. Jagmohan, in turn, initiated a series of machinations whereby a number of National Conference legislators defected to the Congress, further threatening Farooq's position. Jagmohan eventually dismissed Farooq as Kashmir's chief minister in 1984, claiming without proof that Farooq had lost the support of a majority in the legislature.

Farooq's dismissal—very much a part of an all-India pattern of a threatened Indira Gandhi bent on centralizing and weakening India's federal institutions—turned out to be a critical turning point. While public opinion data are not available, it appears that the dismissal sent a strong message, especially to Kashmiri Muslims, that their democratic and legitimate efforts to create greater political spaces within India may well be thwarted.[5] This growing alienation of Muslims, especially of their urban youth, was not helped by political events that followed. As the 1987 state elections approached (Indira Gandhi was by now dead, replaced nationally by her son Rajiv), Farooq Abdullah, both pressed politically and sufficiently opportunistic, formed an electoral alliance with the Congress Party. This seemingly innocuous electoral opportunism had the profound impact of eliminating any major democratic outlet for Kashmiri Muslims who sought greater autonomy from Delhi. A number of Muslim groups hurriedly came together in an umbrella organization, the Muslim United Front. They, in turn, mobilized the urban youth and their popularity grew. Elections and the aftermath turned out to be bitter. Mobilized and angry youth were confronted by security forces. Many were roughed up. Further alienated, some went across the border to Pakistan to be trained as militants and returned with Kalashnikovs. The National Front—Congress alliance won the election but charges that they had rigged the elections were widespread. Whatever the reality, Kashmir was engulfed by a serious legitimacy crisis.

Meanwhile, the Soviet Union intervened in Afghanistan, the United States rearmed Pakistan, and Pakistani rulers regained a sense of confidence vis-à-vis India that they lost during the 1971 war over Bangladesh. There is ample evidence to indicate that Pakistan trained alienated Muslim youths from Kashmir, and provided arms and resources. Even when the Pakistani government was not directly involved, India's hostile neighbor became both a staging ground and a sanctuary for Kashmiri militants. The number of Kashmiris trained in Pakistan by 1990 was estimated to be in the several thousands.[6]

Following the 1987 elections, Kashmiri Muslims, especially those in the valley (Muslims in Jammu tend to be ethnically distinct), confronted governments in Kashmir and in New Delhi simultaneously as hostile parties. Kashmiri militants and security forces increasingly met each other in growing cycles of militancy and repression. Human rights abuses occurred, and stories of such abuses must have further alienated the Muslim population. When elections were called again in 1989, militant groups boycotted them quite successfully. The more the democratic political process lost its meaning, the more a full-scale insurgency came to be unleashed.

Factionalism among Islamic militants has also increasingly come to the fore.[7] The Jammu and Kashmir Liberation Front (JKLF), a nominally secular group that is nevertheless controlled by Muslim leaders, argues for a sovereign state of Kashmir, including part of the Kashmir controlled by Pakistan, and remains a popular group. The JKLF and other similar separatist groups have sought to work together under an umbrella organization, the All-Party Hurriyat Conference. The Hizbul Mujahideen are modeled after the Mujahids in Afghanistan and argue for accession of Kashmir to Pakistan. While less popular than the JKLF, the Mujahideen receive more support from Pakistan and its hardened militants are better trained and better armed. Other small Pakistani-trained terrorist groups—such as the Lakshar-e-Toiba—do not enjoy mass following but can unleash considerable havoc. The popular separatist groups face the enormous obstacle that neither India nor Pakistan supports the possibility of a sovereign state of Kashmir. By contrast, the militant Mujahideen and others, while a potent armed force, are politically not so popular. The more the Hindus have migrated out of the Kashmir valley, the more the struggle has become one of Kashmiri Muslims versus India. Most Kashmiri Muslims, however, want a sovereign state; they do not want to join Pakistan. Aside from the fact that neither India nor Pakistan favors such an outcome, Kashmiri Muslims face another major hurdle: there are nearly 100 million Muslims in India, of which Kashmiri Muslims constitute only about 5 million.

Fearing their own welfare in India if a Kashmiri Muslim state were established by force (such a move is bound to encourage anti-Muslim sentiments), Indian Muslims have generally refrained from openly supporting the cause of Kashmiri Muslims. The overall situation is thus a near stalemate: most Kashmiri Muslims are by now deeply alienated from India, and while divided among themselves, a majority would probably opt for a sovereign state of Kashmir. Not only will the powerful Indian state not let go of the Kashmiri Muslims, even Pakistan does not support such an outcome. Pakistani-trained militants, however, with arms left over from the Afghanistan civil war, remain a powerful militant force, but one that Indian security forces have successfully fought to a standstill. The state-level elections of 1996 brought Farooq Abdullah back to power, and the 2002 elections a Congress-supported coalition. Both of these governments continued to rule a fairly turbulent region.

Leaving the details of the tragic story aside, what are its analytical implications? It is clear that the roots of the cycle of militancy and repression in Kashmir can be traced back to a power conflict in which a centralizing Indira Gandhi dislodged the elected government of Farooq Abdullah, precipitating a long-term legitimacy crisis. Had political institutions like parties within Kashmir or the Indian federal system been stronger, such centralizing antics of one leader would have been not only difficult to pursue but easier to weather if pursued. The combination, however, of weakening institutions and an unaccommodating national leader helped push normal power struggles down the path of a militancy and repression cycle. The early trajectory of the Kashmir conflict thus broadly fits the analytical argument developed above. That the conflict in Kashmir continues clearly defies the predicted accommodation. Since India's democratic institutions, in spite of some weakening, remain relatively strong and since the leadership of Rao and of his successors—at least until the rise of the BJP—was more flexible than that of Indira Gandhi, how does one explain the persistence of a high-intensity ethnic conflict in Kashmir?

Three different answers (or three components of one answer) are possible to this question, each with different implications for the analytical argument proposed in this essay. The first answer, and the one least compatible with the thesis of this essay, would focus on the distinct values and discourse of Islam, possibly suggesting that political identity based on Islam is felt both more intensely and more comprehensively and thus an Islam-based ethnic movement ought not to be expected to follow the same trajectory as Tamil or Sikh nationalist movements. Such an argument, however, would have the burden of explaining why Muslim nationalism flared up mainly in Kashmir (and not in other parts of India) and why mainly in the 1990s.

A second answer would focus on the role of Pakistan in the Kashmir crisis. Unlike in Tamilnadu and even more than in the Punjab, the argument would be that Pakistan's continuing involvement in Kashmir has prolonged the conflict. While I have not emphasized this explanation, such an argument is compatible with the thesis of this essay insofar as the logic of the argument developed here is essentially political: ethnic movements in federal democracies constitute a political process whereby the central state and mobilized groups discover their relative power balances. Intervention by an external actor then alters the power-balancing process, at least prolonging, if not altering, the overall trajectory.

Finally, the simple answer that is most readily compatible with this essay's thesis is that it is still too early to predict how the Kashmir crisis will end. If Pakistan's role diminishes (a role which, at the time of writing, seems to be actually increasing) and if the BJP government maintains a firm but flexible set of policies, the ethnic conflict in Kashmir may well decline over the next few years. However, if the BJP government attempts to curtail the autonomy of Kashmir, moving farther in the direction of centralization, and/or if Pakistan's role in the conflict escalates, the regional conflict may well be exacerbated.

Conclusion

This volume seeks to understand why territorial cleavages are accommodated better in some states than in others. While the editors of the volume will provide the broader, cross-national generalizations, the Indian case alone also sheds some light on this central question. First, for the most part, Indian federalism works. Sharing of power within the framework of a relatively well-established central state has enabled the accommodation of a number of ethnic groups within Indian democracy. Ever since the linguistic reorganization of the Indian federal system in the late 1950s, it is a notable fact that most of India's large states have accepted the legitimacy of the system. When they have not, the resulting political conflict has been mostly peaceful. The case of Tamilnadu discussed above underlined the general process of how such successful accommodation has been achieved. A well-institutionalized federal democracy both encouraged ethnic demands to emerge and provided firm limits on how far such demands can go. Concessions by secure but accommodating national leaders, in turn, gave ethnic elites what they wanted most, namely, enhanced power. As a result, the ethnic movement lost its radical edge and settled down as part and parcel of politics of peaceful negotiation within a federal structure.

There are other instances in India that do not conform to this happy pattern of successful accommodation. They too teach us some analytical lessons of broader significance. The cases of Punjab and Kashmir analyzed above highlighted how growing deinstitutionalization in the Indian polity and centralizing leadership strategies provided the changed context within which these regional secessionist movements emerged. From the standpoint of this volume, the general point here is that the more a formal federal system functioned in practice as a unitary system, the less was the system's capacity to accommodate ethnic and territorial cleavages. The fact that these two movements gelled around religious rather than linguistic identities, and that they had considerably more access to foreign resources probably helps explain—at least in part—their prolonged militancy. Nevertheless, some combination of boundary-setting repression and concessions helped the ethnic conflict in Punjab settle down. Whether a similar process of successful accommodation will unfold in the near future in India's Kashmir or not will remain an important test for the argument developed in this essay.

NOTES

This chapter is based on an earlier (1997) essay, "Can Democracies Accommodate Ethnic Nationalism?" *Journal of Asian Studies* 56, 2:325–44

1. I use this term *institutionalization* in the manner of Samuel Huntington. See his *Political Order in Changing Societies* (New Haven: Yale University Press, 1968).

2. A growing personalization of power was at the heart of the story; growing political fragmentation in society privileged personalism and, in turn, personalistic leaders damaged the institutions that constrained their discretionary powers. For details, see Atul Kohli, *Democracy and Discontent* (New York: Cambridge University Press, 1990). Also see Paul Brass, *Politics of India Since Independence* (New York: Cambridge University Press, 1990); and Lloyd Rudolph and Susanne Rudolph, *In Pursuit of Lakshimi: The Political Economy of the Indian State* (Chicago: University of Chicago Press, 1987).

3. Other prime ministers, including the current one (in early 2001), Atal Bihari Vajpayee, have not ruled long enough at the time of writing to merit special attention.

4. The contrast between these leaders and Indira Gandhi helps bolster the claim that leadership strategies are indeed somewhat independent of the degrees of institutionalization of state authority.

5. See, for example, the essays by George Fernandez (a well-known Indian political leader who directly participated in Kashmiri affairs) and Riyaz Punjabi (a Kashmiri professor who lived through these events) in Raju Thomas, ed., *Perspectives on Kashmir: The Roots of Conflict in South Asia* (Boulder: Westview, 1992).

6. George Fernandez in 1990 estimated this figure to be in the range of 3,000 to 5,000. Since in his former capacity as India's minister for internal affairs (Janata Government, 1989), he had access to all of Indian and other intelligence services data and since this estimate was provided in a public lecture at Harvard University, one is inclined to give some credence to these estimates. See Thomas, *Perspectives on Kashmir*, 289. Subsequently, even the U.S. State Department has corroborated Pakistan's role in training terrorists. See, for example, Judith Miller, "South Asia Called Major Terror Hub in a Survey by US," *New York Times*, April 30, 2000, A1.

7. For a quick (journalistic) overview of various factions involved in the Kashmir Conflict, see *India Today,* August 14, 2000, 16–24; for a more scholarly account, see Widmalm.

REFERENCES

Barnett, Marguerite Ross. 1976. *The Politics of Cultural Nationalism in South India.* Princeton: Princeton University Press.

Brass, Paul. 1990. The Punjab Crisis and the Unity of India. In *India's Democracy: An Analysis of Changing State-Society Relations,* ed. Atul Kohli, 169–213. Princeton: Princeton University Press.

Kohli, Atul. 1997. Can Democracies Accommodate Ethnic Nationalism? Rise and Decline of Self-Determination Movements in India. *Journal of Asian Studies* 56, no. 2:325–44.

Kohli, Atul, ed. 2002. *The Success of India's Democracy.* Cambridge: Cambridge University Press.

Varshney, Ashutosh. 1991. India, Pakistan and Kashmir: Antinomies of Nationalism. *Asian Survey* 31, no. 11:997–1019.

Weiner, Myron. 1967. *Party Building in a New Nation.* Chicago: University of Chicago Press.

———. 1989. *The Indian Paradox.* New Delhi: Sage.

Widmalm, Sten. 2002. *Kashmir in Comparative Perspective: Democracy and Violent Separatism in India.* London: Routledge.

CHAPTER ELEVEN

Russia

Managing Territorial Cleavages under Dual Transitions

Kathryn Stoner-Weiss

The 1990s was an absolutely crucial decade in the reform of the shape and nature of the Russian state, and center-periphery relations in particular. In the space of approximately a decade, Russia moved from being an unquestionably unitary state under Communist Party rule to a hyperfederation operating within the context of an unruly democracy and a halting economic transition to market economics.

As the Soviet system began to unravel in the late 1980s so too did the two main bulwarks of its vertical system of central control over the periphery—the Communist Party of the Soviet Union (CPSU) and the command economy. Their undoing was in part hastened by the holding of free elections to regional soviets (or legislatures) in the spring of 1990, thus loosening the stranglehold of the CPSU on the machinery of government—the first bulwark of the Soviet system of centralization. The Party itself collapsed following the attempted August 1991 coup against then president of the Soviet Union, Mikhail Gorbachev.

The gradual erosion of the power of central ministries over the economy, the second bulwark of Soviet centralization, was brought about initially through a series of half-baked reforms under Gorbachev also in the late 1980s. Throughout the late 1980s the staffs of the huge bureaucracies that controlled all economic decision making were slashed and the ministries were subjected to a series of ill-conceived reorganizations

(Rutland 1993, 208). This led to a reduced role for planning agencies and federal bureaucracies in regional economies, and contributed to the emerging independent authority of powerful enterprise directors and, as important, newly elected regional governments (Solnick 1998).[1]

Beyond the disintegration of the CPSU and the command economy, however, Boris Yeltsin's political jockeying with Gorbachev in 1990 and 1991 for Russia's supremacy over the unraveling USSR also undoubtedly hastened the devolution of power from USSR to Russian Republic and from Russian Republic to its constituent provinces. Yeltsin's now infamous exhortation to regional leaders within Russia to "take as much autonomy as you can swallow" paralleled his own struggles against Union supremacy and Gorbachev's desperate attempts in 1991 to hold the Soviet Union together.

Yeltsin likely did not anticipate, however, just how much autonomy Russia's regional governments would grab through the 1990s. In 1990–91 the autonomous oblasts of Russia changed their names to "republics" to denote what they considered to be their newly elevated status. Four of five autonomous oblasts (Adigai, Gorno-Altai, Karachia, and Khakassia) similarly declared themselves sovereign and also unilaterally raised their status to that of republic. This set a dangerous precedent. By declaring themselves republics, these autonomous oblasts grabbed increased jurisdiction over their own territories. As a result, the renamed Russian Federation is currently comprised of 21 republics, 49 oblasts and 6 krais, the 2 special status cities of Moscow and St. Petersburg, both of which have oblast status, 10 autonomous okrugs, and 1 autonomous oblast.

The republics were set up ostensibly as ethnic homelands for different nationalities. It was often arbitrary, however, where boundaries were drawn (in the 1930s by Stalin with few changes made until the 1950s) and so the establishment of these autonomous republics (as distinct from Union republics) was somewhat capricious. In 1989, according to the last USSR census, only in 7 of the then 16 autonomous republics did the titular nationality make up the largest ethnic group in the republic. Russians were the most numerous ethnic group in 8 of the autonomous republics in 1989. Nonetheless, republics and the 11 autonomies are thought of as ethnically non-Russian regions, while the oblast and krai level is predominantly ethnically Russian. The latter is where over 80 percent of the population of the Russian Federation lives.

These eighty-nine units vary tremendously in geographic size—with, for example, the republic of Sakha-Yakutia spanning an area greater than the size of modern France, while the Chechen Republic is about half the size of the state of Rhode Island. Population size also varies dramatically among the constituent parts of Russia, such that the city of Moscow counts about 8.6 million inhabitants while the Evenk Autonomous Okrug includes approximately 19,000 (*Rossisskii Statisticheskii*

Ezhegodnik 1999, 54–55). In addition, from east to west, Russia covers eleven time zones and includes in its citizenry as many as a hundred distinct ethnic groups.

Given the diversity of its land and people, the complex and complicated heritage of the Soviet system, and the added complication of a simultaneous economic and political transition initiated in 1992, it is perhaps not surprising that post-Soviet Russian center-periphery relations quickly became contentious and, in some instances, highly conflictual. The two Chechen campaigns (the first beginning in the fall of 1994 and ending with an uneasy peace in 1996 and the second reigniting three years later in the fall of 1999 and still being pursued at time of this writing) are particularly stark examples of the difficult relationships Moscow has had with many of its constituent units. Yet the Chechen experience is not representative of the ways in which ethnic disputes were resolved through the 1990s. Indeed, where Chechnia's demands for increased autonomy from Moscow devolved into violent conflict, several other ethnically non-Russian republics pursued nonviolent means to gain increased policy-making autonomy from Moscow. Contrasting Chechnia's troubled path with that of the Republic of Tatarstan is instructive of the varying ways in which Moscow has attempted to accommodate ethnic disputes, and the factors that may determine these differing outcomes.

Tatarstan and Chechnia, both Muslim republics, were among the first regions of Russia to declare themselves sovereign within the USSR in June 1990. In March 1992, following the collapse of the USSR, the leadership of Tatarstan even went so far as to hold a popular referendum on its status within the Russian Federation. Remarkably, 61 percent of participating voters voted in favor of the republic becoming an independent territory within the newly formed Russian Federation, although it was left unstated exactly what this would mean in practice. Moscow reacted to the referendum and Tatarstan's growing demands for increased autonomy by offering first a series of federative agreements to all of Russia's constituent regions in 1992, which neither Tatarstan nor Chechnia signed. Tatarstan's leadership instead, while still threatening to pursue its own sovereignty, embarked on separate bilateral negotiations with Moscow, culminating in a treaty and series of accompanying agreements in 1994. This effectively established Tatarstan's association with Russia as distinctive from other regions in that it reserved for the republic a special set of rights that other regions did not share—in particular, control over key social and educational programs that enabled the preservation of Tatar ethnicity. As important, through its bilateral treaty with Moscow, Tatarstan also gained increased jurisdictional control over the mineral resources located in its territory.

Although Tatarstan's treaty with Moscow created a dangerous precedent for other regions to pursue similar deals, it also effectively ended secessionist threats from the republic. Since 1994, the republic has pursued its own economic, cultural, and social policies, although largely within the framework of its bilateral treaty.

Chechnia, therefore, presents a notable contrast with Tatarstan in terms of the outcome of its sovereignty project despite a somewhat similar initial starting point.[2] The Chechens are one of dozens of Caucasian nations in the south of Russia. Historically, Russia had a great deal of trouble in governing Chechnia and so brought in a series of external rulers to oversee the region even in the imperial period. This led to a series of revolts by the Chechens, most notably in the nineteenth century, when Russia pursued a long and bloody war with the Chechens.

In 1944, Stalin ordered the Chechen population deported to Kazakhstan and Siberia because he deemed their leadership untrustworthy and suspected them of collaborating with the Germans. In 1956–57 they were rehabilitated and many or most returned to Chechnia, although not all Chechens in Russia live in Chechnia today. The dislocation of the Chechens in this time period, however, has left lingering conflicts. In the late Soviet period, Gorbachev under glasnost permitted the repatriation of some of the North Caucuses peoples and they were granted more independence and some of the trappings of statehood. Arguably these historical factors are the roots of Chechnia's independence movement in the 1990s.

In 1990 the Chechen leadership adopted a decision to separate from the Chechen-Ingushetian territory, thus creating two republics still within Russia when previously there had been one. This unilateral decision upset the Ingush leadership because it created a territorial dispute between the two. In June 1991 the Chechens moved to mark borders with Ingushetia and tensions with the Ingush increased. In August 1991 at the time of the attempted coup against Soviet leader Gorbachev, leaders in Chechnia supported the coup plotters. Russia's newly elected president, Boris Yeltsin, sent a Russian general of Chechen descent, Dzhokhar Dudaev, to Chechnia to reestablish Moscow's control in the republic. This proved to be a terrible mistake on Yeltsin's part. Dudaev, although ethnically Chechen, had lived most of his life outside Chechnia. He was born in Kazakhstan during Stalin's deportation of the Chechens and was the first Chechen general in the Soviet armed forces. Despite this long history of loyalty to the Soviet state, Dudaev broke with Yeltsin and with Russia when Yeltsin decided to appoint a transitional council in Chechnia without Dudaev at its head. Dudaev called for elections in October 1991 in Chechnia and, while the results were suspect, he was proclaimed president of the Chechen Republic.

Events moved rapidly thereafter. In November 1991, Chechnia announced independence from the Soviet Union (not just Russia). There was, however, opposition in Chechnia to Dudaev. The opposition argued that Dudaev was a spoiler who had appropriated the mantle of nationalism for his own personal gain, that he was supportive of warlords who looted and stole from fellow Chechens, and that his interests did not coincide with those of the Chechen people. Conflict among groups and factions within Chechnia ensued. In the late spring of 1992, Dudaev shut down Chechnia's parliament and formally broke with the opposition, declaring himself undisputed leader of the republic.

At the same time, relations with newly independent Russia continued to deteriorate as Dudaev's rhetoric regarding Moscow became increasingly aggressive and shrill and Yeltsin became increasingly intransigent in dealing with Chechnia. In addition, armed conflict broke out between opposition groups in Chechnia with the opposition wanting to remove Dudaev from power. At the time, there were rumors that the Russian military was actively helping Dudaev's opposition, and although Yeltsin continued to deny this, we now know that this was most likely true. By the end of November 1994, there was a failed coup against Dudaev. Moscow seized on this as its opportunity to begin a military operation in Chechnia, ostensibly to end the republic's violent internal turmoil. Thus began the first Chechen war of the twentieth century on December 11, 1994.

Although Yeltsin and his advisers, most notably his defense minister at the time, Pavel Grachev, predicted that this would be a short and easy war that would likely boost Yeltsin's flagging popularity back home, the Russian military executed the operation poorly. Some commanders refused to fight to bring Chechnia back into Russia when faced with crying Chechen women in villages surrounding Grozny, Chechnia's capital. Some Russian troops mutinied and thousands of ill-trained and poorly equipped Russian conscripts were quickly felled by well-armed and well-disciplined Chechen fighters. Russian public opinion strongly opposed the war (with 65 percent reporting their opposition in opinion polls). Russian television provided gruesome coverage of the war on a daily basis, showing dead Russian soldiers and portraying hundreds of mothers from around Russia traveling to the battle zone to try to talk their sons off the front lines.

In the face of bad press, a mounting refugee problem, hundreds of dead Russian soldiers and Chechen civilians, and increased incidents of domestic terrorism in Russian regions neighboring Chechnia, Yeltsin became desperate by 1996 to end a conflict that had humiliated him and the Russian military. The conflict was clearly threatening his chances in the upcoming presidential election in June of that year. Following his miraculous reelection to the Russian presidency in July 1996, Yeltsin commissioned General Alexander Lebed to broker a deal with the Chechen leadership that at least temporarily ended fighting in the republic but that delayed the final decision on the future status of Chechnia relative to Russia for five years. The root, therefore, of the Chechen conflict persisted and the Chechen leadership's pursuit of independence clearly did not evaporate. The Russian military had accomplished none of its objectives in Chechnia aside from managing to assassinate Dudaev in 1997. This, however, appeared to only strengthen the resolve of Chechnia's new president, Aslan Mashkhadov, and the separatist warlords over whom he had only loose control.

From 1997 through 1999, Chechnia descended into virtual lawlessness, with Mashkhadov exercising tentative authority at best throughout the republic. In the summer of 1999, Chechen warlord Shamil Basaev, in an apparent attempt to reignite the conflict with Russia and to spread Chechnia's influence beyond the republic, led an incursion into the neighboring Russian republic of Dagestan. Although he and his group were beaten back by Russian forces, this act, along with bombings of apartment buildings in Moscow in late August 1999, was seized upon by then prime minister Vladimir Putin as reason enough for Russian forces to reenter Chechnia to establish Russian control and tame the restive republic once and for all.

Ironically, where Yeltsin's Chechen melee had almost led to his political undoing, arguably, this second Chechen war helped propel Putin to electoral victory as Russia's second president in March 2000. Unlike the first Chechen war, this second conflict proved highly popular with the Russian electorate. Most likely, this was a result of Basaev's incursion into Dagestan as well as the Moscow apartment bombings, which appeared to bring the Chechen conflict home to average Russians (even those living nine time zones from Moscow).[3] Putin's war over Chechnia's status within Russia, however, has been scarcely more successful than Yeltsin's. Although popular opinion in favor of the war has remained greater than 60 percent, it has dropped since the conflict reignited in the fall of 1999. Putin's control of media coverage of the Chechen conflict has undoubtedly helped to keep public opinion higher than in the first conflict. Nonetheless, at the time of this writing Putin has been similarly unsuccessful in using the Russian military to clarify Chechnia's status within Russia. In April 2002, during his annual state of the nation address, Putin declared the Chechen conflict over, although this is likely news to Chechen fighters and Russian soldiers still mired in combat.

In October 2002 a group of fifty radical Chechen militants took over a theater in central Moscow during a performance of the popular musical, *Nord-Ost.* Approximately 800 Russians were taken hostage. The militants threatened to blow up the theater and kill the hostages if President Putin did not immediately withdraw Russian forces from Chechnia. The fifty-seven-hour siege ended after the Russian military released an airborne version of the painkiller Fentanyl into the theater's ventilation system. In the ensuing chaos, 129 hostages died and purportedly all the hostage takers were killed.

The incident had the effect of heightening the intensity of Russia's siege of Chechnia, while searching for a definitive solution to the conflict. As part of this, a referendum on a Russian-backed constitution affirming Chechnia's status as part of Russia was held within Chechnia in March 2003. The relatively high turnout of Chechen voters (70 percent) and overwhelming vote in favor (almost 90 percent) of the constitution was indicative of the exhaustion of Chechen civilians with the war. Whether it will lead to a stable administration of the province and a true clarification of its status vis-à-vis Russia, however, remains to be seen at the time of writing.

Short of this sort of violent conflict over Chechen independence, however, and Tatarstan's particularly aggressive (although peaceful) push for increased policy-making autonomy, the Russian center has endured challenges to its authority in one form or another from almost all quarters. The cleavages within the Russian Federation cut in a number of ways—center versus peripheries, ethnic Russian regions versus ethnically non-Russian regions, and wealthy regions versus poor regions. There is no single cause for these lines of cleavage. Rather, a number of causes have contributed to the awkward shaping and reshaping of Russia's federal relations. Even in the years leading up to the collapse of the Soviet Union in December 1991, a fundamental clash of views developed concerning the shape of Russian federal relationships. The central authorities, borrowing from the Soviet system, preferred a federal system where the center was clearly preeminent while many regional political officials pushed hard for a far more decentralized system. This clash of views is evident in the peculiar institutional and constitutional framework that developed to manage center-periphery relations in Russia. Undoubtedly also, the introduction of competitive elections did a great deal to force devolution from center to periphery in that elections made regional officials accountable to local interests rather than distant officials in Moscow. This served to seriously damage and eventually destroy the preexisting system of vertical integration and central control that existed during Soviet rule. Moreover, the institutions that developed to manage Russian territorial politics have proven weak and ineffective.

Explaining Conflictual Federal Relations in Russia— Institutional Factors

The tug of war between the central government and the provinces that characterized the period (1990–93) leading up to the adoption of the Russian constitution illustrates the conflicting views regarding what kind of institutional framework would arise to manage Russian territorial conflict. While Moscow sought to impose a highly centralized federal system—that is, a system imposed from above, with the central government being the clear leading power—the provinces advocated a more contractual federal system, where each subnational unit would agree to enter the federation on a negotiated, contractual basis and where the central government's power would be deemphasized relative to that of the federation's constituent parts. A troubled and ineffective institutional framework arose that ultimately satisfied neither of these contradictory views. What follows is an analysis of the genesis and functioning of the main institutions intended to manage territorial differences. These include the office of presidential representative, governors, the constitution of 1993, and the system of bilateral treaties between the center and many of Russia's constituent units.

The introduction of competitive elections at the regional level launched Russia on the difficult path of reform. The 1990 elections of regional soviets (legislatures) injected the notion of political accountability into subnational politics. If elected officials were now going to be held responsible by their electorates for local conditions, then they naturally demanded increased control over matters of prime importance at the subnational level. The regional activism in this early period was also, in part, an immediate reaction to the extreme centralization of the past (where all trade and most interregional contacts were controlled by Moscow). Under the old unitary system, many regions were not able to benefit from their natural material resources (like oil and gas) because they were effectively treated as colonies of the central Soviet state. The proceeds from mineral extraction, for example, went straight to Moscow, with the region and its inhabitants deriving practically no benefit. As their regions suffered from cuts in funding from Moscow, and an increase in policy responsibilities, new regional leaders found this situation intolerable. Finally, the surge in regional demands for more control during this period may also have been a result of the fact that many old Communist Party bosses, who sometimes found themselves still in office following the 1990 elections, wanted increased control in order to enrich themselves and protect their own preferred status in the new political and emerging economic order.

The assertiveness at the level of the twenty-one ethnic republics of Russia (Tatarstan and Chechnia among them) was accompanied by a "war of laws" between the Russian Federation government in Moscow and several republics (where republics would pass legislation directly contravening Moscow's edicts), as well as the financially crippling and widespread withholding of tax revenues from Moscow by both oblast and krai, as well as republic-level governments. In the first nine months of 1993 alone, Moscow reportedly lost 800 billion rubles to the regions.

This was despite the fact that in 1991, in a failed attempt to avoid the erosion of central authority in the provinces, President Yeltsin introduced two institutional reforms that have become an enduring feature of Russian center-periphery politics: the office of presidential representative, as well as head of oblast and krai administrations (commonly referred to as governor and, in the republics, as president).

Presidential Representatives

The position of presidential representative was an overt attempt by Moscow to reintroduce central executive control over the provinces and has been thrice reformed since its inception in 1992. Within a month of his first being elected president of Russia in June 1991, Yeltsin announced his intention to appoint an envoy to every region. This was to ensure that presidential decisions would be reliably implemented and to provide reliable information about the political situation in each region. The office of presidential representative was described by some of its detractors as "the emperor's eyes and ears in the provinces." Significantly, however, Yeltsin claimed that the job of the presidential representative would not be to interfere in the business of local governance. Indeed, the decree that he signed in August 1991 officially creating the position stated simply: "Leaders and officials of ministries, departments, and other organizations of the RSFSR [as it was still then called], and organs of executive power are instructed to assist the RSFSR presidential representatives in the fulfillment of the functions vested in them." These functions were described merely as fulfilling the president's instructions. What this meant in practice was not even clear to many of the men Yeltsin appointed to these positions (Stoner-Weiss 1997a, ch. 3). Some of Yeltsin's appointees, usually already residents of the region to which they were assigned, construed their functions as merely reporting the goings-on of the local legislature and executive. Others, however, claimed that they had the power to remove local political actors from office if they persistently defied Moscow.

In reality, however, the office of presidential representative did not carry with it much influence in local affairs. To the extent that presidential representatives came to have any influence over politics in their provinces, this had little to do with the actual office itself. Rather, in some cases, because he had made his appointments so quickly in the fall of 1991, President Yeltsin inadvertently put former local Communist Party officials into position as presidential representatives—men who had little loyalty to Yeltsin or his new regime.

Presidential representatives under Yeltsin proved to be largely weak and ineffectual (even following a reform in 1997 intended to strengthen the office by better defining its functions). His successor, Vladimir Putin, reformed this office yet again in a renewed attempt to regain control over Russia's restive provinces. In May 2000, Putin installed new presidential representatives in each of seven newly created superdistricts (each encompassing approximately twelve to fifteen oblasts, krais, republics, or autonomies). As with the two previous iterations of this office under Yeltsin, the new representatives of the federal executive have poorly defined responsibilities. It is unclear, for example, to what degree they are supposed to oversee the actions of regional governments in general or merely federal bureaucrats in the regions (Ukaz "O polnomochnom pred-stavitele Prezidenta ...," May 13, 2000, and Samoilov, August 4, 2000). Indeed, this in-stitutional solution to the center's problems in the regions appears to have merely created a further layer of the Russian state without necessarily enhancing its abilities to govern at the regional level. It also may be an attempt to resurrect a system of vertical integration reminiscent more of the Soviet era than of a developing federal democracy. In any event, it is as yet unclear what effect, if any, this new arrangement is having on center-periphery relations in Russia.

Heads of Oblast and Republican Administrations (Governors of Oblasts and Presidents of Republics)

Both Putin and Yeltsin sought to use the position of presidential representative to counter the authority of regional heads of administration. The administration became the executive branch of government in 1991, and its head was initially appointed by President Yeltsin on the recommendation of the local soviets (elected in 1990) until elections could be held. When Yeltsin first made his appointments to these positions beginning in the fall of 1991, he promised that popular elections for governor would be held in December of that year. But fearing that conservative politicians might sweep these elections, thus further weakening Moscow's control over provincial Russia, Yeltsin postponed the elections indefinitely.

While Yeltsin attempted to ensure that the first appointed heads of administration would have their loyalties firmly based in Moscow rather than the regions over which they governed, his efforts often failed. As was true with his appointments to the post of presidential representative, in some cases Yeltsin appointed so many individuals at the same time that his administration lost track of who exactly was coming to power in the provinces. In some cases, previously powerful Communist Party officials, generally considered to be antireform, became governors in their regions. Further, in anticipa-tion of their having to stand for election at some point in the future, many governors gradually shifted their loyalties from Moscow to their local constituents. As a result, many of Yeltsin's own appointees later led their regions' efforts to gain increased au-tonomy from Moscow. The best example of this is the unilateral attempt by the gover-nor of Sverdlovsk oblast, in 1993, to raise the status of his region to that of a republic and to rename the oblast the "Urals Republic." Yeltsin responded by removing the gov-ernor from his position, who then promptly won election as the chair of the regional legislature in the fall of that year. In 1995, he was popularly elected governor (and at the time of this writing remains governor). By the end of 1996, most regions had held at least one gubernatorial election, and at the time of writing most have had at least two and in some cases, three elections for governor.

The office of governor carries with it the right to appoint an entire local cabinet, as well as control over local budget spending and a good deal of local budget revenue. In sum, the governor of an oblast or president of a republic is the undisputed boss of any given region.

The Federative Agreements of 1992

In the spring of 1992, as market reform got under way, the increasingly impoverished central government began pushing more and more policy responsibility to the provincial level. The difficulty was that provincial governments had little funds with which to pay for these new responsibilities. Further, as the struggle for ownership of property slated for privatization intensified, and the propensity of subnational governments to withhold tax revenue from Moscow increased, the lack of transparency regarding the division of powers between Moscow and the constituent units of the federation became an even more pressing issue. The continuing war of conflicting laws between levels of government led to the signing of the March 1992 federative agreements. This set of three agreements (one for each level of the Federation—republics, oblasts and krais, and the autonomies) was supposed to establish which areas were to be of central jurisdiction, which areas were to be shared responsibilities, and which areas were to be specifically assigned to each of the three categories of the constituent units.

Far from alleviating the growing tensions between the oblast and republic levels of the federation, however, the federative agreements simply reinforced the inequalities between ethnically Russian and non-Russian territories. This was because the twenty-one republics were declared "subjects of the federation," whereas oblasts and krais remained "territorial administrative units." Republics were given more control rights over property and trade than were oblasts and krais and were permitted by their agreement with Moscow to create presidencies rather than the (initially) centrally appointed governorships that were established by this time in the oblasts and krais.

Given that in only about one-third of republics did the titular nationality outnumber other groups, in particular, ethnic Russians, this seemed particularly unfair to those oblasts that had as strong an ethnic claim to republic status and its inherent privileges. Further, most of Russia's population lives in oblasts and krais (in which are located autonomies) rather than in republics. Thus, the federative agreements reinforced the perception in the minds of many that "twenty-three million Russian subjects [those living in the republics] will live in a federation, and 124 million [those living in oblasts and krais] will live in a unitary state" (Glezer in Solnick 1995, 52). In sum, far from solving the most pressing problems of center-periphery relations, these agreements exacerbated tensions that already existed between center and peripheries, but also among some ethnically Russian and non-Russian regions. As a partial result, tax withholding persisted and a reported twenty regions stopped remitting taxes to the center altogether by the fall of 1992. This number had increased to thirty regions by 1993 (Wallich 1994, 248).

Despite the special privileges that had accrued to republics in their federative agreement with Moscow, Tatarstan and Chechnia refused to sign this agreement, and two other republics, Bashkortostan, and Sakha, insisted on special clauses granting them additional control over foreign trade and mineral resources before they would accept the deal. The intransigence of these republics, and the continuing tax revolts across many ethnically Russian regions, raised the possibility in 1992 that the very survival of the Russian state was in question. In truth, however, this was probably never really a possibility as it is far from clear that Tatarstan, Bashkortostan, and Sakha in particular would have actually acted on their threats to leave the federation. Rather, these threats appear to have been part of a broader strategy to widen the economic control rights of these wealthy republics over the proceeds from the extraction and sale of oil, gas, and diamonds located on their territories.

The Constitution of 1993

Provincial power was on the rise in the Russian Federation during the summer of 1993 when President Yeltsin convened a constitutional convention in yet another failed attempt to provide Russia with a comprehensive basic law. While the sharp divisions between president and parliament during this time are usually considered the main reason why this constitutional project ultimately failed by August 1993, in fact the insistence of regional leaders (including Yeltsin's own appointed regional governors) on more autonomy over policy, and more control over fiscal matters in particular, greatly contributed to the poor results of this second to last constitutional attempt.

Yeltsin's storming of the Russian parliament in October 1993 led to the adoption of a new constitution and further attempts to refine and redefine the institutions governing Russian center-periphery relations. The 1993 constitution of the Russian Federation was intended to address some of the vagaries of the Russian federal system. It contained two articles (71 and 72) that assigned policy jurisdiction to the various levels of government. Article 71 lists the powers exclusively allotted to the federal government in Moscow, while Article 72 enumerates those areas in which responsibility is to be shared between Moscow and the constituent units of the Federation. Article 71 is so exhaustive, however, that there are few powers left to share with the regions. Indeed, there is no section in the constitution of the Russian Federation that specifically enumerates the powers reserved exclusively for subnational governments, raising the question as to whether the Russian basic law actually constitutes the country as a federation in the Rikerian sense (that is, as a single land with at least two levels of government, each having exclusive jurisdiction in certain areas).

The Bilateral Treaties and Agreements

The ambiguity of the constitution has led some regions and republics to claim some exclusive powers through alternative means. Tatarstan's stubbornness in this regard and its success in extracting from Moscow additional jurisdictional rights through a bilateral agreement were outlined in greater detail in the first section of this essay. It is important to emphasize that this led to the establishment of a dangerous precedent in center-periphery relations. This deal initiated a series of similar agreements signed between Moscow and both oblasts and republics and further sustained the principle of Moscow's unequal treatment of units of the federation.

The examples of the special agreement the center had made with Tatarstan, Bashkortostan, and other republics in 1994 gave rise to further asymmetries in Russian federal relations as forty-six other regions demanded and achieved bilateral treaties and agreements for themselves by 1998. It is indicative of the extent to which some regional leaders were willing, however, to take matters into their own hands when one considers that the constitution of the Republic of Tuva contradicted the Russian constitution on as many as twelve points. These included "a nullification of the federal constitution's guarantee that land would be privatized, the right to overrule a federal declaration of a state of emergency, the right to appoint prosecutors and judges, and to veto top military appointments in the republic" (Solnick 1995, 52–53).

The treaties (*dogovora*) themselves were relatively general statements regarding the nature of the division of powers and shared powers between the particular subject of the federation and federal institutions. All the treaties were slightly different, although they contained some common elements. They were accompanied by a series of agreements (*soglasheniye*), which could be signed any time after the conclusion of the treaties.

The agreements were far more detailed than the treaties with respect to specific policy purviews and were, therefore, rather wildly different for each region depending on particular policy concerns and resource endowments. Sverdlovsk oblast, for example, signed eighteen agreements, ranging from the region's investment policy, to use of natural resources, to health and cultural policies, in addition to its original treaty. In contrast, Kaliningrad signed only three agreements: one on education and science, another on cultural questions, and the third on maintaining law and order in the region (Guboglo 1997, 313–19, 652–90, 642–48).

Further, regions were able to propose additional agreements after they signed their original treaty.[4] Many, but not all, of the agreements were made for a set period of time (generally two to five years). According to the terms of these time-bound agreements, they could be canceled by either party (the region or the federal center) provided that each side provided the other with notice at least six months prior to the expiration of the agreement of their intention to do so. If no such notice was provided, the agreements were automatically renewed for an additional two to five years.[5]

According to the Presidential Decree (No. 370) of March 12, 1996, and a June 24, 1999 law on the treaties, the treaties and accompanying agreements are not to violate the constitution of the Russian Federation; cannot change the status of a subject of the Federation; cannot add to or change what is enumerated in articles 71 and 72 of the constitution; and must respect the supremacy of the constitution. On this basis, in the view of central officials, the treaties and agreements are not intended to be extraconstitutional documents, but are supposed to merely "concretize areas of joint jurisdiction specific to each subject of the Russian Federation, taking into account the specific peculiarities of each region" (Shakhrai 1997, 158).

In reality, however, a number of the treaties and agreements actually either contradicted the constitution or went beyond what was envisioned in articles 71 and 72. For example, areas that in the constitution of the Russian Federation are ascribed to the federal government exclusively (art. 71) appeared as areas of joint authority in many treaties. This type of constitutional violation appeared in the treaties of North Ossetiya (art. 4, point 3), Kabardino-Balkariya, (art. 4, point g), Tatarstan, (art. 3, point 2), and Bashkortostan (art. 4, point 2), where the treaties granted these regions the right to defend state and territorial integrity. Another notable example was the authority both Sverdlovsk and Udmurtiya gained in their treaties over the functioning of enterprises in the defense complex (art. 2, point g of the Sverdlovsk Treaty; and art. 2, part 7 of Udmurtiya's Treaty).[6]

Further, in a number of agreements, areas that are again to be exclusively reserved for the Russian Federation government were included in lists of authorities for subjects of the Federation. For example, participation in international relations, the establishment of relations with foreign states and conducting agreements with them (Tatarstan, art. 2, point 11); the establishment of national banks (art. 2, point 12, Tatarstan; art. 3, point 11, Bashkortostan); and questions of republican citizenship (art. 2, point 8, Tatarstan; art. 3, point k, Kabardino-Balkariya; art. 3, point 1, Bashkortostan).[7]

Finally, areas that in the constitution are identified as spheres of joint jurisdiction between the federal government and the subjects of the Federation at times appeared in the treaties as the apparently exclusive authority of several of the subjects of the Federation. For example, the defense of the rights of citizens (Tatarstan, art. 2, point 1; Kabardino-Balkariya, art. 3, point j; Bashkortostan, art. 3, point 1); formation and use of republican precious metals and stones fund (Yakutiya, art. 1, point j); and a system of state organs, their organization and activities (Tatarstan, art. 1, point 7; Kabardino-Balkariya, art. 3, point g; Bashkortostan, art. 3, point 2) to name but a few areas (Guboglo 1997).

In sum, the treaties and agreements, despite central government declarations to the contrary, were not always based on the constitution and supportive of the principles of the supremacy of federal law, and the establishment of a single political and economic expanse. They served to establish Russia's federal relations more on a contractual than on a national-constitutional basis, carving out far more freedom of action for the subjects of the Federation than the drafters of the 1993 constitution had likely intended. On one level or another, some treaties contradicted the constitution rather directly. Indeed, the treaties and agreements in general contradicted the declared intention of the constitution to render all subjects of the Federation equal to one another.

Although the treaties may have served to calm the more rebellious and demanding regions of Russia (Tatarstan and Sverdlovsk oblast chief among them) in some respects, this came at considerable cost to the federal government. The economic crisis stemming from the August 1998 financial collapse served to underscore the fact that many regions in practice exercised autonomy beyond what was provided for in either the bilateral agreements, the constitution, or existing federal law. That is, the treaties were far from definitive in terms of lending predictability to center-periphery relations, or in ensuring implementation of and adherence to central policy at the provincial level. Thus, if the treaties were a federal strategy intended to restrain further grabs for regional autonomy, or to lend more predictability to center-periphery power relations, then that strategy failed. By spring 2002, after two years in office, President Putin moved to annul twenty-eight of forty-seven treaties and vowed not to sign any more.

More significantly, however, the available empirical evidence from the regional level indicates that the treaties were not the sole means by which regions gained increased autonomy over policy. Not infrequently it was simply taken by republics and oblasts alike.[8] Regions were punished infrequently by central authorities for doing so, although the possible pattern of punishing transgressions requires further study.

Throughout the 1990s, there were abundant examples of regions legislating in direct opposition to federal law and the constitution. These examples range widely across regions of Russia, across time, and across policy areas. For example, in 1996, the Ministry of Justice reported that of the 44,000 regional legal acts it reviewed, including gubernatorial orders, it found that "nearly half [that is, almost 22,000] of them did not correspond with the Constitution of the Russian Federation" (*Izvestiia*, November 4, 1997). A similar report was issued indicating that in the first three quarters of 1998, 30 percent of regional acts were found to violate the constitution and federal law (*Russian Regional Report*, October 1998). In a speech on May 17, 2000, President Putin reported that in the first few months of 2000, the Ministry of Justice reported that 20,000 regional laws (or 20 percent of all regional laws passed so far that year) violated the constitution or federal law.[9]

The kinds of regional violations of federal authority are nontrivial. Reportedly the regions of north Ossetiia, Voronezh, Samara, Arkhangelsk, Irkutsk, Tiumen', and Omsk have all passed legislation restructuring their judiciaries, a right exclusively reserved to the federal government by article 71 of the constitution. Other regions introduced their own land codes in advance of a federal land code. An estimated fifty-one of eighty-nine regions violated provisions of the law on local government such that some regional governors illegally appoint mayors of cities in their regions rather than holding elections for these posts (*Russian Regional Report*, February 5, 1998).[10] Other regions claimed the right to ratify international treaties, and even revise federal borders (*Russian Regional Report*, March 6, 1997).

In a host of regions political leaders (including the mayor of Moscow) maintained restrictions on freedom of movement and choice of a place to live guaranteed by the Russian constitution. Despite the fact that the constitutional court has ruled that such restrictions are clear violations of the constitution, the residency permit system persists in many regions of Russia (including Moscow oblast and the city of Moscow, Adigea, Kabardino-Balkaria, Karachai-Cherkessia, Krasnodar, Stavropol, Voronezh, and Rostov oblasts) (Visotskii 1998, 2). In addition, the mayor of Moscow, Yurii Luzhkov, steadfastly refused to implement the federal government's housing policy (*Russian Regional Report*, January 15, 1998, and May 15, 1997). Still other regions violated both the constitution and Russian electoral law in maintaining immigration quotas or language and educational requirements and age quotas for prospective voters on their territories (Visotskii 1998, 2).

Other common kinds of transgressions included violations of articles 71 and 72 of the constitution that deal with questions of ownership, use, and distribution of natural resources, with subjects of the federation claiming exclusive ownership despite the fact that the federal government had legal jurisdiction. Similarly, regions and republics frequently introduced unconstitutional laws regarding the administration and distribution of federal property located on their territories. Others introduced laws establishing financial, credit, and hard currency regulations—a right reserved exclusively for the federal government in article 71. Finally, some regions have even passed laws regarding the organization and activities of federal executive power (like branches of federal ministries) located on their territories and over whom they had no legal jurisdiction (Visotskii 1998, 2).

According to analysis from the Ministry of Justice, the constitutions and charters of some regions (for example, Ingushetia, Kalmikia, Tatarstan, Bashkortostan, Tyva,

Kabardino-Balkariia and Irkutsk oblast, and Khanti-Mansii autonomous okrug) claimed the supremacy of their laws over federal law. Others even foresaw the possibility of suspending federal law on the territory of the region if it contradicted the constitution or charter of the region (Sakha, Bashkortostan, Tyva, Komi, and Tatarstan) (Visotskii 1998, 2).

Almost immediately after coming to power in the spring of 2000, President Putin decreed that many of the more egregious regional contradictions of federal law be reversed, but many others remained. He also initiated two key institutional reforms, including that of presidential representative (described above) in order to reassert central control over Russia's restive regions. Beyond the reform of the office of presidential representative, Putin also initiated legislation that was later adopted by the state duma enabling the Russian president to dismiss regional heads of administrations (presidents of republics and governors of oblasts) and regional legislatures deemed by the courts to have passed legislation that violates either the constitution of the Russian Federation or federal law. Although this is an undoubtedly powerful instrument on paper, in practice it has proven difficult to use since Putin faces the unpopular scenario of having to dismiss elected authorities in the provinces. This tool is not likely to be used often, if at all, as a result.[11] Moreover, Putin's reforms aimed at strengthening central control over the periphery have met with mixed success. While sporadic reports of regional noncompliance with federal law and the constitution persist, some of the most egregious violations have been reversed. Nonetheless, the institutional framework intended to govern Russian federal relations remains somewhat unstable and problematic in the longer term.

The Institutional and Noninstitutional Causes of Russia's Territorial Conflicts

The preceding section has demonstrated the conflictual and confused nature of Russian center-periphery relations, while outlining the main institutional features of the system of territorial conflict management. What should be evident is how weak many of these new institutions are in ensuring the smooth functioning of shared authority between center and periphery and ameliorating ethnic differences by extension. There remains a tremendous amount of unpredictability in center-periphery relations. What seems clear is that formal institutional arrangements are routinely disregarded or reshaped. The malleability of key institutions designed to govern center-periphery relations (like, for example, the constitution of 1993) is undoubtedly an important cause of the central state's problems in the periphery. Poorly designed or underspecified institutions (like the presidential representative) are also clearly a cause of Russia's difficulties. Further, the constitution, for example, fails to outline clearly what shared jurisdiction actually means in practice and so regions have taken it upon themselves to breathe life into the meaning of this section, although not in any uniform way. Relatedly, the system of bilateral treaties Moscow signed with half, but not all, of Russia's constituent units produced contradictions in federal relations as well as insti-tutionalizing huge asymmetries in regional power. Finally, a weak system of judicial re-view and poor implementation of legal decisions have contributed to the difficulties Moscow faced in taming the periphery in the 1990s.

Beyond these institutional factors, however, important noninstitutional factors share a role in shaping center-periphery conflict. Although some of these are common to all eighty-nine regions of Russia, others are a result of the specific histories of rela-tionships between Moscow and particular regions.

Moscow's troubled relationship with Chechnia, for example, is conditioned by his-torical, geographical, economic, cultural, and international factors. The Chechen peo-ple have a long and unfortunate history of struggle against Russian rulers stemming back to imperial Russia. Their fractious relations with Moscow continued through the Soviet period with mass deportations under Stalin. Perhaps it should not be surprising, given this history, therefore, that Chechnia remains a hot spot in the post-Soviet era.

Geographically and economically, Chechnia is also a special case. It is one of a few Russian republics located on an outer border, which makes it more difficult for Moscow to regulate its trading (particularly arms trading) activities. It is also located in the heart of the North Caucusus, a region of the former Soviet Union fraught with eth-nic and religious conflict. Chechnia was also strategically important to Moscow be-cause major oil pipelines connecting the Caspian Sea to Eastern Europe run across its territory. Indeed, some analysts have argued that if it were not for these pipelines, Moscow would have written off Chechnia long ago.

Finally, the rise of militant Islam in Chechnia has served to emphasize the cultural differences between the Chechens and the Russian government's policies. It has also meant the reported incursion into Chechnia of arms suppliers and mercenaries from organizations in Afghanistan and perhaps Iran and Saudi Arabia. In short, the course of Moscow's relations with Chechnia is complicated and perhaps the potential sources of conflict there in the 1990s are in some ways overdetermined.

Nonetheless, the set of circumstances under which Chechnia's troubled relations with Moscow have unfolded is largely distinct from Moscow's experiences with the other non-Russian republics within its borders. The roots of Moscow's conflicts with the republics of Tatarstan, Bashkortostan, and Sakha (Yakutia), for example, are both cultural and economic in nature. Each of these republics can lay a reasonable claim to a clear and distinct non-Russian ethnic heritage. Tatarstan and Bashkortostan, like

Chechnia, are Muslim republics, although not of the militant, Chechen type. Thus, part of their conflict with Moscow has undoubtedly been a result of their leaderships' genuine desire to forge a culturally distinct ethnic identity that was long-suppressed under Soviet rule.

It would be a mistake, however, to assume that this is the only clear cause of their assertiveness vis-à-vis Moscow. For all three of these republics also have in common vast mineral resources (oil and gas in Tatarstan, oil in Bashkortostan, and diamonds in Sakha). Sakha, for example, is the seat of the Russian diamond industry (and Russia is second in the world in its mining of precious stones), while Tatarstan and Bashkortostan are absolutely key centers for Russia's oil and gas industry. Much of the desire for autonomy in each of these republics has been driven by their leaderships' wish to reap greater benefit from what lies beneath their soil after years of exploitation under Soviet rule. The pattern of regional activism throughout the 1990s provides support for this interpretation of at least the force behind some of Russia's nationalist revival. That is, those regions that have the most valuable economic resource endowments have proven most active in making claims for increased policy autonomy. Dan Treisman, for example, found that "those ethnic regions that had large populations and high industrial output, were major raw materials producers or had high industrial exports were much more separatist" (Treisman 1997, 239).

Other less well-endowed republics of Russia, however, have also been relatively aggressive in their pursuit of increased autonomy, although none have been as aggressive as Chechnia, Tatarstan, Bashkortostan, and Sakha. Buriatia and Tuva, for example, are among the poorest of Russia's twenty-one republics, yet both of them have signed bilateral treaties with Moscow and both have passed constitutions fraught with clauses that contradict the Russian constitution and strongly challenge the sovereign right of Russia to legislate on their territories. The sources of their autonomy drives would appear to be more cultural than economic, therefore—with Tuva having a greater than 63 percent indigenous population, and a distinctive set of cultural, religious, and linguistic attributes (indeed, part of its population is comprised of nomadic herders living as their ancestors have for thousands of years). Buriatia is similarly culturally distinct from the rest of Russia, with a significant part of the population claiming the Buddhist religion, for example (Orttung 2000, 63, 580).

Aside from the non-Russian republics, even ethnically Russian regions have doggedly sought to challenge Moscow's authority. Unlike some of the republics, these claims are more clearly based in economics than in culture or language. There is at least preliminary evidence that the basis for regional activism among ethnically non-Russian regions is economic rather than primordial nationalism in that "regional leaders who were of the titular nationality were not significantly more likely to press separatist demands than those who were Russian" (Treisman 1997, 243).

Beyond common institutional problems, or particularistic historical or cultural causes, Russia's territorial politics are clearly deeply affected by the fact that as the country undergoes a political transition and the evolution of new political institutions, it is simultaneously undergoing key economic changes. In particular, the shift in property rights from public to increasingly private has had a direct impact on how center-periphery relations have played out in the recent past and how they will likely continue in the future.

Elsewhere I have argued that the root of this variation and of regional activism more generally is the simultaneity of the economic and political aspects of Russia's transition (Stoner-Weiss 2001a, 2001b). That is, the economic transition—in particular, the transfer of property rights regimes from public to private through the late 1980s and early 1990s—engendered new social forces that were not incorporated into new institutional frameworks. These interests are untamed and directly challenge what the central state can accomplish. Resistance to central policies then comes not from elected public officials alone in republics and oblasts of the Russian Federation, but also from the small circles of business interests by whom they have been captured and to whom they have often become accountable. These early "winners" from the transition have little interest in promoting central state regulation of their activities. In order to protect their early financial and property gains, they have effectively carved up and captured parts of the state—particularly at the regional level—for personal financial advantage.

As a result, we see regional governments in both republics and oblasts of Russia passing legislation that contradicted the constitution predominantly in ways that affect economic conditions in their regions. For example, the underlying cause of a region establishing a citizenship requirement for voters, or language requirements for elected officials in contradiction to the federal constitution, is undoubtedly to limit and control who is entitled to select regional leaders and also who those regional leaders can be. Regional violations of housing and privatization policies are also designed to ensure that regional assets are controlled by regional interests. Restructuring of judiciaries is another strategy to control mechanisms by which ownership disputes might be resolved, ensuring once again that regional interests are protected and advantaged. The imposition of illegal tariffs and taxes on goods entering many regions is another strategy to ensure that local goods and services are privileged over those from outside the region. Restrictions on freedom of movement through the residence permit system that persists in many regions is a strategy for limiting factor mobility in local production facilities and maintaining the prevailing economic balance of power. Finally, declarations of regional ownership of natural resources are further mechanisms by which regional governments, under the influence of regional economic interests, aim to ensure they benefit the most from what lies under their soil.

Evidence of the influence of regional business circles, versus other social forces, on regional politics and politicians comes from the responses reported in Table 11.1. In a 1999 survey of public officials in seventy-two of Russia's eighty-nine regions, my Russian colleagues and I asked a subsample of top elected political officials in the regions to indicate to what degree social, political, and economic groups and organizations influenced the activities of their administrations.[12] Local and regional business circles were reportedly more influential than any other social or political group or institution, with a mean of 3.84. This is in particularly stark contrast to the influence of social organizations (such as political lobby groups like Soldiers' Mothers) with a mean of 2.13, unions with a mean of 2.48, and political parties with a mean of 2.33.

The penetration of regional economic interests goes beyond the executive into the legislatures of many regions. From detailed analysis of regional electoral data, we know that regional legislatures are frequently filled with deputies elected to represent powerful local economic interests. In 1997, the Central Electoral Commission reported that "in practically all legislative organs of the subjects of the Federation it is possible to meet leaders of strong enterprises and commercial structures of the region. In the Republic of Sakha (Yakutia) it is the leaders of diamond and gold enterprises, in the Republics of Komi and Tatarstan and Tiumen and Sakhalin oblasts it is oil companies. In Cheliabinsk oblast it is metallurgical factories, and in Murmansk oblast, it is the Kol'skii Nuclear Power Station." As the Central Electoral Commission itself notes, this

Table 11.1 The Influences of Societal Groups and Organizations on the Activities of Regional Political Officials

Q. To what degree do the following organizations and groups influence the activity of your administration?

Degree of Influence	Means of All Responses (N = 66)
Local and regional business circles	3.71
Unions	2.58
Political parties	2.12
Social organizations	1.88
Media	3.34
Church	1.98

Notes: Respondents were asked to indicate their response on a 5-point scale: not at all = 1, a little = 2, moderately = 3, a good deal = 4, very strongly = 5. Means were calculated such that the higher the mean, the greater the degree of reported influence. Regional political officials include governors, deputy governors, presidents, and vice-presidents of republics. Means exclude no response.

results in the "strengthening of the influence of economic lobbyists on the economic policies of subjects of the Russian Federation. Aside from this is the threat of confrontation of the regional elite with the federal center in constructing the interests of the regions" (*Vybory* 1997, 637).

In addition, a cross-tabulation from our survey of regional government executives by region of Russia and levels of noncompliance also provides a good initial, although preliminary, indicator of the extent to which business interests may influence regional executives' policy decisions and policy independence from the center. There is strong evidence that those regions that have the most resilient records of noncompliance to federal policy and the federal constitution are regions where the heads of executives (or their deputies) reported significant influence of regional business interests on the activities of their administrations. Some of the most notorious noncompliers (Tatarstan, Yakutia, Bashkortostan, Sverdlovsk oblast, Udmurtia, Buriatia, and Tuva, for example) are also prominent among those regions where our respondents from regional executives indicated the highest degrees of influence of regional business interests on their activities. Asked to indicate on a scale of 1 to 5 (with 1 being "not at all" and 5 being "very strongly") the degree to which their administrations were influenced by regional business interests, executive respondents from Tatarstan, Yakutia, Sverdlovsk, Udmurtia, Buriatia, and Tuva indicated either a 4 or a 5. Correspondingly, executive respondents from those regions that rarely, if ever, appear in national newspapers as noncompliers, like, for example, Kursk, Rostov, Amur, or Ryazan, indicated little to no influence (1 or 2 on the 5-point scale) on the part of business interests on the activities of their administrations.

Moreover, the foregoing should demonstrate that the conflict over the shape of the Russian Federation is determined as much by noninstitutional forces. In many regions of Russia, cultural and religious influences are important causes of friction in relations with federal authorities in Moscow. But the influence in other regions of the externalities of the economic transition and in particular the rise of powerful, but particularistic business concerns are clearly also more important factors in explaining Russian territorial politics than are formal institutions alone. This has important implications for the success of past and possible future remedies for the management of Russia's territorial problems.

Institutional Remedies for Post-Soviet Territorial Crises

What institutional reforms might improve the management of ethnic conflicts along territorial lines? Suggestions for improvement are, of course, easier made than implemented.

First, Russia lacks a functioning federal court system. Although it maintains a constitutional court charged with providing judicial remedies for constitutional disputes—including those between the central government and provincial governments—it still lacks a working system of courts at the provincial level that are beyond the interference of local interests. So, not only must the country ensure constitutional court decisions are implemented (a recalcitrant problem as regional reactions to the ruling on the housing permit system attest), it must also create a system of independent courts and perhaps a system of federal courts akin to the U.S. circuit court system that might better insulate judges from local interference. This, however, is a long-term project as Russia has yet to develop a coherent system of rule of law, including the development of meaningful conflict of interest laws.

Second, to better integrate center and periphery, Russia's political leaders must work to create a truly national political party system. Elsewhere, I have documented the underdevelopment of national political parties at the regional level in Russia (Stoner-Weiss, 2001b, 2002). The situation is such that over 80 percent of deputies sitting in regional legislatures across the country run and win elections as independents. Arguably, this contributes to a lack of integration of Russian political actors. While I am not advocating a resurrection of the Communist Party of the Soviet Union, the establishment of national political parties that are capable of attracting and incorporating regional political and economic interests may well help to better integrate the country. In developed electoral democracies parties assist in ensuring policy implementation by linking national and local political actors. If a representative from the provinces owes his or her electoral victory to the agency of the president or head of the party, "presumably he is willing to do what the President asks without much hesitation, thereby also eliminating the president's cost of bargaining" (Riker 1964, 93–96). While this does not altogether eliminate the high costs of bargaining with local politicians, it can at least lower those costs (Riker 1964, 96). As a result, Martin Shefter notes that parties are "institutions of representation, but also of control" (Shefter 1994, 16). An important task of political parties in Russia and elsewhere, then, is not just the aggregation of interests within society, and their representation in a national legislature, but also the enhancement of the stability and authority of the political system by linking political actors at various levels of the polity. But due to the pervasive and persistent underinstitutionalization of political parties of all ideological stripes outside of Moscow, Russian parties fail to provide these benefits. The adoption of a federal law that requires that all regional governments adopt systems of proportional representation for the election of regional legislatures (with a requirement that a party receive at least 5 percent of the vote to gain representation in the legislature), and the additional requirement that candidates for regional governor or republican president be sponsored by a national political party may help to spur national party development in the periphery. This, in turn, would help to better integrate the country's politicians.

Finally, to support the development of parties and to aid in better and less costly means of vertically integrating the country, Russia should opt for more democracy rather than less (Ordeshook 1996). The best way to promote party development and widen accountability beyond narrow, particularistic economic interests may be to hold more elections—for judges at all levels, for police chiefs, and the like. By eradicating the system of appointments that is often the purview of "captured" regional politicians, lesser Russian public officials may feel themselves more accountable to their electorate than to powerful regional patrons if they themselves were elected.

These three proposals (with the possible exception of the creation of a federal court system), however, are unlikely to be adopted in Russia in the near future. This is again because of the alignment of forces against the development of a coherent and cohesive federal system. That is, many interests in the Russian political establishment derive great benefit from the chaos and politics of uncertainty that prevails in Russian federal relations. In addition, those with stronger ethnic claims also see little value in strengthening the influence of the central state in their internal cultural affairs. As a result, the management of territorial cleavages in Russia is likely to continue to be highly problematic in the coming decade, as it was in the previous one.

NOTES

1. Solnick 1998 provides more information on the breakdown of hierarchical control in Soviet institutions more generally.

2. This brief account of the Chechen conflicts is drawn from Lieven 1998 and Stoner-Weiss 1997b.

3. It should be noted that even at the time of writing, there is no systematic evidence that the apartment bombings in Moscow were perpetrated by Chechens. The fact that the Chechen leadership and Chechen warlords refused to take responsibility for the bombings has led to a rumor that the Russian security forces may have perpetrated the blasts to engender support for a renewed invasion of Chechnia. There is also no evidence, however, to support this theory.

4. For example, Sverdlovsk oblast concluded its agreement on the regulation of land relations and the administration of land on May 29, 1996, although its original treaty with Moscow and other agreements were signed on January 12, 1996. See Guboglo 1997, 870.

5. A statement to this effect appears at the end of all the agreements between Sverdlovsk oblast and Moscow, although no such statement appears at the end of the agreements with Kaliningrad, and only a few other regions' agreements contain this statement. See Guboglo 1997, where many of the existing treaties and agreements are printed.

6. These and almost twenty other areas where many of the treaties violate the constitution are cited in Lysenko 1997, 184–85.

7. Again, more examples can be found in Lysenko 1997, 185, and through careful comparison of the treaties and the constitution.

8. Further study is required to determine whether certain types of regions and republics tend to be more aggressive in seizing policy autonomy from the center. It is clear that this behavior takes place in both oblasts and republics, but in some oblasts and republics more than others.

9. Putin's speech was transcribed by the BBC and reported in Johnson's Russia List, May 18, 2000.

10. The specific reference is to the practice of Novosibirsk's governor, Vitalii Mukha.

11. Indeed, rather than using his new ability to remove errant governors, Putin has succeeded in removing undesirable regional leaders from office only after offering them plum jobs in government in Moscow.

12. It is easier to list which of Russia's eighty-nine regions were not included in the interviewing process than those that were. Because of the danger involved in going to the North Caucasus in the fall of 1999, neither Chechnia nor Ingushetia was included in the sample. In addition, it proved impossible to complete interviews in the city of Moscow, Moscow oblast, or Leningrad oblast. Since we were primarily interested in the relationship between republics and oblasts and krais and the center, none of the ten autonomous okrugs nor the one autonomous oblast were included. The survey was conducted in cooperation with Aleksandr Gasparishvili and Sergei Tumanov of the Opinion Research Center, Moscow State University. We employed the network of interviewers Gasparishvili and Tumanov constructed in the provinces during the 1990s. Teams of interviewers conducted person-to-person interviews of a list of respondents that we provided. On average, interviews lasted forty minutes. More data and information on this survey can be found in Stoner-Weiss 2001a.

References

Glezer, Ilya. 1992. *Moscow News*, no. 7.

Guboglo, M. N. 1997. *Federalizm Vlasti i Vlast Federalizma*. Moscow: Inteltekh.

Izvestiia. November 4, 1997. Report as reproduced in *Russian Regional Report* 2, no. 38.

Justice Ministry Warns Regions That They are Not Complying With Federal Legislation. 1997. In Institute for East West Studies, *Russian Regional Report* 2, no. 9.

Komsomolskaia Pravda. March 14, 1991.

Lieven, Anatol. 1998. *Chechnia: Tombstone of Russian Power*. New Haven, Conn.: Yale University Press.

Lysenko, V. N. 1997. Razdelenie vlasti I opit Rossiiskoi Federatsii. In *Federalizm Vlasti i Vlast Federalizma*, ed. M. N. Guboglo. Moscow: Inteltekh.

Moscow Mayor Spars With Boris Nemtsov Over Housing Reform. 1997. In Institute for East-West Studies, *Russian Regional Report* 2, no. 17.

Newly Elected Governors Grapple With Moscow, Regional Problems. 1998. In *Russian Regional Report* 3, no. 2.

Ordeshook, Peter. 1996. Russia's Party System: Is Russian Federalism Viable? *Post-Soviet Affairs* 12, no. 3:195–217.

Orttung, Robert W., ed. 2000. *The Republics and Regions of The Russian Federation: A Guide to Politics, Policies and Leaders.* New York: M. E. Sharpe for the East West Institute.

Riker, William. 1964. *Federalism: Origins, Operations, Significance.* Boston: Little, Brown.

Rossisskii Statisticheskii Ezhegodnik. 1999. Moscow: Goskomstat, 54–55.

Russian Regional Report. 1998. 3, no. 30.

Rutland, Peter. 1993. *The Politics of Economic Stagnation in the Soviet Union: The Role of Local Party Organs in Economic Management.* New York: Cambridge University Press.

Shakhrai, Sergei. 1997. Rol' dogovornikh protsessov v ukreplenii i razvitii rossiiskogo federalizma. In *Federalizm Vlasti i Vlast Federalizma,* ed. M. N. Guboglo. Moscow: Inteltekh.

Shefter, Martin. 1994. *Political Parties and the State: The American Historical Experience.* Princeton: Princeton University Press.

Solnick, Steven L. 1995. Federal Bargaining in Russia. *East European Constitutional Review,* 4, no. 4:52.

———. 1998. *Stealing the State: Control and Collapse in Soviet Institutions.* Cambridge, Mass: Harvard University Press.

Soobshenie Press-Sluzhbii Prezidenta Rossiiskoi Federatsii, 2000–05–13–002 Ukaz. O polnomochnom presdstavitele Prezidenta Rossiiskoi Federatsii v federal'nom okruge. (Decree on the authority of the representative of the president of the Russian Federation, May 13, 2000).

Stoner-Weiss, Kathryn. 1997a. *Local Heroes: The Political Economy of Russian Regional Governance.* Princeton: Princeton University Press.

———. 1997b. Regionalism and Federalism. In *Developments in Russian Politics 4,* ed. Stephen White, Alex Pravda, and Zvi Gitelman. Durham: Duke University Press.

———. 2001a Whither the State? The Regional Sources of Russia's Stalled Reforms. Mimeo.

———. 2001b. The Limited Reach of Russia's Party System: Under-Institutionalization in Dual Transitions. *Politics and Society* 29, no. 3:385–414.

———. 2002. Central Governing Incapacity and the Weakness of Political Parties: Russian Democracy in Disarray. *Publius* 32, no. 2:125–46.

Treisman, Daniel. 1997. Russia's Ethnic Revival: The Separatist Activism of Regional Leaders in a Postcommunist Order. *World Politics* 49, no. 2.

Visotskii, Pavel. 1998. O konstitutsionnoi zakonnosti v Rossiskoi Federatsii. *Chelovek i pravo*102, no. 13.

Vybopry regionii posle viborov-96. 1997. Moscow: Russian Electoral Commission.

Wallich, Christine. 1994. *Russia and the Challenge of Fiscal Federalism.* Washington, D.C.: The World Bank.

… While Administration Cracks Down on Other Regions. 1998. *Institute for East West Studies, Russian Regional Report* 3, no. 5.

CHAPTER TWELVE

Nigeria

Dilemmas of Federalism

Rotimi T. Suberu

Within days of the political disengagement of the Nigerian military on May 29, 1999, the country became embroiled in violent ethnic and regional conflicts. The fragile foundations of Nigeria's new federal democracy were swiftly brought into the open by the resurgence of state-ethnic and interethnic clashes in the oil-rich Niger Delta region in southern Nigeria; by furious sectarian conflicts over the actual or planned extension of Sharia or Islamic law in the Muslim north; by bloody clashes involving the three principal ethnicities of Hausa, Yoruba, and Igbo; and by the intensification of pressures for the convening of a Sovereign National Conference (SNC) that would constitutionally restructure the country.

These convulsions evoked memories of Nigeria's ghastly Biafran civil war (1967–70) in which at least one million persons perished and engendered profound anxiety about the country's immediate and long-term political prospects. More than the new democratic experiment was endangered by the resurgence of internecine communal conflicts; the viability and survival of Nigeria as a multinational federation appeared to be in question.

Although there are emerging and potential federal experiments elsewhere on the African continent (especially in Ethiopia and South Africa), Nigeria is Africa's sole established federation (Keating 1999, 10). Whereas fully fledged federal experiments have been resisted or rejected for a variety of historical and cultural reasons in many developing multiethnic countries, federalism has long been recognized as the indispensable basis for Nigeria's stability and survival. Thus, among African countries, Nigeria is distinguished by a loose civilian elite consensus in support of federalism (as against unitarism or secessionism), by the maintenance of a formal federal structure for virtually all of the postindependence period, and by the continuing vigorous debate about the reform or renewal of the federal system. Yet, the Nigerian system of federalism is plagued by severe infirmities and contradictions. So much is this the case that the country is often derided or denounced, by Nigerian and non-Nigerian observers alike, as a "unitary state in federal disguise," as a "hollow," "embattled," "subverted," or "failed" federation, or as practicing the "worst form of federalism anywhere in the world" (Adebayo 1993; AM News, January 7, 1996, 14; Naanen 2000, 6; Soyinka 1999, 29; Williams 1980, 100).

Nigeria's checkered federal experience began in 1954, when the British colonial authority and the emergent Nigerian political elites opted for the federalization of the unitary (albeit decentralized) Nigerian colonial state in order to hold together the disparate ethnic, regional, and religious communities that Britain had encased within Nigeria's artificial boundaries. Originally, the federation consisted of three regional units: the northern region (which contained slightly over one-half of the national population and two-thirds of the country's territory), and the western and eastern regions in the south. The three regions were designed to grant political autonomy and security to the Muslim Hausa-Fulani of the north, the religiously bicommunal Yoruba of the southwest, and the predominantly Christian Igbo of the southeast, respectively. These three major ethnicities constitute approximately two-thirds of the country's current 110 to 120 million people. The rest of the population is made up of some 250 or more minorities, who had been inequitably incorporated into the three-region structure. The more prominent of these smaller ethnic communities include the Tiv, Kanuri, and Nupe in the north, and the Ijaw, Ibibio, Efik, Edo, and Urhobo in the south. The egregious regional and ethnic imbalances in the tripartite federal system fueled intergroup insecurity and conflict, derailed Nigeria's first postindependence Republic (1960–66), and helped pave the way for the attempted secession in 1967 of the Igbo-led eastern region. Several additional subunits were subsequently created in Nigeria to give the federal "system a better population and ethnic balance" (Diamond 1987, 211). Today, the federation consists of thirty-six states, a federal capital at the center of the country in Abuja, and 774 constitutionally entrenched local government areas. The states are currently often classified into six more or less informal geopolitical or geocultural zones as shown in Table 14.1.

Table 12.1 *Nigeria's Geopolitical Zones*

Zone	Component States	Predominant Ethnic Composition	Predominant Religious Composition	Population (1991)	Area (km²)
Northwest	Jigawa, Kaduna, Kano, Katisna, Kebbi, Sokoto, Zamfara.	Hausa-Fulani	Muslim	22,913,412	216,165
Northeast	Adamawa, Bauchi, Borno, Gombe, Taraba, Yobe.	Mixed	Muslim	11,900,913	272,395
Northcentral (Middle Belt or Lower North)	Benue, Kogi, Kwara, Nasarawa, Niger, Plateau and the Federal Capital Territory, Abuja.	Mixed	Mixed	12,554,912	242,325
Southwest	Ekiti, Lagos, Ogun, Ondo, Osun, Oyo.	Yoruba	Mixed	17,455,043	78,771
Southeast	Abia, Anambra, Ebonyi,Enugu, Imo	Igbo (Ibo)	Christian	10,774,977	29,525
Southsouth (Niger Delta)	Akwa Ibom, Bayelsa, Edo, Delta, Cross River, Rivers.	Mixed	Christian	12,392,963	84,587

Sources : Adapted from the final 1991 census figures. For the zonal distribution of states, see Federal Character Commission, "Press Briefing on the Activities of the Commission" (Abuja, August 19,1999). *Note* : The 1991 census, which is believed to have understated the country's population by about 10 million, excluded information on the ethnic or religious identities of Nigerians. Because the Igbos have settled in large numbers in various regions of the country, the 1991 census figures for the Igbo southeastern states may actually understate the Igbo population. In any case, official population statistics remain extremely controversial in Nigeria.

The following pages chronicle the vicissitudes of Nigerian federalism as a design for the accommodation of ethnic-territorial cleavages. They document the fatal failure of Nigeria's original regional federalism, and the relative success of the subsequent multistate structure in managing territorial conflict (see also Horowitz 1985, 602–13). While acknowledging the genius of Nigeria's multistate federalism in averting a recurrence of secessionist conflict, however, this chapter also highlights the multiple dilemmas of a federal system that must cope not only with the challenges of territorially based ethnic, religious, and economic conflicts, but also with the contradictions of an oil-centric political economy and the legacies of hypercentralized military rule.

The Evolution and Transformation of Nigerian Federalism

The Rise and Demise of Regional Federalism, 1954–1967

Following British colonial occupation, the Nigerian state was finally established in 1914 through the amalgamation of two contiguous but culturally and administratively disparate colonial territories, the protectorates of northern and southern Nigeria. The subsequent decision to federalize this state in 1954 owed a lot to the country's deep cultural fragmentation, the aggravation of this diversity by sundry colonial policies, and the enormous attraction that federalist guarantees of subnational autonomy had for Nigeria's rising political elite. The adoption of a federal system of three regions derived from the preponderance in each region of a major ethnic group, the emergence and role of the three areas as the main administrative units of the colonial state since 1939, the rough demarcation of the regions by the lateral axis and southward confluence of the country's main Benue and Niger rivers, and the regions' broad coincidence with the three different routes by which the British penetrated and incorporated Nigeria after the 1861 annexation of Lagos. But the tripartite federal structure involved contradictions that would fatally polarize and destabilize Nigeria in the years following the country's independence from Britain in October 1960.

The most serious contradiction was the overwhelming size of the north, which was larger, more populous, and, hence, politically more powerful than the two southern regions (the west and east) combined. Despite southern pressures for the dissolution of the regions into more structurally equivalent units, however, the mutually conservative northern regional elite and British colonial administration insisted on the indivisibility of the north as "the sole defense" against domination of Nigeria by the more modernized south (Diamond 1988, 29). Yet, northern hegemonic domination became the single most important source of ethnic-regional insecurity and instability in the 1960–66 era as the main northern Hausa-Fulani-dominated party, the Northern People's Congress (NPC), decimated its rivals within the region, consolidated its political control of the federal government, and progressively subdued its opponents in the Yoruba-based Action Group (AG) and the Igbo-led National Council of Nigerian Citizens (NCNC), respectively.

The denial of subunits to the nation's non-Hausa-Fulani, non-Yoruba, and non-Igbo ethnic communities was another fundamental flaw of the regional federal system. A 1958 colonial commission on minority problems had advised against the creation of new regions, justifying its position by referring to the difficulty of drawing "a clean boundary which does not create a fresh minority," the high financial and administrative costs of establishing new subunits, and the need to avoid the administrative perpetuation of "differences that might otherwise disappear" (Nigeria 1958). Ethnic minority fears, the commission concluded, should be allayed by the creation of special developmental agencies, the establishment of a strong nonpartisan national police, and the maintenance of a competitive liberal democratic process. As the ruling regional parties began to use their official powers to advance the interests of the majority ethnic groups, however, the frustration of ethnic minority communities developed into a major source of violent conflict and instability in the First Republic. Thus, resistance to NPC rule by the north's largest minority community, the Tiv, exploded into fatal large-scale rioting in the region in 1962 and 1964. Similarly, ethnic minority agitation against Igbo domination produced the first violent secessionist campaign in Nigeria in 1966, the short-lived declaration of the "Delta Peoples Republic" by Isaac Boro and "other frustrated [Ijaw] advocates of creating a Rivers state out of the ... Eastern Region" (Tamuno 1970, 577). Meanwhile, the deepening ethnic minority crisis in the west had been alleviated by the 1963 creation of a midwest state for ethnic minority non-Yoruba communities in the region. The outcome of a politically motivated move by the NPC and NCNC to balkanize the regional base of the AG, the fragmentation of the west (the smallest of the three original regions) not only left Nigeria's ethnic minority problems substantially unresolved, but actually worsened the imbalance in the structural composition of the federation.

Yet another deficiency of Nigeria's regional federalism was the vulnerability of the center vis-à-vis the regions. The three original regions were larger than several independent African states and, indeed, made all pretensions to sovereignty and self-sufficiency. At various times in the 1950s and 1960s, each of the regions had actually threatened secession (Tamuno 1970). The regions enjoyed the loyalty of their respective major ethnic communities, commanded relatively substantial constitutional powers and financial resources, had become internally self-governing before the independence of the federation as a whole, and were run by the federation's more talented politicians and bureaucrats. Although the federal government acquired more prestige and influence in relation to the regions after independence, the lopsided structure of the federation led ironically to the regionalization of federal supremacy. In Dudley's words, "federal super-ordination ... turned out to be Northern dominance" (Dudley 1966, 16–17). Nigeria's regional federalism, built around a few large ethnoregional bastions, worked to abet, and not to moderate, disruptive centrifugal tendencies.

Indeed, the Nigerian experience provides robust confirmation of the thesis regarding the inherent instability of federal systems with very few units. The small number of regions promoted "an extraordinary degree of polarization," prevented the reciprocal insulation of central and regional politics, and robbed the federal system of the fluidity, flexibility, and multiplicity of bargaining coalitions and options found in truly multiunit federal systems (Diamond 1988, 294). Following the 1962–63 decimation of the western regional political class by an expedient coalition of northern and eastern political elites, for instance, the three-player ethnoregional game between the federation's founding regions degenerated into an increasingly bitter bipolar north-versus-east, Hausa-Fulani-versus-Igbo confrontation. This north-east polarization provided the fatal basis for the 1966 ethnomilitary coups and anti-Igbo pogroms, which culminated in the 1967–70 Nigerian civil war.

The basic flaw in Nigeria's regional federalism was that it converted the country's relatively manageable and potentially integrative "multiple ethnic balance of power" into "a federal imbalance" and a threat to national survival (Lijphart 1977, 164; Young 1976, 307). Although each of the three major ethnic groups—Hausa, Yoruba, Igbo—constituted a clear majority in its region, none of these groups accounts for up to 30 percent of the total national population, which includes tens of smaller but still numerically significant communities like the Ijaw, Tiv, Kanuri, Edo, Ibibio, Urhobo, and Nupe. Furthermore, each of the three major groups was historically internally fragmented along territorial, political, or even cultural-linguistic lines, developing an overarching sense of identity only with the introduction of colonialism and regionalism. Instead of making the most of this cultural complexity, however, the system of regional federalism reduced it to a tripolar structure that fueled ethnoregional chauvinism, insecurity, polarization, and secessionism.

Multistate Federalism in Nigeria since 1967

In May 1967, the Nigerian military government announced the dissolution of the regional system into twelve states in a bid to stave off the imminent secession of the eastern region. The redivision failed to achieve its immediate objective, as the eastern region swiftly announced secession in order to forestall its fragmentation into three states—Rivers, East Central, and South Eastern—under the newly announced twelve-state framework. However, the new structure contributed mightily to the defeat of the secessionist campaign and to the stabilization of the federation after the civil war. To be sure, post-civil war Nigeria has been plagued by internecine political instability and conflict, including coups and repressive military rule, ethnic, regional, and religious rifts, and the collapse and abortion of the second and third democratic republics in 1983 and 1993, respectively. However, owing significantly to the ingenuity of the multistate structure (which expanded from 12 states in 1967 to 19 in 1976, 21 in 1987, 30 in 1991, and 36 in 1996), the federation is now relatively less vulnerable to secessionist conflict.

The most important achievement of multistate federalism in Nigeria is the dilution of northern hegemony. In place of a monolithic and hegemonic northern regional government, there are currently nineteen northern state governments representing a plurality of partisan, ethnic, religious, and related interests or constituencies. The fragmentation of the north into several states has made it more unlikely that the entire region would fall under the control of a Hausa-Fulani-based party, which could then project its regional dominance onto the federal arena. Rather, the rise of two or more viable parties in control of state governments in the north since the Second Republic (1979–83) has mitigated southern apprehensions of northern domination, while promoting previously foreclosed opportunities for credible interethnic political cooperation across the north-south divide.

Multistate federalism in Nigeria has also involved the administrative subdivision of the three major ethnic groups, each of which is now currently distributed across no less than five states. This administrative fragmentation has not necessarily precluded the relative political cohesion of each majority group. However, by relegating the majority ethnicities into several relatively small states, which have highlighted important subethnic cleavages within each group, the multistate structure has helped to crosscut and defuse the majoritarian ethnic chauvinisms that had polarized the old regional system, aggravated ethnic minority insecurity, and fueled secessionist tendencies.

Yet another important achievement of Nigeria's multistate federalism has been the accommodation of the minority non-Hausa-Fulani, non-Yoruba, and non-Igbo ethnic communities. The current multistate federalism includes approximately fourteen, mostly ethnically heterogeneous, minority-controlled states. The conciliation of the minorities has encouraged and enabled them to play a critical stabilizing role in the federation. Thus, ethnic minority officers from Nigeria's north (including wartime head of state Yakubu Gowon) played a leading role in the 1967–70 struggle to preserve Nigerian unity. Nigeria's victory in the civil war was also enormously facilitated by the more or less explicit defection of southern minorities in the new Rivers and South Eastern states from the eastern region's secessionist campaign, and by the positive participation of previously alienated eastern ethnic minority activists like Isaac Boro and Ken Saro-Wiwa in the center's suppression of the Biafran secession. Although it has not been possible to give each of Nigeria's hundreds of minorities a state of its own (and strident agitations for new states have persisted in many of the federation's more ethnically variegated or lopsided minority-populated states), multistate federalism has enabled "a variety of ethnic minority states to play an increasingly active role in a more fluid ... polity" (Rothchild 1991, 39).

Nigeria's multistate federalism has also functioned, albeit quite controversially, as an instrument of interregional resource redistribution. The institutionalization of multistate federalism in Nigeria coincided with the transformation of the country's political economy into a geographically concentrated, oil-centric system; from one-third of the value of all Nigerian exports in 1966, oil revenues have expanded to provide 90 percent of export earnings and 80 percent of public revenues at all governmental levels since

1974. By decisively altering the old regional rules for sharing federally collected revenues (which had emphasized the return of such revenues substantially to the region of derivation), Nigeria's military government ensured that the oil revenues were consolidated into a common centrally managed pool, or "federation account." This account is shared by federal law or decree vertically between the center and the subunits and, then, horizontally among the subunits, with interunit equality and relative population (rather than derivation) as the key elements of the horizontal distribution formula. However, although this redistributive federalism ensured a relatively more even geographical distribution of revenues, it increased the financial dependency of the states (and their localities) on the center, spawned a relentless pressure for new subunits as an easy avenue to oil revenues, and fueled a creeping sense of economic dispossession and political alienation in the minority-populated oil-rich sections.

Though the establishment of a multiplicity of subunits with some access to valued resources has contributed to the decentralization and depolarization of territorial conflict, the establishment of a multiplicity of subunits that are not strictly coterminous with ethnic group boundaries has encouraged the development of subunit identities as a cleavage that can potentially compete with, or crosscut, ethnic identities. Recognition must also be given to the disruptive conflicts and discriminatory practices arising from the attempts by groups within subunits to exclude so-called nonindigenes (Nigerians resident in states other than their own) from economic and political opportunities available to indigenes. Indeed, with the proliferation of states has come a severe contraction in the territorial space in which a Nigerian can claim indigeneity or enjoy full citizenship opportunities. Ironically, the discrimination against nonindigenes is partly legitimated by Nigeria's integrative "federal character" doctrine, which enjoins the adequate representation of state and local elites (indigenes) and interests in the composition and conduct of public institutions, including presidential and gubernatorial cabinets, political parties, and the bureaucracy.[1]

But the most contentious feature of Nigeria's multiunit federal system has been the consolidation of central political hegemony, partly in reaction to the enervation of central authority. This centralization has been promoted not only by secessionist tendencies under the old regional system, military rule, the oil economy, and the proliferation of states, but also by the structure of the Nigerian constitutions since the 1979 basic law for the Second Republic. Thanks partly to the military's tight supervision of constitution-making and redemocratization processes, the 1979 constitution and its successors (the 1989 and 1999 constitutions for the Third and Fourth Republics, respectively) did not reverse, but rather legitimated, the federal military government's invasion or monopolization of several subjects of regional or concurrent federal-regional jurisdiction under the First Republic. The affected subjects include the police and prisons, local government, land use, personal income taxation, the distribution of mining rents and royalties, and the powers of the subunits to have their own constitutions. What is more, the constitutional power of the center since 1979 to promote an omnibus schedule of "fundamental objectives and directive principles of state policy" has meant that, the federal division of powers notwithstanding, the autonomous functions of the states will be "determined largely by what the Federal Government voluntarily chooses to leave to the states" (Joye and Igweike 1982, 94). Much of the current agitation for federal constitutional restructuring in Nigeria has focused on this overcentralization.

An Embattled Federal Democracy

Three regionally combustible issues have buffeted Nigeria's federal democracy since May 1999: the extension of Islamic law in the Muslim north; the agitation for resource control in the Niger Delta; and the southern-based clamor for political decentralization, or "true federalism."

The Sharia Imbroglio

Reflecting their precolonial Islamic political heritage, many northern Nigerian Muslims have long inveighed against the country's colonially inherited common law order. The order relegates Islamic law essentially to the status of customary or native law; restricts the jurisdiction of the various local and appellate Sharia and customary courts largely to personal/civil or noncriminal matters; confines these courts essentially to the subfederal level; and subjects their decisions to review in the superior common law federal courts. Although the 1959 northern Nigeria penal code incorporated some elements of Sharia law, the code modified or excluded several sanctions under the Sharia tradition, including flogging, amputation, and stoning to death. The restrictions on Sharia were designed to reassure the departing colonial government, allay the fears of the region's large minority non-Muslims, and preserve the unity of the north vis-à-vis the south. But northern Muslim demands for Sharia have become more expansive and politically explosive with independence in 1960, the dissolution of the north into relatively more religiously homogeneous states since 1967, the international spread of Islamist political ideologies since the Iranian revolution of 1979, and the consolidation of northern Muslim ethnomilitary rule at the federal level during the 1984–99 era.

Thus, in the early 1960s the northern Nigerian government successfully pursued a constitutional amendment that would enable the grand khadi of the northern Sharia court of appeal to sit on the high court of the region (a privilege to which he was technically unqualified) in order to give his advice in appeals involving Muslims. In 1975–78 northern Muslim interests unsuccessfully demanded the establishment of a federal Sharia court of appeal (FSCA) as a replacement for the region-wide northern Sharia court of appeal, which had ceased to exist with the dissolution of the north into six states in 1967, and the establishment of separate state-level Sharia courts of appeal. The Sharia lobby achieved two things under the 1989 constitution for the aborted Third Republic: the establishment of a Sharia court of appeal for the federal capital territory, Abuja, and the extension of the jurisdiction of Sharia courts from questions of personal law to civil proceedings generally. At the same time, however, the federal military government constitutionally restricted the use of Sharia courts to Muslims only, thereby reversing a provision of the Second Republic's 1979 constitution under which consenting non-Muslims could appear before Sharia courts.

In October 1999, the northwestern Muslim state of Zamfara approved legislation extending Sharia fully to criminal matters. The Zamfara government consequently instituted new Islamic courts and codes, including provisions for the flogging, amputation, or stoning of Muslims guilty of "un-Islamic" conduct. Monitoring and vigilante institutions were also established to enhance compliance with the extended Sharia system. The government claimed the extension was justified under a long-standing constitutional provision that empowers the state-level Sharia court of appeal to "exercise jurisdiction in civil proceedings involving questions of Islamic personal law ... in addition to such other jurisdiction as may be conferred upon it by the law of the state" (Federal Republic of Nigeria 1999, 104). But Christians and other critics argued that the extension was in violation of the constitutional prohibition both of a state religion and of degrading or inhumane punishment. Citing numerous instances of alleged rights abuse against Christians in the Muslim north before 1999, the critics also dismissed as "gratuitous fiction" the assurances by the Zamfara government that Sharia law would apply to Muslims only. In fact, non-Muslims reportedly have been punished under the extended Sharia regime for consuming or selling alcoholic beverages (*The Punch,* July 9, 2000, 1–2).

Although it was condemned by the federal government, Zamfara's extension of the Sharia system was more or less copied by several other predominantly Muslim northern states, including Bauchi, Borno, Gombe, Jigawa, Niger, Kano, Kebbi, Katsina, Sokoto, and Yobe. Except for relatively limited or localized incidents of ethnoreligious violence in states like Bauchi, Niger, Borno, and Sokoto, however, these extensions of Sharia law passed largely peacefully.

But the story was different in Kaduna, a state with a substantial indigenous (southern Kaduna) and immigrant (partly Igbo) non-Muslim population, and a history of bloody ethnoreligious conflict. Here, plans to extend Sharia degenerated into horrific violence that claimed some 1,500 lives in February and May 2000. This number excludes the tens of migrant Muslim Hausas that were killed in the Igbo states of Abia and Imo in retaliation for the killing of Igbo migrants in the Kaduna clashes.

The contrasting trajectories and outcomes of the Sharia debacle in Zamfara and Kaduna are worth discussing. Zamfara is an overwhelmingly Muslim Hausa-Fulani state of 2.2 million people, with an estimated Christian population of only 60,000, the majority of whom are migrants from southern Nigeria. Kaduna, unlike Zamfara, is a borderline, rather than core, Muslim Hausa-Fulani northwestern state. Four elements in the Kaduna context were particularly consequential.

First, although the interreligious distribution of Kaduna's (and Nigeria's) population is the subject of much contentious debate, there is undoubtedly a substantial non-Muslim population in the state. According to Abubakar Umar, a liberal Muslim and former military governor of the state, "Kaduna ... is divided equally between Muslims and Christians, population wise" (Umar 2000, 62). Indigenous non-Muslim activists in the Southern Kaduna Peoples Union (SOKAPU) contend that a carefully orchestrated agenda of political gerrymandering (rather than the actual ethnoreligious demographics of the state) is responsible for the allocation of all but two-thirds of local government areas and constituency seats to the Muslim Hausa-Fulani areas (*The Guardian*, January 30, 2000).

Second, Kaduna has long been polarized violently along converging ethnoreligious, regional, socioeconomic, and political fault lines. Such violent polarization consistently has pitted the state's Muslim Hausa-Fulani politicoeconomic power group, which is based mainly in the northern portions of the state, against a constellation of non-Muslim southern Kaduna minority tribes. Both communities, as well as migrants from all over Nigeria, are heavily represented in the capital city of Kaduna, which was also the headquarters of the former northern region. Large-scale conflicts between the two blocs date back to at least the mid-nineteenth century, when "the non-Hausa communities were raided and enslaved by the Hausa Muslims" (Kazzah-Toure 1995, 3). More recently, particularly since the late 1980s, southern Kaduna towns have been embroiled in ethnoreligious bloodletting over the demands of their non-Muslim communities for complete autonomy from the traditional Muslim emirate structure. Such a history of violent ethnoreligious antagonism had led some to characterize Kaduna or southern Kaduna as the "Lebanon" or "East Timor" of Nigeria (Yakusak 1999, 53). It has also led to proposals that the state be split into two new subunits, along ethnoreligious lines.

Third, notwithstanding persistent allegations by the southern Kaduna elements of Muslim Hausa-Fulani hegemonic domination, the non-Muslim elites were somewhat visible in the Kaduna government structure. For instance, the deputy governor of the state, Stephen Shekari, and the deputy speaker of the state legislature, Gideon Gwani, were Christians of southern Kaduna origin. Unlike in Zamfara, therefore, Christian interests opposed to the Sharia system were represented in the Kaduna state government.

A final feature of the Sharia saga in Kaduna was the more or less conflicting roles of the state's executive and legislature in the whole crisis. In the course of 1999, for instance, the state governor, Alhaji Mohammed Makarfi, established two separate consultative committees, each with equal Muslim and Christian representation, to advise the government on ways to promote interreligious harmony, and to fashion a Christian-Muslim consensus on the Sharia issue, respectively (*The New Nigerian,* March 8, 2000, 18). The reports of the two committees were still pending when the February 2000 ethnoreligious riots broke out.

The riots were precipitated largely by the brazen sectarianism of an eleven-member, all-Muslim state legislative committee on the Sharia issue. Three Christian members of the legislature had declined to serve on the committee because of its heavily Muslim composition, and their worst suspicions were confirmed when the committee ultimately recommended the extension of Islamic law in the state. In October 2000, however, Governor Makarfi initiated political and legal reforms that were designed to soften Christian-Muslim conflict in the state. Based largely on the work of the two Christian-Muslim consultative committees instituted by the governor in 1999, these reforms would involve the establishment of new customary courts and chiefdoms for the southern Kaduna tribes, the delegation of the authority to make religion-based by-laws to local councils, the exemption of religiously mixed parts of the state (including several sections of Kaduna city) from the application of any parochial laws as a way of preserving the "cosmopolitan and heterogeneous complexity" of these areas, and the prohibition of the notoriously abusive religious vigilante groups (*Vanguard,* October 19, 2000, 20–21). Although these measures did not satisfy the extremists on both sides of Kaduna's ethnoreligious divide, they were demonstrably effective in relieving the ethnoreligious tension in the state.

The Niger Delta Question

Hostage taking, hijackings, attacks on oil company personnel, destruction of government-owned oil pipelines, sabotage of oil company installations and facilities, deadly skirmishes between alienated youths and central law enforcement agencies, and intergroup conflicts for oil-related resources have become common occurrences in the Niger Delta. The source of conflict in the Niger Delta is obvious, because, though the Niger Delta region has been the economic backbone of the Nigerian federation since the 1970s, the "great majority of people from the minority ethnic groups of the oil producing areas have remained impoverished," while the region as a whole "remains poorer than the national average" (Human Rights Watch 1999, 8). What is more, the region is ecologically endangered, owing to serious negative environmental externalities of oil exploration and production (Onosode 1999, 21).

The economic dispossession of the Niger Delta derives significantly from the over-centralization of the Nigerian federation. Unlike the more decentralist practices in federations like the United States, Canada, Australia, Brazil, and India, all oil revenues in Nigeria are collected by the federal government (Ikporukpo 1996, 164). These revenues, to reiterate, are partly retained by the federal government and partly redistributed to the states and localities on the basis of criteria that largely operate to the advantage of the major ethnic communities and other groups located outside the Delta region.

Though the derivation principle was an important feature of federalism in the First Republic, it has been progressively deemphasized as the oil revenues have expanded. This progressive shift away from the derivation principle reflected the centralizing proclivities of the military, the limited political clout of the minority oil-producing groups vis-à-vis the major ethnic communities, and the need to avoid huge disparities in the resources available to the oil-rich areas, on the one hand, and to the rest of the federation, on the other. Although recent revenue allocation laws have sought to contain the agitation in the Niger Delta via the partial restoration of the derivation principle, the concessions still fall short of the demands, expectations, and needs of the oil-endowed communities. In essence, the amount of federally collected oil revenues returned to the subunits on a derivation basis had declined from 50 percent of on-shore and off-shore mining rents and royalties in the 1960s, through 20 percent of on-shore mining rents and royalties in the late 1970s, to less than 5 percent of oil revenues in the 1980s and 1990s, before it was lately increased to "not less than 13 percent" of these revenues under the 1999 constitution. In addition, a Niger Delta Development Commission (NDDC) was established in 2000, to replace the failed Oil Mineral Producing Areas Development Commission (OMPADEC), as a federal agency for the amelioration of the developmental problems of oil-bearing communities. But recent policies for the alleviation of the problems and grievances of the Niger Delta have been dogged by considerable contradiction and contention. Following a legal action that was initiated by the federal government, for example, the Nigerian Supreme Court in April 2002 proclaimed that off-shore oil revenues could be excluded from the application of the 13 percent derivation rule because the nation's continental shelf belonged to the federation as a whole, and not to the adjoining littoral oil-producing states. The judgment embittered many groups in the Niger Delta.

Agitation, therefore, persists in the Niger Delta over the failure of Nigeria's federal governance to satisfy both the short-term distributive demands and the more concrete economic and political goals of the oil-producing communities. The latter objectives include the restoration of the derivation principle and, even more radically, a constitutional amendment that would grant the governments or communities of the Niger Delta "full control of their respective natural resources" (*This Day,* July 16, 2000, 5). This quest for resource control was most forcefully articulated in the 1990 Ogoni Bill of Rights, the 1998 Kaiama Declaration of Ijaw Youths, and the July 2000 Conference of Niger Delta Governors and Federal Legislators. Because it challenges the fundamental basis of centralized distributive federalism in Nigeria, however, the campaign for resource control has been sternly denounced and repressed by the federal government.

A major instance of such repression involved the police killings in November 1990 of eighty members of the Umuechem community in Rivers State following the murder of three policemen who had participated in police operations against Umuechem on the invitation of Shell Oil Company during the preceding October (Human Rights Watch/Africa, 1995, 9). Another instance was the internationally publicized repression of the Ogoni movement, which peaked with the execution of writer Ken Saro-Wiwa, and eight other Ogoni activists, in November 1995. Yet another involved the killings in December 1998 of tens of Ijaw youths seeking to enforce the Kaiama Declaration on resource control. Finally, in what was denounced "as a military campaign of awesome destructiveness unworthy of a democratic government," the Obasanjo administration in November 1999 unleashed armed troops on Odi town, Bayelsa State, following the murder of twelve federal police officers in the area by militant Ijaw youths (Adebajo 2000, 48).

A Struggle for "True Federalism"

The agitation for resource control in the Niger Delta is the most focused, strident, and violent expression of a relatively more diffuse and quiescent struggle for "true federalism," variously defined, in (mainly southern) Nigeria. Presumably, a true federalism would restore the vertical (federal-regional) distribution of powers under the old regional system, but without that system's egregious horizontal (interregional and interethnic) imbalance. The quarterly meetings of the seventeen southern governors since October 2000 have provided the major platform for the campaign for true federalism in Nigeria. Among the specific demands emerging from these meetings and related forums are the following: a constitutional amendment to permit the establishment of independent state police units; the transfer of more revenues to the states and localities from the federation account and greater transparency in the management of the account by the federal government; the enthronement of true fiscal federalism, with emphasis on the principles of regional resource control and derivation; an acknowledgment of the rights of the northern Muslim states to develop the Sharia system as long as the rights of resident non-Muslims are scrupulously respected; an end to central intervention in local government affairs, basic education, public housing, agriculture, rural development, and related subjects; and the dissolution of centralizing, military-created institutions like the National Judicial Council and the National Primary Education Commission. In addition, many state governments have denounced or resisted the centralization of the national minimum wage structure, the imposition of a national anticorruption law on all levels of government, and the center's exclusive arrogation of the power to declare public holidays. A far more radical demand calls for a return to a modified form of regional federalism that would consolidate the current thirty-six states into about six viable federal regions (Movement for National Reformation 1992; The Patriots 2000).

The southern-based movement for true federalism has often elicited opposition not only from the central government, but also from the landlocked and relatively more economically depressed north, which depends more heavily than the south on the present system of centralized distributive federalism. Indeed, according to one attitudinal survey of the northeast zone, "while the people of the region agree on the desirability of a federal system for a heterogeneous society like Nigeria, they are worried that an over-decentralized federal system could reduce the capacity of the central government to intervene to uplift disadvantaged regions of the country" (International IDEA 2000, 163). Thus, while they have supported the transfer of more federally collected revenues to the subfederal authorities, the northern states are averse to any proposals for regional resource control or the allocation of federal revenues on the basis of derivation.

Indeed, while there is broad, but by no means universal, support in Nigeria for greater decentralization, there are serious concerns and controversies regarding the desirability and viability of specific decentralizing measures. A good example is the debate over the decentralization of Nigeria's unitary police structure. While it reflects popular disenchantment in Nigeria with the country's understrength, corrupt, and ineffectual national police force, the agitation for state police units is severely undermined by several factors. These include public recollections of the politicization and manipulation of local authority police forces by the regional governments in the First Republic; doubts about the capacity of Nigeria's financially weak and dependent state governments to fund and manage independent police units effectively; fears about potentially violent confrontations between separate police formations in a context of weak institutionalization or overpoliticization; and alarm at the excesses and sectarianism of current state-based vigilante groups, including the Bakassi Boys and the Movement for the Actualization of a Sovereign State of Biafra (MASSOB) in the Igbo southeastern states, the Egbesu Boys in the Niger Delta, the Odua Peoples Congress (OPC) in the Yoruba southwestern states, and the Sharia vigilante or monitoring groups in the Muslim north.

The radical proposal for the restructuring of Nigeria into about six regional federating units is even more problematic or unrealistic, and it enjoys little or no support in the northern half of the country. The proposal would involve the reestablishment of pan-Igbo and pan-Yoruba regions, but would create more politically controversial and unsustainable ethnic outcomes in the Niger Delta, the Hausa-Fulani far north, and the middle belt of northern minorities. Its implementation is not only likely to generate opposition from current state-based interests, but also to distort Nigeria's complex ethnic configurations and vitiate the impact of the country's multistate federalism in diluting ethnoregional chauvinism, in promoting a relatively more fluid structure of interethnic relations, and in providing a viable federal authority as a focus for the development of a common Nigerian identity. For these, and related reasons, the proposal for the re-regionalization of Nigeria is seen by critics as a recipe for centrifugal polarization and a deathtrap for Nigerian unity and survival.

Reviewing the Institutional Context

Often in contention in Nigeria today is the legitimacy or efficacy of the country's political institutions as reconstructed and centralized by the military during its long spells of rule from 1966 to 1979 and from 1984 to 1999. The most consequential military-sponsored federalist reforms of the Nigerian political system have involved the shift from a regional to a multistate framework and the elaboration of the doctrine of federal character as a general principle of equitable intersegmental integration. The contribution of the multistate framework to the depolarization of ethnic and regional conflict in Nigeria has been discussed. The more contentious effect of the framework in producing a highly centralized federation has also been highlighted. Suffice it to reiterate here that Nigeria's current thirty-six states, unlike the three or four regions of the 1960–66 era, do not have their own constitutions or local-level police forces, cannot make any constitutional claims to off-shore oil revenues or to the exclusive control of local government affairs, and must operate within a federal constitutional framework in which the central government can legitimately intervene in virtually every matter of public importance.

The centralization of Nigerian federalism is underscored and reinforced by the structure and organization of many of the country's political institutions. The Nigerian constitution, for instance, provides for a unified hierarchy of "superior courts of record" in the federation (Federal Republic of Nigeria 1999, 4–5). At the apex of this judicial structure is the Supreme Court of the federation, which is the final appellate court in the country, and at the base of the unified structure of superior courts are the Sharia and customary courts of appeal in Abuja and in the states. Under the 1999 constitution, the National Judicial Council, which is headed by the chief justice of the Supreme Court, is empowered to make recommendations for appointment into, and to control the finances of, all the courts, including the state-level high courts and Sharia and customary courts of appeal. Such extensive centralization, coupled with the political subversion or manipulation of the judicature under military rule, has generated significant cynicism regarding the legitimacy or arbitral capacity of the judicial system. To be sure, the postmilitary era since 1999 has been characterized by the reassertion of judicial independence, and by the Supreme Court's enforcement of states' rights in such areas as the conduct of local government elections and the management of the federation account. Yet, the capacity of the Court to serve as an instrument of true federalism is constrained by the enormous constitutional powers of the center.

The centralization of the Nigerian political system is reinforced also by the change from the First Republic's Westminster parliamentary system to an American-style presidential system since the 1979 constitution. Originally seen by the military in 1975 as a way of cementing the country's unity through the pan-Nigerian figure of a nationally elected president, the change to presidentialism was eventually endorsed during 1975–77 by two civilian bodies, the Constitution Drafting Committee (CDC) and Constituent Assembly (CA), which drafted and debated the 1979 constitution, respectively. Since then, the military supervisors and promulgators of Nigeria's successive transitions and constitutions have proclaimed presidentialism as an inviolable component of the country's political structure.

Among other consequences, the adoption of presidentialism has entailed a strict separation of powers and personnel between the federal executive and the two federal legislative chambers, namely, the senate and the house of representatives. Under the 1999 constitution, the senate consists of three members from each of the thirty-six states, and one member from the federal capital territory, Abuja, making a total of 109 senators. The house of representatives, on the other hand, consists of "three hundred and sixty members representing constituencies of nearly equal population as far as possible" (Federal Republic of Nigeria 1999, 27). Each senator or representative is elected from a single-member constituency on a plurality or first-past-the-post basis. Both houses of the national assembly also enjoy equivalent policy-making powers, although the senate is responsible exclusively for the confirmation of major federal appointments. The rigid system of separation of powers and plurality-based legislative elections at the federal level in Nigeria is reproduced at the state level, with the important exception that state legislatures are unicameral, not bicameral, institutions.

A major consequence of the election of Nigeria's legislators on a plurality basis from more or less ethnically homogeneous, single-member constituencies has been to turn the country's legislative houses into institutions for the promotion of parochial interests (Horowitz 1985, 638; International IDEA 2000, 58). Similarly, the concentration of executive powers in individual presidential and gubernatorial incumbents has fueled sectional competition to control these positions. The problem is exacerbated by the fixed four-year term of the president and governors, by the ability of an incumbent to win a second term, and by the absence of effective institutional checks on executive political dominance in the Nigerian context. In essence, the intensity of the sectional competition for executive positions in Nigeria would appear to confirm Lijphart's thesis that the presidential system's "one-person executive," unlike the more collective and inclusive executive of parliamentarianism, is a poor instrument of ethnic accommodation (Lijphart 1977) but the situation has been mitigated by reforms.

Presidentialism in Nigeria was designed explicitly to promote interethnic integration, consensus, and accommodation. The election of the political executive takes place in a federation-wide or a statewide contest, rather than from a local parliamentary constituency. More important, a requirement for a minimum territorial spread of support was introduced into the presidential and gubernatorial election formula in order to ensure that an elected executive would be a candidate truly enjoying broad territorial legitimacy; to be successful on the first ballot, a presidential candidate must obtain the highest number of votes, plus "not less than one-quarter of the votes cast ... in each of at least two-thirds of all the states in the Federation and the Federal Capital Territory, Abuja" (Federal Republic of Nigeria 1999, 55). A successful gubernatorial candidate is similarly required to obtain "not less than one-quarter of the votes cast in each of at least two-thirds of all the local government areas in the state" (Federal Republic of Nigeria 1999, 71). In addition, a president or a governor is constitutionally enjoined to exercise his or her "powers of appointment" with due "regard to the federal character of Nigeria," or "the diversity of people within the state," and the need to promote national unity (Federal Republic of Nigeria 1999, 81). The president is specifically required to "appoint at least one minister [member of the federal cabinet] from each state, who shall be an indigene of such a state" (Federal Republic of Nigeria 1999, 61). An indigene of each state of the federation must also be represented in several other important federal executive bodies, including the National Economic Council, the Revenue Allocation Commission, and, of course, the Federal Character Commission. Thus, while presidentialism may often be inimical to ethnic conflict management, the Nigerian experience suggests that presidentialism can be creatively reinvented or adapted to produce more benign ethnopolitical outcomes.

The idea that the composition and conduct of national institutions should reflect Nigeria's plural composition has become a defining feature of the country's federal practice. Its underlying goal is to prevent the kind of ethnoregional domination and insecurity that consumed the First Republic. Thus, before it can be registered by the national electoral agency and function officially as a political party, a political association is constitutionally required to be "open to every citizen of Nigeria irrespective of his place of origin, circumstance of birth, sex, religion or ethnic grouping." The "name, ... symbol or logo" of the association must "not contain any ethnic, religious" or regional "connotation"; "the headquarters of the association" must be "situated" in the "Federal Capital Territory, Abuja"; and the executive committee (or any other governing council) of the association must include members from at least "two-thirds of all the states of the Federation and the Federal Capital Territory, Abuja" (Federal Republic of Nigeria 1999, 86–87).

The close constitutional regulation of party formation, along with the suspension of political party activities for much of the period of military rule, has left Nigeria with an unstable, shallow, contested, chaotic, and artificially deethnicized party system. Yet, while formally fulfilling constitutional requirements, Nigerian political parties have remained ethnic-bound: they have either been sectional in their actual or core support base, or have been fragmented internally along ethnic and regional lines. Of the three parties that were licensed in 1988 to compete in the transition to the new democracy, the northern-led All Nigerian Peoples Party (ANPP) and the Yoruba-based Alliance for Democracy (AD) are formally national, but effectively ethnoregional, organizations. The ruling Peoples Democratic Party (PDP), on the other hand, is a loose federal coalition of disparate ethnic, regional, or state-based political factions that are held together by the share-out of national patronage on the basis of federal character. As one newspaper editorial puts it, "the PDP ... is divided on virtually every public issue... It is difficult to know where the party stands on such ... issues as the Sharia, resource control, fiscal federalism, or even the much talked about issue of a national conference" (*The Comet*, March 7, 2001, 13).

All of this is not to ignore the immense creativity of some of Nigeria's past and current parties in reinventing and extending the concept of federal character. The parties have informally, but rigorously, extended the principle to incorporate strategies for the regional, geopolitical, religious, ethnic, and subethnic balancing and rotation of political offices at both federal and subfederal levels. Thus, key positions in Nigeria (including party chairmanships and presidential and vice-presidential nominations, as well as the headship of strategic ministries or branches of government) are often balanced on a north-south and/or Christian-Muslim basis. There is also the expectation that these positions would rotate among regions, ethnicities, or geopolitical zones from one election to another. These informal strategies help to mitigate the potential superficiality or rigidity of formal rules, advance the quest for national unity through nondomination or balanced intersegmental participation, and promote some measure of interethnic consensus.

For all its efficacy, popularity, and ingenuity, however, the federal character concept is deeply implicated in the centralization of Nigerian federalism since it has "encouraged many Nigerians to view federalism, not as a principle of non-centralized democratic government, but as simply a guarantee of ethnic and religious representation in the institutions of government, no matter how centralized" (Adamolekun and Kincaid 1991, 178).

Analytical Overview

Institutional Factors: Federalism and the Federal Character Principle

Federalism remains the lifeblood of Nigeria's survival as a multiethnic country. But the Nigerian experience suggests that to manage territorial conflicts effectively federal institutions must be vertically and horizontally balanced. Under Nigeria's First Republic, federalism promoted ethnoregional domination, polarization, and alienation, all of which set the stage for democratic collapse, ethnomilitary infighting, and secessionist warfare. Under today's reformed multistate framework, ethnic and regional conflicts have become less polarized, and are distinctively less likely to be a major source of democratic collapse or to degenerate into secessionist warfare. Nigeria's Second Republic collapsed for reasons other than ethnic conflict, and, despite the persistently strident debates about the fragility of Nigerian unity, there has been no major secessionist challenge to the Nigerian federation under the multistate structure.

By exploiting the integrative and accommodative opportunities inherent in Nigeria's complex ethnic diversity itself, the multistate framework has functioned relatively well to provide opportunities for some measure of self-governance to a variety of territorial communities, contain some conflicts within the federation's respective subunits, fragment and dilute the ethnocentrism of the three major groups, alleviate ethnic minority insecurity or fears of intergroup domination, generate potentially crosscutting state-based identities, and decentralize and redistribute economic resources.

For all the controversy and conflict it has generated, the extension of Sharia law in the Muslim north may illustrate the vitality and efficacy of multistate federalism in Nigeria. The federalist accommodation of territorial diversity in Nigeria is demonstrated in the legal pluralism arising from the constitutional provisions that empower the states to establish Sharia (as well as customary) courts for their populations, alongside the federation-wide common law courts. Consequently, states in the Muslim north have been able to institute fairly elaborate systems of Islamic courts without endangering the rights and interests of Christian or animist groups in non-Muslim states, or violating the basic secularity or interreligious neutrality of the common federal arena. The relative success of Nigerian federalism in accommodating the Sharia issue is also underscored by the flexibility that the implementing states have to enact the Sharia system most suited to their peculiar circumstances (for example, Kaduna); by the multiplicity of appellate opportunities that are available in Sharia cases from the lowest Islamic courts through the state-level Sharia court of appeal to the federal Supreme Court; by the formal acknowledgment by the Sharia-implementing states of the supremacy of the Nigerian constitution and the rights of resident non-Muslims; and by the fact that the implementation of the Sharia system is being spearheaded by relatively moderate Muslim political leaders who are apparently committed to Nigeria's federal democracy, as distinct from the northern Muslim fundamentalist elements who seek to create an Islamic Republic of Nigeria (Ostien 2001).

Yet, there can be little doubt that Nigerian federalism is plagued by deep contradictions and conflicts arising mainly from its fiscal overcentralization under the combined impact of "soldiers and oil." The domination of the federal system by the centralized redistribution of federally collected oil revenues has perversely focused the attention of all subunits on this national cake-sharing process. The process generates both intense sectional mobilization for the control of this all important center—particularly the presidency—as well as frustration among regional elites regarding the absence of genuine autonomy in the periphery. The centralized funding of the subunits encourages the country's further political fragmentation and hypercentralization by unleashing sectional pressures for the creation of more such units as a means of obtaining easy access to the oil revenues. Meanwhile, such easy access to oil rents promotes financial irresponsibility at all levels of the federal system, with adverse consequences not only for the country's developmental and democratic prospects, but also potentially for its legitimacy and viability as a multiethnic entity.

Most important, however, the system of centralized distributive federalism has produced deep disaffection and violent agitation in the Niger Delta, whose diverse minority communities have become the hapless milch cows of the federation. In the words of the Nigerian Nobel Laureate in literature, Wole Soyinka (1999, 29), "the oil-producing [areas] … have been treated as vassals to a remote, indifferent and avaricious center, and today we are looking at consequences that involve not simply a confrontation between a region and that center, but murderous confrontations along the length and breadth of the region, a rupture of former harmonious relationships [and] a desperation and intransigence beyond anything that has been witnessed in the nation since the Biafran civil war."

The elitist, quasi-consociational, federal character practices that co-opt sectional representatives into multiethnic governing coalitions have really not been very effective in containing the resentment and violent agitation in the Delta. This is because such vi-olence mainly has involved unemployed or underemployed youths and other alienated, nonelite groups. Moreover, while they have helped to prevent extreme forms of sec-tional bias in political representation or recruitment, federal character practices have not completely removed fears, perceptions, allegations, or actual situations of ethnic, regional, or religious underrepresentation in government. In February 2000, for in-stance, the Federal Character Committee of the senate showed that the south-south (Niger Delta) and the southeastern (Igbo) geopolitical zones were relatively underrep-resented, vis-à-vis the other four zones, in the distribution of political appointments (*The Guardian,* February 18, 2000). Many in the Niger Delta region also point to the fact that, for all its contributions to the nation's economy, the region is the only zone that has yet to produce a head of the federal government, either under military or under civilian rule.[2]

A more salutary impact of the federal character concept has involved its relative suc-cess in generating transcommunal "political appeals and constituencies" in presidential and gubernatorial contests because of the geographic distribution requirement (Diamond 1995, 475). The confidence-building measures of the Kaduna political exec-utive on the Sharia issue may reflect the capacity of this requirement to promote ac-commodative behavior at the gubernatorial level in an otherwise ethnically heterogeneous and conflict-prone state. The Kaduna Sharia crisis of 2000 also illus-trates the extent to which the absence of such incentives in simple plurality legislative elections can promote violent "ethnic demagoguery" in the legislature (International IDEA 2000, 55). Yet reflecting the heavy burden of the country's British colonial history, as well as the strong entrenchment of the idea of direct constituency representation in Nigerian political culture, proposals to reform the system of legislative elections in order to generate more transcommunal appeals remain unpopular in Nigeria (International IDEA 2000, 134–35).

Noninstitutional Factors

The underlying reason why the Sharia issue was turbulent in Kaduna, but relatively quiescent in Zamfara, involves the obvious and enormous differences in the ethnoreli-gious configuration and conflict-history of the two states. Prior to the excision of the state from Sokoto in 1996, the Zamfara area was enmeshed in a controversy over the constitution of new emirate authorities and state units within the boundaries of the old Sokoto emirate, which was the headquarters of the wide-ranging (Sokoto) caliphate in northern Nigeria. But nothing in the history of this overwhelmingly Muslim Hausa-Fulani area is comparable to the long tradition of violent ethnoreligious enmity in Kaduna. What was involved in the Kaduna crisis was not simply the depth of the ethnoreligious and sociopolitical differences between the northern Muslim Hausa-Fulani and the southern non-Muslim minority communities. Equally consequential was the combustible situation engendered by collective recollections of a long-standing history of distrust, disaffection, and violent confrontation between the two groups. In particular, the southern Kaduna peoples referred to their "oppression" by the Muslim elements "for decades," beginning with slave raiding and tribute exaction in the precolonial period, and extending through the colonial era into the present epoch in the form of such provocations as the continuing imposition of emirate rule on the southern Kaduna tribes and their economic and political marginalization by dominant Hausa-Fulani elements at federal and state levels (*The Comet,* September 13, 2000, 5).

The Niger Delta communities, like the southern Kaduna peoples, are among Nigeria's ethnically heterogeneous minority sections, who have always felt marginalized by the major ethnicities of Hausa-Fulani, Yoruba, and Igbo. Although they were conciliated by the state-creation exercises in 1963 and 1967, the Niger Delta communities became progressively disillusioned with their condition in the Nigerian union as new central revenue allocation laws increasingly confiscated the oil revenues from the region; as additional centrally funded states were created primarily to meet the distributive interests of the major ethnic subgroups and not to assuage the problems of ethnic minorities; as the ecological and developmental problems of the Niger Delta deepened; and as a succession of northern Muslim-dominated military governments resorted to repression to contain the growing agitation for political and economic autonomy in the Delta.

A striking feature of the agitation in the Niger Delta was its internationalization, particularly by Ken Saro-wiwa and his cohorts in the Movement for the Survival of the Ogoni People (MOSOP). International involvement in the Niger Delta has included the following: the documentation, publicizing, and condemnation of the excesses of the Nigerian government and the oil multinationals by Euro-American human rights' and environmental groups; the recognition and support from Western governments for the work of crusading ethnic elites, including the granting of political asylum to endangered activists; the imposition of sanctions that were designed to delegitimate military rule in Nigeria, notably the suspension of the country from the Commonwealth of ex-British colonies in 1995, following the executions of Saro-Wiwa and eight other MOSOP activists; and international development assistance to soften the environmental and socioeconomic problems of the Niger Delta.

There can also be little doubt that developments in the Arab world, especially the Iranian revolution, and contacts with the region, including training at the Islamic University in Madina (Saudi Arabia), have influenced the campaign by northern

Muslim elements for the "de-secularization of the Nigerian state, and expanding the scope of Sharia" (Umar 2001, 138). Non-Muslim critics of the Sharia system in Nigeria, especially the Christian Association of Nigeria (CAN) and the southern-dominated print media, have also accused many Muslim nations of encouraging or funding the Sharia movement as part of a scheme to promote the Islamization of the country. Support for such insinuations has been limited largely to the following: the military's surreptitious decision to enlist Nigeria in the Organization of Islamic Conference (OIC) and the Islamic Development Bank (IDB) in 1986–87; the presence of representatives of several Arab or Muslim states (notably, Iraq, Libya, Pakistan, Palestine, Saudi Arabia, Sudan, and Syria) at the public launching of the extended Sharia system in Zamfara in October 1999 and in Kano in June 2000; the ongoing plans to build an international Islamic university in Kano with Libyan financial support; and revelations by Zamfara's Governor Sani, among others, that *Alkalis* (judges) for the Sharia courts would be trained in Saudi Arabia (*The Guardian,* October 24, 1999, 1–2; *The Punch,* June 30, 2000, 1, 16). Yet, unlike in northern Nigeria after 1999, in most Muslim countries the Sharia is confined largely to matters of personal status. At the same time, Western countries and organizations like Canada, Australia, the European Union, and the United Nations Children Fund (UNICEF) have condemned the new Sharia penalties in Nigeria's Muslim states as "inhuman," "degrading," and a violation of some of the United Nations conventions "to which Nigeria is a signatory" (*The Guardian,* January 25, 2001, 1; January 31, 2001, 80). In essence, international involvement in recent internal regional conflicts in Nigeria has been largely benign; it has not contributed significantly or directly to the eruption or intensification of violence.

A United or Divided Nigeria? Elite Perspectives and Incentives

For all the conflicts that beset Nigeria's multistate federalism, the country's central and regional elites have remained broadly committed to sustaining the federation's unity. As revealed by President Olusegun Obasanjo in October 2000, recent discussions between the federal government and "a wide cross-section of the political, traditional and religious leadership of each of the six zones of the federation" confirmed that "not one zone … did not believe in a strong and united Nigeria" (*The Guardian,* October 1, 2000, 105). Instead, a preference for maintaining Nigeria's federal union has been openly expressed by such disparate and often competing territorial groups as the northern Muslim-dominated Arewa Consultative Forum (ACF), the Middle Belt Forum (MBF) of northern Christian minority elites, the conference of Niger Delta Governors and Federal Legislators, *Ohanaeze Ndi Igbo* (the preeminent Igbo sociopolitical organization), and the Yoruba-based *Afenifere.* Although openly separatist movements like MASSOB and factions of the OPC are also active in Nigeria, opinion surveys suggest that a clear majority in each zone of the country, ranging from 58 percent in the Igbo southeast to 87 percent in the northeast, agrees that Nigeria should remain united as one country. Overall, about three-quarters of Nigerians affirm national unity, while an equally overwhelming majority of the citizenry professes firm commitments to both group and national (Nigerian) identities (Lewis and Bratton 2000, 2001). Several factors help explain such overwhelming commitment to Nigeria's federal "unity in diversity," despite the persistence of significant disagreement and disaffection regarding the actual operation of the federal union.

First, for all its flaws and failures, Nigeria's multistate federalism has been relatively successful in promoting intergroup accommodation and in preventing the kind of egregious domination that had completely delegitimated the old regional federalism. Second, the Nigerian federation is historically rooted in a "voluntary will to federate" (Adamolekun and Kincaid 1991, 180). It was not "forced together" but emerged from "a consensus decision reached between Nigeria's nationalist leaders and the British colonial authorities" (Bermeo 2002, 108; Adamolekun and Ayo 1989, 157). Third, all the major alternatives to federalism—unitarism, confederalism, and partition—have been tried in Nigeria with disastrous consequences. The May 1966 unitary decree of Igbo military head of state Aguiyi-Ironsi provoked anti-Igbo riots in the north and accelerated Nigeria's descent into secessionist warfare; an attempt to stave off the war via the confederalist Aburi (Ghana) Accord of 1967 collapsed following conflicting interpretations of the agreement by central and eastern regional military elites. Fourth, Nigeria's complex ethnic configurations make a federal compromise a more feasible and peaceable political option for the country than the extremes of unitarism and separatism. Fifth, all the geopolitical zones in the country, with the exception of the oil-rich Niger Delta, are net economic beneficiaries from the Nigerian union by virtue of their access to redistributed oil revenues. However, the potential economic advantages of union have been largely negated by the mismanagement of the nation's resources, including the U.S.$280 billion that Nigeria has earned from oil revenues since the 1970s, and the country's attendant impoverishment (per capita income in 1999 was a miserable $310). Nonetheless, secessionism is not an economically rewarding option for any section of Nigeria, including the Niger Delta, which would be deeply divided internally and quite vulnerable externally as an independent state. Thus, even as they denounced the "enslavement" of the Ijaw "in the fraudulent contraption called Nigeria," the militant Ijaw youths who proclaimed the 1998 Kaiama Declaration "agreed to ... work for self-government and resource control for the Ijaw people ... within Nigeria" (*The Guardian,* December 28, 1998).

A sixth explanation for the strong support for Nigeria's federal union involves the general belief that some of the country's current political problems "are not inherent in federalism" but derive from a "departure from the practice of true federalism," especially under military rule (*The Guardian*, November 29, 1999; *Newswatch*, April 17, 2000, 23). This belief partly accounts for the rejection of renewed military rule and the general support for federalist reform or renewal in Nigeria (Lewis and Bratton 2001). Finally, support for Nigeria's federal unity also derives from the expectation among the country's leadership and intelligentsia that a single Nigeria, as Africa's demographic and political colossus, could emerge as an influential force in international politics.

Conclusion

Nigeria came into independence in 1960 with a structurally inequitable, triregional, federal system that distorted the country's complex ethnic balance, fueled ethnic and regional polarization, destabilized a fledgling democratic republic, and set the stage for ethnomilitary infighting and secessionist warfare. The reconstruction of this federal system since the eve of the Nigerian civil war in 1967 has produced a radically different federal structure of multiple states in the country. Compared to the old regional federalism, the multistate system has functioned relatively well to provide some measure of political autonomy and security to a wide variety of territorial groups, hold the country together, contain divisiveness within relatively manageable limits, and sustain a broad elite commitment to the preservation of Nigeria as a united multiethnic federation. Although Nigeria has recently witnessed serious regional conflicts over the extension of Sharia law in the Muslim north and the struggle for subnational resource control and greater political decentralization in the south, these conflicts are evidently not secessionist in nature. Rather, the Nigerian experience demonstrates that federalism can be creatively used to tame secessionist tendencies and depolarize intergroup conflicts. All of this, however, is not to underestimate the daunting challenges that currently confront Nigeria in managing a federal system that is troubled by the centralizing legacies of prolonged military rule, by the pathologies of a distributive, oil-centric, political economy, and by disagreements among key regional elites regarding the scope or direction of federal reform.

NOTES

1. The Nigerian constitution tautologically defines state indigeneity on the basis of genealogy rather than residency. Under section 318 of the 1999 constitution, for instance, a person can claim to belong to, or originate from, a state if any of his/her "parents or ... grandparents was a member of a community indigenous to that state."

2. The federal character norms on intersegmental inclusion have been respected or implemented more faithfully under civilian than under military rule. On why civilian governments tend to be more ethnically inclusive or representative than military regimes, see Horowitz (1985).

REFERENCES

Adamolekun, Ladipo, and Bamidele Ayo. 1989. The Evolution of the Nigerian Federal Administration System. *Publius: The Journal of Federalism* 19, no. 1:157–76.

Adamolekun, Ladipo, and John Kincaid. 1991. The Federal Solution: Assessment and Prognosis for Nigeria and Africa. *Publius: The Journal of Federalism* 21, no. 4:173–88.

Adebajo, Adeyeke. 2000. Signposts to Armageddon. *Tell* 27 (March):48.

Adebayo, A. G. 1993. *Embattled Federalism: History of Revenue Allocation in Nigeria.* New York: Peter Lang.

Bermeo, Nancy. 2002. The Import of Institutions. *Journal of Democracy* 13, no. 2:96–110.

Diamond, Larry. 1987. Issues in the Constitutional Design of a Third Nigerian Republic. *African Affairs,* 86, no. 343: 209–26

———. 1988. *Class, Ethnicity and Democracy in Nigeria: The Failure of the First Republic.* London: Macmillan.

———. 1995. Nigeria: The Uncivic Society and the Descent into Praetorianism. In *Politics in Developing Countries: Comparing Experiences with Democracy,* ed. Larry Diamond, Juan J. Linz, and S. M. Lipset. Boulder: Lynne Rienner.

Dudley, Billy. 1966. Federalism and the Balance of Political Power in Nigeria. *Journal of Commonwealth Political Studies* 4, no. 1:16–29.

Federal Republic of Nigeria. 1999. *Constitution of The Federal Republic of Nigeria 1999.* Lagos: Federal Government Press.

Horowitz, Donald. 1985. *Ethnic Groups in Conflict.* Berkeley: University of California Press.

Human Rights Watch. 1999. *The Price of Oil: Corporate Responsibility and Human Rights Violations in Nigeria's oil Producing Communities.* New York: Human Rights Watch.

Human Rights Watch/Africa. 1995. *Nigeria: The Ogoni Crisis; A Case-Study of Military Repression in South-Eastern Nigeria.* New York: Human Rights Watch.

Ikporukpo, C. O. 1996. Federalism, Political Power, and the Economic Power Game: Conflict over Access to Petroleum Resources in Nigeria. *Environment and Planning* 14:159–77.

International Institute for Democracy and Electoral Assistance (International IDEA). 2000. *Nigeria: Continuing Dialogue(s) for Nation Building.* Stockholm: International IDEA.

Joye, Michael, and Kingsley Igweike. 1982. *An Introduction to the Nigerian 1979 Constitution.* London: Macmillan.

Kazzah-Toure, Toure. 1995. Inter-Ethnic Relations, Conflicts and Nationalism in Zango Katab Area of Northern Nigeria: Historical Origins and Contemporary Forms. Paper presented at the Eighth General Assembly of the Council for the Development of Social Science Research in Africa (CODESRIA), Dakar, Senegal, June 26–July 2.

Keating, Michael. 1999. Challenges to Federalism: Territory, Function, and Power in a Globalizing World. In *Stretching the Federation: The Art of the State in Canada,* ed. Robert Young. Kingston: Institute of Intergovernmental Relations.

Lewis, Peter, and Michael Bratton. 2000. *Attitudes Towards Democracy and Markets in Nigeria: Report of a National Opinion Survey, January—February 2000*. Washington, D.C.: International Foundation for Election Systems and Management Systems International.

————. 2001. *Down to Earth: Changes in Attitudes Toward Democracy and Markets in Nigeria*. Washington, D.C.: International Foundation for Election Systems and Management Systems International.

Lijphart, Arend. 1977. *Democracy in Plural Societies: A Comparative Exploration*. New Haven, Conn.: Yale University Press.

Movement for National Reformation, 1992. *A General Brief*. Port-Harcourt: Saros International.

Naanen, Ben. 2000. The Niger Delta and the National Question. Paper presented at the Conference on the Management of the National Question, University of Ibadan, August 28–30.

Nigeria. 1958. *Report of the Commission Appointed to Enquire into the Fears of Minorities and the Means of Allaying Them*. London: Her Majesty's Stationery Office.

Onosode, Gamaliel. 1999. Protecting the Niger Delta. *The Punch* (Lagos), November 1, 21.

Ostien, Philip. 2001. Ten Good Things About Sharia. *Newswatch* (Lagos) July 9, 61–64.

Rothchild, Donald. 1991. An Interactive Model for State-Ethnic Relations. In *Conflict Resolution in Africa*, ed. Francis Deng and William Zartman. Washington, D.C.: The Brookings Institution.

Soyinka, Wole. 1999. The Federal Quest. *The Nigerian Social Scientist* 2, no. 2:27–35.

Tamuno, Tekena, 1970. Separatist Agitations in Nigeria since 1914. *Journal of Modern African Studies* 8, no. 4:563–84.

The Patriots. 2000. A Bill to Amend the 1999 Constitution. *The Comet* (Lagos), January 29–30, 27–34.

Umar, Abubakar. 2000. Healing the Nation's Wounds. *Tell* (Lagos), July 3, 62–65.

Umar, Muhammad. 20001. Education and Islamic Trends in Northern Nigeria: 1970s–1990s. *Africa Today* 48, no. 2:127–50.

Williams, Gavin. 1980. *State and Society in Nigeria*. Idanre: Afrografika.

Yakusak, Ezra. 1999. Southern Kaduna: Nigeria's East Timor. *The Guardian* (Lagos), October 20, 53.

Young, Crawford. 1976. *The Politics of Cultural Pluralism*. Madison: University of Wisconsin Press.

CHAPTER THIRTEEN

Mexico

The Political Foundations of Indigenous Mobilization and Ethnoterritorial Conflict (1975–2000)

Guillermo Trejo

Since the early 1970s, most Latin American countries have experienced a wave of peasant indigenous mobilizations that continues to this day. From earlier concerns related to land tenure, the focus of the peasant indigenous organizations across the region has increasingly shifted to ethnoterritorial concerns. The purpose of this chapter is to analyze the origins and evolution of this wave of indigenous mobilization in Mexico and to explore whether and to what extent the political institutions of centralized federalism in Mexico provided incentives for a more negotiated or violent response to indigenous protest and demands by federal and local elites. The main finding of this chapter is that democratization and economic liberalization opened a window of opportunities for peasant indigenous mobilization, but that the intensity of protest and the likelihood of rebellion were mainly shaped by local political arrangements: levels of electoral competition, electoral calendars, local government repression and human rights violations. A cross-sectional statistical analysis shows that the most intense levels of protest and rebellion were likely to occur in those states dominated by single-party rule, where local governors faced few electoral and constitutional checks and reacted to nonviolent peasant indigenous protest with high levels of police repression. In turn, ethnification, the process by which a social group adopts a discourse based on ethnocultural and territorial demands, was most likely to occur in those states with more intense levels of protest where higher levels of income inequality overlapped with racial mestizo/indian divisions.

The chapter also analyzes responses by federal and local authorities to ethnoterritorial demands. The Mexican experience suggests that negotiating broad constitutional reforms to accommodate ethnoterritorial demands under authoritarian rule is tricky because unchecked authoritarian elites face limited political costs if they betray minority groups. Negotiating these reforms under democratic rule is equally difficult because minority groups have a limited electoral weight in a majoritarian national political marketplace. Nonetheless, the comparison of Oaxaca and Chiapas, two southern impoverished and multicultural states, helps illustrate how, in the context of a federal institutional arrangement, different local political structures and circumstances may open the way for local ethnoterritorial reforms. The challenge posed by the penetration of leftist political parties in Oaxaca provided strong incentives for Partido Revolucionario Institucional (PRI) authoritarian elites to take a more reformist stance and negotiate incremental constitutional changes to accommodate indigenous demands. These experiences suggest that in a democratic and pluralistic federation, indigenous minorities may pave the way to national constitutional reforms only by means of incremental local reform.

Mexico's Ethnic Structure: The Geographic Distribution of Indigenous Populations

Measured in absolute terms, Mexico is the Latin American country with the largest indigenous population. According to 1990 census data, approximately 6.2 million Mexicans, or 7.5 percent of Mexico's total population, belong to indigenous populations.

Mexico's indigenous population is divided into fifty-six major ethnolinguistic groups of varied size. While some ethnolinguistic groups like the Nahua (central Mexico) are larger than a million, other groups like the Triqui (Oaxaca) have less than 15,000 members. Differences in group size present different opportunities for collective action, with larger groups (following the Olsonian logic) less successful than smaller groups.

These groups have significant cultural and linguistic differences. While some indigenous groups live in closed corporate, hierarchical communities ruled by councils of elders, others live in open communities in which religious authorities gave way to civilian elites decades ago. Linguistic differences across groups are also of great significance. For example, the difference between the Rarámuri of Chihuahua and the Tzotzil of Chiapas is as great as the difference between a Teutonic and a Romance language. Cultural and linguistic differences increase the difficulties of group coordination and the development of a pan-Indian identity.

Mexico's indigenous ethnic groups are largely mixed within and across administrative jurisdictions. Most indigenous populations live intermingled with mestizo populations or with indigenous populations from other linguistic groups. Table 13.1 shows the effective number of ethnic groups (ENEG) for every state that has at least one municipality with 10 percent indigenous population (N = 21). While the country as a whole scores a level of 1.2 effective ethnic groups, most indigenous municipalities in the states sampled in Table 13.1 have between 1.8 and 2.5 effective ethnic groups. Fragmentation increases coordination problems and, in some states, diminishes the probability of pan-Indian collective action.

Mexico's fifty-six major ethnolinguistic groups are widely dispersed across state boundaries. For example, the Nahua of central Mexico are dispersed at least across five different states (Puebla, Veracruz, San Luis Potosí, Hidalgo, and Guerrero). By contrast, other groups like the Triqui and the Tzeltal live mostly within the boundaries of Oaxaca and Chiapas, respectively. In fact, Oaxaca (65.67) and Chiapas (41.59) present the high-

Table 13.1 Indigenous Population and Ethnic Groups in Twenty-One Mexican States, 1990

States	Indigenous Population (in percent)	Municipalities with more than 10 percentage Ind. Pop., 1970–1990	Effective Number of Ethnic Groups	Relative Concentration of Ethnic Groups
Campeche	19.1	6	2.32	0.00
Chiapas	26.0	59	2.14	41.59
Chihuahua	2.9	13	2.50	3.27
Durango	1.6	1	2.82	0.73
Guerrero	13.4	32	2.47	5.75
Hidalgo	19.5	29	2.30	5.55
Jalisco	0.5	2	2.47	0.38
México State	3.7	21	2.60	13.25
Michoacán	3.5	14	2.18	5.64
Morelos	1.9	3	1.82	0.00
Nayarit	3.4	2	2.57	1.09
Oaxaca	39.1	389	1.87	65.67
Puebla	14.1	100	2.10	28.58
Querétaro	2.3	2	2.65	0.00
Quintana Roo	32.2	7	2.05	0.00
San Luis Potosí	11.9	17	2.52	5.12

(Continued)

Table 13.1 — Continued

States	Indigenous Population (in percent)	Municipalities with more than 10 percentage Ind. Pop., 1970–1990	Effective Number of Ethnic Groups	Relative Concentration of Ethnic Groups
Sonora	3.1	2	2.15	2.18
Tabasco	3.7	4	2.10	2.02
Tlaxcala	3.4	7	–	0.00
Veracruz	10.7	72	1.99	12.83
Yucatán	44.2	106	1.88	28.27

Source: INEGI, *XI Censo Nacional de Población y Vivienda,* 1990.
Notes: The effective number of ethnic groups (ENEG) is calculated only for those municipalities that at any time between 1970 and 1990 had at least 10 percentage indigenous population. $ENEG = 1/\sum P_i^2$, where P is the population share of each ethnic group. The larger the ENEG, the more ethnically fragmented the state. The relative concentration of ethnic groups is calculated as follows: $ECI = \sum E_i * P_i$, where E_i is a value from 0 to 3 assigned to every group according to the percentage of ethnic groups members living within the state boundaries and P_i is the relative size of each group within Mexico's total indigenous population. The larger the ECI, the greater the number of ethnically concentrated groups within state boundaries.

est levels of the ethnic concentration index (ECI) in the country. This means that for every indigenous linguistic group that lives in Oaxaca or Chiapas, the large majority of that specific group lives within the state boundaries. In contrast, every indigenous group living in central Morelos and Querétaro is most likely to be spread across more than one jurisdiction. For the most part, administrative boundaries in Mexico's federal structure of government do not overlap with ethnic group boundaries. Group cohesion within a single national subunit tends to increase the probability for group collective action, while groups that cross administrative boundaries tend to be less successful with group action.

One of the most politically significant facts about the Mexican ethnic geographical distribution is that indigenous populations taken as a whole do not represent the majority of the population in any one of Mexico's thirty-one states. At the district and municipal levels, however, indigenous populations do have majority status in states like Quintana Roo, Yucatán, Chiapas, and Oaxaca.

Although not all poor households in Mexico are Indian, most Indian households are poor. By almost any social criteria, the indigenous populations of Mexico have the lowest levels of social well-being. According to World Bank data, in 1990, while 17.9 percent of the non-Indian Mexican population lived below the poverty line, 80.6 percent of the Mexican indigenous population was poor (Psacharopoulos and Patrinos, 1993). Similarly, in 1990, while 10 percent of non-Indian Mexicans were illiterate, 40.7 percent of the indigenous population could not read or write. By international standards, this constitutes the most extreme form of economic discrimination faced by any minority group in the world (Gurr 1993). Poverty and illiteracy tend to correlate with risk aversion and help to lower the likelihood of group action.

On simple theoretical grounds, there would be few reasons to expect indigenous populations to act collectively on their group-shared grievances. And yet, indigenous populations have led one of the most impressive waves of social protest experienced during Mexico's transition to democracy and a market economy.

The Ethnoterritorial Movement in Mexico

In the past thirty years, indigenous populations in Mexico have undergone one of the most dramatic processes of social and political transformation since colonial times. One of the most significant outcomes of this process has been the emergence of a national indigenous movement that demands the right to autonomy and self-determination for indigenous peoples.

The movement has followed two parallel tracks. One was advanced by peasant indigenous organizations engaged in a three-decade-long wave of mobilization, demanding land reform, respect for human rights, and the democratization of municipal authority structures. The other track was pursued by the Zapatista Army of National Liberation (EZLN), a guerrilla group of Mayan peasants that declared war on the Mexican federal government in 1994. Although a program calling for indigenous peoples' right to autonomy and self-determination had been devised by some local indigenous movements in the late 1980s, it was not until the insurrection of the EZLN in 1994 that a window of opportunity opened for the national projection of an ethnoterritorial movement.

Peasant Indigenous Protest: The Civilian Path to Ethnoterritorial Claims

The emergence in the mid-1990s of the Congreso Nacional Indígena (Indigenous National Congress—CNI) and the Asamblea Nacional Indígena Plural por la Autonomía (National Pluralistic Indigenous Assembly for Autonomy—ANIPA), two national umbrella organizations bringing together many different regional and local indigenous organizations under the banner of autonomy and self-determination for indigenous peoples, was the result of three decades of peasant indigenous protest.

Figure 13.1 illustrates the long stretch of this wave throughout the whole process of democratic transition in Mexico.[1] The figure captures 3,553 acts of protest reported by the national press between 1975 and 2000 in all municipalities with a population that is at least 10 percent indigenous. The sample includes 898 municipalities from

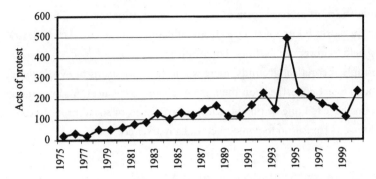

Figure. 13.1 Peasant Indigenous Protest in Mexico, 1975–2000. Source: Trejo 2002.

21 states previously reported in Table 13.1. Acts of protest include public denunciations, marches, meetings, hunger strikes, land invasions, the takeover of government buildings, the kidnapping and lynching of authorities, the invasion of municipalities, and the establishment of rebel autonomous territories and guerrilla attacks.

Average levels of protest increasingly grow from one decade to another: in the 1970s there was one act of protest every ten days, by the 1990s, every other day. Although indigenous public contestation takes a first important hike under the de la Madrid administration (1982–88), the most dramatic peaks occur in 1992 and 1994 under the Salinas administration (1988–94). Levels of protest after the 1994 Zapatista uprising are similar to those recorded in the late 1980s.

Ninety-three percent of all acts of protest reported in Figure 13.1 involved little or no violence. The most prominent acts of large-scale guerrilla activity were undertaken by the EZLN in 1994, when ten days of open confrontation between the Zapatistas and the Mexican armed forces gave way to a long period of peace negotiations and stalemates that continues to this day. Between 1996 and 2000, various guerrilla groups conducted sporadic, local attacks against police forces and the army, mainly in the southern states of Oaxaca and Guerrero and in the Huasteca region of the central state of Hidalgo.

Most acts of peasant indigenous protest are targeted at state and local governments. Yet, in the 1990s, the federal government became as important a target of dissent as state governments, particularly during 1991–92, when the Salinas administration launched a constitutional reform to liberalize land tenure, and during 1997–98, when the Zedillo administration and the EZLN discussed constitutional reforms to grant the right to autonomy and self-determination to indigenous communities. For all practical purposes, municipal authorities have almost disappeared as targets of indigenous collective dissent since the Zapatista insurrection.

Peasant indigenous dissent is mainly driven by political demands. Almost 60 percent of all publicly expressed demands between 1975 and 2000 were political, while 30 percent were economic and 10 percent were ethnic. Political demands focused on the democratization of municipal authority structures and an end to government repression and human rights violations. Economic demands mostly concerned land reform, and the dominant ethnic demands involved constitutional recognition of the right to autonomy and self-determination of indigenous peoples.

Publicly expressed demands by peasant indigenous dissenters have undergone dramatic transformations in the past twenty-five years. Figure 13.2 captures the evolution of economic, political, and ethnic demands between 1975 and 2000. Economic demands experienced a spectacular decline from a historic high of 60 percent in 1975 to 20 percent in 2000. Political demands consistently remained around 50 percent and ethnic demands rose from near nonexistence to nearly 40 percent in 1996–97.

If publicly expressed group demands are indicative of group identities, Mexico's indigenous organizations have introduced a complex menu of class, civic, and ethnic identities since the late 1990s. In fact, indigenous organizations have increasingly channeled economic and political demands into an ethnic program by which land claims have become territorial demands and requests for the democratization of municipal authority structures have been transformed into demands for Indian self-government.

Peasant indigenous protest and publicly expressed demands have varied widely across states and regions. The southern states of Chiapas, Oaxaca, and Guerrero account for almost 64 percent of all acts of protest and the central states of Hidalgo, Puebla, and Veracruz account for almost 20 percent. Yet, these are the most densely populated indigenous regions in the country. Figure 13.3 shows the relative contribution of each state to indigenous collective dissent weighted by its contribution to

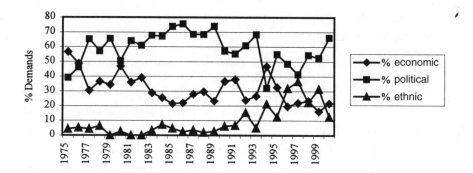

Figure. 13.2 Indigenous Demands in Mexico by Category, 1975–2000. *Source:* Trejo 2002.

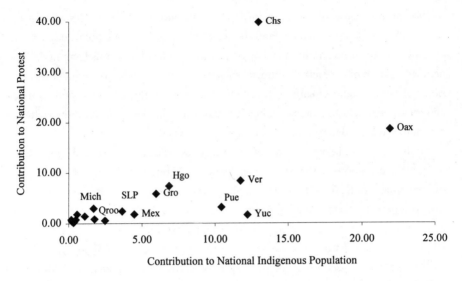

Figure. 13.3 Contribution to Protest and to Indigenous Population by State, 1975–2000 (in percentages). *Source:* Trejo 2002.

overall indigenous population. Although Chiapas has only 13 percent of Mexico's indigenous population, the state contributes 40 percent of all acts of dissent.

On a per capita basis, the largest indigenous states that display intense levels of protest include the southern states of Chiapas and Guerrero, central Hidalgo and western Michoacán. Large states with low levels of per capita protest include Yucatán, Quintana Roo, along with the central states of Mexico and Puebla. Among the states with the smallest indigenous population, Jalisco scores the highest per capita levels of protest and Tlaxcala and Nayarit the lowest.

The ethnification of peasant indigenous demands has also varied widely across states. Among the most densely populated indigenous states, Chiapas, Michoacán, and Guerrero present the most intense experiences of ethnification. Among the states with small indigenous populations, Jalisco and Querétaro stand out as the two cases of most rapid ethnification in the 1990s.

Guerrilla Warfare: The Zapatista Track to de Facto Territorial Power

As illustrated in Figure 13.2, the right to autonomy and self-determination for indigenous peoples became one of the leading demands of Mexico's indigenous movement only when the EZLN made it its number one priority in the second round of peace negotiations with the federal government in 1996. Between 1995 and 1996 the EZLN underwent a dramatic strategic shift from espousing the traditional economic demands of Marxist-Leninist guerrillas to embracing an ethnoterritorial program. While the main issue in the first round of peace negotiations in 1994 was the allocation of federal funds to indigenous communities, the right to autonomy and self-determination became the dominant theme in the second round of peace negotiations in 1996. Since 1996, the EZLN tied the fate of peace negotiations to a constitutional reform that guarantees the right to autonomy and self-determination to indigenous peoples in the whole country.

How did the EZLN turn to ethnicity within such a short time span? In the aftermath of the Zapatista rebellion three interrelated events marked the history of the Zapatista movement in the years ahead: (1) the EZLN's support of Amado Avendaño, the candidate of the left, in the 1994 gubernatorial election; (2) a massive wave of land invasions conducted by the rank-and-file of the independent peasant indigenous movement and the Zapatista supporters; and (3) an unprecedented wave of invasions of municipal palaces and attacks against municipal authorities.

Although the electoral challenge presented by the Zapatista-supported candidate, Amado Avendaño, provided a severe blow to PRI hegemony in the state (Sonnleitner 2001), the electoral fraud that allowed for a PRI victory in the gubernatorial election in 1994 led the Zapatistas to boycott every election since. Peasant indigenous organizations took advantage of the window of opportunity opened by the Zapatista rebellion and the federal and local elections to launch the largest wave of land invasions in modern Chiapas history. Almost 1,500 private plots were invaded in 1994. At the same time, the military insurrection of the EZLN opened a window of opportunity for local organizations to express their accumulated grievances against local authorities, and almost 40 percent of the state's municipal palaces came under dissident control.

After the first round of negotiations between the federal government and the Zapatistas had failed, in the aftermath of the 1994 electoral fraud and the massive wave of land and municipal palace invasions, the Zapatistas decided to launch a new strategy. In December 1994, Zapatista rank-and-file took over thirty-eight municipal palaces and established, through civil disobedience and sheer force, rebel territories ruled by Zapatista municipal or regional authorities. These de facto governments constitute a situation of multiple sovereignties (Tilly 1979). Although these autonomy arrangements theoretically involve one-third of Chiapas's municipalities, only some of these autonomy governments operate fully; the rest exist only as "imagined autonomies."

Zapatista autonomous municipalities and regions are de facto local governments that claim legitimate jurisdiction over newly defined territories within constitutionally specified municipal boundaries. Rebel authorities and council members deny the authority of constitutionally elected mayors, governors, and the president of Mexico and declare themselves accountable only to their Zapatista base communities and to the EZLN commanders in chief (Burguete 1998). Therefore, Zapatista authorities deny access to their territory to any local, state, or federal authority or member of the police or the Mexican army and have closed all agencies, schools, and hospitals under the jurisdiction of constitutionally elected authorities. Community members refuse to pay taxes, participate in any electoral competition, pay electricity or water bills, and receive any government programs or subsidies. Zapatista governments are charged with the collection of taxes, the provision of public goods, and the administration of communal resources, civil and penal justice, public security, and educational and health services for their communities.

Unlike many other ethnoterritorial movements around the world, the Zapatista rebel authorities have always emphatically declared that autonomy, whether municipal or regional, will never lead to secession. Instead of harboring secessionist ambitions, the Zapatista rebels suggest that the main objective of de facto autonomous governments is to create truly representative and accountable local authorities, which were lacking for almost a century under the PRI's hegemonic control. Echoing both a severe critique of local PRI authorities and a romanticized view of community authority structures, Zapatista community members of the autonomous municipality of *Tierra y Libertad* in Las Margaritas declared that "in these territories our autonomous authorities rule and will continue to do so because we need them, because they respect us, because we know them, because they obey us and because we know how to obey them."[2]

Municipal territories with dual sovereignties are deeply divided societies dominated by a deep and ubiquitous *master cleavage* cutting across almost every aspect of life: the Zapatista/anti-Zapatista divide. This division determines all aspects of social and political life in these regions. Each camp has its own political authorities (constitutionally elected versus rebel authorities), army (paramilitary groups versus EZLN), political party (PRI versus PRD), human rights organization, and so on. In fact, each side enjoys unusually high levels of social organization and intragroup trust. Violence in some municipalities with dual sovereignties has dramatically increased since 1995, particularly in the highlands, northern, and eastern parts of Chiapas. Whereas, in past years, indigenous communities and organizations mobilized against the federal government, since 1995 intercommunal violence has sharply increased, particularly between the rank-and-file of the EZLN and different PRI-sponsored armed groups. The 1997 massacre of forty-five Tzotziles in Acteal, Chenalhó, is perhaps the most dramatic outcome of the intercommunal conflict that characterizes these contested territories.

Explaining Protest, Rebellion, and the Ethnification of Demands

What are the factors that account for the origins of peasant indigenous protest, rebellion, and ethnification? The aim of this section is to provide some preliminary statistical accounts to explain *when* and *where* and *under what conditions* indigenous peoples undertake peaceful or violent forms of dissent.

Accounting for the Origins and Timing of Peasant Indigenous Protest and Ethnification

Dominant explanations of indigenous protest in Latin America explain its timing as a response to the collapse of import substitution industrialization (ISI) in the 1970s (Stavenhagen 1992); as a reaction to the neo-liberal policy shift in the 1980s (Le Bot 1994; Harvey 1998); as a response to the globalization of the world economy (Castells 1997); or as a response to democratization coupled with a neo-liberal policy shift in agriculture (Yashar 1998).

Does the collapse of ISI, the neo-liberal policy shift, or the transition to democracy explain the origins and development of the wave of peasant indigenous protest in Mexico? Does neo-liberalism encourage the adoption of ethnic identities?

ECONOMIC FACTORS

To assess the impact of neo-liberalism on the wave of peasant indigenous protest and the process of ethnification, one should first distinguish between macroeconomic and microinstitutional variables. The three most relevant macroeconomic variables are economic growth, inflation, and unemployment. Since unemployment figures are poorly elaborated in Mexico, I concentrate on GDP growth and inflation. Simple correlation analyses show that indigenous protest is practically unrelated to inflation and only weakly associated with GDP growth (Trejo 2002).

If agricultural growth is the first symptom of an agricultural crisis, Figure 13.4 lends some support to those authors suggesting that mobilization was triggered by the ISI agricultural crisis of the 1970s and 1980s, for it shows a negative relationship between the rate of growth of agricultural production and peasant indigenous protest in the 1975–96 period. The crisis of rural populism began in the late 1960s and, after a brief interruption during the oil boom, resumed between 1982 and 1989, when most ISI-linked rural programs and policies were dismantled. The crisis of ISI and the lack of any alternative agricultural policy under neo-liberalism jeopardized the life chances of much of the indigenous population and consequently increased their general propensity to mobilize.

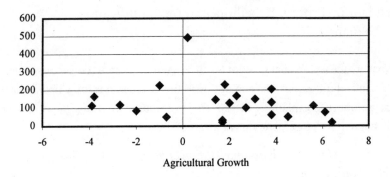

Figure. 13.4 Peasant Indigenous Protest Explained by Agricultural Growth, 1975–1996

More than aggregate macroeconomic variables and policy transformations, microinstitutional reforms, particularly the liberalization of land tenure, seem to be a key explanatory factor in peasant indigenous protest and ethnification. If one compares levels of protest five years before and after the liberalization of land tenure (1991–92), protest doubled on average after the constitutional reform was passed. The spectacular crisis of Mexico's agriculture, together with the liberalization of land tenure, predisposed the peasant indigenous populations toward dissent.

The year 1992 marks a turning point for most peasant indigenous organizations in Mexico: not only did mobilization levels reach unprecedented levels but, more important, large numbers of Indian peasants strategically shifted from class to ethnic identities. Figure 13.5 shows levels of ethnification of peasant indigenous demands five years before and five years after the 1991 national debate around the liberalization of land tenure. For many peasant indigenous organizations the reform of article 27 signaled the collapse of peasant identities and, as ethnic identities were gaining international recognition in the wake of the 500th anniversary of the conquest of the Americas, many peasant indigenous leaders strategically began a historical switch toward ethnicity.

POLITICAL FACTORS

Although the liberalization process begun in the late 1970s opened a national window of opportunity for social dissent, the uneven process of subnational democratization shows different local dynamics. As I argue in the next section, it was not the most rapidly democratizing states that experienced the most intense levels of indigenous contentious collective action but, instead, those lagging in their democratization process.

Elections are good predictors of the timing of protest and rebellion. As illustrated in Figure 13.1, the slope of the protest curve becomes steeper as levels of electoral competition increase, from 1976 to 1982, 1988, 1994, and 2000. When explaining the timing of

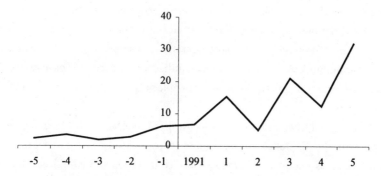

Figure. 13.5 Ethnic Demands before and after Land Liberalization (in percentages). *Note:* Although the constitutional reform to Article 27 was approved in 1992, I use 1991 as baseline. *Source:* Trejo 2002.

the Zapatista uprisings, most analysts suggest that rebels took up arms as the North American Free Trade Agreement (NAFTA) came into effect. Yet, one should not overlook the fact that 1994 was an electoral year. Electoral years are magnets for protest and rebellion because the unusual media attention that comes with competitive elections increases the costs of repression for incumbent governments and increases the benefits of public dissent.

Another political factor that may help to account for the timing of indigenous protest and ethnification is the constitutional reform of indigenous-related affairs. In 1991, the Mexican government introduced a constitutional amendment to provide for the constitutional recognition of Mexico's indigenous peoples. In 1996, the government signed an agreement with the EZLN granting the right to autonomy and self-determination to indigenous peoples, opening a national debate on the feasibility of constitutional reform. It follows that both indigenous protest and the ethnification of peasant indigenous demands experienced historical peaks in 1992 and 1997.

Accounting for Regional Variation in Peasant Indigenous Protest and Ethnification

If the neo-liberal policy shift in agricultural policy and the liberalization of land tenure opened a window of opportunity for indigenous dissent, why did Mayan Indians in Chiapas take to the streets while Mayan Indians in Yucatán remained passive? If political liberalization and the enactment of constitutional reforms on indigenous-related affairs showed a more flexible national political elite, why did Huichol Indians in Jalisco seize this opportunity while Huicholes and Coras in Nayarit did not? Finally, why did Nahua Indians in Guerrero respond to the country's severe agricultural crisis by embracing ethnicity while Nahua Indians in Hidalgo remained loyal to peasant identities?

Economic explanations alone cannot persuasively cope with questions derived from intracountry variations, nor do political explanations that put the explanatory weight of indigenous protest on the process of democratization alone. To make sense of intra-country variation, students of Latin American indigenous movements have resorted to organizational factors, that is, the indigenous people's capacity to solve collective action problems.

Did changing political institutions of centralized federalism in Mexico have any connection with the differences in protest and rebellion scores across Mexican states? To account for cross-regional variation in social contestation and ethnification, I concentrate on the political institutions of federalism and local political practices: local constitutions, elections and electoral calendars, and the governor's responses to social dissent in terms of human rights violations and government repression.

Protest, rebellion, and ethnification are the three dependent variables to be explained. The economic variables tested in the model include level of development, poverty, and income inequality. Based on the literature, I would expect protest and rebellion to be negatively associated with economic development (Fearon and Laitin 1997) and positively associated with poverty and inequality (Gurr 1993; Mueller and Seligson 1987).

Political variables related to Mexico's centralized federalist structures include first a measurement of local democratization. Following the main trends in the literature (Gurr and Moore 1997; Cleary 2001), I expect to observe the highest levels of protest and rebellion in the most authoritarian states.

A second political variable is the constitutional powers of governors. Following Huntington's (1963) maxim that revolutions are the stuff of inflexible institutions, I would expect the most intense levels of protest and rebellion to occur where governors are less subject to horizontal or vertical checks.

The third political variable included in the model is the electoral calendar. In federal systems where national, state, and local elections may take place simultaneously, the political stakes are often higher. In Mexico, electoral calendars vary widely across states. Based on information reported by De Remes (2000), I construct an index of federal concurrence according to the electoral calendars followed across Mexican states. I distinguish among three cases: (1) high concurrence, when federal elections concur with at least two local elections (governor, local legislature, or municipal elections); (2) mild concurrence, when federal elections concur with one local election; and (3) null concurrence, when there is no concurrence at all. I construct a second index of state-level concurrence between gubernatorial, legislative, and municipal races. I would expect levels of protest and rebellion to increase together with electoral concurrence.

I use three ethnodemographic variables as proxies of the organizational factors. These three variables refer to the proportion, cohesion, and concentration of indigenous populations. Following Fearon and Laitin (1997) and Gurr (1993), I would expect protest and rebellion to be positively associated with the relative size, cohesion, and concentration of indigenous populations.

I use linear multiple regression models to conduct a preliminary testing of these hypotheses, as summarized in Tables 13.2 and 13.3. Results from the protest equation suggest that the model explains 35 percent of the variation in levels of indigenous protest across states. Economic variables turned out to be statistically insignificant under different specifications of the protest model. Considering the high degree of correlation between the GDP per capita, the Gini coefficient, and the marginality index, after testing for several specifications of the model, I opted for the measurement that provided the best fit: GDP per capita. As reported in Table 13.2, not only is the per capita GDP statistically insignificant, it shows a different sign (+) from the predicted one (-). Municipal-level data are required to reject the hypothetical impact of economic variables.

Political-institutional variables showed the expected signs under all specifications of the model and turned out to be a powerful set of factors in explaining cross-regional variation in protest levels. As reported in Table 13.2, the most consistently significant political variable under different specifications was the level of local democratization. The negative sign suggests that as democratization in a state is bolstered, levels of peasant indigenous mobilization are most likely to decrease. That is, in those states with higher levels of electoral competition, where different political forces are duly represented in the local legislature and where governors respect human rights, levels of indigenous contentious action tend to decrease. The flip side of this is that levels of peasant indigenous mobilization tend to increase in those states where local elites are incapable of accommodating indigenous demands and, constrained by weak institutional checks, confront mobilization with state repression.[3]

The second political variable that turned out to be statistically significant in the model was the electoral cycle. More specifically, regression results suggest that in those states in which local and state elections overlap with national elections, levels of peasant indigenous mobilizations are likely to increase. As discussed earlier, elections open a window of opportunity for social movement leaders to express group grievances at relatively low costs. If federal concurrence is taken as a proxy of centralized power over local affairs, the conclusion would be that more intense protest is likely to take place if state and federal incumbent governments are in need of electoral support.

Organizational variables turned out to be statistically insignificant, except for the proportion of indigenous population. Like the economic variables, the size of

indigenous population, the effective number of ethnic groups, and group concentration were highly correlated. After testing for different specifications, I ran the final
model with indigenous population, which turned out to be statistically significant.
Results suggest that higher levels of contestation were not undertaken by the most indigenous states but by mixed ones.

To account for the likelihood of rebellion, I used the same set of variables as in the
protest model, except that I added protest as a potential explanatory variable. As illustrated in Table 13.2, results from the final rebellion equation suggest that the model
explains 78 percent of the variance in the likelihood of rebellion across states.
Economic factors in the rebellion equation turned out to have the expected signs—
GDP per capita (-), poverty (+), and inequality (+). To avoid problems of multi-
collinearity, however, in the final analysis I opted for using GDP per capita. Holding
all other variables constant, we can say that an increase of 1,000 1990 U.S. dollars in a
state's GDP per capita would decrease the probability of rebellion by 0.46 points on a
6-point scale.

Results among the political variables are mixed. Although the political power of the
governor and the elected concurrence of municipal and state-level elections turned out
to be statistically insignificant factors, democracy and federal concurrence are strong
predictors of rebellion. The democracy index is statistically significant at the one percent level and we can say that, ceteris paribus, for every additional point in the democracy index, the probability of rebellion decreases by 1.15 points on a 6-point scale.
Likewise, for every additional point in the federal concurrence index, rebellion increases by 0.47 points, holding every other variable constant. If we bring together the
democracy and centralization indicator, one would expect a greater chance of rebellion
in states ruled under local authoritarian conditions and where federal authorities over-
shadow local authorities.

If we compare the effect of GDP per capita and democracy on the likelihood of rebellion, we can safely conclude that the reason why a rebellion took place in Chiapas
and not, say in neighboring Oaxaca is because of political and not economic reasons.
For example, if from one day to another the government had discovered huge reserves
of oil in Chiapas in 1990 and Chiapas's GDP per capita had reached a similar level as
the one of the oil-rich southern state of Tabasco (the sample's wealthiest state in 1990),
Chiapas would have gone from level 6 in the 6-point scale of guerrilla activity to 4.4.
In contrast, if from one day to another opposition parties had flooded Chiapas in
1990 and the government had become more accountable to the people and improved
its human rights record, say, at the level of Querétaro (the sample's most democratic
state in the 1988–95 period), guerrilla activity in the state would have gone from level

Table 13.2 *Explanatory Factors of Peasant Indigenous Protest and Rebellion in Mexico, 1975–2000*

Variable X	Protest Model		Rebellion Model	
	Coefficient	t-statistic	Coefficient	t-statistic
Intercept	-7.935	-0.734	1.154	2.12
Economic				
GDP per capita	0.003	0.863	-0.0004*	-2.05
Political				
Democratization index	-5.046*	-2.244	-1.151**	-6.60
Governor power index	7.825	0.996	—	—
Federal election	4.985*	1.907	0.464*	2.371
State election	6.074	1.738	—	—
Protest				
Ethnocultural				
Indigenous N	-0.356*	-2.110		
ENEG				
Ethnic concentration				
N	21		21	
Adjusted R²	0.355		0.778	
SE	8.064		0.715	

Notes: Protest was measured as the per capita number of protests taking place in the Twenty-One states of the sample between 1975 and 2000. Rebellion was measured, following the coding scales of rebellion of the Minorities at Risk project (Gurr and Moore 1997) on a scale from 0 to 6, assigning a ranked number for every state in the 1990–2000 period.

I use the 1989 per capita GDP to measure development. I use the 1990 marginality index (MI) developed by Mexico's National Population Council (CONAPO) as an indicator of poverty levels. The MI is a composite index, including education, health and housing indicators per municipality. I use a state-level Gini index calculated by Hernández Valdez (2000), based on the 1995 Income-Expenditure Survey as an indicator of income inequality.

I use a democratization index developed by Hernández Valdez (2000) to measure state-level democratization in the 1988–97 period. The index captures three dimensions of democracy: (1)local legislative electoral competition, (2)the distribution of seats in local legislatures, and (3) human rights violations.

I borrow Blanco's (2001) index of gubernatorial power, constructed on the bases of the constitutionally defined horizontal and vertical powers of governors. Horizontal powers are the provisions governors enjoy vis-à-vis local congresses and the judiciary and vertical powers refer to the governor's powers vis-à-vis municipal governments and the electorate.

For the size of indigenous population per state. I use the percentage share of indigenous population as of 1995. Ethnic heterogeneity is measured as the effective number of ethnic groups. Ethnic concentration is measured through the ethnic concentration index, also explained in Table 13.1.

* Statistically significant at the 0.05 level.
** Statistically significant at the 0.01 level.

6 to 0.86. In other words, had there been a multiparty democracy in Chiapas in the early 1990s, a guerrilla uprising would never have taken place, even if the state had remained as poor as it was.

To explain cross-regional variations in levels of ethnification, a preliminary analysis was conducted using the percentage of ethnic demands expressed in all acts of public dissent during the 1990s. As model 1 in Table 13.3 shows, ethnification was more likely to take place in states with high levels of protest. However, model 2 adds a second statistically significant variable. I created an index of inequalities, by multiplying the Gini index by the ENEG. Since the ENEG records the existence of mestizo and indigenous groups, this multiplicative variable represents a measurement of income and racial differentials. Model 2 suggests that in those places where greater income and racial inequalities overlapped, ethnic identities were more likely to emerge.

Centralized Federalism and Local Government Responses to Indigenous Dissent

While statistical models help us identify the macrostructural and macropolitical determinants of protest, rebellion, and ethnification, they nevertheless have little to say about the processes of strategic interaction between government elites and indigenous dissenters movement organizations use to solve their collective action problems and transform group grievances into contentious action. The purpose of this section is to explore in greater depth the historical role federal and state government elites have played in shaping peasant indigenous movements' strategies of dissent. Chiapas and

Table 13.3 *Explanatory Factors of the Ethnification of Peasant Indigenous Demands, 1990s*

Variable X	Model 1		Model 2	
	Coefficient	t-statistic	Coefficient	t-statistic
Intercept	-36.280	-1.655	-15.402	-1.342
Gini index	34.133	1.294		
Protest	1.976**	2.563	1.951**	2.607
ENEG	11.285	1.829		
Gini × ENEG			19.207*	2.095
N	20		20	
Adjusted R²	0.240		0.279	
SE	7.7		7.5	

Note: Ethnification was measured as the percentage of the state's peasant indigenous movement's demands that were couched in ethnic terms during the 1990s.
* Statistically significant at the 0.1 level.
**Statistically significant at the 0.05 level.

Oaxaca provide examples of how even small differences in the career ambitions of local politicians, local political arrangements, and past conflict can lead one state into rebellion and conflict and another one down a path of contingent but peaceful negotiation.

Federal and State Responses before 1994: Assimilation, Co-optation, and Repression

The Federation. For most of the twentieth century, the Mexican federal government pursued a policy of nation building aimed at the assimilation of a diverse indigenous ethnic mosaic into a mestizo hegemonic project. While formally a democratic federation since 1821, Mexico has been under authoritarian regimes for most of its independent life. Scholars of Mexican federalism characterize the Mexican case in the twentieth century as one of centralized federalism, in which federal executives overshadowed the powers of senators, governors, and municipal presidents (Díaz Cayeros 1995). Presidents are relatively weak vis-à-vis congress (Weldon 1999), but relatively strong vis-à-vis the senate and the states (Marván 1997). Presidents prevail over other federal players mainly because of their constitutionally defined administrative capacities in the collection and distribution of resources. Unlike many federal systems, the Mexican central government controls most taxation policies, the application of labor codes, the definition of minimum wages, land redistribution, and education and health policies. Although market-oriented governments have decentralized education, health, and poverty alleviation programs in recent years, state governments only operate the programs. The PRI's nearly sixty years of electoral hegemony (1929–88) facilitated the political construction of a centralized "federal" state.

The main objective of revolutionary nationalism—the official cultural ideology of the postrevolutionary Mexican state—was to forge a mestizo melting pot under the PRI banner. Under this national hegemonic arrangement, prehispanic indigenous cultures would serve as the historical myth of Mexican nationalism, but indigenous identities among the current indigenous population would be heavily discouraged (Gutiérrez 1999). Like the Napoleonic state, Mexican presidents since the 1930s used the centralized and corporatist hierarchies, as well as the resources of the federal bureaucracy and the PRI, to encourage the adoption of class identities and national-level loyalties. Rural and educational policies served to turn Indians into Mexican peasants under PRI tutelage.

Since the 1930s, the federal government constantly encouraged peasant indigenous populations to join the rank-and-file of the PRI's National Peasant Confederation (CNC) and to base their demands on material rather than cultural grounds. As peasants, indigenous populations could aspire to land reform and rural credit, but, as Indians, resources were nearly unattainable. Indigenous policies of bilingual education, on the other hand, encouraged the assimilation of indigenous populations with the mestizo mainstream. Indigenous policy makers saw the teaching of autochthonous languages as the most effective means of castelianizing indigenous populations (Gutiérrez, 1999). Bilingual indigenous elites could also serve as middlemen or cultural brokers, facilitating state control over indigenous communities.

The PRI's policies of assimilation had different effects across states, depending on local political structures and differences in center-periphery elite bargaining. Until at least 1994, the central elites delegated the power to deal with indigenous dissident leaders to local elites. The cases of Chiapas and Oaxaca illustrate how slightly different political structures and levels of electoral competition shaped different responses of local elites to similar initial mobilization trends.

Chiapas has witnessed more peasant indigenous protest than any other state in the past twenty-five years. Between 1975 and 1993, 30 percent of all acts of peasant indigenous protest took place in Chiapas. After 1994, more than 50 percent of all protest took place there. Average levels of protest grow from decade to decade: in the 1970s there was one act of protest every two weeks, in the 1980s every week, and in the 1990s every other day. Although public demonstrations jumped first under the administration of General Absalón Castellanos (1982–88), the most dramatic peaks took place in 1992 and 1994 under the administration of Patrocinio González (1988–94).

As in the rest of the country, original demands in the 1970s were mainly about land reform. Throughout the late 1970s, land represented half of all demands made by Chiapas's peasant indigenous organizations, dominated by class demands and identities. In the 1980s, however, peasant indigenous organizations increasingly embraced a civic discourse, demanding the democratization of municipal authority structures, respect for human rights, and an end to government repression. In the late 1980s, more than in any other state in the country, peasant indigenous organizations began a slow evolution from demanding a universalistic program of civic and human rights to one of group-specific ethnic rights.[4]

This process of exponential protest and ethnification was led by regional and local organizations that emerged from a complex process of religious competition between Catholic and Protestant churches. As the Protestant strategy of reconversion (translating Bibles into indigenous languages and organizing literacy groups, health clinics, and rural cooperatives) proved highly profitable in the Chiapan religious marketplace in the 1950s and 1960s, the Catholic Church reacted by imitating the Protestant strategy in the 1970s and 1980s. The unintended result was the emergence of a dense network of communal organizations and local leaders that spread mainly across the highlands and northern, eastern, and central Chiapas (Trejo 2000). Some of the leaders forged by the government would eventually break with state tutelage and join the emerging peasant indigenous movement. In fact, some of the communal networks and leaders that emerged from these processes of political and religious competition would eventually become the organizational infrastructure on which the state's indigenous movement and the EZLN were built.

Although by 1977 central elites had already initiated the political liberalization of Mexico's authoritarian regime, local elites in Chiapas, like in the rest of the country, reacted to initial peasant indigenous protest with government repression. But elites in Chiapas went further than any other local political class. Seventy percent of all peasant indigenous acts of protest were, sooner or later, matched by a subsequent act of police repression against independent peasant organizations and leaders. Fueled by historical myths of an Indian insurrection or a caste war in the state, local elites in Chiapas reacted violently to peasant indigenous mobilization throughout the 1980s. Police repression proved to be ineffective in deterring peasant indigenous dissent. Thus, after 1982, General Castellanos inaugurated what eventually became the Chiapas-style land reformism, by which governors would buy land from landowners and distribute it to the campesinos. Critics suggest that Chiapas's authorities generally overcompensated landowners by paying a political rather than market price for the land (Reyes Ramos 1998) and that most land ended up in the hands of PRI-affiliated peasants (Villafuerte et al. 1999). The slowdown of agricultural production in the 1980s together with land overpopulation and the accumulated deficit in land distribution motivated many opposition peasants to protest. The vicious cycle of protest, repression, and protest initiated in the late 1970s was consolidated under the general's administration.

Although mobilization and repression diminished in the first years of the administration of Patrocinio González, when the Salinas administration began dismantling traditional programs of rural support and as reforms leading to the liberalization of land tenure were openly discussed, peasant indigenous protest began to rise again . With no land to offer to opposition peasants, González reacted more aggressively to peasant indigenous protest than his predecessor. While, on average, General Castellanos responded with subsequent acts of repression to 40 percent of all acts of dissent, in the case of González, 50 percent of all acts of indigenous protest were subsequently followed by government repression. Between 1991 and 1992, mobilization and repression grew exponentially, leading to the Zapatista rebellion in 1994.

The liberalization of land tenure had two effects in Chiapas. First, the experience of peasant indigenous movements in the 1980s revealed that the Chiapan political system was incapable of offering institutional means of channeling peasant indigenous grievances and demands. Not only had opposition parties made few inroads in the indigenous areas of the state, but most important, the PRI held tight control over all elected positions in the state. It is in these years, as prospects for economic development were jeopardized by the 1992 liberalization of land tenure, that some members of the rank-and-file of the Chiapas peasant indigenous movement decided to join the guerrilla forces of the EZLN that had been operating in the Lacandón jungle since 1983. Second, it was also around 1992 that peasant indigenous organizations strategically shifted their demands toward an ethnic discourse. By 1992 ethnic demands had already surpassed economic concerns in Chiapas—in distinction from all the other states in the country.

Oaxaca. Throughout the wave of indigenous protest, Oaxaca has persistently scored intermediate levels of protest. On average, in the 1970s there was one act of peasant indigenous protest every seven weeks in Oaxaca, one every two weeks in the 1980s, and one every ten days in the 1990s. Indigenous protest took off under the administration of Pedro Vázquez Colmenares (1980–86), showing a first dramatic peak in 1983, the year of the political and violent turmoil over the control of the municipality of Juchitán, and slowed down the rest of the administration. Mobilization remained almost at the same level during the administration of Heladio Ramírez (1986–92) and experienced the greatest hike between 1992 and 1998 during the administration of Diódoro Carrasco.

Initial demands of peasant indigenous organizations in the 1970s were mainly about land reform. In the 1980s, however, after peasant indigenous organizations made inroads into local electoral politics and were met with severe repression, they replaced economic demands (30 percent) with civil and political concerns (70 percent); mobilizations in the early 1980s evolved into anticacique and prodemocracy movement that attempted to gain control over municipal governments (Hernández Navarro 1999). In the late 1980s and 1990s, as economic demands gave way to ethnic demands in many other states, in Oaxaca ethnicity never really displaced political and material demands from the top of the social agenda. The highest levels of ethnic demands were reached in 1987, when Governor Ramírez tried to introduce a local constitutional reform to provide cultural rights to Oaxacan indigenous peoples; in 1994 and 1995 when reforms to the electoral code to accommodate indigenous customary laws and traditions were being debated; and in 1997 when the Zapatistas and the federal government negotiated the right to autonomy and self-determination for indigenous peoples. Yet, on average, ethnicity never went beyond 10 percent.

Initial peasant indigenous mobilizations in Oaxaca were met with government repression. Between 1975 and 1980, half of all acts of protest in the state were matched by subsequent acts of police repression. After an initial repressive start-off, the administration of Vázquez Colmenares had to open up to political negotiation in the second half of his administration after the Juchitán crisis of 1983. From then on, while the Chiapas local elite followed a path of partial land reform cum police repression, local elites in Oaxaca followed a path of partial political reformism cum police repression. Governor Ramírez, a Mixteco Indian, on the one hand would ineffectively fight central elites in his attempt to introduce constitutional reform to recognize ethnocultural rights to indigenous peoples in Oaxaca and, on the other, would react to peasant indigenous protest like governors did in the 1970s, by matching 53 percent of all acts of protest during his administration with subsequent police repression.

Mobilization in Oaxaca was first led by peasant organizations that emerged as a reaction to the agricultural crisis of ISI and then by indigenous organizations headed by Indian leaders who were trained in the peasant movements of the 1970s. As in Chiapas, the Catholic and Protestant churches in Oaxaca played an important role in the initial phases of organization and mobilization.[5]

Although peasant indigenous protest in the 1980s in Oaxaca followed a trend similar to that in Chiapas, the intensity of protest, the radicalization of demands, and the levels of violence were always lower than in Chiapas.[6] This is largely explained by the nature of the Oaxaca political system. Although the state governor in Oaxaca holds greater institutional powers than his Chiapas counterpart, opposition parties in Oaxaca made earlier and more decisive inroads than in Chiapas. Despite high levels of government repression, continuous political bargaining with opposition parties since the early 1980s and with indigenous social leaders opened important channels of political communication and nonviolent participation. In the aftermath of the Zapatista rebellion, this previous history of limited political bargaining allowed local elites to introduce preventive institutional reforms to avoid a rebel contagion from Chiapas.

Federal and State Responses after 1994: The Politics of Multiculturalism

The Federation. The uprising of the Zapatistas in 1994 dealt a severe blow to the politics of assimilation, co-optation, and repression followed by federal and local elites in Mexico. While in the first round of peace negotiations in 1994 economic demands dominated the Zapatista rhetoric at the negotiation table, in the second round of negotiations in 1995–96, demands for autonomy and self-determination became the cornerstone of the peace process. Peace negotiations in San Andrés Larráinzar, Chiapas, focused on: (1) indigenous rights and culture; (2) democracy and the political representation of indigenous peoples; (3) land reform and economic and social development; and (4) women's rights. In 1996, after a few months of intense negotiations on the first issue, the Zapatistas and the government signed the San Andrés Accords, guaranteeing a series of rights to indigenous peoples, in the name of autonomy and self-determination. The federal government was supposed to draft a legal initiative based on the accords and submit it to congress for constitutional reform. Provided that President Zedillo enjoyed a PRI majority in congress, the accords would become constitutional law almost by presidential decree. Zedillo never drafted the law because he became convinced that the constitutional translation of the San Andrés Accords would open the door for the "Balkanization" of the country.

To avoid the collapse of the peace process, a multiparty legislative commission created in 1995 (COCOPA—Comisión de Concordia y Pacificación) drafted an initiative, calling for the redefinition of the Mexican nation and for the transformation of Mexico's federal pact to allow for the political accommodation of indigenous rights to autonomy and self-determination.[7]

President Zedillo did not embrace the initiative though representatives of all major political parties, including the PRI, had drafted it. The Zapatistas, in contrast, quickly embraced the initiative. The peace negotiation resulted in a stalemate, the Zapatistas returned to the jungle, and Zedillo expanded the military presence in every conflict-ridden indigenous region, while encouraging local solutions to indigenous demands.

In *Oaxaca*, in August 1995, the state legislature passed a legal reform by which communities could opt between two electoral systems to select their municipal authorities: traditional party competition in open elections through secret ballot, or indigenous customary practices and laws, where the participation of political parties would be prohibited by positive law. For the 1995 municipal election, 72 percent of the state's 570 municipalities opted for selecting their local authorities on the basis of indigenous customary practices.[8]

Although most members of the national indigenous movement and the EZLN saw the Oaxaca reform as a case of limited communalism, they nonetheless pointed at the reform as evidence that providing indigenous communities with special group rights would not result in secessionist ambitions. Local independent indigenous movements also celebrated the 1995 reform as a first step toward further autonomy arrangements in the future. Both the federal government and local elites in Oaxaca also cheered the reform as proof that limited action may suffice in satisfying indigenous demands for autonomy and self-determination.

Why did state elites in Oaxaca opt for institutional reforms that partially satisfied the demands of the independent indigenous movement in the state? After the first "rebel territories" were established in Chiapas in December 1994, different peasant indigenous organizations in Oaxaca, Guerrero, Hidalgo, and Veracruz started discussing the possibilities of establishing their own rebel territories. PRI local elites in Oaxaca preventively accelerated the introduction of legal reforms to accommodate local communal customary practices. One of the key aims of the reforms was to lower the probability of rebel contagion across borders. However, the reform would also serve as a guarantee that the growing power of the left opposition among indigenous voters in the state would be curtailed. By accepting the reform, the PRI closed the doors of municipal institutions to all political parties and hoped to maintain control of local communities through informal networks of cacique rule and state-distributed resources. An econometric analysis conducted by Guerra (2000) shows that those communities with higher levels of PRI hegemony were more likely to have opted for customary law, while those communities with higher levels of party competition remained loyal to the party system. As a Hernández Navarro put it, "the state government approved the [reform] in order to keep the indigenous communities from allying with the [left] opposition" (1999, 159). A final motivation for the reform was the political ambition of a young technocratic governor who tried to use the reform to position himself as a key contender for the PRI presidential campaign of 2000 (Elizarrarás 2002).

The indigenous reform in Oaxaca has had mixed results. In several municipalities reforms opened the way for more participatory communal politics; in others, communal practices curtailed the political participation of women and young men in local decision making; in still others, informal control by local caciques linked to the PRI was strengthened. Overall, in those municipalities that adopted customary laws to select their local authorities abstentionism increased substantially in subsequent gubernatorial and federal elections (Elizarrarás 2002). The fact remains, however, that whatever inherent virtues or drawbacks the Oaxaca reform may have, the very process of negotiation of legal changes signaled the existence of institutional channels for social and political contestation in the state.

In *Chiapas*, interim governor Roberto Albores (1997–2000) followed a two-track strategy. First, following the Oaxaca model, Albores introduced a series of constitutional and legal reforms to accommodate indigenous group rights. The second track, however, moved away from the Oaxacan experience. To confront the potential spread of Zapatista rebel territories, local PRI politicians resorted to the "privatization" of government repression by sponsoring or protecting armed civilians in their growing strife against Zapatista autonomous municipalities.

The constitutional reform track included a reform in Chiapas's constitution that introduced substantive changes, recognizing Chiapas as a pluricultural state; specifying the nine indigenous ethnic groups that the state should protect; promising that the government would protect and promote indigenous customary laws and traditions; encouraging political parties to name indigenous candidates to compete in those municipalities and electoral districts of indigenous majority; establishing penal sanctions against racial discrimination; demanding equal access to judicial courts for indigenous populations; and providing bilingual education wherever necessary. Many of these changes placed Chiapas, together with Oaxaca, at the forefront of pro-Indian state constitutions. However, for most indigenous organizations in Chiapas, these changes came at least a decade late. Since their focus had shifted to more fundamental reforms to the federal constitution, these local changes passed unnoticed.

Governor Albores also promoted a long-requested program of remunicipalization and created eight new municipalities. As suggested by local observers, however, the new municipalities were all established next to Zapatista autonomous municipalities mainly to manage the resources that the Zapatistas had rejected (Burguete and Leyva 2000). In fact, confronting the Zapatista-controlled territories had been one of the key objectives of the Albores administration. Albores ordered the dismantling of at least half a dozen Zapatista autonomous municipalities. During his administration PRI municipal authorities and local deputies sponsored anti-Zapatista armed civilians (the so-called paramilitaries) that operated almost freehandedly between 1997 and 2000. Intercommunal conflict in these years skyrocketed in the highlands, the northern Chol region, and eastern Chiapas. During these years, some regions of Chiapas practically slipped into small civil wars in which hundreds of families were displaced and mass murders, like Acteal, took place.

Redefining the Nation-State under a Democratic Regime?

On July 2, 2000, with the presidential victory of the opposition candidate Vicente Fox, Mexico's protracted transition to democracy came to an end. A month later, on August 20, a former PRI senator, Pablo Salazar, became the first opposition candidate to defeat the PRI in a gubernatorial race in Chiapas. The simultaneous opposition victory in the 2000 presidential election and in the gubernatorial race in Chiapas opened up a unique window of opportunity for the resumption of peace negotiations between government authorities and the Zapatistas.

In his inaugural speech, President Fox announced that his first government action would be to send the COCOPA law initiative to congress. By sending the law initiative to the senate, the president hoped to resume peace negotiations with the Zapatista rebels. Far from an ideological commitment of a right-wing president to Mexico's indigenous peoples, the midterm congressional elections of 2003 may explain Fox's action. For the first three years of his term, President Fox will have to rule without a majority from his National Action Party (PAN)in congress. Passing a constitutional reform that would grant indigenous peoples the right to autonomy and self-determination would have certainly provided the most prestigious progressive credentials to a right-wing president, allowing him, at the same time, to negotiate second-generation economic reforms that would consolidate Mexico's market-oriented economic model. If successful, Fox would have been able to consolidate the party realignment initiated in July 2000.

In Chiapas, Governor Salazar announced in his inaugural speech that reconciliation would be the main policy objective of his administration. From the outset Salazar knew that his political future would mainly depend on sowing the seeds for reconciliation in the state. To that purpose he created a Commission for Reconciliation charged with the difficult task of rebuilding social relations in those municipalities in which pro- and anti-Zapatista forces were engaged in fierce disputes over land, territory, and peoples.

The main challenge for the president and the governor was that neither of them had a majority in their respective congresses. Moreover, to pass his constitutional reform initiative Fox had to strike important deals with nineteen PRI governors (out of thirty-two states) and members of his own party. To make his reconciliation program work, Salazar also had to strike important deals with PRI mayors that then dominated two-thirds of the municipal presidencies in the state.

The negotiation of the "Indian law" became the first Mexican experience in more than seventy years of a constitutional reform under a democratic regime. Under conditions of divided government in which an opposition party (the PRI) controlled two-thirds of the state legislatures, the approval of a constitutional reform that would for all practical purposes redefine the nature of Mexican federalism was no easy task. Rather than directly lobbying governors and local and national legislators, the two parties most interested in the approval of the reform, the EZLN and President Fox, decided to take their case to the streets and the media. On one side, the Zapatistas organized an "epic" two-week march that took the commanders in chief of the EZLN and Subcommander Marcos from Chiapas into Mexico City and then into congress. On his side, President Fox launched a massive media campaign to show his support for the COCOPA initiative and his commitment to the Indian cause, but he never designed a serious lobby campaign to secure a majority in congress. Following a plebiscitarian logic, the president assumed that his enormous first-year popularity and his media campaign would force all legislators to approve his reform.

Senators from the major political parties in Mexico, led by the president's right-of-center National Action Party (PAN) and the PRI, drafted and passed an Indian law that turned out to be substantially different from the COCOPA initiative. Although the law approved by congress did, indeed, recognize important rights for indigenous populations, the heart of the law did not fully recognize the right to autonomy and self-determination and the actual recognition and implementation was left to be negotiated with state legislatures. In the best tradition of revolutionary nationalism and corporatism, the law was substantive in social provisions but weak in political-institutional transformations.

The Zapatistas condemned the constitutional reform, withdrew any contacts that had been established with federal authorities, and went back in the jungle. Since the resumption of peace negotiations had been strategically conditioned to the approval of the COCOPA initiative, the peace process went back into a new, now democratic, stalemate.

Reconciliation in the state of Chiapas has been a rather Herculean task. The Commission for Reconciliation suffered a severe blow at the beginning of the administration when the two-decade-long conflict between members of the Emiliano Zapata Peasant Organization (OCEZ) and PRI supporters in the municipality of Venustiano Carranza scaled up again and nine PRI-affiliated peasants were assassinated. For the most part, the Commission has been able to sign reconciliation agreements with one side, but not with the others (i.e., Tila) and some of the displaced populations that have been taken back to their communities (i.e., Acteal) still face an uncertain future. Reconciliation is even more difficult because the governor has spent most of his time trying to sort out political battles with congress and the judiciary and trying to bring a once all-mighty state police under control. Now that the Zapatistas are back in the jungle, the prospects for reconciliation are even less likely.

International experience shows that successful negotiations of guerrilla warfare and of autonomy arrangements for ethnic minorities are more likely to take place under democratic regimes than under authoritarian rule.[9] Democracies provide rebel minorities and elites with greater incentives for negotiation than authoritarianism. Nonetheless, the Mexican example shows the enormous complications involved in the negotiation of minority rights under majoritarian institutions, particularly in the early stages of democratic consolidation when actors are just beginning to establish the new rules of political cooperation.

Conclusion

One of the most peculiar aspects of the wave of peasant indigenous mobilization in Mexico is the strong cross-regional variation displayed since the early 1980s. Although economic factors may explain the *timing* of indigenous mobilizations, preliminary statistical analyses show that the political institutions of centralized federalism under authoritarian rule defined to a large extent the *geography* and intensity of indigenous mobilization. In fact, one of the main findings of this chapter is that the wide cross-regional diversity in mobilization and conflict levels is not only related to sociodemographic factors, but mainly to local political arrangements and elite responses to initial social contestation.

The uneven process of democratization across regions had a long-lasting impact on the development of indigenous mobilizations. In those states with authoritarian local constitutions, strong PRI hegemony, and high levels of electoral concurrence, regional elites enjoyed the institutional and political foundations for autocratic rule. Repression, rather than negotiation, was the typical response of government elites to initial indigenous mobilizations and economic demands in these states. Repression led to higher mobilization and increased social protest led, in turn, to the escalation of repression. The most extreme outcome of these cycles of protest and repression was the uprising of the EZLN in Chiapas in 1994. In other states, where regional elites were constrained by party competition and more democratic local constitutions, peasant indigenous demands were partially met through negotiation and accommodation. Nonetheless, even in the most democratic states, local elites proved incapable of coping with the evolving demands of a peasant indigenous movement that, in two decades, evolved into a powerful interest group whose demands already transcended mere economic concerns and have been channeled through a program of ethnocultural and territorial rights.

The new political geography that resulted from the presidential elections in 2000 opened a window of opportunities for the dramatic transformation of Mexico's centralized federalist structures and for the redefinition of the Mexican nation as a pluriethnic society. Although the first attempt at transforming the Mexican constitution and resuming peace negotiations proved to be unsatisfactory for many of the parties involved in the conflict, the advantage of a democratic regime is that parties and social forces can rethink their original strategies and try again. The main challenge for Mexico's emerging democratic regime will be to persuade members of the EZLN and the national indigenous movement that transforming national and local institutions to further their collective interests can be done through democratic means.

As peace negotiations between the EZLN and the administration of Vicente Fox went into a "democratic stalemate," a wave of local constitutional reforms on indigenous-related affairs began across states. The EZLN and the speakers of Mexico's emerging national indigenous movement have closed the door to any potential participation of their member organizations in negotiating any local constitutional reform. The question remains as to whether the EZLN and the CNI will have the capacity to preclude any participation of local organizations in these reforms and whether local elites will push these reforms even without the participation of the most vocal indigenous organizations in their states.

As this chapter made evident, federalism, even under authoritarian and centralized rule, opened windows of opportunities for local reformism. Despite the persistence of local authoritarian pockets of power in some states, Mexico's "new federalism" under democratic rule opens many doors for exploring innovative, creative, and incremental change in the states. Contrary to the perception of the Zapatistas and of some prominent members of Mexico's new indigenous national elite, local reforms would not necessarily preclude the emergence of a pan-Indian movement in Mexico. Successful experiences of local reformism pushed from below may very well pave the way for future rounds of national constitutional reforms. As paradoxical as it may sound, exploring a federalist solution of combining local and national reforms in an *incremental* and *simultaneous* fashion may very well be a more effective way of negotiating radical ethnoterritorial transformations in an increasingly pluralistic and democratic federation.

NOTES

Rosario Aguilar and Rolando Ochoa provided invaluable research assistance for this project. I am grateful to Valerie Bunce, Miguel Centeno, Alain de Remes, Robert R. Kaufman, Susan Stokes, and Deborah Yashar for insightful suggestions. Nancy Bermeo and Ugo Amoretti provided excellent guidance throughout the project. I nonetheless remain responsible for errors and omissions.

1. Data are taken from the OIMSREG data set. OIMSREG is a newly created data set based on reports by 7 Mexican national newspapers, covering 21 Mexican states and 898 municipalities, 1975–2000. See Trejo (2002).

2. Cited in Burguete (1999).

3. Although governor's power turned out to be only weakly significant, it shows the expected sign: the more authoritarian the institutional powers of the governor, the higher the probability of protest.

4. Rich case studies on peasant indigenous movements in Chiapas can be found in González Esponda 1989; Morquecho 1992; Mattiac, 1998; and Harvey 1997.

5. See Hernández Navarro (1998, 1999), Norget (1999), and Hernández Díaz (1998).

6. Note that although a guerrilla group, the Popular Revolutionary Army (EPR), emerged in the state in 1996, there is no clear link between the independent peasant indigenous movement of Oaxaca and the guerrillas. This stands in sharp contrast to the case of the EZLN in Chiapas, where the Zapatista rank-and-file grew out of tactic fragmentations from the independent peasant indigenous organizational networks.

7. For a thorough legal analysis of the "COCOPA law initiative," see Cossío Díaz et al. (1998).

8. See Recondo (1999) and Guerra (2000).

9. See Arnson (1999) and Ghai (2000).

REFERENCES

Arnson, Cynthia, ed. 1999. *Comparative Peace Processes in Latin America.* Stanford: Wilson Center Press and Stanford University Press.

Blanco, Oscar. 2001. El poder de los gobernadores en el ámbito local. Tesis de licenciatura, Mexico City, CIDE.

Burguete, Araceli. 1999. Poder local y autonomía indígena en Chiapas: rebeliones comunitarias y luchas municipalistas. In *Espacios Disputados: Transformaciones Rurales en Chiapas,* ed. María Eugenia Reyes Ramos et al. Mexico City: UNAM and ECOSUR.

Burguete, Araceli, ed. 1999. Empoderamiento indígena: Tendencias autonómicas en la región Altos de Chiapas. In *México: Experiencias de Autonomia Indígena.* Copenhagen: IWGIA/SI.

Burguete, Araceli, and Xóchítl Leyva. 2001. Nuevos municipios en Chiapas. Manuscript, CIESAS.

Castells, Manuel. 1997. *The Power of Identity: The Information Age.* Oxford: Blackwell.

Cleary, Matthew. 2000. Democracy and Indigenous Rebellion in Latin America. In *Comparative Political Studies* 33, no. 9 (November).

Cossío Díaz, José Ramón, et al. 1998. *Derechos y cultura indígena: Los dilemas del debate jurídico.* Mexico City: Miguel Angel Porrúa.

De Remes, Alain. 1999. Juxtaposition in Mexican Municipal Electoral Contests: The Silent Cohabitation. CIDE, Working Paper, no. 96.

———. 2000. Municipal Electoral Processes in Latin America and Mexico. CIDE, Working Paper, no. 125.

Díaz Cayeros, Alberto. 1995. *Desarrollo Económico e Inequidad Regional: Hacia un Nuevo Pacto Federal en México.* Mexico City: Porrúa.

Elizarrarás, Rodrigo. 2002. Gobernabilídad y autonomía: los municipios de usos y costumbres en Oaxaca. Tesis de licenciatura, Mexico City, ITAM.

Fearon, James, and David Laitin. 1997. A Cross-Sectional Study of Large Scale Violence in the Postwar Period. Manuscript, University of Chicago.

Ghai, Yashi. 2000. Autonomy as a Strategy for Diffusing Conflict. In *International Conflict Resolution After the Cold War,* ed. National Research Council. Washington, D.C., National Academy Press.

González Esponda, Juan. 1989. Movimiento Campesino Chiapaneco, 1974–1984. Tesis de licenciatura, San Cristóbal de las Casas, UNACH.

Guerra, Maira Melisa. 2000. Usos y costumbres o partidos politicos: Una decisión de los municipios oaxaqueños. Tesis de licenciatura, Mexico City, CIDE.

Gurr, Tedd. 1993. *Minorities at Risk: A Global View of Ethnopolitical Conflicts.* Washington, D.C.: United States Institute of Peace.

Gurr, Tedd, and Will Moore. 1997. Ethnopolitical Rebellion: A Cross-Sectional Analysis of the 1980s with Risk Assessments for the 1990s. *American Journal of Political Science* 41, no. 4 (October).

Gutiérrez, Natividad. 1999. *Nationalist Myths and Ethnic Identities: Indigenous Intellectuals and the Mexican State.* Lincoln: University of Nebraska Press.

Harvey, Neil. 1997. *The Chiapas Rebellion: The Struggle for Land and Democracy.* Durham: Duke University Press.

Hernández Díaz, Jorge. 1998. Las organizaciones indígenas en Oaxaca. In *Autonomías étnicas y Estados nacionales,* ed. Miguel A. Bartolomé and Alicia Barbas. Mexico City: CONACULTA.

Hernández Navarro, Luis. 1999. Reaffirming Ethnic Identity and Reconstructing Politics in Oaxaca. In *Subnational Politics and Democracy in Mexico,* ed. Wayne Cornelius, Todd Eisenstadt, and Jane Handley. La Jolla: Center for U.S.-Mexico Studies.

———. 1998. Ciudadanos iguales, ciudadanos diferentes: La nueva lucha India. In *Acuerdos de San Andrés,* ed. Luis Herández Navarro and Ramón Vera Herrera. Mexico City: ERA.

Hernández Valdez, Alfonso. 2000. Las causas estructurales de la democracia Local en México, 1989–1998. *Política y gobierno* 7, no. 1.

Huntington, Samuel. 1963. *Political Order in Changing Societes.* New Haven, Conn.: Yale University Press.

Le Bot, Yvon. 1994. *Violence de la modernité en Amerique latine: Indianité, société et puvoir.* Paris: Karthala.

Marván, Ignacio. 1997. *¿Y después del presidencialismo? Reflexiones para la formación de un nuevo regimen.* Mexico City: Océano.

Mattiace, Shannan. 1998. Peasant and Indian: Political Identity and Indian Autonomy in Chiapas. Ph.D. dissertation, University of Texas at Austin.

Montemayor, Carlos. 1997. *Chiapas: La rebelión indígena de México.* Mexico City: Océano.

Morquecho, Gaspar. 1992. Los indios en proceso de organización. Tesis de licenciatura, San Cristóbal de las Casas, Universidad Autónoma de Chiapas.

Muller, Edward N., and Mitchell Seligson, 1987. Inequality and Insurgency. *American Political Science Review* 81, no. 2.

Norget, Kristin. 1999. Progressive Theology and Popular Religiosity in Oaxaca, Mexico. In *Latin American Religion in Motion,* ed. Christian Smith and Joshua Prokopy. New York: Routledge.

Olson, Mancur. 1966. *The Logic of Collective Action: Public Goods and the Theory of Groups.* Cambridge, Mass.: Harvard University Press.

Psacharopoulos, George, and Harry Patrinos. 1993. *Indigenous People and Poverty in Latin America: Empirical Analysis.* Washington, D.C.: The World Bank.

Recondo, David. 1999. Usos y costumbres y elecciones en Oaxaca: Los dilemas de la democracia representativa en una sociedad multicultural. *Trace* (December).

Reyes Ramos, María Eugenia. 1998. Los Acuerdos Agrarios en Chiapas: una política de contención social. In *Espacios Disputados: Transformaciones Rurales en Chiapas,* ed. María Eugenia Reyes Ramos et al. Mexico City: UNAM and ECOSUR.

Rubin, Jeffrey. 1997. *Decentering the Regime: Ethnicity, Radicalism, and Democracy in Juchitán, Mexico.* Durham, N.C.: Duke University Press.

Sonnleitner, Willibald. 2001. *Los indígenas y la democratización electoral: Una década de cambio político entre los tzotziles y tzeltales de Los Altos de Chiapas (1988–2000).* Mexico City: IFE and COLMEX.

Stavenhagen, Rodolfo. 1992. Challenging the Nation-State in Latin America. *Journal of International Affairs* 34, no. 2 (winter).

Tilly, Charles. 1978. *From Mobilization to Revolution.* Reading, Mass.: Addison-Wesley.

Trejo, Guillermo. 2002. Organizaciones Indígenas, Movimientos Sociales y Represión Gubernamental (OIMSREG). México, 1975–2000. *Database.* Mexico City: CIDE.

———. 2000. Religious Competition, State Action and the Renaissance of Indigenous Identities in Chiapas: A Micro-Analytic Approach to Ethnic Identity Formation. CIDE, Working Paper, no. 136.

Villafuerte, Daniel, et al. 1999. *La tierra en Chiapas: Viejos problemas nuevos.* Mexico City: Plaza y Janés.

Weldon, Jeffrey. 1999. Political Sources of Presidencialismo in Mexico. In *Presidentialism and Democracy in Latin America,* ed. Scott Mainwaring and Matthew S. Shugart. Cambridge: Cambridge University Press.

Yashar, Deborah. 1998. Contesting Citizenship: Indigenous Movements and Democracy in Latin America. *Comparative Politics* 31, no. 1 (October).

CHAPTER FOURTEEN

Turkey

Roots of the Turkish-Kurdish Conflict and Prospects for Constructive Reform

Michele Penner Angrist

The Turkish state has failed to accommodate successfully its Kurdish population. Since the founding of the Turkish Republic in 1923—and, more notably, since Turkey's transition to competitive politics in 1950—conflict between the Turkish state and its Kurdish population has meant that Kurdish citizens (concentrated largely in the southeast) have not enjoyed the political and civil liberties that have been available to most Turks. Much of the southeast has lived under emergency rule for long periods of time. Turkish authorities have "Turkicized" Kurdish placenames, banned the use of Kurdish languages, and placed constitutional restrictions on activities evocative of Kurdish ethnic identity. In their efforts to control the southeast, Turkey's security forces have carried out widespread search-and-arrest operations, forcible population transfers, and the evacuation and razing of villages—all under allegations of practices of torture and summary executions. Indeed, in large part due to state harassment and repression of Kurds, Freedom House awards Turkey a political rights score of only 4 and a civil rights score of only 5.[1]

An extremely high level of violence has characterized the relationship between the Turkish state and its Kurdish citizens in the southeast in the past two decades. In 1984, the Kurdistan Workers' Party (PKK) launched a guerrilla war against the state with the goal of creating an independent Kurdish state. That war, which neared conclusion only in 1999 with the capture by Turkish authorities of PKK leader Abdullah Öcalan, is widely estimated to have cost nearly 40,000 lives.

Finally—and not surprisingly, given the limitations on Kurds' civil and political liberties and the extent of the violence that has transpired—high levels of disaffection with the political system exist among Kurdish residents of southeastern Turkey. Citing a confidential official Turkish document, Eric Rouleau reported that in the early 1990s, the number of PKK "fighters," "sympathizers," and "active supporters" in the southeastern provinces was approximately 375,000—a figure that represents one-fifth of the adult population of the region (1993, 122). In 1995 general elections, the pro-Kurdish HADEP Party, which is generally understood by analysts to be aligned with the PKK, won more than 40 percent of the vote in two southeastern provinces and more than 20 percent of the vote in six others.

This essay analyzes the causes of the Turkish-Kurdish conflict and considers the proposition that decentralizing and other institutional reforms would enable Turkey to manage it more successfully. It asserts that three institutional characteristics of the Turkish Republic have played lead roles in generating, exacerbating, and prolonging the conflict. These are the formation of a highly centralized, unitary state; the attachment of an assimilationist Turkish nationalist ideology to the state; and the long shadow that the Turkish military has cast over civilian politicians in recent decades.

As the shape of state and regime institutions are the primary factors motivating the conflict, prospects for managing the conflict more peacefully will depend on altering the ways in which the Turkish center relates to its Kurdish periphery. The set of politically feasible institutional reforms that will likely contribute to more peaceful conflict management includes demilitarizing the conflict, creating space within which civilian politicians can consider nonmilitary approaches to resolving the conflict, granting Kurds significant linguistic and cultural concessions, and devolving some significant measure of decision-making authority to the local level. More radical alterations in the center-periphery relationship (i.e., autonomy and federalism) are politically unrealistic. As no change in the status quo will be forthcoming if Turkish decision makers believe it will lead to a renewed, strong separatist movement, the essay closes with a discussion of the likelihood that a more accommodating approach to the Kurdish minority would encourage secessionist tendencies. In light of intra-Kurdish divisions, the nature of the Turkish party system, and international factors, it answers in the negative.

Most of Turkey's 66 million citizens are ethnically Turkish. The Kurdish population is the country's sole significant ethnic minority.[2] It is also the only minority that is territorially concentrated and that makes territorially based political claims.[3] Accurate data illuminating the size of Turkey's Kurdish population do not exist: estimates range from between 8 and 12 million, or 13 to 20 percent of the total population. Though many have migrated westward toward Turkey's major metropolises (Istanbul, Ankara, Izmir),[4] most Kurds live in the southeast portion of the country, where they constitute more than 60 percent of the population in eight of Turkey's nearly eighty provinces, and 20 to 60 percent of the population in seven additional provinces (Gunter 1990, viii).

How deep are the differences that characterize the Turkish-Kurdish cleavage? Kurds constitute a major Middle Eastern ethnic group distinct from their Turkish, Arab, and Persian neighbors. However, Kurds' physical characteristics do not differ dramatically from Turks'. That is to say, facial features and skin, hair, and eye color do not provide reliable markers of ethnicity. Neither does religion constitute a substantial fault line. Like the majority of Turks, most Kurds are Sunni Muslims—though the two communities subscribe to different schools of Islamic legal jurisprudence.[5] Instead, the key distinguishing characteristic dividing Turkey's Kurds from Turkey's Turks is language: Kurds speak a mother tongue that is thoroughly distinct from Turkish. Stemming from linguistic specificity are trajectories of literature, folklore, and other kinds of cultural production that are distinctly Kurdish rather than Turkish.

Turkey's Kurdish population has never been homogeneous, however. Though a majority are Sunni Muslim, a substantial segment of the population subscribes instead to Alevism. Others belong to various dervish orders, further augmenting the Kurds' religio-spiritual internal diversity. Linguistic differences also divide the community: Turkey's Kurds speak two of three major Kurdish dialects (Zaza and Kurmanji). Strongly individualistic tribes and clans have characterized Kurdish social structure. Finally, historically hostility has existed between seminomadic and nomadic Kurdish tribes on the one hand, and sedentary Kurds engaged in agricultural pursuits on the other.

In part because these cleavages have rendered collective action difficult, Turkey's Kurds never possessed a state of their own during the modern era.[6] Instead, for 400 years prior to World War I, the Kurdish communities of the Middle East fell under the control of either the Ottoman-Turkish or the Persian empires. The geopolitical upheaval that followed the war saw the majority of Kurds come under the control of three new republics: Iran, Iraq, and Turkey. In the Turkish case, the upheaval took the form of an independence war between 1920 and 1923, during which time Mustafa Kemal Atatürk led the denizens of the Anatolian peninsula and what remained of the Ottoman army in a successful bid to resist foreign invasion and plans for partition. This effort secured the borders of contemporary Turkey. The southern and eastern borders of the new republic enfolded about half of the Kurdish population of the Middle East.

Soon after the founding of the Turkish Republic in 1923, Turkish state builders came into conflict with the Kurdish communities of the southeast. The years 1924 to 1938 saw the creation and consolidation of a centralized, secular, Turkish nationalist state. These processes triggered numerous localized revolts against the central state on the part of Kurdish tribes. The Turkish army forcefully put down the revolts, and policy makers followed up with resettlement schemes and other laws designed to dissolve Kurdish ethnic identity.

During the 1940s and 1950s, though serious grievances and political dissent still were present in the southeast, overt, armed conflict between the center and its Kurdish periphery did not take place. The Kurdish question did not preoccupy decision makers in the Turkish capital, Ankara. Turkish political elites spent these years navigating the country through World War II and managing a transition from one-party dictatorship to competitive party politics. Social mobilization and political polarization dominated Turkish affairs during the 1960s and 1970s. A violent, radical, leftist movement emerged, in turn provoking actors on the extreme right to counterorganize. Growing levels of political violence coupled with party system fragmentation and a turn toward a norm of unstable, short-lived, coalition governments marked these decades.

In the context of these developments, the question of Kurdish rights reappeared in the political arena as Kurdish activists began pressing political claims. While many did so by joining extant leftist groups, explicitly pro-Kurdish political organizations also began to emerge. Faik Bucak founded the Kurdish Democratic Party of Turkey in 1965. Kurdish intellectuals created the Revolutionary Cultural Society of the East (DDKO) in 1969. The 1970s saw the creation of a number of other, mostly leftist, Kurdish groups; their political impact, however, was limited by internal divisions and splintering.[7] Two exceptions to this phenomenon stand out, however. The first is Abdullah Öcalan's Kurdistan Workers' Party (PKK), which was founded in 1978 and would prosecute a long war against the Turkish state beginning in 1984. The second is Kemal Burkay's Kurdistan Socialist Party (PSK), founded in 1979, which opposed the PKK and is still active in exile today. Though some violence did characterize center-Kurdish relations during the 1960s and 1970s, it was minimal when compared with the levels of intra-Turkish, left-right violence that dominated the political stage.

By the 1980s, left-right violence no longer plagued Turkey.[8] Violence surrounding the Kurdish question exploded, however. In 1984, the PKK launched an armed rebellion in the southeast, initially with the goal of creating an independent, socialist, Kurdish state. The PKK pulled the Turkish armed forces into a grinding war that reached a hiatus only in 1999, when Turkish authorities captured Öcalan. The war cost billions of dollars and saw tens of thousands of lives lost and hundreds if not thousands of villages destroyed, their inhabitants evacuated, their fields and herds destroyed. Though nearly all relevant actors view the PKK as a terrorist group that must not be accommodated, in the 1990s the PKK's ability to enmesh Turkey in a costly and inconclusive internal war drove Turkish decision makers to begin asking what kinds of reforms might ameliorate the conflict.

Today, although the war in the southeast is on the wane, the problem of accommodating Kurds into the Turkish political community remains. The task is complex not only due to the bitterness that is a legacy of the war but also because Turkey's Kurds are as politically diverse as they are socially heterogeneous. Burkay's PSK (in exile in Europe) advances a leftist political agenda but does not condone violence. For two decades, Öcalan's PKK also pressed a leftist agenda but espoused very violent methods. At the same time, many conservative Kurdish elites sided with the Turkish state in the conflict with the PKK, helping to arm whole villages in the southeast in order to defend them against PKK attacks and/or infiltration.[9] In the 1990s, a right-wing, religious nationalist Kurdish group, Hizbollah, also began to confront the PKK violently in the southeast.

In the realm of elections, Kurds gave their support to a wide range of political parties during the 1990s. The leftist, pro-Kurdish HADEP Party won significant numbers of votes in southeastern provinces. The Islamist Virtue (formally Welfare) Party also did well in southeastern provinces, while it picked up large portions of the Kurdish migrant vote in western Turkey. At the same time, Turkey's two main center-right parties performed reasonably well in the southeastern provinces, typically attracting the support of Kurdish landowners or tribal chiefs with promises of patronage rewards.

This overview of the conflict and its contours complete, the essay now turns to a discussion of three central institutions of the Turkish Republic and their role in shaping the Turkish-Kurdish conflict: state centralization, Turkish nationalism, and the powerful political role of the Turkish military. The centralization of power that the state achieved in the early twentieth century undermined the authority of local leaders, and numerous Kurdish tribal revolts against this turn of events took place in the southeast. The revolts reinforced the conviction of the Republic's Kemalist founders that if their new state was to be a strong one, it would have to be built on a foundation of Turkish nationalism. The aggressive, assimilatory policies that flowed from this conviction worsened the confrontation between the state and the Kurds, laying the groundwork for a reappearance of overt, violent conflict in the contemporary period. In the 1980s and 1990s, the consequences of the constitutionally sanctioned political prerogatives of the military escalated the conflict and blocked Turkey's political parties from taking pragmatic steps aimed at ameliorating it.

System Type: The Triumph of Center over Periphery

The first institution that in part accounts for the origins and evolution of the Turkish-Kurdish conflict is the highly centralized, unitary nature of the new state that was built by Mustafa Kemal (Atatürk) and his associates in the early 1920s. The political system created by Kemal was a republic; sovereignty was located in the nation. At the outset, the constitution located executive and legislative authority in a unicameral parliament whose members were elected according to majoritarian rules every four years and were bound to represent not only the constituency that elected them but also the Turkish nation as a whole.[10] Until 1950 this parliament was constituted in authoritarian fashion, with Kemal's ruling party monopolizing or near-monopolizing the body. After 1950, competitive elections were instituted. Members of parliament elected the president, who then designated the prime minister and approved the prime minister's cabinet. No effective checks, judicial or otherwise, existed on the power of the legislature. In addition, Kemal's regime built up a strong, centralized state bureaucracy that was designed to implement in every Turkish province decisions taken by parliament.

This system type's causal impact stems from the fact that it represented the culmination of a gradual but dramatic departure from the decentralized political arrangements that had governed Turkish territory previously. Prior to 1923, the lands that today constitute Turkey were part of the Ottoman Empire. During the seventeenth and eighteenth centuries, the authority of the central Ottoman government over affairs in the periphery, or provinces, was quite thin. In return for the payment of taxes and the contribution of fighting forces to the center when needed, powerful tax-farming local elites called *âyan* dominated governance in the provinces.[11] It was the *âyan* rather than centrally appointed officials who controlled civil and financial administration in the Ottoman periphery (Özbudun 1976, 31).

By the turn of the nineteenth century, however, the empire's marked military decline relative to its European neighbors drove central Ottoman officials to alter this scenario radically. Seeking to collect increased tax revenues to pay for a new, modern army, the center resolved to end its dependence on the *âyan* as middlemen between it and its subjects.[12] It set out to abolish tax-farming and to tax and administrate the provinces directly. During the nineteenth century, a series of reformist sultans and bureaucrats in the imperial capital of Istanbul succeeded in substantially centralizing political-administrative power in the empire. In the early twentieth century, the Committee for Union and Progress (CUP) regime (1908–18) and that established by Kemal continued the centralization of power, while secularizing the public sphere as well.

Of course, the central government's campaign to augment its power threatened the *âyan* and other provincial political elites, who had a vested interest in the decentralized status quo and vigorously opposed the centralization initiative.[13] In most of the Turkish provinces (everywhere but the southeast), the response of the central government to peripheral opposition unfolded in two phases. Between 1812 and 1820, the center used armed force to destroy the *âyans'* provincial armies, establishing Istanbul's monopoly over the use of serious force. After 1820, center-periphery political conflict continued but was no longer managed through the use of force. Instead, the central government found itself building a new set of political institutions that granted the periphery political voice in return for its (grudging) acceptance of a much larger political-administrative role for the center in local affairs.[14] Beginning in the 1840s, a provincial administrative council system was developed wherein elected local notables governed the periphery together with officials appointed by the center.[15] At the center, a parliamentary institution evolved as a mechanism for managing center-periphery conflict. A bipolar pattern of competition emerged in Ottoman parliaments, with advocates of increased central state power squaring off against those who sought to maximize local autonomy.

This was not *democratic* conflict management. The rules of the game decisively favored the Ottoman sultan and the executive branch, which did not hesitate to take decisions in an authoritarian fashion when necessary. Yet Ottoman decision-making institutions were evolving in ways that allowed provincial elites to express their opinions on policy issues—opinions that the center often did take into account. As a result, centralization proceeded relatively smoothly and did not encounter serious obstacles thrown up by actors in the periphery.

The exception was the southeast, where the majority of Ottoman subjects happened to be Kurdish. This region's difficult, often mountainous terrain was remote from the capital, low on infrastructure, and inhabited by numerous armed nomadic and seminomadic tribes. Here the center could *not* achieve a monopoly on the use of force beyond the major towns and their immediate, settled, environs. As a result, as the Ottoman state pursued its centralizing reforms, it was forced to contend with a series of violent tribal rebellions in the southeast as local leaders resisted its efforts to alter the status quo (Bozarslan 1988). These rebellions unfolded throughout the nineteenth century and into the twentieth. They represented a constant headache for the central government, which was seeking to shore up an empire that was rapidly hemorrhaging territory.[16] The modalities of nineteenth-century center-periphery conflict—as it played out in southeastern Anatolia—meant that the center came to be increasingly suspicious and distrustful of the region's population, much of which was ethnically Kurdish.

The Growth of Assimilationist Turkish Nationalism

In the closing decades of the nineteenth century and the opening decades of the twentieth, rebellions by Kurdish tribes continued to frustrate the efforts of the Ottoman central government to impose its authority in the southeast. Center-local contestation over the appropriate locus of political authority remained pivotal to the conflict and to the rebellions. Increasingly, however, the rebellions began to take on Kurdish nationalist overtones.[17]

In the late nineteenth and early twentieth centuries, nationalism was becoming an increasingly potent political force in the region. Nationalism had a particularly destructive impact on the multiethnic Ottoman Empire as many of its numerous subcommunities—including the Greeks, Serbs, and Armenians—fought to secede from the empire and establish independent states of their own. Nationalist ideals made their way into the Kurdish community as well. Educated Kurds in the army and liberal professions began to articulate Kurdish nationalism. Over time, these intellectuals teamed up with local leaders on the ground in the southeast—often with religious leaders[18]—in order to spread Kurdish nationalist ideas widely among the masses.

Two additional nationalisms further fueled Kurdish nationalists' fervor. To the east, Armenian nationalists sought an independent state, the borders of which Kurds feared would overlap with the territory they themselves inhabited. To the west, the central Ottoman government was becoming increasingly secular and Turkish nationalist in its ideology. This evolution began during the regime of the Committee for Union and Progress Party and continued under Kemal's leadership, climaxing in 1923 and 1924, when Kemal declared Turkey a republic and abolished the (Islamic) institutions of the sultanate and caliphate. For centuries, Turks and Kurds had experienced fraternity and sociopolitical parity and primacy as fellow Muslims in an Islamic empire. Secularization removed the social glue that held these communities together, and the center's Turkish nationalist turn threatened the Kurds with second-class political status.

Now a clash of nationalisms reinforced a situation of ongoing center-periphery conflict. The result was a recipe for serious confrontation. The increasingly secular and Turkish nationalist center was anxious about and suspicious of a long-rebellious and now increasingly Kurdish nationalist southeast. Likewise, local Kurdish elites in the southeast did not wish to yield to augmented central government control—especially now that the center increasingly denigrated Islam and privileged Turkish ethnicity.

Geopolitical context intensified the nationalisms, mutual hostility, and political res-oluteness of both sides. For in the 1910s and 1920s, the center was trying desperately to hold the empire together. During the CUP era, the central government struggled with a series of serious threats to the empire's European territories. All the while, anti-CUP political agitation and outright rebellion were continuing among the Kurds of the southeast—a trend that was angering and distressing to the CUP. Though many Kurds served the government during World War I, the CUP reacted to Kurdish activism with stiffened Turkish nationalist commitments and an assimilationist agenda. By the end of the war, the CUP had resolved to separate Kurdish tribal chiefs from their followers and to resettle Kurds in western Anatolia to be merged into the Turkish majority (McDowall 1996, 105).

As Kemal and his allies rose to power at the center on the heels of the CUP's and the Ottoman defeat in World War I, the geopolitical context grew even more dire, further worsening the Turkish-Kurdish conflict. These were the empire's last and darkest hours, during which time Kemal led a war of independence against Allied attempts to occupy and partition what remained of the Ottoman Empire. His goal was to defend what was left of the empire's non-Arab, Muslim territories in Thrace and the Anatolian peninsula. The Kurdish-inhabited areas of what today is Turkey constituted the southeasternmost portion of that territory. As a result, Kemal set about recruiting Kurdish leaders to his cause, emphasizing Muslim (rather than Turkish) unity and promising that Kurds would enjoy equality with Turks. In this effort he was quite successful: by the end of 1919, more than seventy Kurdish tribes and a number of influential urban Kurdish notables had declared their support for Kemal (McDowall 1996, 130).[19]

Still, Kurdish nationalist consciousness was growing, and the Kurdish population was not homogeneously in support of Kemal's efforts. The most dramatic evidence of this unfolded in the fall of 1920. As Kemal's movement faced an Armenian offensive in the east and a Greek invasion in the west, the (Kurdish) Koçgiri tribe of the Dersim region launched a rebellion against and demanded autonomy from the provisional government that Kemalist forces had created in Ankara.[20] Kemal's government played for time over the winter, moving forces in to quash the rebellion in the spring of 1921.

The Koçgiri rebellion, coming as it did at one of the darkest moments of the independence war, fueled the Kemalists' conviction that Kurdish nationalism represented a serious threat to the new state that they were struggling to build. In their eyes, that state would require not only a strong central government but also an ideology that snuffed out Kurdish ethnic identification. This became clear beginning in 1923 after Kemal's forces had successfully secured the borders of what we know today as Turkey. Between 1920 and 1923, due to the exigencies of the war, Kemal had been solicitous of Kurdish political and military support and had given lip service to the Kurdish nation and its aspirations. In 1923, with the war won, an assimilationist, Turkish nationalist ideological agenda began to characterize the regime.[21]

This agenda amounted to official denial of the existence of a Kurdish ethnic minority within Turkey's borders, combined with policies designed to dissolve Kurdish identity, fully assimilating the population into a Turkish nation-state. Turkish delegates refused to acknowledge the Kurdish minority during the 1923 negotiations at Lausanne, where the provisions of the 1920 Sèvres Accord (which had held out the distinct possibility of an independent Kurdish state) were rewritten in light of Kemal's military victories.[22] In 1923, Turkification policies began in the southeast: many of the region's administrative positions were filled with Turks rather than Kurds, and Kurdish place-names were replaced with Turkish ones. The 1924 Turkish republican constitution banned the use of Kurdish in official settings and public places. Also in 1924, a law was passed permitting the government to expropriate Kurdish property in order to give it to Turkish speakers who were willing to resettle in the southeast.

Thus not only was Mustafa Kemal's Turkish Republic a highly centralized, secular state, it was a state possessed of a determined Turkish nationalism.[23] This combination produced a vicious cycle wherein continued Kurdish rebellion in the southeast strengthened the Turkish nationalist resolve of the center, which used increasingly repressive measures in an attempt to eradicate the Kurdish problem, which resulted in further Kurdish rebellion. In August 1924 the Koçgiri tribes rebelled once again. In September, some 500 Kurdish officers and soldiers in the Turkish army mutinied at Beyt Şabab. Yet the event that truly galvanized the center occurred in 1925, when Sheikh Said led 15,000 Kurdish tribesmen in a revolt that required 52,000 members of the Turkish army to quell.[24] In McDowall's words, "Sheikh Said's revolt marked the beginning of 'implacable Kemalism' " (1996, 198).

In its wake, central authorities became even more determined to destroy Kurdish ethnic identification and were willing to use considerable force to do so. Though education was one mechanism the regime hoped to use to "reinvent" its Kurdish citizens, it utilized darker tools as well. Foremost among these were operations in which the Turkish armed forces deported Kurdish citizens, expropriating their immovable property and forcing them to resettle in western Turkey, where the majority of the population was Turkish. These policies in turn sparked continuous small-scale revolts and other unrest in the Kurdish southeast throughout the late 1920s.

The response of the center intensified, and the conflict came to a climax in the late 1930s. In 1934, the extent of the center's assimilatory zeal was revealed with the passage of Law 2510, which formally identified areas of Turkey (with non-Turkish majorities) that were to be completely evacuated, their inhabitants resettled in other, Turkish-majority "zones" for the purpose of linguistic and cultural assimilation. The law gave the state full power to carry out these resettlement plans. Its intent was "to disperse the Kurdish population, to areas where it would constitute no more than 5 per cent of the population, thus extinguishing Kurdish identity" (McDowall 1996, 207).

In 1935 the government set out to apply this law in the Dersim region (Tunceli province). Dersim drew the government's focus because it was a "notoriously defiant" area of the republic that had succeeded for more than a half century in frustrating the imposition of central governmental authority (McDowall 1996, 207). Determined to preserve their autonomy, a number of Dersim's tribes launched a rebellion in 1937–38 to resist the state's assault. Ultimately they were defeated by the Turkish army, whose reprisals included the deployment of air force squadrons to bomb the rebels into submission.[25] This would be the last of the confrontations between various Kurdish tribes and the young Kemalist state.

The damage, however, was done. The centralization and secularization of the Turkish state had triggered substantial rebellion among the Kurdish tribes of the southeast. The rebellions jeopardized the mission of centralizing Turkish state builders, driving them to attach an aggressive Turkish nationalist ideology to the new state and to seek to destroy Kurdish identity, which they perceived as a threat to the state. The Turkification campaigns that followed worsened Turkish-Kurdish relations further. Continued Kurdish revolts intensified the center's response. Though by the end of the 1930s those revolts had ended, the brutality of the center's response (sources report the loss of life of many innocents) constituted a bitter backdrop against which Kurdish claims and demands would reappear in the 1960s and 1970s.

One final point remains to be made about the state's Turkish nationalist policy agenda. The Turkification campaigns were implemented largely by the military. "Of the major nineteen military engagements in which the Turkish armed forces participated from 1924 to 1938, all but two were against or connected with efforts to suppress Kurdish rebellions and nationalism" (Olson 1989, 127). As a result, Turkish nationalist ideology came to be most strongly held by the military institution. This fact became a serious obstacle blocking paths to possible Turkish- Kurdish accommodation in later decades.

The Military's Political Shadow

After a hiatus in the 1940s and 1950s, in the 1960s and 1970s Kurdish activists began to confront the state once again. They spoke out against the Kemalist regime's denial of the Kurds' existence and its attempts to make that denial a reality, and they called for the restoration of Kurdish cultural rights. The renewed conflict between the regime and its Kurdish minority worsened over time, occasioning large-scale violence during the 1980s and 1990s, when the PKK launched a sustained guerrilla insurrection in the southeast, initially with the goal of creating an independent Kurdish state. For the past two decades, the political role of the Turkish military has prevented the Turkish regime from finding a workable, long-term solution to the renewed conflict with the Kurds. This is the third institutional feature of the Turkish Republic identified as crucial to the evolution of the Turkish-Kurdish conflict.

The military's political role has its roots in the troubled nature of the transition to democracy that Turkey began in 1950.[26] That is, the military gradually has obtained substantial legal rights to intervene in civilian politics. The Turkish military achieved these rights in the course of three successive, short-lived coups (in 1960, 1971, and 1980) that were launched as "corrective" measures when, in the military's eyes, the behavior of civilian politicians and parties jeopardized the health of the Turkish body politic.[27] On each coup occasion, the military presided over constitutional changes that granted it incrementally more influence in the realm of civilian decision making.

The most important mechanism projecting the military's voice into civilian political affairs is the National Security Council (NSC), a deliberative body composed of top military and civilian officials. Whereas the 1961 constitution conceived the council as a platform enabling the military to voice its opinion on national security matters, constitutional amendments in 1973 augmented the NSC's role to one of making recommendations to the government, while the 1982 constitution dictated that cabinets must give priority consideration to NSC recommendations (Sakallioğlu 1997, 157).[28] Also, until very recently, the number and clout of military NSC members increased at the expense of the body's civilian members. Since 1983, when the military last handed government back to civilian politicians, the NSC has played a formidable, constitutionally sanctioned political role.

The shadow cast by the military over Turkey's civilian politicians was twofold: it had considerable legal power, and the threat constantly loomed that it would carry out yet another coup. This state of affairs had two key consequences for how the Kurdish conflict unfolded. First, it radicalized many Kurds and exacerbated the conflict. Historically the institution most committed to the Turkish nationalist rejection of Kurdish claims, the military ensured that Turkish governments' policy response to the PKK insurrection would be to characterize the Kurdish problem as one of terrorism (rather than minority rights) and to react to the problem exclusively with repression. No Turkish government would entertain the demands and grievances of moderate, nonviolent Kurdish groups or interlocutors. Turkish citizens who publicly recognized the Kurdish nation or suggested that it might be treated differently were prosecuted for advocating separatism and for undermining article 3 of the 1982 constitution, which stated that "The Turkish State, with its territory and nation, is an indivisible entity." The military intended to solve the problem by defeating the PKK on the battlefield.

As the Turkish military response to the PKK's insurrection unfolded, it proved to be extremely destructive, violent, and increasingly arbitrary. In order to deny the guerrillas crucial local intelligence and provisioning support, the government's campaign came to include the evacuation and burning of villages and the destruction of surrounding fields and herds. In its determination to stamp out the PKK, the military allegedly committed widespread human rights abuses and took the lives of innocent noncombatants. Moreover, many sources indicate that the military has turned a blind eye to right-wing, extragovernmental, anti-PKK terrorist groups who have assassinated numerous PKK activists and sympathizers.[29]

With avenues to dialogue with the state blocked and as the brutality and arbitrariness of the military's campaign in the southeast became clear, Turkey's Kurdish population became increasingly radicalized and pro-PKK during the late 1980s and the 1990s (Gürbey 1996, 17; Barkey and Fuller 1998, 45). This is important because in the early years of the conflict, the PKK did not enjoy substantial support in the southeast. It had made a practice of murdering Kurds who were associated with rival organizations or who were loyal to the state. This was a practice that repulsed many, and in 1987 the PKK (wisely) chose to stop it. Afterward, as the authorities' transgressions increased, popular support for the PKK mounted as Kurds concluded that the PKK represented their only hope for positive change. Increased popular support in turn strengthened the PKK's military position by providing its fighters with increased local intelligence, protection, and provisioning.

Second, not only did the military's presence in civilian decision-making processes exacerbate the Kurdish problem, it also prevented Turkey's political parties from taking pragmatic steps to solve the problem. Subsequent to the transition to competitive party politics in 1950, Turkish parties have shown substantial interest in garnering votes in the southeast—an interest that has often led them to entertain possibilities for changes in state policy toward the Kurdish population. As it courted Kurdish votes in the 1950 election campaign, for example, the opposition Democrat Party promised to loosen cultural restrictions and lessen state repression in the southeast. Prior to elections in 1973, RPP leader Bülent Ecevit toured Kurdish regions and promised to pay attention to "the problems of the east" (Gunter 1990, 19). When 1991 election results demonstrated the PKK's popularity,[30] the leaders of the coalition government that subsequently took shape "rushed to the south-east straight after the election," promising to uphold human rights and liberalize troublesome aspects of the anti-PKK campaign (McDowall 1996, 430).

The military's political role, however, has quietly placed a firm limit on party leaders' ability to move Kurdish policy in more creative and accommodating directions. The case of Suleyman Demirel, leader of the center-right True Path Party (DYP) and prime minister of Turkey from 1991 to 1993, is illustrative. Upon becoming prime minister Demirel publicly acknowledged "the Kurdish reality," promised to tend to economic development in the southeast, and

> seemed by 1992 ... ready for some compromises and concessions. But the main impediment to change remained the military. Demirel, a former six-time prime minister twice deposed by the armed forces (in 1971 and in 1980), was unlikely to risk being deposed a third time by opening talks with the PKK. Meanwhile, General Doğan Güres, chief of the general staff, repeatedly vowed to crush the guerrillas (Marcus 1993, 245).

Demirel backed away from his accommodating tone and toed the military's policy line.

When Demirel became president in 1993, Tansu Çiller succeeded him as head of the DYP and as prime minister. Early on, Çiller showed a willingness to consider reconfiguring Turkish policy, proposing among other things that Kurdish-language broadcasts be permitted on state-owned television and that Turkey look to Spain's handling of the Basque issue as a problem-solving model for its conflict with the Kurds. Both Demirel and the military chief of staff rebuked her. Faced with their criticism, she backed off, yielding control over Kurdish policy to the military (Barkey and Fuller 1998, 137–38).[31]

The search for electoral support gives Turkey's political parties significant incentives to take a more open, less repressive policy approach to Kurdish activism. Turkish parties have proved to be capable of quite a lot of pragmatism, and many party leaders have shown an inclination to change the tone of the (non-)debate surrounding Kurdish political claims. But the military has cast a long shadow over the parties. To safeguard their hold on power and to prevent the reoccurrence of a coup, parties repeatedly have deferred to the military's preferences about how to manage the conflict. The shadow of the military thus has been an obstacle to the emergence of a more pragmatic response to the Kurdish community's political claims.

Socioeconomic and International Factors

This essay emphasizes the causal impact of three institutional factors on the origins and evolution of the Turkish-Kurdish conflict: a centralizing state, the assimilationist Turkish nationalism that came to be attached to the state, and the shadow cast by the Turkish military over civilian politicians. Two additional, noninstitutional factors deserve mention, however. These are socioeconomic stimuli and the demonstration effects of the relationship that unfolded between the neighboring Iraqi state and *its* Kurdish minority. While neither is as causally weighty as the institutional factors, both influenced the shape that the conflict took on in the contemporary period (i.e., the leftist PKK insurrection that began in 1984).

Three socioeconomic factors are relevant. First, the provinces of the southeast are undoubtedly Turkey's poorest.[32] In the 1990s, per capita income in the Kurdish provinces was only approximately 40 percent of the national average. Moreover, the gap between living standards in western Turkey and those in the southeast has widened during the past half century. In that time, relative deprivation in the southeast added to the substance of Kurdish political discontent. This could be seen in mass demonstrations that broke out in the southeast in the late 1960s: Bozarslan points out that the demands protestors made (e.g., calls for increased investment and more schools, dispensaries, and infrastructure) concerned civil and social rights rather than ethnicity per se (1992, 99).

Second, the political environment created by the socioeconomic crises that Turkey experienced in the 1960s and 1970s nurtured the emergence of a radical Kurdish movement. Beginning in the 1950s as Turkey industrialized, mass migration from rural to urban areas took place (including Kurdish migration away from the southeast), leading to the emergence of a sizable national urban working class for the first time. Economic growth and job creation did not keep pace with this demographic shift, however, and the result over time was the growth of a large, young, urban population facing an uncertain future. An economic downturn in the 1970s saw many new social forces—labor, students, and unemployed youth—mobilized into a number of radical leftist groups that used violence for their political ends. The PKK's institutional roots lie in this environment. Ideologically and methods-wise, the leftist PKK was a product of the extremism and political violence that characterized Turkey in the late 1960s and 1970s. A majority of the PKK's fighting forces in the 1980s and 1990s were drawn from the ranks of unemployed and underemployed Kurdish youth.

A third socioeconomic circumstance also helped determine that contemporary Kurdish activism would take on a leftist form. In the poor, southeastern, Kurdish-majority provinces of Turkey, social structures largely revolved around very unequal land distribution and labor-repressive agriculture. Large (Kurdish) landowners typically "owned" one or more villages in the sense that the peasants resident in them depended on the landlords for employment and protection. Given the scarcity of local industrial jobs and educational opportunities, those at the bottom of the social ladder had few other options than to remain under the economic, social, and political thumb of their landlords. Those who founded the PKK resented these conditions and set out to change them.

Socioeconomic conditions therefore seem crucial to explaining why the contemporary manifestation of the Turkish-Kurdish conflict took the form it did. Poverty increased discontent in the southeast. A violent political left emerged in Turkey in the 1960s and 1970s. Together with the southeast's oppressive social structure, these factors help to explain why, when Kurdish activists challenged the Turkish state in the contemporary period, these activists were *leftist* activists. When it commenced its insurrection in 1984, the PKK possessed a radical leftist ideology. It sought to separate from Turkey in order to create an independent, socialist Kurdish state in which the power of the "feudal, collaborationist, and comprador" Kurdish large landlords would be broken.[33]

Still, socioeconomic conditions are not the prime causal factor. In order to mobilize support, PKK founder Abdullah Öcalan relied on the litany of Kurdish grievances that stemmed from the consequences of state centralization and the implementation of aggressive Turkish nationalist policies earlier in the century. Also, as was indicated earlier, the PKK would not have grown in strength and popular support had the Turkish military not pushed the government's policy response to the PKK in an unyielding and repressive direction. Measures to improve socioeconomic conditions in the southeast, while they would be welcome and useful, are unlikely to be sufficient to effect successful political accommodation of the Kurds.

The international factor deserving of mention is the impact on Turkish politics of the ongoing struggle between Iraq and its rebellious Kurdish minority. In 1961, Iraq's Kurds launched a revolt against that country's young republican regime. In 1970, Iraq and its Kurdish population signed an agreement that was to provide the latter with autonomy. The agreement not withstanding, the Iraqi-Kurdish conflict would prove to be protracted and ugly. The Iraqi Kurds' persistence in challenging Baghdad and their (admittedly qualified) victories—including the achievement of semiautonomous status following Iraq's defeat in the Gulf War—have resonated with Turkey's Kurds, emboldening them to challenge Ankara and to make demands for autonomy and independence.

Paradoxically, in the late 1980s and the 1990s, Iraq's conflict with its Kurds contributed to a healthier political climate surrounding the Kurdish question in Turkey. On two occasions, the first in 1988 and the second in 1991, Iraqi Kurds fled into Turkey seeking refuge from the regime of Saddam Hussein. In both instances, Ankara was forced to provide assistance to the refugees and to condemn Baghdad for its treatment of its Kurdish citizens. These events have forced Turkish leaders to acknowledge publicly the existence of the Kurdish minority. Given that, until the 1990s, much of officialdom actively denied the presence of an ethnic Kurdish minority within Turkey's borders, this represents an important step forward along the road to political accommodation (Bozarslan 1992, 106; Barkey and Fuller 1997, 66).

Would Changes in Political Institutions Matter?

The Turkish Republic is and has always been a centralized, unitary state. During the 1990s, however, many actors openly began to rethink the desirability and even the viability of the status quo. Prolonged, violent conflict pitting the Turkish state against its Kurdish minority population has triggered unprecedented public questioning of current arrangements.[34] The conflict has inflicted an enormous human and financial toll on Turkey. It also has harmed Turkey's reputation internationally. As the costs mounted, nearly every decision maker whose actions bear on the future course of the conflict publicly entertained the proposition that improved management of the Turkish-Kurdish cleavage will require some degree of institutional reform of the state. Many spoke of solutions involving decentralized, autonomous, or federal arrangements.

This essay has argued that although socioeconomic and international factors have shaped the Turkish-Kurdish conflict in important ways, the shape of state and regime institutions lies at the heart of the conflict. It follows that prospects for managing the conflict more peacefully will depend on altering the ways in which the Turkish center relates to its Kurdish periphery. The following considers the set of politically realistic reforms that are likely to contribute to more successful accommodation. These include demilitarizing the conflict, creating political space within which civilian politicians can consider alternative approaches, granting Kurds significant linguistic and cultural concessions, and devolving some decision-making authority to the local level. More radical alterations in the center-periphery relationship (e.g., autonomy or federalism) are politically unrealistic. Indeed, no change in the status quo will be feasible if Turkish decision makers believe it will lead to a renewed, strong separatist movement.[35] The essay thus closes with an assessment of the likelihood that a more accommodating approach to the Kurds will encourage secessionist tendencies, concluding in the negative.

The first step toward meaningful reform of the center-periphery relationship would be to end the government's militarized approach to managing the conflict.[36] This reform implicitly points to another that must also take place. The shadow cast over civilian politicians by the military must be shortened, allowing the former more political space in which to entertain new approaches to managing the Kurdish question. To shorten the military's shadow, Turkey's parties will have to cooperate with one another to reduce the military's political prerogatives. Unfortunately, events of the past half century suggest that the parties are not likely to do so anytime soon. After all, it was unstable coalition governments and other regrettable consequences of Turkish parties' behavior that opened the door for the coups through which the military originally obtained its prerogatives.

Still, there is reason to believe that the future will not necessarily look like the past. In December 1999, the European Union (EU) agreed to name Turkey as a candidate for membership. To become a member, Turkey will have to reform its political economy to conform with key EU membership criteria, including demonstrating stable democratic institutions and the rule of law. This implies eliminating the military's political role. Importantly, all but one of Turkey's six major parties support EU accession (Öniş 2000). Over the medium to long term, therefore, the material, political, and psychic rewards of EU membership could act as a force that coaxes Turkey's parties through the cooperative maneuvers that will be required if the military is to be eased out of its current position of influence.[37] Three hopeful precedents along these lines—wherein Turkey's parties mustered sufficient consensus to amend the constitution in ways that further democratized the political system—were set in 1995, 1999, and 2001.[38]

What new policy approaches should civilian politicians and party leaders be considering? Minimally, the state's attachment to an unyielding Turkish nationalist ideology will have to be softened, perhaps becoming reconfigured to emphasize civic unity rather than a mythical, shared Turkish national identity. Practically, this entails granting Kurds substantial cultural and political rights. These include the right to speak Kurdish, to develop Kurdish languages and culture, to produce Kurdish-language broadcasts and publications, to educate (privately, at least) in Kurdish, and to form political parties whose platforms are devoted to Kurdish affairs. The EU requires its members to protect their minority populations, thus Turkey will have to implement such reforms if it wishes to become a member. Importantly, with an eye toward earning EU approval, in October 2001 Turkish politicians amended the constitution in such a way as to allow the use of Kurdish languages in broadcasts and published materials.[39]

Because cultural and political concessions do not address the ways in which state centralization has contributed to the Turkish-Kurdish problem, however, these reforms are unlikely to suffice to ensure more peaceful future management of the conflict. It was the rise of a powerful, centralizing Turkish state that first spawned violent conflict between the state and its Kurdish-inhabited southeast territory in the 1920s and 1930s. Subsequently, the fact that Ankara appoints all governors, civil servants, security officials, and nearly all administrators to all of Turkey's provinces has, in the southeast, alienated the local population from those who govern them.[40] The way in which the state prosecuted the war against the PKK exacerbated this alienation. To alleviate resentment in the region and begin building Kurdish confidence in the state administration, some significant degree of decision-making authority (e.g., in the areas of health, education, and cultural policy) will have to be devolved to locally elected officials and bodies.[41] In addition, policies designed to recruit and appoint more local residents to civil service bureaucracies and security apparatuses on the ground in the southeast would be helpful.

How politically feasible would these reforms be? What can be said about the levels of popular support that exist for these proposed remedies to the conflict? Unfortunately, because the Kurdish question is not yet debated either widely or frankly in the Turkish political arena, almost no data exist to answer these questions. Turkish political elites began to acknowledge the Kurdish issue publicly only in the early 1990s. Throughout that decade, citizens who spoke out about the conflict were punished routinely by the authorities. The topic remains taboo, and little to no public opinion data have been collected regarding citizens' views about the conflict and how best to resolve it.

One exception to this is a 1995 study published by the Turkish Union of Chambers of Commerce and Industry based on interviews with over 1,000 self-identified Turkish Kurds.[42] One of the questions posed concerned the types of political reforms for the amelioration of the conflict that respondents supported. In order of most to least drastic, 11 percent favored the creation of an independent Kurdish state, 36.1 percent favored a federal solution, 11 percent favored granting "autonomous" status to Kurdish regions, and 16.6 percent favored implementing local administrative reforms in Kurdish areas (TOBB 1995, 40).[43]

Even less is known about the preferences of the non-Kurdish majority of Turkey's citizens. To the author's knowledge, no recent public opinion polls have probed Turks' views about how to solve the problem. Thus, to generate a very general view of the political landscape, Table 14.1 outlines the policy solution that each of Turkey's six major parties might be expected to support[44] and reports the parties' performances in the 1999 general election.

As Table 14.1 suggests, proposals for power devolution beyond decentralization are unrealistic. In Gunter's words, "to most Turks … a federation would be an anathema, a major way station along the road to separatism" (1997, 134). Fear of secession and an insistence on preserving Turkey's existence as a unitary state are deeply embedded in the policy perspectives of military and civilian decision makers as well as much of the general public. For this reason, proposals for autonomy for the southeast or for a federal arrangement between Turks and Kurds will be politically unworkable.

Because the fear of secession is powerful and will constrain the universe of feasible policy change in Turkey, it is important to ask whether *any* reform of the relationship between center and periphery is likely to increase the probability that a powerful movement for Kurdish secession will emerge. The literature on federalism tells us that, depending on a set of intervening variables, devolving power either can help states manage ethnic conflict better, or can make matters worse, leading to more strident calls

Table 14.1 Policy Prescriptions and Party Support, Turkey, 1999

Policy Prescription	Parties in Support[a]	Parties' Performance in the 1999 General Election (in percent)
Status quo/policy of military repression in sutheast	MHP	18.1
Repress terrorists but develop the southeast socioeconomically	DSP	22.3
Augment Kurds' civil and political rights	DYP, ANAP	12.1, 13.3 (Total 25.4)
Augment Kurds' civil and political rights, and decentralize	FP, CHP	15.5, 8.9 (Total 24.4)
Turkish-Kurdish federal state	None	n/a
Allow Kurdish areas to secede from Turkey	None	n/a

[a]The MHP is the Nationalist Action Party, a right-wing Turkish nationalist party. The DSP, or Democratic Left Party, and the CHP, the Republican People's Party, are Turkey's two, main, center-left parties. The DYP, or True Path Party, and ANAP, the Motherland Party, are Turkey's two, main center-right parties. The FP, or Virtue Party, was Turkey's Islamist party and successor to Necmettin Erbakan's Refah (Welfare) Party. The FP was banned by Turkey's Constitutional Court in June 2001 and has been succeeded by the Felicity Party.

for secession and independence. This literature suggests that prospects for secession in the case of the Turkish-Kurdish conflict are slim, both in the short and the long terms.

In the short term, fears of secession would seem to be unfounded for two reasons. First, no major Kurdish figure or group is calling for secession. Over the course of the 1990s, as global and domestic political trends moved against it, the PKK—long the most important of the radical Kurdish groups—steadily moderated its stated political goals. While the PKK was avowedly secessionist in 1984, by the early 1990s it was calling for a federal solution to the conflict. Today, with its leader in prison, PKK objectives appear to have become even less far-reaching, emphasizing cultural concessions and the need to strengthen Turkey's democracy.

Second, available data suggest that most of Turkey's Kurds do not want to secede. McDowall (1996, 440) cites a 1992 poll that showed that 70 percent of Kurds interviewed stated that they did not want independence from Turkey.[45] Rouleau (1993) argues that most observers believe that granting Turkey's Kurds normal democratic civil and political rights would likely settle the violent conflict. Finally, the 1995 Turkish Union of Chambers of Commerce and Industry study cited earlier found that of those

Kurds who answered the question (concerning their preferred political solution to the conflict), only 12 percent wanted an independent Kurdish state (TOBB 1995, 40).

This positive short-term prognosis can only be partially reassuring to Turks concerned about secession, however, because the potential secession-fueling dynamics unleashed by power devolution schemes may take time to appear. Still, there are at least three reasons to argue that decentralizing reform need not create a slippery slope toward secession in the Turkish case over the long term.

First, if the Turkish government turned away from the confrontational policies that have encouraged diverse Kurds to find common political ground, the considerable divisions present among Turkey's Kurds likely would resurface. As described earlier, the Kurdish community manifests important religious, linguistic, socioeconomic, and political heterogeneity.[46] Indeed, Kurds did not speak with one political voice in the 1980s and 1990s. One of the PKK's main organizational rivals, Kemal Burkay's Socialist Party of Kurdistan (PSK), rejected the use of armed struggle and refused to join the Kurdish Parliament in Exile (KPE) that was established under the influence of the PKK in 1995. In the 1990s, Kurds voted not only for pro-Kurdish political parties but also for left and right establishment parties as well as for Islamist parties. Bozarslan (1996, 148) argues that intra-Kurd political pluralism would become more pronounced in a liberalized political environment. There are thus serious reasons to doubt that Kurdish elites would find themselves united in support of a secessionist—or any other—policy.

Second, Turkey's party system shows signs that it would be able to integrate the southeast's Kurdish electorate into the political system rather than encourage the formation of a Kurdish nationalist party that mobilized regional resources in the direction of secession.[47] Turkish electoral law has generally required parties to organize in half or more of all provinces in order to be eligible to compete in national elections. As a

Table 14.2 Regional Differences in Party Support, Turkey, 1991–1999

Party	1991 National		1994 Local		1995 National		1999 National	
	Turkey	Kurdish provinces	Turkey	Kurdish provinces	Turkey	Kurdish provinces	Turkey	Kurdish provinces
SHP	20.8	33.7	13.6	14.2	–	–	–	–
CHP	–	–	4.6	2.8	10.7	5.7	8.9	6.9
DSP	10.8	2.8	8.8	0.9	14.6	3.2	22.3	5.2
ANAP	24.0	22.5	21.0	19.0	19.7	16.3	13.3	11.1
DYP	27.0	20.8	21.4	22.1	19.2	16.2	12.1	13.8
RP/VP	16.9	16.6	19.1	27.3	21.4	27.2	15.5	18.6
MHP	–	–	8.0	5.3	8.2	5.8	18.1	9.2
HADEP	–	–	–	–	4.2	19.5	4.7	22.5

result, Turkish parties are national parties, and many have established a substantial presence in the southeast. Table 14.2 shows the performance of Turkey's major parties both nationally as well as in the Kurdish-inhabited southeastern provinces in four recent elections.[48]

In the 1995 elections, the explicitly pro-Kurdish HADEP Party won only 19.5 percent of the vote in Kurdish provinces, while the two mainstream center-right parties (ANAP, DYP) each took 16 percent of the vote, and the Islamist Welfare Party (RP) took 27.2 percent.[49] While it is true that the electoral fortunes of ANAP, DYP, and the Islamist Virtue Party (VP) declined in the Kurdish provinces in 1999, these declines mirrored national-level political losses for those parties.[50] They remain well-positioned to compete effectively in the southeast. If the Turkish government were to take a more accommodating approach to Kurdish demands, support for the pro-Kurdish HADEP Party might weaken and the center-right establishment parties could improve their performance. In other words, it is far from inevitable that Kurds will vote en masse for Kurdish parties in the future.

Finally, in the foreseeable future, the international environment is not one that will be friendly to the possibility of Kurdish secession from Turkey. Syria, Iraq, and Iran would not look kindly on the formation of an independent Kurdish state, for such a turn of events might motivate their own Kurdish minority communities to press political claims more vociferously. Turkey, Syria, and Iran met often during the mid-1990s "to consider how to meet the common threat of a Kurdish state in northern Iraq" (Gunter 1997, 96). Would-be secessionists will have to contemplate the risk of reprisals from these states. The probable international economic ramifications of secession would also seem to be unpalatable. Secession would create an independent Kurdish state with little industry and few natural resources, surrounded by hostile neighbors. If, on the other hand, the southeast remains part of Turkey, the Kurds preserve their access to the large Turkish market, a market that is likely to eventually become part of the EU.

Conclusion

This essay argues that the shape of state and regime institutions is the primary causal force that has molded the conflict between the central Turkish state and its Kurdish periphery in the southeast. State centralization, the emergence of an assimilationist Turkish nationalism, and the political shadow cast over civilian actors by the military created, exacerbated, and prolonged the antagonism between center and periphery. On the basis of this analysis, the essay asserts that prospects for more successful accommodation of the Turkish-Kurdish cleavage hinge on implementing several institutional reforms. Specifically, Turkish decision makers must shorten the military's political shadow, abandon the policy of meeting Kurdish claims only with repression, reconfigure the content of Turkish nationalism so that it does not negate Kurdish identity, grant Kurds political and cultural rights, and devolve some decision-making powers to the local level.

More radical alterations in the center-periphery relationship, such as proposals for Kurdish autonomy or for a Turkish-Kurdish federation, are politically unrealistic because they trigger deep-seated Turkish fears about the possibility of fueling a Kurdish secessionist movement. The essay argues that the reforms it advocates should *not* create secessionist momentum because secession does not appear to be the preference of most Kurds, because diversity within the Kurdish community should preclude effective collective action, because Turkey's party system shows signs that it could successfully integrate the Kurdish electorate into national politics, and because the international political and economic environment is one that would be unfriendly to a secessionist Kurdish state.

NOTES

I wish to thank the following individuals for their comments on the original draft of this essay: Nancy Bermeo, Ugo Amoretti, Henri Barkey, Larry Diamond, the other participants of the *Divided or United* workshop, Reşat Kasaba, Hakan Yavuz, and James Meyer.

1. These are Freedom House's 1999–2000 designations, taken from www.freedomhouse.org. The scores correspond to a scale of 1 to 7, with 1 being the designation earned by the world's freest countries, and 7 that earned by those deemed least free. Freedom House cites the Turkish authorities' actions vis-à-vis Islamist political activists as the other main detractor from Turkey's potential rankings.

2. Turkey's population contains small numbers of numerous other ethnic groups, including Albanians, Greeks, Arabs, Circassians, and Laz. For a detailed cataloguing of Turkey's ethnic makeup, see Andrews 1989.

3. Turkey's other significant minority population is its Alevi community. Whereas the religious orientation of most Turks is Sunni Islam, Alevism is a branch of Shi'ite Islam. Alevis make up between 15 and 20 percent of Turkey's population, spanning both the Turkish and Kurdish ethnic groups. The Alevi minority and its preferences impact Turkish party politics in important ways, but the community is geographically dispersed and does not make territorially based political demands or claims.

4. In addition, approximately half a million Kurds have settled in Western Europe.

5. Most Turks belong to the Hanefite school, while most Kurds belong to the Shafii school.

6. Further adding to the difficulties of united political action is the fact that the Middle

East's Kurds inhabit harsh, mountainous physical terrain that is geographically remote from the capitals of the political units that hold sovereignty over them.

7. These include the KUK (Kurdistan National Liberators), the PPKK (Peşeng-Kurdistan Vanguard Workers' Party), Rızgari (Kurdistan Liberation Party), Ala Rızgari, and Kawa. For background on the leaders and histories of the numerous Kurdish organizations in Turkey, as well as a very helpful "family tree" that maps their emergence, transformations, and splinters, see Ballı 1991.

8. Civil peace was largely the result of government actions taken during the period of military rule that Turkey experienced between 1980 and 1983.

9. This occurred under the auspices of the Village Guard program. In villages that were dominated by participating Kurdish elites, the Turkish government armed and paid salaries to young Kurdish men who were charged with keeping PKK activists out of the villages. By 1996, 67,000 so-called village guards were in the employ of the state.

10. Turkey's political system took on the characteristics described here from the founding of the Republic in 1923 until 1960, when major constitutional changes were undertaken in response to perceived flaws in the system.

11. For more details on political arrangements during this period, see İnalcık 1964, Shaw 1969, and Karpat 1972.

12. Under the tax-farming status quo, the *âyan* pocketed a considerable amount of surplus, which represented the difference between the sum they paid the central government for their farms and the total revenue they were able to collect from the Ottoman subjects who resided in their farm territories.

13. For the masses, centralization's main impact was to lessen significantly the role provincial elites had played as mediators between them and the state. For Ottoman subjects under the control of particularly rapacious *âyan*, this came as a relief. However, Ottoman scholars concur that most of the *âyan* had positive relations with the Ottoman subjects under their jurisdiction, and that they portrayed themselves to the masses as figures that protected them from a rapacious central government. These subjects likely were ambivalent at best about centralization. Explicit mass *reaction* to centralization did not occur until the 1920s, 1930s, and 1940s, when the center's tax collectors and rural police intruded increasingly directly and painfully into the masses' daily lives. Kemal's hostility to public manifestations of Islamic piety further alienated the masses. They registered their discontent by supporting a series of opposition parties that attempted to break the power monopoly held by Kemal's Republican People's Party.

14. For a fuller discussion of this phenomenon and arguments about its repercussions for the development of Turkish democracy, see Angrist 2000.

15. For more details on the provincial administrative council system, see Shaw 1969, Davison 1966, and Shaw and Shaw 1977.

16. At its zenith, the empire had controlled much of North Africa, the Arabian peninsula, the Fertile Crescent, and southeastern Europe. By the turn of the twentieth century, it had lost much of its European lands to a rising tide of nationalism, foreign intervention, and secession, and its North African holdings to European colonization.

17. Among the most noteworthy unfolded in 1880, when Shaykh Ubayd Allah led a rebellion that at its peak included 20,000 fighters, with the goal of forming an autonomous Kurdish principality that was loyal to the Ottoman sultan but free from the grip of centrally appointed Ottoman officials. McDowall (1996, 53–56) notes that many regard Ubayd Allah as "the first great

Kurdish nationalist" but concludes that, "while using the vocabulary of contemporary European nationalism," Ubayd Allah more probably was seeking to reestablish local control over Kurdish territory.

18. Religious figures were receptive to this movement aimed at mobilizing opposition to the center in part because the center had been pursuing secularization, thus threatening their social and political stature.

19. The patronage resources available to the new Turkish state-in-the-making helped Kemal in his attempt to recruit Kurdish leaders to his cause. For example, the Kemalist regime could appoint local Kurdish chiefs as members of the new parliament. The state also could help Kurds acquire secure and legal title to property left behind in southeastern Anatolia by fleeing Armenians during and immediately after World War I (Olson 1989, 36–37).

20. The Kurds of the Dersim region were a largely Alevi, Kurmanci-speaking subset of the Kurdish population that lived in the northwesternmost area of the Kurdish southeast (present-day Tunceli province)

21. Kemalist Turkish nationalism is somewhat difficult to characterize. It was a qualified civic nationalism to the extent that Turkish constitutions have defined "Turks" as all the citizens of Turkey. In addition, nonethnically Turkish citizens who identified themselves as Turks, spoke Turkish, and assimilated into the official Turkish culture were not discriminated against. Turkish nationalism was an ethnic nationalism in that it glorified (and, indeed, manufactured "truths" about) the Turkish race's language and history. Turkish nationalism was also an ethnic nationalism in its absolute intolerance of citizens' self-identification as any other ethnicity. Kurds were the primary victims of state repression carried out in the name of constructing a single, indivisible Turkish "nation."

22. International actors allowed Turkey this denial out of expediency and in light of the Kemalists' success in repulsing Greek, Armenian, and French invasions. Kemal's victories demonstrated that his government was the preeminent political authority in Anatolia. Britain's interests were especially pivotal. The United Kingdom sought to achieve stability along the northern border of its Iraqi protectorate (a region inhabited by Kurds and where Turks had been fomenting unrest). Between 1921 and 1923, the United Kingdom had contemplated helping Kurds revolt against Kemal with a view to establishing an independent Kurdish state on Iraq's northern border. As Kemal's victories showed his regional authority in increasingly clear light, the United Kingdom decided to negotiate a deal directly with Kemal as the surest way to achieve a stable border. In return for border peace between Turkey and Iraq, the United Kingdom ceased insisting upon some form of political autonomy for the Kurds. For more details, see McDowall 1996, 138–43.

23. For other statements as to the causal significance of Turkish nationalism for the Kurdish conflict, see Gunter 1990, 126, and Gürbey 1996, 10.

24. Sheikh Said was a religious leader who commanded the loyalty of a significant number of Zaza-speaking, Sunni Muslim, Kurdish tribes, mainly west of Lake Van and north of the city of Diyarbakır. Notably, most of the Kurmanci-speaking, Alevi Kurdish tribes of the Dersim region (present-day Tunceli province) did not join in the revolt.

25. For more on the Dersim uprising, see Watts 2000.

26. For the first two decades following the founding of the Turkish Republic in 1924, Mustafa Kemal and his successors ruled the country through a dictatorial single party, the Republican People's Party (RPP). The RPP faced substantial and near-constant opposition, however, and in

the late 1940s it yielded to pressures for political pluralization. In 1950 the opposition Democrat Party (DP) won free and fair elections and was allowed to take power.

27. In 1960 the army moved against the ruling Democrat Party, which, in the late 1950s as its electoral support steadily eroded, began to clamp down on democratic freedoms and civil liberties, backtracking on the democratic bargain that had allowed it to come to power in the first place. The military interventions of 1971 and 1980 came on the heels of widespread political violence and the inability of Turkey's increasingly fragmented and ideologically polarized party system to combat it.

28. In many other respects as well, the 1982 constitution bears the military's political stamp. It outlaws all activities deemed threatening to three fundamental principles that organize the Turkish political community: republicanism, secularism, and Turkish nationalism. Article 4 prohibits the amendment of articles 1–3, in which these principles are set out. Practical effects of the constitution included banning the Kurdish language and significantly restricting the freedom of speech, press and media freedoms, political party and union activities, and associational life. Apart from the nonamendability of articles 1–3, however, procedures for amending the constitution were not particularly restrictive. Indeed, in 1995, a set of constitutional amendments was passed that liberalized the conditions under which parties, unions, and associations could operate.

29. For more details, see Gunter 1997, 68–73.

30. In this election, candidates of the first pro-Kurdish political party, the People's Labour Party (HEP), won a majority of seats in Kurdish provinces. The HEP was understood to be a party that was sympathetic to the PKK.

31. Many others have noted this phenomenon, including Bozarslan 1996. The same pattern would be repeated when Necmettin Erbakan, leader of the (now-outlawed) Islamist Refah Party, became prime minister in 1996. For details, see Gunter 1997, 87.

32. The reasons for this are many and include their remoteness and isolation; the destruction of the region's Armenian communities early in the century—communities that had accounted for a significant portion of the southeast's entrepreneurial middle class (McDowall 1996, 202); the fact that Kurds with capital tended to invest it in western Turkey, where the expected returns were greater; and governmental neglect.

33. The quote is an excerpt from a PKK program as published in Gunter 1990, 59. Kurdish landlords perceived the PKK as a serious threat to their position, and as a result many cooperated with the Turkish authorities in combating the PKK through the Village Guard program.

34. Published examples include the study on the Kurdish question commissioned by TÜSES, the Turkish Foundation for Social, Economic, and Political Research (Gürsel 1996). The report on Turkish democratization published by TÜSİAD, Turkey's primary businessmen's association, includes a section that outlines suggested reforms designed to ameliorate the Kurdish conflict (TÜSİAD 1997). For a Kurdish perspective, see the proceedings of a conference organized by the Istanbul Kurdish Institute (Istanbul Kürt Enstitüsü 1996).

35. Though the PKK initially sought secession, it ratcheted down its political demands in the 1990s, stating that it sought to form a Turkish-Kurdish federation instead.

36. At the time, the February 1999 capture of PKK leader Öcalan appeared to make such a turn of events less likely. Prior to his capture, the war's mounting costs had contributed to a growing consensus that a military "solution" to the conflict did not exist. Even the military had shown signs of acknowledging this. When captured, however, Öcalan instructed his cadres to desist from

further attacks inside Turkey. The latter complied, significantly reducing the intensity of armed conflict in the southeast. This hiatus in the violence has allowed hardliners within the Turkish military and political establishments to claim victory for the militarized policy and resist reforms aimed at more substantially accommodating Turkey's Kurdish community. Because the fundamental issues driving the Turkish-Kurdish conflict have yet to be addressed, however, the conflict will continue, as should the search for workable political accommodation.

37. This said, one should not underestimate the challenges involved. The five parties that support EU accession do so for very different reasons, reasons that reveal the depth of the policy gulfs that separate them. The center-left parties believe that EU membership will strengthen and defend Turkey's secular foundations, particularly against the perceived threats from Islamist politicians. The center-right parties are most interested in the commercial and business opportunities that EU membership holds out. The Islamist Virtue Party (and the pro-Kurdish HADEP, a seventh, marginal party) hope that EU membership would force Turkey to protect the civil and political rights of citizens who have Islamist or Kurdish sympathies—rights that often are currently denied.

Turkey's ties to NATO, by contrast, do not appear to offer the kinds of incentives and pressures for constructive reforms that the prospect of EU membership does. Turkey is already a NATO member, and has been since the early 1950s. While this is counted among the reasons why the Turkish military never directly held power for very long during its three twentieth-century coups, NATO tolerated the indirect influence the military has wielded over politics during the 1980s and 1990s. Analysts of Turkey's possible future political trajectories do not invoke NATO as a source of pressure for change.

38. The 1995 amendments substantially widened individuals' and groups' civil and political liberties and made some changes to Turkey's antiterror law. It was passed at least in part in order to persuade the European Parliament to ratify the agreement bringing Turkey into Customs Union with the EU. The 1999 amendment removed military judges from Turkey's state security courts' three-judge panels. In October 2001, Turkey's parliament and president approved a package of constitutional reforms that included altering the composition of the NSC such that civilian members would outnumber military members 9 to 5. Many see this as a first step toward limiting the military's influence on the council.

39. Critics who believe this amendment does not go far enough point out that the state retains the ability to ban Kurdish broadcasts if national security or public safety is deemed threatened. In the meantime, education in Kurdish remains prohibited, and the state prosecutor's office is working to have the pro-Kurdish HADEP Party closed down.

40. See Barkey and Fuller 1998, 197–98, for a more detailed discussion of state centralization in Turkey.

41. Interestingly, many Turkish politicians have been calling for nationwide decentralizing reforms, not as a solution to the Kurdish conflict, but instead as a remedy for more general problems associated with the extremely centralized nature of the Turkish state. Öniş's investigation of the parties' programs going into the 1999 general elections revealed six of seven parties to be "strongly in favor of" decentralization, with the position of the seventh characterized as "mixed" (2000, 297).

42. It should be noted that this report has come in for significant criticism. Due to the sensitive nature of the issue domestically, the criticisms of some have been less dispassionate than that of others (see Turgut 1996 for a sample of the former, and Sakallıoğlu 1996 for an example of the

latter). Many question the accuracy of the report's empirical findings and diagnoses of the problem. Still, it is the only source of its kind, and, for that reason, its results are noted here.

43. The total number of respondents was 1,267. 5.4 percent said no solution existed to the problem; 10.1 percent answered in a category called "other"; and 9.8 percent did not answer the question at all. The results need to be treated with caution, for the study's authors note that follow-up interviews revealed that respondents had widely varying understandings of what the terms *federalism* and *autonomy* meant. For example, many respondents failed to offer accurate definitions of federalism, instead describing a situation in which the Turkish government simply allowed Kurds more freedom and autonomy in living their daily lives (TOBB 1995, 41).

44. These characterizations are based on public statements made by party leaders during the late 1980s and the 1990s. The roughness and indirect nature of this measure needs to be stressed. Many of these parties include members whose views on the Kurdish matter are not consonant with the public statements of their leaders. In addition, the Turkish political class has never seriously entertained a change from the policy dictated by the military. Thus, party leaders' statements have been made in an atmosphere in which leaders know that they will not have to follow through with action. Still, the political climate has been such that any public statements contrary to the status quo can be politically costly, thus the statements may represent to some significant extent party leaders' true preferences.

45. Indicative of the depth of secession fears among Turks, however, is the poll's finding that 89 percent of the Turks interviewed stated that they believed Kurds wanted independence.

46. Barkey and Fuller aptly point out that the side-taking necessitated by the manner in which the state-PKK war unfolded has further divided Kurdish society in the southeast (1998, 43).

47. For helpful discussions of the relationships between party systems and the viability of federalism, see Stepan 1999, Ordeshook 1996, and Ordeshook and Shvetsova 1997.

48. Data for the 1991, 1994, and 1995 elections were taken from Kirişci and Winrow 1997, 142. The 1999 data were calculated by the author, who is grateful to Ali Çarkoğlu for sharing his personal data set of raw 1999 election results broken down by province. The author attempted to match as closely as possible Kirişci and Winrow's methodology. The latter counted 18 provinces as "Kurdish" in their 1995 results. The author reports results for 17 of those 18 provinces in the 1999 "Kurdish" column. These are Adıyaman, Ağrı, Bingöl, Bitlis, Diyarbakır, Elazığ, Erzincan, Hakkarı, Malatya, Mardin, Muş, Tunceli, Şanlıurfa, Van, Batman, Sırnak, and İğdir.

49. Moreover, in the same election, HADEP did not successfully attract the votes of Kurdish émigrés in western Turkey, who tended to vote for Refah instead.

50. ANAP and DYP suffered from uninspiring and scandal-plagued leaders and corruption charges. The performance of the Islamist Party suffered in 1999 in part because, in the wake of the state's banning of the Refah Party, many voters believed its successor Virtue Party would meet the same fate.

REFERENCES

Andrews, Peter Alford, ed. 1989. *Ethnic Groups in the Republic of Turkey.* Wiesbaden: Dr. Ludwig Reichert Verlag.
Angrist, Michele. 2000. Political Parties and Regime Formation in the Middle East: Turkish Democratization in Comparative Perspective. Ph.D. diss., Princeton University.

Ballı, Rafet. 1991. *Kürt Dosyası.* Istanbul: Cem Yayınevi.

Barkey, Henri J., and Graham E. Fuller. 1997. Turkey's Kurdish Question: Critical Turning Points and Missed Opportunities. *Middle East Journal* 51, no. 1:59–79.

———. 1998. *Turkey's Kurdish Question.* Lanham, Md.: Rowman and Littlefield.

Bozarslan, Hamit. 1988. Les révoltes kurdes en Turquie Kémaliste (quelques aspects). *Guerres mondiales et conflits contemporains* 38, no. 151: 21–36.

———. 1992. Political Aspects of the Kurdish Problem in Contemporary Turkey. In *The Kurds: A Contemporary Overview,* ed. Philip G. Kreyenbroek and Stefan Sperl, 95–114. London: Routledge.

———. 1996. Political Crisis and the Kurdish Issue in Turkey. In *The Kurdish Nationalist Movement in the 1990s: Its Impact on Turkey and the Middle East,* ed. Robert Olson, 135–53. Lexington: University of Kentucky Press.

Constitution of the Republic of Turkey: Law No. 2709 of 7 November 1982 As Amended to Law No. 3361 of 17 May 1987. 1994. In *Constitutions of the Countries of the World,* ed. Albert P. Blaustein and Gisbert H. Flanz. Dobbs Ferry, N.Y.: Oceana.

Davison, Roderic H. 1966. The Advent of the Principle of Representation in the Government of the Ottoman Empire. In *Beginnings of Modernization in the Middle East,* ed. William R. Polk and Richard L. Chambers, 93–108. Chicago: University of Chicago Press.

Gunter, Michael M. 1990. *The Kurds in Turkey: A Political Dilemma.* Boulder: Westview.

———. 1997. *The Kurds and the Future of Turkey.* New York: St. Martin's.

Gürbey, Gülistan. 1996. The Development of the Kurdish Nationalist Movement in Turkey Since the 1980s. In *The Kurdish Nationalist Movement in the 1990s: Its Impact on Turkey and the Middle East,* ed. Robert Olson, 9–37. Lexington: University of Kentucky Press.

Gürsel, Seyfettin, et al. 1996. *Türkiye'nin Kürt Sorunu.* Istanbul: Türkiye Sosyal Ekonomik Siyasal Araştırmalar Vakfı.

İnalcık, Halil. 1964. The Nature of "Traditional" Society: Turkey. In *Political Modernization in Japan and Turkey,* ed. Robert E. Ward and Dankwart A. Rustow, 42–63. Princeton: Princeton University Press.

Istanbul Kürt Enstitüsü. 1996. *Kürt Sorunu ve Demokratik Çözüm Önerileri.* Istanbul: Avesta Yayınları.

Karpat, Kemal H. 1972. The Transformation of the Ottoman State, 1789–1908. *International Journal of Middle Eastern Studies* 3:243–81.

Kirişci, Kemal, and Gareth M. Winrow. 1997. *The Kurdish Question and Turkey: An Example of a Trans-state Ethnic Conflict.* London: Frank Cass.

Marcus, Aliza. 1993. Turkey's Kurds After the Gulf War: A Report from Turkey's Southeast. In *A People Without a Country: The Kurds and Kurdistan,* trans. Michael Pallis; ed. Gerard Chaliand, 238–47. London: Zed.

McDowall, David. 1996. *A Modern History of the Kurds.* London: I. B. Tauris.

Olson, Robert. 1989. *The Emergence of Kurdish Nationalism and the Sheikh Said Rebellion, 1880–1925.* Austin: University of Texas Press.

Ordeshook, Peter C. 1996. Russia's Party System: Is Russian Federalism Viable? *Post-Soviet Affairs* 12, no. 3:195–217.

Ordeshook, Peter C., and Olga Shvetsova. 1997. Federalism and Constitutional Design. *Journal of Democracy* 8. no. 1:27–42.

Öniş, Ziya. 2000. Neoliberalization, Globalization and the Democracy Paradox: The Turkish General Elections of 1999. *Journal of International Affairs* 54, no. 1:283–306.

Özbudun, Ergun. 1976. *Social Change and Political Participation in Turkey.* Princeton: Princeton University Press.

Rouleau, Eric. 1993. The Challenges to Turkey. *Foreign Affairs* 72, no. 5:110–26.

Sakallıoğlu, Ümit Cizre. 1996. Historicizing the Present and Problematizing the Future of the Kurdish Problem: A Critique of the *TOBB* Report on the Eastern Question. New *Perspectives on Turkey* 14 (spring):1–22.

———. 1997. The Anatomy of the Turkish Military's Political Autonomy. *Comparative Politics* (January):151–66.

Shaw, Stanford J. 1969. The Origins of Representative Government in the Ottoman Empire: An Introduction to the Provincial Councils, 1839–1876. In *New York University Near Eastern Round Table I, 1967–1968,* ed. R. Bayly Winder. New York: New York University.

Shaw, Stanford J., and Ezel Kural Shaw. 1977. *History of the Ottoman Empire and Modern Turkey,* Volume II: *Reform, Revolution, and Republic: The Rise of Modern Turkey, 1808–1975.* Cambridge: Cambridge University Press.

Stepan, Alfred. 1999. Federalism and Democracy: Beyond the U.S. Model. *Journal of Democracy* 10, no. 4:19–34.

TOBB. 1995. *Doğu Sorunu: Teşhisler ve Tespitler.* Ankara: Aydoğu Ofset.

Turgut, Mehmet. 1996. *"Doğu Sorunu" Raporu Üzerine.* Istanbul: Boğaziçi Yayınları.

TÜSİAD. 1997. *Perspectives on Democratisation in Turkey.* Istanbul: TÜSİAD.

Watts, Nicole. 2000. Relocating Dersim: Turkish State-Building and Kurdish Resistance, 1931–1938. *New Perspectives on Turkey* 23 (fall):5–30.

CHAPTER FIFTEEN

Federalism, Nationalism, and Secession

The Communist and Postcommunist Experience

Valerie Bunce

Michael Hechter (2000, 2) has introduced his recent book on nationalism with the observation that "while the politics of class has been retreating in the wings, the politics of ethnicity has been moving into the limelight." This generalization applies unusually well to developments over the past several decades in the former Soviet Union and east-central Europe. While communism eradicated class, at least in a purely Marxist sense, it managed to substitute in its place, largely by accident, an unusually potent political force: the nation (see, especially, Verdery 1994). Indeed, it was the nation and nationalist movements that were largely responsible for bringing down communism in the eastern half of Europe a decade ago (see, especially, Bunce 1999b; Beissinger 2002). This was the case not just in heterogeneous contexts, such as the Soviet Union, where national minorities mobilized against the state and the regime, but also in homogeneous societies, such as Poland, where a nationalist movement, though formally entitled a workers' movement, liberated the country from both Soviet and socialist hegemony.

If nationalism undermined regimes throughout the eastern half of Europe, it was also responsible for dismembering three of the region's states: Yugoslavia, beginning in mid-1991, the Soviet Union six months later, and Czechoslovakia at the end of 1992. With the end of Yugoslavia came the return of war to the European stage—after a forty-six-year hiatus. Again, the core issue was contestation over the definition of the nation and the boundaries of the state. And once more, class conflict served as a mere bystander.

The tides of nationalism did not fully subside, however, once communism and the Soviet, Yugoslav, and Czechoslovak states exited from the European stage. In a few of the successor regimes, such as Poland, nationalism provided the political support necessary for navigating the difficult transition to democracy and capitalism. By contrast, in other countries, nationalism served as the basis for violent conflicts between the center and secessionist peripheries—most notably within the new states of Russia, Serbia and Montenegro, Moldova, and Georgia (see, for example, Lieven 1998; King 2000a). Finally, while less influential than expected, given the economic stresses of postcommunism and the widely assumed relationship between prolonged economic downturns and democratic breakdowns (but see Bermeo 2003), illiberal nationalists managed in some countries—for instance, Croatia, Slovakia, Romania, and Russia—to mobilize popular support, thereby undermining the democratic project. In each case, they have done so by touting the superiority of the numerically dominant nation and by cataloguing severe threats to its survival posed by both minorities and international forces—perceived variously as separate dangers and as collaborative campaigns (Tismaneanu 1998; Shenfield 2001).

In the eastern half of Europe, therefore, nationalism has played a variety of roles: dismembering states and founding new ones; investing and disinvesting in state capacity; supporting and undermining old dictatorships and new democracies. Despite the diversity of its effects, however, there is nonetheless one consistent theme regarding the relationship between nationalism and the state after the socialist era. The boundaries of the twenty-seven states that now comprise the region as a result of state dissolution a decade ago have managed to remain in place—though the future of Serbia and Montenegro is still in some question. Thus, while nations in this part of the world have often been restless, nationalism, like all social movements, has been cyclical (Tarrow 1994; Beissinger 2002). Indeed, the "cult of culture" (King 2000a, 229) has fewer followers today than it had a decade ago—at least in the postcommunist context.

The purpose of this chapter is to use the communist and postcommunist experience (supplemented, where helpful, by cases outside the region) to explore the rise of nations and nationalism and their consequences for the sustainability of regimes and states. Of particular interest is how the institutional design of politics in multinational contexts—or the contrast between unitary and federal systems—affect national identities, secessionist demands, and the durability of regimes and states. The presumption here is that political institutions distribute resources and incentives. In doing so, they shape the political identities of groups, their goals, and their behavior—which in turn can support or disrupt the institutional landscape. This is hardly a controversial claim. It lies at the heart, for example, of recent research on such varied topics as electoral politics, political protest, the consequences of parliamentary versus presidential government, and even the causes of revolution (Stepan and Skach 1993; Shugart and Carey 1992). It is also a central premise underlying continuing debates about the nation and nationalism (see Anderson 1991; Horowitz 1981, 1985, 1994; Hechter 1977, 1987, 2000; Brubaker 1996; Lijphart 1996; Bunce 1999b).

In the first part of the chapter, I provide a brief survey of the terrain of study by defining key terms and attendant theoretical considerations. The particular focus will be on the nation, nationalism, secession, and the state—concepts central to this chapter and book, the subject of considerable research, and, at the same time, as underdefined as they are perhaps overdetermined. In the remainder of the chapter, I examine the impact of federalism on the nation, nationalism, and the durability of the state in three regime settings, all drawn from the former communist world: state socialism (or dictatorial systems), regimes in transition from state socialism, and democratic orders. Put simply, then, I am varying the institutional design of both the regime and the state.

What emerges from this discussion are the following arguments. First, in spite of its goals, state socialism undermined itself, largely because it constructed and then empowered nations. Second, in the federal versions of state socialism, the weakening of the regime was accompanied by a fragmentation and then dissolution of the state. Indeed, the combination of federalism and state socialism bound these two developments together. Third, in new, multinational democracies in the postsocialist region, secessionist pressures on the state have been greatest where the state is federal in form. However, in all of these cases federalism emerged as the "culprit," largely because of two factors accompanying federalism: continuation of a national federal state from the communist past and the absence of a consensus around the liberal political project.

Defining Terms: The State and the Nation

We can begin setting the conceptual stage by defining the state (see, for example, Herbst 2000; Silberman 1993; Migdal 1988). The state is a political entity combining two monopolies: a spatial monopoly and a monopoly over the exercise of legitimate coercion. What distinguishes a state from other political constructs, therefore, is the existence of spatially bounded political authority—or what was defined at Westphalia in the seventeenth century as the geographically bounded maintenance of political order. States vary, of course, in levels of contestation over boundaries and over the exercise of political authority within those boundaries. In weak states, contestation is high; in strong states, a monopoly is in place. Finally, there is no necessary correlation between international recognition of statehood and the strength of the state. Indeed, during the cold war era, juridical statehood was often granted even when states failed to meet the minimal conditions of a spatial and coercive monopoly (Jackson and Rosenberg 1982). This practice continued, moreover, even as the cold war ended.

The second term is the nation, which can be defined as a shared understanding among a large group of people that they have a common cultural identity that distinguishes them from other groups (see, especially, Hobsbawm 1992; Greenfeld 1992; Gellner 1983; Young 1976, 1993). That identity comes about through shared historical experiences that have produced common cultural symbols and common institutions. A shared language, religion, or ethnicity is neither a necessary nor a sufficient condition for the formation of a nation—though these considerations have often been influential in nation building since the final quarter of the nineteenth century, when the idea of the nation diffused from the northwest quadrant of Europe, where states were in place, to southern and eastern Europe, where empires were the norm (Hobsbawm 1992). Moreover, there is no necessary correlation between the boundaries of the state and the boundaries of the nation. States can have many nations; nations do not necessarily have states; and nations can straddle many states. Finally, nations are not objective formations; rather, they are intersubjective. But their intersubjectivity is premised upon an unusual principle: commonality not just among those who know each other and interact repeatedly, but also among strangers who are presumed in theory to share the same identity. In this way, the nation is a product of both interaction and imagination (see, especially, Anderson 1991).

There is, of course, a continuing debate about the origins of nations, with different positions staked out by primordialists, constructivists, and instrumentalists (see, especially, Young 1993; Esman 1994). However, in my view, while the nation, or the political community, often has primordialist origins, it is, nonetheless, always constructed through shared experiences and the cues of commonality that arise when political authority is consolidated. Thus, the nation is always a political, cultural, and social construct, but it is neither a given, nor a stable construct. Instead, it is "forever assembled, dismantled and reassembled" (Wolfe 1982, 391, quoted in Danforth 1995, 26). The fluidity and the forms of national identity reflect the impact of four factors: geographical proximity (enhanced by the development of settled agriculture), the consolidation of political authority, the density of intragroup interaction, and through these arenas of interaction the continuing struggle among people over power, money, and cultural symbols.

Nationalism and Secession

Nationalism enters the scene when the nation, or at least political leaders claiming to speak on behalf of the nation, define a political project that demands expanded sovereignty on behalf of the national community. In practice, these demands take variable forms (which is where I disagree with Hechter 2000). They can involve calling for greater autonomy of the nation within an existing state, or they can involve secession—to join another state or found a new one. Such demands, moreover, can take cultural, economic, and political forms—for example, recognition of the minority language as an official language, expanded representation of members of the nation in economic leadership posts, or creation of a separate representative assembly. What unites all of these goals, however, is one theme: using politics to legitimate difference and to expand autonomy.

There are several generalizations that are important for understanding nationalism. One is that nationalist leaders do not necessarily have nationalist followers. Nationalist leaders, in short, may presume to speak for the nation, but they may not be leading a social movement embracing a nationalist agenda (on this point, see, especially, Gagnon 2003). Moreover, the leaders themselves may not be nationalists, but, rather, use nationalism as a mechanism for defeating their rivals and maintaining their political power. Thus, nationalism can substitute for, say, a liberalization of politics, which, in an authoritarian system, constitutes a threat to incumbent elites. What I have just described, for example, is Serbia during the reign of Slobodan Milosevic, where nationalist rhetoric substituted for both nationalism and liberalism.

Second, majorities, as well as minorities, can be nationalists—despite the pronounced emphasis on minority nationalism in the literature to the point where the noun presumes the adjective. Here, we must remember that Poles were every bit as nationalist in 1989 as Slovenes, yet it was only in the latter case that nationalism equaled secession. Just as important is the fact that the nationalist rhetoric of the majority can construct nationalist responses on the part of minorities. This is one interpretation, for example, of the rise of Slovak nationalism within interwar Czechoslovakia (Leff 1988).

Third, nationalism is a sentiment that unites as well as divides people. Again, the Polish case is highly instructive. In the unusually homogeneous context of Poland, nationalism functioned to bring Poles together in pursuit of the common objectives of ending state socialism and Soviet domination. Success in both areas then brought with it two more advantages. One was to create a legitimate regime—a development that stabilized democracy, empowered the state, and thereby created a mutually supportive relationship between the new regime and the old state. The other was to expand Polish tolerance for the economic difficulties involved in stabilizing the economy and under-going a transition to capitalism. Nationalism, in short, lengthened political horizons (see, especially, Abdelal 2001). It was a form of political capital.

Finally, while the specific demands of nationalists vary, the common theme is a challenge to the territorial reaches of state authority and sovereignty. This, plus the variable consequences of nationalism for democracy and dictatorship, means that nationalism is best understood as a spatial, not an ideological project (in contrast to the arguments of Banac 1984; and see Lustick 1990 on the political importance of territory). As such, nationalism can be combined with support for either liberal or illiberal political projects, and it can be exclusivist or inclusivist, depending upon the definition of the nation and its spatial reach.

The last term is secession—the departure of a region or regions from the state (Hechter 1992; Meadwell 1994; Buchanan 1991). This situation typically arises through a three-stage process, wherein political leaders of a spatially concentrated nation, eyeing a mixture of threats and expanded opportunities in the political environment, begin to demand major changes in the political and economic relationship of the region to the center. What then commences is bargaining between central and regional leaders, with bargaining understood loosely to include demands, promises, and threats. In the final stage, bargaining leads to either maintenance of the boundaries of the state (sometimes by expanding regional autonomies) or shrinkage of those boundaries through the subtraction of a region or regions from the state.

There are some important generalizations we can make about secession. First, the roots of secession are virtually always national in form. Thus, regions lacking a distinctive national identity rarely challenge the boundaries of the state (for evidence on this point, see Beissinger 2002). Classes, for example, do not threaten to leave the state; nations do. Second, secessionist demands in most cases tend to emerge from bargaining, rather than serving as the point of departure for bargaining. In the Yugoslav case, for example, it was only through continuing conflicts between the Slovene and Serbian leaders that the Slovene League of Communists defected to the Slovene opposition and that both parts of Slovene society came to argue in concert in support of independent statehood. Third, secessionist demands lead to violence for two reasons: because those demanding secession have weapons at their disposal, and, even more commonly, because the center, jealous of its territory and its authority, resists secessionist demands and uses its coercive power to prevent the departure of the region from the state. Fourth, it is a mistake to infer preferences from outcomes in struggles over the boundaries of the state. For example, neither Czechs nor Slovaks wanted to end Czechoslovakia and, indeed, neither did the Slovak leadership. Rather, this was a threat used to gain concessions from the leader of the Czech lands—who then decided, for reasons of power and his economic policy agenda, to accede to the request. Similarly, while citizens in the Baltic states and their leaders wanted to leave the Soviet Union by 1990, the same cannot be said for, say, Kazakhstan, Belarus, and, arguably, the Russian Federation. Yet, as the state fragmented, all the republics felt compelled to leave. Secession, therefore, can occur in the absence of a nationalist project supporting independent statehood.

Finally, the common wisdom is that secession is to be avoided at all costs, because it unleashes violence, because national and state boundaries can never be perfectly aligned, and because there are in the world today far more nations than there are states. Indeed, it is precisely because of these concerns that Michael Hechter has entitled his recent book, *Containing Nationalism,* and why the "long peace" in Europe during the cold war (at least in Western Europe) has often been attributed in part to the stability of European state boundaries (see Gaddis 1986; Woodward 1995). However, it can be argued that there is another side to this story. First, two of the three socialist states that divided did so peacefully—as did, for example, Norway and Sweden more than eighty years before. Second, it can be argued that the breakup of the Soviet Union made democracy possible in Russia, Ukraine, Moldova, and the Baltic states—as did the breakup of Yugoslavia in the cases of Slovenia and Macedonia in particular and the dissolution of Czechoslovakia in the case of the Czech Republic. The logic here is that, with the dissolution of the state, the most liberal regions of these states—reflecting developments within these regions over the last decade of state socialism—were freed from the political constraints imposed by their less liberal neighbors and, indeed, by what had become heightened contestation over the future and the form of the regime and the state itself. In this sense, state dissolution did not just bring national and state boundaries into closer alignment; it may also have prevented continuing conflicts over regime transition, which could have led to war, while opening up the possibility that some of these new states at least were sufficiently free of dictatorial entanglements that they could become democratic orders.

Much has been made of the Europeanization of West Germany during the postwar period and the ways in which this process of embedding Germany in a larger set of Western European institutions secured the democratic experiment by rendering the state semisovereign (see, for example, Katzenstein 1987). However, from the perspective of Europe's eastern half, this story needs to be complicated in two ways. First, there are reasons to argue that the subtraction of East Germany in the immediate cold war period also invested in West German democracy (Bernhard 2001)—a process similar to what we see fifty years later in Yugoslavia, the Soviet Union, and Czechoslovakia. Second, recent democratization in the case of east-central Europe can be seen as a two-, rather than one-stage process. In the first stage, expanded sovereignty—or liberation from the Soviet bloc—was central to democratization. With the subsequent movement eastward of the European Union and NATO, however, the German example is replayed: reductions in state sovereignty in the service of democratic consolidation.

State Socialism and Federalism

As already noted, there is a substantial body of work supporting the claim that the design of political institutions, in distributing resources and incentives, plays a powerful role in shaping the identities and the behavior of both mass publics and political elites. It would be wrong to draw the implication, however, that those elites powerful enough to design political institutions can then calibrate the consequences of institutional choice. There are two problems here. One is that the context of institutions matters a great deal, because most social settings are dense with institutions, which may operate at cross-purposes with each other, and because contextual considerations shape the forms and the supply of incentives and resources. Thus, the same institutions can be placed in different settings and have very different results—as Robert Moser has argued, for example, with respect to electoral systems (see, especially, Moser 1999). Second, from a longer-term perspective, institutions serving one purpose—say, the consolidation of an empire—can over time have quite different effects—for example, the unraveling of centralized political control. Institutional design, in short, has powerful, but—in part because of that—often unpredictable and, for the dominant groups within the system, sometimes undesirable effects.

This was certainly the case, for instance, with respect to the design of state socialism—a distinctive type of dictatorship, combining state ownership of the means of production, central planning, governance by a Leninist party, isolation from the global economy, and an ideology committed to rapid socioeconomic transformation. On the face of it, the concentration of economic and political resources in the hands of the party—or a centralized and fused political and economic monopoly—would seem to have been ideally suited to reproduce the system. However, it was precisely this monopoly that over time proved to be the undoing of these economic and political regimes, given, for example, growing intraparty conflict, declining capacity of the party to control its lower reaches and, more generally, the society, growing capacity of the periphery to stake out autonomy from the core, and, finally, declining economic performance, which in these fused systems had necessarily politically destabilizing consequences. Precisely because of its institutional design, therefore, and precisely in opposition to elite goals, state socialist systems deregulated themselves. Absent the monopoly that defined and defended them, these systems then ended (Bunce 1999b; Solnick 1998b).

We can now take these observations about the power of institutions and focus on the concern of this chapter. How did the institutional design of state socialism affect the identities and the resources of the nations that resided in east-central Europe and the former Soviet Union? Here, it is instructive to look at two kinds of institutional settings. The first is domestic and concentrates on the contrast between federal and unitary states, with the Soviet Union, Yugoslavia, and Czechoslovakia examples of the former, and the remaining states in the state socialist region examples of the latter. As in other contexts, so in this one federalism was defined as a system that: (1) claims to be federal in its constitution; (2) features two sets of political-administrative units, distinguishing the center from a set of smaller, geographically defined subunits; and (3) shared policy responsibilities between the center and the subunits in combination with policy arenas featuring a division of powers between the two. As a result, the exercise of power, the making of policy, and political representation are all segmented in federal systems, and citizens in such systems are governed simultaneously by both the center and the particular subunit within which they reside. Sovereignty, therefore, is dual, as well as interlinked.

What was distinctive about state socialist federations—and remains so for Belgium and India, but not for either the American or the German federations—is that they were national in form; that is, the subunits were constituted (and this was their rationale for existence) on the basis of the territorial concentration of a particular minority community, the name of which provided the name of the subunit. For example, within the Soviet Union, the Ukrainian republic was named after the Ukrainians that constituted it, the Estonian republic after Estonians, and the like. National and administrative boundaries, therefore, correlated. As a result, citizens within state socialist federations had three identities: a national identity, an administrative identity (which was not necessarily their national identity), and an ideological identity. But the correlation between the first two was far from perfect, given, on the one hand, the tendency of ethnic groups to be shared among republics and even among states, and, on the other, the failure of most groups, who had some claims to a shared and distinctive history, language, religion, and/or ethnicity, to be given an administrative unit of their own. To take one example: the Roma were well represented in a number of states in the region and in some cases constituted a large percentage of the population (as in, say, Czechoslovakia), but in no case were they given a republic.

Several other details about these federations are also essential for the discussion that follows. First, it was the most heterogeneous of the states in the region—that is, those states where the second largest nation exceeded 20 percent of the population—that became national federations. Other states, having smaller minority populations, were unitary. Second, while Yugoslavia was a symmetric federation, the Soviet Union and

Czechoslovakia were not. In the latter two cases, the institutional resources of the republic representing the largest nation within the state—or Russians and Czechs, respectively—were limited in comparison with those of the other republics making up the federation. Third, the size of the constituting community relative to the rest of the population within the subunit varied widely. For example, there was no majority nation in either Kazakhstan or Bosnia, whereas the Armenians and the Slovenes constituted a very large percentage of their republics in the Soviet Union and Yugoslavia, respectively. Finally, in the Soviet Union and Yugoslavia, there were subunits within subunits, each of which was defined in terms of a titular minority community. However, these "lesser" units had "lesser" rights than the units designated republics (though this was altered by the 1974 Yugoslav constitution, thereby empowering both Vojvodina and Kosovo). Moreover, especially in the Soviet case, these lower-level units were usually numerically dominated not by the titular nation, but, rather, by another nation—often the dominant nation within the country as a whole. To draw upon American slang: the autonomous regions, counties, and the like in the former Soviet Union were often formed through gerrymandering—a process that in this context did not guarantee electoral results so much as guarantee Russian dominance. The formation of the republics in Central Asia in the 1920s, moreover, was also a product of gerrymandering—in this instance, multiplying nations and drawing administrative boundaries in ways that divided and ruled—to the benefit of the Slavic areas of the Soviet Union and the power of the Communist Party.

Goals of National Federalism

The Yugoslav, Soviet, and Czechoslovak federations were designed with two goals in mind (see Slezkine 1994). One was purely pragmatic and more short-term: to use institutional investments in the nation—including in many cases the development of a written language, but in all cases political boundaries, recognition of the local language, and creation of local schools, media, a Communist Party, secret police, and academy of sciences—in order to expand the territorial reach of the socialist state and the socialist project. National federalism, therefore, was central to state building and regime building in multinational contexts. This was particularly important where there had been a history of conflict among nations within the state, where the revolution had involved such conflicts and the growth in secessionist demands, and where the state was large and thinly populated and, thus, highly constrained in its capacity to project political authority across space (see, especially, Herbst 2000 on Africa; also see Stoner-Weiss 1999; Smith 1999; Harris 1999). This is a particularly accurate description, for example, of the Soviet Union—the inventor of national federalism.

National federalism, therefore, was a mechanism of incorporation, co-optation, and socialization, though the precise forms this process took varied across republics (see Laitin 1998). Indeed, it was precisely because of the weakness of the regime and the state that Czechoslovakia became a federation after the Soviet invasion in 1968. Federalism was a way to recognize and co-opt the Slovak nation and thereby limit the political and economic dominance of the Czech lands—the center, it must be remembered, of protests against the regime from 1967 to 1968.

The other goal was more long-term. It was to deepen central control over the periphery through administrative policies that secured the economic and political hegemony of the party and through social and economic policies that over time would even out the socioeconomic disparities among republics and among the nations that constituted those republics. The assumption here was, first, that combining federalism with state socialism would enhance administrative compliance and the overall performance of the system, since nations would be appreciative of their gains, since the republican parties controlled those nations, and since central-level party organizations controlled in turn the republican parties. The key, in short, was combining investments in the nation with the economic and political monopoly of the party and the economic and political dependence of lower-level party units on upper-level units. Second, it was assumed that achievement of high levels of socioeconomic development across-the-board would pave the way for a statewide shift of identities from local to purely ideological; that is, from being a Kazakh to being a Soviet citizen embracing Soviet identity and Soviet ideology. Communist rulers, therefore, were much like modernization theorists in the West—another group that fell out of favor once their ideas and their designs were superseded by developments in the real world. They both assumed that national identities and nationalist movements would wither away in the face of education, urbanization, and economic growth.

The Soviet Bloc as a Federation

We can now turn to a second important setting—in this instance, international, rather than domestic—where institutional design also shaped national identities and national resources: the Soviet bloc. When Stalin consolidated control over what came to be called the "People's democracies" of east-central Europe after the Second World War, he decided to leave nation-states in place rather than treat the new regimes to his west as integral parts of the Soviet federation (with the Baltic states, Moldova, and an expanded Ukraine serving as exceptions). With the export of Stalinization in "ready-to-wear fashion" to state socialism's periphery (see Brus 1977), Stalin and then Khrushchev built a regional bloc of states that duplicated in factual form the Soviet model. Indeed, the logic at the regional realm was remarkably similar to the logic of national federalism in the domestic realm; that is, to recognize nations and empower them through boundaries and economic, political, social, and cultural institutions, but within an administrative structure that rendered these nations dependent upon the local party for power and privilege and that party in turn dependent upon the center for the same.

Thus, national and state boundaries were left intact in east-central Europe, but it was Moscow that controlled the parties that governed these states. It was precisely this dependence—spatially tiered in the bloc as in the socialist federations—that was to harmonize national, territorial, and socialist identities, that was to promote the socialist project, and that was to maximize the control of the center over the periphery. This was the case whether the center was, say, the Soviet Union within the bloc or the Politburo and the Central Committee in the Czechoslovak, Yugoslav, or Soviet capitals.

In the short run, the goals driving the establishment of federalism—and its regional equivalent, the Soviet bloc—seemed to have been met. The boundaries of the bloc, each of its member states, and the boundaries of the socialist federations were all well defined and well defended; the capacity of the center to control the periphery was considerable at the domestic and regional levels; and the institutional design of these domestic and regional federations appeared to further the goals of socialist transformation. However, central to this story was the construction of nations. As Charles King (2000b, 164) has observed: "Communists were not always nationalists, but they were without exception nation-builders." In some instance, of course, national identity was already in place prior to the socialist experiment—for example, majority populations in much of east-central Europe and in the Baltic states. This is hardly surprising, since an important investment in national identity—as we learned from the Western European experience—is the existence of a state. However, in many other cases, particularly republics within the federations, the demarcation of political boundaries and their salience for political and economic flows, the introduction and empowerment of political, social, and cultural institutions, and the creation of local elites were all instrumental in constructing nations that had before been merely groups variously defined by ethnicity, religion, and/or language—and, indeed, not always having even these familiar markers.

Through deliberate and defining policies, therefore, state socialism constructed national identities, though the nation was expected to share the stage with an ideological identity that was to supersede it in importance over time. The key question then became whether those nations would be able to reconcile their national with their ideological identities; whether they would use the considerable resources at their disposal to comply with the center or to carve out zones of autonomy; and whether the center would be able to maintain its control over a territory united by ideology and by the economic and political dependence of the periphery on the core, but segmented by national identity. Put simply, was investing in the nation in fact investing in the regime and the state—not just in the short term, but also in the longer run?

Even prior to their formal demise from 1989 to 1992, state socialism, socialist federations, and the Soviet bloc all exhibited trends that counseled skepticism. First, the actual size of the Soviet zone of influence in east-central Europe declined over time, given the departure of both Yugoslavia and Albania and the growing recalcitrance of Romania, beginning in the late 1960s. Second, rebellions in east-central Europe—that is, in East Germany, Czechoslovakia, Hungary, and, repeatedly, Poland—testified in every case to the power of nationalism. This was especially the case, given the particular assets enjoyed by the periphery of state socialism. Occupying the borderlands of the empire, three issues, central to the survival of the empire, were joined together: liberation of the nation, liberation of the regime, and liberation of the state. These revolts also testified to the limits of Soviet imperial control, as did the telling statistics regarding the growing economic and military burdens of east-central Europe on the Soviet Union (Bunce 1984–85). Third, at least some of the popular rebellions in these communist states involved demands for greater national and regional autonomy within the state—as with the Slovaks within Czechoslovakia from 1967 to 1968, the Croats within Yugoslavia in the early 1970s, and the Kosovar Albanians, again within Yugoslavia, at the beginning of the 1980s.

There were some warning signals, therefore, that policies constructing nations in the state socialist setting could deconstruct the regime, the state, and the bloc. In this sense, the costs of national federalism—and its regional equivalent, the Soviet bloc—seemed to increase over time.

The Demise of State Socialism

By the mid-1970s, evidence was accumulating that state socialist regimes were in serious trouble. For example, the growth of corruption, the decline in economic performance, periodic mass protests, and the growing economic burdens of Eastern Europe on the Soviet Union all indicated that communist parties at home and the Soviet leadership within the bloc were losing their capacity to control both politics and economics. Perhaps the greatest testimony to the mounting problems of state socialism, however, were two developments during the Brezhnev era. The first was "stability in cadres," or the slowdown in the circulation of elites, within the Soviet Union and within Eastern Europe as well. Just as this indicated the political weakness of Brezhnev, so it generated considerable anger among party officials denied promotions. Stuck in place, moreover, these officials began to carve out considerable economic and political autonomy. In this way, republics became empowered within federations and the Eastern European regimes became empowered within the Soviet bloc.

The second development was Brezhnev's decision in the early 1970s to open up the bloc to Western trade and capital. This was a radical decision, because it ended one of the defining features of state socialism: isolation from the global economy. Isolation was central to maintenance of the party's ideological, spatial, and economic monopoly. The logic behind the decision, however, was conservative: to avoid painful domestic economic reforms that would antagonize already restless publics and elite stake-holders in the system. The impact of this decision, however, was opposite to what was intended. As external debts grew, economic performance worsened and Eastern European burdens on the Soviet Union expanded. The fusion of politics and econom-ics in these systems meant that these economic problems became necessarily political problems. By the early 1980s, then, both the regimes and the bloc were in the process of rapid political and economic deregulation—a process that was only enhanced by the blocwide effects of leadership succession and struggles over power and policy priori-ties. In the context of the Soviet bloc and socialist federations, deregulation was not just economic and political; it was also spatial. In this way, the weakening of the regime was necessarily accompanied by fragmentation of federal states and the Soviet bloc.

With institutional breakdown, the national identities, forged by the institutional de-sign of state socialism, were converted into nationalist movements. Again, it was the weakening of the regime, or the deregulation of its economic and political monopoly, that provided the political opportunities necessary for nations to demand states. Central to this process was another cost of federalism and the Soviet bloc. With the cen-ter weakening, the party fragmenting, and the chains of dependence breaking, subunits combining boundaries with leaders, institutional resources, and national identity—whether, say, Poland within the bloc, Slovenia within Yugoslavia, or Lithuania within the Soviet Union—began to move in divergent directions. Thus, struggles over the regime, economic and political, were joined with struggles over the state. And neither the regime, the state, nor the Soviet bloc could contain either these struggles or differ-entiation among units.

As a result, the Soviet Union fissured along republican lines, as did Yugoslavia and Czechoslovakia. At the regional level, the collapse of state socialism began in the pe-riphery with the Polish roundtable, soon to be followed by the Hungarian roundtable and then massive protests in East Germany and Czechoslovakia. What is striking about this process is that, like the domestic federal cases, so within the bloc institutional re-sources and the confluence of national and territorial divisions of power were critical, because in a time of regime weakening they joined demands for a new regime with assertions of national sovereignty. In packaging politics and economics along territorial lines, then, both socialist federations and the Soviet bloc joined ideological with spatial struggles. The end results were new regimes and new states. The boundaries of those new states, and, indeed, the patterns of nationalist mobilization, reflected nearly perfectly the boundaries of the republics within the federal systems and the states within the Soviet bloc.[1]

The Limits of National Federalism as an Explanation

The previous discussion provided us with five generalizations about federalism, state socialism, and regime transition. First, in the communist region, there were three federal systems, and all three of these were national in form. Second, the countries having the largest minority populations within the region (relative to the size of the dominant nation) were precisely those countries that had federal orders, that is, the Soviet Union, Yugoslavia, and Czechoslovakia. Third, the Soviet bloc was based upon correlations between political and national boundaries and a radial, bilateral, and asymmetric economic and political relationship between the Soviet Union and Eastern Europe. As a result, the bloc functioned at the regional level much as federations functioned in the domestic arena. Fourth, national federalism had the effects of constructing and thereby empowering nations and states-in-the-making within the state. The equivalent at the regional level was strengthening national identities within Eastern Europe and empowering these states, despite the emphasis, for example, on a common socialist identity, bloc integration, and Soviet domination. Finally, when the center's control over the periphery weakened in both economic and political terms, the dominant nations of those Eastern European countries that were members of the bloc mobilized against the regime and, thus, the Soviet Union. At the same time and for similar reasons, nations within the federal systems mobilized against the equivalent constraints on their autonomy, that is, both the regime and the state. As a result, the Soviet bloc, socialist federations, and communist regimes all unraveled. Ideological and spatial fragmentation, therefore, went hand-in-hand.

These arguments leave us, however, with two questions, which will be the focus of the final portion of this chapter. First, if the most diverse countries within the region were federal, then how can we disentangle the impact of diversity versus federalism on the dissolution of the state? Put simply, was the problem the size and territorial concentration of minority communities, the institutional design of the state, or a combination of the two? This question is particularly hard to answer, since the state socialist region featured no examples of "a-national federalism," that is, federal systems like the American, West German, Brazilian, and Argentine models that are purely spatial in form and are administratively agnostic with respect to the relationship between national and political boundaries (Gibson and Calvo 2001).

Second, to what degree is the relationship between national federalism and state dissolution a function of a dictatorial context? For example, it might be argued that national federalism undermined the state, because it combined spatial cleavages with the absence of democratic rights. As a result, contestation over the regime—or a demand for expanded rights and liberalized political procedures—was joined with contestation over the boundaries of the state. By contrast, in a democratic context, the combination of democratic rights and national federalism might very well invest in the durability of both democracy and the state by providing civil liberties and political rights, but in an administrative context that recognizes the concerns of minorities and empowers those minorities through segmented state institutions. In such circumstances, the legitimacy of the regime is tied to the legitimacy of the state, as in dictatorial contexts, but in a manner that sustains rather than undermines both. Indeed, this is precisely the logic behind arguments that advocate various forms of federalism and consociationalism in multinational democratic contexts, though neither approach to stabilizing politics in a democratic context was designed with the problem of national diversity in mind (see, especially, Roeder 2000a on this point; also see Lijphart 1996).

Diversity versus Federalism

There are in fact several good reasons to privilege the institutionalist claim, that is, that it was national federalism, not diversity in and of itself, that constructed nations during state socialism and that in a time of regime weakening produced dismemberment of the Soviet, Yugoslav, and Czechoslovak states. First, the socialist region as a whole had—and, indeed, continues to have—an enormous number of minority groups, many of which were territorially concentrated, but lacked their own institutional identities. However, it was precisely those groups having such identities and thereby resources—and virtually only those groups—that mobilized against the regime and the state. This is clear, for example, if we look at the absence of nationalist protests launched by minorities in the unitary states within the region—for example, Hungarians in Romania, Turks in Bulgaria, and the Roma in Hungary and Romania (see, especially, Barany 2001 on the Roma).

The same pattern appears, when we compare the mobilization rates of minorities within federal systems. During the last years of the Soviet Union, those who protested did so primarily on nationalist grounds, and those protesters, in turn, were for the most part members of nations that had their own administrative units (Beissinger 2002). Indeed, even after the dissolution of the Soviet Union, demands for greater political autonomy within the Russian Federation have tended to come primarily from those groups allocated republics, autonomous regions, and the like (Treisman 1997). By the same token, while Slovaks were quick to protest within Czechoslovakia, both the Roma and the Hungarians were not. A final example comes from the former Yugoslavia and allows us to speak in another way to the question at hand by highlighting the political consequences of changes over time in institutional resources. Nationalist protests in Kosovo grew only after the implementation of the 1974 constitution, that is, following the death of Tito in 1980 when the powers of this autonomous province were upgraded to nearly equal that of a republic. From that time, protests in Kosovo follow a relatively predictable pattern. When politics within Serbia became more conflictual, the Serbian authorities became more aggressive within Kosovo and Kosovars in turn mounted more protests against Serbian domination. Just as interesting, given the importance of the Yugoslav National Army to the violent end of that state, is another factor shaping developments in Kosovo, that is, whether the Kosovo Liberation Army had access to weapons. With the collapse of the Albanian state in 1997–98, such weapons became readily available.[2]

When combined, these examples suggest that national federalism, not the mere presence of minority populations, even if they are geographically concentrated, is critical for generating secessionist demands on the state—at least in a dictatorial context when the regime is losing control. This is hardly surprising, once we recognize the importance of institutional resources for all kinds of protest activity (see, for example, Tarrow 1994; Yashar 1999). Without such resources, groups cannot take advantage of any expanded opportunities for change that present themselves.

The institutionalist interpretation is also supported by some other considerations. One is that the new states that formed *all* did so along republican lines. Serbia and Montenegro might be considered an exception, but even here, the external boundaries do indeed date from the socialist era, reflecting a decision by the Serbian leadership to carry out a last-minute coup d'état against Montenegro, Kosovo, and Vojvodina. As a result, the Serbian elite aggregated and arrogated borders in anticipation of the dissolution of the regime and state. However, as subsequent events demonstrated, the old administrative and national boundaries simply became the new internal fault lines of Serbia and Montenegro. At the same time, just as state boundaries in the region have been stable since January 1993 (when the final federal system, Czechoslovakia, dissolved into two states), so contestation over boundaries in the region has been a process largely taking place within and not between states (with Armenia and Azerbaijan constituting exceptions). Just as significant is the fact that most of these conflicts have occurred within those republics, now states, that inherited national-territorial divisions from the state socialist era.

A final consideration supporting the institutionalist interpretation comes from outside the postcommunist region. If we look at other countries which were declining dictatorships, which had minority communities, but which were either unitary or federal (but in no cases with the national "adjective"), we find an unvarying pattern. Each of these states survived regime transition intact. At most, secessionist pressures grew (as in the Spanish transition, taking place within a unitary state); at the least, they never materialized (as in federal Argentina and Brazil).

When combined, all of these considerations carry one message. What made national federalism so powerful as an agent of change was its capacity to define and redefine the boundaries of politics. National federalism was able to do so, moreover, precisely when the other defining features of politics were becoming blurred. It organized politics—that is, political identities, political agendas, and political boundaries—in disorganized times. But the key to all these developments was the combination of national cleavages with federalism.

National Federalism and Democracy

This leads us to the second question. If national federalism undermines both the regime and the state in authoritarian settings, especially as the center's control over politics weakens, then does the same argument hold when the regime in question is democratic in form? We can begin to answer this question by focusing on those countries in the postsocialist region that have minorities constituting more than 10 percent of the population and that are coded at the least as "partly free" by Freedom House (see Bunce 1999a; Freedom House 1997). This produces eleven cases in the region: the federal states of Russia, Moldova, Georgia, and Bosnia, and the unitary states of Slovakia, Macedonia, Ukraine, Latvia, Estonia, Bulgaria, and Romania. What emerges from this comparison is a straightforward conclusion. Secessionist demands, contestation over state boundaries, and violent confrontations along national lines have all been more frequent in the national federal setting than in its unitary counterpart. However, this is not to suggest that intranational relations within the unitary democracies have been smooth—as the Croatian and Slovak cases demonstrate, though less well now than, say, five years ago.

The impact of national federalism remains, moreover, once we take alternative explanations into account. For example, some likely candidates to explain differences in secessionist demands and violence are the territorial concentration of minority populations, whether those populations are minorities at home, but majorities next door, and, finally, their relative size (see, for example, Horowitz 1985, 1994; Brubaker 1996; Hechter 1987). One might expect, for example, that greater conflicts would occur where minorities are more concentrated, have an adjacent majority homeland, and constitute a larger percentage of the population. However, none of these considerations seem to have explanatory power. Thus, all of these countries feature compact minorities. Moreover, while Bosnia might testify to the problems of majority homelands (as might Kosovo), Ukraine, Latvia, and Estonia, with their large Russian minorities, and Romania and Slovakia, with their large Hungarian minorities, suggest that these problems can be negotiated in ways that maintain, if imperfectly, the regime and the state. Finally, those countries having the largest minorities are Bosnia, Macedonia, Latvia, and Estonia, that is, countries demonstrating quite variable degrees of international cooperation and conflict.

The one consideration that does seem to be important, however, and that demands a more nuanced interpretation of the impact of national federalism is what can be termed the institutional point of departure. Here, it is helpful to go outside the region and look at two countries that seem to have been successful in combining democratic governance with national federalism: Spain and India.[3] The Spanish case is instructive for our purposes, because Spain is a new democracy and the identities of the Basques and the Catalonians were well developed prior to democratization. For these reasons, many analysts were concerned that, with the death of Franco, the Spanish state would fissure along national lines. The Indian case is important, because we can assess the longer-term consequences of national federalism, we have some knowledge about the formative years of Indian democracy and sovereign statehood, and democratization was preceded by a nationalist movement and combined with independence, state building, and, given the formation of Pakistan, state subtraction.

While these two cases vary in their details and, thus, speak to different aspects of our concerns in this chapter, they nonetheless share one illuminating commonality: the introduction of democracy took place in the context of a unitary state. This was critical, because it gave those leaders managing the transitions involved the political flexibility to assuage the concerns of minorities by redrawing in appealing ways the internal boundaries of the state. It is interesting to note in this regard that political conflicts within these states have often been over rights of minorities to get their own subunits rather than minorities with or without territorial institutions demanding to leave the state.

What was also critical were several other factors: a consensus around democratic governance in both cases; a capable state (as indicated by, for example, its capacity to tax and spend); and, in the Indian case in particular, a popular leader and an inclusive definition of the nation, both emerging from the independence movement (Belmont and Varshney 2000). These considerations were important, because they took some incendiary issues off the political agenda and thereby prevented national issues from combining with issues related to the future of the regime and the state. As we saw earlier, it was precisely this combination that made national federalism in the state socialist context so combustible. Moreover, because these two countries were well defined democracies, individual rights were well developed. This also reduced the political tensions surrounding the rights of nations.

Conclusion

This survey of national federalism in democratic settings leaves us with one conclusion. If new democracies inherit a national federal structure, they tend to be more vulnerable to secessionist pressures. This is particularly the case where civil liberties and political rights are less well defined and fully implemented and where a popular and elite consensus around democracy is less well defined. When democracy is weak and states segmented, then both the regime and the state are less secure. Indeed, their respective fates are closely tied. In this way, the costs of national federalism, so pronounced under state socialism, seem to continue after state socialism has departed from the scene. Thus, inventing national federalism was costly insofar as the regime and the state were concerned. The same can be said, at least in the postsocialist context, for continuing this design of the state. Whether this generalization holds outside the region remains to be seen, though the Indian and Spanish cases are illuminating. But at least one study suggests that the experiences of the postsocialist region are typical, not deviant (Roeder 2000b).

NOTES

1. Space limitations prevent me from addressing an important issue: why the breakup of Yugoslavia was violent, whereas the dissolution of both Czechoslovakia and the Soviet Union was peaceful. Suffice to note here that institutional differences between Yugoslavia, on the one hand, and Czechoslovakia and the Soviet Union, on the other, were critical. More specifically, the greater decentralization of Yugoslavia, the combination in Serbia of considerable institutional resources, but limited political power (a pattern opposite to the position of Russians in the Soviet Union and Czechs in Czechoslovakia), and, finally, the intervention of the Yugoslav military in the dissolution of the state were all critical in creating violent conflicts (see Bunce 1999b).

2. It might be countered, however, that Vojvodina represents a counterexample. However, minority representation in that province is smaller relative to that of Kosovo's; access to weaponry is far more limited; and Vojvodina did not serve as the target of Serbian nationalism.

3. I have chosen not to look at Belgium or Canada because they are long-standing democracies and states. On the Belgian case, see, especially, Martiniello 1995, and on the Canadian case, Meadwell and Martin 1996.

REFERENCES

Abdelal, Rawi. 2001. *Economic Nationalism after Empire: A Comparative Perspective on Nation, Economy and Security in Post-Soviet Eurasia.* Ithaca, N.Y.: Cornell University Press.

Anderson, Benedict. 1991. *Imagined Communities: Reflections on the Origins and Spread of Nationalism.* London: Verso.

Banac, Ivo. 1984. *The National Question in Yugoslavia.* Ithaca, N.Y.: Cornell University Press.

Barany, Zolton. 2001. *The East European Gypsies: Regime Change, Marginality and Ethnopolitics.* Cambridge: Cambridge University Press.

Beissinger, Mark. 2002. *The Tides of Nationalism: Order, Event and the Collapse of the Soviet State.* Cambridge: Cambridge University Press.

Belmont, Katharine, and Ashutosh Varshney. 2000. Nationalism and Secession: Comparing India and Sri Lanka. Paper presented at the conference on Powersharing and Peacemaking, La Jolla, December 8–9.

Bermeo, Nancy. 2003. *Ordinary People in Extraordinary Times: The Citizenry and the Collapse of Democracy.* Princeton: Princeton University Press.

Bernhard, Michael. 2001. Democratization in Germany: A Reappraisal. *Comparative Politics* 33 (July):379–400.

Brubaker, Rogers. 1996. *Nationalism Reframed.* Cambridge: Cambridge University Press.

Brus, Wlodzimierz. 1977. Stalinism and the People's Democracies. In *Stalinism: Essays in Historical Interpretation,* ed. Robert Tucker, 77–110. New York: Norton.

Buchanan, Allan. 1991. *Secession: The Morality of Political Divorce from Fort Sumter to Lithuania and Quebec.* Boulder: Westview.

Bunce, Valerie. 1984–85. The Empire Strikes Back: The Transformation of the Eastern Bloc from a Soviet Asset to a Soviet Liability. *International Organization* 39 (winter):1–46.

——— . 1999a. The Political Economy of Postsocialism. *Slavic Review* 58 (winter):756–93.

——— . 1999b. *Subversive Institutions: The Design and the Destruction of Socialism and the State.* Cambridge: Cambridge University Press.

Danforth, Loring. 1995. *The Macedonian Conflict: Ethnic Nationalism in a Transnational World.* Princeton: Princeton University Press.

Esman, Milton. 1994. *Ethnic Politics.* Ithaca, N.Y.: Cornell University Press.

Freedom House. 1997. The Comparative Survey of Freedom. *Freedom Review* 28 (January–February):3–14.

Gaddis, John Lewis. 1986. The Long Peace: Elements of Stability in the Postwar International System. *International Security* 10 (spring):99–142.

Gagnon, Valere P. 2003. *Culture and International Politics.* Unpublished book manuscript, Ithaca College, Ithaca, N.Y.

Gellner, Ernest. 1983. *Nations and Nationalism.* Oxford: Basil Blackwell.

Gibson, Edward, and Ernesto Calvo. 2001. Federalism and Low-Maintenance Constituencies: Territorial Dimensions of Economic Reform in Argentina. *Studies in Comparative International Development* 35 (winter):51–82.

Greenfeld, Liah. 1992. *Nationalism: Five Roads to Modernity.* Cambridge: Cambridge University Press.

Harris, James R. 1999. *The Great Urals: Regionalism and the Evolution of the Soviet System.* Ithaca, N.Y.: Cornell University Press.

Hechter, Michael. 1977. *Internal Colonialism: The Celtic Fringe in British National Development, 1536–1966.* Berkeley: University of California Press.

———. 1987. *Principles of Group Solidarity.* Berkeley: University of California Press.

———. 1992. The Dynamics of Secession. *Acta Sociologica* 35:267–83.

———. 2000. *Containing Nationalism.* Oxford: Oxford University Press.

Herbst, Jeffrey. 2000. *States and Power in Africa: Comparative Lessons in Authority and Control.* Princeton: Princeton University Press.

Hobsbawm, Eric. 1992. *Nations and Nationalism since 1780: Programme, Myth, Reality.* 2d ed. Cambridge: Cambridge University Press.

Horowitz, Donald. 1981. Patterns of Ethnic Separatism. *Comparative Studies in Society and History* 23 (April):165–95.

———. 1985. *Ethnic Groups in Conflict.* Berkeley: University of California Press.

———. 1994. Democracy in Divided Societies. In *Nationalism, Ethnic Conflict, and Democracy,* ed. Larry Diamond and Marc Plattner, 35–55. Baltimore: Johns Hopkins University Press.

Jackson, Robert H., and Carl G. Rosenberg. 1982. Why Africa's Weak States Persist: The Empirical and the Juridical in Statehood. *World Politics* 35 (October):1–36.

Janos, Andrew C. 2000. *East Central Europe in the Modern World: The Politics of the Borderlands from Pre- to Postcommunism.* Stanford: Stanford University Press.

Katzenstein, Peter. 1987. *Policy and Politics in West Germany: The Growth of a Semi-Sovereign State.* Philadelphia: Temple University Press.

King, Charles. 2000a. *The Moldovans: Romania, Russia and the Politics of Culture.* Hoover: Hoover Institution Press.

———. 2000b. Post-Postcommunism: Transition, Comparison, and the End of "Eastern Europe." *World Politics* 53 (October):143–72.

Laitin, David. 1998. *Identity in Formation: The Russian-Speaking Populations in the Near Abroad.* Ithaca, N.Y.: Cornell University Press.

Leff, Carol Skalnik. 1988. *National Conflict in Czechoslovakia: The Making and Re-making of a State, 1918–1987.* Princeton: Princeton University Press.

Lieven, Anatol. 1998. *Chechnya: Tombstone of Russian Power.* New Haven: Yale University Press.

Lijphart, Arend. 1996. The Puzzle of Indian Democracy: A Consociational Interpretation. *American Political Science Review* 90 (June):258–68.

Lustick, Ian. 1990. Becoming Problematic: The Breakdown of a Hegemonic Conception of Ireland in Nineteenth Century Britain. *Politics and Society* 18:39–83.

Mainwaring, Scott, and David Samuels. 2000. Federalism, Constraints on the Central Government, and Economic Reform in Democratic Brazil. Unpublished manuscript, February 2000.

Martiniello, Marco. 1995. The National Question and the Political Construction of Ethnic Communities in Belgium. In *Racism, Ethnicity and Politics in Contemporary Europe,* ed. Alex G. Hargreaves and Jeremy Leaman, 131–44. London: Edward Elgar.

Meadwell, Hudson. 1994. Transitions to Independence and Ethnic Nationalist Mobilization. In *Politics and Rationality,* ed. William James Booth, Patrick James, and Hudson Meadwell, 191–213. Cambridge: Cambridge University Press.

Meadwell, Hudson, and Pierre Martin. 1996. Economic Integration and the Politics of Independence. *Nations and Nationalism* 2:67–87.

Migdal, Joel. 1988. *Strong Societies and Weak States: State-Society Relations and State Capabilities in the Third World.* Princeton: Princeton University Press.

Moser, Robert. 1999. Electoral Systems and the Number of Parties in Postcommunist States. *World Politics* 51 (April):359–84.

Riskin, Steven M. 2000. Three Dimensions of Peacebuilding in Bosnia: Findings from USIP-Sponsored Research and Field Projects. *Peaceworks* 32, 1–47. Washington, D.C.: U.S. Institute of Peace.

Roeder, Philip. 2000a. Longterm Stability of Powersharing and Divided-Power Constitutions. Paper presented at the conference on Powersharing and Peacemaking, La Jolla, December 8–9.

———. 2000b. The Robustness of Institutions in Ethnically Plural Societies. Paper presented at the annual meeting of the American Political Science Association, Washington, D.C., August 31–September 3.

Shenfield, Stephen. 2001. Foreign Assistance as Genocide: The Crisis in Russia, the IMF, and Interethnic Relations. In *Carrots, Sticks and Ethnic Conflict: Rethinking Development Assistance,* ed. Milton Esman and Ronald Herring, 175–209. Ann Arbor: University of Michigan.

Shugart, Matthew, and John Carey. 1992. *Presidents and Assemblies: Constitutional Design and Electoral Politics.* Cambridge: Cambridge University Press.

Silberman, Bernard. 1993. *Cages of Reason: The Rise of the Rational State in France, Japan, the United States, and Great Britain.* Chicago: University of Chicago Press.

Slezkine, Yuri. 1994. The USSR as a Communal Apartment, or How a Socialist State Promoted Ethnic Particularism. *Slavic Review* 53 (summer):414–52.

Smith, Gordon. 1999. State-Building in the New Russia: Assessing the Yeltsin Record. In *State-Building in Russia: The Yeltsin Legacy and the Challenge of the Future,* ed. Gordon B. Smith, 3–16. Armonk, N.Y.: M. E. Sharpe.

Solnick, Steven. 1998a. Gubernatorial Elections in Russia, 1996–1997. *Post-Soviet Affairs* 14.

———. 1998b. *Stealing the State: Control and Collapse of Soviet Institutions.* Cambridge, Mass.: Harvard University Press.

———. 2000a. Is the Center Too Weak or Too Strong in the Russian Federation? In *Building the Russian State: Institutional Crisis and the Quest for Democratic Governance,* ed. Valerie Sperling, 123–57. Boulder: Westview.

———. 2000b. Putin and the Provinces. Program on New Approaches to Russian Security, Policy Memo Series, no. 115, Davis Center, Harvard University.

Stepan, Alfred. 2000. Russian Federalism in Comparative Perspective. *Post-Soviet Affairs* 16 (April—June):133–76.

Stepan, Alfred, and Cindy Skach. 1993. Constitutional Frameworks and Democratic Consolidation: Parliamentarism versus Presidentialism. *World Politics* 46 (April): 1–42.

Stoner-Weiss, Kathryn. 1997. *Local Heroes: The Political Economy of Russian Regional Governance.* Princeton: Princeton University Press.

———. 1999. Central Weakness and Provincial Autonomy: Observations on the Devolution Process in Russia. *Post-Soviet Affairs* 15 (January):15–42.

Tarrow, Sidney. 1994. *Power in Movement.* Cambridge: Cambridge University Press.

Tismaneanu, Vladimir. 1998. *Fantasies of Salvation: Democracy, Nationalism and Myth in Postcommunist Europe.* Princeton: Princeton University Press.

Treisman, Daniel. 1997. Russia's Ethnic Revival: The Separatist Activism of Regional Leaders in a Postcommunist Order. *World Politics* 29 (January):212–49.

Verdery, Katherine. 1994. Nationalism in Romania. *Slavic Review* 52 (summer):179–203.

Weber, Eugen. 1976. *Peasants into Frenchmen: The Modernization of Rural France, 1870–1917.* Stanford: Stanford University Press.

Wolfe, Eric. 1982. *Europe and the People without a History.* Berkeley: University of California Press.

Woodward, Susan. 1995. *Balkan Tragedy: Chaos and Dissolution after the Cold War.* Washington, D.C.: The Brookings Institution.

Yashar, Deborah. 1999. Contesting Citizenship: Indigenous Movements and Democracy in Latin America. *Comparative Politics* 31 (January): 23–42.

Young, Crawford. 1976. *The Politics of Cultural Pluralism.* Madison: University of Wisconsin Press.

———. 1993. The Dialectics of Cultural Pluralism: Concepts and Reality. In *The Rising Tide of Cultural Pluralism: The Nation-State at Bay?* ed. Crawford Young, 245–78. Madison: University of Wisconsin Press.

CHAPTER SIXTEEN

Federalism and Democracy

Beyond the U.S. Model

Alfred Stepan

For those of us interested in the spread and consolidation of democracy, whether as policy makers, human rights activists, political analysts, or democratic theorists, there is a greater need than ever to reconsider the potential risks and benefits of federalism. The greatest risk is that federal arrangements can offer opportunities for ethnic nationalists to mobilize their resources. This risk is especially grave when elections are introduced in the subunits of a formerly nondemocratic federal polity prior to democratic countrywide elections and in the absence of democratic countrywide parties. Of the nine states that once made up communist Europe, six were unitary and three were federal. The six unitary states are now five states (East Germany has reunited with the Federal Republic), while the three federal states—Yugoslavia, the USSR, and Czechoslovakia—are now twenty-two independent states. Most of postcommunist Europe's ethnocracies and ethnic bloodshed have occurred within these postfederal states.

Yet in spite of these potential problems, federal rather than unitary states are the form most often associated with multinational democracies. Federal states are also associated with large populations, extensive territories, and democracies with territorially based linguistic fragmentation. In fact, every single long-standing democracy in a territorially based multilingual and multinational polity is a federal state.

Although there are many multinational polities in the world, few of them are democracies. Those multinational democracies that do exist, however (Switzerland, Canada, Belgium, Spain, and India), are *all* federal. Although all these democracies, except for Switzerland, have had problems managing their multinational polities (and even Switzerland had the Sonderbund War, the secession of the Catholic cantons in 1848), they remain reasonably stable. By contrast, Sri Lanka, a territorially based multilingual and multinational unitary state that feared the "slippery slope" of federalism, could not cope with its ethnic divisions and plunged headlong into a bloody civil war that has lasted more than fifteen years.

In addition to the strong association between multinational democracies and federalism, the six long-standing democracies that score highest on an index of linguistic and ethnic diversity—India, Canada, Belgium, Switzerland, Spain, and the United States—are all federal states. The fact that these nations chose to adopt a federal system does not *prove* anything; it does, however, suggest that federalism may help these countries manage the problems that come with ethnic and linguistic diversity. In fact, in my judgment, if countries such as Indonesia, Russia, Nigeria, China, and Burma are ever to become stable democracies, they will have to craft workable federal systems that allow cultural diversity, a robust capacity for socioeconomic development, and a general standard of equality among their citizens.

Consider the case of Indonesia, for example. It seems to meet all the indicators for a federal state. It has a population of over 200 million, and its territory is spread across more than 2,000 inhabited islands. It has great linguistic and ethnic fragmentation and many religions. Thus it is near the top in virtually all the categories associated with federalism. If Indonesia is to become a stable democracy, one would think that it would have to address the question of federalism or decentralization. Yet at a meeting of Indonesian political, military, religious, and intellectual leaders that I attended after the fall of Suharto, most of the participants (especially those from the military) rejected federalism out of hand because of secessionist conflicts at the end of Dutch colonial rule. Indonesia should at least consider what I call a *federacy* to deal with special jurisdictions like Aceh or Irian Jaya. A federacy is the only variation *between* unitary states and federal states. It is a political system in which an otherwise unitary state develops a federal relationship with a territorially, ethnically, or culturally distinct community while all the other parts of the state remain under unitary rule. Denmark has such a relationship with Greenland, and Finland with the Aaland Islands.

A Misleading Picture of Federalism

In seeking to understand why some countries are reluctant to adopt federal systems, it is helpful to examine what political science has had to say about federalism.

Unfortunately, some of the most influential works in political science today offer incomplete or insufficiently broad definitions of federalism and thereby suggest that the range of choices facing newly democratizing states is narrower than it actually is. In large part, this stems from their focusing too exclusively on the model offered by the United States, the oldest and certainly one of the most successful federal democracies.

One of the most influential political scientists to write about federalism in the past half century, the late William H. Riker, stresses three factors present in the U.S. form of federalism that he claims to be true for federalism in general (Riker 1975). First, Riker assumes that every long-standing federation, democratic or not, is the result of a bargain whereby previously sovereign polities agree to give up part of their sovereignty in order to pool their resources to increase their collective security and to achieve other goals, including economic ones. I call this type of federalism *coming-together federalism*. For Riker, it is the only type of federalism in the world.

Second, Riker and many other U.S. scholars assume that one of the goals of federalism is to protect individual rights against encroachments on the part of the central government (or even against the "tyranny of the majority") by a number of institutional devices, such as a bicameral legislature in which one house is elected on the basis of population, while in the other house the subunits are represented equally. In addition, many competences are permanently granted to the subunits instead of to the center. If we can call all of the citizens in the polity taken as a whole the *demos*, we may say that these devices, although democratic, are *demos-constraining*.

Third, as a result of the federal bargain that created the United States, each of the states was accorded the *same* constitutional competences. U.S. federalism is thus considered to be constitutionally *symmetrical*. By contrast, *asymmetrical* arrangements that grant different competencies and group-specific rights to some states, which are not now part of the U.S. model of federalism, are seen as incompatible with the principled equality of the states and with equality of citizens' rights in the postsegregation era.

Yet although these three points are a reasonably accurate depiction of the political structures and normative values associated with U.S. federalism, most democratic countries that have adopted federal systems have chosen not to follow the U.S. model. Indeed, American-style federalism embodies some values that would be very inappropriate for many democratizing countries, especially multinational polities. To explain what I mean by this, let me review each of these three points in turn.

Coming-together versus Holding-together

First of all, we need to ask: How are democratic federal systems actually formed? Riker has to engage in some concept stretching to include all the federal systems in the

world in one model. For example, he contends that the Soviet Union meets his definition of a federal system that came about as the result of a "federal bargain." Yet it is
clearly a distortion of history, language, and theory to call what happened in Georgia,
Azerbaijan, and Armenia, for example, a federal bargain. These three previously independent countries were conquered by the 11th Red Army. In Azerbaijan, the former nationalist prime minister and the former head of the army were executed just one week
after accepting the "bargain."

Many democratic federations, however, emerge from a completely different historical and political logic, which I call *holding-together federalism.* India in late 1948,
Belgium in 1969, and Spain in 1975 were all political systems with strong unitary features. Nevertheless, political leaders in these three partially multinational polities came
to the decision that the best way—indeed, the only way—to hold their countries together in a democracy would be to devolve power constitutionally and turn their
threatened polities into federations. The 1950 Indian constitution, the 1978 Spanish
constitution, and the 1993 Belgian constitution are all federal.

Let us briefly examine the holding-together characteristics of the creation of federalism in India to show how they differ from the coming-together characteristics cor-
rectly associated with the creation of American-style federalism. When he presented
India's draft constitution for the consideration of the members of the constituent assembly, the chairman of the drafting committee, B. R. Ambedkar, said explicitly that it
was designed to maintain the unity of India—in short, to hold it together. He argued
that the constitution was guided by principles and mechanisms that were fundamentally different from those found in the United States, in that the Indian subunits had
much less prior sovereignty than did the American states. Since they had less sovereignty, they therefore had much less bargaining power. Ambedkar told the assembly
that although India was to be a federation, this federation was created not as the result
of an agreement among the states, but by an act of the constituent assembly (India,
Constituent Assembly 1951.) As Mohit Bhattacharya, in a careful review of the constituent assembly (Bhattacharya 1992), points out, by the time Ambedkar had presented the draft in November 1948, both the partition between Pakistan and India and
the somewhat reluctant and occasionally even coerced integration of virtually all of the
568 princely states had already occurred. Therefore, bargaining conditions between relatively sovereign units, crucial to Riker's view of how and why enduring federations are
created, in essence no longer existed.

Thus one may see the formation of democratic federal systems as fitting into a sort
of continuum. On one end, closest to the pure model of a largely voluntary bargain, are
the relatively autonomous units that come together to pool their sovereignty while
retaining their individual identities. The United States, Switzerland, and Australia are

examples of such states. At the other end of the democratic continuum, we have India, Belgium, and Spain as examples of holding-together federalism. And then there is what I call putting-together federalism, a heavily coercive effort by a nondemocratic centralizing power to put together a multinational state, some of the components of which had previously been independent states. The USSR was an example of this type of federalism. Since federal systems have been formed for different reasons and to achieve different goals, it is no surprise that their founders created fundamentally different structures. This leads us to our next point.

Demos-constraining versus *Demos*-enabling

Earlier, I described American-style federalism as *demos*-constraining. In some respects, all democratic federations are more *demos*-constraining than unitary democracies. There are three reasons for this. First, unitary democracies have an open agenda, as Adam Przeworski points out (Przeworski 1986), while in a federal democracy the agenda of the *demos* at the center is somewhat restricted because many policy areas have been constitutionally assigned to the exclusive competence of the states. Second, even at the center there are two legislative chambers, one (in theory) representing the one person—one vote principle, and the other representing the territorial principle. Third, because jurisdictional disputes are a more difficult and persistent issue in federal than in unitary systems, the judiciary, which is not responsible to the *demos*, is necessarily more salient and powerful.

Riker sees the *demos*-constraining aspect of federalism (and the weak politywide political parties normally associated with federalism) as basically good (Riker 1982, 247–53), because it can help protect individual rights from being infringed by the central government's potential for producing populist majorities.[1] But when examined from the point of view of equality and efficacy, both of which are as important to the consolidation of democracy as is liberty, the picture becomes more complicated. The deviation from the one citizen—one vote principle that federalism necessarily implies may be seen as a violation of the principle of equality. Overrepresentation in the upper house, combined with constitutional provisions requiring a supermajority to pass certain kinds of legislation, could, in certain extreme cases, lead to a situation in which legislators representing less than 10 percent of the electorate are able to thwart the wishes of the vast majority. This raises serious questions for the efficacious and legitimate functioning of democracy. If one were interested only in creating a system that best reflects the *demos* and that functions as an effective democracy, a case could be made that the democratic values of participation, decentralization, and equality would be better addressed in a unitary system that has decentralized participation than in a federal system. But if a polity has great linguistic diversity, is partly multinational, and is very large, its chances of being a democracy are much better if it adopts a federal system.

If federal systems were forced to adhere to the Rikerian model, multinational democracies would be faced with a stark choice: if they wished to adopt a federal system to reduce ethnic, religious, or linguistic tensions, they could do so only at the risk of severely constraining majority rule. But if we look at the federal systems that actually exist in the world, we see that not all federal systems are *demos*-constraining to the same degree. American-style federalism is *demos*-constraining, and Brazil is the most *demos*-constraining federation in the world. Yet the German federal system is much more *demos*-enabling than that of the United States, and India's is even more *demos*-enabling than Germany's. We can, in fact, construct a continuum, ranging from federal systems that are *demos*-constraining to those that are *demos*-enabling. Where a particular federal system lies on this continuum is largely determined by the nature of the party system, which I discuss elsewhere, and by three constitutionally embedded variables: (1) the degree of overrepresentation in the upper chamber; (2) the policy scope of the territorial chamber; and (3) the sorts of policy issues that are off the policy agenda of the *demos* because they have been allocated to the states or subunits.

Overrepresentation in the Territorial Chamber. I think it is fair to argue that the greater the representation of the less populous states (and therefore the underrepresentation of the more populous states), the greater the *demos*-constraining potential of the upper house will be. The United States and Brazil follow the same format: in both countries, each state gets the same number of senators. Since Wyoming had a population of 453,000 and California had a population of 30 million in 1990, this meant that one vote for a senator in Wyoming was worth 66 votes in California. In Brazil, the over-representation is even more extreme. One vote cast for senator in Roraima has 144 times as much weight as a vote for senator in São Paulo. Moreover, Brazil and Argentina are the only democratic federations in the world that replicate a version of this over-representation in the lower house. With perfect proportional representation, São Paulo should have 114 seats. It actually has 70. With perfect representation, Roraima should have one seat. It actually has eight. The Brazilian constitution, inspired by the ideology of territorial representation, specifies that no state can have more than 70 seats in the lower house (thereby partially disenfranchising São Paulo) and that no state can have fewer than 8.

Yet the principle of equal representation of each state in the upper house is not democratically necessary and may even prove to be a disincentive to multinational polities that contemplate adopting a federal system. Many democratic federations have quite different formulas for constructing their upper houses. In Germany, the most populous states (or *Länder*) get six votes in the upper chamber, those of intermediate size get four, and the least populous get three. Austria, Belgium, and India are still closer to the one person—one vote end of the continuum. If multilingual India had followed the U.S. pattern, it would not have been able to do some things that were absolutely crucial for political stability. Between 1962 and 1987, India created six new culturally distinctive states in the northeast, mostly carved out of Assam, a conflict-ridden region bordering Burma and China. If India had followed the U.S. model, these new states, containing barely one percent of India's population, would have had to be given 25 percent of all the votes in the upper chamber. The other Indian states would never have allowed this. Thus something democratically useful—the creation of new states, some of which were demanding independence by violent means—would have been difficult or impossible under the U.S. principle of representing each state equally.

The range of variation among the world's federal democracies can be seen in Table 16.1. This table also illustrates what I said above about most federal democracies choosing not to follow the U.S. model. The United States, along with Brazil and Argentina, which follow the same model, is an outlier on this continuum. The first line measures the degree of inequality of representation according to the Gini index. The values range from 0, which indicates perfect one person±—one vote representation, to 1, which indicates that one subunit has all of the votes in the upper house. Belgium's upper house has a Gini index value of close to 0. Austria's is not much higher. India's is .10. Spain's is .31. The U.S. Gini index value is almost .50, and Brazil's is .52. This means that the best-represented decile in the United States has 39 percent of the votes in the Senate; in Brazil, the best-represented decile has 43 percent of the votes; in India, it only has 15 percent. The variations are immense. On this indicator, the United States is clearly on the *demos*-constraining end of the continuum.

Policy Scope of the Territorial Chamber. Now let us turn to our second variable, the competences of the territorially based chamber. My proposition is that the greater the competences of the territorial house, the more the *demos*—which is represented on a one person—one vote basis in the lower house—is constrained. In the United States, the lower house has a somewhat more important role than the Senate in budget initiation, but if one takes into account the Senate's constitutionally exclusive prerogatives to advise and consent on judicial, ambassadorial, and major administrative appointments, the two houses come fairly close to policy-making parity. On this variable, Brazil has the most *demos*-constraining system in the world. There is no area that the Brazilian senate does not vote on, and there are twelve areas where it has exclusive competence, including authority to set limits on how much states can borrow.

As we can see in Table 16.2, however, other federal democracies do not give the upper house as much policy scope as they give the lower house.

Table 16.1 Continuum of the Degree of Overrepresentation in the Upper Houses of 12 Modern Federal Democracies

Gini index of inequality[a]	Belgium .015	Austria .05	India .10	Spain .31	Germany .32	Canada .34	Australia .36	Russia[b] .43	Switzerland .45	U.S.A. .49	Brazil .52	Argentina .61
Ratio of best represented to worst-represented federal unit (on basis of population)	Austria 1.5/1	Belgium 2/1	Spain 10/1	India 11/1	Germany 13/1	Australia 13/1	Canada 21/1	Switzerland 40/1	U.S.A. 66/1	Argentina 85/1	Brazil 144/1	Russia 370/1
Percentage of seats of best-represented decile	Belgium 10.8	Austria 11.9	India 15.4	Spain 23.7	Germany 24.0	Australia 28.7	Canada 33.4	Russia 35.0	Switzerland 38.4	U.S.A. 39.7	Brazil 41.3	Argentina 44.8

Source: Stepan, "Federalism and Democracy: Beyond the U.S. Model," *Journal of Democracy* 10, no. 4: 19–34.
Note: Complete information on all federal countries is contained in the Alfred Stepan-Wilfrid Swenden federal data-bank. We are grateful to Cindy Skach and Jeff Kahn for having provided us with the data on India and Russia, respectively. Other data were taken from *Whitakers Almanac* (London: J. Whitaker, 1977); *The Europa World Year Book* (London: Europa, 1995); and Daniel J. Elazar, ed., *Federal Systems of the World*. For the constitutional provisions on second chambers, see S.E. Finer, Vernon Bogdanor, and Bernard Rudden, *Comparing Constitutions* and A.P. Blaustein and G.H. Flanz, *Constitutions of the Countries of the World* (Dobbs Ferry, New York: Oceana, 1991).
[a]The Gini coefficient equals zero if the composition of the upper chamber is fully proportional and equals one if one subunit has all the votes in the second chamber. Arend Lijphart was among the first authors to use the Gini coefficient as a measure of inequality for the composition of second chambers. See Arend Lijphart, *Democracies: Patterns of Majoritarian and Consensus Government in Twenty-one Countries* (New Haven, Conn.: Yale University Press, 1984), 174.
[b]The status of Russia as a democracy is the most questionable of the 12 countries in the table. The data are included for comparative purposes.

Table 16.2 *Continuum of the Upper Chamber's Constitutional Prerogatives to Constrain a Majority at the Center*

Least Constraining →→→→→ Most Constraining

India	Spain	Germany	United States	Brazil
The territorial chamber has no constitutional powers to protect subunit autonomy against a 60-day central intervention. Upper chamber has capacity to review or deny "President's Rule" only after 60 days. Largely a revisionary chamber.	Major power is granted by Article 155 of the Constitution, which precludes intervention by the center unless it has received approval by an absolute majority of the upper house. Plays no role in constructive vote of no confidence or normal legislation. Largely a revisionary chamber;	Plays no role in constructive vote of no confidence. Can play a potential veto role only in that part of the legislative agenda that directly relates to center-subunit issues. Power has grown somewhat over the last 20 years. Conflicts between the two chambers are resolved in closed door meetings.	Extensive capacity to block a democratic majority. Senate has the same voting rights on all legislation as the "one person-one vote" chamber. Has exclusive competence to confirm or deny all major judicial and administrative appointments. A committee chairman alone can at times block important nominations.	Excessive for the efficacious and legitimate functioning of democratic government. The extremely disproportional upper chamber must approve all legislation. The Senate has 12 areas of exclusive lawmaking prerogatives. Senators representing 13 percent of the total electorate can block ordinary legislation supported by senators representing 87 percent of the population.

449

The German, Spanish, and Indian systems are less *demos*-constraining, because their upper houses are less unrepresentative and less powerful. While in Brazil senators representing 13 percent of the total electorate can block ordinary legislation (and in the United States, a committee chairman alone can at times block important nominations), in Germany important bills are seldom vetoed by the upper chamber. How can we account for such a difference? First of all, the upper chamber cannot participate in the two most important legislative votes, those for government formation and government termination. This power is the exclusive competence of the lower chamber. Second, the upper chamber can delay, but not veto, bills that do not directly involve the *Länder*. Third, on the approximately 50 percent of the bills that the upper chamber can theoretically veto because they do relate directly to the *Länder*, it seldom does so after closed-door reconciliation meetings are held in the joint committee representing both houses.

In Spain, Belgium, India, and Austria, as well as in Germany, only the lower house participates in no-confidence votes. In many countries, the upper house is largely a revisionary chamber, although it has a major role in anything having to do with federal intervention. In Spain, for example, if the government wishes to take action against a regional government that is in contempt of the constitution, the decision must be approved by two-thirds of the upper house. This, in my view, is entirely appropriate.

The Degree to Which Policy-making Authority Is Constitutionally Allocated to Subunits. The third constitutionally embedded variable on which democratic federations differ greatly is the powers that are given to the *demos* at the center versus the powers that are constitutionally allocated to the states. Table 16.3 presents a continuum showing the balance of policy-making authority between subunits and central governments in several countries.

The 1988 Brazilian constitution is so extensively detailed that a great deal of ordinary legislation can be passed only by a supermajority. In Brazil, many specific provisions on state and municipal pensions, state banks (all the states have banks), and the right of states to tax exports were constitutionally embedded. This is extremely *demos*-constraining. When too many issues are constitutionally embedded, the result is profoundly undemocratic, because these issues cannot be decided by a normal majority. Almost everything of importance in Brazil is constitutionally embedded. In order to change the constitution, 60 percent of the members of both houses (both those present and those absent) must vote in favor of an amendment *twice*. In a country the size of a continent, with bad transportation, it is hard even to get 60 percent of the legislature to show up.

At the opposite end of the continuum (see Table 16.3), India has a very *demos*-enabling constitution. At the time of its drafting, its authors were painfully aware that

Table 16.3 *The Degree to Which Policy Making is Constitutionally Allocated to Subunits of the Federation*

Least ──► Most

India	Germany	Spain	United States	Brazil
Does not constrain demos.	Federal Law explicitly given precedent over Land Law.	Major constraints on majority at the center derives from the statutes of autonomy.	Constitution is extremely difficult to amend but is parsimonious, so the vast majority of legislation can be passed as ordinary legislation.	1988 Constitution is so detailed about states rights that much ordinary legislation can only be passed by exceptional majorities.
Capacity to respond to minority desires by redrawing the boundaries of states. Probably should constrain the ease with which the majority can intervene in states. Since 1994 Supreme Court decisions give somewhat more protection to subunits from imposition of "President's Rule" from the center.	Wide areas where lawmaking powers are either explicitly given to the center or are concurrent responsibilities. More tax money is spent by the Lander then by the center. Many federal programs are decentralized so as to be administered by the Lander, while lawmaking and policy oversight remains the prerogative of the center.	Occasional bargaining process if center needs votes of regional party during process of government formation.	Power is horizontally shared at the center between three branches. Power is vertically devolved and shared in "marble-cake" federalism between the federal and the state governments.	States and municipalities had such extreme control over export taxes and banking that central government's fiscal and trade policy in 1989–96 was impeded. Some centralization of tax and bank policies in 1996–97 but extremely costly to the center.
Residual power with center.	Most powers are concurrent.	Residual power with center.	Residual power with states.	Residual power with states.

451

there were more than fifteen languages spoken in the country that at least 20 million people could claim as their mother tongue. The boundaries of the states did not correspond with linguistic boundaries. To get the government closer to the people, the framers of the Indian constitution had to respect the linguistic principle, so they decided (art. 3) that the lower house, by a simple majority vote, could eliminate any state, carve new states out of existing ones, or change their names. That is the sort of provision that a holding-together federation can write. In a states'-rights federation like the United States, such a provision would be absolutely impossible. But if it had not been possible in India, the failure to realize the "imagined communities" of the country's hundreds of millions of non-Hindi speakers might have led to secession in a number of places.

The U.S. constitution is even more difficult to amend than the Brazilian constitution, but it is parsimonious, so the vast majority of legislation can be passed by ordinary majorities. In Spain, the main constraint on the majority at the center derives from the statutes of autonomy, which deal primarily with questions of culture and language. In Germany, many federal programs are administered by the *Länder,* but lawmaking and policy oversight remain the prerogative of the center.

Constitutionally Symmetrical versus Asymmetrical

Let us now turn to a final point concerning the U.S. model. The U.S. constitution, as discussed above, establishes a form of symmetrical federalism, which is bolstered by a certain normative disinclination on the part of Americans to accept the concept of collective rights. With the exception of Switzerland (where none of the political parties strictly represents any one linguistic or religious group), all of the multinational democracies are constitutionally asymmetrical: in order to hold the multinational polity together, they assign different linguistic, cultural, and legal competences to different states. Under the symmetrical American model, many of the things that are most essential in a multinational context cannot be accomplished. With the possible exception of the special case of Switzerland, *all* federations that are constitutionally symmetrical—Austria, Germany, Australia, the United States, Argentina, and Brazil—are mononational. India, Belgium, Canada, and Spain are multinational and their federations are all asymmetrical. (The Russian Federation is also asymmetrical, but, constitutionally, it does not yet work as a democratic federation.)

The concept of collective rights is in tension with the traditional American way of thinking about such matters, which is based on individual rights. It is true that a polity cannot be a democracy unless the individual rights of all citizens are enshrined in the constitution and a countrywide system of horizontal and vertical controls is credibly established to support these rights. Whatever rights the national subunits may possess, they cannot constitutionally or politically violate the rights of individual citizens. The enforcement of individual rights can be an obligation of both the center and the subunits, but the center cannot completely delegate responsibility for the establishment and maintenance of democratic rights and continue to be a democracy. Alexis de Tocqueville is very clear on this point. He admired the robust local associationalism of U.S. democracy but pointed out that the rule of law in the entire polity had to be guaranteed and enforced by the center.

In multinational polities, however, some groups may be able to participate fully as individual citizens only if they acquire, as a group, the right to have schooling, mass media, and religious or even legal structures that correspond to their language and culture. Some of these rights may be described as group-specific collective rights. Many thinkers in the liberal tradition assume that all rights are individual and universal and view any deviation from individualism and universalism with suspicion, but this assumption is open to question.

Let me conclude with four observations, partly drawn from studies of the historical development of democracy, about democratic group-specific rights,[2] to use a term coined by the Canadian political philosopher Will Kymlicka (Kymlicka 1995). First, individuals are indeed the primary bearers of rights, and no group rights should violate individual rights in a democratic polity. In democratic multinational federal states, this means that something like a bill of individual rights should be promulgated by the federal center, and any laws and social policies that violate it must fall outside the constitutionally guaranteed policy scope of the subunits.

Second, while individual rights are universal, it is simply bad history to argue that in actual democracies all rights have been universal. Frequently, the struggle to reconcile the imperatives of political integration with the legitimate imperatives of cultural difference has led countries to award certain minorities group-specific rights, such as those given to French-speaking Quebec in Canada, to cultural councils in Belgium, and to Muslim family courts in India. The key point is that it is the obligation of the democratic state to ensure that no group-specific right violates individual or universal rights.

Third, while individuals are the bearers of rights, there may well be concrete circumstances in which individuals cannot develop or exercise their full rights unless they are active members of a group that struggles for some collective goods common to most of its members. If, for example, the Catalans had not been given certain group-specific rights involving the public status of their own language, I doubt whether as individuals they could have become full democratic citizens of Spain. Similarly, I do not think Kurds will become full democratic citizens of Turkey unless they are granted certain group-specific rights (such as the right to Kurdish newspapers and radio stations in the southeast of Turkey, where Kurds are a majority).

Finally, although such group-specific rights may not be consistent with some nineteenth-century tenets of Anglo-Saxon liberal democracy or with the French idea of citizenship in a nation-state, they are consistent with a polity in which group rights do not violate individual rights, and they permit effective democratic citizenship and loyalty to be extended throughout the polity. They offer, in fact, one of the few ways to craft democracy successfully in the difficult and populous world of multinational states.

The Limits of the U.S. Model

The U.S. model of federalism, in terms of the analytical categories developed in this essay, is coming-together in its origin, constitutionally symmetrical in its structure, and *demos*-constraining in its political consequences. Despite the prestige of this U.S. model of federalism, it would seem to hold greater historical interest than contemporary attraction for other democracies.

Since the emergence of nation-states on the world stage in the aftermath of the French Revolution, *no* sovereign democratic nation-states have ever come together in an enduring federation. Three largely unitary states, however (Belgium, Spain, and India), have constructed holding-together federations. In contrast to the United States, these federations are constitutionally asymmetrical and more *demos*-enabling than *demos*-constraining. Should the United Kingdom ever become a federation, it would also be holding-together in origin. Since it is extremely unlikely that Wales, Scotland, or Northern Ireland would have the same number of seats as England in the upper chamber of the new federation, or that the new upper chamber of the federation would be nearly equal in power to the lower chamber, the new federation would not be *demos*-constraining as I have defined that term. Finally, it would obviously defeat the purpose of such a new federation if it were constitutionally symmetrical. A U.K. federation, then, would not follow the U.S. model.

The fact that since the French Revolution no fully independent nation-states have come together to pool their sovereignty in a new and more powerful polity constructed in the form of a federation would seem to have implications for the future evolution of the European Union (EU). The EU is composed of independent states, most of which are nation-states. These states are indeed increasingly becoming functionally federal.

Were there to be a prolonged recession (or a depression), however, and were some EU member states to experience very high unemployment rates in comparison to others, member states could vote to dismantle some of the economic federal structures of the federation that were perceived as being politically dysfunctional. Unlike most classic federations, such as the United States, the EU will most likely continue to be marked by the presumption of freedom of exit.

Finally, many of the new federations that could emerge from the currently nondemocratic parts of the world would probably be territorially based, multilingual, and multinational. For the reasons spelled out in this essay, very few, if any, such polities would attempt to consolidate democracy using the U.S. model of coming-together, *demos*-constraining, symmetrical federalism.[3]

NOTES

This chapter was originally published as an article in *Journal of Democracy* 10 (Oct. 1999): 19–34.

1. As Riker acknowledges, however, federalism may also give the majority in the subunits the power to limit the freedom of some of the citizens (as the history of the southern United States shows), making it difficult for the federal government to protect them.

2. For a powerful argument by a distinguished legal theorist that group rights are often a precondition of individual rights, see Joseph Raz, *The Morality of Freedom* (Oxford: Clarendon, 1986), 193–216. For a political and philosophically acute discussion of these issues in India, see Rajeev Bhargava, "Secularism, Democracy, and Rights," in *Communalism in India: Challenge and Response*, ed. Mehdi Arslan and Jannaki Rajan (New Delhi: Manohar, 1994), 61–73.

3. The tentative arguments made in these concluding paragraphs will be developed analytically and empirically in much greater depth in *Federalism, Democracy and Nation*, a book being written by Juan J. Linz and myself.

REFERENCES

Bhattacharya, Mohit. 1992. The Mind of the Founding Fathers. In *Federalism in India: Origins and Development*, ed. Nirmal Mukarji and Balveer Arora, 81–102. New Delhi: Vikas.

India, Constituent Assembly. 1951. *Debates: Official Report*, vol. II, 31–44. New Delhi: Manager of Publications.

Kymlicka, Will. 1995. *Multicultural Citizenship: A Liberal Theory of Minority-Rights*. Oxford: Clarendon.

Przeworski, Adam. 1986. Some Problems in the Study of the Transition to Democracy. In *Transitions from Authoritarian Rule: Comparative Perspectives,* ed. Guillermo O'Donnell, Philippe C. Schmitter, and Laurence Whitehead, 47–63. Baltimore: Johns Hopkins University Press.

Riker, William H. 1975. Federalism. In *Handbook of Political Science,* ed. Fred Greenstein and Nelson W. Polsby, 5:93–172. Reading, Mass.: Addison-Wesley.

———. 1982. *Liberalism Against Populism: A Confrontation Between the Theory of Democracy and the Theory of Social Choice.* San Francisco: W. H. Freeman.

CHAPTER SEVENTEEN

Conclusion: The Merits of Federalism

Nancy Bermeo

By asking how territorial cleavages are best accommodated, the essays in this collection focus on one of the most consequential issues of our time. Ethnic violence is much more common now than interstate violence and tends to be longer lasting as well (Fearon and Laitin 1999, 1, Licklider 1995; Walter 1997). Since 1945, ethnic violence has played a major role in half of all wars, turned over 12 million people into refugees, and caused the death of at least 10 million more (Welsh 1993, 43; Horowitz 1985, xi). Since there are probably fewer than twenty ethnically homogeneous states in the world today (Welsh 1993, 45), and territorial conflict may emerge from regional as well as ethnic identity, we can safely conclude that the lessons learned here are relevant throughout the world.

In looking for answers to our research questions, our authors searched a broad range of terrain, covering five continents, varied levels of economic development, radically different regimes, and unitary as well as federal states. Despite this diversity, the chapters yield a number of common themes.

Depth of Difference

One of the more surprising themes regards the association between accommodation and depth of difference. As we began this project, we assumed that our cases would verify the widespread notion that material and cultural differences would be harder to accommodate if they overlapped. A venerable group of scholars had found associations in a variety of case studies (Melson and Wolpe 1970; Treisman 1997, 218), and it was logical to expect that more differences would translate into more points of disagreement and, consequently, more problematic accommodation.

As compelling as this argument seemed initially, the effects of difference do not explain much of the variation in our cases. No consistent pattern emerges from differences on either economic or cultural dimensions. Discerning whether differences were singular or multiple seems to give us little purchase on which cleavages are most problematic.

Economic differences are not consistently associated with failed or successful accommodation. Problematic cleavages emerged in relatively poor areas such as the north of Ireland, the south of Nigeria, and the Kurdish region of Turkey, but they emerged in relatively wealthy areas too. The Basque Country has been one of the wealthiest regions in Spain for decades. The northern regions are the site of Italy's strongest separatist movement but they are the country's wealthiest regions as well. Quebec is not the wealthiest province in Canada but it is very far from the poorest and its separatist movement emerged only after the region had caught up with the rest of the country in economic terms. The territorial conflict associated with the Flemish nationalist movement intensified only in the 1960s, just as traditionally disadvantaged Flanders overtook Wallonia in terms of gross regional product per capita. Separatist actions in Russia were strongest among "advanced groups in advanced regions" (Treisman 1997, 234).

To point out that regional economic development is not a consistent predictor of accommodation is not to argue that economic differences do not matter. A long history of discrimination and exploitation provides both the incentive for mobilization and the shared experience that can strengthen a people's sense of solidarity. Economic difference can matter greatly—but it seems not to matter in a consistent way.

State attempts to remedy economic differences seem to have unpredictable effects as well. Catholics in the north of Ireland were not won over by the programs of the British welfare state (Keating) and Corsican loyalty to France remains problematic despite the fact that transfers from Paris make the island the country's wealthiest region in terms of per capita budget (Smyrl). In Eastern Europe, the Soviets hoped that regional development programs would bolster regional loyalties to both a central state and to the bloc itself, but their hopes were apparently vain (Bunce).

Going beyond our cases and into the broader literature on separatism, we see once again that transfers alone do not always dampen separatist desires. Treisman's comparative work on Russia found that regions dependent on central subventions were not significantly less separatist once raw materials production and exports factors were taken into account (Treisman 1997, 240). Horowitz found a similar result in the third world in the 1970s. As he put it, "it may seem paradoxical that a poor region benefiting from association with more prosperous regions should want to terminate the arrangement. Yet the desire recurs" (Horowitz 1981, 177). Central governments that seek to accommodate territorial cleavages by decreasing economic difference often fail to do so. Here, again, we are not arguing that transfers from central governments to poorer peripheries never have positive, binding effects. We are arguing instead that their effects are unpredictable.

The effects of cultural differences, whether multiple or singular, are no more consistent than the effects of economic difference. Our cases do offer numerous examples where multiple cultural differences clearly exacerbated conflict. Keating's comparison of territorial cleavages in the United Kingdom shows us that the political divide with the north of Ireland was greatly exacerbated by Catholic versus Protestant divisions—a difference that was absent in the cases of Scotland and Wales. Likewise, Suberu teaches us that the horrific violence in the state of Kaduna derived in large part from the overlapping and converging ethnoreligious and socioeconomic cleavages between Muslim Hausa-Fulanis and a whole range of poorer, urbanized non-Muslim groups. Stoner-Weiss, similarly, attributes the deadly separatist struggle in Chechnia, in part, to the coincidence of ethnic, religious, and economic differences dividing Chechens and Russians.

Yet, there are facts that emerge from our cases that show that accommodation and depth of difference are not related in a straightforward way. One of the bloodiest cleavages analyzed in our project involves Kurds and Turks. Their struggle has cost over 40,000 lives thus far. Yet, as Angrist explains, what divides "Turkey's Kurds from Turkey's Turks is language" alone. The groups are indistinguishable by physical characteristics and the majority of both peoples are Sunni Muslims. In continental Western Europe, similarly, the most problematic cleavage is the one between Basques and Spaniards. Yet Basques and Spaniards share the same religion and physical characteristics. If ethnic difference alone were at the root of the accommodation failure, we would see the same degree of failure in a Basque-French divide. Yet, the Basques in France are not nearly as alienated (Raento1999, 220). Difference is obviously important in these cases. It is literally a life and death issue—but it is also singular. Deep and multifaceted differences can make for bloody conflict but single differences can make for deadly violence too.

Another complexity highlighted by our cases concerns the activation of deep differences. Kohli's essay points out that deep divisions have one meaning in one period and a very different meaning a short while later. Muslim Kashmiri leaders maintained "a working arrangement" with non-Muslim political elites in New Delhi from the 1950s until the mid-1980s. Throughout this period, Kashmiri nationalism "remained relatively mild" in dramatic contrast to what we see today. Timing mattered greatly in Turkey too. Kurds and Turks lived, for centuries, in "fraternity" as "fellow Muslims" and only became divided in the second decade of the twentieth century (Angrist).

In Russia, on the other hand, deep divisions faded in importance faster than many predicted. After the Soviet Union disintegrated, the three "most assertively separatist regions in Russia were Tatarstan, Chechnya, and Bashkortostan" (Treisman 1997, 231). Their Muslim identity fueled fears of a multifront religious war. Yet, as our case study shows, the separatist movement in Tatarstan disappeared as soon as elites worked out a bilateral agreement with Moscow. Bashkortostan also worked out a bilateral agreement with federal authorities and is no longer a separatist threat. The chairman of the constitutional court recently named Tatarstan and Bashkortostan "the calmest and most stably developing" republics (Radio Free Europe, August 4, 2001, 1). Multifaceted cleavages can make for long-lasting struggles but sometimes they make for no lasting struggles at all.

Each of the territorial cleavages analyzed in our project is the fruit of some difference marking the boundaries between one community and another. But whether the difference has one dimension or many is not a good predictor of accommodation success or failure. Whether the difference is essentially religious, linguistic, or economic does not predict much either. As compelling as the hypothesis about depth of difference seemed at first, it was not borne out by our cases. Other, recent, comparative studies have drawn similar conclusions: Treisman found no association between ethnic difference and separatist activity in Russia (Treisman 1997, 244–45), and a broad, cross-national study by Fearon and Laitin found that neither linguistic nor religious difference predicted ethnic violence (1999, 2). Varshney's work in India illustrates that ethnic conflict is not related to sociological differences per se but to the organization of associational life (Varshney 2001). Another cross-national study by Saidemann and Ayres found that separatist movements in the 1990s were more likely to emerge from groups that had "*fewer* ethnic differences with their host state" (2000, 1139).

The conclusion we reach with our cases here is that differences are an essential part of every accommodation challenge but that the implications of difference and multiple differences are not consistent enough across time or space to be the stuff of any credible generalizations. Differences matter but the way they matter depends on how they combine with other contextual factors. One such factor is the history of interaction between cleavage groups. Another is the international context in which cleavage conflict is played out.

Foreign Allies and Resource Groups

Our project revealed few surprises on the question of international context. Sometimes international forces work through legitimate channels to help publicize and resolve an accommodation crisis peacefully. Suberu mentions that human rights groups performed this role in Nigeria. Sometimes, international actors give rebels and would-be rebels access to weapons and training that make accommodation crises more violent and more difficult to resolve. Kohli details how weapons from the Afghan war aided the Sikh rebellion and how Pakistani resources aided Kashmiri Muslims. Bunce shows likewise how the collapse of Albania helped the Kosovo Liberation Army. Neither the negative nor the positive examples are numerous enough or detailed enough for us to draw any conclusions that would go beyond existing literature (Lake and Rothschild 1998). The fact that so few of our authors gave any attention to international factors suggests that most of our particular sets of cleavage conflicts are rooted more in domestic history.

History of Interaction

The identities that lie at the root of territorial cleavages are the fruit of history. Indeed, the term *shared history* is integral to most definitions of ethnicity and identity more broadly (Gurr and Moore 1997, 1081; Smith 1991, 12). The nature of a group's past interactions with dominant and neighboring "others" is a key determinant of its present positions. As Horowitz reminds us, the leaders of ethnic groups make their decisions based on calculations of group interest—but interest is inevitably "alloyed with enmity" and "offset by apprehension" (Horowitz 1981, 167). The intensity of enmity and the depth of apprehension are products of history.

Despite wildly diverse details, the case histories related by our authors share several commonalities. These commonalities set two generalizations in stark relief. The first concerns what happens when the history of interaction is marked by oppression and violence rather than compromise. The second concerns the venues in which interaction takes place.

Compromise versus Coercion

The histories related here illustrate quite clearly that compromise is preferable to oppression as a formula for coping with territorial cleavages. This conclusion is obvious from a moral perspective, but in practical political terms, the conclusion holds as well. Table 17.1 sorts all of the major territorial identity groups included in our project by level of recent violence.

Table 17.1 Cleavage Groups, Terrorism, and Violence

Accommodation			
Failed ◄──────────────────────────────────► Successful			
Recent/Ongoing Mass Violence	Ongoing Acts of Terrorism	Violence Ended	No Violence
Chechens	Basques/ETA	Sikhs	Catalans
Chiapas/Indians	Irish/IRA	Tamils	Flemish
Kashmiri Muslims	Corsicans/FLNC		Oaxaca/Indians
Kurds			Northern Italians
			Québécois
			Scots
			Swiss/French
			Swiss/Italian
			Welsh

Each of the most problematic cleavages analyzed here—meaning each cleavage that has been characterized by mass violence in recent times—emerges from a context of highly oppressive historical interaction. The Kurds, as Angrist explains, were victims of property expropriation, forced resettlement, constant surveillance, and even aerial bombings before the current nationalist movement emerged in the 1960s. The Chechens' bloody interactions with Moscow began during the time of imperial Russia and continued through the Soviet period with mass deportations under Stalin. The minority peoples of southern Kaduna date their victimization by northern Muslims from the time of slave raiding in the eighteenth century. The violent nature of the indigenous movement in Chiapas seems to have also been the fruit of extraordinary coercion. The harsh experience of "peasant indigenous movements in the 1980s revealed that the Chiapan political system was incapable of offering institutional means of channeling peasant indigenous grievances" (Trejo). In Kashmir too, Muslim interactions with non-Muslim rulers were fraught with violence from at least the time of Sikh rule in 1819. Even when the core of Kashmir was tranquil, the Jannu region was often fraught with communal conflict and population flight (Punjabi 1992, 132–51).

Historical interactions that are marked by mass civil and physical oppression have highly negative long-term consequences. The term *mass* is important here, for the targeting of leading militants is not likely to have the effects that mass coercion has (Lichbach 1987, 266–97; Gurr and Moore 1997, 1084). Persecuting leaders creates martyrs, but persecuting whole peoples creates movements. As Steve Van Evera puts it, "the experience of warring or oppressed peoples, filled as it is with tales of sacrifice for the common good, creates a stronger we-feeling than the experiences of people who escape these tragedies" (Van Evera 2001, 21).

The legacies of coercion are often more negative and longer lasting than its perpe-trators realize. Margaret Thatcher's hard-line in Northern Ireland "gave Sinn Feín a massive boost within the Catholic community and provided a recruiting bonanza for the IRA" (Keating). New Dehli's harsh reaction to Tamil opposition to the imposition of Hindi as the national language only polarized relations further (Kohli). Even in-transigence (as opposed to outright coercion) can turn a moderate movement in a more radical direction. As Hooghe reminds us, the nineteenth-century Flemish move-ment was confined to urban intellectuals and focused mainly on individual language rights. It was only radicalized and popularized by "the intransigence of the French-speaking elite" (Hooghe).

Of course, the legacies of intransigence, coercion, and even war may not last forever. As Table 17.1 illustrates, our project includes many cases where enmity seems to have been reduced. Conflict continues, but only through nonviolent means. In each of these more successful cases, central authorities offered minorities some sort of compensa-tory and inclusive compromise. These moments of compromise mark historical switchpoints that make for new and more successful accommodation formulas.

The merits of compromise emerge with clarity across a broad range of cases. The treatment of Catholics and conservatives in the aftermath of the Swiss civil war pro-vides an early and particularly graphic example. The Catholic and conservative cantons that attempted secession were defeated decisively in 1847, but the constitution that was drafted on the eve of their defeat limited the competencies of the new state and shunned majoritarianism in an effort to accommodate the vanquished (Bäechtiger and Steiner).

In Oaxaca, Mexico, in a radically different case, inclusive institutional reform had similar, positive effects: the 1995 state legislature broke national precedent and met a long-standing indigenous demand for the recognition of indigenous political practices in the selection of local government leaders. Nearly three-quarters of the state's mu-nicipalities voted to ban political parties, scotch municipal elections, and use an in-digenous selection process instead. Critics feared that the concession would bring on violence and secession. Yet, the indigenous movement in Oaxaca remains unarmed, and the establishment of rebel territories on the Chiapas model is no longer discussed.

Two of our Indian cases show the same pattern, though they differ dramatically from one another and from the cases just discussed. When Tamil nationalists mobilized against what they saw as northern Hindi domination in the early 1950s, political actors in New Delhi feared separatism and argued for repression. When Nehru gave the Tamils a separate state instead, the drive for separatism died down. The separatist movement among Sikhs in the Punjab dragged on for years as Indira Gandhi refused concessions and used armed force. When Rajiv Gandhi came to power and held elections instead, violence dropped dramatically (Kohli). Violence rose again when Rajiv had to backtrack on a number of concessions, but his successor's decision to hold a series of elections has brought the major Sikh party to power, decreased violence, and forced Sikh separatism off-stage (Kohli).

Concessions to the peoples of the Niger Delta ended Nigeria's first violent secessionist campaign in 1966 (Suberu) and even brought former separatists on to the central government's side in later struggles. Concessions from Moscow ended the drive for separatism in Tatarstan as well (Stoner-Weiss).

Compromise is often feared as a slippery slope that will only increase violence and end in secession. Our case studies show that compromise is likely to decrease violence and to dampen separatist drives instead. Our research thus bolsters arguments offered by Diamond (1999, 53) and Horowitz (1985, 625). As Bunce argues, the threat of separation is often a ploy. Politicians often threaten secession when they will settle for something else. The histories related here suggest that autonomy and inclusion are usually effective substitutes. In any case, the term *separatist* has many meanings—even for those who call themselves "separatists." As Smyrl teaches us, only a small minority of Corsicans who see themselves as separatists actually want "outright independence." In Quebec, most separatists sought "continued association" with Canada and the last referendum was written to reflect this (Simeon). Compromise is not a slippery slope but smart politics, instead.

Of course there are cases where violent, separatist movements endure even after authorities have made inclusive concessions. The ETA in the Basque Country and the FLNC in Corsica exemplify the phenomenon. But they also exemplify groups with narrow constituencies. These are small, clandestine organizations that use the force of arms because they lack the force of numbers. They lack broad popular support precisely because concessions from the central state have given their cleavage group viable alternatives to violence. Their marginality legitimates our defense of compromise and inclusiveness.

There were periods in which the IRA had a broader base of support than either of these groups. But the relative popularity of the IRA legitimates our defense of compromise and inclusiveness too. As Keating's essay demonstrates, the central government in London was not successful in creating an inclusive formula for accommodation until the Good Friday Agreement of 1998. Since the partition of Ireland in 1921 left northern Catholics in a permanent minority, the majoritarian mechanisms that meant regional hegemony for Basques and Corsicans meant only continued exclusion for the Catholic Northern Irish. Credible inclusion of the Catholic community required nonmajoritarian, consociational institutions. These have finally been put in place, though how long they will last is highly questionable. Whatever the longevity of these new institutions, we know that the alternatives to violence that have been offered the Catholics have fallen far short of true self-government for over eighty years and that the proponents of violence have reaped the benefits. The fact that previous compromises offered by London were ineffective in stopping anti-Catholic violence fed support for the IRA as well. The historical contrast between the IRA and other violent groups suggests not simply the merits of compromise but of full, institutional inclusion.

The merits of inclusionary compromise are illustrated further by the case of Quebec. Separatist movements rarely attract majority support, especially in an advanced democracy, yet, as Simeon's essay reminds us, the *Québécois* separatist movement came within one percentage point of victory in the 1995 referendum. The movement has always been nonviolent and is thus dramatically different from the IRA, but both movements benefited from existing barriers to group self-government. In Canada, the federal system has allowed the people of Quebec substantial autonomy and, as Simeon argues, it is federalism that has kept the separatist movement entirely peaceful. But the institutional constraints on a further deepening of provincial autonomy provide the separatists with their principal raison d'être. As Amoretti, Simeon, and Weaver have shown, Canada's federal system has strong majoritarian elements. Though French speakers are a clear majority in Quebec, they constitute small minorities in other provinces. Since fundamental legal changes in the autonomy accorded Quebec require consent from a majority of the legislatures of Canada's ten provinces (plus a majority in the national legislature) the possibilities for expanding autonomy within the existing majoritarian constraints are decidedly limited. Simeon shows that the movement for separatism expanded precisely when these constraints were made manifest through legislative defeat, that is, after the "exclusion" of 1982 and after the failure of the Meech Lake Accord. What the Canadian and the Northern Irish cases show us is that the institutional nature of the center's inclusionary compromise matters greatly. Institutional change can compensate for a conflictual history of interaction but some institutional changes are better than others.

Venues for Interaction

The conclusion of the previous section connects us to the second generalization that emerges from our study of the history of interaction, for just as some institutional changes are better than others, some settings for interaction are better than others too.

Successful accommodation always seems to involve some sort of venue for linkage wherein potentially problematic territorial groups become integrated with a larger whole. These linkage mechanisms provide the channels through which positive historical interaction occurs. Sometimes, linkage mechanisms are constitutionally legitimated state institutions wherein territorial groups forge a strong link with central authorities by exercising authority at the center themselves. Switzerland's many consensual institutions exemplify this sort of linkage.

More often, though, the mechanisms through which territorial groups interact with central authorities are less formalized and therefore more precarious. In many of our cases, interaction and linkage took place historically through nationally popular political parties and through the resources these parties offered in exchange for support. Nationally popular parties can be extremely useful as a means of integration for the reasons laid out in Stepan's essay. However, it is risky to use political parties as the primary venue for interaction because party fortunes vary much more frequently than formal constitutional provisions. The availability of resources varies too. If a state's accommodation formula depends on a particular party configuration and pay-off system, successful formulas for accommodation can become untenable overnight.

We see this pattern clearly in a broad range of our cases. Amoretti's essay teaches us that Italy was able to accommodate substantial territorial cleavages for decades through a party and patronage system that worked against the mobilization of regional differences. The Christian Democratic Party provided the setting for regional elites to share power and transfers from the central state. Potential regional cleavages were overshadowed by the left-right divide and neutralized by vast resources from the center. The history of center-regional interaction was amicable until the end of the cold war and the beginning of European Union budget constraints made the old accommodation formula unworkable. The Northern League rose from the ruins of the old system.

Keating's essay shows how a similar dynamic transformed the historical interaction between Scotland and the central authorities in the United Kingdom. For decades, British parties served as informal "brokers" for Scottish interests and elites. Until the 1980s, Scotland was rarely run by non-Scots and rarely run by a party for which it had not voted. The election of Thatcherite Conservatives, with little or no support in Scotland, changed the equilibrium. Just as the traditional party-based venue for interaction disintegrated, the EU emerged, "positing an alternative external support system for Scottish autonomy." Though the specifics of the relationship with the EU differed greatly, regionalist movements in Italy and the United Kingdom were clearly boosted by the decline of an old party system and the rise of the EU.

We see pieces of this picture again in countries as diverse as Belgium, India, and Mexico. In Belgium, the material transfers that were key to accommodation in the postwar period became untenable under the harder budget constraints of the EU. These constraints eventually forced center elites to substitute the transfer of power for the transfer of funds. This substitution, in turn, began the transition from consociationalism to federalism and to a new formula for accommodation. Happily, the new formula was inclusive and successful.

In India, as in Italy, the accommodation of territorial differences was greatly facilitated by the hegemony of a single party, the Congress Party. When the balance of the party system began to shift, under Indira Ghandi, a less secure center became more intransigent and more willing to use military force as part of its accommodation formula. The use of coercion proved highly problematic.

In Mexico, we see an accommodation formula that depended even more on the hegemony of a single political party in what was, for decades, a single-party regime. When the PRI began to be threatened by new parties, sectors of its leadership turned to increased military force. This proved counterproductive and reinforced the foundations of the guerrilla movement in Chiapas.

All of these examples illustrate two related points. The first is about the connection between historical interaction and institutions. As social scientists, we tend to divide historical and institutional explanations into two discrete categories. Our essays show that this division is artificial. Historical interactions inevitably have institutional components. Interactions usually take place within institutions, but even when they take place in the street or in combat, coercive institutions inevitably play a key role.

The second point these essays bring to light is that the institutional venues of historical interaction matter greatly. In our most successful examples of accommodation, interaction takes place in formal decision-making venues: territorial cleavage groups have been included in legitimate governmental institutions and allowed some degree of autonomy. In our least successful examples of accommodation, cleavage groups are the subjects of violence rather than inclusion and they become purveyors of violence themselves. In our cases where violence is limited to terrorists, the central state has made concessions toward inclusion but these fall short of what mobilized sectors of the cleavage group desire.

The salience of institutions in our discussion of historical interaction brings us to the question of what sort of institutional arrangements make the successful accommodation of territorial cleavage most likely. Do federalist institutions facilitate accommodation better than unitary institutions?

Federalism versus Unitarism

A small sample of cases from current press reports could easily be the foundation of a critique of federalism. The persistence of ETA, the long and deadly struggle in Kashmir, and the tragedies emerging from the breakup of Yugoslavia suggest that federalist formulas for accommodation are at best ineffectual and at worst, deeply damaging. If we were to generalize from these cases, the contest would be between scholars who maintain that federalism simply does "not have much effect on political life"

(Riker 1975, 159) and scholars who argue that "ethnically based federalism and regional autonomy should be avoided" (Snyder 2000, 40).

Though our project confirms that federalism is no panacea for divided states, it presents a surprisingly consistent, positive message about the merits of federalism as a means of managing cleavages. Though some of our authors' essays offer cautionary tales, the individual components of the project add up to a strong argument for federalism.

Despite the diversity of our cases, the majority of our authors draw the conclusion that federalist arrangements facilitate successful accommodation. Our study of Belgium concludes that "federalism is better equipped to accommodate subnational demands"; that it is more "effective" than consociationalism for "contending with territorial conflict"; and that the formal move to federalism in 1993 was accompanied by "the ebbing" of both "disruptive, territorial protest and of exclusive identities."

Our study of Nigeria—a very different case—draws a similar conclusion. "Federalism has long been recognized as the indispensable basis for Nigeria's stability and survival," despite the grave challenges of governing three major ethnicities and 250 assorted minorities. Federalism has helped to "contain divisiveness within relatively manageable limits, and sustain a broad elite commitment to the preservation of Nigeria as a united" entity. The conclusion of our chapter on India is also positive: Kohli writes that federal power sharing within the relatively well-established Indian state "enabled the accommodation of a number of ethnic groups" and helped keep "political conflict" "mostly peaceful." "The more a formal federal system functioned in practice as a unitary system, the less was the system's capacity to accommodate ethnic and territorial cleavages" (Kohli).

In Mexico, even under semiauthoritarian conditions, federalism allowed some regional elites to compromise with the local leaders of indigenous movements long before the central government was willing to do so. The dramatic difference between the indigenous movements in Oaxaca and Chiapas is explained by this dynamic. In Oaxaca, local elites changed key laws, empowered indigenous leaders early on, and helped avoid armed struggle. In Chiapas, local elites proved as intransigent as central elites and helped provoke armed struggle. The difference between Oaxaca and Chiapas has much to do with the autonomy derived from federalism.

Our study of Canada concedes that federalism helps to perpetuate "the very cleavages it is designed to manage," but concludes that "federal institutions have proved effective" in the management task. For Quebec, federalism "has helped ensure that ... nationalism has remained peaceful and highly democratic and that the Canadian unity debate has been conducted with remarkable civility."

Spain and Russia are presented as relatively problematic cases, but here too a federalist accommodation formula appears beneficial. Beramendi and Maíz argue that the "openness, asymmetry, and lack of institutionalized cooperation" in Spanish federalism has led to a hazardous "expansion in the number of regionalist and cryptonationalist parties," and that federalism's capacity to provide a stable institutional solution is decreased by the presence of different nationalisms. Yet, they also teach us that Spain's federal institutions "were integral to the new constitution's initial success" during the transition to democracy and that they facilitated the accommodation of several national identities. Currently, they conclude that "Spanish federalism has been relatively successful in maintaining and nurturing dual, compatible identities" and in ensuring that the number of citizens embracing "exclusive identities" is not "high enough to allow any credible push toward secession."

In a parallel with the Spanish case, Stoner-Weiss links Russia's problems to an open constitution and bilateralism. The Russian constitution, like the Spanish, left many potentially divisive issues aside and bilateral treaties have evolved to compensate for this lack of specificity. Stoner-Weiss argues that bilateralism exacerbates the ineffectiveness of an already weak center and results in a "tremendous amount of unpredictability in center-periphery relations." Yet, even flawed federalism seems to have made a positive contribution to the little stability Russia enjoys. Events in the Republic of Tatarstan exemplify how even the most problematic center-periphery relations can be eased by federal structures. Though a full 61 percent of the republic's voters endorsed becoming "an independent territory," in a March 1992 referendum, a bilateral treaty giving the Muslim Republic special controls over social and educational programs, plus increased control over mineral resources, "effectively ended secessionist threats" (Stoner-Weiss). The treaty increased asymmetry, but prevented the violent dissolution of the state.

The situation in Chechnia was, of course, not resolved peacefully, but Stoner-Weiss reminds us that the "Chechen experience is not representative" of center-periphery relations in the rest of the Russian Federation. The Russian Federation embraces eighty-nine potentially problematic autonomous units and over a hundred distinct ethnic groups. Yet, only a single republic half the size of Rhode Island has launched a secessionist struggle. Forty-six regions followed the example of the Tatars, negotiating bilateral treaties and eschewing both violence and secession. Federalism allowed them this option.

The options offered by federalism may explain why federalist accommodation is becoming increasingly popular as a solution to the management of cleavages in unitary states. Federalism is catching on in all but one of the unitary states we studied. The system which has emerged today in the United Kingdom, in which "devolved assemblies pursue their own policies, while the minority nations continue to be represented" at the center is, according to Michael Keating, "a form of de facto federalism." In France, Marc Smyrl foresees a "quasi-federal arrangement" to create a territorial assembly in Corsica empowered to make legislation in line with the island's "special conditions." In Italy, the devolution of regional powers that began in the 1970s developed into a national referendum endorsing gradual federalization in the fall of 2001.

The single exception to the trend toward federalism is Turkey. In Turkey, central authorities are convinced that any devolution of power to the Kurdish region will bring on secession. The material presented in the preceding chapters suggests that they are wrong. Our comparative materials illustrate that separatist movements decline when concessions are made. Angrist's evidence from the Kurdish region of Turkey itself suggests that only a minority of Kurds want full independence anyway.

The general consensus in favor of federalism is echoed in three of our general essays as well. R. Kent Weaver's comparison of federalist electoral systems dispels a series of negative predictions about the effects of federalism on party systems. He finds "little evidence ... that federalism has an *independent* effect on the degree of fragmentation in a legislature," and no clear relationship between federalism and the growth of anti-system parties. He finds a strong affinity between federalism and disproportional upper chambers, but argues that this provides better checks and balances for minorities and protection for small units that were once independent.

Ferrán Requejo makes a strong case not simply for federalism but for asymmetric federalism. His essay thus stands as a counterweight to arguments against bilateralism. He argues that the quality of democracy in plurinational states is incompatible with symmetrical models of power distribution and that the rights of minorities require a number of "institutional external protections" that only asymmetry can provide.

Alfred Stepan argues for asymmetrical federalism too. Federalism in general helps "countries manage the problems that come with ethnic and linguistic diversity." But under the symmetrical model of federalism, "many of the things that are most essential in a multinational context cannot be accomplished." Like Requejo, Stepan argues that minorities in plurinational states "may be able to participate fully as individual citizens only if they acquire ... group-specific collective rights." But he goes beyond linking asymmetry to the quality of democracy and links it to the longevity of democracy as well. He argues that if a polity is large, linguistically diverse, and multinational, "its chances of being a democracy are much better if it adopts a federal system."

Stepan, like Simeon, recognizes that federalism is Janus-faced and that it may offer special opportunities for divisive nationalists. Valerie Bunce focuses on how these opportunities emerged in the Soviet bloc and offers us a sobering counterpoint to the consensus emerging from our other essays. Reminding us that territorially concentrated minorities in federalist systems were the only minorities that challenged state boundaries in the new regimes of postcommunist Eastern Europe, she concludes, "if new democracies inherit a national federal structure, they tend to be more vulnerable to secessionist pressures."

The key to reconciling Bunce's conclusion with the more positive conclusions emerging from the rest of our project lies in the term *inherit*. With the possible exception of Russia, none of the countries we analyze in our other essays inherited their federal systems from an immediately preceding regime. Russia is a special case in that it went through a process of "defederation" and "refederation." After the Soviet Union disintegrated, Russia convinced nineteen out of twenty-one republics to sign a federal treaty in March 1992. The constitution that enshrined federalism was decidedly more centralist and less popular but still won endorsement by referendum in a majority of Russia's republics in December 1993 (Smith 1995b, 170).

In all the states that Bunce discusses, federalism was the legacy of imposed rule and of a past era shaped by a dictatorial party. The countries that broke away from the Soviet Federation had their federal status imposed upon them by the very "odd empire" centered in Moscow at the end of World War II (Suny 1991, 111–26; Smith 1995b, 157–58). Yugoslavia had its Soviet-model constitution imposed on it by a dictatorial Communist Party in a constitutional assembly in which non-Communists had no voice. Its first federal constitution was "closely modeled on the Soviet federal constitution of 1936" and the product of a constitutional assembly in which non-Communists had no voice (Binns 1989, 122). In Czechoslovakia, federalism was imposed by the Soviets in 1968 in the aftermath of a brazen military invasion. Its purpose was to weaken the relative power of the Czech region where the liberalizing forces behind the Prague Spring were based.

Federalism had radically different roots in the countries considered by our other authors. Nigeria and India had colonial pasts and in this respect were similar to the countries of the Soviet bloc, but federalism in both Nigeria (Suberu) and India (Stepan) was the fruit of domestic elite consensus. It was supported by a colonial power but not imposed and not inherited. Nigeria's current democracy inherited federalism from a military government but military governments inherited federalism from civilians. In all of our other cases, federalism emerged from domestic elite bargaining and consensus. Even in the Swiss case, where secessionist cantons were forced back into the federation after losing a civil war, the original federation had deep, voluntaristic roots.

There are sound theoretical and empirical reasons for expecting that imposed federal systems would be less suited to successful accommodation. The roots of the word *federal* lie in the Latin term *foedus*, meaning covenant or compact. Just as a lasting covenant must be voluntary, lasting federalism needs to be voluntary too. Federalism is not simply an institutional arrangement but a process as well. Daniel Elazar was correct to argue that federalism requires "a sense of partnership … manifested through negotiated cooperation … and based on a commitment to open bargaining" (Elazar 1987, 67). A sense of partnership cannot be imposed.

The contrast between the effects of federalism in Eastern Europe and elsewhere highlights the importance of considering the origins of federal systems when making projections about their effects. Federal systems that are imposed by outside forces are always troubled and usually short-lived. Table 17.2 lists all the major examples of failed federalism outside communist Europe in the past half century. Every federalist system that either split apart or turned toward unitarism was one that was forced upon regions by an outside, usually colonial, power. This pattern is not the fruit of coincidence, but, rather, a strong signal that origins matter.

Alfred Stepan addresses the question of federalism's origins in his essay and delineates two distinct forms of covenant and the two forms of federalism to which they give rise. The differences he outlines between *coming-together* systems and *holding together* systems are indeed important. However, our project as a whole points to a third form of system that emerges from a different dynamic. Bunce's essay highlights a subtype we might call *forced-together federalism*, in which a federal arrangement emerges not from domestic consensus but from direct or indirect imposition by an outside actor.[1] When for any reason, constraint from the outside actor decreases, the federal arrangement is likely to collapse. Forced-together federalist systems produce different effects and have different implications for accommodation and democracy. Federalist arrangements do

Table 17.2 Failed Federalism outside Postcommunist Regimes in the Twentieth Century

Federation	Foreign Pressure	Longevity	Dissolution
British West Indies Federation	Britain	1958–62	Peaceful[a]
British Central African Federation	Britain	1953–63	Rioting[b]
Burma	Britain	1948–62	Armed resistance/military coup[c]
Cameroon	Britain	1961–72	Pres. Ahidjou unilaterally abolishes federation[d]
Congo	Belgium	6/1960–9/1960	Col. Mobuto stages coup[e]
Ethiopia	UN Resolution	1952–62	Eritrean civil war after emperor centralizes[f]
Indonesia	Netherlands	1949–50	Sukarno declares unitary republic[g]

(Continued)

Table 17.2 — Continued

Federation	Foreign Pressure	Longevity	Dissolution
Libya	Allies/UN	1951–63	PM Fakimi/King Idris abolish federation[h]
Mali Federation	France/Domestic Elites	1959–60	Fr. Sudan (Mali) tries to centralize, Senegal withdraws[i]
Malaysia-Singapore	Britain/Domestic Parties	1963–65	Rioting/expulsion of Singapore[j]
Pakistan	Britain	1947–71	Civil war/separation of Bangladesh[k]

[a]The federation had the support of some domestic political elites but was less popular with the public. When the idea of federation was defeated by a landslide in a referendum in Jamaica, the collapse began.

[b]The federation included northern and southern Rhodesia plus Nyasaland. It was designed "without any consultation or cooperation being sought with the Africans." Africans were "bitterly opposed to the whole idea." Ursula Hicks, *Federalism: Failure and Success* (London: Macmillan, 1978), 77.

[c]The constitution of 1947, which came into effect with Burman independence in 1948, was federalist in nature but left many ethnic groups dissatisfied. Within months fighting ensued in Karen areas and in other areas which resented Burman domination. Disorder gave a rationale to coup makers in 1962. Josef Silverstein, *Burmese Politics. The Dilemma of National Unity* (New Brunswick: NJ Rutgers, 1980).

[d]Ahidojou came from East Cameron, which was much larger in terms of population, land, and wealth than West Cameroon. The whole existence of Cameroon was, ironically, a legacy of pre–World War I German colonialism. East and West Cameroon were legacies of Allied divisions of the German colony. See Augustine Wamala, "Federalism in Africa: Lessons for South Africa," in *Evaluating Federal Systems* (Boston: M. Nijhoff, 1994), 251–67.

[e]The leaders of the new state were divided over whether federalism was desirable. The Belgians imposed a federalist constitution and the country broke into separatist and civil wars almost immediately.

[f]As a former Italian colony, Eritrea was joined to Ethiopia by a U.S.-sponsored UN resolution.

[g]Federalism was widely thought to be a divide and rule tactic aimed to save Dutch hegemony. Those who seek federalism in Indonesia today are still struggling against this legacy.

[h]The UN Commissioner sought the federation of three regions controlled by Italy before World War II: Tripolitania, Fazzan, and Cyrenaica. Resistance to federalism was strongest in Tripolitania, but it was approved by a handpicked commission of local elites from each region. Cyrenaica's Amir became king of the new federalist state and eventually abolished federalism after oil was discovered in his region. Parties were banned shortly after independence. Helen Chapin Metz, ed., *Libya: A Country Study* (Washington, D.C.: U.S. Government Printing Office, 1989), 34–41.

[i]Both nations were part of the French Community when the federation was formed. Senegal became independent in June 1960 and withdrew from the federation on August 20, claiming Sudan was attempting to centralize power.

[j]Britain sought federation as a bulwark against a communist government after decolonization. Security concerns were so great that the British retained control of the armed forces and military affairs. The merger was hotly contested by communist parties in both states and by others who feared domination of the Malays by ethnic Chinese. The two nations' prime ministers supported it until ethnic rioting and aggression from Indonesia made it too politically costly for Malaysia's PM.

[k]In Pakistan, it was federal borders rather than federal institutions that were imposed. M. A. Jinnah,, Pakistan's founding father, envisioned a federal state that would include the whole of Bengal, the whole of the Punjab, Kashmir, the Rann of Kutch, Sind, Baluchistan, and the Northwest Frontier. Pakistan ended with much less than this and as a divided state with two vastly different wings separated by the Indian states of Bihar and Uttar Pradesh. The date of Pakistan's first federalist constitution was 1947. The Pakistanis rewrote it in 1957, but provincial autonomy was rescinded by a third constitution in 1962 and then restored by yet another constitution in l969 (Hicks 1978, 109–18).

seem to assist in the successful accommodation of territorial cleavages but only if they are the product of domestic covenants.

If federalist systems are to be the product of covenants rather than coercion, policy makers will need to be convinced that federalism really does have the beneficial effects highlighted here. Yet, without more comparative work, we cannot be certain if the patterns we observe in these cases are observable elsewhere. Nor can we be certain of the conditions under which these beneficial effects are produced. We can verify our conclusions with more single-country case studies, but we shall also require cross-national comparison with the broadest possible range of cases. The comparison will have to include unitary states as well, of course, but as of now, systematic comparison of unitary versus federal systems is still surprisingly rare. To get us started on the task ahead, I use the remainder of this essay to examine how our generalization about the relative superiority of federalism fares with a larger set of cases.

Federalism versus Unitarism: A Broader Comparison

If federalism really is beneficial for the accommodation of territorial cleavages, the positive assessments our authors have made in our project thus far should be replicated in other cases as well. The data in Phase I of Ted Robert Gurr's Minorities at Risk (MAR) project give us the opportunity to examine the relative merits of federalism with a larger set of cases. Gurr's data set focuses on the 1980s and deals with minorities on every continent. Though the MAR project does not concern federalism, it provides highly detailed information on the whole set of minority groups fitting specified criteria. The project offers data on every minority group that suffered from or benefited from systematic discriminatory treatment, mobilized in defense of their self-defined interests at some time between 1945 and 1989, lived in a nation whose population exceeded one million in 1985 and constituted either one percent of their country's population or numbered over 100,000 themselves (Gurr 1993, 5–9). The MAR data set in Phase I contains 233 such cases. We eliminated four subsets of these before undertaking our comparison. First, we set aside all seventy-four sub-Saharan African cases, in part because of the unavailability of data, but also because the state-minority dynamic was likely to be unique where extreme heterogeneity meant that the majority of a population can claim minority status (Herbst 2001). We then eliminated a subset of forty-one minorities who were not territorially concentrated, three nomadic minorities who were not settled in any particular country, and three other minorities whose territorial concentration was unknown. The final set of cases subject to comparison numbered 112. Forty-six of these minorities reside in federal states and sixty-six reside in unitary states.

The MAR data provide us with a broad range of information to supplement our detailed case studies. Inevitably, particular classifications and codings might be subjects for debate. Yet there are good reasons to assume, as David Laitin and Jim Fearon do, that the MAR data provide the means for "a serviceable first-cut" (1999) at our research question. We can safely assume that debatable codes and classifications, to the extent that they exist, are randomly distributed across our unitary and federal cases. We can also assume that the subject of the MAR project—minorities who have already mobilized—provides a useful subset of minorities for us to investigate. Though it might have been interesting to have information on minorities that lacked either the capacity or the incentive to mobilize, the "already mobilized" provide the greatest accommodation challenge and are worthy of attention in themselves.

The questions we examined with these data focus on whether successful accommodation of territorial cleavages is more likely under federal systems. As we stated in the Introduction, successful accommodation does not involve the elimination of all conflict. Successful accommodation involves the elimination of violent conflict and the lessening of conditions that might provide incentives for violence in the future.

If the diffusion of power intrinsic to federalism does in fact benefit territorially concentrated minorities, we would expect minorities in federal states to engage in fewer acts of armed rebellion, to experience lower levels of economic and political discrimination, and to harbor lower levels of grievance concerning political, economic, and cultural policy. Most of these expectations are borne out by the data. Though we have to be extremely cautious given our small number of cases, on each of these six dimensions of accommodation, federal regimes score better than unitary regimes (see Table 17.3).[2]

Federal systems provide more layers of government and thus more settings for peaceful bargaining. They also give at least some regional elites a greater stake in existing political institutions. With these incentives we would expect fewer armed rebellions in federal states. In fact, the mean armed-rebellion score for federal states is less than half that for unitary states.[3] When federal and unitary dictatorships are compared, federal systems look even better: the score for armed rebellion is significantly greater in unitary dictatorships than in federal dictatorships.

If we look at the behavior of minorities in democracies we see a different pattern—at least initially. The armed-rebellion score for minorities in federal democracies is slightly higher than that in unitary democracies. Yet a closer look reveals that the result is driven entirely by rebellions in India. If we exclude India as an outlier, the rebellion score for minorities in federal democracies drops to about half the score for unitary democracies.[4] The divergent Indian case deserves a great deal more attention, but it is significant that no minority in any other developing-world federal democracy was engaged in armed struggle in the 1980s.

Table 17.3 Accommodation of Minorities in Federal versus Unitary States, 1980s

Measures of accommodation	All States		Dictatorships		Democracies	
	Federal	Unitary	Federal	Unitary	Federal	Unitary
Armed rebellion	1.13	3.14	0.92	4.36	1.59	1.20
Political discrimination	1.54	1.95	1.42	2.05	1.67	1.88
Economic discrimination	1.33	2.00	1.00	1.79	1.61	2.24
Political grievances	1.67	3.11	1.08	3.16	2.29	2.92
Economic grievances	1.87	2.56	1.00	2.14	2.72	3.28
Cultural grievances	1.96	2.32	1.73	2.41	2.28	2.20
N	46[a]	66[b]	26	37[c]	18[d]	25

Source: Ted Robert Gurr, Minorities at Risk: A Global View of Ethnopolitical Conflicts (Washington, D.C.: United States Institute of Peace, 1993).
Notes: Here and in Tables 17.4 and 17.5, lower numbers mean better accommodation. Numbers are means for aggregates of all groups with scores for the measure. Each coded minority group is one observation. If a case had no score on a measure, it was excluded. Six cases in countries that underwent regime change between 1984 and 1986 were excluded when data were sorted by regime type. Measures of accommodation were assessed with the following variables from MAR Phase 1: REBEL80, POLDIS, ECODIS, POLRITXX, SOCGRIXX and ECOGRIXX. For descriptions of coding rules see Gurr 1993. Minorities who were not territorially concentrated were excluded. The dictatorship and democracy categories exclude Brazil, El Salvador, Guatemala, and the Philippines (two cases), all of which changed from dictatorship to democracy in the mid-1980s. The democracy category includes Argentina, Bolivia (two cases), Honduras (two cases), and Turkey, which were democratic for most of the 1980s; it also includes Mexico and Malaysia (two cases), which were semidemocratic in the 1980s. The dictatorship category includes Thailand (two cases), which was authoritarian until 1988.
[a] For the measures armed rebellion and political grievances, N = 45.
[b] For the measure armed rebellion, N = 65; for the measure economic discrimination, N = 63.
[c] For the measure armed rebellion, N = 36; for the measure economic discrimination, N = 34.
[d] For the measures armed rebellion and political grievances, N = 17.

Is federalism associated with reduced political discrimination? There is ample reason to expect that it would be, especially for "minorities" that are numerically dominant in a certain region. In these cases, representatives in regional governments might suffer sanctions if they did not protect "minority" rights. The MAR data suggest that political discrimination is, in fact, lower in federal regimes. Furthermore, this difference holds among both democracies and dictatorships. The evidence is only suggestive and must be weighed with caution. Perhaps due in part to the small number of cases, only the difference between federal and unitary dictatorships is statistically significant, but all observed differences run in the direction favoring federalism.[5]

A similar pattern emerges when we compare perceived levels of economic discrimination. These were also decidedly lower in federal than in unitary states. Statistically significant differences favoring federalism emerge for democracies, dictatorships, and both regime types combined. Economic discrimination levels seem lower in federal states.[6]

One would expect lower levels of political and economic discrimination to be associated with lower levels of grievance, and this expectation is also confirmed, for the most part, by the data. The bottom half of Table 17.3 compares grievance levels in three issue areas: political rights other than autonomy, economic rights, and cultural rights. Levels of grievance concerning both political and economic rights were significantly lower among minorities in federal states. Levels of grievance concerning cultural rights were lower in federal states too, though the divergence from the levels in unitary states was not statistically significant.

Assessing grievance levels in dictatorships is probably impossible because people are forced to conceal their preferences to avoid persecution. Grievance measures for democracies, however, are less problematic. Although the small number of federal democracies and lack of statistical significance requires that we view these results with extreme caution, minorities in federal democracies seem better off than their counterparts in unitary democracies in terms of both political and economic grievances. Minority grievances concerning cultural and social rights, however, appear slightly higher in federal democracies. The sources of this discontent are not clear and the small magnitude of the difference may mean that the levels of grievance are essentially the same, but it is intriguing that this is the only dimension of accommodation on which federal democracies fall short.

These data provide us with only a first cut at systematic comparison, but they do suggest that federal systems might indeed facilitate accommodation better than unitary systems. Since the MAR data reinforce the generally positive assessments of federalism that emerge from our case studies, two very different sorts of evidence point us toward the same conclusion.

Alternative Explanations?

But are we mistaking the effects of federalism for the effects of something else? Although this question merits lengthy investigation, two alternative hypotheses warrant our immediate attention. The first relates to regime stability. It stands to reason that stable regimes might be better at accommodating minorities than unstable regimes. If federal regimes are more stable than unitary regimes, it is possible that our results are being driven by regime stability rather than by federalism per se.

In fact, federal states were more stable than unitary states in the period captured by the MAR data set. In 1980, when the MAR data begin, the average age of federal regimes was 20.5 years, while the average age of unitary regimes was only 14.4 years. Although the small number of countries per category makes generalization problematic, the relative superiority of federalism remains even if we control for regime longevity (see Table 17.4).

These data suggest that stability, *in itself,* does not determine a regime's capacity for accommodation—federalism seems to have an independent effect. Since regimes in federal states seem to last longer than regimes in unitary states, it is possible that federalism contributes to regime stability. The fact that minorities in federal states are less likely to resort to armed struggle may help to explain why.

The effects of federalism appear to be independent of regime stability, but are they independent of wealth? It makes sense that wealthier countries would be better able to accommodate minorities because they have more resources to meet public demands. In fact, when we compare federal versus unitary countries in terms of per capita GDP, we see immediately that federal states are significantly wealthier than unitary states. There were only eighteen federal states in existence in the 1980s and only fourteen in our data set (due to our focus on countries with territorially concentrated minorities), but this small group includes some of the world's richest countries. For the countries we studied, the mean per capita GDP of federal states exceeds that of unitary states by approximately $3,000.

Sorting our cases into three categories by wealth helps us refine our thinking about federalism's effects (see Table 17.5).

Once again we need to be cautious, given the small number of cases in each category, but some suggestive patterns emerge. For states with a per capita GNP of $6,000

Table 17.4. *Regime Duration and Minority Accommodation in Federal versus Unitary States in the 1980s*

Measures of accommodation	Twenty Five Years or Longer		Less Than Twenty Five Years		Less Than Fifteen Years	
	Federal	Unitary	Federal	Unitary	Federal	Unitary
Armed rebellion	0.76	1.28	1.69	4.05	3.38	4.25
Political discrimination	1.26	2.07	1.88	1.93	1.50	1.76
Economic discrimination	1.14	2.00	1.75	1.84	1.25	1.80
Political grievances	1.46	3.19	1.63	2.99	1.75	3.02
Economic grievances	1.78	2.78	2.44	2.43	1.38	2.46
Cultural grievances	1.82	2.69	1.63	2.03	1.50	2.13
N	8	9	4	20	2	15

Source: Gurr 1993.
Notes: Analysis excludes countries that changed regime type during the 1980s. Regime duration is calculated as the number of years between the most recent coup and 1980 (for authoritarian regimes) or the number of years between the change to democracy and 1980, (for democratic regimes). Each country is one observation. Country averages were determined for each measure of accommodation and then an average across countries was determined

Table 17.5 Per Capita Gross Domestic Product and Minority Accommodation in Federal versus Unitary States in the 1980s

Measures of accommodation	Greater Than $6,000 Federal	Greater Than $6,000 Unitary	Less Than $6000 Federal	Less Than $6000 Unitary	Less Than $3,000 Federal	Less Than $3,000 Unitary
Armed rebellion	0.72	1.81	1.07	3.26	3.78	3.80
Political discrimination	0.84	1.50	2.19	2.22	2.25	2.14
Economic discrimination	0.76	1.83	2.20	2.09	2.17	1.85
Political grievances	1.17	3.33	2.15	3.16	2.33	3.25
Economic grievances	1.32	3.22	3.45	2.51	2.29	2.56
Cultural grievances	1.78	2.53	1.92	2.21	1.92	2.26
N	6	6	8	27	2	18

Source: Gurr 1993.
Notes: GDP is the average from 1980 to 1989 and is measured in purchasing power parity (PPP) terms at 1985 international prices. The average is for those years for which data are reported on Penn World Tables 5.6, available online at pwt.econ.upenn.edu variable RGDPL. Each country is one observation. Country averages were determined for each measure of accommodation and then an average across countries was determined.

or above, federal states appear better at accommodation on all measures. Yet when we look at cases below the $6,000 threshold, federalism's effects are not so uniform. Unitary states score higher than federal states on the two dimensions of accountability most directly related to economic life: economic discrimination and economic grievances. Among the poorest states, in which per capita GDP falls below $3,000, federal states score lower than unitary states in terms of both economic and political discrimination. Thus federalism appears to have clear advantages at a certain level of development, but below that level its advantages over unitarism are less uniform.

Admittedly, our data for the poorest countries are particularly problematic: coding was probably especially difficult due to a lack of sources and there are only two federal cases in this subset of data anyway. However, the evidence we have suggests that federalism might be more advantageous in some sorts of polities than in others. Whether this conclusion would be verified with different sorts of evidence remains a wide open question. On the one hand, the conclusion is reinforced by the fact that all of our least successful examples of cleavage accommodation come from the poorest countries among our case studies. On the other hand, our detailed analyses of these same countries suggest that federalism is overall beneficial.

The suggestion that federalism is most advantageous above a certain developmental threshold deserves much more attention in future research, but it brings us back full circle to the question of context with which we began. We should not expect any institutions to have the same effects in dramatically different contexts. Expecting uniform results from federalist institutions is particularly unwise because federalism involves a constellation of institutions that can each take majoritarian or consensual forms.

Our research project was built around assumptions about the importance of sociological and historical context and these assumptions were borne out by the project's essays. For each of our case studies, the role of federal (and unitary) institutions was always depicted as mediated rather than all determining. Though socioeconomic differences (alone and in combination) did not have uniform effects across our cases, no one denied that they affected each case. The history of interaction between groups and the center affected each case too and in more uniform ways. The international context of each division mattered as well: if actors across borders provided resources for conflict, conflicts were more likely to endure.

The authors of our chapter on Switzerland describe the importance of context succinctly. They conclude that institutions structure actors' choices but do not determine them. In Switzerland, the far-reaching delegatory powers and multiple veto points intrinsic to federalism did prevent conflicts between religious and linguistic groups from becoming "disruptive" but, our authors insist, "other noninstitutional factors ... contributed" to success as well (Bäechtiger and Steiner).

In poorer countries, the noninstitutional underpinnings of federalism may often be absent. The trust and sense of security elites need to make the kind of inclusive covenants that viable federalism requires are rare in conditions of scarcity. Other reinforcing institutions, such as strong countrywide parties, civilian-dominated militaries, and independent judiciaries may be absent too. How they can develop requires further research.

Further research is also needed to confirm the central conclusions that emerge from the project's essays. Stated simply these are: (1) neither singular nor overlapping socioeconomic differences explain much of the variation in accommodation; (2) accommodation seems to be strongly related to historical interaction; (3) coercive and oppressive interactions create the foundation for future violence; (4) compromise weakens the proponents of violence and creates the foundation for successful accommodation; (5) countrywide political parties are good venues for inclusion but they are best if combined with more permanent and inclusive government institutions; (6) majoritarian formulas for decision making are riskier for accommodation than consociational formulas; and finally, (7) federal arrangements are associated with successful accommodation but they cannot be imposed and require efficacious states to work best. If this collection serves to stimulate more systematic comparative work on any of these generalizations, or on other aspects of cleavage accommodation in federal and unitary states, it will have served its purpose.

NOTES

1. In *Arguing Comparative Politics,* Stepan discusses "putting together federalism" and the uniqueness of federations formed from coercion (2001, 323–24). My concept of forced-together federalism differs in its emphasis on outside actors and in its emphasis on system frailty.

2. Despite the small number of cases, the differences in means are significant at the 10 percent level or better using a two-tailed t-test in each category except political discrimination ($p = .102$) and cultural grievance ($p = .248$).

3. $p < .001$.

4. The mean for federal democracies when India is excluded is .667 but the difference in armed-rebellion scores for federal versus unitary democracies is not statistically significant when measured either with or without Indian cases. This is perhaps due to the small number of federal democracies in existence in the 1980s.

5. One-tailed t-tests on the differences in means on the political discrimination measure result in the following p-values: overall ($p = .05$); dictatorship ($p = .04$); democracy ($p = .29$).

6. One-tailed t-tests on the differences in means on the economic discrimination measure result in the following p-values: overall ($p = .004$); dictatorship ($p = .01$); democracy ($p = .04$).

REFERENCES

Binns, Christopher. 1989. Federalism, Nationalism and Socialism in Yugoslavia. In *Federalism and Nationalism,* ed. Murray Forsyth. New York: St. Martin's.

Brown, Michael E. 1993. Causes and Implications of Ethnic Conflict. In *Ethnic Conflict and International Security,* ed. Michael Brown. Princeton: Princeton University Press.

Diamond, Larry. 1999. Size and Democracy: The Case for Decentralization. Unpublished manuscript, Chapter 4, now published as *Developing Democracy: Toward Consolidation,* Baltimore: Johns Hopkins University Press.

Elazar, Daniel J. 1987. *Exploring Federalism.* Tuscaloosa: University of Alabama Press.

Fearon, James D., and David D. Laitin. 1999. Weak States, Rough Terrain and Large-Scale Ethnic Violence Since 1945.Working paper available at www.stanford.edu/group/ethnic..

Gurr, Ted Robert. 1993. *Minorities at Risk: A Global View of Ethnopolitical Conflicts.* Washington, D.C.: United States Institute of Peace Press.

Gurr, Ted Robert, and Will H. Moore. 1997. Ethnopolitical Rebellion: A Cross-Sectional Analysis of the 1980s with Risk Assessments for the 1990s. *American Journal of Political Science* 41 (October):1079–1103.

Heston, Alan, Robert Summers, and Bettina Aten. Penn World Table Version 5.6, Center for International Comparisons at the University of Pennsylvania.

Horowitz, Donald L. 1981. Patterns of Ethnic Separatism. *Comparative Studies in Society and History* 23 (April):165–95.

———. 1985. *Ethnic Groups in Conflict.* Berkeley: University of California Press.

Lake, David, and Donald Rothchild. 1998. *The International Spread of Ethnic Conflict.* Princeton: Princeton University Press.

Lichbach, Mark. 1987. Deterrence or Escalation? The Puzzle of Aggregate Studies of Repression and Dissent. *Journal of Conflict Resolution* 31 (June):266–97.

Licklider, Roy A. 1995. The Consequences of Negotiated Settlement in Civil Wars, 1945–1993. *American Political Science Review* 89 (September):681–90.

Melson, Robert, and Howard Wolpe. 1970. Modernization and the Politics of Communalism: A Theoretical Perspective. *American Political Science Review* 64 (December):1112–30.

Minorities at Risk Project, Phase I dataset. Center for International Development and Conflict Management. Available at www.minoritiesatrisk.com.

Punjabi, Riyaz.1992. Kashmir: The Bruised Identity. In *Perspectives on Kashmir: The Roots of Conflict in South Asia*, ed. Raju G. C. Thomas. Boulder: Westview.

Radio Free Europe/RL Tatar-Bashkir Service. 2001. rferl.org/bd/tb/reports/weekly/index.html. Accessed on August 4.

Raento, Paulina. 1999. The Geography of Spanish Basque Nationalism. In *Nested Identities: Nationalism, Territory and Scale*, ed. Guntram H. Herb and David H. Kaplan. Lanham, Md.: Rowman and Littlefield.

Riker, William H. 1975. Federalism. In *Handbook of Political Science: Governmental Institutions and Processes*, vol. 5, ed. Fred I Greenstein and Nelson W. Polsby. Reading, Mass.: Addison-Wesley.

Saidemann, Stephen, and R.William Ayres. 2000. Determining the Causes of Irredentism: Logit Analyses of Minorities at Risk Data from the 1980s and 1990s. *Journal of Politics* (November):1126–44.

Silverstein, Josef. 1980. *Burmese Politics: The Dilemma of National Unity.* New Brunswick, N.J.: Rutgers University Press.

Smith, Anthony.1991. *National Identity* Reno: University of Nevada Press.

Smith, Graham 1990. *The Nationalities Question in the Soviet Union.* London: Longman.

———. 1995a. Mapping the Federal Condition: Ideology, Political Practice and Social Justice. In *Federalism: The Multi-ethnic Challenge*, ed. Graham Smith. London: Longman.

———. 1995b. Federation, Defederation and Refederation: From the Soviet Union to Russian Statehood. In *Federalism: The Multi-ethnic Challenge*, ed. Graham Smith. London: Longman.

Snyder, Jack. 2000. *From Voting to Violence: Democratization and Nationalist Conflict.* New York: W. W. Norton.

Stepan, Alfred C. 2001. *Arguing Comparative Politics.* Oxford: Oxford University Press.

Suny, R. 1991. Incomplete Revolution: National Movements and the Collapse of the Soviet Empire. *New Left Review* 189 (September—October)111–25.

Treisman, Daniel S. 1997. Russia's Ethnic Revival: The Separatist Activism of Regional Leaders in the Post Communist World. *World Politics* 49 (January):212–49.

Van Evera, Stephen. 2001. Primordialism Lives! *APSA-CP* 12 (winter):20–22.

Varshney, Ashutosh. 2001. Ethnic Conflict and Civil Society: India and Beyond. *World Politics* 53 (April):362–98.

Welsh, David. 1993. Domestic Politics and Ethnic Conflict. In *Ethnic Conflict and International Security*, ed. Michael E. Brown. Princeton: Princeton University Press.

About the Contributors

Ugo M. Amoretti is a researcher in political science at the University of Genoa, Italy. His research interests focus on federalism, democracy, ethnic conflicts, Italian politics, and political economy. His articles have appeared in such journals as *South European Society & Politics, Journal of Democracy, and Rivista Italiana di Scienza Política.*

Michele Penner Angrist is an assistant professor of political science at Union College in Schenectady, New York. Her research interests span political parties, political development, and regime change in the Middle East, the Islamic world, and beyond.

André Bächtiger is a research assistant at the Institute of Political Science at the University of Bern (Switzerland) and a Ph.D. candidate in political science. In the academic year 2002–3 he was a visiting scholar at the Department of Political Science at the University of North Carolina at Chapel Hill. His research interests are political deliberation, institutionalism, and democratization. His Ph.D. is on favorable conditions for deliberation in real-world politics.

Pablo Beramendi is a Senior Research Fellow at the Institutions, States and Markets Unit, Wissenschaftszentrum für Sozialforschung, Berlin. He has recently earned his Ph.D. (Decentralization and Income Inequality) at Nuffield College, University of Oxford, and CEACS, Juan March Institute, Madrid. Broadly described, his research interests are focused on the study of the relation between political actors, political institutions, redistribution, and inequality.

Nancy Bermeo is a professor of politics at Princeton University, where she writes on regime change and the relationship between political institutions and group conflict. Her publications include *Civil Society Before Democracy*, co-authored with Philip Nord (Rowman & Littlefield, 2000); *Unemployment in the New Europe* (ed., Cambridge University Press, 2001); and *Ordinary*

People in Extraordinary Times (Princeton University Press, 2003). She is a member of the Club of Madrid and vice-president of the Democratization section of the American Political Science Association.

Valerie Bunce is a professor and chair of government at Cornell University. Her research examines the causes of ethnic cooperation and conflict and variations in democratization and economic reform in east-central Europe and the former Soviet Union. She served as president of the American Association for the Advancement of Slavic Studies in 2001 and vice-president of the American Political Science Association 2001–2.

Liesbet Hooghe is an associate professor of political science at the University of North Carolina at Chapel Hill. Her principal areas of interest are comparative politics, European integration, ethnic conflict, nationalism, and federalism. Her most recent publications are *The European Commission and the Integration of Europe: Images of Governance* (Cambridge University Press, 2002) and, co-authored with Gary Marks, *Multi-Level Governance and European Integration* (Rowman & Littlefield, 2001).

Michael Keating is a professor of regional studies at the European University Institute and a professor of Scottish politics at the University of Aberdeen. He was previously on the faculties of the universities of Strathclyde and Western Ontario. His main interests are in urban and regional politics and minority nationalism and his most recent books are *Plurinational Democracy: Stateless Nations in a Post-Sovereignty Era* (Oxford University Press, 2001) and *Culture, Institutions and Economic Development*, co-authored with John Loughlin and Kris Deschouwer (Edward Elgar, 2003).

Atul Kohli is the David Bruce Professor of International Affairs at Princeton University. His research interests span the study of politics, political sociology, and political economy of development, with a special interest in India. He is the author and editor of nine books and has published some forty essays.

Ramón Máiz is a professor of political science at the University of Santiago de Compostela, Spain. His fields of research include comparative policies of ethnic and nationalist regulation, nationalist movements and discourse, and indigenous mobilization in Latin America. Among his recent works are *Identity and Territorial Autonomy in Plural societies*, co-edited with William

Safran (London: Frank Cass, 2000); *Construcción de Europa, Democracia y globalización* (Santiago de Compostela: USC Press); and "Politics and the Nation: Nationalist Mobilization of Ethnic Differences" in *Nations and Nationalism* 9, no. 2 (2003): 195–212.

Ferran Requejo is a professor of political science and head of the Ph.D. program in political and social sciences at the Universitat Pompeu Fabra in Barcelona. His main fields of research are theories of democracy, federalism, political liberalism, social democracy after World War II, and multinational democracies. He is a member of the executive committee of the European Consortium for Political Research and was awarded the *Rudolf Wildenmann Prize* (ECPR) in 1997. Among his recent works are *Democracy and National Pluralism* (ed., Routledge, 2001); "Federalism and National Groups," *International Social Sciences Journal* (2001); "National Pluralism and Federalism: Four Political Scenarios for Spanish Plurinational Democracy," *Perspectives on European Politics and Society* (2001); "Cultural Pluralism, Nationalism, and Federalism: A Revision of Democratic Citizenship in Plurinational States," *European Journal for Political Research* (1999); and *European Citizenship, Multiculturalism and the State* (ed. with U. Preuss, Nomos, 1998).

Richard Simeon is a professor of political science and law, University of Toronto. His recent research and writing has focused on federalism, constitutionalism, and institutional design in Canada and other divided societies, with a recent focus on decentralization in developing countries, especially in Africa. He is a member of the Advisory Council of the Club de Madrid, an association of former heads of state and government in transitional democracies.

Marc Smyrl is on the faculty of law at the Université Montpellier in Montpellier, France. His principal research interest is the role of political choice in the design and performance of institutions.

Jürg Steiner is a professor emeritus of political science at the University of North Carolina and the University of Bern. He is currently Swiss chair at the European University Institute in Florence. His research interests lie in discourse ethics and deliberative politics.

Alfred Stepan is the Wallace S. Sayre Professor of Government at Columbia

University and has previously taught at Yale, Oxford, and Central European University. With Juan J. Linz, he is the author of *Problems of Democratic Transition and Consolidation: Southern Europe, South America, and Post-Communist Europe* (John Hopkins University Press). They are currently working on a book entitled *Federalism, Democracy and Nation*.

Kathryn Stoner-Weiss directs the Russia and Eurasia Project at the Liechtenstein Institute on Self Determination at Princeton University and teaches political science at Columbia University. She is the author of *Local Heroes: The Political Economy of Russian Regional Governance* (Princeton, 1997) as well as numerous articles on contemporary Russian politics. Her new book, *Resisting the State: Reform and Retrenchment in Post-Soviet Russia*, is forthcoming from Cambridge University Press.

Rotimi T. Suberu is a senior lecturer in political science at the University of Ibadan in Nigeria. His research focuses on problems of federalism, ethnic conflict, and democracy in Nigeria. A former fellow at the United States Institute of Peace and the Woodrow Wilson Center, both in Washington, D.C., Suberu has most recently authored *Federalism and Ethnic Conflict in Nigeria* (Washington, D.C.: United States Institute of Peace Press, 2001).

Guillermo Trejo is an assistant professor of political science in the Politics Division at the Centro de Investigación y Docencia Económicas (CIDE) in Mexico City. He specializes in movements of social protest, intercommunal conflict, guerrilla warfare, and ethnicity, with a particular focus on Latin America and Mexico. His research has been published by the *Journal of Latin American Studies, MOST Journal on Multicultural Studies, and Política y Gobierno*.

R. Kent Weaver is a professor of public policy and government at Georgetown University. His major areas of research are comparative political institutions, electoral reform, and comparative public policy. He was co-author and editor of *The Collapse of Canada?* (Brookings, 1992), and co-author and co-editor of *Do Institutions Matter?: Government Capabilities in the U.S. and Abroad* (Brookings, 1993) and *Government Taketh Away: Political Institutions and Loss Imposition in the United States and Canada* (Georgetown, 2003).

Index

Note: Page numbers in *italics* refer to figures and tables.

Hooghe, Liesbet, 15, 463
Horowitz, Donald: on ethnic states, 10; on
  leaders of ethnic groups, 461; on majority
  rule, 11; on secession, 12; on separatist desires,
  459; on violence, 7
Hungary, 429
Hunt, David, 167
Huntington, Samuel, 12

identities: in Belgium, 65–66, 84–85; in Canada,
  97; in Italy, 190; in Nigeria, 334; in Spain,
  143–47; state socialist federations and, 425,
  428–29; in Switzerland, 42; in United
  Kingdom, 172–73
India: accommodation in, 297–98; bicameralism
  and, 235, 240; conflict management in,
  463–64; democracy, national federalism, and,
  435–36; as *demos*-enabling, 446, 447, 450, 452;
  "Emergency" in, 284, 290; ethnic movements
  in, 281–82; federalism in, 297, 442, 444, 468,
  471; history of, 283; leadership strategy in,
  283–85; as multinational federation, 260, 261;
  Muslim nationalism in Kashmir, 292–97;
  political parties in, 467; Sikh nationalism in,
  288–92; Tamil nationalism and, 285–88
indigenous protest. *See* peasant protest
individual rights, collective rights compared to,
  452–54
Indonesia, 442
industrialization: import substitution
  industrialization (ISI), collapse of in Mexico,
  365; territorial divisions and, 5
Ingushetia, 316–17
institutions: accommodation and, 282–83; in
  Belgium, 74–76, 85–86; in Canada, 97, 99–103,
  115–18; context of, 424, 480; in France, 206–9,
  219–21; historical interactions and, 467; in
  Italy, 183–88, 189–93; in Mexico and peasant
  protest, 368–72; in Nigeria, 342–46; resources,
  incentives, and, 418–19; in Russia, 307–18,
  322–24; in Spain, 123–24, 138–43, 147–49; in
  Switzerland, 43; in Turkey, 392–93, 408–9; in
  United Kingdom, 160–71
interaction between minority group and central
  state: compromise *versus* coercion, 461–65,
  462; history of, 11–12; venues for, 465–67
interlocking strategy, 79
international actors: accommodation and, 13;
  Kurdish secession and, 408; Nigeria and,

349–50; resource groups and, 461; Turkey and,
  402. *See also* European Union (EU)
Iran, 408
Iraq, Kurds in, 402, 408
Ireland: characteristics of, 156; government of,
  171–72; history of, 156; home rule in, 158, 159;
  nationalism in, 157; partition of, 159;
  unionism in, 158–59. *See also* Northern
  Ireland
Ireland, Republic of, 159, 169–70
Irish Republican Army (IRA), 163, 464
Irkutsk, 316–17
Italian Communist Party (PCI), 183, 186–87, 190,
  191–92
Italian Socialist Party, 183
Italy: federalism in, 470; financial status of, 458;
  history of, 182–83, 189; institutions in, 183–88,
  189–93; political parties in, 183–85, 186–87,
  189–93, 194, 253, 466; territorial cleavage in,
  181–82, 189–93; violence in, 254

Jagmohan, 294
Jalisco, 362
Jammu and Kashmir Liberation Front, 295
Jospin, Lionel, 217–18
Juchitán, 376
judicial review: in Belgium, 76; in Canada, 100;
  importance of in federal systems, 9; in Italy,
  185; in Nigeria, 342–43; in Russia, 323; in
  United Kingdom, 170
Jura problem in Switzerland, 32, 44–45
Justice Party, 286

Kabardino-Balkariya, 314–15, 316–17
Kaduna, 336–38, 348–49, 459, 462
Kaliningrad, 313
Kalmikia, 316–17
Karachai-Cherkessia, 316
Kashmir: history of nationalism in, 459–60;
  international actors in, 461; Muslim
  nationalism in, 292–97; violence in, 292,
  294–95, 462
Kazakhstan, 423, 426
Keating, Michael: on Northern Ireland, 458, 463,
  464–65; on Scotland, 466; on United
  Kingdom, 16–17, 459, 469–70
Kemal (Atatürk), Mustafa, 389, 392, 395–97
Khanti-Mansii, 316–17
Khrushchev, Nikita, 427–28